# EXPERIMENTAL STUDIES
# OF
# INTERACTIVE DECISIONS

*by*

### AMNON RAPOPORT

*University of Arizona, Tucson, U.S.A.*

*with contributions from*

Nancy Cole
Arthur Coston
Danny Felsenthal
Esther Golan
Richard Helwig
Abraham Horowitz
James Kahan
William Stein
Thomas Wallsten
Eythan Weg
Rami Zwick

## KLUWER ACADEMIC PUBLISHERS
DORDRECHT / BOSTON / LONDON

*MATH*

*sep 12e*

Library of Congress Cataloging in Publication Data

Rapoport, Amnon.
    Experimental studies of interactive decisions / by Amnon Rapoport.
        p.    cm. -- (Theory and decision library.  Series C, Game
    theory, mathematical programming, and operations research)
    Includes bibliographical references.
    ISBN 0-7923-0685-6 (alk. paper)
    1. Decision-making, Group.  2. Game theory.  3. Social psychology.
  I. Title.   II. Series.
  HD30.23.R37  1990
  302.3'4--dc20                                                90-4098


ISBN 0-7923-0685-6

---

Published by Kluwer Academic Publishers,
P.O. Box 17, 3300 AA Dordrecht, The Netherlands.

Kluwer Academic Publishers incorporates
the publishing programmes of
D. Reidel, Martinus Nijhoff, Dr W. Junk and MTP Press.

Sold and distributed in the U.S.A. and Canada
by Kluwer Academic Publishers,
101 Philip Drive, Norwell, MA 02061, U.S.A.

In all other countries, sold and distributed
by Kluwer Academic Publishers Group,
P.O. Box 322, 3300 AH Dordrecht, The Netherlands.

*Printed on acid-free paper*

Printed in the Netherlands

# EXPERIMENTAL STUDIES OF INTERACTIVE DECISIONS

# THEORY AND DECISION LIBRARY

General Editors: W. Leinfellner and G. Eberlein

Series A: Philosophy and Methodology of the Social Sciences
Editors: W. Leinfellner (Technical Universtiy of Vienna)
G. Eberlein (Technical University of Munich)

Series B: Mathematical and Statistical Methods
Editor: H. Skala (University of Paderborn)

Series C: Game Theory, Mathematical Programming and
Operations Research
Editor: S. H. Tijs (University of Nijmegen)

Series D: System Theory, Knowledge Engineering and Problem
Solving
Editor: W. Janko (University of Vienna)

---

## SERIES C: GAME THEORY, MATHEMATICAL PROGRAMMING AND OPERATIONS RESEARCH

Editor: S. H. Tijs (University of Nijmegen)

---

Volume 5

---

**Scope**

Particular attention is paid in this series to game theory and operations research, their formal aspects and their applications to economic, political and social sciences as well as to socio-biology. It will encourage high standards in the application of game theoretical methods to individual and social decision making.

For a list of titles in this series, see final page.

# TABLE OF CONTENTS

## SECTION A:  TWO-PERSON INTERACTION

## SECTION B:  SMALL GROUP INTERACTION

## SECTION C: LARGE GROUP INTERACTION

# ACKNOWLEDGMENTS

The papers included in this volume are mostly joint publications. While preparing them for publication, I was reminded of the many fruitful discussions I had and many pleasant and stimulating days I spent with my colleagues in designing and conducting the experiments, analyzing the data, and making sense of the results. I wish to acknowledge the collaboration of Nancy Cole, Arthur Coston, Danny Felsenthal, Esther Golan, Richard Helwig, Abraham Horowitz, William Stein, Thomas Wallsten, Eythan Weg, and Rami Zwick, and thank them for their contribution to my education in computer programming, experimental design, and theory construction.

Of the seventeen papers collected in this volume nine are the outgrowth of joint work with Jim Kahan. Our collaboration has been long, deep, and extremely valuable to me. I wish to acknowledge Jim's contribution and thank him for his permission to reprint our joint papers. The thanks I present here do not adequately reflect my appreciation of his efforts, support, and friendship.

The author and Kluwer Academic Publishers are grateful to the following journals and institutions for permission to reprint the papers included in this volume:

"Optimal policies for the Prisoner's Dilemma," *Psychological Review*, 1967, **74**: 136-148. Copyright.

"Experimental studies of interdependent mixed-motive games," (with Nancy S. Cole), *Behavioral Science*, 1968, **13**: 189-204. Copyright.

"Decisions of timing in bipolarized conflict situations with complete information," (with James P. Kahan), *Acta Psychologica*, 1974, **38**: 183-203. Copyright.

"Decisions of timing in conflict situations of incomplete information," (with James P. Kahan and William E. Stein), *Behavioral Science*, 1973, **18**: 272-287. Copyright.

"Decisions of timing in experimental probabilistic duels," (with James P. Kahan and William E. Stein), *Journal of Mathematical Psychology*, 1976, **13**: 163-191. Copyright.

"Effects of fixed costs in two-person sequential bargaining," (with Eythan Weg and Dan Felsenthal), *Theory and Decision*, 1990, **28**, 47-72. Copyright.

"A PDP-11/45 program for playing n-person characteristic function games," (with James P. Kahan, Arthur W. Coston, Richard A. Helwig, and Thomas S. Wallsten), *Behavior Research Methods and Instrumentation*, 1976, **8**: 165-169. Copyright.

"Test of the bargaining set and kernel models in three-person games," (with James P. Kahan). In A. Rapoport (Ed.) *Game theory as a theory of conflict resolution*, 1974, pp. 119-160. Dordrecht, Holland: D. Reidel. Copyright.

"Test of the kernel and two bargaining set models in four- and five-person games," (with Abraham D. Horowitz). In A. Rapoport (Ed.) *Game theory as a theory of conflict resolution*, 1974, pp. 161-192. Dordrecht, Holland: D. Reidel. Copyright.

"Standards of fairness in 4-person monopolistic cooperative games," (with James P. Kahan). In S. Brams, A. Schotter, and G. Schwödiauer (Eds.), *Applied game theory*, 1979, pp. 74-94. Würzburg-Wien: Physica-Verlag. Copyright.

"Coalition formation in the triad when two are weak and one is strong," (with James P. Kahan), *Mathematical Social Sciences*, 1980, 1: 11-38. Copyright.

"The power of a coalition and payoff disbursement in three-person negotiable conflicts," (with James P. Kahan). *Journal of Mathematical Sociology*, 1982, 8: 193-225. Copyright.

"Coalition formation in a five-person market game," (with James P. Kahan). *Management Science*, 1984, 30: 326-343. Copyright.

"Relative gain maximization in sequential 3-person characteristic function games," (with Rami Zwick). *Journal of Mathematical Psychology*, 1985, 29: 333-359. Copyright.

"Comparison of theories for payoff disbursement of coalition values," *Theory and Decision*, 1987, 22: 13-47. Copyright.

"Assessment of political power in the Israeli Knesset," (with Esther Golan). *American Political Science Review*, 1985, 79: 673-692. Copyright.

"Dominated, connected, and tight coalitions in the Israeli Knesset," (with Eythan Weg). *American Journal of Political Science*, 1986, 30: 577-596. Copyright.

# INTRODUCTION

This book is about the interplay of theory and experimentation on group decision making in economics. The theories that the book subjects to experimental testing mostly come from the theory of games. The decisions investigated in the book mostly concern economic interaction like strict competition, two-person bargaining, and coalition formation. The underlying philosophy of the articles collected in this book is consistent with the opinion of a growing number of economists and psychologists that economic issues cannot be understood fully just by thinking about them. Rather, the interplay between theory and experimentation is critical for the development of economics as an observational science (Smith, 1989).

Reports of laboratory experiments in decision making and economics date back more than thirty years (e.g., Allais, 1953; Davidson, Suppes, and Siegel, 1957; Flood, 1958; Friedman, 1963; Kalisch, Milnor, Nash, and Nering, 1954; Lieberman, 1960; Mosteller and Nogee, 1951; Rapoport, Chammah, Dwyer, and Gyr, 1962; Siegel and Fouraker, 1960; Stone, 1958). However, only in the last ten or fifteen years has laboratory experimentation in economics started its steady transformation from an occasional curiosity into a regular means for investigating various economic phenomena and examining the role of economic institutions. Groups of researchers in the USA and abroad have used experimental methods with increasing sophistication to attack economic problems that arise in individual decision making under risk, two-person bargaining, public goods provision, public choice, welfare economics, auctions, and markets. For excellent reviews and critical discussions of this rapidly growing body of literature, see Binmore (1987), Plott (1979, 1982, 1986), Roth (1987, 1989), and Smith (1976, 1982, 1989).

The history of experimentation in psychology is rich and old. It would have been quite natural and highly desirable for psychologists to extend their scope of research and assume a major role in the study of economic decision behavior. Psychology professes to be the general study of human behavior. Most psychologists are trained to regard their discipline as an observational science; they do not have to overcome the conditioning of many economists who think of economics as an *a priori* science. Psychologists' knowledge of experimental techniques is comprehensive, and their experience in conducting experiments, analyzing data, and discovering empirical regularities exceeds that of most economists. However, with the exception of research on individual choice behavior — where psychologists like Tversky, Kahneman, and Slovic have played a major role — psychologists have not contributed in any significant way to the growing research in experimental economics. Social psychologists for whom interactive behavior is the core of their discipline, have virtually abandoned the study of economic decisions in small groups to their colleagues in economics and related disciplines.

There are several reasons why psychologists have not taken a leading role in experimental research on economic behavior. Progress can only be made as a result of close and often intricate interplay between theory and experimentation. However, most psychological theories of interactive behavior do not have the rigor and precision of economic theories. Consequently, they are often unsuitable for generating testable hypotheses of substance and driving a systematic and comprehensive line of research. In addition, psychological theories are in general unsympathetic to the optimizing hypothesis and the notion of equilibrium that plays such a major role in economic theory. Finally, and perhaps most importantly, psychologists typically do not know economics, do not study much mathematics beyond calculus, linear algebra, and elementary probability theory, and do not understand economic theory very well (Binmore, 1987).

My attempt to partly correct this situation has influenced the style and content of most of the papers collected in the present volume. Although the papers should appeal to experimental economists, decision theorists, political economists, and other social scientists, they were originally written for psychologists who recognize that the interplay of formal theory and laboratory experimentation is critical for the understanding of interactive behavior and advancing their own discipline. Although I make the common assumptions about the reader's knowledge of experimental design and statistical methodology, no previous knowledge of game theory is assumed. Within the space constraints imposed by most of the journals, I have attempted to present and explain many of the basic concepts and some of the models of game theory in considerable detail.

The volume contains seventeen papers I published in the period 1967-1989. I have arranged them into three broad topics. The papers deal with issues ranging from interactive behavior in iterated mixed-motive conflicts to the formation of coalitions in parliamentary systems. However, there is a common intellectual thread going through all of them. They are all part of an on-going attempt to apply the experimental method to test the descriptive power of game theory and to build a theory of interactive behavior.

## SECTION A

The first two chapters deal with the two-person iterated Prisoner's Dilemma game. Chapter 1 presents a model that attempts to resolve the dilemma by structuring the iterated game as a supergame composed of several subgames that differ from one another in the probabilities each player assigns to the next decision of his or her opponent. Essentially, the game is then modeled as a Markov decision process. Maximization of subjective expected utility may lead to either cooperation or defection. Chapter 2 presents an experimental paradigm for studying interactive behavior in a class of noncooperative interdependent mixed-motive conflicts. It presents experimental data, and then tests a model that extends the decision model developed in Chapter 1.

In a recent survey of game theory, Aumann has argued that "...strictly competitive games constitute one of the few areas in game theory, and indeed in social science, where a fairly sharp, unique 'prediction' is made (though even this prediction is in general probabilistic). It thus invites experimental testing" (1987, p. 462). Chapters 3 through 5 constitute early attempts to meet this challenge. The three chapters are concerned with a class of strictly competitive games, called games of timing, where the problem facing each of the two players is not what action to take, but rather when to take it. All three chapters use the Western duel as their experimental paradigm. Chapter 3 reports data from a sequence of computer-controlled duels with complete information ("noisy duels"); Chapter 4 reports data from a sequence of computer-controlled duels with incomplete information ("silent duels"); and Chapter 5 is concerned with a class of probabilistic duels (both noisy or silent), where a duelist does not know whether his or her opponent is armed, but only knows the probability of such armament. All three chapters test the game theoretical prediction for these classes of duels, and report varying degrees of support.

The last chapter in Section A reports experimental data from two-person bargaining where 1) bargaining takes place in discrete time, 2) bargaining is governed by specific rules, and 3) the preferences of the bargainers regarding the value of the commodity at stake (the "pie") are a function of time. The paper studies the case of equal or unequal fixed bargaining costs when the horizon is infinite. Competitive tests of the subgame perfect equilibrium model and two alternative models incorporating notions of equality and equity provide qualified support for the former model.

## SECTION B

The nine chapters composing Section B address situations of partial conflict of interest that share the following aspects:   1) there are three or more players;   2) communication is allowed and binding agreements are enforceable; and 3) players form coalitions by freely negotiating agreements on how to disburse the gains resulting from the coalition members' joint coordinated efforts.   These situations are modelled as characteristic function games with sidepayments.   These chapters share the goal of exploring several solution concepts proposed for this class of cooperative games, and in particular of examining the psychological premises that underlie the various models.   The experimental results reported in Chapters 8-13 have been summarized and critically discussed in my 1984 book with Jim Kahan, *Theories of Coalition Formation*.   However, that summary focused only on model testing, omitting many important results concerning the bargaining and coalition formation process.

All the experiments in Section B were computer-controlled.   Chapter 7 describes the vocabulary of the computer program and its mode of operation, and presents a protocol from a sample four-person game.   The next two chapters present the first two experiments that were conducted under a simplified version of the computer program. Chapter 8 describes experiments on three-person games where only two-person coalitions are allowed.   Chapter 9 describes experiments on four- and five-person apex games where only two-person coalitions including a distinct player called the Apex, and the single coalition of all the players excluding the Apex player are allowed to form.   Both studies provide strong support for the bargaining set theory.

The next three chapters examine characteristic function games where the bargaining set theory no longer accounts for the results.   A new solution concept is introduced and tested, no longer assuming that the characteristic function representation adequately portrays the players' perceptions of the power of coalitions.   Instead the theory of the power bargaining set employs assumptions about the psychology of the players to derive a representation of the power of coalitions in the game.   Chapter 10 presents data from several four-person games with a monopolist, some allow for the formation of the grand coalition, some do not.   Chapter 11 reports the results from a sequence of superadditive three-person games in which two of the players are relatively weak and one is considerably stronger. Chapter 12 develops the $\alpha$-power model further and tests it successfully with data from nine different studies.

Chapter 13 extends the investigation of coalition formation to characteristic function games in which several coalitions may form simultaneously. It uses market games that arise from trading economies in which the participants are intially supplied with a number of commodities which they can trade among themselves without any restrictions. When the game terminates, the value of each coalition is the worth of the combination of commodities it holds. The investigation is extended in yet another direction in Chapter 14, which examines coalition forming behavior in sequential three-person games in which each player seeks to maximize the rank of his or her total score in a sequence of interdependent characteristic function games with sidepayments. Both of these chapters point to the need to extend the models by specifically incorporating sequential coalition building.

The problem of competitively testing one model against another is a thorny one because some models make point predictions, some make line predictions, and others make area predictions. Chapter 15 describes a first attempt to construct a test procedure for model comparison, which offsets the advantage that the less specific model has over a more specific competitor and provides a measure of error which is intuitively satisfactory.

## SECTION C

The last two chapters are concerned with an extensive investigation of the tenth Israeli parliament (Knesset). Chapter 16 reports data from students, parliamentary correspondents, and Knesset members, who were asked individually to assess the political power ratios of the parties represented in the tenth Knesset, and to judge the ideological proximity between them. Analysis of the power ratio judgments gave rise to individual scales of perceived political power, and analysis of the proximity data yielded individual representations of the parties in a politically interpretable multidimensional Euclidean space. The derived measures were then used to test competitively six indices of voting power: three indices due to Shapley-Shubik, Banzhaf, and Deegan-Packel, that only take into consideration the seat distribution, and three nonsymmetric generalizations of these indices that, in addition, incorporate information about ideological similarities between the parties.

The ideological proximity data from Chapter 16 are then used in Chapter 17 to test a model of coalition formation in parliamentary systems. The model combines two criteria for predicting the coalitions that form in parliamentary systems in which a single party is given a mandate to form a coalition. One criterion — the formation of dominated coalitions — is based solely on the structural properties of the coalition game, whereas the other criterion — the formation of connected coalitions — is based on the ideological constraints imposed on the coalition game as reflected by the desire to form ideologically compatible coalitions.

# REFERENCES

Allais, M.    "Le comportement de l'homme rationnel devant le risque: critique des postulates et axiomes de l'ecole americane." *Econometrica*, **21**, 503-546. (1953)

Aumann, R. J.    "Game Theory."    In T. Eatwell, M. Milgate, and P. Newman (Eds.), *The new palgrave: A dictionary of economics*.    London: Macmillan, pp. 460-482.    (1987)

Binmore, K.    "Experimental Economics."    *European Economic Review*, **31**, 257-264.    (1987)

Davidson, D., P. Suppes, and S. Siegel.    *Decision-making: An experimental approach*. Stanford: Stanford University Press.    (1957)

Flood, M. M.    "Some experimental games."    *Management Science*, **5**, 5-26.    (1958)

Friedman, J. W.    "Individual behavior in oligopolistic markets: An experimental study." *Yale Economic Essays*. **3**, 359-417.    (1963)

Kahan, J. P. and A. Rapoport.    *Theories of coalition formation*.    Hillsdale, NJ: L. Erlbaum.    (1984)

Kalisch, G. K., J. W. Milnor, J. F. Nash, and E. D. Nering.    "Some experimental n-person games."    In R. M. Thrall, C. M. Coombs, and R. S. Davis (Eds.), *Decision processes*.    New York: Wiley, pp. 301-327.    (1954)

Lieberman, B.    "Human Behavior in strictly determined 3 × 3 matrix game."    *Behavioral Science*, **5**, 317-322.    (1960)

Mosteller, F. and P. Nogee.    "An experimental measurement of utility."    *Journal of Political Economy*, **59**, 371-404.    (1951)

Plott, C. R.    "The application of laboratory experimental methods to public choice."    In C. R. Russell (Ed.), *Collective decision making*.    Washington: Resources for the future, pp. 137-160.    (1979)

Plott, C. R.    "Industrial organization theory and experimental economics."    *Journal of Economic Literature*, **20**, 1485-1527.    (1982)

Plott, C. R.    "Laboratory experiments in economics: The implications of posted-price institutions."    *Science*, **232**, 732-738.    (1986)

Rapoport, A., A. Chammah, J. Dwyer, and J. Gyr.    "Three-person non-zero-sum non-negotiable games."    *Behavioral Science*, **7**, 38-58.    (1962)

Roth, A. E. "Laboratory experimentation in economics." In T. Bewley (Ed.), *Advances in economic theory, fifth world congress*. Cambridge: Cambridge University Press, pp. 269-299. (1987)

Roth, A. E. "Laboratory experimentation in economics: A methodological overview." *The Economic Journal*, **98**, 978-1031. (1989)

Siegel, S. and L. E. Fouraker. *Bargaining and group decision making: Experiments in bilateral monopoly*. New York: McGraw-Hill. (1960)

Smith, V. L. "Bidding and auctioning institutions: Experimental results." In Y. Amihud (Ed.), *Bidding and auctioning for procurement and allocation*. New York: New York University Press, pp. 43-64. (1976)

Smith, V. L. "Microeconomic systems as an experimental science." *American Economic Review*, **72**, 923-955. (1982)

Smith, V. L. "Theory, experiment and economics." *Journal of Economic Perspectives*, **3**, 151-169. (1989)

Stone, J. J. "An experiment in bargaining games." *Econometrica*, **26**, 286-297. (1958)

# CHAPTER 1

# OPTIMAL POLICIES FOR THE PRISONER'S DILEMMA

**ABSTRACT.** An optimal model for the Prisoner's Dilemma game is suggested. The model is normative in the sense that given few assumptions about the way the game is perceived by the players, an optimal policy is prescribed to each player maximizing his long-run expected gain. The dilemma is "resolved" by restructuring the game as a supergame composed of several component games such that transitions among them are possible. Dynamic programming is used to derive the optimal policy.

It has been almost a decade since Luce and Raiffa (1957) presented social scientists with the game known as the Prisoner's Dilemma (PD), which until then had received considerable attention from game theorists only. The game is classified as a two-person non-zero-sum noncooperative game, where "noncooperative" indicates that no preplay communication is permitted between the players. The PD game is better known to psychologists as a "mixed-motive" game in which each player must choose between alternatives which are assumed to serve different motives. In the typical PD game two alternatives are available to each player: whether to cooperate, so as to increase total gain of both players, or to compete, so as to increase his own gain at the expense of the other player. Thus, the confrontation is not only between the two conflicting players but also between the conflicting motives within each player (Rapoport & Chammah, 1965).

The general form of the game is represented by the payoff matrix given in Table 1 (Scodel, Minas, Ratoosh, & Lipetz, 1959). There are two players, A and B. Each must choose between C (for cooperation) and D (for defection) on every trial. (To simplify the notation, C and D are not subscripted. Joint decisions are indicated by CC, CD, DC, or DD, where the first letter indicates A's decision.) There are four entries in the payoff matrix. By convention, the first of the payoffs in each entry is that accruing to the row player, A. The payoff matrix is subject to the following rules:

1. $2\lambda_1 > \lambda_2 + \lambda_3$
2. $\lambda_3 > \lambda_1 > \lambda_4 > \lambda_2$

*Table 1. Payoff matrix for PD*

| Player A | Player B | |
|:---:|:---:|:---:|
| | C | D |
| C | $\lambda_1, \lambda_1$ | $\lambda_2, \lambda_3$ |
| D | $\lambda_3, \lambda_2$ | $\lambda_4, \lambda_4$ |

The first rule is introduced to prevent the possibility of more than the one form of tacit collusion - tacit agreement to play CC. If the inequality in the first rule is reversed another form of tacit collusion is possible, namely, an alternation between CD and DC (assuming that the game is repeated). The second rule is introduced to motivate each player to play noncooperatively.

In PD games D dominates C in the game theoretic sense. However, the joint choice DD results in a payoff $(\lambda_4)$ to each player which is smaller than the payoff $(\lambda_1)$ associated with CC; hence the dilemma. For a detailed description of the game see Luce and Raiffa (1957), and Rapoport and Chammah (1965). Reviews of experimental studies of PD are given in Rapoport and Orwant (1962), and Gallo and McClintock (1965).

The dilemma presented by the PD game becomes conceptually challenging when one realizes the difficulty in prescribing rational criteria to resolve it. When rationality is discussed in the context of PD games, a distinction should be made between one play of PD and a sequence of repetitions of the game. When the game is played just once a rational criterion based on the dominance principle is rather compelling. Its acceptance seems almost unavoidable, in spite of the slight feelings of uneasiness caused by noticing that so-called irrational players will both fare better than so-called rational players (Luce & Raiffa, 1957).

The "dominance" argument is considerably weakened when PD is played many times, whether or not the duration of the game is known. It is commonly agreed that a nonambivalent normative prescription of strategy choice is not possible, and that "even consistent strategy choices cannot be explained by rationality or nonrationality of the players [Rapoport & Orwant, 1962, p. 5]." This conclusion has been accepted by most of the investigators who have studied human decisions in PD games. No effort has been made to compare the observed percentage of cooperative responses, much less more refined statistics, to theoretical predictions derived from "normative" models. Most of the models suggested to "explain" the players' decisions in a repeated play of PD (Rapoport & Chammah, 1965; Suppes & Atkinson, 1960) have been descriptive. An important exception is given by the class of second-order classical dynamic models investigated by Rapoport and Chammah (1965, Ch. 10).

It is this general acceptance of the impossibility of prescribing "rational" behavior when PD is played many times in succession that this paper will try to challenge. Without trying to explicate the notion of rationality the author will present a "normative" model for a repeated play of PD. The model is normative in the sense that given some rather weak (it is believed) assumptions about the way the players should perceive their task in a repeated play of PD, an optimal policy is prescribed to each player maximizing his long-run expected gain. Furthermore, we suspect that the suggested way of perceiving the game may not be far away from the player's actual perception of it. Consequently, the model may be tested experimentally and serve as a base line for constructing descriptive models for a repeated play of PD and related interactive processes. It is not expected that the present model will be experimentally corroborated. It is hoped, however, that experimental tests of the model, which will be undertaken in the future, may reveal some constraints on human ability to process information and make decisions. Incorporating these constraints, the investigator will be able to construct another model, a constrained optimal model, which may adequately describe the player's behavior.

The proposed model is not specific to the PD game, but can be generalized to other two-person games played many times in succession. As our main interest is in mixed-motive games, the PD paradigm will be maintained in the exposition of the model. As is shown below, the model is based upon the assumption underlying most of the theories for individual decision-making under uncertainty - the maximization of subjective expected utility. A repeated play of PD is viewed as a supergame composed of several component games, the number of which is not fixed but depends on the amount of information a player considers before making his decision. A component game is determined by the joint choices of the players in the previous trials. The component games differ from one another not in the terms of the payoff matrices defining them, which are the same, but in terms of the player's expectations, stated as subjective probabilities, concerning the other player's decision in every component game.

Thus, instead of playing the same game repeatedly, the players are assumed to play a sequence of different component games, moving from one component game to another and accumulating rewards. The sequential joint decisions of both players constitute a Markovian decision process (Howard, 1960), where transitions from one state (component game) to another generate rewards (the payoffs for each player), and future gains or losses are explicitly considered by each player. Dynamic programming (Bellman, 1957a, 1961) is used to resolve the dilemma by determining an optimal policy for each player, specifying a unique decision to be made in every component game, and maximizing each player's long-run subjective expected gain. Before proceeding with this task the basic characteristics of Markovian decision processes are presented.

## Markovian Decision Processes

Markovian decision processes or Markov processes with rewards have been studied by Bellman (1957b), Bellman and Dreyfus (1962), and Howard (1960). To see what is meant by a discrete-time finite-state Markov process consider a system which at any particular time is in State $i$, $i = 1, 2, ..., N$, where $N$ is finite. The system changes from one state to another. The changes occur at discrete times $t = 0, 1, ...,$ (also called trials), and are governed by a transition probability matrix

$$P = [p_{ij}], \text{ with } 0 \leq p_{ij} \leq 1, \text{ and } \sum_{j=1}^{N} p_{ij} = 1.$$

$p_{ij}$ indicates the transition probability from State $i$ at Time $t$ to State $j$ at Time $t + 1$. As $P$ is assumed to be independent of time an index $t$ is not needed. It is further assumed that the Markov chain is ergodic, that is, every state can be reached from every other state in a finite number of trials. It is not difficult to show that the probabilities that the system is in State $i$ at Time $t$ converge to a limiting state probability distribution as $t \to \infty$, and that this distribution is independent of the initial starting conditions. If $\pi$ is the row vector of limiting state probabilities, $\pi = (\pi_1, \pi_2, ... \pi_N)$, then $\pi P = \pi$.

Supposing the Markov process is extended to more general situations, where a "reward" matrix $R = [r_{ij}]$ is associated with the transitions from one state to another. Assume further that the $r_{ij}$ as well as the $p_{ij}$ are functions only of $i$ and $j$ and not of any history of the system. The $r_{ij}$ are thus random variables with a probability distribution governed by the transition probabilities. As the process makes transitions among the states a sequence of rewards is generated.

Suppose further that while in State $i$ one of $K$ decisions must be made in order for a transition to take place. $K$ is assumed to be finite and constant for each state. The problem to be solved is that of prescribing a sequence of decisions which will maximize the (average) expected reward obtained from an $M$-trial process, given the initial state of the system. $M$ may or may not be finite. Hereafter we shall indicate a decision by a superscript $k$, $k = 1, 2, ..., K$. Thus $p_{ij}{}^k$ indicates the transition probability from State $i$ to $j$ when Decision $k_i$ is made in State $i$. Similarly, $r_{ij}{}^k$ indicates the reward obtained when the system changes from State $i$ to $j$ after Decision $k_i$ has been made. $P$ and $R$ are redefined by $P = [p_{ij}{}^k]$, $R = [r_{ij}{}^k]$.

We define a policy as an ordered $N$-tuple $(k_1, k_2, ..., k_N)$. Bellman (1957b) has proven that average expected reward is maximized when a particular policy is used repeatedly. Thus, instead of looking for a sequence of decisions we look for a particular policy maximizing expected average reward. We refer to this policy as the optimal policy.

THE OPTIMAL POLICY

An iterative technique for getting the optimal policy for a Markov process with rewards has been given by Howard (1960). Define $V_i(M)$ as the expected total reward in the next $M$ trials from a process starting in State $i$ using a fixed policy. By the "Principle of Optimality" of dynamic programming (Bellman, 1957a), $V_i(M)$ satisfies the recurrence relation

$$V_i(M) = \sum_{j=1}^{N} p_{ij}[r_{ij} + V_j(M - 1)]$$

$$= q_i + \sum_{j=1}^{N} p_{ij}V_j(M - 1), \tag{1}$$

where $q_i = \sum\limits_{j=1}^{N} p_{ij}r_{ij}$ is the expected *immediate* reward for State $i$. Note that there is no need for superscript $k$ to appear in Equation 1 because the use of a fixed policy has defined the probability matrix and the reward matrix for this policy (both are square matrices of order $N$, and are submatrices of $P$ and $R$ respectively).

For large $M$ (see Howard, 1960, Ch. 2)

$$V_i(M) = V_i + Mg,$$ (2)

where $g$ is defined by

$$g = \sum_{i=1}^{N} \pi_i q_i.$$ (3)

Equation 2 asserts that the expected reward will be composed of two parts, a transient part $V_i$ which depends only on the starting state, and a steady-state part, $Mg$, resulting from the behavior of the process as $M \to \infty$. $g$, the (average) expected gain of the system for a particular policy, is equal to the sum of expected immediate rewards resulting from this policy weighted by the corresponding limiting state probabilities. Substituting Equation 2 in Equation 1 yields

$$V_i + Mg = q_i + \sum_{j=1}^{N} p_{ij} V_j (M - 1)$$

$$= q_i + \sum_{j=1}^{N} p_{ij}[V_j + (M - 1)g].$$ (4)

As $\sum_{j=1}^{N} p_{ij} = 1$, Equation 4 simplifies to

$$g = q_i + \sum_{j=1}^{N} p_{ij} V_j - V_i,$$ (5)

a set of $N$ linear simultaneous equations in $N + 1$ unknowns (the $N$ $V_i$'s and $g$). As only the relative value of $V_i$ and not its absolute value is important, Equation 5 can be solved by setting arbitrarily $V_N = 0$.

The following iteration cycle is then provided:

1. The value-determination operation. Use $p_{ij}$ and $q_i$ for a given policy to solve Equation 5 for all relative values of $V_i$ and $g$ by setting $V_N = 0$.

2. The policy-iteration routine. For each State $i$ find the Decision $k'$ that

maximizes $q_i{}^k + \sum\limits_{j=1}^{N} p_{ij}{}^k V_j$, using the relative values $V_i$ of the value–determination

operation.    Then $k'$ becomes the new decision in State $i$, $q_i{}^{k'}$ becomes $q_i$, and $p_{ij}{}^{k'}$
becomes $p_{ij}$.    Howard (1960) has proved that each iteration of this cycle leads to a
policy of higher, or at least as large, expected gain.   Furthermore, this cycle will lead to
the optimal policy.

In many dynamic decision tasks (Rapoport, 1966), particularly in situations where
economic or military decisions are made, future expected cost or gain is discounted.
Discounting can be explicitly considered in the analysis of Markovian decision processes.
A quantity $\beta$, $0 \leq \beta < 1$, is defined as the value at the beginning of a transition interval
of a unit sum received at the end of the interval, and an iteration cycle for getting the
optimal policy, given $\beta$, is provided (Howard, 1960).    Typically, $\beta$ is interpreted as the
reciprocal of 1 plus the interest rate that is applicable to the time interval required for a
transition.    When discounting cannot be meaningfully assumed, $\beta$ can be interpreted in
terms of the uncertainty concerning the duration of the process.    Let $\beta$ be defined as the
probability that the process will continue to yield rewards after the next transition.
Then $1 - \beta$ is the probability that the process will stop at its present state.

The optimal policy may also be obtained by solving Equation 3 for each feasible
policy.    Once a policy is determined its limiting state probability distribution can be
obtained by standard techniques (typically, by getting powers of its corresponding $N \times N$
transition probability matrix) and when multiplied by the corresponding expected
immediate reward it will yield the (average) expected gain for this policy.    All expected
gains for all the feasible policies may be calculated in this way.    The optimal policy is
that policy yielding the highest expected gain.    The difficulty with this technique is that
it becomes impractical when the number of states or decisions in each state is large, as
the number of feasible policies is generally given by $K^N$.

## PD as a Markovian Decision Process

If Player A were to maximize his expected *immediate* reward when PD is played
repeatedly, then his decision should always be D.    If A does not think that his decision
together with B's decision on Trial $t - u$, $u = 1, 2, ..., t - 1$, could have any effect on
what B might do on Trial $t$ then again A should play D repeatedly.    To put it
differently, if A does not believe in the possibility of tacit communication with B, and if
he does not believe that by his decision at Time $t - u$ he can transmit information to B,
which will in turn effect B's decision at Time $t$, there is nothing left to him but to play
D.    When a sequence of PD trials is regarded as a sequence of independent joint
decisions, the rational decision to make is D.

The reason that PD is an intriguing game to the players (not to mention social
scientists), and a meaningful paradigm for a variety of actual social and political
phenomena is exactly because the players realize that tacit collusion is possible.    The
players can try to "teach" each other or let themselves "be taught" as information about
their strategies and personalities is transmitted via their decisions.    The important thing

to note is that each player believes that his decision at Time $t - u$ can partly effect what will happen at Time $t$.    The repeated trials are not regarded as independent. Learning takes place and, in addition, each player can partly control the learning of the other player.    To play the game intelligently, each player should consider the effect of his present decision on the future decisions made both by himself and by his adversary. It is unreasonable to assume that A believes that his decision at Time $t - u$ is going to determine uniquely what B will do on Trial $t$ or $t + u$.    It is not unreasonable, however, to assume that A believes that his present decision may partly determine future decisions of B.

It is questionable how far ahead each player can look while making his decision. As changes in B's decisions are likely to take place it might be difficult, time-consuming, and hence unwise of A to get involved in complicated considerations trying to evaluate the effect of his decision together with B's decision at Time $t - u$ on B's decision at Time $t$ or $t + u$, for even a moderate value of $u$.    It seems only natural to start the analysis by assuming that A is only considering the effect of his decision together with B's decision at Time $t - u$ on B's decision at Time $t$.    This assumption is even more justified when data from experimental studies of PD are analyzed, as the time intervals between successive trials typically are not more than a few seconds, and do not permit A to become involved in long considerations.

STATE-CONDITIONED PROPENSITIES

Define the following (state-conditioned) propensities (Rapoport, 1964) for Player B:

$$x_B^1(t) = P(C_t | CC_{t-1}),$$

$$x_B^2(t) = P(C_t | CC_{t-1}, CC_{t-2}),$$

and in general,

$$x_B^u(t) = P(C_t | CC_{t-1}, CC_{t-2}, ..., CC_{t-u}), \quad u = 1, 2, ..., t - 1.$$

Similarly,

$$y_B^u(t) = P(C_t | CD_{t-1}, CD_{t-2}, ..., CD_{t-u}),$$

$$z_B^u(t) = P(C_t | DC_{t-1}, DC_{t-2}, ..., DC_{t-u}),$$

$$w_B^u(t) = P(C_t | DD_{t-1}, DD_{t-2}, ..., DD_{t-u}).$$

$x_B^1(t)$ is the probability that B will choose cooperatively at Time $t$, following a cooperative and rewarded decision at Time $t - 1$ (following CC at Time $t - 1$).    $x_B^u(t)$ is the probability that B will choose cooperatively at Time $t$, following a run of $u$ cooperative and rewarded decisions.    $y_B^u(t)$ is the probability that B will choose cooperatively following a run of $u$ noncooperative and rewarded decisions.    $z_B^u(t)$ and

$w_B{}^u(t)$ are defined in a similar way. The propensities for A are defined analogously, with the roles of A and B reversed.

Note that $x^u(t)$ and $w^u(t)$ are defined similarly for players A and B. However, $y^u(t)$ and $z^u(t)$ are reversed. $y_A{}^u(t)$ is the probability that A will choose cooperatively following a run of $u$ cooperative and nonrewarded decisions, while $z_A{}^u(t)$ is the probability that A will choose cooperatively following a run of $u$ noncooperative and rewarded decisions.

We assume that the propensities are independent of time for both players and suppress the time index. This assumption will be questioned later.

Let us further define $\hat{x}^u$, $\hat{y}^u$, $\hat{z}^u$, and $\hat{w}^u$ as A's estimates of $x_B{}^u$, $y_B{}^u$, $z_B{}^u$, and $w_B{}^u$, respectively. As only A's decisions are going to be discussed, the estimates $\hat{x}^u$, $\hat{y}^u$, $\hat{z}^u$, and $\hat{w}^u$ are not subscripted. They are also assumed to be independent of time. Thus, $\hat{x}^u$ is A's subjective probability that B will choose cooperatively following a run of $u$ CCs. $\hat{y}^u$ is A's subjective probability that B will choose cooperatively following a run of u CDs. $\hat{z}^u$ and $\hat{w}^u$ are defined similarly. $\hat{x}^u$, $\hat{y}^u$, $\hat{z}^u$, and $\hat{w}^u$ will be referred to as A's subjective probabilities (SPs). They are assumed to satisfy the regular axioms of probability theory. The SPs reflect what A thinks that B will do at Time $t$ after a run of the same $u$ joint decisions terminating at Time $t - 1$. It is assumed that A believes that B has a policy in the sense discussed below. Thus A's SPs reflect A's uncertainty with regard to B's policy. All the information gathered by A about B, including the effect of A's past decisions on B's policy, is assumed to be summarized by A's SPs.

PD AS A SUPERGAME

We assume that A considers a PD game played repeatedly as a supergame composed of $h$ (component) games $\Gamma_1$, $\Gamma_2$, ..., $\Gamma_h$. To simplify the presentation we assume $h = 4$ (this assumption will be relaxed later). The four component games are presented in Table 2. The meaning of the entries will become apparent shortly. Suppose that at Time $t$ component game $\Gamma_1$ is played, with the players making simultaneous decisions. Suppose the joint choice of the players is CD, then the resulting payoff $(\lambda_2, \lambda_3, \Gamma_2)$ means that A receives $\lambda_2$ units, B receives $\lambda_3$ units ($\lambda_2$ or $\lambda_3$ may, of course, be negative) and the next component game to be played at Time $t + 1$ is $\Gamma_2$. When $\Gamma_2$ is played, each player can choose again between C and D. Suppose the joint choice of the players at Time $t + 1$ is DD, then the resulting payoff $(\lambda_4, \lambda_4, \Gamma_4)$ means that each player receives $\lambda_4$ units, and the component game to be played at Time $t + 2$ is $\Gamma_4$.

The four component games have the same payoffs in their entries. They differ only with respect to the (first-order) SPs, $\hat{x}^1$, $\hat{y}^1$, $\hat{z}^1$, and $\hat{w}^1$. To understand the role of the SPs suppose that at Time $t$ $\Gamma_1$ is played. Player A knows that by playing C he will either receive $\lambda_1$ and "stay" in $\Gamma_1$ with (subjective) probability $\hat{x}^1$, or with (subjective) probability $1 - \hat{x}^1$ he will receive $\lambda_2$ and "move" to $\Gamma_2$. To maximize his (average) subjective expected gain, A has to somehow weight his expected immediate reward and the future consequences of his decision, where these consequences are controlled both by himself (through the selection of a policy) and by Player B (through the SPs). To give a simple example, supposing that $\hat{x}^1 = 1$, and $\hat{y}^1 = \hat{z}^1 = \hat{w}^1 = 0$. It seems reasonable to expect A to play C repeatedly in component game $\Gamma_1$. For suppose A plays D, then he may expect to get $\lambda_3$, the highest possible payoff, and to get "trapped" in component games $\Gamma_2$, $\Gamma_3$, and $\Gamma_4$, which will yield him either $\lambda_2$ or $\lambda_4$ repeatedly. On the other hand, by playing C, A expects to be "trapped" in component game $\Gamma_1$ with SP equal to one. As component game $\Gamma_1$ will yield him $\lambda_1$ repeatedly, and as $\lambda_1 > \lambda_4 > \lambda_2$, C should be preferred on D.

*Table 2. Payoff matrices for PD composed of four component games*

| | | Game $\Gamma_1{}^a$ | | | | Game $\Gamma_3{}^c$ | |
|---|---|---|---|---|---|---|---|
| | A | | B | | A | | B |
| | | C | D | | | C | D |
| C | | $\lambda_1$, $\lambda_1$, $\Gamma_1$ | $\lambda_2$, $\lambda_3$, $\Gamma_2$ | C | | $\lambda_1$, $\lambda_1$, $\Gamma_1$ | $\lambda_2$, $\lambda_3$, $\Gamma_2$ |
| D | | $\lambda_3$, $\lambda_2$, $\Gamma_3$ | $\lambda_4$, $\lambda_4$, $\Gamma_4$ | D | | $\lambda_3$, $\lambda_2$, $\Gamma_3$ | $\lambda_4$, $\lambda_4$, $\Gamma_4$ |
| | | Game $\Gamma_2{}^b$ | | | | Game $\Gamma_4{}^d$ | |
| | A | | B | | A | | B |
| | | C | D | | | C | D |
| C | | $\lambda_1$, $\lambda_1$, $\Gamma_1$ | $\lambda_2$, $\lambda_3$, $\Gamma_2$ | C | | $\lambda_1$, $\lambda_1$, $\Gamma_1$ | $\lambda_2$, $\lambda_3$, $\Gamma_2$ |
| D | | $\lambda_3$, $\lambda_2$, $\Gamma_3$ | $\lambda_4$, $\lambda_4$, $\Gamma_4$ | D | | $\lambda_3$, $\lambda_2$, $\Gamma_3$ | $\lambda_4$, $\lambda_4$, $\Gamma_4$ |

[a] $P(C) = \hat{x}^1$;  $P(D) = 1 - \hat{x}^1$.
[b] $P(C) = \hat{y}^1$;  $P(D) = 1 - \hat{y}^1$.
[c] $P(C) = \hat{z}^1$;  $P(D) = 1 - \hat{z}^1$.
[d] $P(C) = \hat{w}^1$;  $P(D) = 1 - \hat{w}^1$.

When PD is viewed as a supergame composed of four component games, the repeated joint choices constitute a Markov process with rewards. The (subjective) transition probability matrix and the reward matrix for Player A, $\hat{P}$, and $R$, respectively, can be constructed. They are presented in Table 3. For example, if $\Gamma_3$ is played, A's SPs are $\hat{z}^1$ and $1 - \hat{z}^1$ that decision C will move him to $\Gamma_1$ and $\Gamma_2$, respectively, with corresponding rewards $\lambda_1$ and $\lambda_2$. If he plays D, his SPs of staying in $\Gamma_2$ or moving to $\Gamma_4$ are $\hat{z}^1$ and $1 - \hat{z}^1$, respectively, with the respective rewards $\lambda_3$ and $\lambda_4$. The dashes in matrix $R$ indicate that the rewards for some transitions are not defined. It is seen from matrix $\hat{P}$ that the subjective probabilities of these transitions are zero.

*Table 3.    Transition and reward matrices for PD composed of four component games*

| $t - 1$ | | | $t$ | |
|---|---|---|---|---|
| Decision | $\Gamma_1$ | $\Gamma_2$ | $\Gamma_3$ | $\Gamma_4$ |
| Matrix $\hat{P}$ | | | | |
| Game $\Gamma_1$ | | | | |
| C | $\hat{x}^1$ | $1 - \hat{x}^1$ | 0 | 0 |
| D | 0 | 0 | $\hat{x}^1$ | $1 - \hat{x}^1$ |
| Game $\Gamma_2$ | | | | |
| C | $\hat{y}^1$ | $1 - \hat{y}^1$ | 0 | 0 |
| D | 0 | 0 | $\hat{y}^1$ | $1 - \hat{y}^1$ |
| Game $\Gamma_3$ | | | | |
| C | $\hat{z}^1$ | $1 - \hat{z}^1$ | 0 | 0 |
| D | 0 | 0 | $\hat{z}^1$ | $1 - \hat{z}^1$ |
| Game $\Gamma_4$ | | | | |
| C | $\hat{w}^1$ | $1 - \hat{w}^1$ | 0 | 0 |
| D | 0 | 0 | $\hat{w}^1$ | $1 - \hat{w}^1$ |
| Matrix $R$ | | | | |
| Game $\Gamma_1$ | | | | |
| C | $\lambda_1$ | $\lambda_2$ | – | – |
| D | – | – | $\lambda_3$ | $\lambda_4$ |
| Game $\Gamma_2$ | | | | |
| C | $\lambda_1$ | $\lambda_2$ | – | – |
| D | – | – | $\lambda_3$ | $\lambda_4$ |
| Game $\Gamma_3$ | | | | |
| C | $\lambda_1$ | $\lambda_2$ | – | – |
| D | – | – | $\lambda_3$ | $\lambda_4$ |
| Game $\Gamma_4$ | | | | |
| C | $\lambda_1$ | $\lambda_2$ | – | – |
| D | – | – | $\lambda_3$ | $\lambda_4$ |

Table 4.    Feasible policies for PD and their corresponding expected gain for different payoffs and propensities

| Policies | Propensity and payoff conditions | | | |
|---|---|---|---|---|
| | (1) $\hat{x}^1 = .763,$ $\lambda_1 = 1$ | (2) $\hat{x}^1 = .950,$ $\lambda_1 = 1$ | (3) $\hat{x}^1 = .763,$ $\lambda_1 = 5$ | (4) $\hat{x} = .763,$ $\lambda_1 = 9$ |
| (C, C, -, -) | -4.310 | -0.809 | -2.240 | -0.171 |
| (C, D, C, C) | -3.135 | -0.727 | -1.643 | -0.151 |
| (C, D, C, D) | -2.040 | -0.525 | -0.977 | 0.086 |
| (C, D, D, C) | -2.749 | -0.851 | -1.653 | -0.557 |
| (D, C, C, C) | -3.685 | -2.745 | -2.764 | -1.844 |
| (D, C, C, D) | -3.000 | -2.610 | -2.230 | -1.460 |
| (D, C, D, C) | -2.864 | -3.784 | -2.547 | -1.930 |
| (D, D, C, C) | -2.602 | -1.967 | -1.960 | -1.318 |
| (D, D, C, D) | -1.506 | -1.159 | -1.079 | -0.651 |
| (D, D, D, C) | -2.152 | -1.184 | -1.823 | -1.493 |
| (-, -, D, D) | -0.638 | -0.638 | -0.638 | -0.638 |

The model assumes that PD is played many times and that the number of trials (decisions) is not disclosed to the players.  This assumption is met in many experimental studies of PD (Rapoport & Chammah, 1965; Rapoport & Mowshowitz, 1966).  To put it differently, the model assumes that PD does not have a termination point, or that it is not known to the players.  One advantage of this assumption is that it eliminates the multistage PD paradox (Luce & Raiffa, 1957, p. 95) due to backward induction from a known termination point.  For further advantages of using games of possible infinite length see Shubik (1963).

When PD is viewed as a Markovian decision process with an infinite duration it can be analyzed by the iteration procedure described in the preceding section. Alternatively, all feasible policies for Player A can be evaluated, and his optimal policy can be determined.  What is important to note is that the optimal policy will not necessarily prescribe playing only D in Game $\Gamma_i$.  It will depend on the particular values of $\lambda_i$ as well as on the values of $\hat{x}^1$, $\hat{y}^1$, $\hat{z}^1$, and $\hat{w}^1$.

When there are $N$ states in a Markovian decision process with $K$ decisions in each state, the number of feasible policies is $K^N$.  In the PD, $N = 4$ and $D = 2$.  However, not all 16 policies yield different (average) expected gains.  Actually, there are only 11 different policies.  To see this, denote a policy by an ordered 4-tuple, where each element indicates the decision to be made in one of the four component games. Thus (C,D,D,C) is a prescription to play C in $\Gamma_1$, D in $\Gamma_2$, D in $\Gamma_3$, and C in $\Gamma_4$. All policies starting with (C,C) will "trap" A in component games $\Gamma_1$ and $\Gamma_2$, and hence will yield the same (average) expected gain. There are four such policies: (C,C,C,C), (C,C,C,D), (C,C,D,C), and (C,C,D,D,). We denote all these policies by (C,C,-,-). Similarly, all policies ending with (D,D) will trap A in component games $\Gamma_3$ and $\Gamma_4$. There are four such policies yielding the same expected gain: (C,C,D,D), (C,D,D,D), (D,C,D,D) and (D,D,D,D). We denote all these policies by (-,-,D,D). It is noted that (C,C,D,D) yields the same expected gain as (C,C,-,-) or (-,-,D,D) depending whether A starts in one of component games $\Gamma_1$ and $\Gamma_2$ or in one of component games $\Gamma_3$ and $\Gamma_4$. The resulting 11 policies which yield, in general, different expected gains, are given in the first column of Table 4.

## Method

### COMPUTATION OF EXPECTED GAINS FOR ALL POLICIES

To compute the (average subjective) expected gain, $g$, for each feasible policy, Equation 3 may be used. To use Equation 3, powers of a $4 \times 4$ (subjective) transition matrix corresponding to a given policy have to be computed to get the limiting state probabilities vector $\pi$, a lengthy process. A faster computation method, especially when a computer is available, is given below. Define $\hat{P}_m$ to be a $4 \times 4$ (subjective) transition matrix corresponding to every feasible policy $m$, $m$ = (C,C,-,-), (C,D,C,C),... $\hat{P}_m$ is a submatrix of $\hat{P}$, and there are 11 $\hat{P}_m$'s for each player. Let $R_m$ be the $4 \times 4$ reward matrix corresponding to a policy $m$. The expected immediate reward for component game $\Gamma_i$ under policy $m$ is given by

$$ qr_i m = \sum_{j=1}^{N} \hat{p}_{ijm} r_{ijm}, $$

where $\hat{p}_{ijm} \epsilon \hat{P}_m$ and $r_{ijm} \epsilon R_m$. The expected immediate reward for all component games is given by the (row) vector

$$ q_m = (q\Gamma_1 m, q\Gamma_2 m, q\Gamma_3 m, q\Gamma_4 m) . $$

From $\hat{P}$ construct a new $8 \times 4$ matrix $H$ as follows:

$$H = \begin{bmatrix} \hat{x}^1 - 1 & 1 - \hat{x}^1 & 0 & -1 \\ -1 & 0 & \hat{x}^1 & -1 \\ \hat{y}^1 & -\hat{y}^1 & 0 & -1 \\ 0 & -1 & \hat{y}^1 & -1 \\ \hat{z}^1 & 1 - \hat{z}^1 & -1 & -1 \\ 0 & 0 & \hat{z}^1 - 1 & -1 \\ \hat{w}^1 & 1 - \hat{w}^1 & 0 & -1 \\ 0 & 0 & \hat{w}^1 & -1 \end{bmatrix} ,$$

and define the (row) vector

$$V = (V_1, V_2, V_3, g),$$

where $g$, the last element of $V$, is the (average) expected gain for a policy $m$. Then the $N$ simultaneous equations of Equation 5 with $V_N = 0$ are shown to be equivalent to the (column) vector in Equation 6

$$-q_m' = H_m V' , \tag{6}$$

where $H_m$ is a $4 \times 4$ matrix made of the rows of $H$ corresponding to policy $m$. The solution of Equation 6 is given by

$$V' = H_m^{-1}(-q_m') , \tag{7}$$

from which the value of $g$ is immediately obtained.

EXAMPLES WITH SEVERAL PROPENSITIES AND PAYOFFS

To give an example, suppose that $\hat{x}^1 = .763$, $\hat{y}^1 = .254$, $\hat{z}^1 = .461$, and $\hat{w}^1 = .221$. These are the probabilities (B's propensities) used by a stooge in Experiments II and III, reported in Rapoport and Mowshowitz (1966). The payoffs in these experiments were $\lambda_1 = 1$, $\lambda_2 = -10$, $\lambda_3 = 10$, and $\lambda_4 = -5$. The (average) expected gain, $g$, for each of the 11 feasible policies is given under Condition 1 of Table 4. Thus $g(C,D,D,C) = -2.749$, and $g(D,C,C,D) = -3.000$. The optimal policy is $(-,-,D,D)$ prescribing a repeated noncooperative behavior with $g(-,-,D,D) = -0.638$. The worst policy in terms of $g$, $(C,C,-,-)$, prescribes a repeated cooperative behavior yielding a considerably smaller expected gain, $g(C,C,-,-) = -4.310$. The second best policy is $(D,D,C,D)$ — playing noncooperatively in every component game except $\Gamma_3$. This policy yields an expected gain which is 2.36 times as small as the expected gain of the optimal policy. The third best policy is $(C,D,C,D)$ — a "tit-for-tat" policy — with $g(C,D,C,D) = -2.040$.

The sensitivity of $g$ to the particular values of the SPs is shown by the following example. Suppose that $\hat{y}^1,\hat{z}^1,\hat{w}^1$, and the $\lambda_i$ have the same values as before, but $\hat{x}^1$ = .950. The values of $g$ for all feasible policies for these SPs are given under Condition 2 of Table 4. Inspection of this condition indicates that the optimal policy for these propensities is (C,D,C,D) – a tit-for-tat policy – with $g$(C,D,C,D) = -0.525. The noncooperative policy (-,-,D,D) = -0.638. The cooperative policy (C,C,-,-) is the fourth best policy and not the worst policy as before. Furthermore, the differences in $g$ among the optimal policy, the cooperative policy, and the noncooperative policy are considerably smaller than the corresponding differences in the previous condition. In the previous condition, if A decided to play nonoptimally and to use the cooperative policy instead of the optimal (noncooperative) policy, his expected gain was reduced by a factor of 6.76. In the present condition a shift from the optimal policy to the cooperative policy decreases the expected gain by a factor of only 1.54.

Setting $\hat{x}^1$ = .960 and keeping the same values for $\hat{y}^1,\hat{z}^1,\hat{w}^1$, and $\lambda_i$ as before, yields $g$(C,C,-,-) = -0.591, and $g$(-,-,D,D) = -0.638. With $\hat{x}^1$ = .960 the cooperative policy yields a higher expected gain than the noncooperative policy.

The above examples demonstrate one of the main points of the proposed model, namely, that even slight changes in the SPs may change the order of the policies according to the expected gain that they yield. If the SPs are not assumed fixed throughout a repeated play of PD but allowed to vary, different policies may be prescribed as optimal throughout the game, depending on the particular values of the SPs.

Similarly, the order of the policies as well as their corresponding values of $g$ are sensitive to changes in the payoffs. In PD the payoffs are supposed to represent utilities, and changes in the payoffs thus represent trial-to-trial changes in the utilities. To give an example, suppose that $\hat{x}^1$ = .763, $\hat{y}^1$ = .254, $\hat{z}^1$ = .461, $\hat{w}^1$ = .221, $\lambda_2$ = -10, $\lambda_3$ = 10, $\lambda_4$ = -5, as before, but $\lambda_1$ = 5 instead of 1. The resulting PD game is more "moderate," where the temptation to defect and play noncooperatively is not as strong as before. The expected gains for all feasible policies for the above values of the SPs and the payoffs are given under Condition 3 of Table 4. The last column of Table 4 (Condition 4) gives the expected gains for all policies for the same values of the SPs and payoffs with the exception of $\lambda_1$ = 9.

When $\lambda_1$ = 5 the noncooperative strategy is still the optimal strategy. However, the second best policy is the tit-for-tat policy with $g$(C,D,C,D) = -0.977. The cooperative policy is not the worst policy. When $\lambda_1$ = 9, the optimal policy is the tit-for-tat policy. The cooperative policy is the third best policy, and it yields a higher expected gain than the noncooperative policy.

## Extensions of the Model

It was assumed above that a sequence of PD trials is viewed by A as a supergame composed of $h$ = 4 component games. The assumption concerning the number of component games can now be relaxed. Specifically, the number of component games considered by A, $h$, can be enlarged by allowing for "higher-order" SPs, $\hat{x}^u$, $\hat{y}^u$, $\hat{z}^u$, and $\hat{w}^u$, $u > 1$. Depending on the number of SPs considered by A before a decision is made, the number of component games as well as the corresponding matrices $\hat{P}$ and $R$ can be determined. For example, suppose $\hat{x}^1 < \hat{x}^2 < \hat{x}^3 = \hat{x}^{u\prime}$, $u' = 3, 4, 5, \ldots$, and $\hat{y}^u$, $\hat{z}^u$, and $\hat{w}^u$ are constant for $u = 1, 2, \ldots$. The PD, as viewed by A, includes now six component games. These component games, $\Gamma''_1$, $\Gamma'_2$, $\Gamma_1$, $\Gamma_2$, $\Gamma_3$, and $\Gamma_4$, are presented in Table 5. The payoffs, $\lambda_i$, which are the same for all six games, are omitted. Matrices $\hat{P}$ and $R$ (each is a 12 × 6 matrix) can be set as before, and the expected gains for all feasible policies can be obtained from Equations 6 and 7. As the number of feasible policies is large in this case their expected gains are not given here. We only present the expected gain for the cooperative policy $(C,C,C,C,-,-)$ — playing C in component games $\Gamma''_1$, $\Gamma'_1$, $\Gamma_1$, and $\Gamma_2$, the noncooperative policy $(-,-,-,-,D,D,)$ — playing D in component games $\Gamma_3$ and $\Gamma_4$, and the tit-for-tat policy $(C,C,C,D,C,D)$ for one set of parameters. Suppose $\hat{y}^u = .254$, $\hat{z}^u = .461$, $\hat{w}^u = .221$, $\lambda_1 = 1$, $\lambda_2 = -10$, $\lambda_3 = 10$, and $\lambda_4 = -5$, as before, and $\hat{x}^1 = .763$, $\hat{x}^2 = .905$, and $\hat{x}^3 = .962$. Then, $g(C,C,C,C,-,-) = -0.815$, $g(-,-,-,-,D,D) = -0.681$, and $g(C,C,C,D,C,D) = -0.529$.

A questionable assumption of the proposed model is that the first-order as well as the higher-order SPs are independent of time. This assumption may or may not hold when tested experimentally. There is no direct evidence bearing on it, where measures of SPs are obtained at different stages throughout a repeated play of PD. There is some indirect evidence, however which is concerned not with the SPs but with the actual propensities. In the first experiment reported by Rapoport and Mowshowitz (1966), 19 pairs of college students were run in a typical PD experiment for 300 trials. The analysis indicated that the means of $x^1$, $y^1$, $z^1$, and $w^1$ did not change very much after 50 trials or so. The data further indicated that changes in some of the mean higher-order propensities were small. The means of $y^u$, $z^u$, and $w^u$ were approximately constant throughout the game for $u = 1, 2, \ldots, 5$, while $x^1 < x^2 < \ldots < x^5$.

Even when the SPs are time-dependent the proposed model keeps its merits. Instead of prescribing an overall optimal policy for the PD game it will prescribe a policy relative to the SPs *at Time t*. Thus, when $\hat{x}^u$ is replaced by $\hat{x}^u(t)$ and similarly for the remaining SPs, matrices $\hat{P}(t)$ and $R$ may be obtained as before, yielding an optimal policy at Time $t$. The model has the desired property that when SPs change considerably from one time to another different policies may be prescribed as optimal. A player may behave "optimally" using different policies on different trials throughout the game.

When the termination of PD is indefinite we agree with Shubik (1963) that formal models for games of possible infinite length should include some form of discounting of the future. To quote: "It is my contention that any important model for a deterrence scheme must explicitly or implicitly have taken into account some discounting mechanism on future states [Shubik, 1963, p.7]." For most applications of PD it is reasonable to assume that "there will be a tomorrow" and that tomorrow is not as important as today. As we indicated above, the introduction of a discounting factor into stationary Markovian decision processes causes no problem. What may be difficult is to provide it a meaningful psychological interpretation. We suspect that in most experimental studies of PD the discount factor, $\beta$, could be interpreted as the player's SP that the game will

*Table 5.* *Payoff matrices for PD composed of six component games*

| Game $\Gamma_1{}^a$ | | | | Game $\Gamma_2{}^d$ | | | |
|---|---|---|---|---|---|---|---|
| A | | B | | A | | B | |
| | | C | D | | | C | D |
| C | | $\Gamma'_1$ | $\Gamma_2$ | C | | $\Gamma_1$ | $\Gamma_2$ |
| D | | $\Gamma_3$ | $\Gamma_4$ | D | | $\Gamma_3$ | $\Gamma_4$ |

| Game $\Gamma'_1{}^b$ | | | | Game $\Gamma_3{}^e$ | | | |
|---|---|---|---|---|---|---|---|
| A | | B | | A | | B | |
| | | C | D | | | C | D |
| C | | $\Gamma''_1$ | $\Gamma_2$ | C | | $\Gamma_1$ | $\Gamma_2$ |
| D | | $\Gamma_3$ | $\Gamma_4$ | D | | $\Gamma_3$ | $\Gamma_4$ |

| Game $\Gamma''_1{}^c$ | | | | Game $\Gamma_4{}^f$ | | | |
|---|---|---|---|---|---|---|---|
| A | | B | | A | | B | |
| | | C | D | | | C | D |
| C | | $\Gamma''_1$ | $\Gamma_2$ | C | | $\Gamma_1$ | $\Gamma_2$ |
| D | | $\Gamma_3$ | $\Gamma_4$ | D | | $\Gamma_3$ | $\Gamma_4$ |

[a] $P(C) = \hat{x}^1$; $P(D) = 1 - \hat{x}^1$.
[b] $P(C) = \hat{x}^2$; $P(D) = 1 - \hat{x}^2$.
[c] $P(C) = \hat{x}^3$; $P(D) = 1 - \hat{x}^3$.

terminate. Even if the player is not informed about the duration of the experimental game, he knows that it will not last forever. When the player expects to make many decisions $\beta$ should be very close to one.

## Discussion

The model proposed in this paper tries to "resolve" the dilemma when PD is played many times. It prescribes an optimal policy at Time $t$ relative to the payoff matrix, to the number of SPs, to the method of their measurement, and to their specific values at Time $t$. The policy prescribed by the model is optimal in the sense that it maximizes average gain relative to A's knowledge of the process at Time $t$, assuming that his SPs are not going to change. This is a strong assumption, indeed. Of course, A may anticipate changes in B's policy and hence in his own SPs. B may notice A's policy and change his own policy. However, A does not know what these changes are going to be. They may be in his "favor" or "disfavor." Thus the best thing that A can do is to play his optimal policy relative to the SPs he considers at Time $t$ (assuming that they are not going to change), revising them continuously as he obtains more information about B's decisions.

The problem posed by the PD game is resolved by the present model in a peculiar way. The effects of the interaction between the players, which are the essence of the game, are treated only indirectly via the changes in the SPs. It is probably the main advantage of the present model that it distinguishes between two processes, namely the decision-making process relative to the player's SPs at Time $t$, and the revision of these SPs. Only the first process is treated by the model, assuming that a reliable method for measuring the SPs is available, and that they satisfy the axioms of probability theory. A model for the trial-to-trial changes in the SPs is not presented here.

The separation between the decision-making process at Time $t$ and the trial-to-trial changes in the SPs would not be made if a normative model for nonstationary Markovian decision processes could be constructed. Such a model may be constructed in some cases when specific assumptions about the changes in the SPs are made. Thus if the SPs are assumed to vary periodically in time an optimal policy for a periodic discrete-time Markovian decision process can be found with the iteration procedure suggested by Riis (1965).

The present model resembles the stochastic models for PD investigated by Rapoport (1964) and tested by Rapoport and Chammah (1965) and Rapoport and Mowshowitz (1966). In the stochastic models each player is characterized by a set of propensities, which may or may not be constant throughout the game. Similarly, in the present model the player is assumed to be characterized by a set of SPs, reflecting his uncertainty with regard to the other player's policy. The SPs may or may not be changed throughout the course of the game. The present model, however, differs from the stochastic models in one important respect. The concept separating these models is that of a policy. The stochastic models try to describe the sequence of joint decisions obtained throughout the game. They do not tell the player how best to play it. The present model prescribes an optimal policy maximizing each player's average gain relative to his opinions and beliefs about the other player.

The preparation of this paper and the experimental research to which it refers was supported by National Institutes of Health Grant MH-10006. The author is indebted to Lyle V. Jones, James Kahan, and Anatol Rapoport for helpful comments.

## References

Bellman, R. *Dynamic programming.* Princeton: Princeton University Press, 1957. (a)

Bellman, R. A Markovian decision process. *Journal of Mathematics and Mechanics,* 1957, **6**, 679-684. (b)

Bellman, R. *Adaptive control processes: A guided tour.* Princeton: Princeton University Press, 1961.

Bellman, R., & Dreyfus, S. E. *Applied dynamic programming.* Princeton: Princeton University Press, 1962.

Gallo, P. S., & McClintock, C. G. Cooperative and competitive behavior in mixed-motive games. *Journal of Conflict Resolution,* 1965, **9**, 68-78.

Howard, R. A. *Dynamic programming and Markov processes.* New York: M. I. T. and Wiley, 1960.

Luce, R. D., & Raiffa, H. *Games and decisions.* New York: Wiley, 1957.

Rapoport, Amnon. A study of human decisions in a stationary Markov process with rewards Chapel Hill: Psychometric Laboratory Report No. 48, 1966.

Rapoport, Amnon, & Mowshowitz, A. Experimental studies of stochiastic models for the Prisoner's Dilemma. *Behavioral Science,* 1966, **11**, 444-458.

Rapoport, Anatol. A stochastic model for the Prisoner's Dilemma. In J. Garland (Ed.), *Stochastic models in medicine and biology.* Madison: University of Wisconsin Press, 1964.

Rapoport, Anatol, & Chammah, A. M. *Prisoner's Dilemma: A study in conflict and cooperation.* Ann Arbor: University of Michigan Press, 1965.

Rapoport, Anatol, & Orwant, C. Experimental games: A review. *Behavioral Science,* 1962, **7**, 1-37.

Riis, J. O. Discounted Markov programming in a periodic process. *Operations Research,* 1965, **13**, 920-929.

Scodel, A., Minas, J. S., Ratoosh, P., & Lipetz, M. Some descriptive aspects of two-person non-zero-sum games. *Journal of Conflict Resolution,* 1959, **3**, 114-119.

Shubik, M. Some reflections on the design of game theoretic models for the study of negotiation and threats. *Journal of Conflict Resolution,* 1963, **7**, 1-12.

Suppes, P., & Atkinson, R. C. *Markov learning models for multiperson interaction.* Stanford: Stanford University Press, 1960.

# CHAPTER 2

# EXPERIMENTAL STUDIES
# OF INTERDEPENDENT MIXED-MOTIVE GAMES

**ABSTRACT:** A multistage Prisoner's Dilemma (MPD) game is presented as a paradigm for a special class of interdependent mixed-motive conflicts. The MPD game is composed of several PD subgames (conflicts) which are interconnected in the sense that each joint decision determines, in addition to the payoff for each player, the next subgame (conflict) to be played. Several experiments are reported, using both male and female players. The results show that players are aware of the delicate strategic considerations involved in the game and are affected by the strategy employed by the other player. When the game is perceived as an individual decision task, the percentage of cooperative behavior increases. A normative model for the MPD game is presented. Its failure to account for the observed results is discussed briefly.

The Prisoner's Dilemma (PD) is a two-person, nonzero-sum, noncooperative game, in which "noncooperative" indicates no preplay communication between the players. A typical form of the game is represented by the payoff matrix in Table 1, subject to the following conditions:

1. $2r_{11Z} \geq r_{12Z} + r_{21Z}$

2a. $r_{21S} \geq r_{11S} \geq r_{22S} \geq r_{12S}$

2b. $r_{12O} \geq r_{11O} \geq r_{22O} \geq r_{21O}$

where $Z = S$, $O$ indicates the player, and $r_{khZ}$ the reward to player $Z$, $k$, $h = 1$, $2$.

Full knowledge of the payoff matrix is assumed. Each of the players must choose between alternative 1 (typically, $C$ for cooperation) and 2 (or $D$ for defection). Decisions are made simultaneously and are designated by 11, 12, 21, and 22, the first digit indicating the choice of $S$ (the row player). For a detailed description of the game, see Luce and Raiffa (1957) and Rapoport and Chammah (1965). Experimental studies of sequential PD games have been reviewed by Gallo and McClintock (1965) and Rapoport and Orwant (1962).

A player of a PD game is viewed as a decision-making unit, not necessarily a single person. The player may be a group of persons, a party, a firm, or a nation. The alternatives 1 and 2 are therefore open to a variety of interpretations as they determine a mixed-motive conflict between the players, whose interests may partially conflict and partially coincide. The payoffs (rewards) are supposed to represent utilities.

19

Sequential PD games may thus describe conflicts in which, though the element of antagonism provides the dramatic interest, mutual dependence is an essential part of the logical structure, demanding or at least allowing for some kind of tacit collaboration. It is not surprising then that the PD has been enthusiastically advocated as a reasonable and suggestive, though drastically oversimplified, paradigm for conflicts of interest in interpersonal relations, international affairs, strikes, jurisdictional wars, and so on.

*Table 1.   Payoff matrix for the 2×2 PD game.*

|              |   | Player $O$ | |
|              |   | 1 | 2 |
|--------------|---|---|---|
| Player $S$   | 1 | $r_{11}S, \ r_{11}O$ | $r_{12}S, \ r_{12}O$ |
|              | 2 | $r_{21}S, \ r_{21}O$ | $r_{22}S, \ r_{22}O$ |

There seem to be two major limitations of the PD schema, particularly as presently used by social psychologists. In the first place, experimental PD games have generally allowed for only two alternatives for each player. However, even a casual inspection of the courses of action open to decision makers in many military, interpersonal, and international conflicts, in which interests are divergent and communication is nonexistent or severely restricted, reveals more than just two alternatives. In international conflicts, for example, the decision is not between peace and totally destructive war. There are many steps of escalation.

A second limitation of the PD schema is based upon a distinction we make between conflict and conflict situation. A conflict is completely defined in terms of the set of alternatives available to each player. Thus if $S$ has $m$ labeled choices and $O$ has $n$ labeled choices, and the payoff matrix satisfies conditions I and II, we have an $m{\times}n$ mixed–motive conflict. We say that we have two occurrences of the same conflict when each player maintains his labeled choices in two different occasions, even though the corresponding rewards in the two associated payoff matrices may differ.

By a conflict situation we mean either (1) the same conflict repeated several times in succession (where payoffs may possibly change), or (2) an aggregate of different interdependent conflicts which have to be resolved sequentially. A conflict situation between two players may prevail for a long period (for life, if the players are married to each other), while conflicts refer to incidents in time which are well defined in terms of the choices available to each player.

The restriction of the PD schema to simple, independent conflicts is, we think, a severe limitation. The PD game has not been extended to cover conflict situations consisting of different, interdependent conflicts. Nor has it been extended to conflict situations in which the same conflict is repeated in succession but payoffs may change. When the same conflict is repeated in time, experimenters and model builders have implicitly or explicitly assumed the invariability of payoffs and the independence of the separate occurrences.

The assumption of invariable payoffs seems to us highly restrictive. It excludes conflict situations in which players may take actions that irreversibly change the situation itself by altering the payoff matrix. The assumption is inconsistent with the observation that in many military, economic, and interpersonal conflict situations, for which the PD game is proposed as a paradigm, payoffs are typically affected by what happened to one or both of the players in the time interval between the present and the previous conflict. Furthermore, the assumption does not account for the possibility that different conflicts or different occurrences of the same conflict may be interdependent, in the sense that changes in payoffs, as well as the sequence by which the conflicts are entered, may depend upon the way previous conflicts or occurrences of the same conflict have been resolved. The structure of this case is more complicated and the logic is more subtle, but the case is neither less interesting nor less typical, we contend, than the usual independent mixed-motive conflicts.

In the next section we shall undertake to extend the PD game to a more general paradigm for interdependent (multistage) mixed-motive conflicts. Several experiments will be described later, which investigate how people play the general PD game.

## A Multistage PD Game (MPD)

We first extend the 2×2 PD game to a general PD game (GPD). Let $k$ indicate a row in a $Y \times Y$ payoff matrix, $h$ indicate a column, and $r_{khZ}$ be the payoff to player $Z$, when row $k$ and column $h$ are chosen by the players. The payoff matrix defines a *weak* GPD if it satisfies the following conditions:

1a. $r_{khS} < r_{(k+1)hS}$

1b. $r_{khO} < r_{k(h+1)O}$

2. $r_{(m+1)(m+1)Z} < r_{mmZ}$ ,

$k, h, m = 1, 2, ..., Y - 1.$

The pressures in a weak GPD operate in both directions. On the one hand, there is pressure on each player to choose alternative $Y$ because of the dominance of row $k + 1$ over row $k$ and column $h + 1$ over column $h$. By condition (1), each player is motivated to choose his dominating alternative, $Y$ (and therefore to receive $r_{YYZ}$ ). On the other hand, there is pressure to choose alternative 1 because by condition (2) 11 is the best joint choice, and so the dilemma.

It may be noted that a weak GPD allows for another form of tacit collusion, in addition to an agreement to play 11. To see this, examine the 4×4 weak GPD presented in Table 2.   It is seen that alternation between 14 and 41, or between 23 and 32, will yield an average joint payoff larger than the one obtained from repeatedly playing 11. To prevent this situation a *strong* GPD is defined as a payoff matrix satisfying the following condition, in addition to (1) and (2):

3.   $2(r_{11S} + r_{11O}) > (r_{khS} + r_{hkO}) + (r_{hkS} + r_{hkO})$ ,

$h, k = 1, 2, ..., Y$ ,

$h \neq k$.

*Table 2. Payoff matrix for a 4×4 weak GPD game*

|         |   | Player $O$ | | | | | | |
|---------|---|---|---|---|---|---|---|---|
|         |   | 1 | | 2 | | 3 | | 4 |
|         | 1 | 1, | 5 | -20, | 10 | -15, | 15 | -25, | 20 |
| Player $S$ | 2 | 10, | -1 | 2, | 4 | -10, | 15 | -20, | 30 |
|         | 3 | 20, | -15 | 25, | 0 | -4, | 3 | -15, | 10 |
|         | 4 | 30, | -8 | 35, | -5 | 0, | 0 | -10, | 2 |

In the remaining sections the distinction between weak and strong GPD is not maintained.   It may have some interest to social psychologists studying whether tacit collusions between players, other than that of repeatedly playing 11, are sometimes adopted.

Experimental studies usually employ symmetric (weak or strong) GPD games, satisfying the condition:

4.   $r_{khS} = \begin{cases} -r_{khO}, & \text{for } k \neq h \\ r_{khO}, & \text{for } k = h \end{cases}$ .

Having lifted the limitation on the number of alternatives available to the players, we next remove the second limitation of the PD schema, the one concerning its failure to consider the more general conflict situation.   Payoffs should be allowed to vary when different interdependent conflicts are considered.   This is accomplished by allowing transitions among conflicts in a way that will become clear shortly.   Instead of considering a GPD game played many times, we shall consider a set of $N$ different GPD subgames, transitions among them being possible.   The set of $N$ subgames will be referred to as a multistage (interdependent) game (MPD) denoted by $\Gamma(N)$.

The reformulation of interdependent mixed-motive conflicts as an MPD game may be best demonstrated by an example.   Table 3 represents an MPD game, $\Gamma(3)$, with three subgames $\Gamma_i$, $i$ = 1, 2, 3.   Each subgame satisfies the conditions of a weak GPD. Payoffs differ from one subgame to another.   They have $i$ as a superscript, that is, $r^i_{hkZ}$ denotes the payoff to player $Z$, when row $k^i$  and column $h^i$ in $\Gamma_i$ are chosen simultaneously.   The meaning of the entries in the payoff matrices will become apparent immediately.   Suppose that at time $t$ (time is taken to be discrete) $\Gamma_i$ is played.   Suppose further that the joint choice of the players in $\Gamma_i$ is $1^l 2^l$.   Then the resulting entry means that $S$ receives $r^l_{12S}$, $O$ receives $r^l_{12O}$, and the subgame to be played on time $t$ + 1 is $\Gamma_2$.   When $\Gamma_2$ is played, each player can choose among three alternatives, which do not necessarily include the two alternatives previously available in $\Gamma_l$.   Suppose the joint choice at time $t$ + 1 is $3^2 2^2$, then the resulting entry in the payoff matrix of $\Gamma_2$ means that the reward to $S$ is $r^2_{32S}$, the reward to $O$ is $r^2_{32O}$, and the players jointly "move" to subgame $\Gamma_l$.

The generalization to $\Gamma(N)$ is straightforward.   In subgame $\Gamma_j$, $i$ = 1, 2, ..., $N$, each player has $Y_i$ alternatives, $1^i$, $2^i$, ..., $Y^i$.   If $S$ chooses $k^i$ and $O$ chooses $h^i$ the resulting entry in the payoff matrix, $(r^i_{khS}, r^i_{khO}, \Gamma_j)$, means that $S$ receives $r^i_{khS}$, $O$ receives $r^i_{khO}$, and $\Gamma_j$, $j$ = 1, 2, ..., $N$, is to be played next.   Note that a one-step transition from one subgame to all others is not demanded.   In general, to move from one subgame to another, other subgames may have to be played first.   In Table 3, for example, there is no joint decision that will move the players in one step from $\Gamma_l$ to $\Gamma_3$.   The path from $\Gamma_l$ to $\Gamma_3$ goes through $\Gamma_2$.   We do require, however, some path from $\Gamma_i$ to $\Gamma_j$, i ≠ j, i, j = 1, 2, ..., $N$.   The reason for this restrictive assumption will become clear when a model for MPD is presented.

MPD may be viewed as a simplified paradigm for a set of interdependent mixed-motive conflicts in which a sequence of decisions must be made, with each decision affecting future decisions.   An interesting characteristic of the game lies in the realization that a nonrational decision may be made in one conflict in order to bring the decision maker to a better conflict.   To see this, consider again the MPD game $\Gamma(3)$ presented in Table 3 and assume $r^1_{11Z} > r^2_{11Z} > r^3_{11Z}$.   Suppose the players decide to cooperate by playing $1^i 1^i$, $i$ = 1, 2, 3.   Because of the above assumption it is better for them to lock on $1^l 1^l$ than on $1^2 1^2$ or $1^3 1^3$.   If, however, they happen to play subgame $\Gamma_2$, for example, one or both of them will have to choose $2^2$ or $3^2$ to get to $\Gamma_l$.   Note that decision $2^2$ or $3^2$ in this example may be misinterpreted by the other player to indicate noncooperative intentions.   Thus, it may very well happen that if the players are locked in on $1^2 1^2$, they will find no easy way to get to $\Gamma_l$, as each of them may assume that choosing $2^2$ or $3^2$ will be misinterpreted by the other player and lead to repeated noncooperative play.

Several experiments will be described in the following sections to investigate (1) how people play the MPD in a "free response" situation and whether they are sensitive to its intrinsic strategic points, (2) what effects, if any, the strategy of the other

*Table 3.  Payoff matrices for a MPD game, $\Gamma(3)$*

Subgame $\Gamma_1$

|  |  | Player $O$ | |
|---|---|---|---|
|  |  | $1^1$ | $2^1$ |
| Player $S$ | $1^1$ | $r^1_{11}S,\ r^1_{11}O,\ \Gamma_1$ | $r^1_{12}S,\ r^1_{12}O,\ \Gamma_2$ |
|  | $2^1$ | $r^1_{21}S,\ r^1_{21}O,\ \Gamma_2$ | $r^1_{22}S,\ r^1_{22}O,\ \Gamma_1$ |

Subgame $\Gamma_2$

|  |  | Player $O$ | | |
|---|---|---|---|---|
|  |  | $1^2$ | $2^2$ | $3^2$ |
| Player $S$ | $1^2$ | $r^2_{11}S,\ r^2_{11}O,\ \Gamma_2$ | $r^2_{12}S,\ r^2_{12}O,\ \Gamma_3$ | $r^2_{13}S,\ r^2_{13}O,\ \Gamma_1$ |
|  | $2^2$ | $r^2_{21}S,\ r^2_{21}O,\ \Gamma_1$ | $r^2_{22}S,\ r^2_{22}O,\ \Gamma_2$ | $r^2_{23}S,\ r^2_{23}O,\ \Gamma_3$ |
|  | $3^2$ | $r^2_{31}S,\ r^2_{31}O,\ \Gamma_3$ | $r^2_{32}O,\ r^2_{32}O,\ \Gamma_1$ | $r^2_{33}S,\ r^2_{33}O,\ \Gamma_2$ |

Subgame $\Gamma_3$

|  |  | Player $O$ | | |
|---|---|---|---|---|
|  |  | $1^3$ | $2^3$ | $3^3$ |
| Player $S$ | $1^3$ | $r^3_{11}S,\ r^3_{11}O,\ \Gamma_3$ | $r^3_{12}S,\ r^3_{12}O,\ \Gamma_3$ | $r^3_{13}S,\ r^3_{13}O,\ \Gamma_1$ |
|  | $2^3$ | $r^3_{21}S,\ r^3_{21}O,\ \Gamma_1$ | $r^3_{22}S,\ r^3_{22}O,\ \Gamma_1$ | $r^3_{23}S,\ r^3_{23}O,\ \Gamma_2$ |
|  | $3^3$ | $r^3_{31}S,\ r^3_{31}O,\ \Gamma_2$ | $r^3_{32}O,\ r^3_{32}O,\ \Gamma_2$ | $r^3_{33}S,\ r^3_{33}O,\ \Gamma_3$ |

player may have on their play, and (3) whether the knowledge of playing against a human stooge has any effect on their decisions. An additional purpose is to present and test a model for MPD games. The development of the model has been stimulated by the work of Shapley (1953) on stochastic games, Howard (1960) on Markov decision processes, and Rapoport (1967) on PD games.

## Method

### SUBJECTS

Players in group M were 30 University of North Carolina male undergraduates who volunteered to participate in an experiment on decision making, in order to fulfill an introductory psychology course requirement, and possibly to earn some money. Players in groups F-I, F-II, and F-III were 39 University of North Carolina female undergraduates who volunteered to participate in the experiment for the same reasons. Thirteen female players were assigned to each of three experimental conditions. In two of the conditions, F-I and F-II, another undergraduate woman served as a stooge. In the third condition, F-III, the experimenter, a female graduate student, served as a stooge.

### PROCEDURE

The procedure for group M was as follows. The players were seated at a table in the position of player $X$ and player $Y$. They were separated by a wooden partition which prevented any view of the other player or the other side of the table. On the table in front of the players was a display of an MPD game presented in Table 4. Subgame I was on the left, subgame II in the middle, and subgame III on the right. The experimenter, a male undergraduate, was seated across the table facing the players.

The instructions, which were presented in a written form, are given in full in Cole (1966). The players were told that they were going to play a game which had certain payoffs to each of them. The payoff for a given trial could not be controlled by a given player alone. He was told: "... the payoffs for you, and for the other player, will depend on what the other player does, as well as on what you do."

The directions for the game were as follows:

"On every trial each of you will make a decision by pointing to the $C$ or the $D$ in a particular one of three subgames. Your decision will be made independently of the decision of the other player and will be final (that is, you may not change your mind once you have pointed to either $C$ or $D$).

Your simultaneous joint decisions on every trial will determine (1) the payoff for each of you for the particular trial, and (2) the subgame to be played on the next trial. The payoffs resulting from your joint decisions as well as the next subgame to be played are indicated on the three sheets. [The payoff matrices were then explained by providing several examples. The players were asked to note that in each subgame]... if both of you make the

*Table 4.  Payoff matrices presented to the players*

|  |  | Subgame I | | | Subgame II | |
|---|---|---|---|---|---|---|
|  |  | Y | | | Y | |
|  |  | C | D |  | C | D |
|  | C | 1, 1 (I) | -8, 8 (II) |  | 2, 2 (II) | -6, 6 (III) |
| X |  |  |  | X |  |  |
|  | D | 8, -8 (II) | -7, -7 (I) |  | 6, -6 (III) | -5, -5 (II) |

|  |  | Subgame III | |
|---|---|---|---|
|  |  | Y | |
|  |  | C | D |
|  | C | 4, 4 (III) | -10, 10 (I) |
| X |  |  |  |
|  | D | 8, -8 (I) | -7, -7 (III) |

same choice, both choose C or both choose D, you will play the same subgame on the next trial.  If you do not make the same decision, you will move to the next subgame."

After each choice the experimenter recorded the choices and read off the number of points gained or lost by each player.  Each player recorded his own gain or loss, and totalled it after every block of 50 trials.  The experiment lasted for 200 trials.  The players were told that points would be converted to money at the end of the experiment.  Each point was worth 1/5 cent for group M, 1/2 cent for group F-ll, and 1 cent for groups F-I and F-III. This was done so that players in all conditions would gain approximately the same amount of money. The amount of money gained or lost was respectively added to or subtracted from a fixed sum of $2.00 given to each player at the beginning of the experiment. Players were instructed to "try to win as much money as possible."

At the end of each block of 50 trials, each player was asked "to make estimates of what you think the other player would do in certain circumstances." These estimates were to be given in terms of subjective probabilities; that is, each player was asked to state his probability, given as a number ranging between zero and one, that the other player would play $C$ in each of the three subgames. Players were told that these estimates should reflect their knowledge of the other player, and might change from one block to another as more information was acquired about the other player. The notion of subjective probability was explicated both in terms of odds and relative frequencies. Players were asked to give as exact estimates as possible, and not to restrict them to round numbers.

At the end of the experiment the players were given a questionnaire to answer. They were instructed as follows: "Pretend that this game will be continued for another 100 trials, and you must instruct someone to play the 100 trials for you. You may express your wishes for the play of the 100 trials only by selecting a $C$ or a $D$ in each subgame. Assuming that the other student will continue to play as in the past, circle the choice in each subgame which you believe to be the best for you to play."

The player circled the appropriate $C$ or $D$ in each subgame, thus determining a policy – an ordered 3-tuple $(k^I, k^{II}, k^{III})$ $k = C, D$. He was asked then to consider all eight possible policies which were written in the questionnaire, and to rank-order them in terms of their desirability, assuming that the game were to continue for 100 more trials.

Instructions for groups F-I and F-II were exactly the same as those given to group $M$. The "real" player was allowed to arrive first and was seated at the table in the position of player $X$. Shortly afterwards, the stooge arrived and was seated in Player $Y$'s position. The rest of the procedure was exactly the same as described above. When the experiment was over and the questionnaire filled out, the stooge asked to be excused on the pretense of having an appointment, while player $X$ stayed and answered a few informal questions about the game.

Instructions to group F-III were slightly different. Players were told that the game to be played was a two-person game, but that "the experimenter will play for the second player by following a prearranged schedule of play from a chart." It was made clear to the players that they were going to play against a prespecified strategy, which would not depend upon their play. They were further told that they would see this prespecified strategy at the completion of the game. The task was thus an individual decision-making task in a two-person game context not only from the experimenter's point of view (as in groups F-I and F-II) but also from the player's own point of view.

The stooge in all F conditions used a prespecified, unconditional strategy. In groups F-I and F-III the stooge played $C$ in subgames I, II, and III with (actual) probabilities $a = .20$, $b = .40$, and $c = .90$, respectively. In group F-II the stooge's probabilities were $a = .40$ for subgames I, II, and III respectively. Thus, the differences between groups F-I and F-II were in the probabilities used by the stooge, while the differences between groups F-I and F-III were in the information provided to the player about the stooge. The stooge's decisions for each subgame and each trial were predetermined by using the probabilities *a*, *b*, and *c*, and a table of random numbers.

## Results and Discussion

GROUP M

Rapoport and Chammah (1965) and Rapoport and Mowshowitz (1966) reported a "lock-in" effect wherein subjects tended to settle into repeated play of 11 or of 22. The result of a lock-in effect in this MPD would be a decrease in the number of transitions among subgames as more practice is gained with the game. This indeed happened. The mean number of transitions among subgames was 20.20, 11.67, 9.20, and 7.00, for blocks 1, 2, 3, and 4, respectively, each of them including 50 trials. The corresponding standard deviations were 8.59, 8.73, 9.51, and 8.83. The decrease in the mean number of transitions is significant $F(3, 42) = 9.54$, $p < .01$, using one-way analysis of variance with repeated measures.

Table 5 presents several statistics describing the behavior of group M. The table presents the means (*CC*, *CD*, *DC*, and *DD*) and standard deviations (S.D.) of the percentage of every joint decision for every subgame and every block of 50 trials. The mean percentage and standard deviation of every joint decision summed over subgames is also presented.

The prominent finding is the presence of the "lock-in" effect – an increase in $\overline{CC}$ and $\overline{DD}$ as a function of practice in the game and a decrease in the unilateral responses, *CD* and *DC*. The size of the effect is of the same order of magnitude as that reported by Rapoport and Chammah (1965) and Rapoport and Mowshowitz (1966). A closer inspection of Table 5 shows that the time changes in the mean percentage of joint decisions depend, in the case of *CC* on the particular subgames. *CC* in subgames I and II decreased with practice, while *CC* in subgame III largely increased. The rank order of the *CC* responses in block 4 is as expected. Most of the *CC* responses were made in subgame III, yielding the highest gain per trial, and lastly in subgame I, yielding only one point per trial for every *CC*. Players who decided to cooperate, tactily of course, did so in most cases by playing *CC* in subgame III.

For the joint decision *DD* the results are different. One may expect the players who decided to play *D* consistently to lock in on *DD* in subgame II, the subgame yielding the lowest loss per trial, 5 points. This, however, was not the case as more than half the *DD* responses in block 4 occurred in subgame I.

The lock-in effect is better understood when group M is divided into 3 subgroups – players who locked in on *CC* in block 4 (at least 45 *CC* responses out of 50), players who locked in on *DD* in block 4, and players who did not show the lock-in effect. From the 6 pairs of players who locked in on *CC*, 5 locked in on *CC* in subgame III and only one pair in subgame II. From the 4 pairs who locked in on *DD* only one pair

*Table 5.*    *Percentage of joint decisions for every subgame and every block of trials (Group M)*

|  | | Block | | | | | | | |
| --- | --- | --- | --- | --- | --- | --- | --- | --- | --- |
| | Subgame | 1 | | 2 | | 3 | | 4 | |
| Joint Decision | | mean | S.D. | mean | S.D. | mean | S.D. | mean | S.D. |
| | I | 2.7 | 3.1 | 0.3 | 0.0 | 0.9 | 2.2 | 0.7 | 1.6 |
| CC | II | 12.1 | 15.3 | 1.1 | 1.7 | 1.5 | 3.7 | 7.1 | 24.8 |
| | III | 9.7 | 14.1 | 28.1 | 38.7 | 33.5 | 43.2 | 37.3 | 45.4 |
| | Total | 24.5 | 27.3 | 29.5 | 38.5 | 35.9 | 42.7 | 45.1 | 46.2 |
| | I | 8.1 | 4.8 | 4.5 | 5.3 | 3.7 | 6.1 | 2.5 | 5.1 |
| CD | II | 6.8 | 4.7 | 4.8 | 5.4 | 3.7 | 5.7 | 2.5 | 4.7 |
| | III | 7.5 | 4.4 | 3.2 | 4.0 | 2.5 | 3.4 | 2.0 | 3.4 |
| | Total | 22.4 | 12.3 | 12.5 | 13.5 | 9.9 | 14.7 | 7.0 | 12.5 |
| | I | 6.4 | 4.4 | 2.9 | 3.2 | 2.1 | 3.2 | 2.3 | 3.2 |
| DC | II | 6.9 | 5.0 | 3.1 | 3.2 | 2.4 | 3.3 | 1.9 | 3.1 |
| | III | 5.5 | 3.5 | 4.3 | 3.5 | 3.5 | 3.8 | 2.7 | 3.5 |
| | Total | 18.7 | 11.6 | 10.3 | 7.8 | 8.0 | 11.1 | 6.9 | 7.9 |
| | I | 10.8 | 9.5 | 15.3 | 15.5 | 17.9 | 29.0 | 22.1 | 30.4 |
| DD | II | 12.1 | 9.3 | 17.1 | 16.1 | 13.6 | 21.9 | 13.7 | 20.2 |
| | III | 11.4 | 7.3 | 15.3 | 18.3 | 14.7 | 21.7 | 5.2 | 9.0 |
| | Total | 34.3 | 20.7 | 47.7 | 35.2 | 46.2 | 39.7 | 41.0 | 40.5 |

played *DD* in subgame I, the others shifted from playing *DD* in subgame I to subgame II.

Of special interest is the pair of players who locked in on *CC* in subgame II. These players competed strongly on blocks 1, 2, and 3, as is reflected by the low percentage of *CC* for these blocks - .18, .06, and .00, respectively. On the first trial of block 4 both players started playing cooperatively in subgame II, the subgame in which they happened to stay on the last trial of block 3. Being afraid, as they later reported, that a *D* decision might be misinterpreted by the other player to indicate competitive tendencies, both players continued playing *C* for all 50 trials, although they realized that only one $D$ decision by either of them was needed to move them from subgame II to III and thus double their gain.

GROUP F

The results of group M suggest that MPD can be played without too many difficulties by college students, that players can distinguish among the different subgames and generally play according to some strategy, and that the game is "interesting" in the sense that it reveals strategic considerations operating in multistage mixed-motive conflicts. Our next step, following similar developments in the study of repeated independent 2×2 PD games, is to investigate whether and to what extent the behavior of the players can be affected by using a pre-specified strategy of a stooge. Studies concerned with 2×2 PD games using a stooge (Bixenstine, Potash, and Wilson, 1963; McClintock, Harrison, Strand, and Gallo, 1963; Minas, Scodel, Marlowe, and Rawson, 1960) have generally yielded negative results. Changes in the stooge's percentage of $C$ did not affect the player's percentage. On the other hand, studies by Oskamp and Perlman (1965) and Sermat (1964) have suggested that players play more cooperatively against a conditional strategy of a stooge than against an unconditionally cooperative one. In our studies two different unconditional strategies are compared to each other, the one used with group F-I and the other with group F-II.

The second relevant comparison is between groups F-I and F-III. Here the differences in play, if any, are those resulting from differences in the MPD game perceived as a two-person game and the game perceived as an individual decision-making task under uncertainty, where the player actually knows that she is facing a stooge playing according to a prespecified but unknown probabilistic strategy.

Table 6 gives the means and standard deviations of the total number of points lost by the players for the three F groups. The players in group F-III made significantly more points than those in group F-I, $t(24) = 2.27$, $p < 0.05$. Group F-II also made more points than group F-I although the difference did not reach significance, $t(24) = 1.61$ , $p < .20$.

Table 6.    Means and standard deviations of total number
            of points lost by the players (Group F)

|  | Group | | |
|---|---|---|---|
|  | F-I | F-II | F-III |
| mean | -138.8 | -68.1 | -69.3 |
| S.D. | 75.6 | 139.2 | 80.1 |

Table 7 presents the means and standard deviations of the *C* responses for every group, every subgame, and every block of 50 trials. As the players played against prespecified strategies, joint decisions are not analyzed. For every group the mean percentages of *C* summed over blocks were compared to one another. None of the subgame differences for all 3 groups reached significance. The players in each group played the same percentage of *C* in each subgame.

*Table 7.* Percentage of C responses for every subgame and every block of trials
(Group F)

|  |  | Block | | | | | | | |
|  |  | 1 | | 2 | | 3 | | 4 | |
| Subgame | | | | | | | | | |
| Group | | mean | S.D. | mean | S.D. | mean | S.D. | mean | S.D. |
| F-I | I | 42.8 | 22.3 | 42.5 | 17.2 | 39.7 | 24.2 | 38.0 | 27.2 |
|  | II | 36.1 | 29.6 | 40.8 | 21.5 | 36.8 | 26.4 | 33.7 | 33.7 |
|  | III | 40.2 | 28.2 | 34.7 | 29.9 | 25.6 | 30.5 | 27.7 | 32.7 |
|  | Total | 40.3 | 23.2 | 43.5 | 18.5 | 34.5 | 22.4 | 36.8 | 23.7 |
| F-II | I | 44.8 | 21.0 | 30.1 | 23.6 | 35.1 | 23.7 | 34.1 | 26.9 |
|  | II | 49.3 | 14.0 | 24.6 | 25.9 | 24.4 | 19.6 | 25.5 | 25.4 |
|  | III | 43.1 | 15.4 | 34.6 | 21.9 | 31.1 | 18.4 | 33.4 | 23.0 |
|  | Total | 47.2 | 14.3 | 31.2 | 20.2 | 30.8 | 18.3 | 32.9 | 22.1 |
| F-III | I | 53.9 | 14.7 | 46.5 | 20.1 | 50.9 | 21.7 | 49.6 | 22.3 |
|  | II | 59.1 | 22.6 | 48.7 | 15.8 | 54.0 | 26.7 | 43.8 | 24.5 |
|  | III | 48.2 | 21.2 | 49.0 | 31.0 | 44.8 | 34.5 | 40.5 | 33.6 |
|  | Total | 55.2 | 17.7 | 51.5 | 20.1 | 52.0 | 25.5 | 46.6 | 24.2 |

The mean percentages of *C* were, therefore, summed over subgames and the effects of blocks and groups were tested by a two-way analysis of variance with repeated measures. The group effect was significant $F_{(2, 36)} = 3.48$, $p < .05$, as well as the block effect, $F_{(3, 108)} = 3.20$, $p < .05$, and the interaction between blocks and groups, $F_{(6, 108)} = 3.80$ $p < .05$. Among individual groups only the difference between groups F-I and F-II was significant, $t_{(24)} = 2.21$, $p < .05$. The significant block effect indicates a decrease in the mean percentage of *C*, as can be seen from Table 7. As for the significant interaction effect, Table 7 reveals that while group F-III had a higher mean percentage of $C$ than F-I and F-II for all four blocks, group F-II showed a higher level of cooperation for the remaining blocks.

Differences between groups F-I and F-II should be reflected most clearly in the probability estimates of the stooge's future $C$ responses in each subgame. The estimates were made four times, after each block. The mean estimates and the corresponding standard deviations are presented in Table 8 for each group, each subgame, and each block, together with the actual probabilities ($a$, $b$, and $c$). Inspection of Table 8 shows that the mean estimates of each group correspond fairly closely to the actual probabilities in each subgame, with the high probabilities (.90) underestimated and the low ones (.20) overestimated. Individual differences, however, are rather large, judging from the large standard deviations that remain stable over blocks of trials.

*Table 8.  Probability estimates (Group F)*

| Group | Subgame | Block 1 mean | 1 S.D. | 2 mean | 2 S.D. | 3 mean | 3 S.D. | 4 mean | 4 S.D. | Actual Probabilities |
|-------|---------|------|------|------|------|------|------|------|------|---------------------|
| F-I   | I       | .31  | .25  | .30  | .23  | .24  | .18  | .26  | .28  | a = .20 |
|       | II      | .39  | .23  | .48  | .22  | .47  | .28  | .46  | .23  | b = .40 |
|       | III     | .64  | .29  | .72  | .28  | .79  | .17  | .86  | .15  | c = .90 |
| F-II  | I       | .45  | .21  | .36  | .21  | .46  | .17  | .37  | .18  | a = .40 |
|       | II      | .50  | .26  | .64  | .29  | .63  | .28  | .73  | .22  | b = .90 |
|       | III     | .36  | .18  | .37  | .18  | .35  | .12  | .31  | .15  | c = .40 |
| F-III | I       | .32  | .20  | .42  | .26  | .35  | .20  | .27  | .20  | a = .20 |
|       | II      | .43  | .20  | .42  | .23  | .53  | .27  | .40  | .21  | b = .40 |
|       | III     | .64  | .26  | .69  | .28  | .66  | .31  | .83  | .15  | c = .90 |

A measure of the goodness of the estimates is that of the absolute value of the difference from the actual probabilities. For each player, this absolute difference, $d_i$, was recorded for each subgame $i$, $i$ = I, II, III. Then $D_w = \sum_i d_i$ represents a measure of the accuracy of estimates in each block $w, w$ = 1, 2, 3, 4. Analysis of variance with repeated measures was used to test the effect of blocks and the differences among the three groups. The block effect was significant, $F(3, 108) = 4.37$, $p < .05$, while the group effect, $F(2, 36) = .15$, and the interaction effect, $F(6, 108) = 1.10$, were not significant. The three groups did not differ from one another with respect to the accuracy of their estimates, and they significantly improved in their estimates.

The relation between the accuracy of estimates on one hand, and the percentage of $C$ responses and total number of points lost on the other hand was investigated. A measure of overall goodness of estimation is provided by $\delta = \Sigma D_w$ for each player. The correlations between $\delta$ and the number of points lost were $-.41$, $-.30$, and $-.36$ for groups F-I, F-II, and F-III respectively, none of these values reaching significance. The correlations of $\delta$ and the percentage of $C$ responses were $-.05$, $-.19$, and $-.57$ for groups F-I, F-II, and F-III respectively, only the last correlation being significant, $p < .05$. Thus only for group F-III did the higher accuracy of the estimates raise the level of cooperation shown by the players.

It may be concluded from the above results that the two different stooge's strategies used with groups F-I and F-II led to differences in the perception of the other player as reflected in the estimates (Table 8), but did not affect the player's level of cooperation (Table 7) or the total number of points lost. The differences between the experimental conditions of groups F-I and F-III did not affect the mean estimates (Table 8) as expected, but led to significant differences in the level of cooperation and number of points lost. Players in group F-III played more cooperatively and won more points than players in group F-I.

Two reasons for the differences between groups F-I and F-III are tenable. The first is that the experimenter rather than the chart is in a sense the opposing player for group F-III, and players are expected to cooperate with the experimenter. The second possible reason is that the removal of a competitor alters the experimental situation so that the strong competitive disposition which many players exhibit is not aroused. When the competitor is removed the player may perceive the game as more of an individual problem-solving task and less of a competitive interaction of two players. It is noted, however, that the amount of cooperation of group F-III is too small to presume that all of the competitive aspect of the MPD game resides in the two-person interaction.

## A Model for MPD

DESCRIPTION OF THE MODEL

In this section a model for MPD is presented. It prescribes an optimal stationary policy for MPD, relative to the player's perception of his adversary stated in terms of subjective probabilities. By applying it to the responses of the players in the present study, its potential descriptive value will be investigated.

The model is an extension of a previous model for 2×2 PD games (Rapoport, 1967), and the reader is referred to that paper for background material, further details, and more examples. The model will be presented in its general form and then tested with the particular MPD used in the present study. To simplify the presentation only player $S$ will be considered, although the model applies equally well to player $O$.

To construct the model, probabilities have to be explicitly introduced into the MPD game.   We assume that $S$ has a subjective discrete probability distribution over the alternatives available to $O$ in each subgame.   Specifically, $p(h^i)$ is defines as $S$'s (subjective) probability that $O$ will choose his $h^{ith}$ alternative *whenever* $\Gamma_i$ is played; $p(h^i)$ is assumed to be a well-defined probability measure, satisfying

$$p(h^i) \geq 0, \text{ and } \sum_{h=1}^{\gamma i} p(h^i) = 1 \quad .$$

The strength of the above assumption should be recognized, for the problem of assessing subjective probability distributions is very difficult.   First, there is the problem of the measurement technique.   Different techniques, in general, lead to different results. Second, in many conflicts of interest there will be no "objective" evidence on which to base the assessment of such probabilities, as some of the conflicts may be completely novel.   In these situations the subjective probabilities may be interpreted in terms of $S$'s personal beliefs (or the betting odds) regarding $O$'s future choices, with which $S$ wishes to be consistent.   Finally, the assumption that $p(h^i)$ remains unchanged on different plays of $\Gamma_i$ seems questionable, unless $\Gamma_i$ has been played for a large number of trials and $p(h^i)$ has stabilized.

When probabilities are introduced, MPD is a Markov decision process (Howard, 1960).   To show this we slightly change notation.   In the MPD game let $p_{ij}^{kh}$ indicate $S$'s (subjective) probability that the joint choice $k^i h^i$ in $\Gamma_i$ will move him to $\Gamma_j$.   ($p_{ij}^{kh} = p(h^i)$ when $S$ chooses $k^i$ and the entry $(k^i h^i)$ determines a transition to $\Gamma_j$.)   $S$'s subjective probability that his decision $k^i$ will move him to $\Gamma_j$ is given by $p_{ij}^k$, defined by

$$p_{ij}^k = \sum_{h=1}^{\gamma i} p_{ij}^{kh} \quad ,$$

for all entries $(k^i h^i)$ in the payoff matrix, determining a transition to $\Gamma_j$.   Similarly, $r_{ij}^{kh}$ indicates the reward to $S$ when $k^i$ and $h^i$ are chosen simultaneously and the process moves to subgame $\Gamma_j$.   The *expected* reward associated with a transition from $\Gamma_i$ to $\Gamma_j$ when $k^i$ is chosen is given by

$$r_{ij}^k = \sum_{h=1}^{\gamma i} r_{ij}^{kh} p_{ij}^{kh} / p_{ij}^k$$

for all entries $(k^i k^i)$ in the payoff matrix determining a transition to $\Gamma_j$. By equating "state $i$" with "subgame $\Gamma_i$," substituting expected rewards for actual rewards, and keeping the same notation, it is easily shown that MPD is a finite-state discrete Markov decision process.

By requiring the Markov chain underlying the MPD game to be single and ergodic we simulate "transient" and "absorbing" subgames as well as multiple-chain structures. This elimination is not as restrictive as it may seem, since extensions can be developed for these cases. We shall not, however, undertake to do this here.

The expected rewards and transition probabilities, $r_{ij}^k$ and $p_{ij}^k$ respectively, are in general not specified by the payoff matrix of $\Gamma_i$, but they can be easily calculated. For example, consider subgame $\Gamma_3$ presented in Table 3, and assume $r_{11S}^3 = 20$, $r_{12S}^3 = -10$, and $r_{13S}^3 = -40$. Assume further that $S$'s (subjective) probabilities are given by the vector $p(3) = (.2, .1, .7)$, where $p(i) = (p(1^i), p(2^i), ..., p(Y^i))$. In words, $S$'s probabilities that $O$ will choose column $1^3$, $2^3$, or $3^3$, are .2, .1, and .7 respectively. When $S$ chooses $1^3$, he will remain in $\Gamma_3$ with probability of .3 (.2 + .1), and expected reward of 10 $(0.2 \times 20 + 0.1 \times (-10))/(.2 + .1)$. These values are entered in the appropriate entries of the transition and reward matrices, $P$ and $R$ respectively.

A policy is indicated by an ordered $N$-tuple $(k^1, k^2, .... k^N)$. Blackwell (1962) has proved that average expected reward in nonterminating Markov decision processes is maximized when a particular policy is pursued repeatedly. We shall refer to this policy as the optimal (stationary) policy. An iterative procedure for obtaining the optimal policy in Markov decision processes is the policy-iteration algorithm of Howard (1960). As we are interested not only in the average expected reward associated with the optimal policy but also in the average expected rewards provided by all policies, we shall compute them directly.

The number of all policies is finite, but generally very large. It is given by $Q = \Pi_{i=1}^N Y_i$, though it may be smaller when some of the policies are equivalent. Let us number all policies successively and denote a policy by $m$, $m = 1, 2, ..., Q$. Every policy $m$ determines an $N \times N$ transition probability submatrix $P_m$, $P_m \subset P$. Similarly, every policy $m$ determines an $N \times N$ reward submatrix $R_m$, $R_m \subset R$. The immediate expected reward for decision $k^i$ determined by policy $m$ is given by $q_{im}^k = \sum_{j=1}^{N} p_{ijm}^k r_{ijm}^k$, where $p_{ijm}^k \in P_m$, and $r_{ijm}^k \in R_m$. (Note that superscript $k$ can actually be suppressed, as policy $m$ uniquely defines the alternative chosen in $\Gamma_i$.) It can be shown (Howard, 1960) that the average expected reward for a nonterminating Markov decision process under policy $m$ is given by

$$g_m = \sum_{i=1}^{N} \pi_{im} q_{im}^k.$$

where $\pi_m = (\pi_{1m}, \pi_{2m}, \dots, \pi_{Nm})$ is the limiting state probability distribution under policy $m$. In words, $g_m$ is equal to the sum of immediate, expected rewards resulting from policy $m$ multiplied by the corresponding limiting state probabilities. To determine $g_m$, $\pi_{im}$ can be computed directly from $P$ and multiplied by $q_{im}^k$. A somewhat faster computational method, especially when $N$ is large, is given in Rapoport (1967). When $S$ adopts a policy $m$, MPD can be summarized by the following steps:

(1) Subgame $\Gamma_i$ is entered.

(2) $S$ chooses alternative $k^i$ from among the $Y_i$ available alternatives; $k^i$, which is determined by policy $m$, is a function of $\Gamma_i$ only.

(3) With (subjective) probability, $p_{ij}^k$, a subset of alternatives is chosen from among the $Y_i$ alternatives available to $O$ determining: (a) the next subgame to be played, $\Gamma_j$; and (b) the expected reward associated with the transition, $r_{ij}^k$, added to $S$'s total reward.

(4) Subgame $\Gamma_j$ is entered, and steps (1) to (3) are repeated.

To give an example for the computation of average expected rewards provided by all policies, the MPD game $\Gamma(3)$ represented in Table 9 will be analyzed. The (subjective) probability vectors are given in Table 9. Matrices $P$ and $R$, the transition probability matrix and the reward matrix, respectively, computed directly from Table 9, are presented in Table 10. Following the method described in Rapoport (1967), they have been used to obtain the average expected reward, $g_m$, for every policy $m$. All policies together with their associated $g_m$'s are presented in Table 11. The table shows that the number of different policies in 15 and not 18 (2 × 3 v3). This is because several seemingly distinguishable policies are actually equivalent. Inspection of Table 9 shows that playing $1^l$ in $\Gamma_l$ and $1^2$ in $\Gamma_2$ would "trap" $S$ in these two subgames. Subgame $\Gamma_3$ would not be entered and a choice of an alternative in $\Gamma_3$ is irrelevant. There are, therefore, three equivalent policies (1, 1, 1), (1, 1, 2) and (1, 1, 3), yielding the same average expected reward denoted by (1, 1, *). (We suppress superscript $i$, as the position of a chosen alternative indicates the corresponding subgame.) Similarly, policies (1, 3, 1) and (2, 3, 1) are equivalent – trapping $S$ in subgames $\Gamma_2$ and $\Gamma_3$ – and are denoted by (*, 3, 1).

Table 11 shows that the optimal policy for $\Gamma(3)$ is (1, 1, *) with $g_l = 1.120$. Playing cooperatively will trap the players in $\Gamma_l$ and $\Gamma_2$ and result in an average expected reward of 1.120 units per trial for player $S$. The worst policy is (*, 3, 1) with $g_5 = -8.893$. It is of some interest to note that (2, 3, 3) – choosing the dominating alternative in each subgame (or playing noncooperatively) – is not the optimal policy for $\Gamma(3)$. As a matter of fact it is one of the worst policies in this example. Although playing noncooperatively will always maximize immediate expected reward, it will not maximize, in general, average expected reward in nonterminating MPD games.

*Table 9. Payoff matrices for $\Gamma(3)$ with specified subjective probabilities*

Subgame $\Gamma_1$    $p(1) = (.9, .1)$

|  |  | Player $O$ | |
|---|---|---|---|
|  |  | 1 | 2 |
| Player S | 1 | 3,  3, $\Gamma_1$ | -10, 10, $\Gamma_2$ |
|  | 2 | 10, -10, $\Gamma_2$ | -5, -5, $\Gamma_3$ |

Subgame $\Gamma_2$    $p(2) = (.6, .2, .2)$

|  |  | | Player $O$ | |
|---|---|---|---|---|
|  |  | 1 | 2 | 3 |
| Player S | 1 | 8,  8, $\Gamma_2$ | -10, 10, $\Gamma_1$ | -20, 20, $\Gamma_1$ |
|  | 2 | 10, -10, $\Gamma_2$ | 1,  1, $\Gamma_2$ | -10, 10, $\Gamma_3$ |
|  | 3 | 20, -20, $\Gamma_3$ | 10, -10, $\Gamma_3$ | -8, -8, $\Gamma_2$ |

Subgame $\Gamma_3$    $p(3) = (.1, .1, .8)$

|  |  | | Player $O$ | |
|---|---|---|---|---|
|  |  | 1 | 2 | 3 |
| Player S | 1 | 10,  10, $\Gamma_3$ | -20, 20, $\Gamma_2$ | -40,  40, $\Gamma_2$ |
|  | 2 | 20, -20, $\Gamma_1$ | 8,  8, $\Gamma_3$ | -36,  36, $\Gamma_2$ |
|  | 3 | 40, -40, $\Gamma_1$ | 36, -36, $\Gamma_1$ | -30, -30, $\Gamma_3$ |

*Table 10.  Transition probability and reward matrices for $\Gamma(3)$ in Table 9*

|  | | Matrix $P_t$ | | | | | | Matrix $R_t$ | | |
|---|---|---|---|---|---|---|---|---|---|---|
|  | Sub-game | $k^i$ | $\Gamma_1$ | $\Gamma_2$ | $\Gamma_3$ | | Sub-game | $k^i$ | $\Gamma_1$ | $\Gamma_2$ | $\Gamma_3$ |
| | $\Gamma_1$ | 1 | 0.9 | 0.1 | | | $\Gamma_1$ | 1 | 3.0 | -10.0 | |
| | | 2 | | 0.9 | 0.1 | | | 2 | | 10.0 | -5.0 |
| $t-1$ | $\Gamma_2$ | 1 | 0.4 | 0.6 | | $t-1$ | $\Gamma_2$ | 1 | -15.0 | 8.0 | |
| | | 2 | 0.2 | 0.2 | 0.6 | | | 2 | -10.0 | 1.0 | 10.0 |
| | | 3 | | 0.2 | 0.8 | | | 3 | | -8.0 | 17.5 |
| | $\Gamma_3$ | 1 | | 0.9 | 0.1 | | $\Gamma_3$ | 1 | | -37.8 | 10.0 |
| | | 2 | 0.1 | 0.8 | 0.1 | | | 2 | 20.0 | -36.0 | 8.0 |
| | | 3 | 0.2 | | 0.8 | | | 3 | 38.0 | | -30.0 |

*Table 11.  All policies with their average expected reward for $\Gamma(3)$ in Table 9*

| $m$ | Policy | $g_m$ | $m$ | Policy | $g_m$ |
|---|---|---|---|---|---|
| 1 | (1, 1, *) | 1.120 | 8 | (2, 1, 1) | 0.502 |
| 2 | (1, 2, 1) | -2.952 | 9 | (2, 1, 2) | 0.738 |
| 3 | (1, 2, 2) | -0.881 | 10 | (2, 1, 3) | -0.632 |
| 4 | (1, 2, 3) | -1.417 | 11 | (2, 2, 1) | -8.922 |
| 5 | (*, 3, 1) | -8.983 | 12 | (2, 2, 2) | -5.902 |
| 6 | (1, 3, 2) | -2.736 | 13 | (2, 2, 3) | -8.390 |
| 7 | (1, 3, 3) | -1.944 | 14 | (2, 3, 2) | -5.132 |
| | | | 15 | (2, 3, 3) | -8.364 |

## TEST OF THE MODEL

An average expected reward may be calculated for each of the eight policies available to each player in groups M and F, given his estimates (subjective probabilities). The estimates given by each player at the end of block 4 were used to calculate the average expected reward for each policy, and then to rank the policies accordingly. This ranking will be referred to as the *optimal ranking*. Note that the policy ranked first is the optimal policy prescribed by the normative model.

In addition to the optimal rankings provided under the model, each player ranked on the questionnaire all eight stationary policies (for the following 100 trials), in order of their desirability against the other player. This ranking will be referred to as the *chosen ranking*. Spearman's rank-order correlations were computed for each player in each of the four groups between his chosen ranking and the optimal ranking. The correlations were in most cases essentially zero. The means of these correlations were -.19, +.14, -.05, and +.09 for groups F-I, F-II, F-III, and M respectively. It is evident that the chosen rankings at the end of the experiment did not correspond to the optimal rankings prescribed by the model.

It may be argued that it is not meaningful to the players to rank all eight policies when perhaps only a few have actually been used. Thus, a better measure might be either the player's selection of a best policy (the policy ranked number 1 in his chosen ranking) or the policy actually played on the last 50 trials.

Of the players in groups F and M, only a few more than would be expected by chance selected as their best policy that policy prescribed by the model. Similarly only 13 of 69 players played the last 50 trials according to the policy which was ranked best in the optimal ranking. Further tests of the model are reported in Cole (1966). Thus even when considering only the top policy, most of the players did not play according to the model.

There may be several reasons for the failure of the normative model. The first, and one often raised, is that players just do not play the MPD game rationally, and hence normative models should not be considered in the first place. It is not our purpose to discuss this answer here or to consider alternative explications of the notion of rationality. However, we do not find this argument sufficient to rule out the possibility of using normative models as a base line for constructing constrained optimal models (Rapoport, 1966) that may adequately describe the player's behavior.

A second possible reason for the model's failure may lie in the probability estimation phase. The technique used for measuring the subjective probabilities was extremely simple. The estimation task was not an integral part of the experiment, and no incentive was provided to the players for making good estimates. Although the mean estimates in the three F groups approached the actual probabilities, this should not be regarded as evidence for the adequacy of the technique, mainly because of the large individual differences that did not decrease as more practice was gained with the game.

Another possible reason for the model's failure is associated not with the technique for measuring subjective probabilities but with their interpretation by the player. The model calls for unconditional estimates, stated in terms of subjective probabilities over the other player's future choices. There are indications that, when asked to make his estimates, the player actually substitutes conditional estimates for unconditional ones. *S* estimates *O*'s future choices in each subgame conditional on the policy that he (*S*) is planning to take, and not unconditionally as required by the model.  This substitution seems to be almost unavoidable in the MPD game as well as in other PD games.  It will often lead to the failure of the model, especially when the players lock in on $CC$.

The difficulty is demonstrated most clearly when, for example, the players are supposed to lock in on $CC$ in subgame $\Gamma_j$.  In this case $S$ will most likely think that $O$ will almost surely continue playing $C$ in $\Gamma_j$ (with probability close to 1.00); and, in fact, he is very likely to be right, providing that he ($S$) will continue to play $C$.  $S$ knows very well that if he shifts to $D$, $O$ will not continue playing $C$ in $\Gamma_j$ for many more trials.  Thus if $S$ decides to discontinue playing $C$ in the future, his estimate that $O$ will continue to play $C$ in $\Gamma_j$ will decline sharply.  Note, however, that using the estimate as unconditional, the model will in most cases (depending on the rest of $S$'s estimates) prescribe playing $D$ in $\Gamma_j$.  It can be shown, then, that players who lock in on $CC$, trust each other, and do not plan to change their decision, will usually be classified as non-optimal by the model.

We must see now if the realities of the MPD game can be reconciled with the model.  In any situation other than that of using a stooge, the probabilities of $O$'s future choices will be subject to change depending on $S$'s contemplated future play.  Even when a stooge is used, but $S$ does not know it, or does not suspect that the stooge is using a stationary policy, the probabilities of $O$'s future choices will be subject to change.  Thus, the probability of constructing a model for MPD without explicitly considering $S$'s contemplated future play seems unlikely, and it seems doubtful whether unconditional estimates in the MPD context have any meaning at all.

A possible solution which preserves the relative simplicity of the individual decision-making situation and the normative flavor of the model, yet handles the interaction between the players more explicitly and perhaps more adequately, is to have the players make conditional estimates as they have been doing anyway.  By this approach, $S$ would make separate estimates of $O$'s future play conditional on each possible policy for $S$.  Then for each set of estimates the average expected reward of each policy could be calculated by the model.  That policy for which the model gave the largest average expected reward, when the estimates were conditional on its continuation in the future, would be considered the optimal policy.  In other words, this approach demands that instead of getting estimates for constructing the matrix $P$ and then obtaining from it every submatrix $P_m$ corresponding to every policy $m$, every submatrix $P_m$ will be estimated directly.  Whether or not this approach is feasible, in terms of $S$'s comprehension of and ability to do this estimation task in experimental studies of mixed-motive conflicts, is a question for future research.

The exploration of a limited normative model for the MPD has led to the explication of many subtleties of the expanded Prisoner's Dilemma which should not be ignored even when dealing only with the repeated, independent PD.  The model allowed for the clear statement of interdependence in the MPD with the weakness noted above in the estimation of probabilities.  The expansion to the MPD increases the applicability of the PD paradigm, and the existence of a satisfactory model of play would further enhance its usefulness.

This research effort was supported in part by NIH Grant MH-10006; during stages of planning and data collection, the second author was an NIF fellow under Grant MH-

8258. The authors are indebted to Lyle V. Jones and Charles W. Greenbaum for many helpful comments.

## References

Blackwell, D. Discrete dynamic programming. *Ann. Math. Statist.*, 1962, **33**, 719-726.

Bixenstine, V. E., Potash, H. M., and Wilson, K. V. Effects of level of cooperative choice by the other player on choices in a Prisoner's Dilemma game. Part 1. *J. Abnorm. Soc. Psychol.*, 1963, **66**, 308-313.

Cole, Nancy S. A test of a normative model for a modified Prisoner's Dilemma game. Unpublished master's thesis, University of North Carolina, 1966.

Gallo P. S., and McClintock, C. G. Cooperative and competitive behavior in mixed-motive games. *J. Conflict Resolut.*, 1965, **9**, 68-78.

Howard, R. A. *Dynamic programming and Markov processes.* New York: M.I.T. and John Wiley, 1960.

Luce, R. D., and Raiffa, H. *Games and decisions.* New York: John Wiley, 1957.

McClintock, C. G., Harrison, A., Strand, S., and Gallo, P. S. Internationalism-isolationism, strategy of the other player, and two-person game behavior. *J. Abnorm. Soc. Psychol.*, 1963, **67**, 631-635.

Minas, J. S., Scodel, A., Marlowe, D., and Rawson, H. Some descriptive aspects of two-person non-zero-sum games. II. *J. Conflict Resolut.*, 1960, **4**, 193-197.

Oskamp S., and Perlman, D. Factors affecting cooperation in a PD game. *J. Conflict Resolut.*, 1965, **9**, 359-374.

Rapoport, Amnon. A study of human control in a stochastic multistage decision task. *Behav. Sci.*, 1966, **11**, 18-32.

Rapoport, Amnon. Optimal policies for the Prisoner's Dilemma. *Psychol. Rev.*, 1967, **74**, 136-148.

Rapoport, Amnon, and Mowshowitz, A. Experimental studies of stochastic models for the Prisoner's Dilemma. *Behav. Sci.*, 1966, **11**, 444-458.

Rapoport, Anatol, and Chammah, A. M. *Prisoner's Dilemma: A study of conflict and cooperation.* Ann Arbor: University of Michigan Press, 1965.

Rapoport, Anatol, and Orwant, Carol. Experimental games: A review. *Behav. Sci.* 1962, **7**, 1-37.

Sermat, V. Cooperative behavior in a mixed motive game. *J. Soc. Psychol.*, 1964, **62**, 217-239.

Shapley, L. S. Stochastic games. *Proc. Nat. Acad. Sci.*, 1953, **39**, 1095-1100.

# CHAPTER 3

# DECISIONS OF TIMING IN BIPOLARIZED CONFLICT SITUATIONS WITH COMPLETE INFORMATION

**ABSTRACT:**    Games of timing constitute a sub-class of two-person, constant-sum, infinite games, where the problem facing each player is not what action to take, but rather when he should take action.    The theoretical structure of games of timing with complete information and equal accuracy functions is described.    An experimental paradigm of such games is presented by a computer-controlled, two-person, infinite game that simulates the Western-style duel.

Ten pairs of male subjects participated in three sessions each in a duel experiment. Each pair played 420 duels in which both players had the same accuracy function, but the starting number of bullets available to each player in the dyad was varied systematically.    The results of this experiment are analyzed and discussed in terms of variables that relate to predictions arising from the mathematical theory of duels.

Within the general game-theoretical framework (von Neumann and Morgenstern 1944), a major classificatory system may be described in terms of four binary dimensions:    (1) whether the number of players is two or more than two (two-person vs *n*-person games), (2) whether the interests of the players are diametrically opposed or are partially opposed and coincident (constant-sum vs nonconstant-sum games), (3) whether the players can agree on joint courses of action or must act independently of each other (cooperative vs noncooperative games), and (4) whether the set of courses of action (pure strategies) available to a player is finite or infinite.    In terms of this classification it is evident that some game categories have received extensive treatment by behavioral scientists (see e.g., Guyer and Zabner 1969, 1970, for extensive bibliographies), whereas others have not.    In particular, experimental research on constant-sum games has been largely neglected for at least two reasons.    It has been claimed that the interests of two players are rarely diametrically opposed.    Rather, in most real-life situations the parties have partially opposed, partially common interests.    Secondly, it has been argued that two-person constant-sum games are experimentally uninteresting, because the solution to these games, the minimax principle, is known.

Neither of these reasons should be uncritically accepted.    Granted that the majority of conflict situations are of the mixed-motive type (Gallo and McClintock 1965), many military, economic, and psychological conflicts are probably best characterized as constant-sum games.    With regard to the second argument, the existence of mathematically optimal solutions of constant-sum games in no way implies that human decision makers will follow such a strategy.    Despite their simplicity, the assumptions of rationality and information that underlie the minimax theorem do not hold experimentally. Thus, critics of game theory (e.g., Ellsberg 1956; Coddington 1967) have lodged the complaint that the minimax principle is not valid because it does not allow a player to exploit weaknesses in strategy of his opponent, such as are very likely to occur in real

43

situations.    Therefore, it is of considerable psychological interest to examine actual game
behavior    in    carefully    conducted    experiments,    to    compare    it    with    mathematically
prescribed  behavior, and  search  for  systematic  differences  that  may  be  meaningfully
interpreted in light of psychological phenomena.

Studies of constant-sum games (e.g., Brayer 1964; Lieberman 1960, 1962; Messick
1967) have made it clear that game theory *per se* is unfit as a descriptive theory of
decision behavior in finite constant-sum games presented repeatedly in normal (matrix)
form (but see Fox 1972). Alternative assumptions ought to be made, present assumptions
should be modified, or specific parameters have to be introduced in subsequent attempts
to    construct    more    descriptive    theories.      Nevertheless,    the    role    of    game    theory    is
important, not only in exposing the purely logical scheme of game-like situations
(Rapoport 1959), but also in providing a measure of how players depart from certain *a
priori*, widely accepted, established standards of decision behavior, and in providing a
skeleton for the construction of more adequate theories.

## Games of Timing

The present experiment undertakes to study decision behavior in two-person, constant-
sum, noncooperative games with infinitely many strategies.  To our knowledge, there has
been no previous experimental work on infinite constant-sum games; this lacuna is
probably due to the complexity of the mathematics of infinite games and to technical
difficulties in setting up experimental games with infinitely many pure strategies.    For
our experiment we have selected one particular variety of constant-sum infinite games,
which consists of games in which the pure strategies for the two players are the possible
times during which certain actions may be taken.    Unlike games in matrix form, the
players' problem is not to choose a single strategy, but rather each player has one or
more specified actions and his strategy involves a decision, either deterministic or
probabilistic, as to when to perform them, sometime between a starting time (arbitrarily
set at 0) and a terminal time (arbitrarily set at 1).    The longer the player waits before
acting, the greater the probability of his act being successful.  Games of this nature are
called "games of timing."

In more formal terms, a two-person constant-sum game, either finite or infinite, is
defined as a triplet $[X, Y, K]$, where $X$ is the complete strategy space for player $A$, $Y$ is
the complete strategy space for player $B$, and $K$ is a real-valued function of $X$ and $Y$,
whose values are interpreted as the expected payoffs from $B$ to $A$. In games of timing
a pure strategy is a real number in the closed interval [0. 1], and represents the choice
of a time to perform a specific action.    The payoff function has the following
properties:

$$\text{(i)} \quad K(\xi, \eta) = \begin{cases} L(\xi, \eta), & \text{if } \xi < \eta \\ \Phi(\xi), & \text{if } \xi = \eta \\ M(\xi, \eta), & \text{if } \xi > \eta \end{cases}.$$

(ii) Each of the functions $L(\xi, \eta)$ and $M(\xi, \eta)$ is jointly continuous in $\xi$ and $\eta$.

(iii) $L(\xi, \eta)$ and $M(\xi, \eta)$ are both monotone-increasing in $\xi$ for each $\eta$, and monotone-decreasing in $\eta$ for each $\xi$.

$K(\xi, \eta)$ is a function of two variables, $\xi$ and $\eta$, each of which ranges over the interval $[0, 1]$, and strategy spaces $X$ and $Y$ consisting of all cumulative distribution functions. Thus, $K(X, Y)$ represents the expected yield to player $A$ for the pure strategies $\xi$ and $\eta$, respectively, where $\xi$ is randomized by $A$ according to a cumulative distribution function $x$, and $\eta$ is independently randomized by $B$ according to a cumulative distribution $y$. The variables $\xi$ and $\eta$ indicate the times when the two players act. The monotonicity of the functions $L(\xi,\eta)$ and $M(\xi,\eta)$ and the discontinuity of the payoff function at $\xi = \eta$ have the following interpretation when each player may act only once: if player $B$ is going to act at a fixed time $\eta$, player $A$ improves his chances of success by deferring his action as long as possible, provided he acts before $B$ does. However, if player $A$ waits until after player $B$ acts, he may lose if $B$ is successful; hence the discontinuity at $\xi = \eta$. Once $B$ has acted and failed, $A$'s chances of success increase with time. The analogous statements apply for player $B$, since he benefits whenever the payoff to player $A$ decreases (Karlin 1959: 32).

Two classes of games of timing may be distinguished. Class 1 consists of games of timing with complete information. The idea of complete information is to be understood here in the sense that the actions of each player and their consequences become immediately known to his opponent. Class 2 consists of all games of timing not in class 1. In such games a player's acts are not always known to his opponent. In almost all cases the optimal strategies are unique, which simplifies their determination, adds to their attractiveness, and makes them particularly useful as cornerstones for building descriptive models.

One of the clearest examples of games of timing is the showdown duel, as often seen in the movies and on television. In this duel, each of two players has a gun with one bullet, and, starting at opposite ends of town (time 0), they slowly walk towards each other. The closer they are, the more accurate their fire. The decision each must make is when to draw his gun and fire at the other duelist. If one fires too soon his chances of missing are great and his opponent, who still has a bullet, may shoot at his leisure, with a sure chance of hitting. If, on the other hand, one waits too long, the other may fire with good chances of a hit. Games of class 1 can be considered *noisy duels*, where each duelist is informed immediately when his opponent fires. By contrast, a subset of class 2 games are *silent duels*, where the duelists have guns equipped with silencers, so that one player does not know when the other has shot unless, of course, he is hit. In the present paper we shall discuss only noisy duels.

Games of timing have not only theoretical interest or entertainment value, but also practical significance. We need not restrict ourselves to considerations of duels, either western or military, but can extend the model without undue stretching to other areas of bipolarized conflict. Consider, for instance, two competing mail-order firms preparing a Christmas catalogue mailing. The firm that gets its catalogue into the mail first has an advantage over the other firm, for customers will place orders before seeing what the competition has to offer. However, if the catalogue is mailed too soon customers will not yet have made plans for Christmas purchases, and the catalogue is likely to be filed away unnoticed. For another business example, consider the case of two competing swimsuit manufacturers. It is advantageous to be the first to release the year's model line, so that customers may have fewer competing alternatives to choose from. However, if the model is released too soon, the buyers (unless from California or Florida) are not interested yet and when the summer season arrives, the line, already familiar in the stores, will not have the "new look" that the competitor, who waited, can claim in its advertising.

Certain political decisions may also be modelled by games of timing. If two members of the same political party are competing for the party's nomination for a particular office, strategic considerations are paramount in deciding when to declare candidacy. The candidate who announces first has the advantage of an early start on his publicity and can get a jump on his competitor. On the other hand, if a candidate declares candidacy too early, his campaign may peak too soon, his expenses may become too high, and the opponent, who entered later, may overtake him.

The reader may think of other bipolarized conflicts, in areas as diverse as business, advertising, politics, and military planning, whose basic characteristics may be plausibly modelled by games of timing. In such conflict situations the actions which the two players may take are given in advance, but the timing of the actions is left to the strategic decisions of the players. Each player wishes to delay his decision as long as possible, but he may be penalized for waiting. Clearly such conflict situations may involve repeated, identical actions rather than a single one, as in the above examples. Thus, in the duel, whether noisy or silent, each duelist may have many bullets. There may be supplements to the Christmas catalogues which are released at various times. Politicians may choose when to file in the primaries of several states.

## The Optimal Strategy for Noisy Duels

The assumptions underlying constant-sum games with perfect information are known (see e.g., Luce and Raiffa 1957; Owen 1968). They assert the existence of a starting point for the game, divide the moves during the game into chance and personal moves, define the information structure as well as the rules of playing the game, and require each player to have a preference pattern over the set of outcomes of the game satisfying the axioms of utility theory. In addition, each player is assumed to be fully aware of the rules of the game and his opponent's utility function, and each is assumed to attempt to maximize his expected utility.

In the noisy duel, each player possesses an accuracy function yielding his (subjective) probability of hit as a function of time (or, equivalently, distance between the players). Let $P_A(\xi)$ denote the probability of a (successful) hit for player $A$ when he fires at time $\xi$, $0 \leq \xi \leq 1$, and let $P_B(\eta)$ denote analogously the probability of a hit for player $B$, where $0 \leq \eta \leq 1$ is $B$'s firing time. It is assumed for both players that $P_Z(0) = 0$ and $P_Z(1) = 1$, for $Z = A,B$. That is, a hit is impossible at time 0 and it is impossible to miss at time 1. Player $A$'s accuracy function is assumed to be continuous and monotone increasing with $\xi$; $B$'s accuracy function is correspondingly assumed to be continuous and monotone with $\eta$. Both $P_A(\xi)$ and $P_B(\eta)$ are assumed known to both players. If one player hits his opponent, the utility for the winner is assumed to be +1 and the utility for the loser is assumed to be -1; if both miss, or if both hit, the utility for each is 0. It is further assumed that if a player fires all of his bullets and misses, his opponent, if he still possesses a bullet, should fire at time 1, when he is sure of a hit.

Under these assumptions, the game-theoretic firing strategy for the noisy duel in which each player starts with a single bullet at time 0 (see e.g., Blackwell and Girshick 1954; Dresher 1961; Karlin 1959) is for both duelists to fire simultaneously at that time $x^*$, which satisfies the equation

$$P_A(x^*) + P_B(x^*) = 1 \ . \tag{1}$$

That is, the duelists should fire simultaneously when the sum of their probabilities of hitting is equal to one. The value of the game is positive or negative, depending on whether $A$ or $B$ has the greater probability of a hit. When the two accuracy functions are equal, the duelists should fire when their accuracies are 0.5; the game is then fair, with an expected value of zero.

If player $B$ does not play optimally, then it is sometimes to player $A$'s advantage to deviate from the minimax strategy in order to exploit $B$'s weakness. Just how great a reduction of security level (see e.g., Luce and Raiffa 1957) player $A$ should risk depends on his personal proclivities towards risk, the value of the game, the amount of information he has acquired about $B$'s strategy in such games, his subjective appraisal of $B$'s personality and intellectual ability, etc. If player $A$ knows $B$'s strategy, the problem ceases to be game-theoretic and becomes one in individual decision making. It can be shown that if $B$ fires too early all of the time, then $A$'s best strategy is not to deviate from optimality, which means, in effect, not firing until point blank range. If $B$ uses a pure strategy and fires too late, then $A$'s optimal strategy is to wait until just before $B$ fires, beating him to the draw by the smallest possible time. In general, if $B$ uses a known mixed strategy, an optimal policy for $A$ can be derived from standard results in decision theory (e.g., DeGroot 1970).

Consider now the case where each duelist has one or more bullets, assuming equal and linear accuracy functions for both players, $P_A(\xi)=P_B(\eta)=t$. Supposing players $A$ and $B$ start at time $t=0$ with $m$ and $n$ bullets, respectively, and at time $t$ they remain with $i$ and $j$ bullets left. Then it can be shown (Blackwell and Girshick 1954) that:

(i) the value of the game is $(m-n)/(m+n)$.
(ii) Whenever it arises that

$$t = 1/(i + j) \ , \tag{2}$$

the player with more bullets should fire once at that time. If he fails to fire, his opponent should fire immediately. In the case of equal number of bullets remaining, both players should fire simultaneously at the prescribed time given by equation (2). As a bullet is fired and misses, the duelists should play optimally for the game with the remaining number of bullets.

For example, if $A$ starts with $m = 1$ and $B$ starts with $n = 3$, then $B$ should fire once at $t = 0.25$, and again at $t = 0.33$. Both players should fire simultaneously at $t = 0.50$, assuming, of course, that both $B$'s previous bullets have missed. If $B$ fires early, $A$ should not change his strategy. But if $B$ does not fire when he should, $A$ should fire as soon as he notices $B$'s lapse, or, if $B$'s strategy is predictable, just before $B$ does fire.

## Method

A duel was implemented on a PDP-8 computer using two teletypes and two TV display units. Each display unit showed the same two figures moving towards each other on a line. The figure on the left represented one duelist (player A), and that on the right the other duelist (player $B$). The computer program allowed parameters to be specified by the experimenter, which might differ from one player to another, for the assignment of different accuracy functions, different approach times of the duelists, different starting number of bullets available to the duelists, different number of repetitions of the same duel, different payoff functions, and different series of parameter sets within an experimental session. Also at the option of the experimenter, the constantly changing probabilities of a hit may or may not be displayed to either or both duelists. For the current experiment, the probabilities of a hit and the number of bullets remaining to each duelist were fully displayed, thus making the game a noisy duel.

SUBJECTS

Twenty University of North Carolina male undergraduates were recruited as subjects for a paid decision making experiment via announcements placed on bulletin boards around campus. They were run in ten pairs, and friends did not participate together.

PROCEDURE

Subjects were placed in separate rooms, each with a teletype and TV display, and were given a set of instructions to read. The instructions described the experimental setup, explained the nature of a noisy duel, and told the subjects that the purpose of the experiment was to study "how people make decisions in a conflict situation involving time pressure when the resources of the two persons involved are limited."

To actually play the game, subjects were instructed as follows:

"In this experiment, you are a duelist named $A$ $(B)$ and your opponent is named $B$ $(A)$. You will participate in many duels which differ from one another in the number of bullets given to each duelist. The probability of $A$ hitting $B$ and of $B$ hitting $A$ will be displayed on the TV screen. The probability of $A$ hitting $B$ is displayed in the upper *left* corner of the screen. If, for example, the screen says 35, then if $A$ fires from this distance he will hit $B$ 35 times out of 100. Immediately below this number is shown the number of bullets $A$ has left to fire at $B$. Similarly, the information for player $B$ is represented in the upper *right* corner of the screen. The upper number shows the probability of $B$ hitting $A$ and the lower number shows how many bullets are left to $B$.

The teletype will print the number of the duel (for this set) and will then print READY?. When you are ready to start, press "Y" for "yes". Immediately after both duelists have typed "Y" the duel will start. The only response you will make during a duel is to fire bullets, and you do this by typing your opponent's name (either $A$ or $B$). Each time you type his name, you fire one bullet. You may fire bullets one at a time, or as many at a time as you wish, pressing the key with the name of your opponent once for each bullet you wish to fire, until you have no more bullets left. Whenever you fire, the number of your bullets will decrease by one. This will be noted on the TV screen. Thus, you can tell when your opponent has fired (and missed) by noting that the number of bullets for him on the screen has decreased by one. A duel terminates immediately if a hit is scored."

Further instructions explained more clearly that the nature of the problem facing the subject was one of timing: when should he fire each bullet in order to maximize his individual gain. Before starting the task, it was assured that both subjects understood the nature of the game and the rules for playing it.

Subjects participated in three identical experimental sessions, spaced approximately one week apart. Each session lasted for approximately two hours, during which seven games, each of 20 independent duels (trials), took place. Thus, each subject completed 140 trials per session, for a grand total of 420 duels. The number of starting bullets for each game, $m$ and $n$, was varied according to the schedule presented in Table 1. The accuracy functions were given by $P_A(\xi) = P_B(\eta) = t$.

*Table 1.    Number of starting bullets by game and player*

|         |          |          |          | Game     |          |          |          |
|---------|----------|----------|----------|----------|----------|----------|----------|
|         | $G_{11}$ | $G_{22}$ | $G_{12}$ | $G_{21}$ | $G_{13}$ | $G_{31}$ | $G_{33}$ |
| $m$     | 1        | 2        | 1        | 2        | 1        | 3        | 3        |
| $n$     | 1        | 2        | 2        | 1        | 3        | 1        | 3        |
| $m + n$ | 2        | 4        | 3        | 3        | 4        | 4        | 6        |

The probabilities of a hit, which were the same for both players, were shown on the TV display. They changed linearly in steps of 0.02 as a function of time (or, equivalently, distance), starting at 0 and ending at 1.00. When no hit was scored, a duel lasted 65 sec.

For each experimental session, the experimenter allocated \$4.00 to each subject. A win for one player resulted in that player gaining 10 cents of his opponent's money. A draw involved no transfer of funds. At the end of the experimental session subjects were paid half of their earnings, with the remainder paid in a lump sum at the termination of the last experimental session.

## Results

The game-theoretic model for the noisy duel implies several testable predictions concerning firing strategies. The present section is organized around these predictions. To clearly state them and to simplify the ensuing presentation of results, a system of notation and terminology is first presented.

A *game*, denoted by $G_{mn}$, is formally defined by the ordered pair $(m, n)$ where $m$ and $n$ are the numbers of starting bullets given to $A$ and $B$, respectively. The seven different games played in the experiment are presented in Table 1. A *position of player* $Z$, denoted by $Q_{ij}$, is defined by the ordered pair $(i, j)$, where $i$, $i \geq 1$, is the number of bullets remaining to player $Z$ at some firing time $t$, and $j$, $j \geq 1$, is the number of bullets remaining to his opponent at the same time. If $Z = A$, then $i = 1, ...,m$ and $j = 1, ...,n$; whereas if $Z = B$, then $i = 1, ...,n$ and $j = 1, ...,m$. Firing times are analyzed in terms of $Q_{ij}$ because the optimal strategy, as presented earlier, is stated in terms of $i$ and $j$ and not $m$ and $n$. "Position" is a psychologically meaningful variable, measuring the relative power of a player at a given moment in time.

There are nine distinguishable positions that may arise in the seven different games played in the present experiment: $Q_{11}$, $Q_{12}$, $Q_{13}$, $Q_{21}$, $Q_{22}$, $Q_{23}$, $Q_{31}$, $Q_{32}$, and $Q_{33}$. In positions $Q_{11}$, $Q_{22}$, and $Q_{33}$, the number of bullets available to each player is the same, and we shall say that the players are *symmetric* with respect to power. In positions $Q_{12}$, $Q_{13}$, and $Q_{23}$, player $Z$ has fewer bullets than his opponent and will be referred to as the *weak* player. In the remaining cases, $Q_{21}$, $Q_{31}$, and $Q_{32}$, player $Z$ is the *strong* player. Clearly, if one player is strong at a given position, his opponent is necessarily weak.

Not all nine positions may occur in all games. In game $G_{11}$, for example the only position a player may encounter is $Q_{11}$. Both players will be in position $Q_{11}$ on the same trial only if they fire simultaneously. In game $G_{22}$, on the other hand, four positions are possible for each player during the course of a single trial, namely, $Q_{11}$, $Q_{12}$, $Q_{21}$, and $Q_{22}$. (Clearly, either position $Q_{12}$ or $Q_{21}$ but not both may occur for player $Z$ on a given trial.) Only in game $G_{33}$ are all nine positions realizable.

The case $i > 0$ and $j = 0$ is of no interest, for then $Z$ is assumed to simply wait until he hits his opponent with certainty at time $t = 1$. With only two or three exceptions, this assumption was satisfied by all of our subjects on every instance where the case $j = 0$ arose.

If $i = j = 0$, a draw is scored and the duel terminates. This event might occur if the two players both fire their last bullets in so close an interval that $Z$'s opponent fires before he is aware that $Z$ has fired and missed. Moreover, simultaneous firing is not restricted to the last bullet only. For this reason, when $Z$ fires any of his bullets at time $t$, his position is actually calculated at time $t - \Delta$, where $\Delta$, $\Delta > 0$, is introduced to account for the time it takes the computer to transmit a signal from his opponent's teletypewriter to his TV display and teletypewriter plus his reaction time. Thus, if $Z$ fires at time $t$ and his opponent had fired at time $t - \epsilon$, $\epsilon < \Delta$, then at times $t - \epsilon$ and $t$, $Z$ is considered to be in the same position, even though the opponent's firing has actually changed the players' relative power. Although $\Delta$ should have been calculated separately for each player, as individuals vary in reaction time, individual reaction times were not measured. Instead, after measuring transmission time and carefully examining individual data, the maximum $\Delta$ was found to equal approximately 1/2 sec for all players.

There were three sessions in the experiment, denoted by $S$, $S = 1,2,3$. In general, players are denoted by $Z$, $Z = A,B$. If we have occasion to refer to a particular dyad from the ten who served in the experiment, or to refer to a particular individual subject, we shall write it explicitly, e.g., "pair 7" or "player $B$ of pair 5".

With the above terminology, let $t_Z(m,n;i,j;S)$ denote player $Z$'s mean firing time in game $G_{mn}$ and position $Q_{ij}$ during session $S$. Recall that not all $G_{mn}$ by $Q_{ij}$ combinations are possible. The frequency for which $t_Z(m,n;i,j;S)$ is computed is the number of trials player $Z$ fired while in position $Q_{ij}$ in game $G_{mn}$ during session $S$. We denote this number by $N_Z(m,n;i,j;S)$, where $0 \leq N_Z(m,n;i,j;S) \leq 20$ for every $(G_{mn},Q_{ij},S)$ combination that may obtain.

Following the logic of this notational system, we define the mean firing time for a particular position in a particular session over all games where this position might occur, as

$$t_Z(i, j; S) \sum_{G_{mn}} t_Z(m, n; i, j; S)\, N_Z(m, n; i, j; S)/N_Z(i, j; S),$$

where $N_Z(i, j; S) = \sum\limits_{G_{mn}} N_Z(m, n; i, j; S)$ is the number of trials on which player $Z$ fired while in position $Q_{ij}$ during session $S$. Thus, $t_A(1,1;2)$ is the mean firing time of player $A$ in session 2 when in the position where both players have one bullet left. Whereas this statistic would be computed over all seven games, $t_A(1,2;2)$, for example, would be based only on observations in the four games in session 2 for which position $Q_{12}$ is realizable for player $A$, namely, $G_{12}$, $G_{22}$, $G_{13}$, and $G_{33}$. To represent the mean firing time for a given position and a given game over all three sessions, let

$$t_Z(m, n; i, j) = \sum_{S} t_Z(m, n; i, j; S)\, N_Z(m, n; i, j; S)/N_Z(m, n; i, j)\ ,$$

where

$$N_Z(m,\ n;\ i,\ j) = \sum_S N_Z(m,\ n;\ i,\ j;\ S)\ .$$

Finally, let

$$t_Z(i,\ j) = \sum_{SG_{mn}} t_Z(m,\ n;\ i,\ j;\ S)\ N_Z(m,\ n;\ i,\ j;\ S)/N_Z(i,\ j),$$

where averaging is done over all sessions $S$ and all games $G_{mn}$ for which position $Q_{ij}$

may obtain, and where $N_Z(i,j) = \sum_S \sum_{G_{mn}} N_Z(m,n;i,j;S)$.

To measure within-subject variability, let $s_Z(m,n;i,j;S)$ denote the standard deviation of firing time of player $Z$ in position $Q_{ij}$ of game $G_{mn}$ during session $S$. $s_Z(m,n;i,j;S)$ measures the variability around $t_Z(m,n;i,j;S)$. Using notation in the same way as for the mean firing time, the within-subject standard deviations of $t_Z(i,j;S)$, $t_Z(m,n;i,j)$ and $t_Z(i,j)$, are donated by $s_Z(i,j;S)$, $s_Z(m,n;i,j)$, and $s_Z(i,j)$, respectively.

To represent group data the index $Z$ will be suppressed. We shall let $t(m,n;i,j;S)$ denote the (unweighted) mean firing time of all players in position $Q_{ij}$ of game $G_{mn}$ during session $S$, $N(m,n;i,j;S)$ denote the number of trials for which $t(m,n;i,j;S)$ is computed, and $s(m,n;i,j;S)$ denote the corresponding standard deviation. Whether data are averaged over all twenty players, or separately over the ten $A$ players and the ten $B$ players, will become clear from the context. Similarly, we define the (unweighted) group statistics $t(i,j;S)$, $t(m,n;i,j)$ and $t(i,j)$ with their corresponding incidences of occurrence and standard deviations.

Given this notational system, several game-theoretic predictions may now be stated precisely. Our purpose is not only to statistically test these predictions, but also to assess discrepancies between observed and predicted results and, if possible, to explain them in psychological terms.

FIRING TIME

When $i = j$ the model predicts simultaneous fire at $1/(i + j)$. On the other hand, when $i \neq j$ only the strong player, having more bullets, should fire at $1/(i + j)$. If he does not fire at that time, the weak player should fire at time $1/(i + j) + \epsilon$ where $\epsilon$ is an infinitesimal. In effect, then, the same firing time is prescribed for a given firing position for both the strong and the weak players. The model predicts that position only should be relevant in determining firing time; the assigned role of the player (either $A$ or $B$) and the experimental session should be of no importance.

   A  mean  discrepancy  from  prediction  score,  $1/(i + j) - t_Z(i, j; S)$  was  computed  for
each  subject  in  each  position  of  each  session,  collapsed  over  all  games  for  which  a
particular  position  is  defined.    To  examine  the  effect  of  position,  session,  and  role,  a
9×3×2 analysis  of  variance  with  repeated  measures  on  two  factors  was  performed  on  the
mean  discrepancy  from  prediction  scores,  which  were  roughly  normally  distributed.    The
analysis  yielded  a  highly  significant  position  effect  ($p < 0.001$)  as  expected.    Neither  of
the  other  two  main  effects,  nor  any  of  the  interactions  were  significant  at  $\alpha = 0.05$.
   Since  only  the  position  effect  was  significant,  results  may  be  collapsed  over  sessions
and  roles  to  facilitate  scrutiny  of  this  effect.    The  frequencies,  group  means  of  firing
time,  mean  deviation  from  prediction  scores,  and  between-subject  standard  deviations  of
firing  time  were  computed  separately  for  each  position  over  the  twenty  players.    They
are  presented  in  Table  2.    Column  5  of  Table  2  shows  that,  except  for  position  $Q_{11}$,  the
observed  means  are  higher  than  the  predicted  firing  times.    This  discrepancy  appears  to
be  systematic  in  that,  with  only  one  exception,  the  lower  the  predicted  firing  time  the
larger  the  mean  discrepancy  from  prediction  score  for  $i + j < 5$.

Table 2.   Frequencies,  mean  firing  times,  deviation  from  prediction  scores,  and  standard
          deviations  of  firing  time  by  position

| Position | $i+j$ | $N(i,j)$ | $t(i,j)$ | $\frac{1}{i+j} - t(i,j)$ | $s(i,j)$ |
|---|---|---|---|---|---|
| $Q_{11}$ | 2 | 1715 | 0.475 | 0.025 | 0.087 |
| $Q_{12}$ | 3 | 901 | 0.388 | -0.054 | 0.062 |
| $Q_{21}$ | 3 | 1593 | 0.378 | -0.045 | 0.063 |
| $Q_{22}$ | 4 | 911 | 0.362 | -0.112 | 0.068 |
| $Q_{13}$ | 4 | 462 | 0.331 | -0.081 | 0.064 |
| $Q_{31}$ | 4 | 999 | 0.335 | -0.085 | 0.058 |
| $Q_{23}$ | 5 | 220 | 0.282 | -0.082 | 0.061 |
| $Q_{32}$ | 5 | 220 | 0.298 | -0.098 | 0.055 |
| $Q_{33}$ | 6 | 697 | 0.262 | -0.096 | 0.055 |

GAME EFFECTS

Subjects  have  been  shown  to  have  fired  later  than  predicted  by  the  model.    It  is  natural
to  ask  if  this  phenomenon  holds  for  a  given  position  in  different  games.    The  minimax
strategy  asserts  that  firing  time  should  be  a  function  solely  of  the  two  accuracy
functions,  and  the  number  of  bullets  $i$  and  $j$.    In  particular,  firing  time  should  not  be
affected  by  the  number  of  starting  bullets,  $m$  and  $n$,  nor  should  it  be  influenced  by  the

history of the game from time 0 until firing time $t$. Psychologically, this model may prove untenable. Resources already spent may be of paramount importance in determining decision behavior. Grand strategies involving all or some of a player's bullets may be formulated and performed without regard to the earlier outcomes or the opponent's performance. Also, if the minimax model is strictly followed, then certain firing positions which in fact do arise should not occur. In particular, since simultaneous fire is prescribed in the case of equal numbers of bullets, positions in which the players are asymmetric should not arise in these instances.

To test the prediction $t_Z(m,n;i,j) = t_Z(i,j)$ for all $i$ and $j$, regardless of the values of $m$ and $n$, firing times for each position must be compared among the various games for which this position is defined. Table 3 presents the frequencies, group means, and group standard deviations of firing time by game and position. For asymmetric games, in order to maintain role equivalence, the means are collapsed for games $G_{21}$, and $G_{12}$ and for $G_{31}$ and $G_{13}$ by the strength of the player.

Six game by role analysis of variance tests were performed separately on $t_Z(m,n;i,j)$ for positions $Q_{11}$, $Q_{12}$, $Q_{21}$, $Q_{22}$, $Q_{13}$, and $Q_{31}$ over all games for which each of these positions is defined. No significant effects were found for the role of the player in any of the six tests, substantiating earlier results. Of all the game effects, only the one for position $Q_{11}$ was significant at $\alpha = 0.05$. To further test this particular position, a set of planned comparisons was used, based on $m + n$, the sum of starting number of bullets of both duelists. Of the set used, only the comparison between $G_{11}$ ($m + n = 2$) on one hand, and $G_{12}$ plus $G_{21}$ ($m + n = 3$) on the other, was significant ($p < 0.02$). All other comparisons, including games $G_{11}$, $G_{12}$, and $G_{21}$ ($m + n < 3$) against the remaining games ($m + n > 3$), were nonsignificant. For position $Q_{11}$, game $G_{11}$ had a firing time of 0.516 while in all of the other games it was between 0.429 and 0.460. It is interesting to note that for game $G_{11}$ the mean firing time is later than predicted, in keeping with results for other positions and other games. The discrepancy in position $Q_{11}$ from the earlier analysis is now clearer: where players start with more than one bullet, the last bullet is fired too soon.

Although the analyses of variance were not significant, it should be noted that, in general, for all positions, the greater the number of starting bullets, $m+n$, the earlier the mean firing time for a given position. For some positions, it was impossible to fire too soon because previous bullets were fired so late that the optimal time was already past. This corresponds to the significant findings for position $Q_{11}$. One possible reason for firing later bullets too soon is that players might be planning series of more than one shot at a time. Such a sequence might be to fire two or more bullets in a row, without regard for prior results. Such behavior would tend to lower the mean firing time for position $Q_{11}$ when $m + n > 2$. We term such behavior *volleying*. Volleying is defined operationally as firing two shots within an observed change in probability of 0.02 or less. The maximum time interval that could be enclosed was 2.5 sec; the majority of observed cases were within half of that time. Volleying was examined only for firing the second and last bullets together. Using this definition, volleying occurred overall in 540 out of a possible 1569 instances, or 34.5%. However, incidence of occurrence was distributed unevenly across dyads, with a range observed of from 5.3% to 74.5% among the ten dyads.

*Table 3.*  *Frequencies, means, and standard deviations of firing time by position, original relative strength, and game*

| Position | Original relative strength | Games | $m+n$ | $N(m, n; i, j)$ | $t(m, n; i, j)$ | $s(m, n; i, j)$ |
|---|---|---|---|---|---|---|
| $Q_{11}$ | symmetric | $G_{11}$ | 2 | 682 | 0.516 | 0.093 |
| | weak | $G_{21}, G_{12}$ | 3 | 259 | 0.456 | 0.069 |
| | strong | $G_{21}, G_{12}$ | 3 | 281 | 0.448 | 0.069 |
| | symmetric | $G_{22}$ | 4 | 211 | 0.460 | 0.080 |
| | weak | $G_{31}, G_{13}$ | 4 | 93 | 0.447 | 0.055 |
| | strong | $G_{31}, G_{13}$ | 4 | 102 | 0.440 | 0.068 |
| | symmetric | $G_{33}$ | 6 | 87 | 0.429 | 0.077 |
| $Q_{12}$ | weak | $G_{21}, G_{12}$ | 3 | 476 | 0.385 | 0.062 |
| | symmetric | $G_{22}$ | 4 | 103 | 0.389 | 0.068 |
| | weak | $G_{31}, G_{13}$ | 4 | 254 | 0.395 | 0.050 |
| | symmetric | $G_{33}$ | 6 | 68 | 0.376 | 0.070 |
| $Q_{21}$ | strong | $G_{21}, G_{12}$ | 3 | 887 | 0.375 | 0.062 |
| | symmetric | $G_{22}$ | 4 | 213 | 0.405 | 0.068 |
| | strong | $G_{31}, G_{13}$ | 4 | 368 | 0.375 | 0.055 |
| | symmetric | $G_{33}$ | 6 | 125 | 0.366 | 0.069 |
| $Q_{22}$ | symmetric | $G_{22}$ | 4 | 708 | 0.370 | 0.069 |
| | symmetric | $G_{33}$ | 6 | 203 | 0.335 | 0.055 |
| $Q_{13}$ | weak | $G_{31}, G_{13}$ | 4 | 400 | 0.339 | 0.060 |
| | symmetric | $G_{33}$ | 6 | 62 | 0.280 | 0.064 |
| $Q_{31}$ | strong | $G_{31}, G_{13}$ | 4 | 948 | 0.335 | 0.058 |
| | symmetric | $G_{33}$ | 6 | 51 | 0.321 | 0.065 |
| $Q_{23}$ | symmetric | $G_{33}$ | 6 | 220 | 0.282 | 0.061 |
| $Q_{32}$ | symmetric | $G_{33}$ | 6 | 220 | 0.298 | 0.055 |
| $Q_{33}$ | symmetric | $G_{33}$ | 6 | 697 | 0.262 | 0.055 |

If volleying causes the lowering of firing time in position $Q_{11}$ when $m + n > 2$, it would be expected that the more volleying occurred for a given dyad, the lower would be the mean firing time for that particular situation. To test this hypothesis, a correlation was computed between the proportion of volleys on the one hand, and the weighted sum of firing times for position $Q_{11}$, except for game $G_{11}$, on the other, yielding a value of $r=-0.67$, which is significant at $\alpha = 0.05$.

WITHIN-SUBJECT VARIABILITY

With regard to within-subject variability, the model predicts a fixed firing time for each position, i.e., $s_Z(m, n; i, j; S) = 0$ for each player and each realizable $(G_{mn}, Q_{ij}, S)$ combination. When the rate of change of the probability of a hit is as rapid as in the current experiment, (probability was stepped up by 0.02 per 4/3 sec), some within-subject variability is to be expected. Variability may also arise if a duelist attempts to conceal his fixed firing time so that his opponent may not consistently precede him, if he becomes involved in long-term planning intended to confuse or throw his opponent off balance, or if he simply wishes to relieve boredom.

The question, therefore should not be whether $s_Z(m, n; i, j; S) = 0$ or $s_Z(m, n; i, j; S) > 0$, for the latter is necessarily the case in duels played in real time, but whether or not it is affected by the player's position or by the experimental session. If subjects' behavior approaches optimality, within-subject standard deviations should decrease with practice over sessions. To test this prediction, a 9×3×2 position by session by role analysis of variance with repeated measures was performed on the within-subject standard deviations, which were distributed unimodally though not normally. Both position and session main effects were significant ($p < 0.001$), while neither the role effect nor any of the interactions were significant at $\alpha = 0.05$. This finding contrasts with the earlier analysis of the mean firing times, where the position effect was significant but the session was not. The means of $s_Z(m, n; i, j; S)$ by session and position are shown in Table 4.

*Table 4.*     *Means of within-subject standard deviations of firing time by session and position*

|         |          |          |          |          | Position  |          |          |          |          |
|---------|----------|----------|----------|----------|----------|----------|----------|----------|----------|
| Session | $Q_{11}$ | $Q_{12}$ | $Q_{21}$ | $Q_{13}$ | $Q_{31}$ | $Q_{22}$ | $Q_{23}$ | $Q_{32}$ | $Q_{33}$ |
| 1       | 0.070    | 0.039    | 0.044    | 0.034    | 0.029    | 0.056    | 0.028    | 0.031    | 0.032    |
| 2       | 0.044    | 0.033    | 0.036    | 0.031    | 0.024    | 0.032    | 0.021    | 0.020    | 0.024    |
| 3       | 0.041    | 0.031    | 0.030    | 0.030    | 0.024    | 0.030    | 0.028    | 0.021    | 0.024    |

It is apparent from an examination of Table 4 that the significant session effect is mostly attributable to a reduction in standard deviations between the first and second sessions. Within-subject variability around individual mean firing time was reduced by practice, and might have been further reduced if more than three sessions were played. Apparently, subjects explored the game environment in the first session, and settled down to less variable firing strategies in later sessions. It should be re-emphasized that this exploration did not affect the mean firing time, but only the standard deviation.

The interpretation of the significant position effect is less straightforward. Table 4 shows that the means of the within-subject standard deviations, like the mean firing times reported in Table 2, decrease as $i + j$ increases. This result may be partially due to the general tendency for the mean and standard deviation of frequency distributions to be positively correlated. As for the actual magnitude of the within-subject standard deviations, it appears from Table 4 that there is a grouping of positions with respect to the means of $s_Z(i, j; S)$ with $Q_{11}$ being in a group by itself, $Q_{12}$, $Q_{21}$, and $Q_{22}$ being in a second group, and the remaining five positions forming a third group. Notice that $Q_{11}$, the first group, is possible in all seven games, $Q_{12}$ and $Q_{21}$ are realizable in four games, and $Q_{22}$ is possible in three games. For the third group, $Q_{13}$ and $Q_{31}$ are possible in two games, while $Q_{23}$, $Q_{32}$, and $Q_{33}$ are only possible in $G_{33}$. Thus it appears that the more games a position is defined for, the larger is the within-subject standard deviation for that position.

Support for the above hypothesis is provided by the following analyses. Recall that for position $Q_{11}$ there were significant differences among mean firing times, depending on which game was played. This would inflate the within-subject standard deviation for that particular position. Results not fully reported here show that within-subject standard deviations $s_Z(m, n; i, j; S)$ computed separately for each game are considerably smaller than $s_Z(i, j; S)$, the means of which are reported in Table 4, and do not differ substantially from one another.

BETWEEN-SUBJECT VARIABILITY

A fourth implication of the minimax model concerns between-subject variability. The model predicts $s(m, n; i, j; S) = 0$ for every $(G_{mn}, Q_{ij}, S)$ combination that may arise. Note that between-subject variability is not logically implied by the absence of within-subject variability. Even if $s_Z(m, n; i, j; S) = 0$ for each player $Z$, there might still be positive between-subject variability because of individual differences in mean firing time. Previous research on decision behavior in finite games, constant-sum as well as nonconstant-sum, has typically yielded marked individual differences which, especially in the latter case, often increase rather than decrease with practice. Hence, in addition to assessing the magnitude of the between-subject standard deviations, we wish to determine whether they were affected by the various firing positions and, more importantly, by the session. If players' behavior approaches the same pure strategy, optimal or not, then both $s(m, n, ; i, j; S)$ and $s_Z(m, n; i, j; S)$ should decrease over sessions.

Table 5 presents results showing reduction in between-subject variability over sessions. For every firing position, $s(i, j; 1) > s(i, j; 2) > s(i, j; 3)$, with the single exception of $s(1, 2; 2)$. With regard to the effect of position on between-subject variability, Table 5 shows, with a few exceptions, the same inverse relationship between $s(i, j;S)$ and $i + j$ that has been reported above for mean firing time.

*Table 5.*    *Between-subject standard deviations of firing time by session and position*

| Session | $Q_{11}$ | $Q_{12}$ | $Q_{21}$ | $Q_{13}$ | $Q_{31}$ | $Q_{22}$ | $Q_{23}$ | $Q_{32}$ | $Q_{33}$ |
|---|---|---|---|---|---|---|---|---|---|
| 1 | 0.109 | 0.065 | 0.074 | 0.080 | 0.068 | 0.080 | 0.072 | 0.065 | 0.066 |
| 2 | 0.072 | 0.066 | 0.063 | 0.057 | 0.052 | 0.065 | 0.059 | 0.051 | 0.050 |
| 3 | 0.069 | 0.048 | 0.049 | 0.049 | 0.050 | 0.051 | 0.043 | 0.037 | 0.046 |

INTRA-DYADIC CORRELATIONS

According to the optimal model, the mean firing times of the two duelists in the same position should coincide. Since no variability around the mean firing time is prescribed, the correlation over dyads between $t_A (m, n;i, j;S)$ and $t_B (m, n;i, j;S)$ should be undefined for each pair of players and each realizable $(G_{mn}, Q_{ij}, S)$ combination. Alternatively, intra-dyadic behavior may be examined from considerations of exploitation of nonoptimality. It was pointed out in the introductory section that if a player responds nonoptimally, firing too late at time $t$, his opponent could exploit this "weakness" by withholding his fire until time $t - \epsilon$. Since it is conceivable that in an iterative duel, where inter-trial conditions remain the same, players will attempt to exploit perceived weaknesses of the opponent, it might be expected that the more optimal player would "track" the firing time of his less optimal opponent, if the latter, in fact, fired too late. Since individual differences are expected, this would result in each pair of players asymptoting on a common (to that pair) firing time, and a correlation of 1.0 between mean firing times of the first bullet. If the firing time of the less optimal player is too early, then proper exploitation is not to track. However, since it has already been shown that subjects fired too late for all but position $Q_{11}$, that they fired too late in that position in game $G_{11}$, and that within-subject variability was nonzero, it is to be expected that within-pair correlations between mean firing times of first bullet should be close to one.

Table 6 presents the correlations between mean firing times of the first bullet fired. Results are presented by game and session. Correlations were computed between mean firing times of the first bullet only, because it was assumed that on a given trial a player best recalls the firing times of his opponent's first bullet in the preceding trials. In addition, volleying, which occurred frequently, would make analysis of later bullets less interpretable. Table 6 shows that the within-pair correlations are uniformly positive and high, all significant ($p < 0.001$), and, with one exception, above 0.91, thus supporting the "tracking" hypothesis or any other hypothesis which yields mutual copying behavior.

Table 6.    *Intra-dyadic correlations between mean firing times of first bullet by session and game*

| Session | $G_{11}$ | $G_{22}$ | $G_{12}$ | $G_{21}$ | $G_{13}$ | $G_{31}$ | $G_{33}$ |
|---------|----------|----------|----------|----------|----------|----------|----------|
| 1       | 0.978    | 0.945    | 0.950    | 0.965    | 0.985    | 0.955    | 0.916    |
| 2       | 0.970    | 0.987    | 0.964    | 0.956    | 0.958    | 0.953    | 0.753    |
| 3       | 0.966    | 0.961    | 0.963    | 0.946    | 0.928    | 0.908    | 0.946    |

## SEQUENTIAL DEPENDENCIES

One of the major difficulties in the application of game-theoretic results to the analysis of experimental data obtained from matrix games is that, rather than being played only once, such games are typically repeated in time.    Although the payoff matrix remains unchanged over trials, the temporally iterated games are not perceived as independent by the subjects (see e.g., Rapoport and Chammah 1965; Rapoport and Mowshowitz 1966). The development of an overall strategy for supergames comprising iterations of nonconstant-sum games, or for segments of such supergames, is not unreasonable.    Such a strategy may be expected to emerge when players possess the knowledge that the same physical situation will be repeated, that reprisals on later trials are possible and even likely, and that the pattern of decisions along repeated games may be used to communicate otherwise unarticulated collusion.

In a supergame composed of iterations of constant-sum games, an overall strategy of playing optimally in the minimax sense at each trial is itself optimal in the supergame (Luce and Raiffa 1957).    The implication for the present experiment is obvious:    if the optimal strategy is employed by both players, successive trials within the game should be independently played.    Neither the outcomes nor the firing times of either of the two players on the preceding trials should affect a player's behavior.

To test the effect of previous outcomes on firing time, a conditional mean firing time was computed separately for each player and each position for those trials following runs of at least one win, two wins, three or more wins, one loss, two losses, and three or more losses.    Trials following a draw and the first trial in a game were not included. All inferential statistics performed on these data revealed no significant differences, thus supporting the game-theoretic prediction.

To further investigate interdependencies between firing times on successive trials, two correlations were computed for each player, each session, and each game.    The first, an intra-subject correlation, was between the firing time of player $Z$'s first bullet on trials $s$ and $s-q$, where $q$ is the minimum number of trials previous to trial $s$ on which player $Z$ fired in a situation where his opponent still had bullets remaining.    For a majority of situations, $q$=1. The second correlation is inter-subject; it is between $Z$'s firing time of his first bullet on trial $s$ and his opponent's firing time of his first bullet on trial $s$-$q$, where $q$ is defined as before. Again, only firing times for the first bullet were considered for reasons given in the discussion of intra-dyadic correlations. Given seven games and three sessions, at most 42 correlations could be computed for each player, for a total of 840 correlations. Twenty of these correlations were undefined because of zero variability around mean firing time for one of the players.

The percentage of significant correlations ($\alpha$ = 0.05) between $Z$'s firing time of his first bullet on trial $s$ and his first bullet on trial $s$-$q$ was only slightly higher than the expected 5 percent; 56% of all correlations were positive, and for only one out of the twenty players was the proportion of positive correlations significantly higher than 0.50. However, the examination of the correlations between a player's firing time of his first bullet on trial $s$ and his opponent's first bullet on trial $s$-$q$ yielded different results. In this case, 14% rather than the expected 5% of the correlations were significant.

A breakdown of the significant correlations by game and by session is presented in Table 7. The table shows that most of the significant correlations (35 out of 66) occurred on the first session, that the number decreased with practice for five out of the seven games, and that the symmetric games $G_{11}$, $G_{22}$, and $G_{33}$, accounted for two-thirds of all the significant correlations.

*Table 7. Number of significant correlations ($\alpha$ = 0.05) between firing times of first bullet on successive trials by game and session*

| | Game | | | | | | | |
|---|---|---|---|---|---|---|---|---|
| Session | $G_{11}$ | $G_{22}$ | $G_{12}$ | $G_{21}$ | $G_{13}$ | $G_{31}$ | $G_{22}$ | Sum |
| 1 | 5 | 10 | 2 | 2 | 3 | 5 | 8 | 35 |
| 2 | 4 | 1 | 1 | 3 | 3 | 2 | 2 | 16 |
| 3 | 2 | 7 | 0 | 0 | 0 | 1 | 5 | 15 |
| Sum | 11 | 18 | 3 | 5 | 6 | 8 | 15 | 66 |

## Discussion

One of the purposes of this study was to identify behavioral regularities in a particular steady-state time-dependent bipolarized conflict situation, and to compare these regularities with prescriptions arising out of game theory. The salient features of the results may be briefly summarized with respect to this purpose.

Our results show that, in general, players fired their first bullets later than the prescribed time, and then fired their later bullets a short time thereafter, mostly sooner than prescribed. In other words, the range of firing time was more compressed than the optimal policy would prescribe. This effect was more pronounced for those players who volleyed, or fired bursts of shots rather than spacing shots one at a time. Within-subject variation was present, but was reduced over experimental sessions. With respect to intra-dyadic interaction, it was found that the two players in a particular dyad matched each other's mean firing time with remarkable accuracy. In general, there was no great degree of trial-to-trial matching of firing time, but there was some tendency, particularly on the first experimental session, for players to match the firing time of their opponent on the previous trial.

Consider together the low inter-trial correlations, the high intradyadic correlations, and the generally low within-subject standard deviations of firing time in individual games. These three findings in conjunction lead to the conclusion that players within a dyad rapidly reached a consensus of some appropriate firing time and then held to a time consistently throughout a game. Small differences within a session were essentially random, thus resulting in the low inter-trial correlations, except for the first experimental session, when the consensual time was being established.

The failure of the minimax model in prescribing firing times is attributable to almost any of the assumptions of the model. However, certain assumptions which are questionable in terms of the psychology of the player suggest themselves as being liable to scrutiny.

Although the game was designed to be constant-sum, it is entirely possible that there might have been personal costs and gains idiosyncratic to various subjects that made the game nonconstant-sum. For example, a win might have been particularly gratifying and a loss shrugged off, or a win taken for granted and a loss mortifying, particularly in asymmetric games, where the strong player's expectation was to win and the weak player's expectation was to lose. Evidence that expectations may influence perceptions of outcomes is shown in studies (e.g., McClintock and McNeel 1966; Messick and Thorngate 1967) demonstrating the importance of relative gain as a determinant of choice strategies in experimental games. However, it can be shown (Karlin 1959) that if the *ordinal* properties of the game are maintained, such that winning is worth more than a draw which is worth more than losing, then the optimal strategies in effect do not change.

Another assumption open to question is equality of the objective probability of a hit, as displayed to the subjects, with their subjective probabilities. An S-shaped subjective probability function or some other function which decreases the probabilities below 0.5, is in reasonable agreement with certain salient features of the results, in particular the late firing time of the first bullet. Since all of the predicted first bullet firing times $1/(i+j)$ are smaller than or equal to 0.5, a subjective probability distribution which underestimates the true probability of success would cause firing to occur at higher objective levels of probability, as occurred in the present experiment. This explanation concurs with that of Herman et al. (1962) who, in an individual decision making task of timing, showed that subjects underestimated the true hit probability for early stages in the task. The decision making literature on this question is not conclusive, however. Often (e.g. Erlick 1964; Pitz 1965) studies have shown overestimation of low and underestimation of high probabilities. Further research needs to be done in both gaming and decision making tasks to clarify this question.

Firing at different times for different games, although in the same position, can best be accounted for in terms of an individual bullet vs whole game strategy explanation. Recall that there was a tendency to fire from a given position later, the more bullets there were to begin with in the duel. For position $Q_{11}$, this resulted in an overall mean firing time below the optimal time; for other positions this probably did not occur because the firing time for the first bullet in a sequence was already too late for the prescription of later bullets. It appears that, rather than consider each bullet separately as the game theory solution would prescribe, subjects often considered the action to be taken as a whole, chose an appropriate time to fire, and then concentrated their actions in a short time interval. Such a decision strategy telescopes multiple decisions into a single choice and puts less pressure on the player. Once a time for action is chosen, it is "do or die" at that point. The apparent neatness of such a solution is likely to be a satisfactory resolution to the player's decision task. Another reason for such behavior might come from a common fallacy concerning probability of disjoint events. It is very likely that the average subject would regard the probability of one successful bullet out of three, each fired with a probability of 1/3, to be fairly close to 1 instead of the objective value of 19/27. With this bias, a maximization procedure would be to bunch all of the bullets within a short timespan.

The close tracking of one member of a dyad with his partner does fall within game theoretic predictions, given that the other tends to fire too late. Whether or not subjects will continue to track, even if the other fires too early, cannot be ascertained from the present experiment. This suggests that one path for future studies in games of timing might involve the use of experimental confederates playing programmed strategies, to test the extent of how much the subject is influenced away from optimality by the behavior of his opponent.

Relaxation of the restriction of equal accuracy functions would be of interest, especially when the more accurate duelist has fewer bullets than this opponent. This would allow the study of the effects of different types of power, as measured by available resources and efficiency, of those resources. The whole area of class 2 games, including "silent" duels has been explored theoretically, but not experimentally. Class 2 games might be better suited to immediate psychological interpretations than noisy duels. There is a wealth of information to be gained from systematic exploration of decision behavior in these and other bipolarized conflict situations.

This research was supported in part by a PHS Grant No. MH-10006 from the National Institute of Mental Health and in part by a University Science Development Program Grant No. GU-2059 from the National Science Foundation. The authors wish to thank Arthur W. Coston for program development, David G. Clark for his help in data collection and data analysis, and Edward S. Johnson, Anatol Rapoport, William E. Stein, and Thomas S. Wallsten for many valuable suggestions.

## References

Blackwell, D. and M. A. Girshick, 1954. Theory of games and statistical decisions. New York; Wiley.

Brayer, A. R., 1964. An experimental analysis of some variables of minimax theory. Behav. Sci. 9, 33-44.

Coddington, A., 1967. Game theory, bargaining theory, and strategic reasoning. J. Peace Res. 1, 39-45.

Degroot, M. H., 1970. Optimal statistical decisions. New York: McGraw-Hill.

Dresher, M., 1961. Games of strategy: theory and applications. Englewood Cliffs, N. J.: Prentice-Hall

Ellsberg, D., 1956. Theory of the reluctant duelist. Amer. Econ. Rev. 11, 909-923.

Erlick, D. E., 1964. Absolute judgments of discrete quantities randomly distributed over time. J. Exp. Psychol. 67, 475-482.

Fox, J., 1972. The learning of strategies in a simple, two-person, zero-sum game without saddlepoint. Behav. Sci. 17, 300-308.

Gallo, P. S., Jr. and C. G. McClintock, 1965. Cooperative and competitive behavior in mixed-motive games. J. Conflict Resolution 9, 68-78.

Guyer, M. and M. Zabner, 1969. Experimental games: a bibliography (1965-1969). Ann Arbor, Mich.: Mental Health Research Institute Communication No. 258, November 1969.

Guyer, M. and M. Zabner, 1970. Experimental games: a bibliography (1945-1964). Ann Arbor, Mich.: Mental Health Research Institute Communication No. 265, February 1970.

Herman, L. M., G. N. Ornstein and H. P. Bahrick, 1962. Probabilistic information processing systems: Displays and operator performance. Paper presented in the IRE International Congress on Human Factors in Electronics. Long Beach, Calif., May 3-4, 1962.

Karlin, S., 1959. Mathematical methods and theory in games, programming, and economics, vol. 2. Reading, Mass.: Addison-Wesley.

Lieberman, B., 1960. Human behavior in a strictly determined 3 x 3 matrix game. Behav. Sci. 4, 317-322.

Lieberman, B. Experimental studies of conflict in some two-person and three-person games. In: J. H. Criswell, H. Solomon and P. Suppes (eds.), Mathematical methods in small group processes. Stanford, Calif.: Stanford Univ. Press, 203-220.

Luce, R. D. and H. Raiffa, 1957. Games and decisions: introduction and critical survey. New York: Wiley.

McClintock, C. G. and S. P. McNeel, 1966. Reward level and game playing behavior. J. Conflict Resolution 10, 98-102.

Messick, D. M., 1967. Interdependent decision strategies in zero-sum games: A computer-controlled study. Behav. Sci. 12, 33-48.

Messick, D. M. and W. B. Thorngate, 1967. Relative gain maximization in experimental games. J. Exp. Soc. Psychol. 3, 85-101.

Owen, G., 1968. Game theory. Philadelphia: Saunders.

Pitz, G. F., 1965. Response variables in the estimation of relative frequency. Percept.

Mot. Skills *21*, 867–873.

Rapoport, Am. and A. Mowshowitz, 1966.   Experimental studies of stochastic models for
the Prisoner's Dilemma. Behav. Sci. *11*, 444–458.

Rapoport, An., 1959.   Critiques of game theory.   Behav. Sci. *4*, 49–66.

Rapoport, An. and A. M. Chammah, 1965.   Prisoner's Dilemma:   a study in conflict and
cooperation.   Ann Arbor, Mich.: Univ. of Michigan Press.

Von Neumann, J. and O. Morgenstern, 1944.   Theory of games and economic behavior
(1st ed.).   Princeton: Princeton Univ. Press.

# CHAPTER 4

# DECISIONS OF TIMING IN CONFLICT SITUATIONS
# OF INCOMPLETE INFORMATION

**ABSTRACT:** Games of timing constitute a subclass of two-person, zero-sum, infinite games, where the problem facing the player is not what action to take, but rather when he should take action. The minimax solution to games of timing with incomplete information and equal accuracy functions is presented. An experimental paradigm of such games is provided by a computer-controlled two-person, zero-sum, infinite game that simulates the Western style silent duel. Ten pairs of male subjects each participated for three sessions in a silent duel experiment. Each pair played 450 duels in which both players had the same accuracy functions, but the starting number of bullets available to each player in the dyad was varied systematically. The results of this experiment are analyzed and discussed in terms of variables that relate to predictions arising from the mathematical theory of silent duels. Differences between results from the silent duel and previous research on noisy duels (Kahan & Rapoport, 1971) are discussed.

Whereas a large portion of the mathematical literature of game theory has been concerned with zero-sum games (Luce & Raiffa, 1957), social scientists interested in studying conflict behavior have shown almost no interest in such games. The bulk of the experimental research on dyadic interaction has been confined to nonzero-sum games, such as prisoner's dilemma and chicken (Rapoport & Chammah, 1965; 1966), which are experimentally administered as payoff matrices that typically provide each player with only two or three pure strategies.

It has been argued that nonzero-sum games may better serve the social scientist's purposes since, as in most real life situations of conflict, they provide the players with partially opposed, partially common interests. This argument has been critically examined by Kahan and Rapoport (1971) in their attempt to revive interest in experimental studies of zero-sum games. In order to shift emphasis from studying behavior in very simple conflict situations to studying decisions of timing, they introduced an experimental paradigm for games of timing, a class of two-person zero-sum games in which each player's space of strategies is the real number interval $[0,1]$. Unlike matrix games, in which a choice of a pure strategy represents the selection of a specific course of action, the choice of a pure strategy in games of timing represents the selection of a time to perform a prespecified action. Similarly, whereas a mixed strategy in matrix games is a probability distribution over a set of mutually exclusive and collectively exhaustive courses of action, in games of timing it is a density function over the time to perform a specified action. The paradigm employed by Kahan and Rapoport, also used in the present study, allows experimental investigations of the timing of decisions in a strictly competitive environment.

Although games of timing may be interpreted in psychological and economic terms, they are most clearly interpreted as tactical problems (Karlin, 1959; Restrepo, 1957). In this context, a game represents a contest between two players trying to achieve the same objective. When one of them succeeds, he wins one unit, his opponent loses the same unit, and the contest is over. The initial resources of the players are limited and are not necessarily equal. Within the time interval $0 \leq t \leq 1$ each player can make only a fixed number of attempts to reach the objective, and each attempt may fail or succeed. At time $t = 0$ every attempt fails, at time $t = 1$ every attempt succeeds, and at any other time every attempt succeeds with some probability, which depends on the player making this attempt and on the time at which the attempt is made. An intriguing example is the Western duel, in which the two duelists start ($t = 0$) at opposite ends of town and walk toward each other, guns drawn and pointing. Each duelist has a fixed number of bullets known to himself and his opponent. The closer they are to each other, the more accurate is their fire. The problem is to decide when to fire each of the bullets, for to fire too early is to risk missing the target and depleting one's resources, while to wait is to risk having already been hit by the opponent before one has fired.

More formally, games of timing are played on the unit square in which the choice of a pure strategy represents the choice of a time to perform a specific action. When each player has only one action at time $t = 0$, each must choose a time in the interval $[0, 1]$ at which to act. If player $A$'s action is successful, then $A$ gains +1 unit and player $B$ gains -1 unit, and conversely if $B$ succeeds. Mutual successes or mutual failures result in zero payoff for both players. The payoff function of this game is defined (Karlin, 1959) as

$$(1) \qquad K(\xi,\eta) = \begin{cases} L(\xi,\eta), & \text{if } \xi < \eta \\ \phi(\xi,\eta), & \text{if } \xi = \eta \\ M(\xi,\eta), & \text{if } \xi > \eta \end{cases}$$

where $\xi$ is the time that player $A$ acts and $\eta$ is the time that player $B$ acts. Each of the functions $L(\xi,\eta)$ and $M(\xi,\eta)$ is monotone-increasing in $\xi$ for each $\eta$ and monotone-decreasing in $\eta$ for each $\xi$. Each of these two functions is jointly continuous in $\xi$ and $\eta$. In terms of our experimental paradigm, given that one player fires at a fixed time, his opponent's odds of a successful shot increase as the time increases, or, alternatively, as the distance between the duelists decreases. In the more general case, if player $A$ starts with $n$ bullets, firing his $k$th bullet at time $\xi_k$, $k = 1, \ldots, n$, then $\xi = (\xi_1,\xi_2, \ldots, \xi_n)$, satisfying the restriction $0 \leq \xi_1 \leq \ldots \leq \xi_n \leq 1$, is a vector describing his pure strategy. Similarly, $B$'s pure strategies correspond to vectors $\eta = (\eta_1, \eta_2, \ldots, \eta_m)$, with $0 \leq \eta_1 \leq \ldots \leq \eta_m \leq 1$, where $m$ is the number of $B$'s bullets at time $t = 0$.

Two classes of games of timing have been distinguished (Karlin, 1959). In class I are games of timing of complete information, where when either player acts, his action and its consequences are immediately known to his opponent. In terms of equation (1), $L(\xi,\eta)$ is a function of $\xi$ alone, and $M(\xi,\eta)$ is a function of $\eta$ alone. The paradigmatical example of this class of games is known as a noisy duel, for in this class each player knows when the other has fired each of his bullets. Class II consists of all games of timing not in Class $I$, i.e., games in which either $L$ or $M$ or both explicitly depend on both $\xi$ and $\eta$. In such games, a player's acts or its consequences are not necessarily known to his opponent. The duel studied in the present experiment is a subclass of Class II, where each duelist knows the starting number of bullets his opponent has (at time $t = 0$), but he does not know (at $0 < t \leq 1$) how many unsuccessful bullets his opponent has already fired. Hence, this type of game is known as a silent duel.

The relevance of silent duels to realistic conflict situations and hence to behavioral scientific investigation is not limited to problems of tactics. Consider a case described by Karlin (1959) of two publishing companies competing for a contract with an author who is considering writing a book. The timing, i.e., the time for the publisher's representative to appear ready with the contract and various inducements, represents the set of pure strategies. Too early a contract offer may meet with failure since the author is not far enough along in his work to be interested in a publishing decision. On the other hand, a late bid may also fail; the competitor may have gotten there first. If the publishers' representatives are too overworked to make more than one visit, and if the two publishing houses do not tell each other of their activities, then the situation is analyzable as a one bullet $vs.$ one bullet silent duel.

Congressional voting policies provide another example of a silent duel. Here, consider two factions competing for the vote of a key congressman. To approach him too late risks that he has committed himself to vote for the other side; to approach him too early risks his not being ready to commit himself. The problem is again one of timing: When is the best time to make the secret visit to his office?

### Optimal Strategy for Silent Duels

As in our previous study (Kahan & Rapoport, 1971), our goal is to develop descriptive models based on behavioral regularities and on systematic deviations between observed and optimal decisions of timing. To do that, we present the optimal strategies for the silent duels employed in our experiment. The derivation of the general solution to the silent duel is too involved to be presented here; the reader is referred to Karlin (1959) or Restrepo (1957) for rigorous expositions.

We first provide the solution to the silent duel where each duelist has only one bullet and they are equally good marksmen. The payoff function of this duel, as defined by equation (1), reduces in this case to

$$K(\xi,\eta) = \begin{cases} \xi - (1 - \xi)\eta , & \text{if } \xi < \eta \\ 0 , & \text{if } \xi = \eta \\ -\eta + (1 - \eta)\xi , & \text{if } \xi > \eta . \end{cases}$$

It can be shown (Karlin, 1959; Owen, 1968) that the optimal strategy is for player $A$ to hold his fire until his probability of hitting $B$ is 1/3, and then fire according to the density function $1/4t^3$. The same optimal strategy is prescribed for player $B$.

For the more general case, where player $A$ starts with $n$ bullets and player $B$ starts with $m$ bullets, the optimal strategy is obtained by solving a set of simultaneous integral equations. In all cases, both players wait some time before firing at all, and then fire according to different density functions for each bullet, depending on the values of $n$ and $m$.

The present experiment considers two special cases, both assuming that players have equal accuracy functions with $P_A(t) = P_B(t) = t$. The first is the equal number of bullets case, where $m = $ n (Dresher, 1961; Karlin, 1959). For $k = $ m, $m - 1, \ldots , 1$, minimax solution is to fire the $(m - k + 1)th$ bullet with the density function

$$(2) \qquad f(t) = \begin{cases} (4kt^3)^{-1}, & \text{if } (2k + 1)^{-1} \leq t \leq (2k - 1)^{-1} \\ 0 , & \text{otherwise .} \end{cases}$$

In the second special case one duelist starts with one bullet and his opponent starts with $m$ bullets. In this nonsymmetric situation, the player with $m$ bullets should fire according to different density functions for each bullet, and, with some finite probability should save his last bullet to time $t = 1$. The player with one bullet should fire his single shot according to a density function made of composite parts corresponding to the firing time intervals for the $m$ bullets of his opponent. A computer program was written to determine the optimal strategies, following Karlin (1959, pp. 153-161). For the case of $n = 1$ and $m = 3$, examined in the present experiment, the program yielded the density function

$$(3A) \qquad f(t) = \begin{cases} 0 , & \text{if } 0 \leq t < a_1 \\ .0786/t^3, & \text{if } a_1 \leq t < a_2 \\ .1165/t^3, & \text{if } a_2 \leq t < a_3 \\ .2736/t^3, & \text{if } a_3 \leq t \leq 1 \end{cases}$$

for player $A$, and the density functions

$$f_1(t) = \begin{cases} .2266/t^3, & \text{if } a_1 \leq t < a_2 \\ 0 , & \text{otherwise} \end{cases}$$

$$(3B) \qquad f_2(t) = \begin{cases} .3112/t^3, & \text{if } \quad a_2 \leq t < a_3 \\ 0 , & \text{otherwise} \end{cases}$$

$$f_3(t) = \begin{cases} 0 , & \text{if } 0 \leq t < a_3 \\ .5320/t^3, & \text{if } a_3 \leq t < 1 \\ .4587 , & \text{if } t = 1 , \end{cases}$$

for player $B$, where $f_k(t)$ refers to the density function for the $k$th bullet of player $B$, $k = 1, 2, 3$, and for both players, $a_1 = .2338$, $a_2 = .3251$, and $a_3 = .5740$. It is easily verified that each of the functions in equations (3) is a well-defined density function.

The optimal strategies for the two special cases described above have certain implications easily testable with experimental data. In particular, when $m$ = n, but not when $m \neq n$, equation (2) implies that the optimal strategy for firing time depends only on the number of bullets currently in possession, and not on the original number of bullets. Another property of the optimal strategy for the case $m$ = n, one which allows comparison of firing times in noisy and silent duels, concerns mean firing time. It can be shown that when the starting number of bullets, $m$, is the same in both noisy and silent duels, the prescribed mean firing time of the $k$th bullet, $k$ = 1, ... , m, for the silent duel is identical to the prescribed fixed firing time in the noisy duel.

There are several parallels in the prescriptions of firing strategy when a comparison is made between noisy and silent duels on the one hand, and between two-person, zero-sum, finite games with and without saddlepoints on the other hand. In noisy duels and in games with saddlepoints the optimal policy is to play a pure strategy, while in silent duels and in zero-sum games without saddlepoints, a randomization of strategies is prescribed. In the former case, if his opponent does not play optimally, a player may gain more than the value of the game, while in the latter case, a player's optimal strategy yields him a fixed value no matter what strategy is pursued by his opponent. In the case of finite games, previous research has shown that zero-sum games with saddlepoints are played optimally (Lieberman, 1960; 1962), but that subjects do not perform optimally in zero-sum games without saddlepoints (Brayer, 1964; Messick, 1967; Kahan & Goehring, 1973), unless, perhaps, they are provided with a rich informational situation (Fox, 1972). Therefore, we may predict that subjects in the present experiment will perform less optimally than those in Kahan and Rapoport (1971).

## Method

A duel was implemented on a PDP-8 computer using two teletypes and two cathode ray display units. Each display unit showed the same two figures moving toward each other on a line. The figure on the left represented one duelist (player $A$), and that on the right the other duelist (player $B$). The computer program allowed parameters to be specified by the experimenter, which might differ from one player to another, for the assignment of different accuracy functions, whether those were displayed or not, different approach times of the duelists, different starting number of bullets available to the duelists, different number of repetitions of the same duel, different payoff functions, and different series of parameter sets within an experimental session. For the current experiment, the probabilities of a hit were displayed but the number of bullets remaining to each player were not, thus making the situation a silent duel.

### SUBJECTS

Twenty male University of North Carolina undergraduates were recruited as subjects in a paid decision making experiment via announcements placed on bulletin boards around campus. Appointments were set up for subjects in ten pairs; friends did not participate together. No subject had participated in a prior duel experiment.

PROCEDURE

Subjects were placed in separate rooms, each with a teletype and a TV display, and were given instructions to read. The instructions described the experimental setup, explained the nature of a silent duel, and told the subjects that the purpose of the experiment was to study decision making in a conflict situation involving time pressure. They were then given instructions as follows:

"In this experiment, you are a duelist named $A$ $(B)$ and your opponent is named $B$ $(A)$. You will participate in many duels which differ from one another in the number of bullets given to each duelist. The probability of $A$ hitting $B$ and of $B$ hitting $A$ will be displayed on the TV screen. The probability of $A$ hitting $B$ is displayed in the upper left corner of the screen. If, for example, the screen says 35, then if $A$ fires from this distance he will hit $B$ 35 times out of 100. Similarly, the information for player $B$ is represented in the upper right corner of the screen. The number shows the probability of $B$ hitting $A$.

Each of the duelists has a silencer on his gun. Hence, you will always know how many bullets you have left to fire, but you will not know how many bullets your opponent has left. In particular, you will never know whether or not your opponent has fired all of his bullets. The computer will tell you, however, how many bullets each duelist has when the duel starts.

The teletype will print the number of the duel (for this set) and will then print READY? When you are ready to start, press "$Y$" for "yes." Immediately after both duelists have typed "$Y$" the duel will start. The only response you will make during a duel is to fire bullets, and you do this by typing your opponent's name (either $A$ or $B$). Each time you type his name, you fire one bullet. You may fire bullets one at a time, or as many at a time as you wish, pressing the key with the name of your opponent once for each bullet you wish to fire, until you have no more bullets left. A duel terminates immediately if a hit is scored."

Further instructions explained more clearly that the nature of the problem was one of timing: When should a player fire each bullet in order to maximize his individual gain? Before starting the task, it was assured that both subjects understood the nature of the game and the rules for playing it.

Subjects participated in three separate identical experimental sessions, spaced approximately one week apart. Each session lasted for approximately two hours. During each session, five series (games) of 30 independent duels (trials) were played, for a total of 150 trials in each session. Thus, each subject completed 450 duels, all against the same opponent. The number of starting bullets for each problem was typed at the beginning of each problem on both teletypewriters. It was varied according to the schedule presented in Table 1. At the outset of each experimental session, the experimenter allocated $4.00 to each subject. A win for a player resulted in that player gaining .10 of his opponent's money; a draw involved no transfer of funds. At the end of the experimental session subjects were paid half of their resultant earnings, with the remainder being paid in a lump sum at the termination of the third, last, experimental session.

*Table 1.  Number of starting bullets by game*

|  | Game | | | | |
| --- | --- | --- | --- | --- | --- |
|  | 1 | 2 | 3 | 4 | 5 |
| $n_A(0) = n$ | 1 | 2 | 1 | 3 | 3 |
| $n_B(0) = m$ | 1 | 2 | 3 | 1 | 3 |

## Results

### NOTATION

The optimal strategy for the silent duel, as given in equations (2) and (3), yields testable predictions concerning interdependency of trials, shape of the observed frequency distribution of firing time, and effects of practice and the values of $m$ and $n$ on firing strategy.  In order to unambiguously state and test these predictions and to simplify the ensuing presentation of the results, a system of terminology and notation is first presented.

Let $n_z(0)$ denote the number of bullets player $Z$, $Z = A,B$, has when the duel starts at time $t = 0$.  $n_A(0)$ and $n_B(0)$ are always known by both players.  A game is defined by the ordered pair $(n_A(0), n_B(0))$ and denoted by the letter $i$, $i = 1, \ldots , 5$.  A game is symmetric if $n_A(0) = n_B(0)$; it is nonsymmetric otherwise.  As is seen in Table 1, games 1, 2, and 5 are symmetric while games 3 and 4 are not.  If $n_z(0) < n_{z'}(0)$, where $Z,Z' = A,B$, player $Z$ is called the *weak* player and $Z'$ is called the *strong* player.

Let $n_z(t)$ denote the number of bullets available to player $Z$ at firing time $t$, $0 \leq t \leq 1$.  A *position* of player $Z$ at time $t$ is defined in terms of three numbers always known to the player: $n_z(t)$, $n_z(0)$, and $n_{z'}(0)$.  A player's position indicates where he is at any time in the duel with respect to how many bullets he has remaining and with how many he and his opponent each started.  As the dependent variable of the duel is player $Z$'s firing time, interest and discussion are restricted to the case $n_z(t) > 0$.  Position is used to define a player's state because, as shown in the introductory section, this determines the optimal firing strategy for a particular player at time $t$.  In the five games played in the present experiment there are ten distinguishable positions.  These are denoted by the letter $j$, $j = 1, \ldots , 10$, and are presented in Table 2.

*Table 2. Definition of position in terms of $n_Z(t)$ and $n_Z(0)$*

|          | Position |   |   |   |   |   |   |   |   |    |
|----------|---|---|---|---|---|---|---|---|---|----|
|          | 1 | 2 | 3 | 4 | 5 | 6 | 7 | 8 | 9 | 10 |
| Game     | 1 | 2 | 2 | 5 | 5 | 5 | 3,4 | 3,4 | 3,4 | 3,4 |
| $n_Z(t)$ | 1 | 1 | 2 | 1 | 2 | 3 | 1 | 1 | 2 | 3 |
| $n_Z(0)$ | 1 | 2 | 2 | 3 | 3 | 3 | 1 | 3 | 3 | 3 |
| $n_{Z'}(0)$ | 1 | 2 | 2 | 3 | 3 | 3 | 3 | 1 | 1 | 1 |

The three experimental sessions are denoted by the letter $d$, $d = 1, 2, 3$. If we have occasion to refer to a particular dyad of the ten who participated in the experiment, or to refer to a particular individual subject we shall write it explicitly, e.g., dyad 9, or player $5B$ (player $B$ of dyad 5).

With the above terminology, let $t_{jdr}(Z)$ denote the event of player $Z$'s firing time on trial $r$ in position $j$ during session $d$, where $r$ is some integer between 1 and 30, $j = 1, \ldots, 10$, and $d = 1, 2, 3$. Of interest is $f_{jd}(Z)$, the observed frequency distribution of firing time of player $Z$ in position $j$ during session $d$, and the mean, $t_{jd}(Z)$, and standard deviation, $s_{jd}(Z)$, of that frequency distribution. Another statistic employed is the number of times $Z$ fired while in position $j$ during session $d$, $N_{jd}(Z)$, where $0 \leq N_{jd}(Z) \leq 30$. If $Z$ never fired on any trial in position $j$ during session $d$, then $N_{jd}(Z) = 0$, whereas if he happened to fire in this position on every trial, then $N_{jd}(Z) = 30$.

To represent group data, the index $Z$ is suppressed. Thus, $f_{jd}$ is the observed frequency distribution summed over all 20 subjects, with mean $t_{jd}$ and standard deviation $s_{jd}$. Clearly, $s_{jd}$ measures both intersubject and intrasubject variability. To test predictions which concern intrasubject variability only, we shall also need the frequency distribution of $s_{jd}(Z)$. Only the mean of this distribution, denoted by $s_{jd}$, will be referred to.

PRESCRIBED FIRING TIME

The various silent duels played in the present experiment terminate as soon as one of the players is hit by his opponent. If in game 1 player $Z$ decides to fire his single bullet at time $t$, but player $Z'$ precedes him and hits him at time $t'$, $t' < t$, player $Z$'s decision is not revealed and cannot be recorded as data. Thus, even if both players fire optimally according to the density functions (2) and (3), the observed distribution of firing time will be biased due to truncation toward early firing time compared to the prescribed distribution. Consider, for example, game 1 where the optimal policy results in a mean firing time of 0.5. If each of the two players randomly selects a firing time according to the density function (2) at the beginning of each trial, on a certain computable percentage of trials the firing time selected by $Z$ will be later than the one selected by $Z'$ and $Z$ will be hit before he can fire. Consequently, the observed mean of $Z$'s firing times in game 1 will be lower than .5.

To allow a comparison of observed and predicted results, the truncation bias toward early firing time should be corrected. The derivation of the truncated density functions of firing time in the silent duels played optimally is given in the appendix of Rapoport, Kahan, and Stein (1972). The corrected means and standard deviations of firing time for each of the ten positions are presented in Table 3, along with the uncorrected means and standard deviations of the density functions defined in equations (2) and (3). Table 3 shows that the effect of truncation is to lower the means and to decrease the standard deviations. The effect is not substantial, however. Except for position 7, the difference in means is less than .026 and the difference in standard deviations is less than .031. As is shown by Rapoport *et al.* (1972), the general shape of the density function of firing time for each of the ten positions is not affected by truncation.

*Table 3.*    *Corrected and uncorrected means and standard deviations of firing time for optimal play*

| Position | Means | | Standard deviations | |
|---|---|---|---|---|
| | Corrected | Uncorrected | Corrected | Uncorrected |
| 1 | .474 | .500 | .142 | .157 |
| 2 | .474 | .500 | .142 | .157 |
| 3 | .247 | .250 | .036 | .037 |
| 4 | .474 | .500 | .142 | .157 |
| 5 | .247 | .250 | .036 | .037 |
| 6 | .165 | .167 | .016 | .016 |
| 7 | .388 | .453 | .168 | .197 |
| 8 | .835 | .854 | .165 | .160 |
| 9 | .412 | .415 | .067 | .068 |
| 10 | .271 | .272 | .025 | .025 |

ROLE AND SESSION DIFFERENCES

The minimax model predicts no differences in mean firing time attributable to the role of the player (A or $B$) in the symmetric games, and no differences across games resulting from player $A$ being strong in game 4 and weak in game 3, with the reverse being true for player $B$. Similarly, as the three sessions were exact replications of each other, there should be no differences due to sessions. Practical and psychological considerations lead one to expect no role effect if players are randomly assigned, but there is the possibility of a session effect attributable to learning, as subjects may play more optimally in later sessions due to increased familiarity with the game and perhaps, due to experience, a more realistic appraisal of the hit probabilities.

To test for role and session effects, two multivariate analyses of variance were performed, one on the ten mean firing times (one for each position) and one on the ten intrasubject standard deviations of firing time. The statistical model employed was a repeated measures design, with two independent variables, role and session. For the analysis of standard deviations, neither the main effect nor the interaction effect were significant ($\alpha = .05$). For the analysis of the means, the interaction and the role effect were nonsignificant as expected, but there was a significant main effect for session (multivariate $F_{20,18} = 3.11$, $p < .009$). Univariate $F$-tests were significant for seven out of ten positions, the exceptions being positions 4, 6, and 10. Examination of the means across sessions in Table 4 shows clearly that for every position there is a decrease in mean firing time from session 1 to session 2 to session 3. Because of this significant session effect, further analyses will examine each session separately; because role was not significant, these analyses will be collapsed over that variable.

GAME DIFFERENCES

The prescribed firing strategy in symmetric games is independent of the starting number of bullets, $n_z(0)$ and $n_{z'}(0)$. Thus, we have the prediction that, in symmetric games, for positions with the same number of bullets, i.e., for equal $n_z(t)$, $t \neq 0$, there should be the same mean and standard deviation of firing time. Specifically, there should be no differences in the means and standard deviations among positions 1, 2, and 4, and between positions 3 and 5. To test these hypotheses, repeated measures analyses of variance were done on the means and intrasubject standard deviations of firing time, with position and session as the independent variables. In no case were there any significant differences in the tests of standard deviations, despite the apparent decrease for positions 2, 3, and 5, reported in Table 4. For the comparison among the means of positions 1, 2, and 4, both the main effects for session ($F_{2,18} = 10.83$) and position ($F_{2,18} = 24.93$) were significant ($p < .001$) but the interaction was not. For the comparison between the means for positions 3 and 5, the session effect was again significant ($F_{2,18} = 6.63$, $p < .007$), the position by session interaction was nonsignificant, and the position effect was marginally nonsignificant ($F_{1,9} = 3.34$, $p < .101$). We are inclined to accept the latter difference from the optimal prediction as real, although the difference is probably not as strong as in the earlier case. Examination of the relevant

Table 4.    Observed and predicted mean firing times and means of intrasubject standard deviations by position and session

| $j$ | Predicted means | Observed means | | | | Predicted SD | Observed standard deviations | | | |
|---|---|---|---|---|---|---|---|---|---|---|
| | | $t_{j1}$ | $t_{j2}$ | $t_{j3}$ | $t_{j\cdot}$ | | $s_{j1}$ | $s_{j2}$ | $s_{j3}$ | $s_{j\cdot}$ |
| 1 | .474 | .562 | .484 | .438 | .493 | .142 | .134 | .149 | .139 | .150 |
| 2 | .474 | .467 | .429 | .371 | .417 | .142 | .181 | .176 | .131 | .166 |
| 3 | .247 | .360 | .324 | .294 | .326 | .036 | .112 | .077 | .058 | .089 |
| 4 | .474 | .399 | .353 | .320 | .356 | .142 | .207 | .159 | .160 | .179 |
| 5 | .247 | .325 | .295 | .266 | .294 | .036 | .097 | .076 | .064 | .083 |
| 6 | .165 | .270 | .256 | .242 | .256 | .016 | .081 | .066 | .064 | .072 |
| 7 | .388 | .384 | .348 | .317 | .349 | .168 | .132 | .108 | .087 | .113 |
| 8 | .835 | .552 | .474 | .462 | .491 | .165 | .238 | .214 | .227 | .229 |
| 9 | .412 | .399 | .349 | .320 | .354 | .067 | .098 | .084 | .075 | .092 |
| 10 | .271 | .320 | .298 | .276 | .298 | .025 | .078 | .067 | .067 | .073 |

means in Table 4 shows that the firing time in position 1 was consistently higher than that for position 2, which in turn was higher than that for position 4. Similarly, the firing time for position 3 was higher than that for position 5 for all three sessions. Thus, relative to the optimal strategy, the more bullets a player started out with, the sooner was he likely to have fired all of them.

One possible reason for this phenomenon is that, rather than separately assigning firing times to each bullet as the optimal strategy prescribes, subjects may formulate a grand strategy of firing all of their bullets, in which bullets may be fired in groups rather than singly. This type of behavior may be conveniently termed volleying. For experimental purposes, volleying is defined as firing two bullets within an observed change of .02 or less in the displayed probability. This corresponds to a maximum real time interval of 1.5 seconds. On trials coded as volleying trials, the mean interbullet interval was well under 0.9 seconds. The proportion of volleying trials varied considerably over subjects, ranging from .161 to .791 in the one bullet left situations in games 2 and 5 (positions 2 and 4), and from .231 to .767 in the two bullets left situation of game 5 (position 5).

If volleying is a contributing factor for the symmetric game differences, then the difference in mean firing time should be more pronounced for subjects with higher proportions of volleying than for subjects with lower proportions of volleying. To test this hypothesis, the proportion of volleying in the two bullets left case was compared to the difference $t_3 - t_5$ collapsed over sessions, and the proportion of volleying in the one bullet left case was compared to the overall difference $t_2 - t_4$. The values for those two correlations were .317 and .375, respectively.   Although the correlations are in the appropriate direction, they are not significantly ($\alpha$ = .05) different from zero.

SEQUENTIAL EFFECTS

Subjects' firing time may well have been influenced by the outcomes on previous trials. Intertrial effects, frequently termed recency or sequential effects in the psychological literature, are nonoptimal in the silent duel.   However, having been repeatedly observed in other decision making and learning experiments, they may also be expected in the present study.   To test the effect of strings of wins or losses on firing time in succeeding trials, the trials of each subject were classified according to whether the subject had won or lost the preceding trial.   This bipartite division was further broken down depending on the number of consecutive outcomes of the same type that had occurred, ranging from 1 to 3 or more.   In this analysis, the first trial of each set and the trials following drawn games, which occurred when all bullets fired were unsuccessful, were excluded from consideration.

A position (1 through 10) by type of sequence (win or loss) by length of sequence (1, 2, 3+) three-way analysis of variance was performed on the individual mean firing times.   Significant $F$ ratios were found for position main effect ($F_{9,18}$ = 141.38, $p < .001$) and for length of sequence main effect ($F_{2,18}$ = 9.56, $p < .001$).   All other effects were not statistically significant.   The position main effect is expected from previously reported results, but the length of sequence main effect is of interest, particularly in view of the failure to find a significant difference due to the type of sequence or to find any interactions.   The observed means of firing time after one, two, and three or more outcomes of the same type in a row were .367, .372, and .390, respectively, showing a very minor, yet significant tendency to fire later after short runs of outcomes of the same type.

INTRADYADIC RELATIONSHIPS

A tracking effect was reported in the noisy duel experiment (Kahan & Rapoport, 1971), where the mean firing times of both members of a particular dyad were very closely related to each other.   A similar effect might also be expected in the present experiment, but would be harder to detect, as player $Z$ may only know when $Z'$ is successful, and even then $Z$ does not know which bullet was fired.   Evidence weakly consistent with tracking behavior is the lack of any role effect reported in earlier analyses and the significant length of sequence effect reported immediately above.   Regardless of whether the sequence was one of wins or losses, the same tendency to fire later was observed. When we consider that a win sequence for one member of a dyad is necessarily a loss sequence for his opponent, then the length of sequence effect becomes indicative of some tracking behavior.

Since a pure strategy of a fixed firing time is prescribed for the noisy duel and the observed variability around individual mean firing times in that duel (Kahan & Rapoport, 1971) was small, tracking behavior could be adequately assessed by correlating the intradyadic mean firing times only. In the silent duel, where relatively large variability around mean firing time is predicted (see Table 3), both measures of central tendency and dispersion should be correlated to properly investigate tracking. To provide a test of tracking behavior, correlations were computed among the observed means and intrasubject standard deviations of firing time for each of the three experimental sessions separately, and for the symmetrical games only (positions 1 through 6). The correlations of interest are the ones for the same position and for each of the two statistics. These correlations are presented in Table 5 for each session separately.

*Table 5.* *Intradyadic correlations for means and intrasubject standard deviations of firing time in symmetric positions*

| | Correlations over | | | | | |
|---|---|---|---|---|---|---|
| Position | Means | | | Standard deviations | | |
| | Session 1 | Session 2 | Session 3 | Session 1 | Session 2 | Session 3 |
| 1 | .832 | .865 | .915 | .528 | .209 | .553 |
| 2 | .097 | .663 | .421 | .104 | .834 | .058 |
| 3 | .679 | .960 | .971 | .430 | .579 | .717 |
| 4 | -.089 | .280 | .347 | -.136 | .648 | .420 |
| 5 | .290 | .865 | .873 | .201 | .855 | .537 |
| 6 | .733 | .722 | .953 | .788 | .560 | .795 |

Table 5 shows that 34 out of 36 correlations are positive, and 21 out of 36 are above .55 ($p < .05$ by a one-tailed test). The correlations seem to increase over sessions for the means, indicating greater coordination over time. The incongruent correlation for the standard deviation of firing time for position 2 in session 3 is due to data from player 7A, whose standard deviation of firing time was one-third the value of the next smallest standard deviation. When dyad 7 is removed from the analysis, the correlation increases from .058 to .510. The correlations reported in table 5 suggest that not only did players in the same dyad tend to have the same mean firing times, they also tend to have similar dispersions around these means.

Inspection of Table 5 further indicates that the highest correlations occur for the first bullet fired, positions 1, 3, and 6. This is a puzzling finding, since it is in positions 3 and 6 that the amount of information about the opponent's firing time seems to be at its minimum.   One possible interpretation of this finding is that it might be easier to determine or recall the firing time of the opponent's earlier hits than his later ones.   A player might tend to pay considerable attention and remember vividly those trials on which he was hit by an early shot of his opponent, presumably assumed to have been his first shot.   Early shots might have gained prominence since they typically left the losing player in the embarrassing position of ending the duel with all of his bullets still unexpended.

DISTRIBUTIONS OF FIRING TIME

Figures 1 through 10 display the observed frequency distributions of firing time, $f_{j3}$, summed over all subjects.   The values of $N_{j3}$ are also included.   Because of the significant session and position effects for mean firing time, the frequency distributions are shown separately for each position for the third session only.   The theoretical distributions, corrected for the truncation bias, as derived by Rapoport *et al.* (1972), are shown along with the observed frequency distributions.   Except for positions 7 and 8, the theoretical distributions are positively skewed, having very similar shapes.   The difference in position 7 is due to the optimal strategy being a composite function based on the number of bullets the opponent has at time $t = 0$, whereas the difference in position 8 results from the strong player saving his last bullet in the nonsymmetric games (games 3 and 4) until time $t = 1$ with probability .413.

Having already shown that the observed means and standard deviations of firing time differ from the ones prescribed (see Table 4), it is not at all surprising that the observed and predicted distributions differ too.   Due to the very large number of observations the difference is highly significant in all ten cases ($p < .01$ by the Kolmogorov–Smirnov test).   Examining the ten figures, it is seen that in most cases the observed frequency distribution is flatter than the predicted distribution, that the righthand tails of the observed and predicted distributions roughly correspond to each other, with a possible shift in mean, but that the lefthand tails do not.   In all ten positions the observed mean starting time of firing precedes the predicted time, and there is a gradual rise in relative frequency before the mode is reached rather than a jump at the mode followed by a sharp decline.

Of special interest is position 8, the only one for which the optimal prescription is to hold fire until time $t = 1$ with some finite probability.   Inspection of Figs. 1, 2, 4, 7, and 8, which portray the frequency distributions for positions with only one bullet left, supports this prediction.   There is a noticeable rise in relative frequency of firing at the end of the game in position 8, and, with the exception of one or two subjects in position 2, not in any of the other four positions.

Discrepancies between observed and prescribed frequency distributions may be found in individual data or may be caused by averaging over subjects, some of whom may fire according to the prescribed negative power functions, but be using different means.   The interpretability of the results portrayed in Figs. 1 through 10 is severely limited unless the extent of individual differences is determined.   Figure 11 presents the observed frequency distributions of firing time $f_{13}(Z)$ for each of the 20 subjects separately.   Relative frequencies are grouped in intervals of size .10.   It may be seen

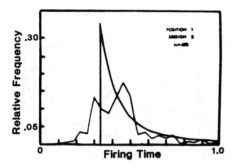

Fig. 1. Observed and predicted frequency distributions of firing time for position 1.

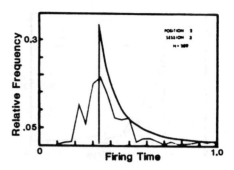

Fig. 2. Observed and predicted frequency distributions of firing time for position 2.

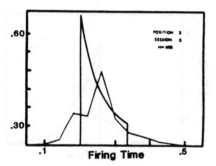

Fig. 3. Observed and predicted frequency distributions of firing time for position 3.

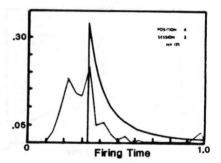

Fig. 4. Observed and predicted frequency distributions of firing time for position 4.

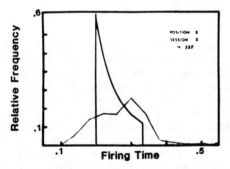

Fig. 5. Observed and predicted frequency distributions of firing time for position 5.

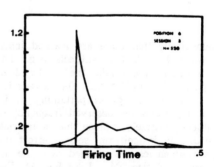

Fig. 6. Observed and predicted frequency distributions of firing time for position 6.

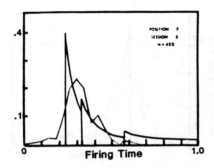

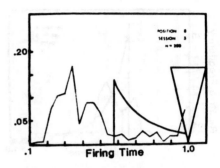

*Fig. 7. Observed and predicted frequency distributions of firing time for position 7.*

*Fig. 8. Observed and predicted frequency distributions of firing time for position 8.*

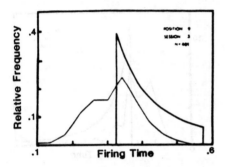

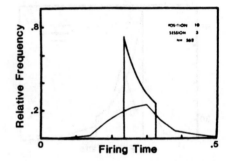

*Fig. 9. Observed and predicted frequency distributions of firing time for position 9.*

*Fig. 10. Observed and predicted frequency distributions of firing time for position 10.*

immediately that there are marked individual differences with regard to firing time in position 1. A few subjects (e.g., 1*A*, 1*B*, 3*B*, 4*A*, 4*B*, 6*B*, 8*A*) possess frequency distributions not unlike the predicted distribution displayed in Fig. 1, whereas others (e.g., 2*A*, 2*B*, 5*A*, 9*A*, 9*B*, 10*A*) possess flatter, almost symmetric, frequency distributions.

Additional results pertaining to individual differences are provided in Fig. 12, which presents the observed frequency distribution of firing time for position 6 for each subject separately. Since the multivariate analysis of variance test for mean firing time yielded an insignificant session effect for position 6 (as well as for positions 4 and 10), the frequencies are summed over the three sessions. Firing frequencies are grouped in intervals of size .04. Like Fig. 11, Fig. 12 shows marked individual differences with respect to both measures of central tendency and variability.

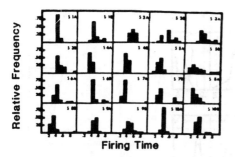

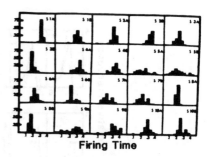

*Fig. 11. Observed frequency distributions of firing time for individual players, position 1, session 3.*

*Fig. 12. Observed frequency distributions of firing time for individual players, position 6, over sessions.*

Notwithstanding the large individual differences and the significant discrepancies between predicted and observed frequency distributions for firing time, there are certain similarities worth mentioning. The optimal firing strategy prescribes waiting a fixed amount of time, which differs from one position to another, before starting to fire. Most of the individual frequency distributions presented in Figs. 11 and 12 clearly show this waiting phenomenon, although it is seldom the same as the prescribed time. Also, as predicted, there is a sharp rise in the observed frequency distributions of most of the subjects, and typically the observed distribution declines less rapidly than it rises.

A detailed examination of individual results for the remaining eight positions yields similar results. Individual differences are large and, with a few noticeable exceptions, the minimax model provides an inadequate description of the data. Interestingly, these exceptional cases, rather than being distributed randomly over subjects, sessions, and positions, are located in the results of a few subjects. Figure 13 portrays the predicted and observed frequency distributions for each of the ten positions of subject 6A; the results are summed over the three experimental sessions. For positions 1, 2, 4, 7, and 8 they are grouped in intervals of size .10, whereas for the remaining positions the size of the intervals is .04. Subject 6A is our best; the average discrepancy between observed and prescribed frequency distribution is minimal for him. Figure 13 shows that the fit of the minimax model, which yields parameter-free predictions, is remarkable for most of 6A's positions.

## Discussion

A cursory inspection of the experimental literature on decision behavior in two-person, zero-sum, finite games (see Guyer, 1967; Rapoport & Orwant, 1962, for two excellent critical reviews of this literature) tends to support predictions derived from the theory of games when the size of the payoff matrix is small, 2×2 or 3×3, the game has a

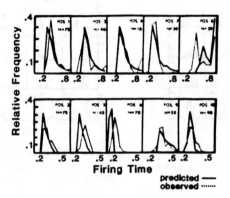

*Fig. 13. Observed and predicted frequency distributions of firing time for each position for player 6A.*

saddlepoint, and a pure strategy is consequently prescribed to each of the players. Adherence to minimax prescriptions does not occur if a mixed strategy is called for (Fox, 1972). Subjects tend to mix their strategies, but not in the proportions prescribed by the theory. Analogous, though tentative conclusions may be drawn from the games of timing studied in both our previous and present duel experiments. When fixed firing time was predicted in our first noisy duel study, no effects due to session or sequence were found. In the present silent duel study subjects maintained a wide, fairly constant variability around the mean firing time for a particular position as predicted, and the shapes of the observed frequency distributions of firing time did not markedly differ from the ones prescribed by the theory for many of the firing positions. However, significant, frequently quite substantial, effects have been reported for session, game, and sequence.

   Moreover, consistent discrepancies between predicted and observed mean firing times have been discovered, leading to a rejection of the minimax model. Consider the five positions, 1, 3, 6, 7, and 10 of firing the first bullet in a duel. Table 4 shows that the differences between $t_{jl}$ and the corresponding predicted firing times are .088, .113, .105, -.004, and .049, for positions 1, 3, 6, 7, and 10, respectively. With the exception of position 7, for which the difference is negative but very small, the differences for the remaining positions are substantial, indicating late firing time of the first bullet during the first experimental session. Consider now the mean firing times for session 1 again for the three positions of firing the last bullet 2, 4, and 8. The differences between $t_{jl}$ and the prescribed firing times are now -.007, -.075, and -.283, for positions 2, 4, and 8, respectively, indicating an early firing time of the last bullet. Positions 5 and 9, the intermediate positions on which the second of three bullets was fired, yielded the respective differences of .078 and -.013 between $t_{jl}$ and the corresponding prescribed firing times. Note that the difference between $t_{51}$ and the corresponding predicted firing time must be positive, since the observed mean firing time of .270 for the first bullet (position 5) was larger than the predicted time of .247 for the second bullet (position 6) in this game, and obviously, there is no way of firing the second bullet before the first.

The following picture then emerges regarding the firing strategy employed during the first session. Subjects tended to fire their first bullets too late relative to the prescribed firing time. Then, if the first bullet missed, the remaining bullets were fired in quick succession. The volleying phenomenon reported in the preceding section is consistent with this interpretation. It suggests that many of the subjects employed a very simple firing strategy of first deciding when to act, then acting all at once with small intervals between successive actions. The time when to act first is a function of the relative powers of the two members of the dyad, as reflected in $n_z(0)$ and $n_{z'}(0)$, and of the opponent's firing time of his first bullet on previous trials. The significant position effect and the high intrasubject correlations between $t_{j1}(Z)$, reported in Table 5, are consistent with this interpretation. The correlations for the first bullet positions (1, 3, and 6) are seen to be significant and high, whereas the correlations for the remaining positions (2, 4, and 5) are considerably smaller and nonsignificant.

The average firing strategy on sessions 2 and 3 is quite similar to the one on session 1. The principal difference is due to the overall decrease in $t_{jd}$ over sessions which, on the average, results in small discrepancies between predicted and observed mean firing times of the first bullet. The discrepancies between $t_{j3}$ and the corresponding predicted firing times are -.036, .047, -.077, -.071, and .055, for positions 1, 3, 6, 7, and 10, respectively. The mean of these five differences is .002, and the absolute values of these discrepancies are smaller than the ones for session 1 for four out of five positions. The volleying phenomenon is even more pronounced for sessions 2 and 3 than for session 1, and, with one exception, the intradyadic correlations between the mean firing times are higher for the first bullet positions (1, 3, and 6) than for the second and third bullet positions (2, 4, and 5).

EFFECTS OF INFORMATION

When applied to games of timing, the game theoretic model embodies four principal elements: (1) the preference structure of each of the players, (2) the actions each player may take during the duel, (3) the relative power of each player as reflected in $n_A(0)$, $n_B(0)$, $P_A(t)$, and $P_B(t)$, and (4) the information structure of each player regarding his opponent's power and firing strategy. A simple preference structure has been assumed for each player. Then, fixing equal accuracy functions for both players by the experimental design and providing each player complete knowledge of his opponent's power, the effects of relative power on firing strategy have been studied by manipulating $n_A(0)$ and $n_B(0)$. Effects of information gathered during the experiment on intradyadic relationships, but not on firing strategy, have been studied by letting the same dyad play a sequence of identical iterations of the same game, then computing the intradyadic correlations between the mean firing times for a given position.

The effects of information about the opponent's actions on firing strategy may also be tested. To implement the test, a player's information structure should be treated as an independent variable. Then, letting various groups of subjects or even the same group of subjects play a game of timing as either a noisy or silent duel, observed properties of firing strategies employed in the two conditions would be compared to each other. It has been precisely to allow this comparison that the same experimental procedure has been employed in our noisy and silent duel studies.

In terms of the minimax prescription of mean firing times, a meaningful comparison holds only for the symmetric games i.e., positions 1 through 6 in the silent duel study and positions 1, 2, 5, 3, 6, 9, respectively, in the noisy duel study. Only when $n_A(0) = n_B(0) = m$, and assuming no truncation effect in the silent duel, are the predicted mean firing times the same for both noisy and silent duels. When results in the silent duel are adjusted for the effect of the truncation artifact, the predicted mean firing times for the silent duel are somewhat lower than the corresponding means for the noisy duel. Table 3 shows that the difference between the two is negligible, .026 for positions 1, 3, and 4, .003 for positions 3 and 5, and .002 for position 6. In addition to mean firing times, the minimax model predicts zero intrasubject standard deviations for each firing position in the noisy duel, but positive and frequently large standard deviations (see Table 4) for the silent duel. Moreover, neither session nor role effects are prescribed nor are sequential effects due to runs of wins or losses on previous trials.

A comparison of the statistical tests performed in the noisy and silent duels shows no role effect for either type of duel, no session effect for the mean firing time in the noisy duel, but a strong session effect for that variable in the silent duel. The latter result suggests that the silent duel is considerably more difficult for the subjects than the noisy duel, requiring much more learning. Indeed, an inspection of the mean firing times for the silent duel presented in Table 4 suggests that subjects may not have reached asymptotic behavior even at the end of the third session.

The difference between the level of difficulty of the two types of duel may be attributed to the different rates of gathering information about the opponent's firing strategy, which is slower for the silent than for the noisy duel. In position 1 information about the opponent's behavior is gathered at a rate of about twice as slow for the silent as for the noisy duel because about one-half of the bullets are seen. But for positions 2 and 5, this rate is considerably slower because even fewer of the bullets are seen, and a player cannot know which of his opponent's bullets have hit him. This factor is reflected in the differences in $s_{jd}(Z)$ between the two types of duel. As Table 6 shows, the mean intrasubject standard deviations are considerably larger for the silent than for the noisy duel. The larger the variability around the opponent's mean firing time for a given position, the slower is the rate of learning of his firing strategy.

The values of $s_{jd}(Z)$ for the silent duel, which are presented in the upper part of Table 6, have been abstracted from Table 4 of the present paper; the corresponding results for the noisy duel appear in Table 5 of Kahan and Rapoport (1971). Standard deviations are reported for each session separately due to the significant session effect for $s_{jd}(Z)$ found in the noisy though not in the silent duel. This discrepancy with regard to session effects is consistent with the minimax model in showing that when playing noisy duels subjects approach a pure strategy, whereas in playing the same games as silent duels they do not.

Since no significant session effect for the mean firing time was found in the noisy duel study, the over sessions means are presented. Because of the significant session effect, Table 6 shows both the over sessions means and the means for the third, last,

*Table 6.*     *Mean firing times and means of intrasubject standard deviations for noisy and silent duels*

| Session | | Position | | | | | |
| --- | --- | --- | --- | --- | --- | --- | --- |
| | | 1 | 2 | 3 | 4 | 5 | 6 |
| | | Standard deviations | | | | | |
| Noisy | 1 | .070 | .039 | .056 | .034 | .028 | .032 |
| | 2 | .044 | .033 | .033 | .031 | .021 | .024 |
| | 3 | .041 | .031 | .030 | .023 | .028 | .024 |
| Silent | 1 | .134 | .181 | .112 | .207 | .097 | .081 |
| | 2 | .149 | .176 | .077 | .159 | .076 | .066 |
| | 3 | .139 | .131 | .058 | .160 | .064 | .064 |
| | | Means | | | | | |
| Noisy | (over sessions) | .475 | .388 | .362 | .331 | .282 | .262 |
| Silent | (over sessions) | .493 | .417 | .326 | .356 | .294 | .256 |
| Silent | (session 3) | .438 | .371 | .294 | .320 | .266 | .242 |

session for the silent duel study.  The differences between the respective overall means are small, not exceeding .036 in absolute value, and unsystematic.  This comparison, however, may be misleading because of the significant session effect for mean firing time in the silent duel.  If the overall means for the noisy duel are compared to the corresponding means in the third session of the silent duel there appears a clear tendency to fire earlier in the symmetric positions of the silent duel.  Even when the truncation bias is taken into consideration, the means for the third session of the silent duel remain below those for corresponding noisy duel positions.  Although there is no theoretical reason for this result, it might arise out of the different psychological perspectives that result from firing and missing.  In the noisy duel, when a player has fired all of his bullets and missed, he knows for a certainty that he has lost the duel, as his opponent can wait until a miss is impossible before firing.  This could lead to a relative conservatism about firing. On the other hand, in the silent duel, a player out of bullets has not necessarily lost the duel. Therefore, he can afford to be less conservative in his firing strategy. Although the mathematical derivation of optimal strategies does not justify this line of reasoning, it is one that is likely to occur to subjects.

As stated earlier, our goal is to develop descriptive models based on behavioral regularities and on systematic deviations between observed and prescribed decisions of timing in a class of pure conflict situations which have not been investigated before. The silent duel experiment described in the present paper and the noisy duel experiment that preceded it provide basic data that may be used in the construction of such models.

The future direction of this line of research is investigation of other species of decisions of timing in pure conflict, leading to theoretical explanatory principles based on psychological considerations. A variety of experiments can be conducted, employing the same paradigm, depending upon the particular independent variables the investigator has under consideration. For example, two possible experimental directions extend the range of applicability of the minimax model and obtain better understanding of conflict behavior. One allows for unequal accuracy functions and the other permits only incomplete information about the opponent's initial resources.

This research was supported in part by PHS Grant No. MH-10006 from the National Institute of Mental Health and in part by University Science Development Program Grant No. GU-2059 from the National Science Foundation. The authors wish to thank Arthur W. Coston for programming assistance, Sandra G. Funk and David G. Clark for their help in data collection and analysis, and Thomas S. Wallsten for many useful remarks.

## References

Brayer, A. R., An experimental analysis of some variables of minimax theory. *Behav. Sci.*, 1964, *9*, 33-44.

Dresher, M., *Games of strategy: Theory and applications.* Englewood Cliffs, N. J.: Prentice-Hall, 1961.

Fox, J., The learning of strategies in a simple, two-person zero-sum game without saddlepoint. *Behav. Sci.*, 1972, *17*, 300-308.

Guyer, M., A review of the literature on zero-sum and non-zero-sum games in the social sciences. Ann Arbor, Mich: Univ. of Mich., Mental Health Research Institute Communication No. 220, 1967.

Kahan, J. P., & Goehring, D. J., Responsiveness in two-person zero-sum games. *Behav. Sci.*, 1973, *18*, 27-33.

Kahan, J. P., & Rapoport, Am., Decisions of timing in pure conflict I: The noisy duel with equal accuracies. Chapel Hill, N. C.: The L. L. Thurstone Psychometric Laboratory, Report No. 102, 1971.

Karlin, S., *Mathematical methods and theory in games, programming, and economics*, Vol. II. Reading, mass: Addison-Wesley, 1959.

Lieberman, B., Human behavior in a strictly determined 3x3 matrix game. *Behav. Sci.*, 1960, *5*, 317-322.

Lieberman, B., Experimental studies of conflict in some two-person and three-person games. In J. H. Criswell, H. Solomon, and P. Suppes (Eds.). *Mathematical methods in small group processes*. Stanford: Stanford Univ. Press, 1962, pp. 203-220.

Luce, R. D., & Raiffa, H., *Games and decisions*. N. Y.: Wiley, 1957.

Messick, D. M., Interdependent decision strategies in zero-sum games. *Behav. Sci.*, 1967, *12*, 33-48.

Owen, G., *Game theory*. Philadelphia: Saunders, 1968.

Rapoport, Am., Kahan, J. P., & Stein, W. E., Decisions of timing in pure conflict III: The silent duel with equal accuracies. Chapel Hill, N. C.: The L. L. Thurstone Psychometric Laboratory, Report No. 108, 1972.

Rapoport, An. and Chammah, A. M., *Prisoner's Dilemma: A Study in conflict and cooperation*. Ann Arbor, Mich.: Univ. Michigan Press, 1965.

Rapoport, An., & Chammah, A. M., The game of chicken. *Amer. Behav. Scientist*, 1966, *10*, 10-28.

Rapoport, An., & Orwant, C., Experimental games: A review. *Behav. Sci.*, 1962, *7*, 1-37.

Restrepo, R., Tactical problems involving several actions. In M. Dresher, A. W. Tucker, and P. Wolfe (Eds.). *Contributions to the theory of games*, Vol. III. Princeton: Princeton Univ. Press, 1957, 307-335.

# CHAPTER 5

# DECISIONS OF TIMING IN EXPERIMENTAL PROBABILISTIC DUELS

**ABSTRACT.** The paradigm of the 2-person, zerosum, infinite game as a model of bipolarized conflicts in real time is extended to the probabilistic duel, where a player does not know with certainty whether or not this opponent is armed, but only knows the probability of such armament. Twenty dyads participated in a computer-controlled probabilistic duel experiment, ten of them playing a noisy version (where all bullets fired are public knowledge) and ten playing a silent version (where unsuccessful fire is unknown to the opponent). Several game-theoretic implications were tested, some of which demonstrate the efficacy of the theory of games of timing as an explicatory mechanism for decision behavior in experimental duels.

Except for a few studies, gaming experiments investigating 2-person interactions have employed essentially one paradigm, which defines a 2-person finite game as an $r \times c$ payoff matrix, in which $r$ is the number of alternative courses of action (pure strategies) available to the Row player, $c$ is the number of courses of action available to the Column player, and each of the cells of the matrix contains two numerical entries, representing the payoffs to Row and Column, respectively. Very seldom do $r$ or $c$ exceed 3; typically, both are equal to 2. Only recently has there been an attempt to explore new paradigms for investigating decision behavior in 2-person conflict situations in which the number of pure strategies, rather than being finite and typically small, is infinite.

A series of studies (Kahan and Rapoport, 1974, 1975; Rapoport, Kahan and Stein, 1973) have addressed themselves to the problem of investigating decision behavior in 2-person conflict situations occurring in real time in situations in which the interests of the two players are diametrically opposed. These studies have utilized a standardized format which is easy to administer, fun to play, and allows meaningful comparison of results.

Employing the terminology of game theory, these studies examine decision behavior in games of timing, a subset of 2-person, zerosum, infinite games, in which the choice of a pure strategy represents the choice of a time to perform a prespecified action. To describe the structure of these studies, introduce terminology, and specify the goals of the present study, a brief characterization of games of timing is warranted.

GAMES OF TIMING

Games of timing constitute a class of 2-person, zerosum, infinite games in which each player's space of pure strategies is the real interval $[0, 1]$. A game represents a contest between two players, called $A$ and $B$, trying to achieve the same objective. Within a time interval $0 \leq t \leq 1$ each player can make a fixed number of attempts to reach his objective. Each attempt taken by either player either fails or succeeds; when a player's attempt succeeds, he wins one unit, his opponent loses one unit, and the contest terminates. When none of the attempts succeed or when both players' attempts succeed simultaneously, the game terminates in a draw, with each player winning zero units. At time $t = 1$ every attempt succeeds; at $t = 0$ every attempt fails; and at $0 < t < 1$, an attempt succeeds with some probability, denoted $p_z(t)$, $Z = A,B$, which depends on the player making the attempt and the time at which the attempt is made. The probability function $p_z(t)$ is called player $Z$'s *accuracy function*, and is usually assumed to be monotomically increasing in $t$.

Consider a special case, where each player can act only once, and must choose a time in the interval [0, 1] at which to take that action. This game is defined by the payoff function for player $A$ (Karlin, 1959).

$$K(\xi,\eta) = \begin{cases} L(\xi,\eta), & \text{if } \xi < \eta, \\ \phi(\xi), & \text{if } \xi = \eta, \\ M(\xi,\eta), & \text{if } \xi > \eta, \end{cases} \tag{1}$$

where $\xi$ is the time that player A acts and $\eta$ is the time that player B acts. Because the game is zerosum, player B's payoff function is $- K(\xi,\eta)$. Each of the functions $L(\xi,\eta)$ and $M(\xi,\eta)$ is monotone-increasing in $\xi$ for each $\eta$ and monotone-decreasing in $\eta$ for each $\xi$. Each of these two functions is jointly continuous in $\xi$ and $\eta$.

Further specifications of the basic characteristics of games of timing and differentiations among various classes of games may be made by considering various categories of assumptions of the players' information structure. Three categories are suggested: (i) assumptions concerning the information each player possesses about the exact times of his opponent's actions; (ii) assumptions concerning the knowledge each player has of his opponent's accuracy function; and (iii) assumptions concerning the information provided to each player at time $t = 0$ about his opponent's initial resources. It is also assumed that both players conform to the regular game-theoretic assumptions regarding preference patterns (Luce and Raiffa, 1957). Specifically, each player is assumed to have preference over the outcomes of the game satisfying the axioms of utility theory, with the preference patterns of both players being strictly opposed to each other; each is assumed to be fully aware of the rules of the game and the utility function of his opponent; and each is assumed to attempt to maximize his expected utility.

If each player possesses complete information about the initial resources, the accuracy function, and the exact time of action of his opponent, the game of timing is said to have *complete information*. Complete information is understood here to mean that the actions of each player and their consequences become known to his opponent as soon as they are executed. If the initial resources, the accuracy function, or the exact times of action of at least one of the players are not revealed to his opponent, the game is said to have *incomplete information*. In this case some or all of the information regarding his opponent may become known to the player at some later time or may never become known.

Information about the opponent's time of action serves to divide games of timing into "noisy" situations, where all of the opponent's actions become known as they occur, or "silent" situations, where unsuccessful attempts are not communicated. Differences along this dimension of information have formed the basis for previous studies of games of timing (Kahan and Rapoport, 1974; Rapoport, Kahan, and Stein, 1973).

The literature concerned with games of timing has assumed complete knowledge of the parameters of both accuracy functions by each of the players. Presently, this assumption seems necessary for obtaining mathematically tractable solutions; however, if such games are to serve as a useful model for the basic characteristics of a variety of bipolarized conflicts evolving in real time, the assumption that both accuracy functions are fully known must eventually be relaxed. One way of weakening it is by assuming that each player possesses only probabilitic information about the parameters of his opponent's accuracy function. For example, suppose that player $B$'s accuracy may be described by a power function $p_B(t)$ $t^c, c > 0$. It is not unreasonable to assume that although player $A$ may not know the exact value of $c$, his knowledge about that parameter may be approximated by some probability distribution.

The third assumption about the player's information structure concerns knowledge of the opponent's initial resources. With regard to this assumption two different categories of games of timing may be distinguished. In the first category, which we term *deterministic games of timing*, each player possesses complete information about his opponent's initial resources. For example, if $A$ can make $n$ separate attempts to achieve his objective at the time interval $[0, 1]$, and $B$ can make $m$ such attempts, it is assumed that the values of $n$ and $m$ are known to both players. Most of the mathematical literature concerned with games of timing, and all previous experimental laboratory studies have dealt with deterministic games. In the second category, which we term *probabilistic games of timing*, each player has only partial information about his opponent's initial resources, summarized by a discrete probability distribution. Thus, if player $A$ can make $n$ attempts at the time interval $[0,1]$ and player $B$ can make $m$ such attempts, the game is probabilistic when it is assumed that $n$ and $m$ are random variables, and that player $A$ possesses probabilities $q_A(x) = Pr(m = x)$ and player $B$ possesses probabilities $q_B(x) = Pr(n = x)$, where $x = 0,1,...$; $q_A(x) \geq 0$, $q_B(x) \geq 0$, and

$$\sum_x q_A(x) = \sum_x q_B(x) = 1.$$ In the special case of $m = n = 1$, treated in the present paper, we define $P \equiv q_A(1)$ and $Q \equiv q_B(1)$.

## DUELS

A visualizable and easily demonstrable example of games of timing, which may encompass all the classes mentioned above, is the Western duel. A simulated version of the duel constitutes the experimental paradigm employed by Kahan and Rapoport (1974, 1975; Rapoport et al., 1973) in a series of computer-controlled experiments. In this version of the Western duel the two players start at time $t = 0$ at opposite ends of a straight street and steadily walk toward each other, guns drawn and pointing. At $t = 0$

each duelist has a fixed number of bullets, $n$ for player $A$ and $m$ for player $B$. The accuracy functions are assumed to be known by each of the duelists. The closer the duelists are to each other, the more accurate is their fire. The duelist's problem is to decide when to fire each of his bullets. To fire too early is to risk missing the opponent and depleting one's limited resources, whereas to hold one's fire is to risk being hit.

We may distinguish between *noisy duels*, in which each duelist is informed immediately when his opponent fires, and *silent duels*, in which both duelists are assumed to possess guns equipped with silencers, so that a player never learns when his opponent has fired and missed. Whether a duel is deterministic or probablistic is independent of the noisy-silent dichotomy.

Noisy or silent duels model basic characteristics of bipolarized conflicts evolving in real time. Examples of deterministic duels taken from business, political science, and psychology are given by Karlin (1959), Kahan and Rapoport (1974), and Rapoport et al. (1973). To demonstrate how a probabilistic duel may serve a similar purpose, consider a modification of Karlin's illustrative example (1959) of two publishing companies competing for a contract with an author who considers writing a book. The times for the publisher's representative to appear ready with a contract and various inducements represent his pure strategies. It is reasonable to assume that the probability of signing a contract increases monotonically in time. Too early an attempt may fail since the author is not far enough along in his work to be interested in a publishing decision. A late bid, however, may also fail, as the competitor has gotten there first. If the two publishing companies do not inform each other of their activities, and if each may make only a single attempt for a contract, this example is analogous to the one bullet vs one bullet deterministic silent duel. We may modify Karlin's example by noting that if a publishing company is not informed of its competitor's activities, it is typically not informed of the competitor's intentions. In particular, it will not know with certainty whether the competitor intends to attempt to get a contract. If the publishing company assesses the probability that the competitor will make such an attempt, the example becomes a probabilistic silent duel.

PRESCRIBED STRATEGIES FOR PROBABILISTIC SILENT DUELS

Consider first the probabilistic silent duel in which players $A$ and $B$ possess a single bullet at time $t = 0$ with probabilities $P$ and $Q$, respectively, and no bullets with probabilities $1 - P$ and $1 - Q$. For the sake of simplicity, linear and equal accuracy functions are assumed hereafter; i.e., $p_A(\xi) = \xi$ and $p_B(\eta) = \eta$, where $0 \leq \xi \leq 1$ and $0 \leq \eta \leq 1$. (The imposition of linearity makes computation tractable, with no loss of generalization.) Since the game is zerosum, the value to player $A$ is 1 if he alone survives, $- 1$ if player $B$ alone survives, and 0 if both survive or neither survives.

To determine the expected value of a game, the payoff function (1) must be considered separately for the four cases: (i) each duelist has a single bullet, (ii) only player $A$ has a bullet, (iii) only player $B$ has a bullet, and (iv) neither player has a bullet. The probabilities of these four mutually exclusive and collectively exhaustive cases are $PQ, P(1 - Q), (1 - P)Q$, and $(1 - P)(1 - Q)$, respectively. In the light of Eq. (1), one must consider separately the cases in which $A$ fires first $(\xi < \eta)$, $B$ fires first $(\xi > \eta)$, or both players fire simultaneously $(\xi = \eta)$. Case (iv) has zero payoffs for both players of course, and need not be considered further.

Suppose $\xi < \eta$. If case (i) obtains, either player $A$ wins with probability $\xi$, or player $B$, who fires later, wins with probability $(1 - \xi)\eta$, or neither player wins with probability $(1 - \xi)(1 - \eta)$. Multiplying each probability by the corresponding value (for $A$) yields the expected payoff under case (i):

$$\xi(+1) + (1 - \xi) \eta(-1) + (1 - \xi) (1 - \eta)0 = \xi - \eta + \xi\eta .$$

If case (ii) obtains, either player $A$ wins with probability $\xi$, or neither player wins with probability $(1 - \xi)$. Player $B$, not having a bullet, of course cannot win. The resulting expected payoff is, therefore, $\xi$. Analogously, the only event under case (iii) whose probability differs from zero is $B$ winning the duel, which occurs with probability $\eta$, yielding an expected payoff $- \eta$. Combining the expected payoffs and multiplying them by the probabilities of cases (i), (ii), and (iii), yields

$$L(\xi,\eta) = PQ(\xi - \eta + \xi\eta) + P(1 - Q)\xi - (1 - P)Q\eta = PQ\xi\eta + P\xi - Q\eta. \qquad (2)$$

Consider $\xi > \eta$. If case (i) obtains, either player $B$ wins with probability $\eta$, or player $A$, who fires later, wins with probability $(1 - \eta)\xi$, or neither wins with probability $(1 - \eta)(1 - \xi)$. The resulting expected value is

$$(1 - \eta)\xi(+1) + \eta(-1) + (1 - \eta)(1 - \xi)0 = \xi - \eta - \xi\eta.$$

Since the expected payoffs under cases (ii) and (iii) are not changed, we obtain

$$M(\xi, \eta) = PQ(\xi - \eta - \xi\eta) + P(1 - Q)\xi - (1 - P)Q\eta = -PQ\xi\eta + P\xi - Q\eta. \qquad (3)$$

Consider that both players fire simultaneously, i.e., $\xi = \eta$. The expected payoffs under cases (ii) and (iii) are again unaffected. If case (i) obtains, either player $A$ wins with probability $\xi(1 - \eta)$, or player $B$ wins with probability $\eta(1 - \xi)$, or they draw with probability $\xi\eta + (1 - \xi)(1 - \eta)$. this results in the following expected payoff in case (i):

$$\xi(1 - \eta)(+1) + (1 - \xi)\eta(-1) + 0 = 0.$$

Taking $\xi = \eta$,

$$\phi(\xi) = P(1 - Q)\xi - (1 - P) Q\eta = (P - Q)\xi. \qquad (4)$$

Combining (2)–(4) results in the payoff function for the probabilitic silent duel

$$K(\xi,\eta) = \begin{cases} PQ\xi\eta + P\xi - Q\eta, & \text{if } \xi < \eta, \\ (P - Q)\xi, & \text{if } \xi = \eta, \\ -PQ\xi\eta + P\xi - Q\eta, & \text{if } \xi > \eta. \end{cases} \tag{5}$$

Without loss of generality assume $Q \geq P$. Karlin (1959, pp. 289–290) has shown that the solution to (5) is given by the following density functions for the optimal firing times $\xi^*$ and $\eta^*$:

$$f(\xi) = \begin{cases} 0, & \text{if } 0 \leq \xi < 1/(1 + 2P), \\ 1/[2P(1 + P)\xi^3], & \text{if } 1/(1 + 2P) \leq \xi \leq 1, \end{cases} \tag{6}$$

for player $A$, and

$$g(\eta) = \begin{cases} 0, & \text{if } 0 \leq \eta < 1/(1 + 2P), \\ (1 + Q)/[2Q(1 + P)^2\eta^3], & \text{if } 1/(1 + 2P) \leq \eta < 1, \\ (Q - P)/[Q(1 + P)], & \text{if } \eta = 1, \end{cases} \tag{7}$$

for player $B$. The density function for the player with the greater probability of having a bullet has a discrete mass at $t = 1$. Also, the time at which either player should start considering firing is a fucntion of the smaller probability, $P$, alone. The value of the game is $(P - Q)/(1 + P)$.

The means, $E(\xi)$ and $E(\eta)$, and variances $\sigma^2(\xi)$ and $\sigma^2(\eta)$, of $f(\xi)$ and $g(\eta)$, respectively, are obtainable in closed form:

$$E(\xi) = 1/(1 + P), \tag{8}$$

$$E(\eta) = [Q(1 + 2P) - P^2][Q(1 + P)^2], \tag{9}$$

$$\sigma^2(\xi) = ((\log_e[1/(1 + 2P)])/2Q(1 + P)) - (1/(1 + P))^2, \tag{10}$$

and

$$\sigma^2(\eta) = (1 + Q)\left[\frac{P^3(Q - P) - PQ(1 + P)}{Q^2(1 + P)^4} - \frac{\log_e[1/(1 + 2P)]}{2Q(1 + P)^2}\right] \tag{11}$$

## PRESCRIBED STRATEGIES FOR PROBABILISTIC NOISY DUELS

To determine the form of the payoff function for the probabilistic noisy duel, one may proceed in a manner similar to before. It should be recalled that in the noisy duel, unlike the silent duel, if each player possesses a bullet at time $t = 0$ and the one who fires first misses, his opponent can win with certainty by waiting until $t = 1$ to fire. It is then possible to show that the payoff function (1) reduces to the form

$$K(\xi,\eta) = \begin{cases} PQ(1 - \xi - \eta) + P\xi - Q\eta, & \text{if } \xi < \eta, \\ (P - Q)\xi, & \text{if } \xi = \eta, \\ -PQ(1 - \xi - \eta) + P\xi - Q\eta, & \text{if } \xi > \eta. \end{cases} \qquad (12)$$

The solution to (12), under the assumption $1 > Q \geq P$, consists of the following two density functions for the optimal firing times $\xi^*$ and $\eta^*$:

$$f(\xi) = \begin{cases} 0, & \text{if } 0 \leq \xi < (1 + P^2)/(1 + P)^2, \\ (1 - P)/[2P(2\xi - 1)^{3/2}], & \text{if } (1 + P^2)/(1 + P^2) \leq \xi \leq 1, \end{cases} \qquad (13)$$

for player $A$, and

$$g(\eta) = \begin{cases} 0, & \text{if } 0 \leq \eta < (1 + P^2)/(1 + P)^2, \\ (1 - P)(1 + Q)/[2Q(1 + P)(2\eta - 1)^{3/2}], & \text{if } (1 + P^2)/(1 + P)^2 \leq \eta < 1, \\ (Q - P)/[Q(1 + P)], & \text{if } \eta = 1, \end{cases} \qquad (14)$$

for player $B$. As in the silent case, the earlier firing time is a function of $P$ alone, and the better-armed duelist (in a probabilistic sense) should hold fire until $t = 1$ with some positive probability. The value of the game is the same as for the probabilistic silent duel, i.e., $(P - Q)/(1 + P)$.

The means of (13) and (14) are given by

$$E(\xi) = \frac{1 - P}{2P} \left[ \frac{1}{2} \int_x^1 \frac{d\xi}{(2\xi - 1)^{1/2}} + \frac{1}{2} \int_x^1 \frac{d\xi}{(2\xi - 1)^{3/2}} \right] = \frac{1}{1 + P}, \qquad (15)$$

where $x = (1 + P^2)/(1 + P)^2$, and

$$E(\eta) = \frac{(1 - P)(1 + Q)}{2Q(1 + P)} \left[ \frac{1}{2} \int_x^1 \frac{d\eta}{(2\eta - 1)^{1/2}} + \frac{1}{2} \int_x^1 \frac{d\eta}{(2\eta - 1)^{3/2}} \right] + \left[ \frac{Q - P}{Q(1 + P)} \right]$$

$$= [Q(1 + 2P) - P^2]/[Q(1 + P^2)] . \qquad (16)$$

The variances of the players' distributions are given by

$$\sigma^2(\xi) = [P^2(1 - P)]/3(1 + P)^3 , \qquad (17)$$

and

$$\sigma^2(\eta) = [4P^3Q(Q + 1) - P^4(4Q + Q^2 + 3)]/[3Q^2(1 + P)^4]. \qquad (18)$$

A comparison of Eqs. (6)–(9) to Eqs. (13)–(16) shows that although the density functions for the probabilistic silent and noisy duels are different from each other, their means are not. The variances as shown in equations (10), (11), (17), and (18) are different for the two types of duel.

The game-theoretic model yields parameter-free predicted distributions of firing time, which are readily testable in probabilistic duels played in the laboratory. A few properties of the optimal firing strategies warrant a special discussion. Equations (6), (7), (13), and (14) show that in both probabilistic silent and noisy duels, when $Q \geq P$, player $A$'s density function depends only on $P$, whereas player $B$'s density function depends on both $P$ and $Q$. The asymmetry with respect to the information about the opponent's initial resources expressed by $P$ and $Q$ should affect player $B$'s firing strategy, but not player $A$'s. Once player $A$ knows that $Q \geq P$, only the exact value of $P$ is of importance to him; he should adhere to the same firing strategy for any value of $Q$. Knowledge of the particular value of both $P$ and $Q$ is relevant to player $B$, however, since both affect his firing strategy. In particular, if player $B$ follows the game-theoretic strategy, the discrete mass of his density function at $t = 1$ should decrease in magnitude as $P$ approaches $Q$.

A second comment concerns the comparison of firing strategies in noisy and silent duels. Although the prescribed density functions of firing time differ from the silent to the noisy duel, the predicted mean firing times, values of the games, and the magnitude of jump at $t = 1$ do not. This result is reminiscent of a similar finding in deterministic duels. If both players start with an equal number of bullets, the optimal mean firing times for the deterministic noisy and silent duels are the same, though the variances are not. One of the attractive features of the game-theoretic model is that, in addition to prescribing firing strategies for various types of duels, it predicts quantiative invariances over 2-person, zerosum, infinite games differing from each other in the players' information structure. These invariances will be tested below.

## Method

Both the noisy and silent probabilistic duels were implemented on a PDP-8 computer controlling two teletypes and two cathode ray display units. The DUEL program allows the experimenter to specify parameters determining the accuracy functions of the duelists, the number of bullets available to each player, the payoff functions, the number of repetitions of each duel, the approach time, and the extent of information each player has about his opponent. The experimental environment has been previously described in detail for both noisy (Kahan and Rapoport, 1974) and silent (Rapoport et al., 1973) duels; details of the procedure and instructions are to be found in those sources. Only those differences in procedure that characterize our particular experiments are elaborated below.

## SUBJECTS

Forty University of North Carolina male undergraduates were recruited as subjects in a paid decision making experiment via announcements posted on bulletin boards around campus.   Appointments were set up for subjects in pairs; friends did not participate together.   No subject had participated in a prior duel experiment.   Ten of the dyads played the probabilistic noisy duel, and the other ten played the silent version.

## PROCEDURE

The experimental procedure followed that of the previously published duel experiments. Subjects observed two figures moving toward each other on a cathode ray display.   Also shown on the display were the probabilities of successful fire for each player.   Subjects fired by hitting a key on their teletypewriters.   The probabilistic nature of the duel was conveyed by the following instructions:

> "At the beginning of each duel, duelist A is assigned one bullet with probability $a$ (and no bullets with probability $1 - a$).   Similarly, duelist B is assigned one bullet with probability $b$ (and no bullets with probability $1 - b$). For example, suppose $a = .8$ and $b = .8$.   This means that if this duel is to be repeated many times, duelist A will be assigned a single bullet on approximately 80 out of 100 duels (and no bullets on approximately 20 out of 100 duels), and similarly for duelist B.   If $a = .6$ and $b = .9$, say, it means that duelist A will be assigned a single bullet on approximately 60 out of 100 duels of this type, whereas duelist B will be assigned a single bullet on approximately 90 out of 100 duels of this type."

The probabilities for the seven sets of duels were presented to the subjects in a table virtually identical to Table 1.   The table was accompanied by the following instructions:

> "Consider this table labelled 'Probabilities of Having a Single Bullet for Each Set of Duels.'   The table shows that for the first set of 20 duels the probability of being assigned a single bullet is .8 for both duelists A and B.   For the fifth set of 20 duels, for example, A's probability is .8 whereas B's probability is .5, and so on.   This information should prove useful to you in deciding when to fire."

Implementation of the probabilistic duel was done by entering the appropriate probabilities for each set of duels into the computer.   For each duel, a random number was generated to determine independently whether or not each player would have a bullet.   Before the duel commenced, each player was notified whether or not he had a bullet.   On the average, subjects experienced the appropriate probabilities of having a bullet, although the actual number of bullets per set of duels and the specific trial number on which a player was armed varied from player to player.[1]

Table I.    Probabilities of Having a Single Bullet for Each Set of Duels

| Set | No. of duels | Prob. A has a bullet | Prob. B has a bullet |
|-----|--------------|----------------------|----------------------|
| 1 | 20 | 0.8 | 0.8 |
| 2 | 20 | 0.3 | 0.3 |
| 3 | 20 | 0.8 | 0.3 |
| 4 | 20 | 0.3 | 0.8 |
| 5 | 20 | 0.8 | 0.5 |
| 6 | 20 | 0.5 | 0.8 |
| 7 | 20 | 0.5 | 0.5 |

Each of the seven sets of duels (games) was played for 20 trials, for a total of 140 duels per dyad per experimental session.    A duel where no hits were scored required approximately 50 seconds to complete; of course, a hit shortened the duel.    Probabilities of a hit (identical for both players) were displayed on both cathode ray displays, and changed linearly from 0 to 1 in steps of 0.04.    A typical experimental session took 2 hr to complete, including playing and preparation time.    The only difference in procedure between the noisy and silent versions was that, for the noisy duel only, an opponent's firing and missing was signaled by a bell ringing on the subject's teletypewriter.

Subjects participating in the noisy duel played two separate identical sessions, spaced approximately one week apart, for a total of 280 duels.    Subjects in the silent duel played three sessions, for a total of 420 duels.    This difference was because previous experiments (Kahan and Rapoport, 1974; Rapoport et al., 1973) have shown that asymptotic behavior is reached at a later state for silent than for noisy duels.

For each experimental session, $4.00 was allocated to each of the players in a dyad.    A win for a player resulted in his gaining 10 cents of his opponent's allocation; there was no transfer of funds in the event of a drawn duel.    Subjects were paid their gains in one payment at the termination of their final experimental session.

---

[1]Because of an error in the random number tables, the actual total number of bullets received was smaller than the probabilities P and Q would have indicated.    This difference, however, was not statistically significant for any individual player in a given session; each of those players receiving fewer than his expectation might individually count himself as unlucky, but not discard the experimentally induced probabilities.

## Results

*Position.* The firing strategies for probabilistic duels yield several testable predictions.[2] To describe them, let $p_s$ denote the probability that a given player has a bullet at $t = 0$, and let $p_o$ denote the probability that this player's opponent has a bullet. $p_s$ and $p_o$ are always known by both players. A position of a player is defined as the ordered pair $(p_s, p_o)$. A position is *symmetric* if $p_s = p_o$; it is *asymmetric*, otherwise. In an asymmetric position, the player is said to be *strong* if $p_s > p_o$, and *weak* if $p_s < p_o$.

In the present experiment there are seven positions, one for each game set, defined in the left-hand portion of Table II. For the symmetrical positions, players $A$ and $B$ occupy the same position for the same game. Thus, positions 1, 2, and 4 obtain for both players for game sets 1, 7, and 2, respectively. When the positions are asymmetric, then on successive game sets player $A$ is first weak and then strong, while player $B$, of course, is the opposite. Thus, position 3 obtains for game 6 for player $A$ and for game 5 for player $B$, with the games reversed for the respective players for position 4. Similarly, position 6 obtains in game 4 for player $A$ and game 3 for player $B$, with the games reversed in position 7 for the players.

*Prescribed firing time.* Position is used to define a player's initial state because, as shown in the introductory section, position alone determines the prescribed firing strategy for a particular player. Table II presents the various theoretical solutions for the noisy and silent probabilistic duels. For each position, the value of the game is given, followed by the prescribed starting time, i.e., that value of $t$ before which neither player should fire. Then the mean and standard deviation of the firing times are given, along with the discrete mass of probability of firing at $t = 1$. Note that because the probability of successful fire is a linear function of time, the two measures yield identical results in the following analysis.

Because of the structure of the DUEL program, the various duels played in the present experiment terminate as soon as one of the players is hit by his opponent. Thus, if in a particular silent duel a player decides (at time $t = 0$) to fire at time $t$ ($0 < t$), and his opponent decides to fire at a particular time $t'$, $t < t'$, then, if the first player hits, his opponent's strategy (and firing time) will not be realized. Also, in the noisy duel, if the player misses at time $t$, then his opponent will not fire at $t'$ ($t < t'$) as planned, but rather, will hold fire until $t = 1$, as the first player has no threat remaining to force an earlier action. Thus, even if both players adhere to the prescribed strategies of Eqs. (6), (7), (13), and (14), the observed frequency distribution of firing time will be biased due to truncation toward early firing time.

---

[2]The prescribed firing strategies, Eqs. (6), (7), (13), and (14) are derived for the case where the players choose $\xi$ and $\eta$ and then a different random device is used for each of them to determine whether or not to assign him a bullet. In our experimental design each player had been told whether or not he had a bullet before the duel started. Since it does not matter when he fires if he does not have a bullet, each player 'should' assume he always has one. The prescribed firing strategies are therefore not affected.

Table II.    Uncorrected and Corrected Prescriptions for Silent and Noisy Probabilistic
             Duels, by Position

Silent probabilistic duels

| Position | $p_s$ | $p_o$ | Value of game | Start firing | Uncorr. mean | Uncorr. SD | Uncorr. mass at $t = 1$ | Corr. mean | Corr. SD | Corr. mass at $t = 1$ |
|---|---|---|---|---|---|---|---|---|---|---|
| 1 | 0.8 | 0.8 | .000 | .385 | .556 | .152 | .000 | .533 | .141 | .000 |
| 2 | 0.5 | 0.5 | .000 | .500 | .667 | .133 | .000 | .652 | .128 | .000 |
| 3 | 0.5 | 0.8 | -.200 | .500 | .667 | .133 | .000 | .649 | .126 | .000 |
| 4 | 0.8 | 0.5 | +.200 | .500 | .750 | .185 | .250 | .724 | .181 | .207 |
| 5 | 0.3 | 0.3 | .000 | .625 | .769 | .104 | .000 | .762 | .102 | .000 |
| 6 | 0.3 | 0.8 | -.385 | .625 | .769 | .104 | .000 | .758 | .101 | .000 |
| 7 | 0.8 | 0.3 | +.385 | .625 | .880 | .138 | .481 | .867 | .141 | .444 |

Noisy probabilistic duels

| Position | $p_s$ | $p_o$ | Value of game | Start firing | Uncorr. mean | Uncorr. SD | Uncorr. mass at $t = 1$ | Corr. mean | Corr. SD | Corr. mass at $t = 1$ |
|---|---|---|---|---|---|---|---|---|---|---|
| 1 | 0.8 | 0.8 | .000 | .506 | .556 | .086 | .000 | .532 | .056 | .000 |
| 2 | 0.5 | 0.5 | .000 | .556 | .667 | .111 | .000 | .647 | .101 | .000 |
| 3 | 0.5 | 0.8 | -.200 | .556 | .667 | .111 | .000 | .641 | .097 | .000 |
| 4 | 0.8 | 0.5 | +.200 | .556 | .750 | .173 | .250 | .711 | .164 | .173 |
| 5 | 0.3 | 0.3 | .000 | .645 | .769 | .098 | .000 | .759 | .095 | .000 |
| 6 | 0.3 | 0.8 | -.385 | .645 | .769 | .098 | .000 | .755 | .093 | .000 |
| 7 | 0.8 | 0.3 | +.385 | .645 | .880 | .135 | .481 | .864 | .139 | .433 |

To account for this bias, the theoretical distributions of firing time corrected for truncation were computed using the technique described in Appendix A. This technique can be modified to correct for the same bias in deterministic duels. The rightmost part of Table II presents the corrected means, standard deviations, and discrete probability masses at $t = 1$. Those numbers form the appropriate prescriptions with which to compare the data. Table II shows that the bias due to truncation does not exceed 0.04, and that it is of approximately the same magnitude for noisy and silent duels. The differences between the mean firing times for the silent and noisy duels for a given position are practically zero; they never exceed 0.013.

*Role and session differences.*[3]     No differences are predicted in the means or standard deviations of firing time attributable to role (*A* or *B*) or session.   Practical considerations and previous experimental results suggest no role differences, particularly in the symmetric games.   For the asymmetric games, however, a role difference might arise because players experience particular positions at different times.   For instance, player *A* is in position 3 in game set 6, whereas player *B* is in that position for game set 5.   If both players were to behave differently in the later game set than in the earlier one, the result would be a role difference in the examination of position 3.

Examination of role and session effects was by multivariate analysis of variance separately for noisy and silent duels, and separately for means and standard deviations of firing time.    Subjects' data were transformed into specific tests for role and session contrasts, and tested in multivariate fashion (McCall and Appelbaum, 1973) separately for each position.   A Type I error rate of $\alpha = .05$ was maintained for these analyses.

Of the 42 tests for means, 2 were significant.   One was a role difference for position 1 of the silent duel ($F_{1,9} = 7.73$, $p < .021$), and the other was for session for position 5 of the silent duel ($F_{2,8} = 5.26$, $p < .035$).   Note that the single role difference was for a symmetric game.   Of the 42 tests for standard deviation, 3 were significant. There was a session effect for position 1 of the noisy duel ($F_{1,9} = 6.68$, $p < .029$), and there were role effects for positions 4 and 5 of the silent duel ($F_{1,9} = 6.08$, $p < .036$ and $F_{1,9} = 11.60$, $p < .008$, respectively).     There being no systematic pattern to these significances, we attribute them to chance; further aggregate results will be collapsed over these variables.

*Means and standard deviations.*   The prescribed means and standard deviations of firing time for all positions for both noisy and silent duels (Table II) may be compared to the aggregate data over subjects, roles, and sessions shown in Table III.   Note that the standard deviations in this table are the mean individual standard deviations over subjects, and not the aggregate standard deviations.   The first point of interest is that the results for silent and noisy duels are quite close to one another, both for means, where the prescriptions are practically identical, but also for the standard deviations, where prescriptions differ widely for some positions.   Thus, subjects behaved similarly in both types of duel.

The observed standard deviations are almost uniformly too small; subjects grouped their fire more closely than prescribed.   In other words, firing behavior was more consistent over trials than the game-theoretical policy would dictate.   This finding, in conjunction with the high mean firing times (about .7), suggests that players could fairly well judge when an opponent would fire if armed, and silent duels were in reality similar to noisy ones.

---

[3]In the calculation of all statistics, the firing of a bullet by a player in a noisy duel after an unsuccessful attempt by his opponent was not included.   In this instance, the appropriate behavior is to abandon previous plans and wait until $t = 1$ before firing. This strategy was followed by all the subjects all of the time except for one or two isolated instances.

*Table III.* Means and Standard Deviations of Observed Firing Time Compared to Prescribed Values, by Position

| Position | Silent duel | | | | Noisy duel | | | |
|---|---|---|---|---|---|---|---|---|
| | Mean | d.o.[a] | SD | d.o. | Mean | d.o. | SD | d.o. |
| 1 | .626 | -.107 | .079 | +.062 | .642 | -.110 | .075 | -.019 |
| 2 | .672 | -.020 | .078 | +.050 | .704 | -.057 | .088 | +.013 |
| 3 | .662 | -.013 | .060 | +.066 | .681 | -.040 | .063 | +.034 |
| 4 | .704 | +.020 | .092 | +.089 | .726 | -.015 | .078 | +.086 |
| 5 | .757 | +.005 | .068 | +.034 | .761 | -.002 | .072 | +.023 |
| 6 | .682 | +.076 | .044 | +.057 | .694 | +.061 | .049 | +.044 |
| 7 | .774 | +.093 | .095 | +.046 | .770 | +.094 | .087 | +.052 |

[a]The d.o. score is obtained by subtracting observed from predicted scores. Thus a negative score indicates a mean or standard deviation that is too high, while a positive score indicates a score that is too low.

Figure 1 compares the prescribed and observed mean firing times for 34 separate dueling situations from four independent studies. The results portrayed in this figure will be discussed later. At present we consider only the 14 position means for the probabilistic duels, shown by position labels written in parentheses. Figure 1 clearly illustrates the similarity between the position means in the noisy and silent probabilistic duels, prescribed by the game-theoretic model. Also, the relationship between the observed and prescribed means is manifested. The best-fit line through the 14 data points for the probabilistic duel in Fig. 1 has a slope of 0.529; the correlation between the prescribed and observed means is .876. The prediction can thus account for 77% of the variance in mean firing time across positions. The nature of the relationship is linear, except that the range of actual firing time is considerably more constricted than the prescribed range. Thus, the previously shown tendency to compress the distribution of firing time within positions is repeated between positions; subjects tended to fire sooner than prescribed for high prescribed values, and later than prescribed for low prescribed values.

*Correlations.* On the basis of previous studies, we expected the two members of a particular dyad to behave in a similar fashion with respect to mean and standard deviation of firing time. To determine whether this phenomenon obtained in the present experiment, within-dyad correlations of the mean firing time and standard deviation of firing time were calculated separately for both duels. These correlations are presented in Table IV. the overall picture is one of moderately positive relationships. Of the 28 correlations presented, only 3 are nonpositive, 2 for means and 1 for standard deviations.

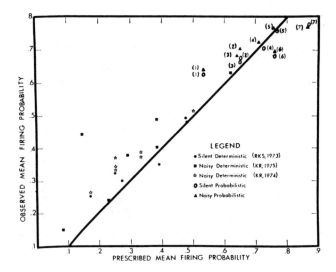

*Fig. 1. Prescribed versus observed means of firing time for first bullet fired, over four studies.*

For a one-tailed test (positive correlations) at $\alpha$ = .05, a value of $r$ = .55 is critical. Using this criterion, 7 of the 14 correlations of means and 2 of the 14 correlations of standard deviations were significant. However, considering all of the correlations as a whole, the most likely conclusion is that they are drawn from a positive population.

Because the two members of the dyad were not independent, subsequent correlations were based on the dyadic scores averaged over pairs within a dyad. Table V presents the position by position correlations of mean and standard deviation of firing time. A positive correlation indicates that the later a dyad fired in a given position (or the more dispersed their firing), the later it would fire in another position (or the more it would disperse its firing). Correlations for the silent duel are presented above the main diagonal and the correlations for the noisy duel are presented below the main diagonal.

Employing a test-wise significance level of $\alpha$ = .05, a correlation of +.55 is required for the directed hypothesis of positive relationship. This criterion yields 31 of the 42 correlations for the means as significant (16 for the silent duel and 15 for the noisy duel). All 42 correlations are positive. For the noisy duel, all correlations not involving position 7 are significant, while none involving that position reach criterion; nonetheless, because all position 7 correlations are positive, it is not advisable to accept the null hypothesis of zero correlation. For the silent duel, the pattern is more diffuse, but position 5 appears to be the least well correlated. The interpretation of these results is clear: There exists a general tendency for dyads to fire early or late relative to each other, and this tendency exists over different positions.

*Table IV.   Within-Dyad Correlations of Mean and Standard Deviation of Firing Time, by Position*

| Position | Silent duel | | Noisy duel | |
|:---:|:---:|:---:|:---:|:---:|
| | Corr. of means | Corr. of SD's | Corr. of means | Corr. of SD's |
| 1 | .903 | .186 | .403 | .078 |
| 2 | .505 | .229 | .780 | .322 |
| 3 | .887 | .435 | .589 | .499 |
| 4 | .589 | .254 | .271 | .363 |
| 5 | .026 | .652 | -.242 | -.350 |
| 6 | .589 | .583 | .908 | .121 |
| 7 | .017 | .049 | -.233 | .503 |

The correlations for standard deviations, like those of the means, are also uniformly positive, but of lower value.   Here, 21 of 42 correlations reach criterion (12 for silent duel and 9 for the noisy duel).   No particular pattern is evident for the standard deviations.   These data indicate that, just as dyad members will consistently fire early or late relative to each other over positions, so will they also group or disperse their fire consistently relative to each other.

*Frequency distributions.*   Given that the means and standard deviations of firing time differ from the prescribed values, the underlying frequency distributions must also be different.   Nevertheless, it is instructive to compare the shapes of the curves for the mathematically derived and empirically produced frequency distributions.   These comparisons are portrayed in Fig. 2 for the silent duel and Fig. 3 for the noisy duel. The data are displayed by position, collapsed over all subjects within an experimental condition.   In calculating the prescribed distribution, the truncation effect (see Appendix A) was taken into account.

Considering first the silent duel, one is immediately struck by the goodness of fit between the prescribed and observed curves for some of the positions.   In particular, for positions 4 and 7, the prescribed holding of fire until the end of the duel is manifested, although to a lesser degree than prescribed.[4]   The instances of one player with a

---

[4]The drop in the empirical curve at the very end is an artifact of the experimental procedure.   If a subject did not fire at all during the duel, he could not win and the computer terminated the duel at time $t = 1$, leaving no reaction time for the pure 'sure thing' fire.   Subjects avoided this mishap by firing just before the duel terminated.

*Table V.* *Correlations across Positions of Mean and Standard Deviation of Firing Time for Silent (above the Main Diagonal) and Noisy (below the Main Diagonal) Probabilistic Duels*

Mean firing time

Position

| Position | 1 | 2 | 3 | 4 | 5 | 6 | 7 |
|---|---|---|---|---|---|---|---|
| 1 | | .80 | .61 | .48 | .31 | .74 | .54 |
| 2 | .80 | | .81 | .74 | .52 | .95 | .79 |
| 3 | .76 | .93 | | .83 | .28 | .81 | .66 |
| 4 | .81 | .92 | .81 | | .62 | .82 | .69 |
| 5 | .80 | .72 | .66 | .75 | | .66 | .62 |
| 6 | .80 | .90 | .77 | .87 | .86 | | .85 |
| 7 | .17 | .46 | .22 | .37 | .15 | .52 | |

SD of firing time

Position

| Position | 1 | 2 | 3 | 4 | 5 | 6 | 7 |
|---|---|---|---|---|---|---|---|
| 1 | | .45 | .66 | .71 | .52 | .41 | .30 |
| 2 | .33 | | .42 | .63 | .42 | .75 | .12 |
| 3 | .41 | .68 | | .79 | .89 | .73 | .58 |
| 4 | .67 | .85 | .61 | | .77 | .81 | .33 |
| 5 | .07 | .53 | .07 | .48 | | .80 | .63 |
| 6 | .34 | .86 | .64 | .70 | .39 | | .46 |
| 7 | .92 | .52 | .52 | .82 | .20 | .46 | |

probability 0.5 of having a bullet (positions 2-4) are all characterized by virtually parallel curves of similar amplitude; the difference between the curves represents the previously reported difference in mean value. The curves involving one player with a probability 0.3 of having a bullet (positions 5-7) appear to have the appropriate mode; the incidence of early fire for all three cases distorts both the means and the standard deviations. Finally, position 1 does worst of all. These results for position 1 compare with position 1 of the silent deterministic duel (Rapoport et al., 1973) in that subjects fired later than prescribed, and had more dispersed fire.

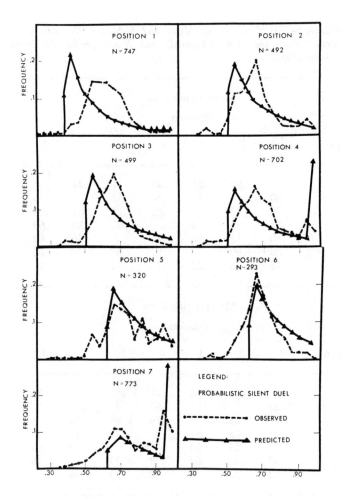

*Fig. 2. Prescribed and observed relative frequency distributions for all positions (silent duel).*

Turning to the noisy duel (note the change in abcissa values between Figs. 2 and 3), the overall view is not nearly as favorable as for the silent duel. In general the noisy duel calls for a peak of fire that subjects did not match, even though the observed standard deviations were smaller than the prescribed ones. Again, the holding of fire for positions 4 and 7 is manifested. For all three of the positions with a probability 0.5

of having a bullet (positions 2–4), there is a bimodal distribution that is not accounted for by the model. As in the silent duel, there is a slight tendency to fire too early for positions 5–7, but these positions, which actually have the least information for the players, provide the best fit. Again, position 1 fares least well.

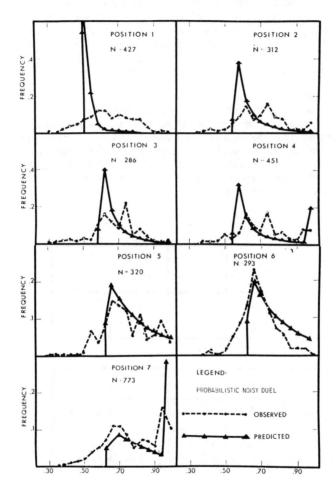

*Fig. 3. Prescribed and observed relative frequency distributions for all positions (noisy duel).*

*Individual differences.*   Some of the discrepancies between observed and prescribed distributions of firing time, particularly the incidence of early firing time in positions 5-7, may be attributed to individual differences.   The significant within-dyad correlations also indicate the worth of examining individual dyads' performance.   Because of the consistency over positions, only selected positions will be examined.   Of interest is the question of whether good fits of the model result from a collection of individually good fits, or whether subjects considered en masse produce results better than any single individual.   Frequency distributions were calculated for each dyad separately for position 1 (an unsatisfactory fit), position 2 (a satisfactory fit in a symmetrical position), and postion 7 (a relatively satisfactory fit in an asymmetrical position).   These results are portrayed in Figs. 4, 5, and 6, respectively.

As Fig. 4 shows, most dyads did choose one peak time of concentration for their fire, but the value of that peak ranged considerably from dyad to dyad.   For subjects who did concentrate their fire on a single value, that value was as likely to be early as late; the overall spread, plus the tendency to have a steeper slope to the left of the peak (as the model prescribes), led to the observed high mean firing time.   In the silent duel, dyads 4, 5, and 8, and to a lesser extend dyad 9, produced appropriately shaped distributions, albeit all with different modes.   For the noisy duel, dyads 1, 4, 7, and 9 had appropriately shaped distributions.

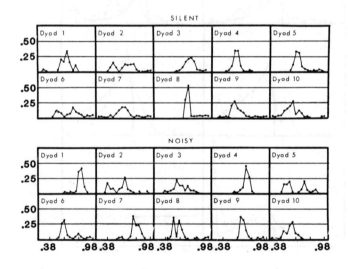

*Fig. 4.   Observed relative frequency distributions for individuals dyads, Position 1.*

Figure 5 presents the data for position 2, where the overall fit was superior to that of position 1.   Considering individual dyads, performance appears to be either fairly close to prescribed or very different.   In the silent duel dyads 1, 3, 4, 5, 7, and 8 all show resemblance to the prescribed distribution, and the range of modes is much closer than for position 1.   Much of the observed discrepancy from prediction can be attributed to the behavior of dyads 2 and 6.   Similarly for the noisy duel, dyads 2, 4, and 6-9 provide first-order approximations to the prescribed distribution.   The range of modes is greater here than in the silent duel, however, thus explaining the lesser fit for the noisy duel for position 2 (Figs. 2 and 3, above).

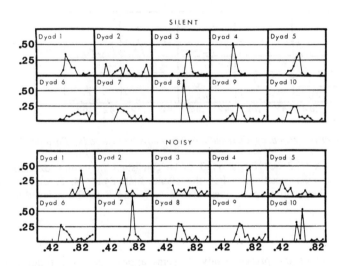

*Fig. 5.   Observed relative frequency distributions for individuals dyads, Position 2.*

Considered next is the asymmetric position 7, which prescribes holding fire until time $t = 1$ with a positive probability.   Figure 6 shows that some of the dyads do have some grouping of fire at the end of the duel, although it is always less than prescribed. The prescribed mode is less in evidence than it was in position 2; it would appear here that the overall grouping is better than any individual dyad.   Dyad 4 provides the best approximation to the prescribed distribution, with dyads 5 and 6 also producing appropriately shaped distributions.   For the noisy duel, many dyads show the appropriate bimodal distribution, although the range of the first peak varies considerably over dyads. Appropriately shaped distributions come from dyad 7 in particular, with dyads 1, 4, and 9 also having good approximations.

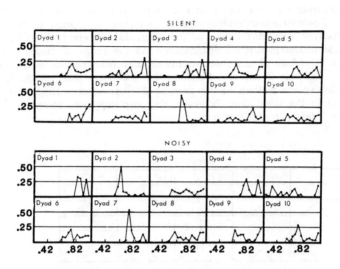

*Fig. 6. Observed relative frequency distributions for individuals dyads, Position 7.*

Overall, there is a tendency for a dyad to be consistent in its approximation to the prescribed distribution over positions. For the silent duel, dyads 4, 5, and 8 provided good approximations; their counterparts were dyads 4, 7, and 9 in the noisy duel.

## DISCUSSION

In discussing the results of the present study it seems appropriate to distinguish between group and individual results, and to further differentiate between measures of central tendency and dispersion. With respect to group, but not individual results, the present study provides support for the parameter-free game-theoretic solution as a first-order approximation to observed behavior in situations of bipolarized conflict, where the decision is when to act rather than what action to take. Whether or not this solution may serve as a basis for constructing a theory of behavior in such situations is an open question.

The utility of the game-theoretic solution is best shown examining results from previous duel studies as well as the present instance. Figure 1 presents the observed and predicted mean firing probabilities for the first bullet in all situations explored in the four duel studies (Kahan and Rapoport, 1974, 1975; Rapoport et al., 1973; the present study). Data in all instances are collapsed over roles and sessions. For all studies except one, firing probability is equivalent to firing time, i.e., $p_z(t) = t$. In Kahan and Rapoport (1975) the weak player had the accuracy function $p_z(t) = t^2$.

Figure 1 shows that the relationship between observed and prescribed mean firing probabilities is well described by a straight line with slope of slightly less than 1. The correlation between the 34 pairs of observed and predicted means is +.959. The best-fit line would cross the line of equality between prescription and observation at about .65. For the lower prescribed probabilities (including all the values in the previous studies), the subjects are conservative, firing at a mean probability later than that prescribed by the model. For higher probabilities, subjects fire earlier. It is likely that these different results for the later probabilities are due to a ceiling effect. At high probabilities, the function relating objective to subjective probability is systematically distorted; highly likely events are seen as even more likely than they actually are. For instance, most individuals, including psychologists, regard a probability of .95 as virtually a sure thing. Subjects in duel experiments commonly expressed anger if high-probability shots missed.

Additional support for the game-theoretic model is provided by examining the position means for the silent and noisy duels. As shown in Fig. 1, the means for noisy and silent duels are very close to each other for each of the seven positions. Contrary to the model's prediction, however, the observed standard deviations are also relatively close; for this measure, prescribed values can be widely separated for the same position. A partial explanation for this phenomenon lies in the late firing times for probabilistic duels. For higher probabilities of success, more of the bullets in the silent duel will be observed, thus reducing the operational difference between the two types of duel. In effect, both become noisy duels. In this context, it is interesting to note that the observed mean standard deviations, being too low, were more appropriate for noisy than for silent duels, as would be implied by this line of discussion.

A closer examination of individual frequency distributions shows that the smaller observed standard deviations resulted not because of a modal firing peak higher than prescribed, but because of a restricted range of firing. The restricted range reflects the difficulty on the part of subjects of conceptualizing the random firing strategy that probabilistic duels necessitate. Although subjects will show some variation from trial to trial in order that their opponents cannot predict their behavior perfectly, the concept of a strategy as a systematic probability distribution from which firing times are selected randomly is certainly beyond their level of mathematical sophistication. A more typical strategy is to select a general time of firing (or accuracy probability), and consistently remain within a small range of that time. In this context, it is interesting to note that if each subject is seen as a separate randomization, in the fashion of data collection for Thurstonian paired-comparisons (Bock and Jones, 1968), the resulting data over subjects provide a better fit to the prescribed model than does any single subject.

There are two findings with respect to individual differences which contradict the game-theoretic solution and, taken together, provide some insight into the nature of how the subjects approached this task. First, the behavior of one member of a dyad provided an excellent predictor of the behavior of the other member. The correlations of within-dyad performance reported in Table IV demonstrate this fact. In addition, data not reported here show that the sequential bullet-by-bullet correlations are high. That is, subjects tend to have similar firing times for a particular bullet and one fired immediately earlier, whether by self or by the opponent.    Second, there were quite consistent individual dyadic differences that perseverated over positions.    At first thought, these two findings might seem contradictory; if individual characteristics determine performance on this task to such a great extent, why do randomly constituted dyads produce similar behavior on the part of both members?    Furthermore, if these pairs of players do perform similarly, overall performance should tend more to a common mean, washing out the effect of between-position dyadic similarity.

A plausible explanation is that subjects would follow one another, and arrive at a common definition of an appropriate strategy, and then employ this strategy in an equilibrium state.    Because of the relative unfamiliarity of the task, there would not be much exploratory behavior away from that equilibrium state.    Furthermore, the effect on a player's payoff of a nonoptimal strategy is not great if his opponent also uses a similar nonoptimal strategy; the foundation of the game-theoretic prescription presupposes optimally performing opponents.    That is to say, this game is not sensitive to mutually occurring deviations from the prescribed policy.    Thus, although not adhering to the prescribed strategies, both players are achieving outcomes not far removed from the minimax value, and thus are not greatly motivated to seek better strategies.

Another possible cause for the general tendency for conservative play comes from a consideration of optimal fire in the light of nonoptimal opponents.    If one's opponent fires too early, then one should not change strategy, but if one's opponent fires late, then it is appropriate to change strategy toward later firing oneself.    Thus, if two players both tend to fluctuate in a quasi-random manner and in general follow each other, then an efficient strategy would be to attend more to upward moves of firing time than to downward moves.    Overall, this would produce the observed conservative firing times. In addition, the later firing time reduces the uncertainty in the game, as a shot taken at a late time is likely to prove conclusive.

The present series of duel studies are subject to an inherent limitation that occurs when interactions are freely studied (Messick, 1967).    Because in such situations two different individuals are free to introduce variables into the system, it is impossible to isolate characteristics of a single decision making entity that determine the state of the system.    The remedial step is to construct further experiments in which one of the duelist's strategies are known to the experimenter beforehand, and to examine the effect of differing strategies on the part of one duelist on the behavior of his opponent.    The outcomes of this series of experiments, in conjunction with the knowledge gained from the free-interaction studies heretofore performed, may provide the necessary information for the construction of a behavioral theory of decision making in timing conflicts.


## APPENDIX A

This Appendix presents derivations of the truncated firing time densities, assuming that the minimax strategies are employed by both members of the dyad.    Two cases are considered:    the probabilistic silent duel and the probabilistic noisy duel.

THE PROBABILISTIC SILENT DUEL

Let $\xi^*$ and $\eta^*$ denote the firing times of players $A$ and $B$, respectively, assuming each has a bullet. The density functions of these random variables, $f$ and $g$, are given in Eqs. (6) and (7). We now define the *observed firing times*:

$$O_A = \begin{cases} \xi^*, & \text{if } A \text{ has a bullet and fires it,} \\ +\infty, & \text{otherwise.} \end{cases}$$

$$O_B = \begin{cases} \eta^*, & \text{if } B \text{ has a bullet and fires it,} \\ +\infty, & \text{otherwise.} \end{cases}$$

Let $D$ denote the time at which the duel terminates. We shall use $F$ and $G$ to denote the distribution functions corresponding to the minimax densities $f$ and $g$, respectively.

We now proceed to compute the distribution function of $O_A$. By representing the event $\{O_A \leq x\}$ as the union of three mutually exclusive events, we may easily compute its probability.

$F(x)$, $x \leq 1$:

$\Pr[O_A \leq x] = \Pr[\xi^* \leq x, \; \xi^* \leq \eta^*, \text{ both } A \text{ and } B \text{ have bullets}]$

$\qquad + \Pr[\xi^* \leq x, \; A \text{ has a bullet, } B \text{ does not}]$

$\qquad + \Pr[\xi^* \leq x, \; \eta^* < \xi^*, \; B \text{ misses at } \eta^*, \text{ both } A \text{ and } B \text{ have bullets}].$

$$\Pr[\xi^* \leq x, \; \xi^* \leq \eta^*] = \int_0^x \Pr[\eta^* \geq \xi^* \mid \xi^* = \xi] f(\xi) d\xi$$

$$= \int_0^x \left[ \int_\xi^1 g(\eta) d\eta \right] f(\xi) d\xi$$

$$= F(x) - \int_0^x G(\xi) f(\xi) d\xi .$$

$\Pr[\xi^* \leq x] = F(x)$:

$\qquad \Pr[\xi^* \leq x, \; \eta^* < \xi^*, \; B \text{ misses at } \eta^*]$

$$= \int_0^x \left[ \int_0^\xi (1 - \eta) \, g(\eta) \, d\eta \right] f(\xi) d\xi$$

$$= \int_0^x G(\xi) f(\xi) d\xi - \int_0^x \left[ \int_0^\xi \eta g(\eta) \, d\eta \right] f(\xi) d\xi.$$

Weighting these three quantities by their probability of occurrence, we obtain the following expression for $\Pr[O_A \leq x]$: $PF(x) - PQ \int_0^x [\int_0^\xi \eta g(\eta) d\eta] f(\xi) d\xi$.

Using formulas (6) and (7) this may be simplified to

$$\Pr[O_A \leq x] = PF(x) \left\{ 1 - \frac{(1 + Q)(1 + 2P)}{2(1 + P)^2} \right\} + \frac{1 + Q}{12(1 + P)^3} \left[ (1 + 2P)^3 - \frac{1}{x^3} \right].$$

From this we may compute the density of $O_A$, as well as the conditional density of $O_A$, given that $A$'s bullet was observed: $d\Pr[O_A \leq x]/\Pr[O_A \leq 1]$. After some simple algebra, we see that this conditional density is of the form

$$(d_1/x^3) + (d_2/x^4), \qquad \text{for } 1/(1 + 2P) \leq x \leq 1,$$

and vanishes otherwise, where $d_1 = c_1/e_1$, $d_2 = c_2/e_1$, and these constants are given by:

$$c_1 = (1/2(1 + P))\{1 - ((1 + Q)(1 + 2P)/2(1 + P)^2)\}$$

$$c_2 = (1 + Q)/4(1 + P)^3,$$

$$e_1 = P\left\{ 1 - \frac{(1 + Q)(1 + 2P)}{(2(1 + P)^2)} \right\} + \frac{(1 + Q)}{12(1 + P)^3} [(1 + 2P)^3 - 1].$$

For player $B$, we may obtain in a similar manner,

$$\frac{d\Pr[O_B \leq y]}{\Pr[O_B \leq 1]} = \begin{cases} \dfrac{c}{y^3} + \dfrac{c}{y^4}, & \dfrac{1}{1 + 2P} \leq y < 1, \\[2ex] \dfrac{Q - P}{e_2(1 + P)^2}, & y = 1, \\[2ex] 0, & \text{otherwise} \end{cases}$$

where

$$c = (1 + Q)/4(1 + P)^3 e_2$$

and

$$e_2 = ((Q(1 + P) + (Q - P))/2(1 + P)^2) + ((1 + Q)/12(1 + P)^3)[(1 + 2P)^3 - 1].$$

THE PROBABILISTIC NOISY DUEL

In the noisy duel, only the first bullet fired will yield information about the minimax densities, (13) and (14). Therefore, this is the only bullet that will be recorded when collecting the data. We shall now define $O_A$ and $O_B$ as the *observed firing time* for players $A$ and $B$, respectively:

$$O_A = \begin{cases} \xi^*, & \text{if } A \text{ has a bullet and fires before } B, \\ + \infty, & \text{otherwise.} \end{cases}$$

$$O_B = \begin{cases} \eta^*, & \text{if } B \text{ has a bullet and fires before } A, \\ + \infty, & \text{otherwise.} \end{cases}$$

To compute the probability of the event $\{O_A \leq x\}$, for $x < 1$, we write:

$$\Pr[O_A \leq x] = \Pr[A \text{ fires before } x \text{ and } (A \text{ has 1 bullet, } B \text{ has no bullets)}]$$

$$+ \Pr\{A \text{ fires before x, } A \text{ fires before } B, (A \text{ has 1 bullet, } B \text{ has 1 bullet})].$$

We shall use $F$ and $G$ to represent the distribution functions corresponding to the densities $f$ and $g$ given by (13) and (14). Now,

$$\Pr[O_A \leq x] \ P(1 - Q) \ \Pr[\xi^* \leq x] + PQ \ \Pr[\xi^* \leq x, \ \xi^* < \eta^*]$$

$$= P(1 - Q) \ F(x) + PQ \int_0^x \Pr[\eta^* > \xi | \xi^* = \xi] f(\xi) d\xi$$

$$= P(1 - Q) \ F(x) + PQ \int_0^x [1 - G(\xi)] f(\xi) d\xi$$

$$= PF(x) - PQ \int_0^x G(\xi) f(\xi) d\xi . \tag{19}$$

By using (13), (14), and the following identity: For $1/2 < x \leq 1$:

$$\int_{(1+P^2)/(1+P)^2}^{x} \frac{dt}{(2t - 1)^2} = \frac{1}{2} \left[ \left( \frac{1 + P}{1 - P} \right)^2 - \frac{1}{2x - 1} \right],$$

we may write

$$\Pr[O_A \leq x] = \frac{P(1 - Q)F(x)}{2}$$

$$+ \frac{1}{2} \left[ \left( \frac{1 + P}{1 - P} \right)^2 - \frac{1}{2x - 1} \right] \left( \frac{1 - P}{2} \right)^2 \left( \frac{1 + Q}{1 + P} \right). \tag{20}$$

By differentation, we may obtain the conditional density of $O_A$, given that $A$'s bullet was observed.

$$d\Pr[O_A \leq x]/\Pr[O_A \leq 1]$$

$$= \left\{ \frac{P(1 - Q)f(x)}{2} + \frac{1}{(2x - 1)^2} \left( \frac{1 - P}{2} \right)^2 \left( \frac{1 + Q}{1 + P} \right) \right\} / \Pr[O_A \leq 1] .$$

Since the density $f$ has zero mass at 1, $\Pr[O_A \leq 1]$ may be computed from (20) with $x = 1$.

The computation for $O_B$ is very similar, with the main differene that $g$ does permit positive mass at 1. In fact, interchaning the roles of $A$ and $B$ in (19), we immediately obtain ($y < 1$)

$$\Pr[O_B \leq y] = QF(y) - PQ \int_0^y F(\eta)g(\eta)d\eta.$$

Now let

$$\delta(y) = \begin{cases} 0, & \text{if } y \neq 1, \\ 1, & \text{if } y = 1. \end{cases}$$

Then, for $y \leq 1$,

$$\Pr[O_B \leq y] = QG(y) - PQ \int_0^{y-} F(\eta)g(\eta)d\eta - PQg(1)\delta(y),$$

where the notation $\int_0^{y-}$ is used to indicate integration over the interval $[0,y)$.

Using (13) and (14), we obtain, after some algebra:

$$\Pr[O_B \leq y] = \frac{P(1 + Q)(1 - P)}{2(1 + P)} F(y) + \frac{(1 - P)(Q - P)\delta(y)}{1 + P}$$

$$+ \frac{1}{2} \left[\frac{1 - P}{2}\right]^2 \left[\frac{1 + Q}{1 + P}\right]\left[\left[\frac{1 + P}{1 - P}\right]^2 - \frac{1}{2x - 1}\right]. \qquad (21)$$

The conditional density of $O_B$, given that $B$'s bullet was observed, is

$$d\Pr[0_B \leq y]/\Pr[O_B \leq 1]$$

$$= \frac{\dfrac{P(1 + Q)(1 - P)f(y)}{2(1 + P)} + \dfrac{1}{(2y - 1)^2} \left[\dfrac{1 - P}{2}\right]\left[\dfrac{1 + Q}{1 + P}\right]}{\Pr[O_B \leq 1]},$$

$$\text{if } \frac{1 + P^2}{(1 + P)^2} \leq x < 1,$$

$$= \frac{(1 - P)(Q - P)}{(1 + P)\Pr[O_B \leq 1]}, \text{ if } x = 1$$

$$= 0, \text{ otherwise.}$$

where $\Pr[O_B \leq 1]$ is given by (21).

This investigation was supported in part by a PHS Grant No. MH-10006 from the National Institute of Mental Health and in part by a University Science Development Program Grant No. GU-2059 from the National Science Foundation.  The authors wish to thank Arthur W. Coston for programming assitance, Sandra Funk, Robert Schulman, and Jerry Solfvin for their aid in data collection and analysis, and Thomas S. Wallsten for many useful remarks.

## REFERENCES

Bock, R. D., and Jones, L. V.  *The measurement and prediction of judgment and choice.* San Francisco: Holden-Day, 1968.

Kahan, J. P., and Rapoport, A.  Decisions of timing in conflict situations with unequal power.  *Journal of Conflict Resolution,* 1975, **19**, 250–270.

Kahan, J. P., and Rapoport, A.  Decisions of timing in bipolarized conflict situations with complete information.  *Acta Psychologica,* 1974, **38**, 183–203.

Karlin, S.  *Mathematical methods and theory in games, programming and economics,* Vol. II. Reading, Mass.: Addision-Wesley, 1959.

Luce, R. D., and Raiffa, H.  *Games and decisions: Introduction and critical survey.*  New York: Wiley, 1957.

McCall, R. B., and Appelbaum, M. I.  Bias in the analysis of repeated measures designs: Some alternative approaches.  *Child Development,* 1973, **44**, 401–415.

Messick, D. M.  Interdependent decision strategies in zero-sum games.  *Behavioral Science,* 1967, **12**, 33–48.

Rapoport, A., Kahan, J. P., and Stein, W. E.  Decisions of timing in conflict situations of incomplete information.  *Behavioral Science,* 1973, **18**, 272–287.

# CHAPTER 6

# EFFECTS OF FIXED COSTS IN
# TWO-PERSON SEQUENTIAL BARGAINING

**ABSTRACT:** Rubinstein (1982) considered the problem of dividing a given surplus between two players sequentially, and then proposed a model in which the two players alternately make and respond to each other's offers through time. He further characterized the perfect equilibrium outcomes, which depend on the players' time preferences and order of moves. Using both equal and unequal bargaining cost conditions and an unlimited number of rounds, two experiments were designed to compare the perfect equilibrium model to alternative models based on norms of fairness. We report analyses of final agreements, first offers, and number of bargaining rounds, which provide limited support to the perfect equilibrium model, and then conclude by recommending a shift in focus from model testing to specification of the conditions favoring one model over another.

In a recent and selective review of experimental economics, Roth (1986) noted that many of the experiments that have been conducted fall on an imaginary continuum somewhere between experiments designed to test and possibly modify formal economic theories, and those designed to have a direct input into policy-making procedure. Between these two ends of the continuum lie experiments whose main purpose is to collect data in controlled settings on interesting phenomena and to detect systematic regularities in economic behavior. We report below the results of two experiments that lie close to the former end of the continuum. These experiments have been inspired by and designed to test the sequential strategic approach to the 2-person bargaining problem poineered by Rubinstein (1982).

Interest in the two-person bargaining problem started long before Rubinstein proposed his model. Edgeworth (1881) considered it the most basic problem of economics (Rubinstein, 1982). However, since utility theory had not yet been developed, Edgeworth could not proceed beyond identifying the negotiation solution to the problem (Harsanyi, 1977). Zeuthen (1930) and Hicks (1932) proposed models for the bargaining problem that assumed reasonable patterns of concession behavior, thus enabling Zeuthen to produce a theory which was essentially equivalent to that formulated by Nash 20 years later. An important step was taken later with the publication of Nash's three seminal papers (1950, 1951, 1953) in which he presented two complementary approaches to the two-person bargaining problem, known as the axiomatic and strategic (noncooperative) approaches.

Nash's axiomatic approach (in both its fixed and variable threat forms) has served as a reference for axiomatic bargaining theory. In his strategic approach, Nash complemented his axiomatic approach by modeling the bargaining problem as a noncooperative game. Although each of these approaches has certain advantages, both have their drawbacks. The major drawback of the axiomatic approach is its generality and the difficulty of assessing the reasonableness of the axioms, whereas the main problem with the noncooperative method is the need to specify the moves of the bargaining game in complete detail. As pointed out by Myerson (1986), face-to-face bargaining between two individuals is considerably more complex than the bargaining models that Nash and others can study. To achieve tractability, they must make some simplifications that may be viewed as arbitrary, ad-hoc, or too special.

## The Sequential Bargaining Game

Rubinstein (1982) generalized Nash's (1953) noncooperative model in two ways: (i) The bargaining takes place in discrete time and is governed by specific rules; (ii) The preferences of the bargainers regarding the value of the commodity at stake are a function of time. Rubinstein's sequential bargaining game is by now well known:

Two players, called P1 and P2, bargain over the set of feasible agreements $X = [0, p]$ (a "pie" of size $p$). The players have opposing preferences over $X$; if $x \geq y$, P1 prefers $x$ to $y$ if and only if P2 prefers $y$ to $x$. Events in the bargaining procedure are confined to times in the set $N = \{0, 1, 2, ...\}$. Each player, in turn, offers a possible agreement (a proposal on the partition of the pie) and his or her opponent must either agree to the offer or reject it. Acceptance terminates the game, whereas rejection leads to the next period in which the rejecting player makes a counteroffer. The play continues without any predetermined limit on the number of iterations (trials) of the process. Player P1 always moves first. The players are assumed to be indifferent to the path of rejected offers made during the negotiations. There are no rules that constrain them to previous offers they made.

Rubinstein assumes essentially that the parties' preference relations with respect to the "pie" and time maintain strict monotonicity, continuity, stationarity, and the larger the portion of the "pie," the more "compensation" a player needs in order for a delay of one time period to be immaterial to him. He also assumes that the preference structures of both players are common knowledge.

From this general description Rubinstein derived an infinite game tree with perfect information. Since every partition of the pie is supported by a pair of strategies in Nash Equilibrium, he resorted to the subgame prefect equilibrium concept (PE) (Selten, 1975) as a decision rule.

Two sub-families of models have received special attention in Rubinstein (1982):

1. *Fixed bargaining cost*: Player $i$'s preference is derived from the function $y - c_i t$ ($i= 1, 2; t = 0, 1, 2, ...$), i.e., each player bears a (possibly different) fixed cost for each period.
2. *Fixed discounting factor*: Player $i$'s preference is derived from the function $y \cdot \delta_i^t$ ($i = 1, 2; t = 0, 1, 2, ...$), i.e., each player has a (possibly different) fixed discount factor.

From a general theorem Rubinstein derived the following results for the fixed bargaining cost case.

S:   $c_1 < c_2$ (P1 is stronger than P2).   There is a unique partition supported by PE strategies that endows P1 with the whole pie on the first round.

W:   $c_1 > c_2$ (P1 is weaker than P2).   There is a unique partition supported by PE strategies that endows P1 with $c_2$ on the first round.

E:   $c_1 = c_2$ (P1 and P2 are of equal strength).   Every partition in the closed interval $[c_1, p]$ is supported by PE strategies.

When the bargaining costs are fixed, the PE solution is discontinuous on the diagonal $c_1 = c_2$. This discontinuity raises the problem of "just noticeable differences," where nominally different costs are perceived by the bargainers as practically equal. This problem is particularly serious for the PE model when $c_1$ and $c_2$ are very small in relation to $p$. Presumably, one could disconfirm the PE model by conducting experiments where the difference $c_1 - c_2$ is small. However, our interest is not in designing experiments to refute the PE model. Rather, our purpose is to find our cost parameters for which the PE solution can account for sequential bargaining behavior. This purpose has dictated the choice of the cost parameters $p$, $c_1$, and $c_2$ in the two experiments described below.

The present study has been preceded by several experiments designed to investigate bargaining behavior in the sequential bargaining game described above (Güth, Schmittberger, and Schwartze, 1982; Binmore, Shaked, and Sutton, 1985; Neelin, Sonnenschein, and Spiegel, 1988, Ochs and Roth, 1989). Our study differs from these studies in three important respects: First, all these studies have actually tested a finite horizon model proposed by Ståhl (1972), whereas we are concerned with testing Rubinstein's (1982) infinite-horizon model. Athough both these models adopt PE as a rational basis for  solution, players cannot solve the bargaining problem by backward induction when the number of proposals that can be made is infinite, but can do so when this number is finite and very small--as is the case in all these studies. Second, whereas most of these studies tested only the case where the two bargainers have equal time preferences, we are also interested in the case where the time preferences of the two bargainers differ (conditions S and W). Finally, the above experiments can be viewed as employing fixed discount factors in order to generate tastes, whereas we have used fixed cost factors. Bargainers may view these two factors as qualitatively different and, consequently, manifest different bargaining behavior.

## Alternative Models

When the number of stages in the sequential bargaining game is fixed and very small, as in the previous experimental tests of the PE solution, players may use the last stage as an anchor and work backward. But when the number of stages is no longer finite or known, players may have to resort to decision heuristics in order to generate a solution. Players may decide, for example, to ignore the strategic aspects of the sequential bargaining game and focus only on the costs differential, or they may even ignore the difference between $c_1$ and $c_2$ altogether. Hence, considerations of equity and equality, which are known to play a major role in other bargaining tasks, may become prominent.

To account for these possible heuristics, we have formulated two alternative models to the PE solution. The solutions associated with these models constitute "focal points" (Schelling, 1963; Roth, 1986) since they incorporate the notions of symmetry or equality. Each of these solutions has two versions, depending on whether or not Pareto optimality is assumed. The strong versions assume, in addition to Pareto optimality, either nominal equality of a 50-50 split (SES) or net payoffs equality (SEP). Recalling that a bargaining outcome is a pair $(x, t)$ it follows that according to both these models an agreement is predicted on the first round. If one does not assume Pareto optimality, one loses uniqueness as to the time period in which the bargaining is expected to end. In this case, one obtains two similar models (WES and WEP, respectively), whose outcomes are essentially conditioned on the time period in which the bargaining is terminated. All these models ignore the strategic aspect of the bargaining game. In addition, the equal-split models ignore the possible differential tastes of the bargainers.

To illustrate the predictions of the three models, consider the parameters actually used in Experiment 1 below: $p = 30$, $c_1 = 0.10$, and $c_2 = 2.50$. The PE model predicts that the bargaining will terminate on the first period with P1 getting 30. The ES model predicts a 15-15 split, irrespective of the trial number. Finally, the EP model predicts a split of 13.8-16.2 on trial 1, a split of 12.6-17.4 on trial 2, and in general gives P1 the value $x_1$, which is the solution of

$$x_1 - t \cdot c_1 = (30 - x_1) - t \cdot c_2, \, t = 1, 2, \ldots$$

There is a large body of experimental research in psychology that supports models ES and EP. And there is also a smaller body of research in experimental economics suggesting that descriptive theories of bargaining ought to incorporate psychological or sociological information beyond the traditional game-theoretic specification of what constitites "complete" information. One example comes from the work of Roth and his associates (Roth and Malouf, 1979; Roth, Malouf, and Murnighan, 1981; Roth and Murnighan, 1982; Roth and Schoumaker, 1983) on two-person bargaining. Another example is the work of Selten (1972, 1982, 1987) on coalition formation in three-person games in characteristic function form. Yet a third example for the persistence of equal split has been given by Kahneman, Knetsch, and Thaler (1986a, 1986b), who showed, in contrast to traditional economics, that people use well-defined rules in their fairness judgements and are even willing to enforce fairness at some cost to themselves.

Experiment 1

## Method

Eighteen male and female students from the University of Haifa participated in the experiment. The subjects were recruited through notices posted on campus promising monetary payoff for participation in a group decision making experiment. The subjects participated in groups of six in a single experimental session that lasted approximately 90 minutes. The stakes were relatively high: the mean payoff per subject was IS23.00 ($1 = IS1.6), approximately 6 times the student hourly rate.

PROCEDURE

The experiment was controlled by a PDP-11/73 computer with six terminals. Accordingly, the experiment consisted of three sessions each involving six different subjects.

Upon arrival at the laboratory, each subject was randomly assigned an integer between 1 and 6 and then escorted by the experimenter to a cubicle bearing that number. Each cubicle included a computer terminal, a set of written instructions, a IS10.00 note, and pencil and paper.

Each session consisted of 20 bargaining games. The first two games were for practice only. They were intended to familiarize the subject with the structure and nature of the sequential bargaining process and the use of the computer terminal. The remaining 18 games were played for monetary reward.

On each game, the six subjects were partitioned into three bargaining dyads according to conditions S, W, and E above. In all three conditions the dyads bargained over the division of IS30.00 ($p = 30$). The fixed bargaining costs were $c_1 = 0.10$ and $c_2 = 2.50$ in condition S, $c_1 = 2.50$ and $c_2 = 0.10$ in condition W, and $c_1 = c_2 = 2.50$ in condition E. Each condition implemented the sequential bargaining game as described above.

Each player assumed the role of P1 in nine games and the role of P2 in the remaining nine games. In each role, the subject played three games in condition S, three in condition W, and three in condition E. Roles and positions were rotated in a balanced design. Bargaining opponents were also rotated from trial to trial. Thus, each subject completed 18 bargaining games (2 roles x 3 cost conditions x 3 iterations or blocks) without ever knowing the identity of his or her opponent.

The computer displayed the cost parameters, trial number, and role of the subject, printed the transmitted offers, agreements, and rejections, and took care of the accounting. Bargaining dyads were never speeded in any way with the exception of instructing them that the game would be terminated by the experimenter if it lasted for "too many trials." Actually, the computer was programmed to terminate bargaining if the number of trials in the game exceeded a random limit that was distributed uniformly between 9 and 13. The experimenter's role was limited to rendering assistance to the subjects in using the terminals, answering questions about the instructions, paying the subjects, and then dismissing them.

In order to enhance the motivation of the subjects to bargain seriously, two complementary incentive mechanisms were implemented. First, each subject was instructed in writing that he or she could keep the IS10.00 note regardless of whether he or she decided to participate in the experiment. We decided on this unusual procedure to counter the argument that "subjects were not bargaining with their own money." Although the subjects could depart from the laboratory with the IS10.00 note without taking part in the experiment, all opted to participate. Second, we used a relatively large pie on each game, but paid the subject his or her portion of the pie in three games only. In particular, subjects were instructed that at the end of the experiment 3 of the 18 games they played would be chosen randomly, and their final payoff would equal the mean of their individual payoffs on these 3 games.

## Results

Technically, there is no way to realize an infinite game in the laboratory, because it is apparent to the subjects that the game must eventually terminate. Even if the bargainers are not informed of the number of periods to be played, it may be argued that the resulting game may not yield the same equilibria as the infinite game. For example, subjects may form subjective probabilities greater than zero that a given period must be the last, which may play a critical role in determining the nature of the equilibrium outcomes (Roth, 1988).

We instructed the subjects that the bargaining would be terminated if it included "too many trials." We did so in anticipation of queries raised by the subjects regarding the end of the bargaining. Of course, we do not know how the instructions were interpreted by the subjects. However, it is our impression that the random stopping mechanism we devised had practically no effect on the outcomes. The subjects never raised questions regarding the meaning of "too many trials." Of a total of 162 games played in Experiment 1, only 6 had to be terminated prematurely by the experimenter. We may conclude that the players had ample opportunity to exercise their best strategic thinking and that the random termination of the game had no effect, or at most only minor effects, on their bargaining. In the six cases in which the game ended prematurely, we planted the mean outcome for this condition and block of trials for the final offer. We did so in order to take advantage of the orthogonal properties of the experimental design in subsequent statistical analyses.

FINAL OFFERS

Table 1 presents the final offers by cost condition and block within condition. Columns 1, 2, and 3 show the final offers for blocks (iterations) 1, 2, and 3 of condition S, columns 4-6 show the same results for condition W, and columns 7-9 present the same results for condition E. Regardless of condition, the data in Table 1 are the shares of the pie obtained by P1, not the actual payoffs; the costs incurred in the bargaining are ignored. Table 1 uses asterisks to differentiate between two subsets of games: games ending on the first trial and games ending in two trials or more. The second row from the bottom presents the means of the final offers, whereas the bottom row shows the proportion of games that terminated on trial 1.

The final offers in Table 1 were subjected to a multivariate analysis of variance (MANOVA) to test for the effect of the cost condition by block interaction as well as the main effects of the two factors of the design. The $9 \times 1$ random variable consisting of the final offers to P1 in the three iterations of the three conditions was taken to be multivariate normal. No design variables were included. All effects were tested using the appropriate linear hypothesis. This approach takes into consideration any dependencies between allocations to P1 due to the communality of the first player.

The MANOVA yielded a significant interaction effect $F(4, 14) = 4.77$, $p < .02$). The mean final offers show clearly that the interaction is due to different trends of learning over blocks in the three cost conditions. The means increase steadily in condition S, decrease in condition W, and show no discernible trend in condition E. These results are congruent with the PE model. If the players gain from their bargaining experience in the sense of becoming more "rational" or "gamespersons," their final offers should converge in the direction seen in the table.

To check these learning trends, three additional MANOVAs were conducted on the final offers in each condition separately. As suggested above, the effects of practice (block) was significant in conditions S ($F(2, 16) = 6.36$, $p < 0.01$) and W $F(2, 16) = 7.60$, $p < 0.005$), but not in condition E ($F(2, 16) = 1.66$, $p > 0.2$).

## FIRST OFFERS

Our next analysis was intended to discover whether practice in bargaining within a given cost condition affects not only the final offers but also the first offers made by P1. In a sense, first offers are more suitable to examine the effects of practice on "rationality" because they are not "contaminated" by the responses of P2. Also, in studying first offers we encounter no problems of missing data due to prematurely terminated games. We note, of course, that the analysis of first offers is confounded with the analysis of final offers above, because in many games first and final offers coincide.

The first offers in all blocks and cost conditions were subjected to a similar MANOVA as above. Exactly as before, the interaction effect was significant ($F(4, 14) = 5.20$, $p < 0.01$). Subsequent contrasts designed to test for practice effects within each cost condition separately were found to be significant in conditions S ($F(2, 16) = 5.56$, $p < 0.02$) and W ($F(2, 16) = 10.81$, $p < 0.002$), but not condition E ($F(2, 16) < 1$).

The mean first offers in condition S increased with practice: 21.1, 23.4, and 25.9 for blocks 1, 2, and 3, respectively. The mean first offers in condition W descreased with practice: 15.2, 13.0, and 11.2 for blocks 1, 2, and 3. And the mean first offers in condition E showed a declining (but nonsignificant) trend: 17.8, 16.4, and 16.2 for blocks 1, 2, and 3. The practice trends are the same as the ones for the final offers. Comparison of the mean first and final offers shows, as might be expected, that bargaining resulted in P1 lowering his demand. This effect is barely noticeable in

*Table 1.*    *Final Offers by Cost Condition, Block, and Player in Experiment 1*

| Subject | Condition S: $c_1 < c_2$ Block | | | Condition W: $c_1 > c_2$ Block | | | Condition E: $c_1 = c_2$ Block | | |
|---|---|---|---|---|---|---|---|---|---|
| | 1 | 2 | 3 | 1 | 2 | 3 | 1 | 2 | 3 |
| 1 | 15 | 18 | 29 | 16* | 10* | 2.5* | 15 | 16 | 15 |
| 2 | 28* | 29 | 30 | 2* | 2* | 1* | 16 | 16 | 15* |
| 3 | 16* | 16.5* | 18 | 15 | 6.8*† | 4* | 15 | 16 | 16 |
| 4 | 17.5 | 27* | 27.5 | 14* | 13.5* | 10* | 15 | 16.5* | 16.5 |
| 5 | 26* | 22.6*† | 29 | 10* | 1* | 1* | 17.5 | 16.1*† | 15 |
| 6 | 20 | 18 | 27.5 | 15 | 12* | 1* | 14* | 16.5 | 16.5 |
| 7 | 30* | 30 | 30 | 15 | 15 | 15 | 15 | 15 | 15 |
| 8 | 30* | 27.5 | 30 | 10 | 2.5 | 2.5 | 15 | 15* | 15* |
| 9 | 23 | 23 | 24 | 14 | 16 | 15 | 17 | 15 | 16 |
| 10 | 10 | 16 | 23* | 12* | 9* | 10* | 15 | 20 | 15* |
| 11 | 15 | 17 | 17 | 2.5* | 0* | 0* | 5* | 17 | 15 |
| 12 | 30* | 20 | 17.5 | 0* | 10* | 0* | 17.5* | 20 | 20 |
| 13 | 18 | 24 | 27.5 | 14 | 10 | 2.5 | 15 | 15 | 15 |
| 14 | 20 | 25 | 27.5* | 2* | 1* | 0.7* | 15 | 15 | 15 |
| 15 | 24.5* | 29.1* | 30 | 7 | 2.5 | 2.5 | 15 | 15 | 15 |
| 16 | 20.8*† | 20* | 25.6*† | 7* | 1* | 0* | 15 | 15 | 15 |
| 17 | 22 | 29.5* | 30 | 10* | 5* | 15 | 14.8*† | 15 | 15 |
| 18 | 8* | 15 | 15 | 14* | 5* | 0.5* | 15 | 15 | 15 |
| Mean | 20.8 | 22.6 | 25.6 | 10.0 | 6.8 | 4.6 | 14.8 | 16.1 | 15.6 |
| Proportion | .50 | .67 | .83 | .39 | .28 | .33 | .78 | .83 | .83 |

\* Games with two trials or more.
† Prematurely terminated games.

conditions S and E, but is more substantial in condition W, where P1 is the weaker player.

NUMBER OF BARGAINING ROUNDS

The frequency distributions of the number of bargaining rounds are shown on the left-hand side of Table 2 for each condition separately. Thus, for example, of the 54 games played in condition S, 36 ended on trial 1, 1 on trial 2, 8 on trial 3, etc. The frequencies are collapsed over blocks because, as shown below, the effects of practice on the number of bargaining rounds was nonsignificant.

*Table 2.*    *Frequency Distribution of Number of Bargaining Rounds (Trials) by Experiment and Condition*

| Trial | Experiment 1 Condition | | | Experiment 2 Condition | | |
|---|---|---|---|---|---|---|
|  | S | W | E | S | W | E |
| 1 | 36 | 18 | 44 | 26 | 14 | 51 |
| 2 | 1 | 17 | 6 | 1 | 19 | 1 |
| 3 | 8 | 2 | 1 | 10 | 3 | 1 |
| 4 | 1 | 9 | 0 | 0 | 3 | 0 |
| 5 | 3 | 1 | 0 | 7 | 0 | 0 |
| 6 | 1 | 1 | 0 | 1 | 1 | 0 |
| 7+ | 1 | 5 | 1 | 5 | 2 | 0 |
| PT* | 3 | 1 | 2 | 4 | 6 | 1 |
| Total | 54 | 54 | 54 | 54 | 54 | 54 |

*Prematurely terminated game

Two observations are warranted with regard to the frequency distributions in Table 2. First, the distributions vary considerably from one another. If the games do not end on the first trial, there is a strong tendency for them to end on odd trials in condition S and even trials in condition W. These are the trials on which the stronger of the two bargainers makes an offer that the weaker player accepts. Second, the distributions are highly skewed. Consequently, any analysis of the length of bargaining based on the mean number of rounds is misleading. To circumvent this problem, and in line with the predictions of the PE model, we defined a new variable to be 0 if the game terminated in a single trial, and 1 otherwise. The resulting data were then subjected to the usual 3 × 3 MANOVA.

The interaction between the cost condition and block for the first offer to reach agreement was not significant ($F(4, 14) = 1.04$, $p > 0.4$). This means that whatever trends due to practice exist in the various conditions, they have the same slope. Next, we tested the main effects due to cost condition and block. Whereas the block effect was not significant ($F(2, 16) < 1$), there was a strong and significant effect due to cost condition ($F(2, 16) = 0.30$, $p < 0.005$). The proportions of single-trial games were most frequent in condition E and least frequent in condition W. They suggest that in the sequential bargaining procedure bargaining is less protracted when the stronger player makes the first offer than when the first offer is made by the weaker bargainer.

## CONSISTENCY WITHIN SUBJECTS

In discussing or attempting to provide solutions to bargaining problems with multiple equilibria, economists have often suggested that the final outcome depends on the "bargaining ability" of the parties. "Bargaining abiliby" has not been included in the given mathematical description of the game. Rather, it has been assumed to be beyond the scope of game theory. We have made no attempt in the present study to assess the bargaining ability of the subjects. However, we contend that if bargaining ability is a personality trait, relatively stable over time, it should affect the outcomes in the present study. Therefore, we should expect relatively able bargainers to do better than other bargainers who are not so able, and consequently to have positive correlations between the final offers in various blocks of the same cost condition.

Denote the correlation between the final offers in blocks $i$ and $j$ in cost condition $k$ by $r_k(i, j)$, where $i, j = 1, 2, 3; i \neq j$, and $k = S, W, E$. We have no interest in the case $k = E$ because of the multiplicity of equal splits in this cost condition. Computing the correlations between the final offers in Table 1, we obtained $r_S(1, 2) = 0.70$, $r_S(1, 3) = 0.50$, $r_S(2, 3) = 0.76$, $r_W(1, 2) = 0.62$, $r_W(1, 3) = 0.45$, and $r_W(2, 3) = 0.61$. All the six correlations are positive, and, with the exception of one (which is marginally significant), highly significant. They point out the importance of individual differences in bargaining ability, whose nature deserves empirical investigation.

## BARGAINING IN LONG GAMES

Being the weaker of the two players, P2 in condition S or P1 in condition W could expect at best an equal split of $p$. At least one of the two players in condition E could also have such an expectation. Hence, in games with seven trials or more, at least one of the players would expect to end the game with a negative payoff. Table 2 shows that there were seven games in Experiment 1 with seven trials or more that ended naturally. The sequences of payoffs and counterpayoffs to player P1 in these seven games are shown in Table 3. We examined these sequences to understand better the bargaining process.

One player (player 18) assumed the role of P1 in three of these seven games (W/1/18, W/2/18, and W/3/18). Although he was the weaker player, player 18 attempted to force an equal split in two of these games, whereas in the third game he offered a 14-16 split. Table 3 shows that player 18 succeeded on the first game, but failed in the subsequent two games. Indeed, his final share was smaller than the offer made to him on trial 2. The stubbornness of P2 in game S/1/5 and P1 in games W/1/2 and W/1/12 was also ineffective. Rejecting the offer of 2 Shekels on trial 1 in game S/1/5, P2 ended with 4 Shekels and a negative payoff, whereas players P1 in games W/1/2 and W/1/12 accepted the share that was originally offered to them on trial 2. Even a worse fate awaited player P1 in game E/2/11, who started by offering himself 17.5 Shekels, increased this offer on subsequent rounds, and finally and unexpectedly accepted a share of 5 Shekels.

The tenor of these results is quite general. Out of the 15 games in condition S that took more than one offer to reach an agreement, seven resulted in P1 getting at least his nominal first offer, and in all these 15 games P2 lost in real terms by prolonging the bargaining. In condition W, P1 never made an offer in which he would obtain, at most, 0.10 Shekels. This deviation from the PE strategy was profitable for P1 in all the (18) games in which P2 accepted P1's first offer, but in none of the cases in which P1's first offer was rejected. Condition E is less clear cut. In five of the eight games in condition E that ended in a single trial, P2 gained in real terms relative to the first proposal.

*Table 3.*     *Offers and Counteroffers in Games that Terminated in Seven or More Trials: Experiment 1*

| | | | Game (Condition/Block/Subject) | | | | |
| Trial | S/1/5 | W/1/2 | W/1/12 | W/1/18 | W/2/18 | W/3/18 | E/2/11 |
| --- | --- | --- | --- | --- | --- | --- | --- |
| 1 | 28 | 13 | 22.5 | 15 | 15 | 14 | 17.5 |
| 2 | 16 | 2 | 0 | 10 | 8 | 2 | 13.5 |
| 3 | 29 | 10 | 25 | 15.5 | 14 | 13.5 | 20 |
| 4 | 16 | 1.5 | 0 | 10 | 7 | 1 | 12.5 |
| 5 | 29 | 10 | 20 | 15 | 13.5 | 12 | 20 |
| 6 | 16 | 1 | 0 | 11 | 8 | 1 | 15 |
| 7 | 26 | 10 | 17.5 | 14 | 15 | 10 | 25 |
| 8 | | 3 | 0 | | 5 | 0.99 | 5 |
| 9 | | 13 | 12.5 | | | 10 | |
| 10 | | 2 | 0 | | | 0.50 | |

MODEL TESTING

We have already remarked about the significant trends in the mean final offers (Table 1) that favor the PE model. An inspection of the individual rather than mean final outcomes in Table 1 shows in many cases a similar trend. In testing the PE model, we count any agreement (on any round) that gives the weak player a nonpositive payoff (i.e., 2.5 of less) as supporting the model. Table 1 shows that there were 20 such agreements in condition S: 4 in block 1, 5 in block 2, and 11 in block 3. Turning next to condition W, Table 1 shows 4 agreements in block 1, 7 in block 2, and 12 in block 3 that support the PE model. The outcome of all the 27 cases in condition E, where an agreement was reached on the first trial, is congruent with the PE prediction. However, we suspect that this is due more to the prevailing egalitarian norms than to strategic considerations.

The predictions of the four equality models coincide in condition E. However, these models fared considerably worse than the PE model in the other conditions: Model

SES accounted for only four outcomes in condition S and seven outcomes in condition W, whereas the equal payoff models did not account for any outcome in these two conditions.

## Experiment 2

To further explore the predictive power of the PE model, we conducted a second experiment with different values of $c_1$ and $c_2$. Fixed bargaining costs were chosen that, on the one hand, still maintained strong asymmetry in the time preferences of the two bargainers, but, on the other hand, yielded a less extreme ratio of $c_1$ to $c_2$ than that used in Experiment 1. A major purpose of Experiment 2 was to examine the effects of relatively small changes in the bargaining costs on the predictive power of the three models.

### Method

With the exception of the bargaining costs, Experiment 2 was identical to Experiment 1 in the population of subjects and experimental procedure. The bargaining costs were $c_1$ = 0.2 and $c_2$ = 3.0 in conditions S, $c_1$ = 3.0 and $c_2$ = 0.2 in condition W, and $c_1$ = $c_2$ = 3.0 in condition E.

### Results

Of a total of 162 games, 11 were terminated prematurely. As before, we included these games in the analysis of the final offers after implanting for each game the mean outcome for its corresponding block and condition.

FINAL OFFERS

The final offers for Experiment 2 are presented in Table 4. The format of the table is identical to that of Table 1.

The final offers in Table 4 were subjected to MANOVA to test the effects of block, cost condition, and their interaction. As in Experiment 1, the interaction effect was significant ($F_{(4, 14)}$ = 5.10, $p < 0.01$). The mean final outcomes show the same learning trends as before: They increase in condition S from 17.2 in block 1 to 22.1 in block 3, they decrease in condition W from 12.1 in block 1 to 8.4 in block 3, and they exhibit no discernible trend in condition E. Subsequent tests conducted on the final offers in each condition separately show that the practice effects were significant in conditions S ($F_{(2, 16)}$ = 8.63, $p < 0.01$) and W ($F_{(2, 16)}$ = 5.36, $p < 0.02$), but not in condition E ($F_{(2, 16)}$ = 1.31, $p < 0.2$).

Table 4.    Final Offers by Cost Condition, Block, and Player in Experiment 2

| | Condition S: $c_1 < c_2$ | | | Condition W: $c_1 > c_2$ | | | Condition E: $c_1 = c_2$ | | |
|---|---|---|---|---|---|---|---|---|---|
| | | Block | | | Block | | | Block | |
| Subject | 1 | 2 | 3 | 1 | 2 | 3 | 1 | 2 | 3 |
| 1 | 18 | 21.4*† | 18* | 8* | 4.6* | 3* | 15 | 15 | 15 |
| 2 | 18* | 18 | 27 | 15* | 11.5*† | 8.4*† | 15 | 15 | 15 |
| 3 | 13.6 | 30 | 29* | 16.4 | 16.4 | 10* | 15 | 15 | 15 |
| 4 | 13.6 | 17 | 25 | 16.4 | 14* | 0* | 15 | 15 | 15 |
| 5 | 23* | 22 | 22 | 12* | 12* | 5* | 15 | 15 | 15 |
| 6 | 20 | 28.2* | 28* | 6* | 6* | 6* | 15* | 17 | 18 |
| 7 | 14 | 16* | 18* | 15 | 15 | 14 | 15 | 15 | 15 |
| 8 | 15* | 15 | 15 | 10* | 15* | 15 | 15 | 15 | 15 |
| 9 | 15* | 20* | 18* | 10* | 8* | 8.4*† | 15 | 15 | 15 |
| 10 | 15* | 21.4*† | 22* | 15* | 11.5*† | 11* | 15 | 15 | 15 |
| 11 | 16 | 15 | 15 | 15 | 18* | 17 | 15 | 15.4*† | 16 |
| 12 | 15* | 17* | 15 | 16* | 14* | 13* | 15 | 15 | 15 |
| 13 | 23* | 30* | 30 | 6* | 3* | 3 | 15 | 15 | 15 |
| 14 | 20* | 29* | 28 | 14 | 13 | 14 | 15 | 15 | 16 |
| 15 | 20 | 20* | 30 | 12.1*† | 18* | 8.4*† | 18 | 20 | 15* |
| 16 | 20* | 30* | 30 | 10* | 5* | 0* | 15 | 15 | 15 |
| 17 | 13.6 | 13.6 | 13.6 | 13* | 16.4 | 15* | 15 | 15 | 15 |
| 18 | 17.2*† | 21.4*† | 15* | 7* | 6* | 0* | 15 | 15 | 15 |
| Mean | 17.2 | 21.4 | 22.1 | 12.1 | 11.5 | 8.4 | 15.2 | 15.4 | 15.3 |
| Proportion | .44 | .39 | .61 | .28 | .22 | .28 | .94 | .94 | .94 |

\* Games with two trials or more.
† Prematurely terminated games.

FIRST OFFERS

The first offers, including those of the 11 prematurely terminated games, were subjected to the same analysis described above.    Again as before, significant block by cost condition interaction effects ($F_{(4, 14)} = 5.20$. $p < 0.01$) and significant block effects were found in conditions S and W ($F_{(2, 16)} = 8.39$ and 4.07, respectively), but not in E.

The mean first offers in condition S were 18.7, 23.1, and 24.1 for blocks 1, 2, and 3, respectively.  Comparison of these means with the mean final offers in Table 4 shows that bargaining resulted in P1 lowering his demands. Exactly as in Experiment 1, this effect is stronger for condition W; the mean first offers in this condition are 15.5, 14.6, and 13.4 compared to the mean final offers (Table 4) of 12.1, 11.5, and 8.4. There is no difference between the mean first offers and mean final offers in condition E.

## NUMBER OF BARGAINING ROUNDS

The frequency distributions of the number of bargaining rounds in conditions S, W, and E of Experiment 2 are shown on the right-hand side of Table 2. The same two observations made in Experiment 1 with regard to these distributions apply in Experiment 2 with equal force.

Differentiating again between games ending in a single trial and games terminating in 2 trials or more, the effects of block, cost condition, and their interaction were tested by MANOVA. The results duplicated those obtained in Experiment 1: only the main effect due to cost condition was significant ($F(2, 16) = 31.3$, $p < 0.001$). The bottom row of Table 4 shows clearly that single-trial games occurred most frequently in condition E (94% of all games) and least frequently in condition W (between 22% and 28%).

## WITHIN-SUBJECT CONSISTENCY

As in Experiment 1, the correlations between the final offers in different blocks within cost condition were positive and significant ($p < 0.05$): $r_S(1, 2) = 0.57$, $r_S(1, 3) = 0.54$, $r_S(2, 3) = 0.75$, $r_W(1, 2) = 0.78$, $r_W(1, 3) = 0.49$, and $r_W(2, 3) = 0.71$. We interpret these results as additional evidence for consistent individual differences in bargaining ability.

## BARGAINING IN LONG GAMES

Because the cost per trial for the weaker of the two bargainers was increased from 2.5 in Experiment 1 to 3 in Experiment 2, we chose to scrutinize all naturally terminated games with six trials or more. At least one of the players should have expected a negative payoff in any of these games. Table 2 shows that there were nine games with six trials or more. The offers and counteroffers to P1 in these nine games are presented in Table 5.

Unlike Experiment 1, prolonged bargaining in Experiment 2 occasionally benefited the weak player. In two of the three games in condition W, the weak bargainer offered the division predicted by the EP podel. Although P2 rejected this offer, he or she terminated the game by offering a 14-16 (game W/2/4) or 15-15 (game W/3/17) division. In condition S, where P1 is the stronger player, P1 made significant concessions in games S/3/1, S/1/10, S/3/18, and S/2/15. In game S/1/5, P1 increased his or her demand as the game progressed, whereas in game S/1/8 he or she insisted on an equal split.

Quite generally, of the 24 games in condition S that terminated naturally in more than two trials, 7 games ended with P1 keeping the (nominal) share demanded on the first proposal and 23 games ended with P2 losing in real terms. All games in conditions W and E in which P2 chose to deviate from the PE strategy ended in a loss for him or her.

*Table 5.    Offers and Counteroffers in Games that Terminated in Six or More Trials: Experiment 2*

| Trial | Game (Condition/Block/Subject) | | | | | | | | |
| | S/1/5 | S/3/1 | S/1/8 | S/1/10 | S/2/15 | S/3/18 | W/2/4 | W/1/9 | W/3/17 |
|---|---|---|---|---|---|---|---|---|---|
| 1 | 20 | 27 | 15 | 25 | 30 | 30 | 16.4 | 15 | 16.4 |
| 2 | 13.6 | 18 | 10 | 13 | 24 | 0 | 0 | 10 | 1 |
| 3 | 25 | 24 | 15 | 23 | 30 | 24 | 19 | 15 | 30 |
| 4 | 10 | 17 | 10 | 15 | 15 | 0 | 4 | 11 | 0 |
| 5 | 24 | 21 | 15 | 20 | 30 | 30 | 20 | 20 | 30 |
| 6 | 15 | 18 | 12 | 15 | 15 | 0 | 15 | 10 | 5 |
| 7 | 23 | | 15 | 17 | 20 | 25 | 22 | | 30 |
| 8 | | | | 15 | | 0 | 14 | | 15 |
| 9 | | | | | | 15 | | | |

MODEL TESTING

In accordance with the procedure used in Experiment 1, we counted any final outcome that gives the weaker bargainer a nonpositive payoff (i.e., 3.0 or less) as support of the PE model.    Table 4 shows that altogether there were 12 agreements in condition S that supported the PE model: 0, 5, and 7 in blocks 1, 2, and 3, respectively.    The number of agreements supportive of model PE in condition W was 6: 0, 1, and 5 in blocks 1, 2, and 3, respectively.    As before, the frequency of agreements in which the stronger bargainer gets essentially the entire pie increases with practice, although it is lower than in Experiment 1.    As in Experiment 1, the outcomes in condition E are consistent with the PE model, but our reservation regarding this conclusion is the same as in Experiment 1.

Ten of the 54 games in condition S and 8 of the 54 games in condition W ended in an equal split, showing a stronger support for  the ES model in Experiment 2 than 1. The agreement predicted by the EP model was obtained in 5 games in condition S and 4 in condition W.    Clearly, the social norm of equal share (after subtracting the bargaining costs) was adopted by some of the subjects.

COMPARISON OF THE TWO EXPERIMENTS

Experiment 2 was designed not only to replicate Experiment 1, but also to find out whether a relatively small reduction in the ratio of the bargaining cost of the stronger to the weaker bargainer affects the final agreements.    For this purpose, we processed

Experiments 1 and 2 in a two-level one-way MANOVA separately for the first and
final offers. As usual, the cost conditions and block effects were modeled within
subjects. The analysis of the first offers showed no significant experiment by cost
condition by block interaction (F(4, 31) < 1. This indicated that first offers in both
experiments show the same patterns. In fact, we found significant block by cost
condition effect (F(4, 31) = 10.93, $p$ 0.001), and significant block effect for conditions S
and W, but none in E (F(2, 33) = 13.95, $p < 0.001$, F(2, 33) = 14.50, $p < 0.001$, and F (2,
33) < 1, respectively). This replicates our previous conclusion. In contrast to the first
offer analysis, the final offer analysis yielded a significant triple interaction, providing
additional justification for our separate analysis of each experiment (F(4, 31) = 3.06, $p <$
0.04). The different learning slopes in Fig. 1 attest to this result. The block effects
within cost condition in Experiment 2 are modest as compared to those in Experiment 1.
We conclude that the different cost structure in Experiment 2 induced more egalitarian
behavior.

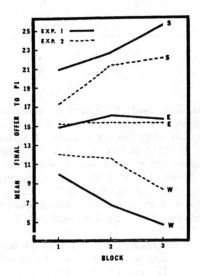

*Figure 1. Mean final offers to player P1 by cost condition and block
(iteration).*

## Discussion

There has been a progression of experiments designed to test the sequential bargaining model developed by Ståhl (1972) and Rubinstein (1982). Güth et al. (1982) started this investigation by restricting the bargaining to a single round. Arguing that the "one-stage ultimatum game is a rather special case, from which it is dangerous to draw general conclusions" (p. 1180), Binmore et al. (1985) extended the investigation to two-round games. Letting the two members of the dyad play the roles of P1 and P2 once, Binmore et al. concluded that the tendency to "play fair" in the first game became a strong tendency to play "like a game theorist" on the successive game. The generality of this conclusion was challenged, in turn, by Neelin et al. (1988), who replicated the results of Binmore et al. in the two-round game but not in games with three or more rounds. Another important extension is the experiment by Ochs and Roth (1989) that allows the discount factors of the two bargainers to be varied independently, and that focuses on the qualitative rather than only on the quantitative predictions of the PE model.

Changing the focus of the research from a small to a large number of trials and from the fixed discounting factor case to the fixed bargaining cost case, the present study constitutes yet another step in this progression. Contrary to the finite bargaining discount experiments, our results provide qualified support for the PE model. They raise the possibility that fixed bargaining costs are very different from discount factors in terms of their effects on bargaining behavior.

Although the experimental work cited above has not been exhaustive, two intermediate conclusions may be drawn at this stage. The first conclusion is a recommendation to shift the emphasis of subsequent research on sequential two-person bargaining from model testing to specification of the conditions that favor one model rather than another. These conditions include, but by no means exhaust, the parameters of the bargaining problem (size of pie, bargaining costs, length of bargaining), bargaining ability (bargaining experience, knowledge of bargaining theory, bargaining "toughness"), prevalence of norms of fairness and justice, and procedural details of the task.

A systematic investigation of the effects of the parameters of the problem has just begun. Binmore et al. showed that a game favorable to the PE model could be constructed by limiting the number of rounds to two. With a larger, yet finite number of rounds, the PE model fails (Neelin, et al., 1988). However, we conjecture that equity norms might be strong even in two-stage fixed but equal discount factor if these are larger than half. In fact, as the discount factor tends to one we expect a stronger tendency for equal split.

Our results show that the bargaining costs also have a strong and systematic effect on the final outcomes when the number of rounds is unlimited and the time-preferences of the two bargainers are different. In particular (see Fig. 1), as the ratio of the fixed bargaining costs of the stronger to the weaker member of the dyad gets smaller, the final outcomes become more egalitarian. This conclusion has been shown to hold with only a small change in the fixed bargaining costs. It holds regardless of whether P1 is the stronger or weaker of the two players. On the basis of these results we hypothesize that, in general, if the bargaining costs are fixed so that $c_1 = c_2 + \epsilon$, the final outcome will approach an equal split as $\epsilon \rightarrow 0$. Parametric studies that manipulate $c_1$ and $c_2$ systematically in a between- or within-subject design are needed to test this hypothesis.

Our second conclusion is also methodological in nature. Because practice in fixed cost bargaining icnreases the frequency of PE agreements, there is a need to manipulate bargaining ability experimentally by either comparing different populations of subjects that differ from one another in their bargaining experience and knowledge or running multiple sessions that provide subjects much more experience with the task than in previous studies. Our results suggest that convergence to a stable division is slower as the bargaining costs of the two players are closer to each other. However, it is possible that convergence will be relatively fast when either $e = 0$ or $e$ is "very large," but considerably slower when $e$ assumes intermediate values.

## Acknowledgement

We wish to acknowledge the help of Ariel Cohen, who wrote the computer programs for the sequential bargaining task, and the assistance of Hamutal Pinnes and Anat Toyster, who supervised the experimental sessions.

## References

Binmore, K., Shaked, A., and Sutton, J. (1985). Testing noncooperative bargaining theory: A preliminary study, *American Economic Review*, 75, 1178-1180.

Edgeworth, F. Y. (1881). *Mathematical psychics*. London: Kegan Paul.

Güth, W., Schmittberger, R., and Schwarze, B. (1982). An experimental analysis of ultimatum bargaining, *Journal of Economic Behavior and Organization*, 3, 367-388.

Harsanyi, J. C. (1977). *Rational behavior and bargaining equilibrium in games and social situations*. Cambridge: Cambridge University Press.

Hicks, J. R. (1932). *The theory of wages*. London: Macmillan.

Kahneman, D., Knetsch, J. L., and Thaler, R. H. (1986a). Fairness and the assumptions of economics, *The Journal of Business*, 59, 285-300.

Kahneman, D., Knetsch, J. L., and Thaler, R. H. (1986b). Fairness as a constraint on profit seeking: Entitlements in the market. *The American Economic Review*, 76, 728-741.

Myerson, R. B. (1986). An introduction to game theory. In S. Reiter (Ed.), *Studies in mathematical economics*. Washington: The Mathematical Association of America, pp. 1-61.

Nash, J. F. (1950). The bargaining problem. *Econometrica*, 18, 155-162.

Nash, J. F. (1951). Non-cooperative games. *Annals of Mathematics*, 54, 286-295.

Nash, J. F. (1953). Two person cooperative games. *Econometrica*, 21, 128-140.

Neelin, J., Sonnenschein, H., and Spiegel, M. (1988). A further test of noncooperative bargaining theory. *American Economic Review*, 78, 824-836.

Ochs, J. and Roth, A. E. (1989) An experimental study of sequential bargaining. *American Economic Review*, 79, 355-384.

Roth, A. E. (1986). Laboratory experimentation in economics. *Economics and Philosophy*, 2, 245-273.

Roth, A. E. (1988). Laboratory experimentation in economics: A methodological overview. *The Economic Journal*, 98, 974-1031.

Roth, A. E., and Malouf, M. W. K. (1979). Game-theoretic models and the role of information in bargaining. *Psychological Review*, 86, 574-594.

Roth, A. E., Malouf, M. W. K., and Murnighan, J. K. (1981). Sociological versus strategical factors in bargaining. *Journal of Economic Behavior and Organization*, 2, 153-177.

Roth, A. E., and Murnighan, J. K. (1982). The role of information in bargaining: An experimental study. *Econometrica*, 50, 1123-1142.

Roth, A. E., and Schoumaker, F. (1983). Expectations and reputations in bargaining: An experimental study. *The American Economic Review*, 73, 362-372.

Rubinstein, A. (1982). Perfect equilibrium in a bargaining model. *Econometrica*, 50, 97-109.

Schelling, T. C. (1963). *The strategy of conflict*. New York: Oxford University Press.

Selten, R. (1972). Equal share analysis of characteristic function experiments. In H. Sauermann (Ed.), *Contributions to experimental economics*, III, J. Tubingen: C. B. Mohr, pp. 130-165.

Selten, R. (1975). Re-examination of the perfectness concept for equilibrium points in extensive games. *International Journal of Game Theory*, 4, 25-55.

Selten, R. (1982). Equal division payoff bounds for three-person characteristic function experiments. In R. Tietz (Ed.), *Aspiration levels in bargaining and economic decision making*, Berlin: Springer-Verlag, pp. 265-275.

Selten, R. (1987). Equity and coalition bargaining in experimental 3-person games. In A. E. Roth (Ed.), *Laboratory experimentation in economics: Six points of view*, New York: Cambridge University Press, pp. 42-98

Ståhl, I. (1972). *Bargaining theory*. Stockhom: Stockholm School of Economics.

Zeuthen, F. (1930). *Problems of monopoly and economics*. London: Routledge.

# CHAPTER 7

# A PDP-11/45 PROGRAM FOR PLAYING N-PERSON CHARACTERISTIC FUNCTION GAMES

ABSTRACT.  NPER II is an on-line PDP-11/45 computer program for studying bargaining and coalition formation processes within the framework of n-person games in characteristic function form.  The extensive vocabulary of the program and its mode of operation are presented nontechnically, followed by an examination of a protocol from a sample four-person game.  Improvements over a previous version of the program and applications to other experimental paradigms investigating coalition formation and bargaining are discussed in the last two sections of the paper.

NPER II is a program written for the PDP-11/45 computer to study bargaining and coalition formation processes within the framework of n-person games in characteristic function form.  This program is a successor to the   system (Kahan & Helwig, 1971; Rapoport & Kahan, 1974) written for the PDP-8, which has been employed in a number of studies on bargaining and coalition formation.  NPER II differs from its predecessor in that it possesses a wider game vocabulary, has better methods of game definition, data storage and retrieval, and bookkeeping, and provides options for types of games not possible previously.  We shall first present a description of NPER II, then a sample game, and shall conclude with a discussion of improvements of the new version over the old, including the generalizability of the basic paradigm that is provided by the program.

## 1.  Playing Games in Characteristic Function Form

An n-person game in characteristic function form is defined by specifying a number of players and a function that assigns a real number (positive integer in the present implementation) to each possible subset (coalition) of the players.  This value assigned to the coalition represents the utility that its members jointly command.  The object of the game is for a player to gain for himself the maximum possible utility through one of the various coalitions of which he is a member.  A coalition is formed when its members agree on how to allocate its value.

When the players are seated, each at individual teletypes in a soundproofed cubicle, NPER II starts a game by telling each player his role in the game (by a letter identification) and by printing out the values for that game.  Consider an example game for four players defined by the values:   A = 10, B = 15, C = 15, D = 10, AB = 30, AC = 35, AD = 25, BD = 40, CD = 35, ABC = 55, ACD = 60, ABD = 60, ABCD = 85.

Consider this game from the point of view of Player A.  Alone he can realize 10 points.  If he forms a coalition with Player B, the two players command 30 points.  Similarly, the coalitions AC and AD command 35 and 25 points together, respectively.  Or, if Player A joins with both Players B and C, the three command 55 points.  Both coalitions ACD and ABD command 60 points.  Finally, if four players combine, this grand coalition of all the players controls 85 points.  Note that Players B and C cannot form a coalition without the presence of Player A. The value of coalitions BC and BCD are technically zero; empirically they are not allowed to form.

In NPER II, the players communicate by typing various statements about how to divide the value of a coalition among its members, in the context of a bargaining process that contains three stages. The first, or negotiation stage, is when players explore the potentials of various coalitions. Different proposals for forming coalitions and allocating the values are made. In this stage, players gain awareness of their relative strengths and weaknesses, and of the stances and expectations of the other players. The second stage, termed the acceptance stage, begins when a set of players indicates general acceptance of a proposal. This acceptance is not binding, but does indicate that serious consideration is being given to the proposal as an outcome for that coalition. During the acceptance stage, the members of the coalition may be interested in modifications of the agreement, and the nonmembers of the coalition are interested in disrupting the proposal to further their own interests. It is in this stage that various strategies and counterstrategies may become quite subtle and complex; and for this reason, it is a psychologically interesting stage. Finally, the third, or ratification stage, terminates the bargaining process. The members of a tentative coalition have considered a proposal, have seen it through acceptance, and are now willing to make a binding commitment. If all players agree upon ratification, the coalition is formed, the players receive their payoffs, and the game is terminated for them. The entire game is terminated when each player is in one, and only one, ratified coalition.

Communication in NPER II is via a set of key words. Upon receiving a request for input from the computer, the player types a key word, followed by parameters if necessary. The computer then checks the legality of the message and transmits its content to the players who are supposed to receive it. Table 1 shows the set of key words used in NPER II, along with their required parameters and their effects on the coalitions addressed and on other coalitions.

The basic key words for bargaining are OFFER, where a player proposes an allocation of points; ACCEPT, where a player makes a tentative commitment to the allocation; and RATIFY, where a player initiates termination of the game. Indeed, it is possible to play the game with only this primitive set of three key words. Any member of a coalition may make an offer; the computer maintains each player's most recent statement regarding each coalition. To enter the acceptance stage, all members of a coalition (including the originator of the OFFER) must ACCEPT it (the originator cannot be the first to ACCEPT his own OFFER). When one player proposes RATIFY, all players in accepted coalitions immediately vote yes or no. Coalitions with unanimous consent are ratified; others are dissolved.

The key words AGREE, REJECT, and AFFIRM give shading to intentions concerning coalitions. AGREE indicates a mild liking of an OFFER and REJECT strong distaste (the proposal can simply be ignored). AFFIRM indicates a reiteration of a player's most recent stand with respect to a coalition. PASS indicates that a player has nothing to say at the present time. SOLO immediately removes a player from the game; he will take what he can get by not joining any coalition. SUGGEST is like OFFER except that (1) it is unofficial and (2) it may be sent to any players, not necessarily including all those in the proposal. REMARK and MESSAGE allow communication

Table 1. Key Words and Their Effects

| Key word | E.g. of paramater | Primary effect | Other effect on this coalition | Effects outside named coalition |
|---|---|---|---|---|
| PASS | (none) | Send null message | (none) | (none) |
| SOLO | (none) | Immediate ratification of player's one-person coalition. | (none) play in this game | Player is removed from further |
| OFFER | A=20, B=18, C=17 | Make a proposal. | Supersedes player's previous OFFER, AGREE, & ACCEPT | (none) |
| SUGGEST | A=20, C=15 to ACD | Make informal | (none) | (none) |
| REJECT | ACD BY C | Erase an offer. | (none) | (none) |
| AGREE | ACD BY C | Show liking for | Same as for OFFER | Erases any ACCEPT made by this player |
| ACCEPT | ACD BY C | Tentative | Same as for OFFER made by this player | Erases any AGREE or ACCEPT |
| (when all players have accepted an offer) | | Game moves to acceptance stage. | (none) | Erases all other positions taken by included players. They may make no new OFFER except to subsets or supersets of the accepted coalition. |
| AFFIRM | ACD | Stand by previous action. | (none) | (none) |
| RATIFY | (none) | Propose move to ratification. | Form coaliton if all members agree to ratification. Coalition is dissolved otherwise. | Concludes game for players in ratified coalitions. |
| REMARK | AC (text) | Send (text) to named player(s). Counts as a communication. | | |
| MESSAGE | A=1, C=3 | Send numbered message(s) to named player(s). Counts as a communication. | | |
| VALUE | (none) | Information: Give all values in the game except those involving removed players. Does not count as a communication. | | |
| VALUE | ACD | Information: Give value of that named coalition. Does not count as a communication. | | |
| STATUS | (none) | Information: Give current statements involving every coalition in the game. Does not count as a communication. | | |
| STATUS | ABC | Information: Give current statements regarding named coalition. Does not count as a communication. | | |
| STATUS | ABOUT AC | Information: Give current statements involving coalitions including named player(s). Does not count as a communication. | | |
| STATUS | BY AC | Information: Give current positions taken by named player(s). Does not count as a communication. | | |

outside the NPER II vocabulary. The former allows free text, while the latter sends experimenter-defined standard messages. If players lose track of the proceedings, the key words VALUE and STATUS keep them up-to-date. All key words other than OFFER, ACCEPT, and RATIFY may be disabled at the experimenter's option.

Figure 1 presents an example game from the point of view of Player B. The game is an example designed to show various features of the program, and does not represent actual data. Except for the numbering of the statements, the figure is an exact replica of the input and output from Player B's teletypewriter. Message 0 is from the computer, and tells the player his own identity and the characteristic function for this game. Our discussion will be guided by the statement numbers in Figure 1, which correspond to moves in the play of this game. The first move of the game is an OFFER from Player A to coalition AC, in which both players A and C receive five more points than each would by participating in no coalition. Player B moves second, and after attempting to address an illegal coalition, makes a three-person OFFER to coalition ACD. Note that, in OFFER statements, the coalition is implied by who is named in the point allocation. Player C chooses to wait one round, so Statement 3 is a PASS on his part. Player D uses his move to send a MESSAGE. Player B receives the message shown on his teletypewriter; he does not know if other players received similar, different, or no messages from Player D. The game continues through move 11, showing the different types of key words and some error messages in response to Player B's errors. Note that in B's REMARK in move 6, the computer reminds him who received his remark; other players do not receive that information.

On move 12, Player D chooses SOLO, which removes him from the game. Player B, on his next move (14), uses the VALUE key word to find out what coalitions remain legal in the game, and then uses STATUS to obtain a record of all current positions in the game. Note that Player B does not see moves 15 and 16; Players A and C have sent communications (SUGGEST, MESSAGE, or REMARK) to each other, but have not included him as a recipient.

In moves 17 through 23, the players again proceed with the game, showing how the computer signals the effect of new moves on previously taken positions and demonstrating how all-accept is signaled. Finally, on move 24, Player C calls for ratification. Both Players A and B vote in favor of ratification (simultaneously and independently) and, with all players now in ratified coalitions, the game terminates. As this game was the only one played in this session, the person who played B is given the sessions' earnings in Statement 25.

## 2.  Computational Features

NPER II is written for the PDP-11/45 in 11TRAN, a language resembling PL/I written at the L. L. Thurstone Psychometric Laboratory. In the program design, emphasis is placed on the subject interface; for example, the program utilizes extensive error checking and validation, dynamic key word abbreviations, and clear, concise messages in easily readable formats. Because of the large number of players allowed, as well as the total possible number of positions that would theoretically be outstanding at one time (on

```
0.    IN THE FOLLOWING GAME YOU ARE PLAYER B
      COALITIONS HAVE THE FOLLOWING VALUES;
      A=10; B=15; C=15; D=10; AB=30; AC=35; AD=25; BD=40; CD=35
      ABC=55; ACD=60; ABD=60; ABCD=85.

1.    A OFFERS AC:                    A=15; C=20

2.    B, GO AHEAD:  OFFER B=25, C=25
      BC IS NOT A VALID COALITION

      B, GO AHEAD: OFFER A=25, B=25, D=10
      B OFFERS ABD:        A=25; B=25; D=10
3.    C PASSES
4.    D SAYS: IF I DON'T GET A GOOD DEAL, I MAY SOLO.
5.    A AGREES ABD BY B;   A=25; B=25; D=10

6.    B, GO AHEAD: ACCEPT ABD BY B
      YOU CANNOT ACCEPT YOUR OWN OFFER UNTIL SOMEONE ELSE DOES

      B, GO AHEAD:  OFFER A=20, B=20
      COALITION DOES NOT SUM TO 30

      B, GO AHEAD: REMARK ACD SORRY, I JUST KEEP MAKING MISTAKES
      B REMARKS TO ACD:  SORRY, I JUST KEEP MAKING MISTAKES
7.    C OFFERS ABC:        A=16; B=17; C=22
8.    D REJECTS ABD BY B: A=25; B=25; D=10
9.    A OFFERS ABC:        A=20; B=15; C=20

10.   B, GO AHEAD: OFFER C=13; A=17, B=25
      B OFFERS ABC:        A=17; B=25; C=13
11.   C AFFIRMS HIS OFFER TO ABC: A=16; B=17; C=22
12.   D SOLOS AND IS REMOVED FROM PLAY
13.   A OFFERS AB:         A=13; B=17

14.   B, GO AHEAD: VALUE
      A=10; B=15; C=15; AB=30; AC=35; ABC=55

      B, GO AHEAD: STATUS
      A OFFERED AC:
      C OFFERED ABC:       A=16; B=17; C=22
      A OFFERED ABC:       A=20; B=15; C=20
      B OFFERED ABC:       A=17; B=25; C=13
      ** SOLOED D:         D=10
      A OFFERED AB;        A=13; B=17

      B, GO AHEAD: SUGGEST A=15; B=21; C=19; TO A
      B SUGGESTS ABC TO A: A=15; B=21; C=19
17.   B, GO AHEAD: AGREE AB BY A
      B AGREES AB BY A:    A=13; B=17
18.   C AGREES AC BY A:    A=15; C=20
19.   A ACCEPTS ABC BY C: A=16; B=17; C=22
      REPLACING HIS OWN OFFER TO ABC

20.   B, GO AHEAD: STATUS
      A OFFERED AC:        A=15; C=20
                          C AGREED.
      C OFFERED ABC:       A=16; B=17; C=22
                          A ACCEPTED.
      B OFFERED ABC:       A=17; B=25; C=13
      ** SOLOED D:         D=10
      A OFFERED AB:        A=13; B=17
                          B AGREED

      B, GO AHEAD: OFFER A=16; C=20, B=19
      B OFFERS ABC:        A=16; B=19; C=20
      REPLACING HIS PREVIOUS OFFER
21.   C ACCEPTS ABC BY B: A=16; B=19; C=20
      REPLACING HIS OWN OFFER TO ABC
      AND HIS AGREE TO A'S OFFER TO AC
22.   A ACCEPTS ABC BY B: A=16; B=19; C=20

23.   B, GO AHEAD: AC ABC BY B
      B ACCEPTS ABC BY B: A=16; B=19; C=20
      REPLACING HIS AGREE TO A'S OFFER TO AB
      ABC NOW ALL-ACCEPTED, NULLIFYING ALL OTHER POSITIONS BY
      THEM
24.   B, PLAYER C CALLED FOR A RATIFICATION VOTE.  DO YOU RATIFY
      THE COALITION ABC: A=16; B=19; C=20
      (Y OR N)?  Y
      C CALLED FOR RATIFICATION
      ABC VOTED TO RATIFY
      ABC ARE NOT IN RATIFIED COALITION AND ARE REMOVED FROM
      PLAY
      !!GAME OVER!!

25.   TODAY YOU HAVE EARNED    19 POINTS
```

*Figure 1.    Player B's protocol of a four-person example game in characteristic function form.  (B's typed messages are underlined.)*

the order of 300,000), data structures are dynamically allocated from free space within the task and are inserted in appropriate linked lists. The essence of NPER II, then, is a computer program composed of a sophisticated parser, an internal structure based on linked lists, and a message formulator and printer.

## 3.   Improvements Over Previous Versions

As stated earlier, NPER II is a revised version of a system used extensively for the past 5 years.   Perhaps an indication of the flexibility of the new program can be gained by reiterating three limitations of the previous version discussed by Rapoport and Kahan (1974), and showing how the present version overcomes these limitations.

The first constraint of the previous program was that a player could accept only one coalition at a time.   In effect, the ACCEPT key word's function was too narrow. In the present version, acceptance has been broken down into AGREE and ACCEPT statements.   An agreement, the weaker version, can now be made to each potential coalition of which a person is a member.   Acceptance is now free to have stronger force.   A player must now accept his own original offer, once others have indicated acceptance of it.   That is to say, where an OFFER was once assumed to be automatically accepted by its author, now it is only assumed to be agreed to.   This loosening of acceptance procedures also allows the program to be expanded so that each player's most recent OFFER to a coalition is outstanding, rather than just one OFFER per coalition.   Thus, particularly in coalitions of size greater than two, the range of possibilities for a player is considerably expanded.

A second limitation of the previous game was that a ratification of a coalition of a subset of players changed the game, as coalitions with members of that subset were then not available to the remaining players.   Thus, only the first coalition ratified could be used as a test of any particular model which assumes simultaneous ratification.   In the present version, the experimenter may lock out ratification for an unlimited time, until all players are in accepted coalitions.   A single ratification statement than serves all accepted coalitions at once, instead of only those players in a particular accepted coalition.

A third limitation was that only one issue could be negotiated at a time.   At present, research trends in the areas of bargaining and decision making indicate increased interest in multi-attribute environments; NPER II has been constructed to play with up to three issues (each specified by its own characteristic function) being negotiated simultaneously.   In the multi-attribute version, the issues are named by the experimenter (typically with color names), and the player must specify, in addition to his key word, which issue he wants to address with his message.   Thus, an agreement in this version might read:   BLUE AGREE ABC BY B.   Here a player agrees to the proposal to coalition ABC made by Player B, in the issue labeled "blue."

## 4. Applicability

NPER II can accommodate all of the research done using the previous system. Coalitions was used in the investigation of games in characteristic function form for three players, both with (Rapoport & Kahan, 1975; Medlin, Note 1) and without (Kahan & Rapoport, 1974, 1975) three-person coalitions, and varieties of four-person games (Funk, 1972; Horowitz & Rapoport, 1974). By simple extension, other work directly investigating n-person games in characteristic function form (e.g., Buckley & Westen, 1973; Maschler, 1965; Riker, 1967; Selten & Schuster, 1968) could be run using NPER II.

In our usage, subjects are paid a linear function of the points they earn. However, by employing special payoff transformations, other experiments that are not already in NPER II format could be replicated. Laing and Morrison (1974) have studied games of status, where a player's payoff depends not on the absolute number of points he has, but rather on the rank order of his total among the totals of all participating players. Their experiments could be replicated by using their characteristic functions as originally presented, but by rewarding subjects on the basis of rank order rather than on absolute quantity.

Much of the social psychological work on coalition formation has used the "Pachisi" paradigm (Caplow, 1968) pioneered by Vinacke and Arkoff (1957). In many of these studies, interest focused on a game where players could combine weights of four, three, and two in a majority-rule constant-sum game. This classical game could be placed in NPER II format by using the following characteristic function: A = 1, B = 0, C = 0, AB = 700, AC = 600, BC = 500, ABC = 900. The values to the multiperson coalitions represent the 4-3-2 weights multiplied by 100. The values to the one-person coalitions represent the fact that, if no coalition forms, Player A (with the largest weight) wins the game. The multiplicative factor of 100 is to round Player A's payoff to zero if coalition BC forms. Subjects are paid a constant sum, which is split in proportion to the points each has at the end of the NPER II game. Such a technique would allow a test of the social psychological hypotheses without the confounding of restricted communication and the artificial separation of payoff and coalition formation that characterize most of the Pachisi studies.

## 5. Reference Note

1. Medlin, S. Effects of grand coalition payoffs on coalition formation in three-person games. Unpublished manuscript, 1975.

## 6. References

Buckley, J. J., & Westen, T. E. The symmetric solution to a five-person constant-sum game as a description of experimental game outcomes. *Journal of Conflict Resolution.* 1973, **17**, 703–718.

Caplow, T. *Two against one: Coalitions in triads.* Englewood Cliffs, N. J: Prentice-Hall, 1968.

Funk, S. G. *Value power and positional power in n-person games.* Unpublished MA thesis, Chapel Hill: University of North Carolina, 1972.

Horowitz, A. D., and Rapoport, Am. Test of the kernel and two bargaining set models in four- and five-person games. In An. Rapoport (Ed.), *Game theory as a theory of conflict resolution.* Dordrecht, Holland: Reidel, 1974. Pp. 161–192.

Kahan, J. P., & Helwig, R. A. Coalitions: A system of programs for computer-controlled bargaining games. *General Systems,* 1971, **16**, 31–41.

Kahan, J. P. & Rapoport, Am. Test of the bargaining set and kernel models in three-person games. In An. Rapoport (Ed.). *Game theory as a theory of conflict resolution.* Dordrecht, Holland: Reidel, 1974. Pp. 119–160.

Kahan, J. P., & Rapoport, Am. *The effect of single-person values on bargaining and coalition formation in three-person cooperative games.* Report No. 139. Chapel Hill, N.C: L. L. Thurstone Psychometric Laboratory, July 1975.

Laing, J. D., & Morrison, R. J. Sequential games of status. *Behavioral Science,* 1974, **19**, 177–196.

Maschler, M. *Playing an n-person game: An experiment.* Economic Research Program Research Memorandum No. 73. Princeton, J.H.: Princeton University, 1965.

Rapoport, Am. & Kahan, J. P. Computer controlled research on bargaining and coalition formation. *Behavior Research Methods & Instrumentation.* 1974, **6**, 87–93.

Rapoport, Am. & Kahan, J. P. *Two- and three-person coalitions in experimental three-person cooperative games.* Report No. 137. Chapel Hill, N.C.: L. L. Thurstone Psychometric Laboratory, April 1975.

Riker, W. H. Bargaining in a three-person game. *American Political Science Review,* 1967, **61**, 642–656.

Selten, R., & Schuster, K. G. Psychological variables and coalition forming behavior. In K. Borch & J. Mossin (Eds.), *Risk and uncertainty.* London: Macmillan, 1968, Pp. 221–245.

Vinacke, W. E. & Arkoff, A. An experimental study of coalitions in the triad. *American Sociological Review,* 1957, **22**, 406–415.

CHAPTER 8

# TEST OF THE BARGAINING SET AND KERNEL MODELS IN THREE-PERSON GAMES

**ABSTRACT.** Twelve groups of undergraduate subjects participated in computer-controlled experiments designed to test the bargaining set and kernel models for $n$-person games in characteristic function form. Each group played four iterations each of 5 three-person games in which $v(A) = v(B) = v(C) = v(ABC) = 0$, and $v(AB) > v(AC) > v(BC) > 0$. The effects of (i) the communication rules governing the negotiations, (ii) the differences among the payoffs assigned to each coalition, and (iii) learning were systematically investigated.

The results are analyzed in terms of the frequencies of different coalition types that were formed, the disbursements of the payoffs, and the characterization of the bargaining process. They show the predominance of coalition $AB$, support the bargaining set and kernel models as predictors of final outcomes, reveal significant effects due to the latter two independent variables but not the former, and provide useful information about the nature of the bargaining process.

## 1. Introduction

The study of coalition formation is a topic of long standing among social psychologists. Observational interest dates at least from Georg Simmel (1902), and experimental evidence dates from the mid-1950s (Vinacke and Arkoff, 1957). Most of the experiments on coalition formation in the triad have followed the Pachisi board format described in Caplow (1968). In this game format, the three players each move counters around a Pachisi board at a rate determined by a chance mechanism in conjunction with experimenter-imposed multiplicative weights. The first player to reach the goal-square on the board is the winner. If two or more players form a coalition, their counters are combined and move as one counter with a multiplicative weight equal to the sum of the weights of the members of the coalition. Each player signals which of the other players he would like to enter into coalition with, and, if there is a mutual choice, a coalition is formed. Allocation of the rewards (typically a fixed reward no matter which person or coalition wins the game) is decided upon by the members of a coalition after it has tentatively formed, in a manner often not reported explicitly (e.g., Vinacke et al., 1966).

It is the contention of the present paper that the experimental paradigm described above is inadequate for the study of coalition formation for two major reasons. First, the paradigm is limited to games with a fixed reward for each coalition. As such, it is insensitive to the fact that different coalitions in real-life may well command different amounts of desirable resources. A decision as to which coalition to join is typically based on such considerations. In political considerations, for example, more than mere majority power gives a ruling coalition power; there is also the question of the legitimacy of that government. In democratic forms of rule, the greater the proportion of citizens represented in the government, the greater the legitimacy of that government. In

147

game-theoretic terms, then, our first objection is that most situations modelled by games are inherently non-zero-sum games. Second, and more importantly, the paradigm strictly separates the process of coalition formation from the division of rewards. Clearly, when the very reason for forming a coalition is to increase one's gains, one will consider the amount of gains that may be won from different coalitions before deciding which coalition to join. Negotiations may occur with different parties simultaneously, and offers may be carefully weighed one against the other, before final decisions are made. This bargaining process is entirely neglected in the Pachisi paradigm. Some recent work (Komorita and Chertkoff, 1973) shows awareness of the problem of negotiations affecting disbursements of payoffs, but even here coalition choice and outcome determination are separated.

The experimental paradigm presented below is designed to overcome these two inadequacies. Thus, coalition formation is scrutinized through examination of negotiated divisions of the rewards jointly available to the members of the coalition. This paradigm necessarily involves somewhat complicated experimental procedures, which were until recently not available within psychological laboratories, and have only become possible with the recent development of the digital computer as an experimental instrument. Prior to such instrumentation, the study of coalition formation through negotiations had only been undertaken in a rigidly narrowed scope. (Riker, 1967; Selten and Schuster, 1968) or as a year-long project without the opportunity for experimental control of psychologically interesting variables or systematic observation of the bargaining process (Maschler, 1965).

The orientation of our experimental paradigm arises from mathematical game theory. Familiarity with the nature, purpose, and principal ideas of game theory in general (see, *e.g.*, Luce and Raiffa, 1957; Rapoport, 1966) is assumed. We begin by a brief review of the mathematical background of $n$-person games, which is less known (but see, *e.g.*, Rapoport, 1970), and continue with a description of the experimental task.

1.1. THEORIES OF $n$-PERSON GAMES

The major mathematical approach to $n$-person games considers them from the point of view of the *characteristic function*. Briefly described, an $n$-person game in characteristic function form is defined by naming all of the possible nonempty subsets of the $n$ players in the game, and assigning a real number value $v(X)$ to each subset so named. The value represents a measure of the utility jointly commanded by that subset in coalition against all of the other players in the game. The term "coalition" is used in a neutral sense, without institutional or structural implications. The assigned real-valued set function $v$, the number and identification of the $n$ players, and the rules governing communication among them completely define the game. A solution to the game is a specification of which coalitions should form, and how the players in each formed coalition should divide among themselves the utility that they jointly control.

The present experiment is designed to investigate a class of characteristic function three-person games which have the special property that $v(A) = v(B) = v(C) = v(ABC) = 0$, and $v(AB)$, $v(AC)$, and $v(BC)$ are all positive but not necessarily equal to one another. Such games may be termed *quota games*, because quotas $\omega_i$ may be assigned to each player such that $v(ij) = \omega_i + \omega_j$ for each of the three possible coalitions $AB$, $AC$, and $BC$, where $i$, $j = A$, $B$, $C$, and $i \neq j$.

Unlike the case of two-person, zero-sum games, where the minimax principle provides a single compelling solution, there exists a multiplicity of solutions of $n$-person games in characteristic function form. Presently, at least five theories for the $n$-person cooperative game may be considered, namely, von Neumann and Morgenstern's *solution* (1947), Shapley's *value* (1953), Aumann and Maschler's *bargaining set* (1964), Davis and Maschler's *kernel* (1965), and Horowitz's *competitive bargaining set* (1973). For the quota games investigated in the present paper, only the bargaining set and kernel theories are of immediate interest. The solution of von Neumann and Morgenstern is unsatisfactory for our purposes as there are an infinite number of solution sets to the quota game. Because $v(ABC) = 0$ in the quota games presented here, the Shapley value does not provide a solution. And in the particular case where $n = 3$, Horowitz's competitive bargaining set theory reduces to the bargaining set theory.

For the particular case of three-person quota games, the two remaining theories — the bargaining set and the kernel — yield the same solution, although from different assumptions. We shall briefly present the principal ideas of both theories, and then show how they relate to the present experiment.

1.2. THE BARGAINING SET

Consider a cooperative $n$-person game in characteristic function form, described by the ordered pair $(v;N)$, where $N = \{1,2,...,n\}$ is a set of $n$ players and $v$ is the characteristic function of the game. The nonempty subsets of $N$ are called *coalitions*; they form the domain of $v$. $v(X)$ is assumed to satisfy two properties:

(i) $v(X) \geq 0$ for each coalition $X$,
(ii) $v\{i\} = 0$ for each one-person coalition.

Let $\mathbf{X}$ be an $m$-partition of $N$, satisfying

$$X_j \cap X_k = \emptyset, \text{ if } j \neq k, \text{ and } \cup_{j=1}^{m} X_j = N.$$

An *outcome* of the game is represented by a *payoff configuration (p.c.)*.

$$(\mathbf{x};\mathbf{X}) = (x_1,x_2,...,x_n;X_1,X_2,...,X_m),$$

where $\mathbf{x} = (x_1,x_2,...,x_n)$ is the vector of utilities gained by each player (called the *payoff vector*), and $\mathbf{X} = (X_1,X_2,...,X_m)$ represents the proposed *coalition structure (c.s.)*.

It is assumed that the members of each coalition $X_j \in \mathbf{X}$ are able to and do make use of all of the utility that they can jointly command, i.e.,

$$\sum_{i \in X_j} x_i = v(X_j), \ j = 1,2,...,m.$$

Furthermore, it is assumed that a rational player does not ask for less than what he could obtain if he were not to participate in any coalition. Thus, a *p.c.* is assumed to satisfy *individual rationality*, *i.e.*,

$$x_i \geq 0, \quad i = 1,2,...,n.$$

A third, key assumption is that every pair of players who are members of the same coalition have to reach a stable outcome representing their strengths and weaknesses. The distinctiveness of the bargaining set theory is how this stability is defined, through the concepts of *objection* and *counter-objection*. Before formally defining these terms, we shall demonstrate them through an example.

Consider a three-person quota game with the characteristic function $v(AB) = 95$, $v(AC) = 90$, $v(BC) = 65$, and $v(A) = v(B) = v(C) = v(ABC) = 0$. Suppose that players $A$ and $B$ have formed a coalition, agreeing on an 80:15 split. The *p.c.* so described is

$$(80, 15, 0; AB, \ C).$$

Player $A$ has a threat, or an objection against $B$. He may point out that he can offer 5 points to player $C$ (which are preferred to the zero points $C$ is getting in the present situation), thus obtaining 85 points (as $v(AC) = 90$), which is more than the 80 he is now slated to receive. Player $A$ can take this action without the consent of $B$. Similarly, $B$ has an objection against $A$. He can offer 15 points to $C$ via coalition $BC$, reserving 50 points for himself. Of these two objections, the latter is *justified*, but the former is not. Justification rests upon whether or not the player objected against has available a counter to the objection. Thus, $A$'s objection against $B$ is unjustified, because $B$ can make a counter-offer, giving $C$ 50 points and keeping 15 for himself. $C$ would prefer the 50 points to the 5 offered him by $A$, and $B$ maintains his 15 points that he had in the original $AB$ coalition. On the other hand, $B$'s objection against $A$ is justified, because there is no way that $A$ can offer $C$ 15 or more points and still maintain his original 80 points.

A coalition is defined as stable when neither member of the coalition has a justifiable objection against the other. For the example presented above, and excluding the case where no coalition is formed, this holds true for the following three *p.c.*'s only:

$$(60, 35, 0; AB, \ C),$$
$$(60, 0, 30; AC, \ B),$$
$$(0, 35, 30; A, \ BC).$$

The definitions of objection and counter-objection may now be formally presented. Let $(\mathbf{x};\mathbf{X})$ be a *p.c.* and let $k$ and $l$ be two members of a coalition $X_j$, $X_j \in \mathbf{X}$. For a coalition $Y$ and a payoff vector for its members, the pair $(\mathbf{y};Y)$ is called an *objection* of $k$ against $l$ in $(\mathbf{x};\mathbf{X})$, if

(i)        $k, l \in X_j, \ k \in Y, \ l \notin Y,$

(ii)       $$\sum_{i \in Y} y_i = v(Y),$$

(iii)      $y_k > x_k, y_i \geq x_i$   for all   $i \in Y.$

In his objection $(y;Y)$, player $k$ claims that he can gain more in the new coalition $Y$, without the consent of $l$, and that this situation is reasonable because the new partners of $k$ in $Y$ get at least what they got in $(x;X)$. Players which are not included either in the original coalition or in the objection are not considered at all, but for three-person games all players are necessarily considered.

For a coalition $Z$ and a payoff vector $z$, the pair $(z;Z)$ is called a *counter-objection* to the objection $(y;Y)$, if

(i)        $l \in Z, \ k \notin Z,$

(ii)       $$\sum_{i \in Z} z_i = v(Z),$$

(iii)      $z_i \geq x_i$   for all   $i \in Z,$

(iv)       $z_i \geq y_i$   for all   $i \in Z \cap Y.$

In lodging a counter-objection, player $l$ claims that he can maintain at least his allocation in $(x;X)$ by giving his new partners in $Z$ at least what they had before in $(x;X)$, and furthermore, if anybody in $Z$ is also a member of $Y$, he gets at least what he would have gotten in $Y$.

An objection is *justified* if no counter-objection to it exists.   Otherwise, it is *unjustified*.   The bargaining set $M_1^{(i)}$ is defined to be the set of all individually rational p.c.'s in which no player has a justified objection against any other member of the same coalition.   The superscript of $M$ indicates individual rationality, and the subscript indicates that objections are made against one player at a time.   Other bargaining sets have been proposed by Aumann and Maschler (1964), but for three-person quota games the results remain unchanged.

Aumann and Maschler showed that the bargaining set model provides a unique set of four p.c.'s in the three-person quota game, one for the case of no coalition $(0,0,0;A,B,C)$ and one for each of the possible coalitions.   The model does not provide a means of selecting which of the four will be chosen, or even a rationale for assuming equal likelihood.

1.3. THE KERNEL

The central concept of the kernel theory (Davis and Maschler, 1965) is that of *excess*. The excess of a coalition $Y$ with respect to a *p.c.* $(\mathbf{x};\mathbf{X})$ is given by

$$e(Y) = v(Y) - \sum_{i \in Y} x_i.$$

$e(Y)$ represents the total amount that the members of $Y$ may gain or lose (depending on whether $e(Y)$ is greater or less than zero, respectively), if they desert the *c.s.* $\mathbf{X}$ and form the coalition $Y$. Clearly, $e(X_j) = 0$, $j = 1,2,...,m$, where $X_j \in \mathbf{X}$.

As before, let $k$ and $l$ be two players in a coalition $X_j$, and let $\tau_{k,l}$ be the set of all the coalitions which contain player $k$ but not $l$, i.e.,

$$\tau_{k,l} = \{Y | k \in Y,\ l \notin Y\}.$$

The *maximum surplus* of $k$ over $l$ with respect to $(\mathbf{x};\mathbf{X})$ is given by

$$s_{k,l} = \max_{Y \in \tau_{k,l}} e(Y).$$

This maximum surplus $s_{k,l}$ is the greatest amount that player $k$ may gain (or the minimal amount he may lose, if $s_{k,l}$ is negative) by withdrawing from $\mathbf{X}$ and entering into coalition $Y$ that does not include $l$, assuming that the other members of $Y$ will be satisfied with receiving the same amount that they had had in $(\mathbf{x};\mathbf{X})$. If the other members of $Y$ are not content with their lot in $(\mathbf{x};\mathbf{X})$, then $s_{k,l}$ may be viewed as the amount that player $k$ has with which to bargain with the other players in $Y$ in order to pursue more reward than his current allocation.

Player $k$ is said to *outweigh* player $l$ with respect to the *p.c.* $(\mathbf{x};\mathbf{X})$ if $s_{k,l} > s_{l,k}$ and $x_l \neq 0$. A coalition is *balanced* if no player in it outweighs the other. The *kernel* of the game, denoted by $\mathbf{K}$, is the set of all individually rational *p.c.*'s having only balanced coalitions. It can be shown that $\mathbf{K} = \mathbf{M}_1^{(i)}$ for the three-person quota games considered in the present study.

Consider again our previous example. Suppose players $A$ and $B$ agree to split the value of their coalition 55:40. The respective *p.c.* is then

$(55,40,0;AB,C)$ .

Coalition $AC$ can gain 35 points if $AB$ is dissolved, but coalition $BC$ can only gain 25 points, so player $A$ outweighs player $B$ in this configuration. By contrast, the maximum surplus coalitions $AB$ or $AC$ have over the *p.c.*

$(0,35,30;A,BC)$

is 60 points, so the coalition is balanced, and this *p.c.* is in the kernel. The same holds for the *p.c.*'s (60,0,30;*AC,B*) and (60,35,0;*AB,C*).

## 1.4. THE COALITIONS GAME

At the Thurstone Psychometric Laboratory of the University of North Carolina, we have created *Coalitions*, a set of programs written for a PDP-8 computer to play bargaining games within the characteristic function framework. Details of the program design and a discussion of its advantages in bargaining experiments may be found in Kahan and Helwig (1971).

The *Coalitions* game explicitly defines three stages in the bargaining process. The first, the *offer stage*, is that time when players explore the potentials of various coalitions. Different offers are made to different possible *c.s.*'s and some ideas towards where a reasonable solution to the game might lie are formed. In this stage, players gain awareness of their relative strengths and weaknesses, and some idea of the expectations of the other players.

The second stage, termed the *acceptance stage*, begins when a set of players indicate a general agreement on a division of the points. This agreement is not binding, but it does indicate that serious consideration of the *p.c.* is in order. During the acceptance stage, the members of a tentative coalition may be interested in modifications of the agreement for that coalition as well as in what other *c.s.*'s might have in store for them. It is in this stage that various strategies and counter-strategies may become their most complex. For the student of bargaining behavior, it is the most interesting stage.

The third stage, or *ratification stage*, terminates the bargaining process. The members of a tentative coalition, having considered an offer and seeing it through acceptance, are now willing to make it a binding agreement. Satisfaction with the proposed coalition and its division of the points is therefore indicated and, by passing into ratification, each party receives its points and the bargaining (and game playing) process is terminated.

In the *Coalitions* game, communication among players takes place through the use of keywords, where a player specifies the type of message he wishes to send (the keyword), followed by the coalition to which it refers, and the allocation of the points to the members of that coalition. The basic keyword in the game is *offer*. A player may offer an allocation of the points to a coalition of which he is a member by stating *offer*, followed by an assignment of the points to both members of the coalition. Upon observing an offer made by another player that involves himself, a player may take a number of actions. First, he may indicate displeasure by sending the keyword *reject*, indicating which potential coalition he is rejecting. Second, he may indicate approval of a proposal by sending the keyword *accept*. Acceptance is understood to be approval to the most recent offer to the particular coalition indicated in the message. The game moves conceptually from the offer stage to the acceptance stage when one player has sent an *accept* of another's *offer*. Third, a player may make a counter-offer to the same coalition by sending an offer of his own. Only the most recent offer to any coalition structure is active at any one time. Fourth, a player may ignore the offer altogether and concentrate on other coalition structures. The offer remains in effect, but in limbo until acted upon.

When a *p.c.* has been in the acceptance stage long enough for at least two complete rounds of messages, it may enter the ratification stage, if a member of the coalition sends the keyword *ratify*. When *ratify* is sent, members of the coalition must immediately either agree to the ratification or veto it. In the former case, the game is ended with that particular *p.c.* is force; in the latter case, the game reverts back to the offer stage.

There are two further keywords used in the present experiment. If a player wishes to make no communication, he sends the keyword *pass*. If he wishes to leave the game with zero points, he sends the keyword *solo*, which immediately transforms the situation to a two-person game, excluding the *solo*-ed player.

One of the purposes of the present study is to test the bargaining set and kernel models by comparing prescribed and observed outcomes in three-person quota games. The various game-theoretic solutions concern themselves only with such outcomes, and not with how they came about. However, to limit the data analysis to this aspect, as previous *n*-person game experiments (*e.g.*, Maschler, 1965; Selten and Schuster, 1968) have done, would be to ignore the richness of the bargaining process leading to ratified outcomes and the possibility of determining how various coalitions are formed. Moreover, investigation of the bargaining process may lead to the discovery of effects of interpersonal bargaining, which may, in turn, result in modifications of mathematical models along psychological principles. In addition to these global goals, in the present experiment we shall also investigate the effects of characteristic functions that provide differing relationships among the three players, and also different means of communication which might have effects on the bargaining process and, consequently, on the outcomes as well.

## 2. Method

### 2.1. SUBJECTS

Subjects were undergraduate males at the University of North Carolina recruited for this experiment via posted advertisement offering monetary rewards for participation in decision-making experiments. Subjects participated in groups of four. In no case were two players in one group close friends, although there were acquaintances who played together.

### 2.2. PLAYING PROCEDURE

Each quartet of players was introduced to the experiment in one three-hour familiarization session. The first hour of this session was given to a written and verbal presentation of the rules of playing the game and how to operate a teletypewriter. The reader is referred to Kahan (1970) for this aspect of the procedure. Following this extensive introduction, subjects played practice games for the remaining two hours under the supervision of the experimenters, who often intervened to suggest lines of play in order to insure that subjects would be familiar with all of the technical details of the *Coalitions* game and the different types of situations that might arise in the course of a game. For this familiarization session subjects were paid $4.50 each.

In the succeeding three weeks, each quartet played three sessions of approximately three hours each, during which a total of twenty games per quartet were played. All games were three-person games, with one player of the quartet acting as a nonparticipating "observer," so that each subject actually played in 15 games. This experimental procedure was employed not only to prevent subjects from knowing which of their compatriots were in which roles, but also to allow subjects time to reflect upon the task and to prevent them from knowing which of the other players were actually present in a particular game. This increased the validity of the assumption of the independence of different games within a quartet.

The incentive to maximize points was provided by paying each subject 5 cents for every point he gained in the 15 games that he played. This resulted in an average gain per subject of $25.00 per experiment, for a rate of somewhat over $2.75 per hour.

## 2.3. EXPERIMENTAL GAMES

Each quartet played five different three-person quota games, four times each. For each of the four iterations of a game, each member of a quartet played each position (including observer) once. The five games, shown in Table I, were chosen to represent different relationships among the quota values for the three players. In Game I there are two relatively poor players in contrast with a wealthy one. In Game II the situation is reversed, with one poor player in relation to two wealthier ones. Games III, IV, and V represent low, moderate, and high differences, respectively, in quota values among all three players. The order of play of the five types of games was randomly selected. Within each game, the order of which player occupied which role was also randomly determined under the restriction that no person would be the observer for two consecutive plays (albeit of different games).

*Table I. Characteristic function and quota values for each game.*

| Characteristic function[a] | Game | | | | |
|---|---|---|---|---|---|
| | I | II | III | IV | V |
| $v(AB)$ | 95 | 115 | 95 | 106 | 118 |
| $v(AC)$ | 90 | 90 | 88 | 86 | 84 |
| $v(BC)$ | 65 | 85 | 81 | 66 | 50 |
| Quotas | | | | | |
| $\omega_A$ | 60 | 60 | 51 | 63 | 76 |
| $\omega_B$ | 35 | 55 | 44 | 43 | 42 |
| $\omega_C$ | 30 | 30 | 37 | 23 | 8 |

[a] $v(A) = v(B) = v(C) = v(ABC) = 0$.

2.4. COMMUNICATION VARIATIONS

Data are reported in the present paper for three separate experiments, each of which used the same five experimental games in the same order. Four quartets, or 16 players, participated in each experiment, for a total of 48 subjects. The differences among the three experiments are accounted for in terms of two communication variables. The first is whether or not secret offers were possible. If secret offers were possible, then one player might suggest to the other a split of their joint reward without the knowledge of the third, whose consent was not needed in any event. The option of allowing the third party to know about the offer is the sole prerogative of the originator of the message; the recipient does not know whether the offer was sent in secrecy or broadcast to all players. An offer, if made secretly, remained secret until it was tentatively accepted, at which time it became public. If secret offers were not possible, all messages were transmitted to all players. The second communication variable was whether or not subjects were allowed to transmit messages in a fixed order, or could speak at will upon request. In the *fixed order* variation, each of the three players communicated one message in turn, in an order fixed for each individual play and not dependent on the relationships of the quotas among the players. Within each experimental game, each player communicated first, second, and third one time. In the *ad lib* variation, subjects hit a special "attention" key on the teletypewriter, and were allowed to communicate messages, one message per request, in the order in which they requested to speak.

The two communication variables were manipulated to yield the following three experimental treatments:

> Exp. 1: no secret messages, speak in order.
> Exp. 2: secret messages allowed, speak in order.
> Exp. 3: secret messages allowed, speak at will.


# 3. Results

The organization of the results section is based on successively deeper examinations of the data. We shall first look at the ratified outcomes, comparing them to the outcomes prescribed by the bargaining set and kernel models, and testing how they were affected by the communication rules governing the game, values of the characteristic functions, and learning. Second, we shall examine the negotiations in the initial phase of the experiment, particularly in the ultimately winning coalition, in order to trace the path of the ratified outcome. Third, we shall analyze selected aspects of the bargaining process. A viewpoint and terminology based on the vocabulary of the bargaining set theory will be employed throughout the present section. Translation to other vocabularies should not be difficult for the industrious reader.

3.1. FINAL OUTCOMES

Tables II, III, and IV present the outcomes (ratified payoff configurations) for each quartet, each game, and each iteration separately, for Experiments 1, 2, and 3, respectively. The last two rows of each table present the mean outcomes computed over the nonzero payoffs, and the corresponding quota values. An inspection of the three tables shows that within quartet differences in the coalition types that were actually formed and in the rewards obtained by their members are of the same type and magnitude as the respective differences among quartets. Also, post-experimental interrogation of the subjects indicated the success of our experimental procedure in preventing subjects from knowing which of the other players were actually present in each play. Hence, different games and repeated plays of the same game within quartet will be assumed independent in some though not all of our subsequent analyses.[1]

When considering the outcomes, the primary variables of interest are the incidence of formation of the various coalitions and the allocations of points for their members. Recall that the bargaining set and kernel models make no predictions as to which coalition should form. From this, it is possible to hypothesize that, given large numbers of independent repetitions of the same characteristic function game, each type of coalition (*AB, AC,* or *BC*) would occur as frequently as the others. In opposition to this "equally likely" hypothesis, the social scientific tradition, through Caplow (1956, 1959) and Gamson (1961), predicts that the two weaker players, *B* and *C*, would combine against the stronger, *A*, resulting in a predominance of *BC* coalitions. Chertkoff (1967) predicts *BC* to *AC* coalitions in the ratio of 2:1, with no *AB* coalitions.

The frequencies of coalition types were tabulated over the five games and three experiments. As no differences due to Experiment were revealed, the frequencies were collapsed over communication differences. As Table V shows, there is a decided tendency for the stronger players to team up and share the largest reward offered. The preeminence of the formation of the *AB* coalition does not occur equivalently over games, however, but differs significantly from game to game ($\chi^2_4 = 32.683$, $p < 0.001$).

Because of the possibility that repeated plays of the same game might bias results, the first play of each game was also examined in similar fashion, with results essentially identical to those repeated.

The deviations of the mean outcome from the predicted quota values are easily computable from the last two rows of Tables II, III, and IV. Overall, these deviations are small, and as later analyses will show, not significantly different from zero. To make results comparable over games and coalition types, define a deviation score for each *p.c.*, whether at the offer, acceptance, or ratification stage, as the number of points proposed to the stronger player in the two-player coalition (i.e., *A* in *AB, A* in *AC,* and *B* in *BC*) minus his quota. Thus, a positive number indicates that the stronger player in a coalition received more than his predicted quota, whereas a negative number indicates that the allocation gained the stronger player less than the prescribed quota value. The majority of all instances of negative deviations indicate *p.c.'s* more egalitarian than the quota predictions; only a few of these instances indicated a disposition to the absolute advantage of the weaker player. Table VI shows the mean deviation scores for the outcomes for each game type and each coalition type separately.

The effects of three factors on the deviation scores were studied: Experiment (with 3 levels), Game (with 5 levels), and Iteration (with 4 levels). The four repetitions of each game constituted the latter factor. Because both the Game and Iteration factors were repeated over quartets, the mean deviation scores were transformed to orthogonal

Table II. Outcomes of Experiment 1.

| Quartet | Game I | | | Game II | | | Game III | | | Game IV | | | Game V | | |
|---|---|---|---|---|---|---|---|---|---|---|---|---|---|---|---|
| | A | B | C | A | B | C | A | B | C | A | B | C | A | B | C |
| 1 | 0 | 47 | 18 | 58 | 57 | 0 | 55 | 40 | 0 | 81 | 25 | 0 | 68 | 50 | 0 |
| | 45 | 50 | 0 | 60 | 0 | 30 | 47 | 48 | 0 | 53 | 53 | 0 | 68 | 50 | 0 |
| | 60 | 0 | 30 | 65 | 50 | 0 | 0 | 49 | 32 | 60 | 0 | 26 | 59 | 59 | 0 |
| | 60 | 35 | 0 | 65 | 50 | 0 | 48 | 47 | 0 | 53 | 53 | 0 | 59 | 59 | 0ᵃ |
| 2 | 55 | 40 | 0 | 0 | 50 | 35 | 50 | 45 | 0 | 0 | 50 | 16 | 68 | 50 | 0 |
| | 70 | 0 | 20 | 0 | 65 | 20 | 60 | 0 | 28 | 36 | 70 | 0 | 70 | 48 | 0 |
| | 0 | 0 | 0ᵃ | 0 | 65 | 20 | 0 | 45 | 36 | 55 | 51 | 0 | 70 | 59 | 0ᵃ |
| | 60 | 0 | 30 | 60 | 0 | 30 | 50 | 0 | 38 | 63 | 43 | 0 | 64 | 0 | 20 |
| 3 | 0 | 30 | 35 | 65 | 50 | 0 | 60 | 0 | 28 | 60 | 46 | 0 | 68 | 50 | 0 |
| | 60 | 0 | 30 | 70 | 0 | 20 | 0 | 40 | 41 | 56 | 50 | 0 | 79 | 0 | 5 |
| | 50 | 45 | 0 | 80 | 0 | 10 | 44 | 0 | 44 | 66 | 40 | 0 | 62 | 56 | 0ᵃ |
| | 50 | 0 | 40ᵇ | 50 | 65 | 0 | 48 | 47 | 0 | 54 | 52 | 0 | 60 | 58 | 0 |
| 4 | 0 | 37 | 28 | 70 | 45 | 0 | 0 | 40 | 41 | 55 | 0 | 31 | 68 | 50 | 0 |
| | 64 | 31 | 0 | 65 | 50 | 0 | 0 | 46 | 35 | 56 | 50 | 0 | 95 | 23 | 0 |
| | 70 | 0 | 20 | 75 | 0 | 15 | 55 | 40 | 0 | 75 | 31 | 0 | 80 | 38 | 0 |
| | 55 | 40 | 0 | 60 | 55 | 0 | 73 | 0 | 15 | 66 | 40 | 0 | 75 | 43 | 0 |
| Mean | 58.2 | 39.4 | 27.9 | 64.8 | 54.7 | 22.5 | 53.6 | 44.3 | 33.8 | 59.3 | 46.7 | 24.3 | 68.9 | 49.5 | 12.5 |
| Quota | 60 | 35 | 30 | 60 | 55 | 30 | 51 | 44 | 37 | 63 | 43 | 23 | 76 | 42 | 8 |

ᵃ Following solo by C.
ᵇ Following solo by B.

*Table III. Outcomes of Experiment 2.*

| Quartet | Game I | | | Game II | | | Game III | | | Game IV | | | Game V | | |
|---|---|---|---|---|---|---|---|---|---|---|---|---|---|---|---|
| | A | B | C | A | B | C | A | B | C | A | B | C | A | B | C |
| 1 | 55 | 40 | 0 | 60 | 55 | 0 | 0 | 45 | 36 | 66 | 40 | 0 | 75 | 43 | 0 |
| | 60 | 0 | 30 | 60 | 55 | 0 | 48 | 47 | 0 | 70 | 36 | 0 | 71 | 47 | 0 |
| | 65 | 0 | 25 | 0 | 55 | 30 | 0 | 40 | 41 | 53 | 53 | 0 | 74 | 44 | 0 |
| | 55 | 40 | 0 | 0 | 55 | 30 | 55 | 40 | 0 | 60 | 0 | 26 | 70 | 48 | 0 |
| 2 | 0 | 35 | 30 | 65 | 50 | 0 | 55 | 0 | 33 | 70 | 0 | 16 | 85 | 33 | 0 |
| | 60 | 35 | 0 | 0 | 60 | 25 | 0 | 50 | 31 | 0 | 50 | 16 | 73 | 45 | 0 |
| | 55 | 40 | 0 | 0 | 58 | 27 | 0 | 46 | 35 | 66 | 40 | 0 | 80 | 38 | 0 |
| | 53 | 42 | 0 | 65 | 50 | 0 | 0 | 45 | 36 | 70 | 36 | 0 | 59 | 59 | 0ᵃ |
| 3 | 52 | 43 | 0 | 0 | 50 | 35 | 0 | 41 | 40 | 0 | 45 | 21 | 80 | 38 | 0 |
| | 48 | 47 | 0ᵃ | 55 | 60 | 0 | 55 | 0 | 33 | 70 | 36 | 0 | 60 | 0 | 24 |
| | 55 | 0 | 35 | 65 | 0 | 25 | 0 | 45 | 36 | 66 | 0 | 20 | 59 | 59 | 0ᵃ |
| | 55 | 40 | 0 | 0 | 55 | 30 | 58 | 0 | 30 | 60 | 46 | 0 | 72 | 46 | 0 |
| 4 | 58 | 37 | 0 | 0 | 50 | 35 | 50 | 0 | 38 | 66 | 40 | 0 | 59 | 59 | 0 |
| | 55 | 40 | 0 | 0 | 60 | 25 | 48 | 0 | 40 | 63 | 43 | 0 | 85 | 33 | 0 |
| | 65 | 0 | 25 | 75 | 40 | 0 | 58 | 0 | 30 | 0 | 35 | 31 | 78 | 40 | 0 |
| | 62 | 33 | 0 | 63 | 52 | 0 | 60 | 35 | 0 | 65 | 41 | 0 | 78 | 40 | 0 |
| Mean | 56.9 | 39.3 | 29.0 | 63.5 | 53.7 | 29.1 | 54.1 | 43.4 | 35.3 | 65.0 | 41.6 | 21.7 | 72.4 | 44.8 | 24.0 |
| Quota | 60 | 35 | 30 | 60 | 55 | 30 | 51 | 44 | 37 | 63 | 43 | 23 | 76 | 42 | 8 |

ᵃ Following *solo* by C.

Table IV. Outcomes of Experiment 3.

| Quartet | Game I | | | Game II | | | Game III | | | Game IV | | | Game V | | |
|---|---|---|---|---|---|---|---|---|---|---|---|---|---|---|---|
| | A | B | C | A | B | C | A | B | C | A | B | C | A | B | C |
| 1 | 48 | 47 | 0 | 0 | 60 | 25 | 55 | 0 | 33 | 80 | 0 | 0 | 73 | 45 | 0 |
| | 55 | 40 | 0 | 0 | 45 | 40 | 55 | 0 | 33 | 0 | 51 | 15 | 70 | 48 | 0 |
| | 60 | 35 | 0 | 65 | 50 | 0 | 58 | 0 | 30 | 58 | 48 | 0 | 60 | 0 | 24 |
| | 70 | 25 | 0 | 55 | 0 | 35 | 55 | 40 | 0 | 76 | 0 | 10 | 59 | 59 | 0ᵃ |
| 2 | 55 | 40 | 0 | 60 | 55 | 0 | 47 | 48 | 0 | 53 | 53 | 0 | 88 | 30 | 0 |
| | 0 | 31 | 34 | 0 | 60 | 25 | 50 | 45 | 0 | 58 | 48 | 0 | 70 | 48 | 0 |
| | 53 | 42 | 0 | 65 | 50 | 0 | 50 | 45 | 0 | 61 | 45 | 0 | 68 | 50 | 0 |
| | 55 | 40 | 0 | 67 | 48 | 0 | 0 | 38 | 43 | 60 | 46 | 0 | 65 | 53 | 0 |
| 3 | 60 | 0 | 30 | 60 | 55 | 0 | 55 | 40 | 0 | 60 | 46 | 0 | 70 | 48 | 0 |
| | 55 | 40 | 0 | 60 | 55 | 0 | 0 | 36 | 45 | 66 | 40 | 0 | 75 | 43 | 0 |
| | 65 | 0 | 25 | 65 | 50 | 0 | 58 | 0 | 30 | 63 | 43 | 0 | 80 | 38 | 0 |
| | 66 | 0 | 24 | 60 | 55 | 0 | 50 | 45 | 0 | 0 | 50 | 16 | 68 | 50 | 0 |
| 4 | 63 | 0 | 27 | 59 | 56 | 0 | 50 | 45 | 0 | 56 | 50 | 0 | 64 | 0 | 20 |
| | 53 | 0 | 37 | 57 | 58 | 0 | 55 | 40 | 0 | 53 | 53 | 0 | 74 | 0 | 10 |
| | 55 | 40 | 0 | 0 | 70 | 15 | 0 | 46 | 35 | 70 | 36 | 0 | 100 | 18 | 0 |
| | 45 | 0 | 45 | 55 | 0 | 35 | 58 | 0 | 30 | 53 | 53 | 0 | 92 | 26 | 0 |
| Mean | 57.2 | 38.0 | 31.7 | 60.7 | 54.8 | 29.2 | 53.5 | 42.5 | 34.9 | 61.9 | 47.3 | 11.8 | 73.5 | 42.8 | 18.0 |
| Quota | 60 | 35 | 30 | 60 | 55 | 30 | 51 | 44 | 37 | 63 | 43 | 23 | 76 | 42 | 8 |

ᵃ Following *solo* by C.

Table V. Frequency of coalition structures by game.

| Game | AB,C | Coalition Structure AC,B | A,BC | A,B,C |
|------|------|------|------|------|
| I | 27 | 15 | 5 | 1 |
| II | 25 | 8 | 15 | 0 |
| III | 17 | 16 | 15 | 0 |
| IV | 35 | 7 | 6 | 0 |
| V | 42 | 6 | 0 | 0 |
| Over game | 146 | 52 | 41 | 1 |

contrasts of these factors and analyzed in multivariate fashion.[2] No main effects, including the grand mean effect (overall difference from zero), or interactions were significant ($\alpha = 0.05$), except the main effect for Game ($F_{4,6} = 14.54$, $p < 0.003$). Consequently, in view of this result and the results for frequency of the c.s.'s presented in Table V, the data are presented collapsed over Experiment and Iteration.

Inspection of Table V and the lower part of Table VI suggests that the five different games may be grouped into two classes, with Games I, IV, and V in one group, and Games II and III in the other. As Table V shows, the number of $BC$ coalitions formed in Games I, IV, and V was 5,6, and 0, respectively, whereas the number of $BC$ coalitions for Games II and III was 15 for each. The lower part of Table VI shows that the stronger player in a coalition received less than his quota in Games I, IV, and V, but obtained more than his quota in Games II and III. The latter overall pattern is shown in the AB coalition case, and not in $AC$ and $BC$, but recall that more than 60% of the final coalitions fell in the former category.

Further evidence concerning the difference between the two classes of games is provided by two measures of the intensity of bargaining activity, namely, the number of messages sent and the time spent per play. These two measures should, of course, be strongly correlated with each other. Multivariate analyses of variance identical to those performed on the deviation scores were performed on these two measures. Significant ($\alpha = 0.05$) effects were found for Game and Iteration only. (For number of messages sent per play, $F_{4,6} = 18.80$, $p < 0.002$ for Game; and $F_{3,7} = 10.75$, $p < 0.005$ for Iteration. For time spent per play, $F_{4,6} = 6.40$, $p < 0.023$ for Game; and $F_{3,7} = 12.61$, $p < 0.003$ for Iteration.) No other significant main effects or interactions were found.

The mean and standard deviation of number of messages sent and time spent (in minutes) per play are shown in Table VII for Game and Iteration. As expected, the two measures are highly correlated. The differences in bargaining intensity for Game follow the results for frequency of coalition type and allocation of points in that Games II and III are distinctly different from the other three games. The Iteration effect, shown in Table VII, is clearly a learning effect. The first time a game is played, much

*Table VI.*   Mean deviation from quota of first offers to the winning coalition, first accepted offers by that coalition, and outcomes by game and coalition type.

| Coalition | Game | | | | | |
|---|---|---|---|---|---|---|
| | I | II | III | IV | V | Over Games |
| **First offers to winning coalition** | | | | | | |
| *AB* | -5.38 | 2.16 | -0.12 | -6.17 | -8.62 | -4.59 |
| *AC* | -4.19 | 4.38 | 5.56 | -4.00 | -11.50 | -0.74 |
| *BC* | -1.00 | -0.67 | 1.87 | -2.00 | a | 0.02 |
| Over coalition | -4.51 | 1.65 | 2.40 | -5.33 | -8.98 | -2.95 |
| **First accepted offers by winning coalition** | | | | | | |
| *AB* | -4.12 | 2.56 | 1.29 | -2.80 | -3.81 | -1.92 |
| *AC* | -2.13 | 5.00 | 8.06 | 1.71 | -11.50 | 1.47 |
| *BC* | -1.00 | 2.07 | -0.87 | 2.33 | a | 0.66 |
| Over coalition | -3.11 | 2.81 | 2.88 | -1.50 | -4.77 | -0.74 |
| **Outcomes** | | | | | | |
| *AB* | -4.33 | 2.36 | 0.65 | -2.03 | -3.74 | -1.88 |
| *AC* | 0.47 | 5.00 | 4.94 | 3.71 | -9.17 | 1.87 |
| *BC* | 1.00 | 2.20 | -0.53 | 3.83 | a | 1.29 |
| Over coalition | -2.33 | 2.75 | 1.71 | -0.46 | -4.42 | -0.52 |

[a] No cases observed.

more time is spent and more messages are sent as the players learn the features of that particular game. By the third and fourth iteration, there is little change in mean bargaining intensity. This does not mean, however, that players returned to the same *p.c.* on repeated iterations of a game; even cursory inspections of Tables II, III, and IV indicate the opposite.

*Table VII. Means and standard deviations of number of messages sent and time spent per play by game and iteration.*

|  | Number of messages | | Time of play (in minutes) | |
|---|---|---|---|---|
|  | Mean | S.D. | Mean | S.D. |
| Game |  |  |  |  |
| I | 20.96 | 13.50 | 18.00 | 14.45 |
| II | 18.92 | 9.79 | 16.15 | 12.76 |
| III | 19.10 | 7.33 | 16.00 | 8.59 |
| IV | 21.63 | 11.18 | 17.75 | 11.27 |
| V | 25.19 | 13.82 | 19.73 | 13.13 |
| Iteration |  |  |  |  |
| 1 | 25.78 | 13.26 | 24.72 | 15.64 |
| 2 | 21.38 | 12.93 | 16.90 | 12.57 |
| 3 | 18.17 | 7.01 | 14.17 | 6.03 |
| 4 | 19.25 | 10.48 | 14.32 | 9.34 |

According to the rules of the game, players had the opportunity of withdrawing from play with zero points by playing *solo*. If a player did use *solo*, the situation was transformed to a two-person cooperative game. Out of 240 plays *solo* occurred a total of nine times, with three quartets employing it once, and three quartets employing it twice. Three *solo*'s occurred in Game I and the remainder in Game V. These outcomes are footnoted in Tables II, III, and IV. In all cases but one (Game I), it was player *C* who chose *solo*. The outcome following a *solo* was generally an equal division of the points between the two remaining players. If these nine cases are not considered, the means for Games I and V become less egalitarian, particularly in Experiment 1, but the overall patterns and significances remain unchanged. The recorded incidence of *solo* lends additional support to the previous interpretation of the final outcomes in terms of the differential saliency of coalition types in different games.

3.2. THE INITIAL PHASE OF NEGOTIATIONS

The deviation from quota score has served as the main dependent variable for assessing the effects of Experiment, Game, and Iteration on the final disbursement of rewards.

Deviation from quota scores may also be computed for the first offer made to the coalition that ultimately became established (the *winning* coalition), and for the offer that was first accepted by both members of that coalition. (The two offers may or may not coincide.) Some insight into how the final disbursement of rewards was determined may be gained from comparing the deviation scores for the first offer made to the winning coalition, and the offer ultimately ratified by that coalition.

A multivariate analysis of variance, identical to the one performed on the deviation scores for the outcomes, was conducted on the deviation scores for the first offer made to the winning coalition. There was a significant grand mean effect ($F_{1,9} = 11.80$, $p < 0.007$), showing that the bargaining set and kernel models, while predicting the outcomes, do not account for the first offers made to the winning coalition. The other significant effect was due to Game ($F_{4,6} = 8.61$, $p < 0.012$). The multivariate Iteration effect was nearly significant ($F_{3,7} = 3.92$, $p < 0.062$), and the univariate linear trend across iterations was highly significant in this case ($F_{1,9} = 10.01$, $p < 0.011$). No other significant main effects or interactions were observed.

A multivariate analysis of variance performed on the deviation scores for the first offer accepted by the winning coalition yielded a significant Game effect ($F_{4,6} = 8.08$, $p < 0.014$). There was also a significant Experiment × Game × Iteration effect ($F_{12,8} = 4.90$, $p < 0.016$), which has no immediate explanation and is probably due to chance. No other significant main effects or interactions were observed. In particular, the grand mean effect, which was significant for the first offer made to the winning coalition, was not significant for the first accepted offer by that coalition ($F_{1,9} = 1.35$, $p < 0.307$).

The upper two parts of Table VI present the mean deviations from quota by Game and type of coalition for the first offer to the winning coalition and for the first accepted offer by that coalition. With minor exceptions, the patterns of deviation from quota between games parallels exactly that of the outcomes, which are shown in the lower part of Table VI.

A comparison of the grand mean effects for the deviation scores ($F_{1,9} = 11.80$, 1.35, and 0.61, for the first offer made to the winning coalition, the first accepted offer by that coalition, and the ultimately ratified offer by that coalition, respectively) shows that the mean overall allocation of rewards approached the quota as play progressed. Examination of Table VI shows that this effect is one of moving away from egalitarian solutions toward the predicted quota values. This tendency is partially attributable to the differential Iteration effect, which is present for first offers made to the winning coalitions, but not for first or final acceptances by those coalitions. It appears likely that players enter the game with some sharing or equity norm but that this norm is rapidly abandoned as the power relationships inherent in the game become realized.

The right-hand column of Table VI shows that the progressively less egalitarian disbursement of rewards holds for each of the three coalition types. In the *AB* winning coalitions the mean difference for player *A* from his quota was -4.59 points for the first offer, -1.92 points in the first accepted offer, and -1.88 points in the ratified coalition. In the *AC* winning coalitions the respective mean differences from the quota for player *A* were -.074, 1.47, and 1.87, showing the same rate of increase as in coalition *AB*. The rate of increase for player *B* in the *BC* winning coalitions was more moderate; his respective mean differences from quota, all of which are positive, were 0.02, 0.66, and 1.29.

A multivariate analysis of variance was also performed on the deviation scores for the first offer made in each play, regardless of to which coalition, winning or losing, it was addressed. The mean deviation scores were significantly different from zero ($F_{1,9} = 311.53$, $p < 0.001$), with the grand mean effect being considerably larger than in the case of the first offer made to the winning coalition. The other significant effects were due to Game, Iteration, and their interaction. In particular, no significant main or interaction effects due to Experiment were found, showing that the two communication variables manipulated in the present study had no effect not only on the outcomes but also not on the initial offers.

## 3.3. THE BARGAINING PROCESS

The bargaining set and kernel models concern only the outcomes, and do not concern themselves with the characterization of the bargaining process. From a psychological viewpoint the latter is of much more interest. The two models may be represented as sets of solutions, each based on different assumptions, of systems of linear inequalities involving the rewards allocated to members of the ratified coalition as unknowns. It is obvious that our human game players do not set up in their minds systems of linear inequalities and solve them in order to determine how to disburse the reward jointly gained by members of a particular coalition. Instead, they employ threats, counter-threats, promises, bluffs, and other negotiation tactics in proceeding to the ratification of a coalition and the disbursement of its reward.

The analysis of the negotiation moves appearing in the game protocols to which we now turn, is divided into two parts. The first part, a static analysis, examines several useful indices of bargaining which may be affected by the Experiment, Game, and Iteration factors. These indices include the number of offers made by each player, the number of accepted offers (tentative coalitions) per play, and the message number of (how many messages were sent before) the formation of the first tentative coalition. The latter part is a dynamic analysis, based upon a model of the bargaining process, which examines the offers sent during a play in light of the offers that precede or follow them.

*3.3.1. Static analysis.* Multivariate analyses of variance, similar to the ones conducted above, were performed on the message number of the first tentative coalition and on the number of tentative coalitions formed during a play. These analyses showed no significant effects involving Experiment, Iteration, or Game for either of the two dependent variables. Again, the type of coalition was not considered as a factor in either analysis. When the message number of the first tentative coalition and the total number of tentative coalitions formed per play were examined according to which coalition was first formed, a different picture emerged. Although the message number of the first tentative coalition did not vary with the type of coalition, it was shown that if coalition $AB$ was the first to form, there were fewer tentative coalitions following it than if either of the other two coalitions formed first. The mean and standard deviation of the number of tentative coalitions per play were 2.22 and 2.03 when coalition $AB$ was formed first, 3.32 and 2.52 when coalition $AC$ was formed first, and 3.15 and 2.64 when coalition $BC$ was formed first, the difference being significant by analysis of variance ($F_{2,237} = 6.25$, $p < 0.002$).

The third index of bargaining to be analyzed was the number of offers sent by each player per play. Table VIII shows the percentages of offers sent by each player to each of the other two players broken down by Game, originator of offers, and target of offer. Table VIII shows that players were more likely to address the stronger of the other two players than the weaker player. This effect, however, seems to be related to the particular game played. It is less prominent in the two all-coalition-active games (II and III) than in the other three games, following the same pattern of differences between the two classes of games detected above. The individual players conformed to this communication preference pattern except for player $A$ in Game I, who showed indifference in making an offer to his two almost equally weak potential partners.

*Table VIII. Percentages of offers by game, originator of offer, and target of offer.*

| From | To | I | II | III | IV | V | Over game |
|------|------|-----|-----|-----|-----|-----|-----------|
| $A$ | $B$ | 54 | 61 | 61 | 70 | 71 | 64 |
| $A$ | $C$ | 46 | 39 | 39 | 30 | 29 | 36 |
| $B$ | $A$ | 66 | 61 | 53 | 71 | 78 | 66 |
| $B$ | $C$ | 34 | 39 | 47 | 29 | 22 | 34 |
| $C$ | $A$ | 69 | 49 | 56 | 59 | 66 | 60 |
| $C$ | $B$ | 31 | 51 | 44 | 41 | 34 | 40 |
| $a$ | Higher | 64 | 56 | 56 | 66 | 71 | 63 |
| $b$ | Lower | 36 | 44 | 44 | 34 | 29 | 37 |

$a$ From $C$ to $B$, $B$ to $A$, and $C$ to $A$.
$b$ From $A$ to $C$, $B$ to $C$, and $A$ to $B$.

3.3.2. *Dynamic analysis.* The use of a dynamic analysis of the bargaining process, which examines messages sent during a play in light of messages that precede or follow them during the same play, requires the specification of a model to classify the various messages and describe the progress of the negotiations. In choosing among various alternatives for modelling the bargaining process, we were motivated by the success of the bargaining set and kernel models in accounting for the outcomes of the present experiment. The constraint on any proposed model that the bargaining process converge to the bargaining set or kernel solutions considerably narrowed the range of alternatives. As a first alternative, extensions of either of the two static models were considered, through providing testable dynamic interpretations to their assumptions. The bargaining set model was chosen over the kernel model because its terminology is more immediately representable in observable responses, and, from a strictly practical viewpoint, because it accounted for the outcomes in another study (Horowitz and Rapoport, 1974), whereas the kernel model did not.

Our proposed model follows the path of a particular *p.c.* from its initial consideration for adoption through its being tested against other alternatives to its final acceptance or rejection. The proposed structure of the bargaining process, the same one considered by Horowitz and Rapoport (1974), is as follows: After preliminary negotiations, the bargaining process enters the stage when a tentative coalition $X$ is formed. The tentative coalition may either result from the initial negotiations among the three players or may follow the dissolution of a previous tentative coalition. Players are assumed to search for justified objections against $X$. If none exist, the coalition is eventually ratified. If at least one justified objection exists, then one of them is selected by a player, and is expressed through an offer (*p.c.*). We denote such an expressed objection, whether justified or unjustified, as $Y_s$.

The rules of the *Coalitions* game dictate that these objections be made serially, $s = 1, 2, \ldots$, and that the payoff vectors be integers rather than real numbers. The identity of the player expressing the objection is not considered here. Thus, for example, if a tentative coalition $X = AB$ is formed, an objection $Y_s = AC$ by $A$ against $B$ may be made by $A$ through an offer to $C$, or by $C$ through an offer to $A$. This requirement is compatible with the definition of objection (Aumann and Maschler, 1964).

If the objection $Y_s$ is justified, the tentative coalition $X$ is immediately dissolved and the objection is accepted, thus resulting in a new tentative coalition, and the beginning of the cycle over again. If, however, the objection is unjustified, the tentative coalition $X$ is retained, and a new objection against $X$, denoted by $Y_{s+1}$, is made. A player may express both unjustified and justified objections. If at least one of the players possessing a justified objection against $X$ eventually expresses that objection, and we assume that he will, it can be shown that, for the class of games considered in the present study, this bargaining model results in convergence to a *p.c.* in the bargaining set.

Not all offers fit within the definition of an objection, either justified or not. The first offer and all other offers before the first acceptance are not objections. Also, if fewer points are offered to a player in a tentative coalition than he would receive in that coalition, the offer is not an objection. The bargaining process model posits that these latter non-objections should not occur; in the present data they occur only rarely.

To exemplify the bargaining process leading to $M_1^{(i)}$, consider Game I. Supposing that after coalition $AB$ is formed with a *p.c.* (55, 40, 0; $AB,C$), $C$ offers 58 points to $A$. Since this is a justified objection by $A$ against $B$, coalition $AB$ is dissolved and the *p.c.* (58, 0, 32; $AC,B$) is formed after $A$ accepts $C$'s offer. Next, for example, $B$ may propose 65 points to $A$, i.e., (65, 30, 0; $AB,C$), which is an objection by $A$ against $C$. However, it is not justified since $C$ may counter-object with an offer such as (0, 33, 32; $A,BC$). Hence the game proceeds with coalition $AC$ remaining intact. Finally, for example, supposing $A$ proposes the *p.c.* (60, 35, 0; $AB,C$). Since this is both a justified and stable objection by $A$ against $C$, $C$ cannot counter-object and no justified objections may be made against it. Thus, it becomes ratified.

The bargaining process model described above fails its most critical test; all games did not end in the predicted quota values. While reserving discussion of this point for later, useful information may be still obtained from examining the bargaining process to discover the sources of discrepancy from the model, which may suggest how to modify it. Within this context, then, we shall test the bargaining process model by examining several statistics relative to the objections.

An enumeration of all offers classifiable as objections was made, and each objection was examined to see whether it dissolved the tentative coalition against which it was addressed (*accepted*) or was unsuccessful in that attempt (*unaccepted*). An objection is said to have been unaccepted if either the tentative coalition to which it was addressed was later ratified, or if the tentative coalition was disrupted by a subsequent objection, involving either the same or a different coalition structure.

Table IX presents the effect of the two types of objections on tentative coalitions for each game separately and over games. Examination of the table shows that justified (J) objections were more effective in dissolving tentative coalitions than unjustified (UJ) ones; 35% of all justified objections disrupted the tentative coalition, as compared to 22% for the unjustified ones. This difference between justified and unjustified objections appears in Games I, II, III, but not in IV and V. This difference between games is particularly pronounced when the fate of the justified objections is examined. In Games I, IV, and V, where *AB* was the dominant coalition, the disrupting justified objections were more likely to be in turn disrupted than not (the corresponding percentages are 31 and 9 for Game I, 23 and 10 for Game IV, and 18 and 9 for Game V). However, in Games II and III a justified objection that was tentatively accepted was as likely as not to be ratified.

*Table IX.  Percentages of objections by game,*
*type of objection, and nature of outcome*

| Game | Objection Type | n | Objection is later Accepted | Unaccepted |
|------|------|------|------|------|
| I     | J   | 65  | 40 | 60 |
|       | UJ  | 125 | 22 | 78 |
| II    | J   | 57  | 32 | 68 |
|       | UJ  | 123 | 15 | 85 |
| III   | J   | 58  | 48 | 52 |
|       | UJ  | 152 | 20 | 80 |
| IV    | J   | 87  | 33 | 67 |
|       | UJ  | 124 | 28 | 72 |
| V     | J   | 119 | 27 | 73 |
|       | UJ  | 72  | 26 | 74 |
| Over  | J   | 386 | 35 | 65 |
| game  | UJ  | 596 | 22 | 78 |

Table X shows the same percentages of objections as Table IX, broken down by iterations instead of by games. The table shows a marked learning effect for the differentiation of justified from unjustified objections. There is no difference in the effect of both types of objections in the first iteration. However, starting with iteration 2, the percentage of justified objections dissolving the tentative coalitions increases slowly (the percentages are 29, 36, 37, and 41 for iterations 1,2,3, and 4, respectively), whereas the percentage of unjustified objections disrupting the tentative coalitions slightly decreases.

The justified and unjustified objections were further broken down by the coalition they were addressed to, by whether the objection was originated by a member of the tentative coalition (an *inside* player) or by the player excluded from it (the *outside* player), and by whether the objection was addressed to the more or less powerful members of the tentative coalition. The number of objections lodged against coalition $AB$ was greater than for the other two coalition types, because more $AB$ coalitions were formed than the other types. Because there was no interaction between the coalition type and the source and target of the objection, results were collapsed over those variables.

*Table X.* Percentages of objections by iteration, type of objection, and fate of objection.

| Objection | | | Objection is later | |
| --- | --- | --- | --- | --- |
| Iteration | Type | $n$ | Accepted | Unaccepted |
| 1 | J | 156 | 29 | 71 |
| | UJ | 181 | 26 | 74 |
| 2 | J | 77 | 36 | 64 |
| | UJ | 129 | 24 | 76 |
| 3 | J | 70 | 37 | 63 |
| | UJ | 140 | 16 | 84 |
| 4 | J | 81 | 41 | 59 |
| | UJ | 148 | 20 | 80 |

Table XI shows the incidence of justified and unjustified objections by Game, source of objection (inside or outside), and target of objection. It can be seen immediately that the outside player made four to five times more objections per game, either justified or not, than an inside player, who made offers to the other member in the tentative coalition in order to better his own position. For the justified objections, but not for the unjustified ones, the stronger player was more likely to be addressed in the objection, regardless of its source. Further inspection of Table XI shows that the latter effect was most pronounced for Games I, IV, and V, where player $A$ had a very clear edge over the other players, but not in Games II and III. In Game III, in which the differences among quota values were the smallest, it was the weaker rather than the stronger player who was more likely to be addressed in the objection, regardless of its source. Unlike the justified objections, the unjustified objections were addressed about evenly to the stronger and weaker players, regardless of the source of the objection.

*Table XI. Incidence of justified and unjustified objections by game, source of objection, and target of objection.*

| | From inside player against | | From outside player against | |
|---|---|---|---|---|
| Game | Stronger Player | Weaker Player | Stronger Player | Weaker Player |
| | *Justified objections* | | | |
| I | 11 | 5 | 38 | 11 |
| II | 8 | 8 | 28 | 13 |
| III | 3 | 11 | 18 | 26 |
| IV | 15 | 4 | 51 | 17 |
| V | 18 | 4 | 80 | 17 |
| Over game | 55 | 32 | 215 | 84 |
| | *Unjustified objections* | | | |
| I | 10 | 11 | 63 | 41 |
| II | 10 | 8 | 49 | 56 |
| III | 15 | 10 | 73 | 54 |
| IV | 8 | 7 | 58 | 51 |
| V | 11 | 9 | 21 | 31 |
| Over game | 54 | 45 | 264 | 233 |

A final examination looks at the success or failure of an objection to disrupt the coalition it is addressed to, based on the actual offer that the objection constitutes. Objections were classified into one of five categories, depending on whether the more powerful player was offered (i) less than 10 points off his quota, (ii) between 5 and 10 points smaller than his quota, (iii) within 4 points of the quota, (iv) between 5 and 10 points greater than his quota, or (v) more than 10 points greater than his quota. Table XII presents a frequency of objections separated by this classification of deviation from quota scores, by Game, and by whether the originator of the objection was an inside or outside player.

Immediate examination of the middle part of Table XII shows that, except for Game V, more objections were in categories (iv) and (v) than in (i) and (ii). In Game - V, for player $C$, who was concerned with most of the objections, there was a maximum limit of 8 points he could give to the more powerful player, which explains in part the difference between Game V and the remaining four games for outside objections. Because of the generally low frequency of inside objections per game, it is not possible to clearly determine between game patterns on total number of objections.

Turning to the percentage of objections accepted, the immediately obvious finding is that inside objections were accepted more than twice as often as outside objections. Of more interest is the finding that (again with the exception of Game V) the percentages of accepted objections constitute a single-peaked, unsymmetric function, with a mode in category (ii) or (iii). This finding holds for outside objections but not for inside objections, showing that, for the former class, objections in the -5 to -10 class (for Game IV) or in the -4 to +4 class (for Games I, II, and III) were more likely to be accepted than objections farther away from the quota, even if these farther away proposals were more in favor of the inside member of the objecting coalition.

The latter analysis suggests that there are two opposing forces which affect the disruption of a tentative coalition. The first and obvious one is the magnitude of temptation to dissolve the coalition, which is a function of the magnitude of increment to the inside player of the objecting coalition. It remains to be seen whether the percentage of accepted objections is a monotonically increasing function of the magnitude of this increment or not. Additional analyses, not reported here, suggest the latter, with the function slowly increasing and then more quickly decreasing as the magnitude of increment to the objecting player is perceived by him as suspiciously large. The second force is directly related to the quota values. Table XII shows that (with the exception of Game V) the viability of an objection decreases as the absolute value of the deviation from quota score increases.

## 4. Discussion

Two separate questions arise in connection with cooperative $n$-person games with more than two players (Rapoport, 1971). The first question, which has been considered to be the more prominent by social scientists interested in coalition formation and bargaining, is: How will the $n$ players organize themselves into coalitions, providing that the rules of the game allow (or require) coalitions? The second question, which has attracted the attention of mathematicians rather than social scientists, is: What will be the final distribution of payoffs? To this brace of questions we add a third one, seldom presented in the literature, which concerns itself with the bargaining process rather than its end result: How does bargaining progress from the initial offer to the final agreement? Within any of these three basic questions, there might arise questions of the effects of different characteristic functions, different modes of communication, and different experimental paradigms.

Table XII.　Analysis of fate of objections by game, origin of objection, and deviation from quota scores.

| Game | Score | Inside objections | | | Outside objections | | | All objections | | |
|---|---|---|---|---|---|---|---|---|---|---|
| | | Acc. | Total | %Acc. | Acc. | Total | %Acc. | Acc. | Total | %Acc. |
| I | <-10 | 1 | 3 | 0.33 | 2 | 10 | 0.20 | 3 | 13 | 0.23 |
| | -5 to -10 | 7 | 10 | 0.70 | 11 | 37 | 0.30 | 18 | 47 | 0.38 |
| | 4 to -4 | 9 | 16 | 0.56 | 13 | 42 | 0.31 | 22 | 58 | 0.38 |
| | 5 to 10 | 3 | 4 | 0.75 | 3 | 38 | 0.08 | 6 | 42 | 0.14 |
| | >10 | 2 | 4 | 0.50 | 2 | 26 | 0.08 | 4 | 30 | 0.13 |
| II | <-10 | 0 | 5 | 0.00 | 1 | 23 | 0.04 | 1 | 28 | 0.04 |
| | -5 to -10 | 3 | 6 | 0.50 | 4 | 23 | 0.17 | 7 | 29 | 0.24 |
| | 4 to -4 | 2 | 4 | 0.50 | 6 | 29 | 0.21 | 8 | 33 | 0.24 |
| | 5 to 10 | 7 | 15 | 0.47 | 8 | 45 | 0.18 | 15 | 60 | 0.25 |
| | >10 | 2 | 4 | 0.50 | 3 | 26 | 0.12 | 5 | 30 | 0.17 |
| III | <-10 | 2 | 5 | 0.40 | 0 | 26 | 0.00 | 2 | 31 | 0.06 |
| | -5 to -10 | 3 | 3 | 1.00 | 3 | 20 | 0.15 | 6 | 23 | 0.26 |
| | 4 to -4 | 10 | 18 | 0.56 | 21 | 54 | 0.39 | 31 | 72 | 0.43 |
| | 5 to 10 | 4 | 7 | 0.57 | 8 | 26 | 0.31 | 12 | 33 | 0.36 |
| | >10 | 1 | 6 | 0.17 | 6 | 45 | 0.13 | 7 | 51 | 0.14 |
| IV | <-10 | 0 | 3 | 0.00 | 5 | 23 | 0.22 | 5 | 26 | 0.19 |
| | -5 to -10 | 3 | 5 | 0.60 | 13 | 31 | 0.42 | 16 | 36 | 0.44 |
| | 4 to -4 | 11 | 15 | 0.73 | 14 | 53 | 0.26 | 25 | 68 | 0.37 |
| | 5 to 10 | 2 | 5 | 0.40 | 8 | 35 | 0.23 | 10 | 40 | 0.25 |
| | >10 | 1 | 6 | 0.17 | 7 | 35 | 0.20 | 8 | 41 | 0.20 |
| V | <-10 | 3 | 6 | 0.50 | 15 | 39 | 0.38 | 18 | 45 | 0.40 |
| | -5 to -10 | 2 | 4 | 0.50 | 6 | 24 | 0.25 | 8 | 28 | 0.29 |
| | 4 to -4 | 7 | 12 | 0.58 | 10 | 65 | 0.15 | 17 | 77 | 0.22 |
| | 5 to 10 | 1 | 2 | 0.50 | 1 | 15 | 0.07 | 2 | 17 | 0.12 |
| | >10 | 3 | 18 | 0.17 | 3 | 6 | 0.50 | 6 | 24 | 0.25 |
| Over game | <-10 | 6 | 22 | 0.27 | 23 | 121 | 0.19 | 29 | 143 | 0.20 |
| | -5 to -10 | 18 | 28 | 0.64 | 37 | 135 | 0.27 | 55 | 163 | 0.34 |
| | 4 to -4 | 39 | 65 | 0.60 | 64 | 243 | 0.26 | 103 | 308 | 0.33 |
| | 5 to 10 | 17 | 33 | 0.52 | 28 | 159 | 0.18 | 45 | 192 | 0.23 |
| | >10 | 9 | 38 | 0.24 | 21 | 138 | 0.15 | 30 | 176 | 0.17 |

### 4.1. INCIDENCE OF DIFFERENT COALITIONS

With regard to the first question, two findings are pertinent. The first is the frequency of coalition structures as presented in Table V. The second is the highly significant difference between the number of tentative coalitions in plays in which coalition $AB$ was the first to form and the number of tentative coalitions in plays in which either coalition $AC$ or $BC$ was formed first. Overall, coalition $AB$ was the ultimate result of the bargaining in more than 60% of all plays, a result that stands in sharp contrast to the hypothesis of equal frequencies and in even sharper contrast to the hypothesis of predominance of $BC$ coalitions (with perhaps some $AC$ coalitions) that results from the social scientific theories currently in vogue. Not only was coalition $AB$ the most frequently ratified, but it was also the most stable during bargaining. That is to say, the $AB$ coalition, in addition to being the most likely to form, was the most likely to survive onslaughts of objections from inside or outside players.

It might be argued that the pre-eminence of the $AB$ coalition results from the highest reward it provides to the players, and that the game is perceived by the subjects as a four-person, zero-sum game. A tacit coalition of subjects against experimenter would result in forming the $AB$ coalition no matter who was player $A$ and who was player $B$. However, we are disinclined to accept this rationale for two reasons. The first is the observed difference in the rate of $AB$ coalitions among different games. This difference was not based on the difference of the $AB$ coalition in potential gain versus the other two coalitions, but rather the differential quota of the $A$ player (whose position is reflected in both the $AB$ and $AC$ coalitions rather than just the former). If the extra value of the $AB$ coalition is the salient feature in its formation, than the frequency of its formation would be greater in Game II than in Game I. Our results in Table V indicate just the opposite. The second reason is that, once the three players tacitly form a coalition against the experimenter, the payoff among the three assumes some characteristics of an $n$-person Prisoner's Dilemma in that, by cooperating all players can do relatively well, but, by defecting, one player can, while remaining anonymous, do even better. Evidence from research on $n$-person Prisoner's Dilemma games (Marwell and Schmitt, 1972; Kahan, 1973) indicates that anonymous $n$-person Prisoner's Dilemma games are even more competitive in tone than their generally competitive two-person counterpart games. Thus, it would appear unlikely that subjects would be so universally cooperative. Once one of the four players in a quartet attempts to exploit the other, then the agreement, being implicit to begin with, would quickly dissolve.

Even before considering the role of the payoff configurations as determining which coalition forms, we can fairly readily explain the differences between the present results and previous data supportive of Caplovian coalition theory and its offshoots. In previous experiments, the characteristic function was zero-sum. Any coalition won a constant value, and, in the absence of a coalition (and in contrast to the political convention model often claimed for such games), player $A$ gained the payoff for himself. In addition, the formation of the coalitions and the dividing of the rewards were not unified, with the former occurring first. In such a situation it appears natural for the two weaker players to stop the stronger from winning all on his own before they consider how to divide up the rewards themselves. Once they have a coalition, player $A$ is not really given the opportunity to intrude into their bargaining processes to make objections, so the $BC$ coalition is ratified.   As the present experiment is nonzero-sum, and as it does give the outside player the opportunity to take part in the negotiations, it is natural that the results should be different.

Despite differences in experimental procedure, Riker's (1967) experiment is sufficiently close in form to the present one that comparisons of data may be meaningfully made.    Riker employed a single quota game with the characteristic function $v(A) = v(B) = v(C) = v(ABC) = 0$, $v(AB) = \$6.00$, $v(AC) = \$5.00$, and $v(BC) = \$4.00$.   Since each point in our experiment was known to the subjects to be worth 5 cents, Riker's characteristic function may be rewritten for purposes of comparison, as equivalent to $v(AB) = 120$, $v(AC) = 100$, and $v(BC) = 80$ in conformity with the functions presented in Table I.    Thus, Riker's quota values become $\omega_A = 70$, $\omega_B = 50$, and $\omega_C = 30$.   This is an equal quota difference game, in which $\omega_A - \omega_B = \omega_B - \omega_C$, directly comparable to our three equal quota difference games, III, IV, and V.    Equal quota difference games may be compared to one another in terms of an index of interplayer distance $\Delta = (\omega_A - \omega_B)/\omega_A$.   In Riker's experiment $\Delta = 0.285$, whereas in our experiment $\Delta$ equals 0.137, 0.317, and 0.447 for Games III, IV, and V, respectively. Thus, Riker's quota game falls between Games III and IV in terms of the index $\Delta$. The percentage of games played by undergraduate students (Groups II and III) in Riker's experiment in which coalition $AB$ was formed was 0.526 (30 of the 57 games in which one of three coalition types, $AB$, $AC$, or $BC$, was formed).    From our Table V, the respective percentages for Games III, IV, and V are 0.354, 0.729, and 0.875, with the percentage of $AB$ coalitions for Riker's experiment falling in the appropriate interval. The same result holds for coalitions $AC$ and $BC$.    The percentages of games in which coalitions $AC$ and $BC$ were formed in Riker's experiment were 0.316 and 0.158, respectively.    The corresponding percentages for Game III are 0.333 and 0.313, for Game IV 0.146 and 0.125, and for Game V 0.125 and 0, with the percentage for Riker's experiment falling in appropriately.

4.2. EFFECTS OF INDEPENDENT VARIABLES

The comparison between Riker's experiment and the present one may be extended to the payoff configurations as well as the coalition structures of the outcomes.   In 22 instances out of 93, the outcomes of Riker's experiment fell exactly in the bargaining set and kernel.    Since his characteristic function involved only numbers divisible by 5, the only games of the present study directly comparable to Riker's game when testing the point predictions of both models are Games I and II.    In these two games, as Tables II through IV show, the final outcomes were included in $M_1^{(i)} = K$ in 19 out of 96 plays.

Moreover, "The average amount won, when player $i$ was a winner, is almost exactly the quota for $i$" (Riker, 1967, p. 648).   The same conclusion has been reached in the present study, as evidenced by the non-significant grand mean effect for the outcomes when measured as deviations from quota scores.

A comparison of several multivariate $F$ values with their associated significance levels reveals an increasing tendency of the p.c.'s to approach $M_1^{(i)} = K$ as the game progresses.    There are four grand mean $F$ values, resulting from the multivariate analyses of the deviation from quota scores, which are pertinent for this comparison. They are $F = 311.53$ ($p < 0.001$) for the first offer made in a play, $F = 11.8$ ($p < 0.007$) for the first offer made to the winning coalition, $F = 1.35$ ($p < 0.307$) for the first tentative coalition formed by the winning players, and $F = 0.61$ ($p < 0.455$) for the outcomes. The corresponding mean deviation from quota scores are -4.31, -2.95, -0.74, and -0.52, respectively. Clearly, these four $F$ values are not mutually independent, since included in the first offers were those made to the winning coalition, many of the first offers made to the winning coalition were also the first to be accepted, and many of the first tentative coalitions were later ratified. A comparison of the associated means shows, however, that as a play unfolded, the $p.c.$'s became progressively less egalitarian, approaching the quota prediction.

Related to the within play learning discussed immediately above is the between play learning reflected in the iteration effect. Again, there are four sets of $F$ values with their associated significance levels, resulting from the multivariate analyses of the deviation scores, that may be examined. For the iteration effect, these values are $F = 11.94$ ($p < 0.004$) for the first offer made in a play, $F = 3.29$ ($p < 0.062$) for the first offer made to the winning coalition, $F = 1.53$ ($p < 0.288$) for the first tentative coalition formed by the winning coalition, and $F = 1.55$ ($p < 0.284$) for the outcomes. The mean deviation scores for the first offers, collapsed over Games and Experiment, were -8.45, -3.28, -2,48, and -3.02 for iterations 1, 2, 3, and 4 respectively, showing that the first offer made the first time a game was played was considerably more egalitarian than first offers made on the second, third, and fourth iterations. Exactly the same type of effect was found for the first offer made to the ultimately winning coalition (the mean deviation scores were -6.73, -1.90, -1.41, and -1.73 in this case), although its magnitude was smaller and its significance only marginal. The iteration effect vanished altogether when the first accepted offers by the ultimately winning coalition and the outcomes were considered. The results of the latter two analyses show that both within play and between play learning occur with regard to the disbursement of rewards, that most of it takes place from the time the first offer is made to the time the first tentative coalition is formed by members of the winning coalition, and that in both cases the overall trend is toward the quota prediction. This observed move toward the quota is a result of the negotiation process, and, more directly, a function of the ability of the players in the coalitions other than the one that has been tentatively accepted making their strengths felt, not only for their own coalitions, but the others as well.

Despite the progressively decreasing deviations between the quota predictions on one hand, and the proposed, tentatively accepted, and ratified $p.c.$'s on the other hand, the significant game effect, unlike the iteration effect, did not vanish. On the contrary, inspection of the multivariate $F$ values for the Game effect in the analyses of the deviation scores shows that they increased as the play progressed. The $F$ values were $F = 6.78$ ($p < 0.021$) for the first offer made in a play, $F = 8.61$ ($p < 0.012$) for the first offer made to the winning coalition, $F = 8.08$ ($p < 0.014$) for the first tentative coalition formed by the winning coalition, and $F = 14.54$ ($p < 0.003$) for the outcomes. As a play developed, the differences among the characteristic functions assumed an increasing importance in determining the disbursement of the reward for members of a particular coalition. In addition to these allocation differences, recall that the incidence of type of final coalition differed across games (Table V) as well as in the percentages of justified and unjustified objections to tentative coalitions (see Table IX).

The most obvious explanation of these effects lies in grouping the five games into two classes. Table I shows that the difference between the two classes is directly related to the index of interplayer distance $\Delta$ discussed above. For Games I, IV, and V, this index assumes the values 0.417, 0.317, and 0.447, respectively, whereas for Games II and III the values of $\Delta$ are 0.083 and 0.137, respectively. The data may be interpreted as showing that when $\Delta$ is large, player $C$ becomes subjectively ineffective, and the $AC$ and $BC$ coalitions are of little interest to the players. Coalition $AB$ so predominates the environment in such games that the three-person game is frequently considered more a two-person game. Player $B$, perceiving the situation more as a two-person game, would be more insistent on an equal share of the results, forcing $A$ to receive less than his quota. However, for games in which $\Delta$ is relatively small (Games II and III), player $C$ is a more relevant participator, the $AB$ coalition is not predominant, and the principal question is which coalition to form. Here player $A$ may exercise his power in the negotiations, receiving his quota and perhaps more.

The evidence reported in Table VII is consistent with the above interpretation. Table VII shows that there are fewer messages in Games II and III than in I, IV, and - V, and that they take less time to complete. As suggested above, since all the three potential coalition structures are active in Games II and III, there is a serious threat of being left out of a coalition if a player gets overly ambitious. Players in such games would not prolong negotiations for fear of disrupting possible alliances with the other players and being left outside of any coalition. On the other hand, in Games I, IV, and V, where the $AB$ coalition is predominant (and particularly in the latter two games), the use of the $AC$ and $BC$ coalition is frequently, though not always, for $A$ and $B$ to jockey around to a final agreement. They will break agreements with each other to establish a later, more advantageous allocation of rewards in the same coalition, if they feel it possible. Hence, more time will be spent bargaining.

We have seen that both game and iteration effects account for the discrepancy between the prescribed quota solutions and the observed p.c.'s expressed in the first offers, first offers made to the winning coalition, and first tentative coalitions formed by the winning coalition. Further information shows that in addition to these two factors, the discrepancies were also affected by who originated the p.c. The originator of an offer may be classified as either the stronger or the weaker player in a coalition. For the first offer made in each play, the mean deviation from quota was -1.36 for a stronger originator, whereas the weaker originator's mean deviation was -6.07. This difference is highly significant by the normal approximation of the $t$ distribution ($z > 3$, $p < 0.001$, for 237 df.). Recalling how deviation from quota scores are computed, the results show that while the stronger player was willing to "shave" 1.36 points on the average from his quota in his first offer, the weaker player proposed an excess of 6.07 points on the average for himself. For the first offer to the winning coalition, the mean deviations from quota were -2.59 and -3.19 for the stronger and weaker players, respectively. The difference between the means is not significant in this case ($z < 1$, for 237 df.), showing that both players are now proposing that the stronger of the two shave his quota by approximately the same amount. However, for the first accepted offers by the winning coalition, the mean deviations were -2.54 and 0.98 for the stronger and weaker players, respectively. The difference between the means is significant ($z > 3$, $p < 0.001$, for 237 df.) but in the opposite direction from the signficant difference found for the first offers, indicating that in the first tentative coalitions players are now making offers more to the liking of the proposed partner. Both players of the ultimately winning coalitions shaved their quotas in their first tentative agreement, though by different amounts. Riker provided evidence showing that players shaved points from their expectations to buy a potential ally and to not be left out with zero rewards. The results reported above show that only the stronger player was willing to shave his quota during the entire game. The weaker player demanded more than his quota in the first offer, then decreased the excess of points he required, and finally also shaved his quota when included in the first tentative coalition formed by the ultimately winning players.

In addition to point shaving, another reason players did not use the quota solution exactly is a tendency to round off values in offers. Recall that the preponderance of exact quota solutions occurred in Games I and II, where the reward is exactly divisible by five for each coalition. Inspection of Tables II, III, and IV shows that 182 out of 240 games played ended in an outcome where one or both players received an amount of points divisible by 5. When this round-off is added to the phenomenon of point shaving, then the results appear even closer to the quota solutions. Other inspections of the data reveal that this use of values divisible by 5 was a ubiquitous phenomenon, with no differences in its frequency of occurrence being found attributable to game, communication conditions, coalition formed, or player making the offer.

Although there were no statistically signficant differences in our measures due to communication conditions, there are interesting trends that deserve comment and might be useful for future research.[3] Table XIII presents the mean deviation scores by type of coalition formed and by Experiment. It can be seen that the first experiment, in which players spoke in formalized order, with no secret offers possible, produced results least like the quota solutions and most towards the egalitarian solution. It is this first condition which is the least like ordinary bargaining, and the most like the typical social scientific traditional experiment. In real life, there are ordinarily ample opportunities for secret communications among potential members of coalitions, and the possession of such confidential information makes more salient for a particular player his strength vis-a-vis the other players. When all communications are public it might be possible for the $B$ and $C$ players to form a coalition not to share their meager rewards, but rather to force player $A$ to give up some of his share (Maschler, 1963). When secret offers are possible, player $A$ can use this fact to restrict his conversations with players $B$ and $C$ so that neither knows what $A$ is negotiating separately with them, thus making this type of coalition formation more difficult and thereby getting player $A$ an outcome closer to his quota.

## 4.3. THE BARGAINING PROCESS

There are several reasons why the answer to our third question, which is concerned with the characterization of the bargaining process rather than its outcome, is necessarily incomplete. One reason has to do with the Coalitions program used to administer the bargaining task. Although providing a common, easy-to-learn language for bargaining and standardization of the negotiation moves, which considerably facilitates their analysis, it does so by forcing players to communicate with one another by using only a small set of legal keywords. Various threats, promises, bluffs, and other intricate negotiation

*Table XIII.*   *Mean deviation from quota of outcomes by coalition type and experiment*

|                | Coalition *AB* | Coalition *AC* | Coalition *BC* |
| -------------- | -------------- | -------------- | -------------- |
| Experiment 1   | -3.49          | -3.35          | -2.58          |
| Experiment 2   | -0.91          | -1.27          | -0.42          |
| Experiment 3   | -1.29          | -0.61          | -1.40          |

tactics are not directly expressable by this highly restricted vocabulary. Added to this is the almost inevitable problem, common to any bargaining experiment, that a large portion of the bargaining process is implicit, especially when the bargainers are experienced, and only a systematic post-experimental interrogation of the players or a talking aloud procedure may reveal its basic structure.

These caveats taken into consideration, the analysis of the bargaining process shows that the theoretical distinction between justified and unjustified objections does have behavioral implications.    Justified objections are more likely to dissolve tentative coalitions than unjustified objections, and, more importantly, the differential effect of these two types of objections steadily increases as more experience is gained with the bargaining task.    Consonant with the distinction between the two classes of games we have discussed, the results (Table IX) show that justified objections are more likely to dissolve the tentative coalitions to which they are addressed than the unjustified objections when all three coalitions are viable (Games II, III, and to some extent I), but not when coalition AB predominates the other two.    It is interesting to note that when justified objections are classified by game, source of objection, and target of objection (Table XI), they conform to the distinction between the two classes of games shown by earlier results.    However, when the unjustified objections are classified in the same manner, they are addressed about evenly to the stronger and weaker players, as can be seen in Table XI.    This, together with the Iteration effect reported in Table X, leads to speculation that justified objections were used by players with some facility and effectiveness in the game, whereas unjustified objections were more frequently lodged by unskilled players.    Further evidence supporting this conjecture comes from the data presented in Table XII, where it is shown that the objections that constituted offers near the quota solution had the highest likelihood of being successful in disrupting the tentative coalitions.    Investigation of this and other related hypotheses awaits further analyses of the bargaining process in subsequent work.

Despite these effects of justified versus unjustified objections, the results cannot be strictly interpreted as supportive of the bargaining process model.    Even in later iterations, most of the justified objections were ignored rather than serving to dissolve the tentative coalitions to which they were addressed.    Two deficiencies of the bargaining process model may account for its failure.    One concerns the size of the set of $p.c.$'s a player is assumed to consider before making an objection, and the other concerns the effect the "distance" between a tentatively accepted offer and $M_1^{(i)}$ should, but does not presently have on its dissolution by a justified objection. These difficiencies have been discussed in detail elsewhere (Horowitz and Rapoport, 1974) and will not be repeated here. A detailed inspection of the game protocols suggests a third weakness. Frequently, when an $M_1^{(i)}$-stable tentative coalition was formed, say between $A$ and $B$, a justified objection by $A$ against $B$ lodged by player $C$ was not accepted by $A$, not because $A$ considered the cost of disrupting the coalition to be prohibitively high, but because he expected $C$ to make one or two more objections, still justified, on the following rounds of negotiations, yielding $A$ a higher gain. It seems that the model's requirement that the first justified objection against a tentative coalition should dissolve it is too restrictive and should be relaxed.

Further research indicated by this study takes on three aspects. First, a more detailed inspection of the bargaining process, for both the present and for future data, is indicated, using modified models as suggested above. Second, there is a need to explore in more detail the various social psychological aspects of this situation, by varying in more ways the communication procedures, and perhaps by introducing experimental confederates to play prescribed strategies that represent bargaining stereotypes (ie., Boulewarism). Such research would help tie the present paradigm more closely to the recorded observations of real bargaining situations. Third, more of the mathematical aspects of $n$-person games need exploring. For instance, the introduction of a non-zero $ABC$ coalition allows the Shapley value to come into play. Findings supportive of one or the other of the various models could suggest underlying psychological variables that determine how individuals make decisions in negotiation environments.

## 5. Notes

This research was supported in part by a PHS Grant No. MG-10006 from the National Institute of Mental Health and in part by a University Science Development Program Grant No. GU-2059 from the National Science Foundation. The authors wish to thank Bruce Taylor and Sandra G. Funk for assistance in data collection, Michael Maschler for his careful reading and insightful comments on an earlier draft of the manuscript, and Abraham D. Horowitz for assistance in data collection, data analysis, and for many valuable discussions.

[1]Ideally, each subject should play each game with a different set of coplayers. The logistics of such a design are, however, beyond the scope of present-day equipment. Nonetheless, the present procedure, where a subject is not only ignorant of the roles played by his coplayers, but also which players are included in a particular game, does establish some degree of independence in the sense that the outcomes are not determined by the players' gains on previous rounds. Of course, games are not strictly independent because of all players' experience with the situation, but this is a variable we shall scrutinize below.

[2]The authors wish to thank Mark I. Appelbaum for his advice concerning the multivariate data analyses.

[3]We are indebted to Michael Maschler for pointing out these particular results.    Our interpretation of them, however, only partly agrees with the one he suggested.

## 6. Bibliography

Aumann, R. J, and Maschler, M., "The Bargaining Set of Cooperative Games" in M. Dresher, L. S. Shapley, and A. W. Tucker (eds.), *Advances in Game Theory*, Princeton University Press, Princeton, N.J., 1964.

Caplow, T., "A Theory of Coalition Formation," *American Sociological Review*, **21** (1956) 489–493.

Caplow, T., "Further Development of a Theory of coalitions in the Triad," *American Journal of Sociology* **54** (1959) 488–493.

Caplow, T., *Two Against One:    Coalitions in Traids*, Prentice-Hall, Englewood Cliffs, N.J., 1968.

Chertkoff, J. M., "A Revision of Caplow's Coalition Theory," *Journal of Experimental Social Psychology*, **3** (1967) 172–177.

Davis, M. A. and Maschler, M., "The Kernel of a Cooperative Game," *Naval Research Logistics Quarterly* **12** (1965) 223–259.

Gamson, W. A., "A Theory of coalition Formation," *American Sociological Review* **26** (1961) 373–382.

Horowitz, A. D., "The Competitive Bargaining Set for Cooperative n-Person Games," *Journal of Mathematical Psychology* (1973).

Horowitz, A. D., and Rapoport, Amnon, "Test of the Kernel and Two-Bargaining Set Models in Four- and Five-Person Games," in A. Rapoport (ed.), *Game Theory as a Theory of Conflict Resolution.    Reidel, Dordrecht, Holland, 1974.

Kahan, J. P. *Coalitions: A System of Programs of Computer-Controlled Bargaining Games: Operating Manual*, L.L. Thurstone Psychometric Laboratory Research Memorandum No. 34, Chapel Hill, N.C. 1970.

Kahan, J. P., "Noninteraction in an Anonymous Three-Person Prisoner's Dilemma Game," *Behavioral Science* **18** (1973) 124–127.

Kahan, J. P. and Helwig, R. A., "Coalitions: A System of Programs for Computer-Controlled Bargaining Games," *General Systems*, **16** (1971) 31–41.

Komorita, S. S. and Chertkoff, J. M., "A Bargaining Theory of Coalition Formation," *Psychological Review* **80** (1973) 149–162.

Luce, R. D. and Raiffa, H., *Games and Decisions: Introduction and Critical Survey*, Wiley, New York, 1957.

Marwell, G. and Schmitt, D., "Cooperation in a Three-Person Prisoner's Dilemma Game," *Journal of Personality and Social Psychology*, **21** (1972) 376–383.

Maschler, M., "The Power of a Coalition," *Management Science* **10** (1963) 8–29.

Maschler, M., *Playing an n-Person Game, an Experiment.    The Econometric Research Program, Research Memorandum No. 73, Princeton University, 1965.

Rapoport, A., *Two-Person Game Theory:    The Essential Ideas*, The University of

Michigan Press, Ann Arbor, 1966.

Rapoport, A., *n-Person Game Theory: Concepts and Applications*, The University of Michigan Press, Ann Arbor, 1970.

Rapoport, A., "Three and Four-Person Games," *Comparative Group Studies* 2 (1971) 191-226.

Riker, W. H., "Bargaining in a Three-Person Game," *American Political Science Review* 61 (1967) 642-656.

Selten, R. and Schuster, K. G., "Psychological Variables and Coalition-Forming Behavior," in K. Borch and J. Mossin (eds.), *Risk and Uncertainty*, Macmillan, London, 1968.

Shapley, L. S., "A Value for n-Person Games," in H. W. Kuhn and A. W. Tucker, (eds.), *Contributions to the Theory of Games*, Vol. II, Princeton University Press, Princeton, J.J., 1953.

Simmel, G., "The Number of Members as Determining the Sociological Form of the Group," *American Journal of Sociology* 7 (1902) 1-46.

Vinacke, W. E. and Arkoff, A., "An Experimental Study of Coalitions in the Triad," *American Sociological Review* 22 (1957) 406-414.

Vinacke, W. E., Crowell, D. C., Dien, D., and Young, V., "The Effect of Information about Strategy in a Three-Person Game," *Behavioral Science* 11 (1966) 180-189.

von Neumann, J. and Morgenstern, O., *Theory of Games and Economic Behavior*, 2nd ed. Princeton University Press, Princeton, N.J. 1947.

# CHAPTER 9

# TEST OF THE KERNEL AND TWO BARGAINING SET MODELS IN FOUR- AND FIVE-PERSON GAMES

**ABSTRACT:** Employing a computer-controlled experimental paradigm for studying coalition formation and bargaining, the present study tests three models for $n$-person games in characteristic function form, namely, the bargaining set and two of its subsets, the competitive bargaining set and the kernel.

Twelve groups of subjects participated in several four-person and five-person Apex games. The effects of group size, order of communication, learning, and values of the characteristic function were systematically investigated. The final outcomes reject the kernel and support the two bargaining set models; they depend upon group size and order of communication.

Models describing the bargaining process, rather than the final outcomes only, are presented, tested, and partially supported. The relationships between the final outcomes of the present study and those of previous studies of Apex games are briefly discussed.

## Introduction

An experimental paradigm has been proposed by Kahan and Rapoport (1974) for investigating coalition formation and bargaining processes in small groups. The paradigm is based on considerations of coalition formation through the negotiated division of rewards, or values, available to each coalition that may be formed. Its orientation arises from $n$-person game theory (see, e.g., Luce and Raiffa, 1957; Rapoport, 1966, 1970; von Neumann and Morgenstern, 1947), in particular from that portion of the theory concerned with formalized models of conflict of interest among $n$ players, which depend only on the respective values of the possible coalitions. Utilization of the paradigm relies heavily upon the development of the digital computer as an instrument of the psychological laboratory for conducting on-line group decision making experiments.

Whereas Kahan and Rapoport (1974) have studied coalition formation and bargaining processes in the triad, the present study, employing their experimental paradigm, has moved a step further to the case $n \geq 4$. Among the various games that may be investigated, we have focused on a psychologically intriguing game, first introduced by von Neumann and Morgenstern (1947, pp. 473-503) and later explored by Davis and Maschler (1965) and Horowitz (1973). The game under consideration, called the *Apex game* by Horowitz (1971), is a cooperative $n$-person game, $n \geq 3$, in which the only coalitions assigned positive values are (*i*) all those coalitions which include a certain player called *Apex*, and (*ii*) the coalition formed by the other $n - 1$ players, called *Base* players.

The apex game may be cast in terms of the characteristic function of the $n$-person game, a real-valued set function assigning a real number $v(X)$ to each nonempty subset $X$ of players, where $X \subseteq N$ and $N = \{1, 2, ..., n\}$. The value $v(X)$ measures the worth or power which the coalition $X$ can achieve when its members act together. For example, consider an Apex game with $n = 5$ in which every coalition may win $c$ units, $c > 0$. Then, assuming that $A$ is the Apex player, and $B$, $C$, $D$, and $E$ denote the four Base players, the characteristic function of this game is $v(AB) = v(AC) = v(AD) = v(AE) = v(ABC) = v(ABD) = v(ABE) = v(ACD) = v(ACE) = v(ADE) = v(ABCD) = v(ABCE) = v(ABDE) = v(ACDE) = v(ABCDE) = v(BCDE) = c$, and $v(X) = 0$ for any other coalition $X$.

The Apex's position may be compared to that of a monopolist, with the only limitation that he must find at least one ally. Only the coalition of all other players against him may defeat him (von Neumann and Morgenstern, 1947). The Base's position poses an intriguing dilemma: he must either cooperate with all other Base players, regardless of their number, or he must join the Apex and possibly some other Base players. If the first course of action is chosen, the Base player risks being frozen out of a winning coalition, if one or more Base players yield to the temptation of extra gain by forming a coalition with the Apex. On the other hand, if he chooses to negotiate with the Apex, the Base must consider the highly competitive environment produced by the Apex's multitude of choices in stating his demand for his share.

The central issue of the Apex game, as well as any other $n$-person cooperative game in characteristic function form, has been stated succinctly by Anatol Rapoport: "Given a particular coalition structure, how will the payoffs accruing to each coalition be apportioned among its members?" (1971, p. 194) Answers to this question may be derived from some of the models proposed for $n$-person cooperative games in characteristic function form, namely, von Neumann and Morgenstern's *solution* (1947), Shapley *value* (1953) and its modifications, Aumann and Maschler's *Bargaining set* (1964), the *kernel* of Davis and Maschler (1965), and Horowitz's *competitive bargaining set* (1973) especially developed for Apex games. In attempting to test these models, we have discarded von Neumann and Morgenstern's solution because of the infinite number of imputations it contains, and because it is formally limited to the coalition of all $n$ players, the *grand* coalition. Shapley's value has been discarded too because it is limited to the grand coalition. We have been left, then, with three models to test, the bargaining set, the kernel, and the competitive bargaining set.

THE COMPETITIVE BARGAINING SET

The basic concepts of the bargaining set and kernel models have been presented and discussed by Aumann and Maschler (1964), Davis and Maschler (1965), Horowitz (1973), Kahan and Rapoport (1974), Rapoport (1970), and will not be repeated here. Since familiarity with the competitive bargaining set model (Horowitz, 1973) cannot be assumed, its principal ideas are presented below.

Consider a cooperative $n$-person game in characteristic function form, which consists of a set $N = \{1, 2, ..., n\}$ of $n$ players along with a characteristic function $v$, assigning the real number $v(X)$ to each nonempty subset $X$ of players, called the coalition $X$. $v(X)$ is assumed to satisfy

(i) $v(X) \geq 0$ for each coalition $X$,

(ii) $v(\{i\}) = 0$ for each one-person coalition.

Let $\mathbf{X}$ be an $m$-partition of $N$ satisfying

$$X_j \cap X_k = \phi, \text{ if } j \neq k, \text{ and } \bigcup_{j=1}^{m} X_j = N.$$

An *outcome* of the game is represented by a *payoff configuration (p.c.)*

$$(\mathbf{x}; \mathbf{X}) = (x_1, x_2, ..., x_n; X_1, X_2, ..., X_m),$$

where $\mathbf{x} = (x_1, x_2, ..., x_n)$ is an $n$-dimensional real vector, called the *payoff vector*, representing the realizable distributions of wealth among the $n$ players, $x_i$ is the amount received by player $i$ in the distribution $\mathbf{x}$, and $\mathbf{X} = \{X_1, X_2, ..., X_m\}$ represents the coalition structure which was actually formed.

A *p.c.* is assumed to satisfy individual rationality, i.e.,

$$x_i \geq 0 \text{ for all } i \in \mathrm{N}.$$

It is further assumed that

$$\sum_{i \in X_j} x_i = v(X_j), \text{ for } j = 1, 2, ..., m.$$

A third, key, assumption is that every pair of players who are members of the same coalition ought to be in equilibrium. The concept of equilibrium is crucial to the competitive bargaining set and is defined in terms of the notions of multi-objection and counter-multi-objection.

Following the notation of Davis and Maschler (1967), let $(\mathbf{x}; \mathbf{X})$ be a *p.c.* and $k$ and $l$ be two members of the same coalition $X_j$, where $X_j \in \mathbf{X}$. Let $Y_1, Y_2, ..., Y_t$ be $t$ distinct coalitions, $t \geq 1$, and let $\mathbf{y}^{(1)}, \mathbf{y}^{(2)}, ..., \mathbf{y}^{(t)}$ be the associated payoff vectors. The set

$$\{(\mathbf{y}^{(1)}; Y_1), (\mathbf{y}^{(2)}; Y_2), ..., (\mathbf{y}^{(t)}; Y_t)\}$$

is called a *multi-objection* of player $k$ against $l$ with respect to the *p.c.* $(\mathbf{x}; \mathbf{X})$, if

(i) $k \in Y_g$,      $l \notin Y_g$,      $k$, $l \in X_j$,      $g = 1, 2, \ldots, t$ ,

(ii) $\displaystyle\sum_{i \in Yg} y_i^{(g)} = v(Y_g)$,   $g = 1, 2, \ldots, t$ ,

(iii) $y_k^{(g)} > x_k$,   $y_i^{(g)} \geq x_i$   for all   $i \in Y_g$,   $g = 1, 2, \ldots, t$.

In his multi-objection, player $k$ claims that he can gain more in any new coalition, $Y_g$, that he may form without the consent of player $l$, and that the new coalition is reasonable because the partners of $k$ in $Y_g$ gain at least what they gained in (x; X).

When $t = 1$, player $k$ may threaten $l$ through a single coalition only. In terms of the terminology of the bargaining set model, $k$ is said to have an *objection* against $l$. Thus, when $t = 1$, the competitive bargaining set notion of multi-objection reduces to an ordinary objection.

For a coalition $Z$ and a payoff vector z to its members, the pair (z; Z) is called a *counter-multi-objection* to k's multi-objection against $l$, if

(i) $l \in Z$,   $k \notin Z$,

(ii) $\displaystyle\sum_{i \in Z} z_i = v(Z)$,

(iii) $z_i \geq x_i$   for all   $i \in Z$,

(iv) $z_i \geq y_i^{(g)}$   for all   $i \in (Z \cap Y_g)$,   $g = 1, 2, \ldots, t$.

In lodging his counter-multi-objection, player $l$ claims that he can protect his share in (x; X) by giving his partners in $Z$ at least what they had before in (x; X), without k's consent. Moreover, if any of l's partners in $Z$ is included in the multi-objection of $k$ against $l$ he would gain at least what he had gained before.

If a counter-multi-objection intersects no more than one of the coalitions $Y_1$, $Y_2, \ldots, Y_t$, it reduces to the notion of *counter-objection* of the bargaining set model.

A multi-objection to a *p.c.* is *justified* if no counter-multi-objection to it exists; otherwise it is *unjustified*. An individually rational *p.c.* is said to be $H_1^{(i)}$-*stable* if for each multi-objection of $k$ against $l$ in (x; X) there exists a counter-multi-objection of $l$ against $k$. The set of all $H_1^{(i)}$-stable *p.c.*'s (which may be empty) is called the *competitive bargaining set* and denoted by $H_1^{(i)}$. The superscript of $H$ indicates individual rationality and the subscript denotes that objections are made by *one* player against *one* player at a time. Both constraints may be replaced, resulting in more severe requirements of stability.

For example, individual rationality may be replaced by coalitional rationality. Formally, a *p.c.* is said to satisfy *coalitional rationality* if for any coalition $W$, $W \subseteq X_j$, $j = 1, 2, \ldots, m$,

$$\sum_{i \in W} x_i \geq v(W).$$

The set of all coalitionally rational *p.c.*'s in which no player has a justified multi-objection against any other member of the same coalition is called the *competitive bargaining set* $H_1$. It can be shown that $H_1 \subseteq H^{(i)}$. For the Apex games considered in the present paper $H_1 = H^{(i)}$.

## COMPARISON OF THE MODELS

The bargaining set is a special case of the competitive bargaining set when $t = 1$. In particular, the *bargaining set* $M_1^{(i)}$ is defined to be the set of all individually rational *p.c.*'s in which no player has a justified objection against any other member of the same coalition. Replacing individual by coalitional rationality yields the bargaining set $M_1$. For the Apex games considered in the present study $M_1 = M_1^{(i)}$.

Horowitz (1973) proved that $H_1^{(i)} \subseteq M_1^{(i)}$. The proof that the kernel of the $n$-person cooperative game in characteristic function form, denoted by $K$, is also contained in $M_1^{(i)}$ is given in Davis and Maschler (1965).

It is worth mentioning that the concepts of objection and counter-objection underlying the bargaining set theory as well as the concepts of multi-objection and counter-multi-objection involve only ordinal comparisons of utilities. Although the kernel, as originally formulated by Davis and Maschler (1965), requires inter-personal comparability of utilities, Maschler, Peleg, and Shapley (1970) have recently suggested an alternative interpretation of the kernel which avoids such comparisons. The assumption of ordinal preferences, which is common to all three models tested in the present paper, considerably enhances their attraction to social scientists interested in coalition formation.

In comparing the bargaining set and the competitive bargaining set models it is noted that the degree of stability and competitiveness in bargaining behavior implied by the former model results from its assumption that only a single objection may be expressed at any one time. Underlying the competitive bargaining set model is another assumption, namely, that since threats or offers are often tacit (see, e.g., Schelling, 1960), their number should not be restricted to one. Rather, threats or offers are assumed to be perceived and considered simultaneously even though their simultaneous implementation may be impossible. The resulting outcome for Apex games is that the competitive bargaining set theory yields a unique solution located at one extreme of the continuum of solutions prescribed by the bargaining set model. The other extreme point is the kernel. For a detailed comparison of the three models with regard to Apex games see Horowitz (1973).

We are faced then with testing three models for the Apex game, $M_1^{(i)}$ and its two extreme points, $H_1^{(i)}$ and K. We expect that within the continuum of solutions prescribed by the bargaining set the actual disbursement of payoffs for a given coalition will depend on the game environment. The game environment consists of some ill-defined variables, which are psychologically important though presently not incorporated in the game theoretic formulation. Included among these variables are the determinateness to form a coalition, the degree of desired stability, and the degree of competitiveness. All of these variables, which cannot be assumed to be mutually independent, may be expected to depend upon the structure of the characteristic function and the type of communication allowed. Horowitz (1973) suggested that as the degree of determinateness to form coalitions gets stronger, the degree of competitiveness is reduced, or the stability requirements are relaxed, the final outcomes will approach the kernel's predictions. And conversely, as the players become more competitive or if they are motivated by a desire for stronger stability, the final outcomes will approach the *p.c.'s* prescribed by the competitive bargaining set.

AN EXAMPLE

Predictions derived from the three models may best be demonstrated by an example. Consider a five-person Apex game with the characteristic function

$$v(AB) = v(AC) = v(AD) = v(AE) = v(BCDE) = 100,$$

and $v(X) = 0$ for any other coalition $X$. This particular Apex game, similar to the games investigated in the present study, is not a full Apex game, as any coalition with an Apex player and two or more Base players is assigned the value 0. This, however, does not affect the predictions of the models concerning the division of the payoff for a two-player coalition.

Since the four two-person coalitions which are assigned 100 points each are symmetric, it is sufficient to consider coalition $AB$. For this coalition there exists a unique $H_1^{(i)}$-stable *p.c.*, namely,

$$(x; X) = (75, 25, 0, 0, 0; AB, C, D, E),$$

as can easily be shown. A multi-objection of $A$ against $B$ with respect to the *p.c.* (x; X) is

$$\{(y_A^{(1)}, y_C^{(1)}; AC), (y_A^{(2)}, y_D^{(2)}; AD), (y_A^{(3)}, y_E^{(3)}; AE)\}$$

where $y_A^{(g)} > 75$, $g = 1, 2, 3$, and therefore $y_C^{(1)}, y_D^{(2)}, y_E^{(3)} < 25$, since $v(AC) = v(AD) = (AE) = 100$. Player $B$ can respond to $A$'s multi-objection by a counter-multi-objection

$$(25, 25, 25, 25; BCDE).$$

Note also that any single objection by $B$ against $A$ with respect to the *p.c.* (x; X) can be countered by the latter player. Also, it is seen that for any $\delta > 0$ the *p.c.*

$$(75 - \delta, \quad 25 + \delta, \quad 0, 0, 0; AB, C, D, E)$$

is not $H_1^{(i)}$-stable, since a multi-objection from $A$ against $B$ in which $y_C^{(1)}$, $y_D^{(2)}$, $y_E^{(3)} > 25$ is justified, i.e., it cannot be met by a counter-multi-objection of $B$.

It can be shown that the only p.c., given the coalition $AB$, which is contained in the kernel of the Apex game, is

$$(50, 50, 0, 0, 0; AB, C, D, E).$$

And finally, the only p.c.'s with the coalition structure $(AB, C, D, E)$ for which no player has an $M_1^{(i)}$-justified objection against any other consist of the continuum

$$(50 \leq x_A \leq 75, \quad 25 \leq x_B \leq 50, 0, 0, 0; AB, C, D, E),$$

where $x_A + x_B = \nu(AB) = 100$.

For the coalition of the four Base players, all three models predict a unique p.c., namely,

$$(0, 25, 25, 25, 25; A, BCDE),$$

as can be easily verified.

Employing the experimental paradigm of Kahan and Rapoport (1974), one of the purposes of the present experiment is to test the three models in Apex games. An additional, equally important, purpose is to develop and test models accounting not only for the final outcomes but also for the bargaining process. Additionally, the present experiment looked at the effects of group size, order of communication among the $n$ players, practice, and ratio of the value of the Apex coalition to the Base coalition on the final outcomes of the game and the bargaining process.

## Method

### SUBJECTS

Sixty undergraduate male students at the University of North Carolina participated in the experiment. They were recruited by advertisements in the student newspaper which promised financial reward. The subjects were divided into 12 groups of five subjects, each group participating in two three-hour sessions.

### DESIGN

A 2×2×2×2 factorial design was employed, with repeated measures on two of the four factors. One factor, $O$, was the order of communication, in which the Apex either communicated before all the Base players ($O_1$) or after them ($O_2$). A second factor, $V$, concerned the value of a coalition between the Apex player and a single Base player, hereafter called the *Apex coalition*. This value was either 72 ($V_1$) or 108 ($V_2$). The value of the coalition of all $n-1$ Base players, hereafter called the *Base coalition*, was always 72 points.    The third factor, $N$, was the size of the group, either a quartet (condition $N_1$, an Apex plus three Base players) or a quintet (condition $N_2$, an Apex plus four Base players).    Each of the eight games defined by the Cartesian product of the three factors $N$, $V$, and $O$ was played twice to yield a fourth factor of runs, $R$, with first ($R_1$) and second ($R_2$) plays as levels.

Three groups of five subjects each were assigned to each of the four $O \times V$ combinations.    Repeated measures on factors $N$ and $R$ were employed.    Each group participated in two three-hour sessions, which typically took place within a single week. The first was a practice session.    In the second session each group played two four- and two five-person Apex games, with a single passive player in the former case, who could observe the bargaining but neither send nor receive any messages.    Players were labelled $A$, $B$, $C$, $D$, and $E$, and were required to send typed messages in alphabetical order. The Apex was therefore player $A$ in condition $O_1$ and player $E$ in condition $O_2$.    The design of the experiment as well as the characteristic functions of the game are presented in Table 1.

*Table 1.   Research design*

| Order | Value | Groups | Size | Characteristic Function |
|-------|-------|--------|------|-------------------------|
| $O_1$ | $V_1$ | 1, 2, 3 | $N_1$ | $v(AB) = v(AC) = v(AD) = v(BCD) = 72$ |
| | | | $N_2$ | $v(AB) = v(AC) = v(AD) = v(AE) = v(BCDE) = 72$ |
| | $V_2$ | 4, 5, 6 | $N_1$ | $v(AB) = v(AC) = v(AD) = 108, v(BCD) = 72$ |
| | | | $N_2$ | $v(AB) = v(AC) = v(AD) = v(AE) = 108, v(BCDE) = 72$ |
| $O_2$ | $V_1$ | 7, 8, 9 | $N_1$ | $v(EB) = v(EC) = v(ED) = v(BCD) = 72$ |
| | | | $N_2$ | $v(EA) = v(EB) = v(EC) = v(ED) = v(ABCD) = 72$ |
| | $V_2$ | 10, 11, 12 | $N_1$ | $v(EB) = v(EC) = v(ED) = 108, v(BCD) = 72$ |
| | | | $N_2$ | $v(EA) = v(EB) = v(EC) = v(ED) = 108, v(ABCD) = 72$ |

Note.    The characteristic functions are the same in the two levels of factor $R$.

## PROCEDURE

The first session started by having the subjects of each group read a set of instructions. Since the instructions are given in Horowitz (1971) and are also summarized in Kahan and Rapoport (1974), they will not be presented here. Essentially, they present the bargaining game as a three-stage process, consisting of an offer stage, in which the potentials of various coalitions may be explored, an acceptance stage, in which a particular *p.c.* is seriously considered, and a ratification stage, in which the agreement on a division of value becomes binding. Communication takes place through the use of six keywords, *offer, accept, reject, ratify, pass,* and *solo,* allowing players to propose various *p.c.'s,* accept, reject or ratify them, make no communication, or withdraw from the game.

The written instructions were followed by a verbal explanation, in which the experimenter reiterated the main rules of the bargaining game. Then each subject entered a separate cubicle containing a teletypewriter connected to a PDP-8 computer to play two example games. While playing the two games under the experimenter's supervision, the subjects were encouraged to ask questions about the rules of the game and the operation of the teletypewriter and to employ all the options provided by the computer program. At the end of the first session they were told that the number of games to be played in the second session was fixed. These additional instructions were provided to discourage the subjects from fast bargaining in order to increase the number of games played and, consequently, the amount of money earned.

Subjects returned a few days later for the experimental session, entered their respective cubicles without communicating with one another, and started immediately to play. The order of the games was randomized for each group, and the Apex role was not assigned more than once to a given subject. Roles were reassigned for each game to prevent sequential effects between games and to assure that experimental effects would be attributed to role and not to bargaining strategies of individual players. An interrogation of the subjects following the second session revealed that subjects did not form any hypotheses about roles assigned to the players in the successive games, nor could they successfully guess the identity of the other players in a particular game.

At the end of the second session, each subject was paid $4.50 for participation in the first three-hour session, plus 5 cents per point earned in the second session, plus a fixed sum of 75 cents per hour in the second session.

The experiment was administered with a set of PDP-8, on-line, computer programs called *coalitions*. A non-technical brief description of the main program is provided by Kahan and Rapoport (1974). For a complete, technical description see Kahan and Helwig (1971).

## Results

The basic data consist of the typed messages sent during the experimental session, starting with the first *offer* or *pass* and ending with the last *ratify*. Conceptually, it is convenient to analyze these data in terms of (*i*) the final outcomes, (*ii*) the initial phase of negotiations, and (iii) the bargaining process. To simplify the ensuing presentation of the results, a system of terminology and notation is first presented. Let $G_{g,r,n}$ denote a game, where $g$, $g = 1, 2, ..., 12$, is the group number, $r$, $r = 1, 2$, is the run number, and $n$, $n = 4, 5$, is the group size. For example, $G_{7,2,4}$ denotes the game played by group 7 in quartet form (condition $N_1$) on the second run (condition $R_2$). An offer is a *p.c.*. When accepted by all its members it is called a *tentative coalition*. The final tentative coalition in a game is called the *ratified coalition*. A tentative coalition is *dissolved* when one of its members rejects it explicitly, or equivalently, enters another tentative coalition. A Base player included in a ratified coalition is a *Base winner*, otherwise a *Base loser*.

The main dependent variable is the number of points, $x_\beta$, allocated to a Base player (or to all the Base players in the case of a Base coalition) in an offer, tentative coalition, or ratified coalition. Since the value of the Apex coalition, as given by the characteristic function, is known (either 72 or 108), the Apex's share, $x_\alpha$, may be obtained by subtraction.

## FINAL OUTCOMES

The final outcomes of the 24 quintet and 24 quartet games are presented in Tables 2 and 3, respectively. Table 2 shows that in 23 of 24 quintet games an Apex coalition was formed, yielding the Base winner a mean of 20.1 points. The range of the Base winner's payoffs was from 18 to 25. The payoffs $x_\beta$ predicted by the bargaining set model fall in the closed interval $18 \leq x_\beta \leq 36$ for both conditions $V_1$ and $V_2$. The competitive bargaining set lies at the one extreme of 18, and the kernel at the other extreme, 36. All the final outcomes fall in the bargaining set $M_1$. In particular, they provide strong support for the competitive bargaining set compared to the kernel.

An Apex coalition was formed in 22 of the 24 quartet games yielding the Base winner a mean of 25.8 points. The range of the Base winner's payoffs was from 18 to 36. The predicted payoffs in $M_1$, $H_1$, and $K$ for the Base winner are $24 \leq x_\beta \leq 36$, $x_\beta = 24$, and $x_\beta = 36$, respectively. As in condition $N_2$, the mean final outcome supports the competitive bargaining set relative to the kernel. The bargaining set is supported by 18 of the 22 final Apex coalition outcomes. Both $M_1$ and $H_1$ are also supported by the results of the two Base coalitions that were formed in games $G_{7,2,4}$ and $G_{8,1,4}$.

To assess the effects of the four experimental conditions on the final outcomes, a $2 \times 2 \times 2 \times 2$ analysis of variance with repeated measures on factors $N$ and $R$ (employing a multivariate approach) was conducted on the Base winner payoffs presented in Tables 2 and 3. The significant group size effect ($F = 53.4$, $p < 0.001$) is not predicted by the kernel model. The competitive bargaining set model, however, predicts a difference of 6 points between quartet and quintet games for the Base winner's payoff; the observed mean difference was 5.7.

The second significant main effect was due to factor $O$ ($F=10.2$, $p<0.02$), with the Base player winning significantly more in condition $O_2$ than in $O_1$. This effect is inconsistent with all three models, since none of them incorporates any consideration of order of communication. The other two main effects, $V$ and $R$, did not contribute significantly to the final outcomes.

The only significant interaction was the two-way interaction $O \times N$ ($F = 6.5$, $p < 0.05$), which accounts for the different effects of order of communication

*Table 2.* *Final outcomes of quintet games*

| $O_1$ | | | | $O_2$ | | | |
|---|---|---|---|---|---|---|---|
| $g$ | $r$ | $x_\alpha$ | $x_\beta$ | $g$ | $r$ | $x_\alpha$ | $x_\beta$ |
| 1 | 1 | 54 | 18 | 7 | 1 | 47 | 25 |
|  | 2 | 54 | 18 |  | 2 | 54 | 18 |
| $V_1$ 2 | 1 | 53 | 19 | 8 | 1 | 0 | $a$ |
|  | 2 | 52 | 20 |  | 2 | 47 | 25 |
| 3 | 1 | 50 | 22 | 9 | 1 | 50 | 22 |
|  | 2 | 53 | 19 |  | 2 | 54 | 18 |
| 4 | 1 | 90 | 18 | 10 | 1 | 86 | 22 |
|  | 2 | 90 | 18 |  | 2 | 83 | 25 |
| $V_2$ 5 | 1 | 90 | 18 | 11 | 1 | 83 | 25 |
|  | 2 | 90 | 18 |  | 2 | 89 | 19 |
| 6 | 1 | 90 | 18 | 12 | 1 | 89 | 19 |
|  | 2 | 88 | 20 |  | 2 | 90 | 18 |
| Mean |  |  | 18.8 | Mean |  |  | 21.5 |
| S.D. |  |  | 1.3 | S.D. |  |  | 3.1 |

[a] Ratified coalition: (9, 21, 21, 21; ABCD)

in quartet and quintet games. This interaction is related to the theoretical predictions in the following way. While outcomes in the quintet games supported the competitive bargaining set, the outcomes of quartet games supported it only when the Apex player communicated first. The means of the quartet games were 22.9 and 29.3 in conditions $O_1$ and $O_2$, respectively. A 0.99 confidence interval computed for condition $O_1$ yielded the range $20.9 \leq x_\beta \leq 24.9$, excluding most of the continuum of the bargaining set and including $H_1$. A similar confidence interval in condition $O_2$ was $26.4 \leq x_\beta \leq 32.2$, covering about two thirds of $M_1$ and excluding $H_1$ as well as $K$.

*Table 3.  Final outcomes of quartet games*

| $O_1$ | | | | $O_2$ | | | |
|---|---|---|---|---|---|---|---|
| $g$ | $r$ | $x_\alpha$ | $x_\beta$ | $g$ | $r$ | $x_\alpha$ | $x_\beta$ |
| 1 | 1 | 48 | 24 | 7 | 1 | 36 | 36 |
|   | 2 | 52 | 20 |   | 2 | 0 | $a$ |
| $V_1$ 2 | 1 | 47 | 25 | 8 | 1 | 0 | $a$ |
|   | 2 | 48 | 24 |   | 2 | 42 | 30 |
| 3 | 1 | 47 | 25 | 9 | 1 | 40 | 32 |
|   | 2 | 47 | 25 |   | 2 | 40 | 32 |
| 4 | 1 | 90 | 18 | 10 | 1 | 80 | 28 |
|   | 2 | 90 | 18 |   | 2 | 78 | 30 |
| $V_2$ 5 | 1 | 83 | 25 | 11 | 1 | 80 | 28 |
|   | 2 | 83 | 25 |   | 2 | 80 | 28 |
| 6 | 1 | 86 | 22 | 12 | 1 | 84 | 24 |
|   | 2 | 84 | 24 |   | 2 | 83 | 25 |
| Mean |  |  | 22.9 | Mean |  |  | 29.3 |
| S.D. |  |  | 2.7 | S.D. |  |  | 3.5 |

$a$  Ratified coalition:  (24, 24, 24; BCD)

THE INITIAL PHASE OF NEGOTIATIONS

The initial phase of negotiations is defined here as the first two rounds of communication, i.e., either the first eight or ten messages in conditions $N_1$ and $N_2$, respectively.  It was extensively analyzed mainly for two reasons.  First, the initial tentative coalition was formed during the first two rounds of negotiations in 47 of 48 games.  Secondly, 25 of the 48 initial tentative coalitions were ratified, indicating that the initial phase of negotiations strongly affected the final outcomes.

The initial phase of negotiations may be divided into three parts that will by analyzed below:  the initial orientation of the Base player, the relation between first offers and final outcomes, and the relations between responses to initial offers and final outcomes.

*Base's orientation.*   On the first round of negotiations a Base player might attempt to either cooperate with the other Base players or form a coalition with the Apex player. A measure of initial orientation of the Base players is provided by the percentage of these players who addressed the Apex with an offer, or accepted an offer he made on the first round of negotiations.   These measures, ranging between 0 and 100, were obtained for each group and subjected to a 2×2×2×2 analysis of variance (using again the multivariate approach) with repeated measures on factors $N$ and $R$.  The analysis yielded a significant group size effect ($F = 14.3$, $p < 0.01$).  Whereas 82% of the Base players in the quintet games negotiated with the Apex on the first round of negotiations (in which each player could send only a single message), only 58% did so in the quartet games.

Another source of significant variation was the two-way interaction $N \times O$ ($F = 10.5$, p<0.01).   When the Apex was the first player that could send a message (condition $O_1$), the percentages of the Base players who negotiated with him were 75 and 77 for conditions $N_1$ and $N_2$, respectively.   When the Apex was the last player to communicate (condition $O_2$), the respective values were 41% and 85%.   The significant interaction is the same as the one found in the analysis of final outcomes. Since neither of the other main effects, $V$, $R$, or $O$, nor any of the interactions were significant, the results point again to the size of the group and order of communication as the two critical variables in Apex games.

*Initial offers.*   Tables 4 and 5 present the initial offers made in each game, the responses to them by Base or Apex on the first or second round of negotiations, and the final outcomes for conditions $N_2$ and $N_1$, respectively.   For each group size results are presented separately for conditions $O_1$ and $O_2$.   The initial offers and the final outcomes are stated as before in terms of $x_\beta$.   The letters $W$ and $L$ indicate that the Base player addressed by the Apex in his first offer was a winner or loser in the game, respectively.

An inspection of the column "Offer by Apex" in both tables for condition $O_1$ reveals a strong run effect in Apex's initial offers; Apex's offer in the second run was never larger than in the first run.   This finding strongly suggests that an Apex player in the second run learned that the Base coalition was unlikely to form, therefore demanding at least what another player in the Apex role had demanded (but not necessarily had accepted) in the first run.

Tables 4 and 5 further show that the distribution of the Apex's initial offers to Base was bimodal, with the major mode falling close to $H_1$, and the minor mode falling close to $K$.   The medians of the Apex's initial offers to Base were within one or two points of $H_1$, and the means were 4.9 and 2.4 points higher than $H_1$ for quintets and quartets, respectively.   A second consistent trend emerged in condition $O_1$ when Apex's initial offer to Base was compared to the final outcome.   The winner Base's final outcome was never larger than his share in the Apex's initial offer.   Stated differently, the bargaining that ensued in condition $O_1$ lowered $x_\beta$ in the direction of $H_1$.   Moreover, the bargaining also reduced the variability around the mean final outcome.

Tables 4 and 5 show that the standard deviation of Apex's initial offers to Base was larger than that of the final outcomes.   This effect is significant as tested by the ratio of the variance for quintets and quartets ($F = 19.6$, $p < 0.01$, and $F = 5.8$, $p < 0.01$, respectively).

*Table 4. Initial offers, responses to initial offers, and final outcomes in quintet games*

| $O_1$ | | | | | | $O_2$ | | | | |
|---|---|---|---|---|---|---|---|---|---|---|
| g | r | Offer by Apex | Base's response | W or L | Final $x_\beta$ | | g | r | Demand by Base(s) | Apex's response | Final $x_\beta$ |
| 1 | 1 | 22 | c.o.l. | L | 18 | | 7 | 1 | 22,27 | c.o.m. 25 | 25 |
|   | 2 | 18 | ign. | L | 18 | |   | 2 | 18,26,36 | acc. 18 | 18 |
| 2 | 1 | 32 | acc. | L | 19 | | 8 | 1 | 19,20,37 | acc. 19 | a |
|   | 2 | 32 | acc. | L | 20 | |   | 2 | 25,30,32 | acc. 25 | 25 |
| 3 | 1 | 22 | acc. | W | 22 | | 9 | 1 | 20,20,26,28 | acc. 20 | 22 |
|   | 2 | 20 | c.o.l. | W | 19 | |   | 2 | 18,18,20,20 | acc. 18 | 18 |
| 4 | 1 | 18 | c.o.m. | L | 18 | | 10 | 1 | 18,20,20,22 | acc. 22 | 22 |
|   | 2 | 18 | acc. | W | 18 | |   | 2 | 20,21,25 | acc. 25 | 25 |
| 5 | 1 | 20 | acc. | L | 18 | | 11 | 1 | 25,25,26,30 | acc. 25 | 25 |
|   | 2 | b | -- | -- | 18 | |   | 2 | 19,23,24,25 | acc. 19 | 19 |
| 6 | 1 | 30 | acc. | W | 18 | | 12 | 1 | 19,28,30,54 | acc. 19 | 19 |
|   | 2 | 20 | acc. | W | 20 | |   | 2 | 14,17,18,25 | acc. 18 | 18 |
| Mean | | 22.9 | | | 18.8 | | Mean | | 24.0 | | 21.5 |
| S.D. | | 5.6 | | | 1.3 | | S.D. | | 7.0 | | 3.1 |

[a] Base coalition formed.
[b] pass.

The results of condition $O_2$, presented on the right-hand sides of Tables 4 and 5, are less regular and different than those of condition $O_1$. A comparison of the initial offers and final outcomes in Table 5 shows that the winner Base obtained on the average 29.3 points, 4.2 points *more* than his average initial demand. This difference between the two means was significant ($t = 2.0$, $p < 0.05$). Quintet games, however, did not exhibit such a significant trend. This finding may be explained in terms of the $N \times O$ interaction, which was significant in the previous analyses. Perhaps due to the

*Table 5.  Initial offers, responses to initial offers, and final outcomes in quartet games*

| $O_1$ | | | | | | $O_2$ | | | | |
|---|---|---|---|---|---|---|---|---|---|---|
| $g$ | $r$ | Offer by Apex | Base's response | $W$ or $L$ | Final $x_\beta$ | $g$ | $r$ | Demand by Base(s) | Apex's response | Final $x_\beta$ |
| 1 | 1 | 28 | c.o.l. | $W$ | 24 | 7 | 1 | 24 | acc. | 36 |
|   | 2 | 20 | acc. | $W$ | 20 |   | 2 | 24 | acc. | $a$ |
| 2 | 1 | 36 | acc. | $L$ | 25 | 8 | 1 | — | off 25 | $a$ |
|   | 2 | 24 | acc. | $W$ | 24 |   | 2 | — | off 32 | 30 |
| 3 | 1 | 25 | acc. | $W$ | 25 | 9 | 1 | — | off 32 | 32 |
|   | 2 | 25 | acc. | $W$ | 25 |   | 2 | 15,24,30 | acc. 15 | 32 |
| 4 | 1 | 18 | acc. | $W$ | 18 | 10 | 1 | 30 | off 20 | 28 |
|   | 2 | 18 | acc. | $W$ | 18 |   | 2 | 30 | acc. 30 | 30 |
| 5 | 1 | 38 | acc. | $L$ | 25 | 11 | 1 | 40 | c.o.m. 28 | 28 |
|   | 2 | $b$ | — | — | 25 |   | 2 | 20,25,25 | acc. 20 | 28 |
| 6 | 1 | 30 | acc. | $L$ | 22 | 12 | 1 | 21,24 | acc. 24 | 24 |
|   | 2 | 28 | c.o.l. | $L$ | 24 |   | 2 | 20,25 | acc. 25 | 25 |
| Mean | | 26.4 | | | 22.9 | Mean | | 25.1 | | 29.3 |
| S.D. | | 6.6 | | | 2.7 | S.D. | | 5.8 | | 3.5 |

$a$  Base coalition formed.
$b$  pass.

relatively few initial offers made by Base to Apex in quartet games in condition $O_2$, the Apex reduced his demand in order to avoid a formation of the Base coalition.

*Responses to initial offers.*   When either a Base or an Apex player was made an offer he had to select exactly one of five possible ways of responding:  (*i*) reject the offer (rej.), (*ii*) ignore the offer by either passing or, if the player was Base, addressing the Base coalition (ign.), (*iii*) counter-offer and demand more than initially offered (c.o.m.), (*iv*) counter-offer and demand less than initially offered, (c.o.l.), or (*v*) accept the offer (acc.).

An inspection of the column labeled "Base's response" of condition $O_1$ in Tables 4 and 5 shows that the Base chose the later two ways in 20 of 22 games (16 acceptances and 4 counter-offers for less points). The two single cases of "resistance" to Apex led to the Base's elimination from the ratified coalition (games $G_{1,2,5}$ and $G_{4,1,5}$).

The particular payoff tentatively accepted by the Base is crucial for his chances to be a winner. The column "$W$ or $L$" in Tables 4 and 5 indicates that a tentative agreement in the higher half of $M_1$ on the kernel's side led finally to the exclusion of the Base player from the ratified coalition. Note the agreements involving, for a Base player, 32 points in quintet games and 36, 38, and 30 points in quartet games. Recall that $K = 36$ points for both quartets and quintets. On the other hand, Base players who accepted a payoff within four points of $H_1$ typically ended the game as winners.

It is instructive to describe two exceptions in which the Base players lost though they accepted initial offers located two points higher than $H_1$. In game $G_{1,1,5}$, the Base player counter-offered for less, 20 instead of 22, and the Apex accepted. Later in the game the Base did not agree to ratify the agreement, demanding 25 points instead of 20. He ended as a loser. In game $G_{5,1,5}$, the original agreement which assigned 20 points for the Base player was disrupted by the Apex. However, in the ensuing negotiations the first Base player passed at a crucial moment after a disruption of another Base coalition, and later he reentered the Base coalition possibly set as a trap by another Base player. It seems that in both games the Base players who had been addressed initially by the Apex could have won if they had been loyal to the Apex through all phases of the negotiations.

THE BARGAINING PROCESS

The two bargaining sets $M_1$ and $H_1$ can be represented as sets of solutions of conjunctive-disjunctive systems of linear inequalities involving the final outcomes as unknowns. The predictions derived from these models, which have been tested above, concern only the final outcomes of the negotiations among the $n$ players. The models are mute with respect to the characterization of the bargaining process which leads to ratification of the tentative coalitions. But, clearly, players do not solve conjunctive-disjunctive systems of linear inequalities in order to form coalitions and disburse their values. Rather, a coalition is ratified and its value is disbursed among its members after a lengthy process of negotiations involving offers, counter-offers, acceptances, rejections, and passes, which reflect only in part the threats, counter-threats, promises, bluffs, and other negotiation steps actually considered by the players. From a psychological viewpoint, it is the bargaining process with all its intricacies rather than the final outcomes which is of primary interest. We attend to an analysis of it in the present section.

The bargaining process may be modelled in several different ways. The alternative chosen here has been motivated by the success of the bargaining set $M_1$ and its extreme point $H_1$ in accounting for the final outcomes of Apex games. If both models provide an adequate description of final outcomes in Apex games, and we are unwilling at this juncture to prefer one or the other, a model of the bargaining process should converge to either $M_1$ or $H_1$ as its final outcome.

Depending whether convergence to either $M_1$ or $H_1$ is sought, the two bargaining models described below amount to testable dynamic interpretations of the bargaining set model and the competitive bargaining set model, respectively. Both $M_1$ and $H_1$ can be described as p.c.'s in which every objection (appropriately defined for each of the two models) has a counter-objection (appropriately defined for each case). If, for a given p.c., a player $k$ can sustain a justified objection against player $l$, a reasonable negotiation move might be for all players included in the objection to accept it. The resulting p.c. may be subjected to further negotiations. If the objection is unjustified, the bargaining continues.

Figure 1 diagrams the proposed structure of the bargaining process. On the first stage of the process a coalition (p.c.) is tentatively formed; it may be either an Apex or a Base coalition. The tentative coalition, denoted by $X$ in Figure 1, may either result from the initial negotiations among the $n$ players or may follow the dissolution of a previous tentative coalition. Players are assumed to search for justified objections against $X$. If none exists, the tentative coalition is eventually ratified. If at least one justified objection exists, an objection to the tentative coalition, denoted by $Y_s$ in Figure 1, is expressed through an offer (p.c.).

The objections involve only integral units and are made one at a time, as dictated by the rules of the game. The identity of the player expressing an objection is irrelevant. Thus, for example, if a tentative coalition $X = AB$ is formed, an objection $Y_s = AC$ by $A$ against $B$ may be made by $A$ through an offer to $C$, or by $C$ through an offer to $A$. This requirement is compatible with the definition of objection (Aumann and Maschler, 1964).

If the objection $Y_s$ is justified, the tentative coalition $X$ is dissolved and the objection is accepted, thus resulting in a new tentative coalition $(X \leftarrow Y_s$ in Figure 1). If, however, the objection is unjustified, the tentative coalition $X$ is retained, and a new objection against $X$, $(s \leftarrow s + 1$ in Figure 1) is made. If a player has only unjustified objections when it is his turn to play, his new objection is necessarily unjustified. However, it is assumed that at least one of the players possessing both justified and unjustified objections against $X$ will eventually express a justified objection. The latter assumption, though admittedly strong, is required to insure convergence.

The proof for Apex games that the bargaining process described above converges to a p.c. in the appropriate bargaining set is too detailed to be presented here. Essentially, it is based on the idea of dividing all the p.c.'s in terms of $x_\alpha$ into five mutually exclusive and collectively exhaustive classes: (1) $0 \leq x_\alpha < c/(n - 1)$, (2) $c/(n - 1) \leq x_\alpha < c/2$, (3) $c/2 \leq x_\alpha \leq c(n - 2)/(n - 1)$, (4) $c(n - 2)/(n - 1) < x_\alpha \leq c$, (5) $x_\alpha = 0$, where $c$ is the value of the Apex coalition. While the first four classes involve the Apex coalition only, the fifth assumes the formation of the Base coalition. The proof proceeds to show that the bargaining process described in Figure 1, assuming $M_1$-justified or $M_1$-unjustified objections, converges in a finite number of stages to the two classes comprising the bargaining set $M_1$, that is, either class (3) or class (5) (with an equal split of the value of the Base coalition). The proof for $H_1$ is quite similar. Stearns (1967) proved convergence of an entirely different transfer scheme to either $M_1$ or $K$ for the general $n$-person game in characteristic function form.

To exemplify the bargaining process leading to $M_1$, consider a four-person Apex game defined for players $A$, $B$, $C$, $D$, where $v(AB) = v(AC) = v(AD) = v(BCD) = 72$.

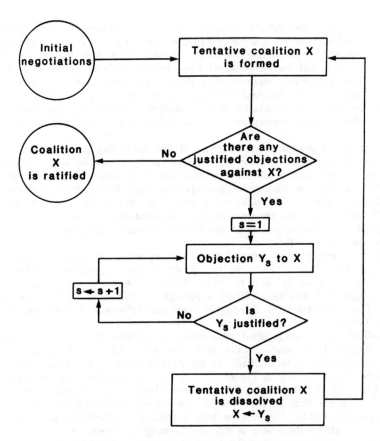

*Figure 1.  A proposed bargaining process converging to the bargaining sets $M_1$ or $H_1$.*

Suppose that after a tentative Base coalition is formed with a *p.c.* (0, 34, 19, 19; *A, BCD*), the Apex player offers 21 points to *C*. Since this offer is an $M_1$-justified objection by *C* against *B* ("Base against Base"), the Base coalition is dissolved and the *p.c.* (51, 0, 21, 0; *AC, B, D*) forms after *C* accepts *A's* offer. The second iteration continues, for example, by an offer from *D* of 62 points to *A*, which is an objection by *A* against *C* (i.e., "Apex against Base"). However, it is not $M_1$-justified because *C* can counter-object. Since the *p.c.* (51, 0, 21, 0; *AC, B, D*) is not $M_1$-stable, the game proceeds. For example, it may continue with a "Base against Apex" objection by *C* against *A* (0, 22, 28, 22; *A, BCD*) made by *B*. Since it is $M_1$-justified it becomes the new tentative coalition. Finally, for example, an objection by *B* against *C*, (72 - $x_B$, 24 ≤ $x_B$ ≤ 27, 0, 0; *AB, C, D*) is both $M_1$-justified and stable, since *C* cannot counter-object. Any such objection should be ratified.

To describe the bargaining process leading to $H_1$, the conditions under which an offer is interpreted as a multi-objection should be specified. The bargaining process model assumes that an objection by player $k$ against $l$ may be viewed as a multi-objection when other objections of $k$ against $l$ are implied and not explicitly stated. A multi-objection may, therefore, be interpreted as a tacit threat accompanying the actual objection. Alternatively, it may be interpreted as an open offer to several potential coalitions involving player $k$. Thus, consider again the previous example. Suppose that players $A$ and $B$ agree on the p.c. (45, 27, 0, 0; $AB$, $C$, $D$), which is $H_1$-unstable. Player $C$ may object to this p.c. by offering 46 points to $A$, i.e., the p.c. (46, 0, 26, 0; $AC$, $B$, $D$). This is an objection of the type "Apex against Base." The multi-objection in this case is assumed to consist of the actual objection plus the implied (tacit) objection (46, 0, 0, 26; $AD$, $B$, $C$). It may be interpreted as a multiple threat of $A$ against $B$. Alternatively, it may be interpreted as if $A$ is proposing 26 points to either $C$ or $D$, indicating no preference between the two. Whatever is the interpretation, since the multi-objection is $H_1$-justified, the bargaining process continues with the dissolution of the Apex coalition, $AB$, until, finally, an Apex coalition is formed in which $A$ gets 48 points.

Any of the following three events disconfirms the two bargaining process models: (i) an unstable tentative coalition not followed at least once by a justified objection, (ii) a justified objection which is ignored, i.e., does not dissolve the tentative coalition to which it is addressed, and (iii) an unjustified objection which is accepted, resulting in a new tentative coalition. The protocols of the 48 games (which appear in Horowitz, 1971) show that each of these violations occurred. With regard to the first event mentioned above, analysis of the protocols shows that of 25 $M_1$-unstable tentative coalitions that were formed, 17 were followed at least once by $M_1$-justified objections but 8 were not. Of 77 $H_1$-unstable tentative coalitions that were formed, 59 were followed by $H_1$-justified objections, but 18 were not.

A frequency analysis of objections in Apex games warrants a distinction among three types of objections: Apex against Base, Base against Apex, and Base against Base. Clearly, when an Apex coalition is tentatively formed, Apex against Base or Base against Apex types of objections may be expressed. If a Base coalition is tentatively formed, only a Base against Base type of objection may be stated.

Regardless of the type of objection, and consistent with the assumptions of the bargaining process models leading to $M_1$ and $H_1$, two cases were distinguished in the classification of the objections presented in Table 6. The first is when players stated only unjustified objections to a given tentative coalition, indicated by $UJ$ in Table 6. The second case is when at least one of the stated objections to a tentative coalition was justified, indicated by $J$. In the former case, the unjustified objections were classified as either accepted or ignored, depending on whether one of them dissolved the tentative coalition or not. The same classification was maintained in the latter case, depending on whether one of the justified objections dissolved the tentative coalition or not.

The two bargaining process models leading to $M_1$ or to $H_1$ may be compared to each other only when the stated objection is of the type "Apex against Base." The two models yield the same predictions when a "Base against Apex" or "Base against Base" objection is stated. Table 6 shows that there were no cases where a player stated an $M_1$-justified "Apex against Base" objection. Of the 69 tentative coalitions for which all

*Table 6.  Frequencies of tentative coalitions followed by unjustified objections only, or by at least one justified objection*

| Who against whom | Objection status | | Objection accepted | Objection ignored |
|---|---|---|---|---|
| Apex against Base | $M_1$ | Only *UJ* | 19 | 50 |
| | | At least one *J* | 0 | 0 |
| | $H_1$ | Only *UJ* | 2 | 25 |
| | | At least one *J* | 16 | 26 |
| Base against Apex | $M_1$ and $H_1$ | Only *UJ* | 7 | 40 |
| | | At least one *J* | 6 | 7 |
| Base against Base | $M_1$ and $H_1$ | Only *UJ* | 9 | 2 |
| | | At least one *J* | 4 | 0 |
| Total | $M_1$ | Only *UJ* | 35 | 92 |
| | | At least one *J* | 10 | 7 |
| | $H_1$ | Only *UJ* | 18 | 67 |
| | | At least one *J* | 26 | 33 |

objections were $M_1$-unjustified, in 50 cases the objections were ignored.  The results for model $H_1$ were even more impressive.  Of the 27 tentative coalitions, in 25 cases the unjustified objections were ignored.  However, of the 42 coalitions against which players expressed $M_1$-unjustified but $H_1$-justified objections, only 16 coalitions were dissolved.  These 16 objections will be discussed in more detail below.  The order of communication significant effect that was found above is reflected in the finding that 13 of these 16 cases occurred in condition $O_1$ and only 3 in condition $O_2$.  And conversely, of the 26 objections that were ignored, thus discounting the bargaining process model leading to $H_1$, only 7 occurred in condition $O_1$ and 19 in condition $O_2$.

A frequency analysis of "Base against Apex" objections shows that of the 13 cases in which players expressed at least one justified objection, only six were accepted.  Of the 47 tentative coalitions against which all the objections made were unjustified, the objections were ignored in 40 cases.  There were seven cases where the Base dissolved the Apex coalition in favor of the Base coalition for an unequal apportionment of its value.  In five of these seven cases the Base disruptor ended as a loser.

There were only 15 tentative coalitions followed by "Base against Base" objections, 13 of which were dissolved. Recalling that the Base coalition was ratified in only three of 48 games, the high percentage of accepted objections provides additional evidence to the instability of the Base coalition. The latter was dissolved by almost any objection, whether justified or not. It is worth noting the relationship between the "Base against Base" objections that were accepted and winning or losing the game. Six of the 9 Base players who dissolved the Base coalition through an unjustified objection ended as losers, whereas all 4 players who dissolved it through a justified objection ended as Base winners.

The frequencies of objections that were either accepted or ignored, summed over the three types, are presented in the lower part of Table 6. The frequencies are shown separately for the two bargaining process models. The null hypothesis of no interaction between the two factors of each table was rejected ($\chi^2 = 5.44$, $p < 0.02$, for model $M_1$, and $\chi^2 = 7.56$, $p < 0.01$, for model $H_1$). Inspection of the frequency tables shows that for both models, when a player had only unjustified objections, an objection was about three times more likely to be ignored than accepted. When he had both justified and unjustified objections, a justified objection was stated and accepted in only approximately half of the cases.

As stated above, there were 16 $M_1$-unjustified but $H_1$-justified "Apex against Base" objections dissolving the tentative coalitions, nine in condition $N_2$ and seven in condition $N_1$. These are portrayed in Figure 2. The bottom axis in each of the two halves of the figure shows the payoff to the Base player in the coalition that was dissolved. The middle axis shows the Base's payoff in the dissolving objections, and the top axis displays the payoffs to Base in the ratified coalitions. Note that in some cases more dissolutions occurred between the middle and top levels. The general pattern of results displayed in Figure 2 indicates that Apex's dissolving objections reduced the large range of payoffs to Base in the tentative Apex coalitions (practically the whole continuum of $M_1$) to a considerably smaller range around $H_1$. Three of the four games in which objections resulted in Base payoffs outside $M_1$ ended in $M_1$ as a result of later disruptions.

## Discussion

### FINAL OUTCOMES

The final outcomes of the Apex games strongly support the bargaining set model; 45 of the 48 final outcomes were included in $M_1$. As noted earlier, for the characteristic functions presented in Table 1, $M_1$ comprises an interval of p.c.'s rather than a unique solution. One may hold the view that stronger predictions, constituting subsets of $M_1$, are not possible, since extra–game–theoretical considerations such as "standards of behavior" in groups of college students, the nature of the communication channels, or the "bargaining abilities" of the players determine particular outcomes within $M_1$. Von Neumann and Morgenstern (1947) presented a similar argument in defending their "solution". But if one is dissatisfied with the multitude of solutions in $M_1$ and wishes to achieve a higher level of predictability, alternative models should be investigated.

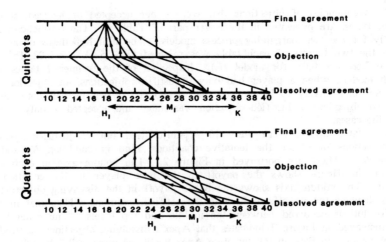

*Figure 2.* *Dissolutions of tentative agreements as a result of $M_1$-unjustified but $H_1$-justified "Apex against Base" objections, in terms of Base's payoff.*

Both the competitive bargaining set and the kernel models predict unique payoff vectors for Apex games, the extreme points of $M_1$. The present experiment was designed to make the range between the two extreme points sufficiently large to allow statistical tests of the models even when the number of groups is relatively small. The final outcomes, however, were unambiguous, requiring no sophisticated statistical analysis of the data. Fourteen of the 48 final outcomes were included in $H_1$ for both group size conditions, whereas its distance from $K$ was approximately five to eight times larger. The analysis of variance results, however, showed that the success of the competitive bargaining set in accounting for final outcomes depended upon the group size and order of communication. Whereas the final outcomes of the quartet games in condition $O_1$ and those of quintet games for both conditions of order of communication supported $H_1$ relative to $K$ and most of $M_1$, the final outcomes of the quartet games in condition $O_2$ were approximately uniformly distributed within $M_1$.

In addition to the competitive bargaining set model, the final outcomes support any other model which makes identical predictions. There is at least one such model. Horowitz (1973) has shown that for Apex games the von Neumann and Morgenstern's main simple solution is identical to what he has called the non-trivial payoff vectors in $H_1$. The final outcomes, therefore, formally support the main simple solution to the extent that they support $H_1$.

Yet, even though both models predict the same final outcomes, they differ from each other in two ways. First, while the competitive bargaining set yields for each winning coalition in the Apex game a unique payoff vector, the main simple solution is only one of a large number of solutions, each of which containing an infinite number of imputations. A second, not less important distinction between the two theories concerns the development of a dynamic theory for the bargaining process. Stearns (1967) as well as the present study present convergence schemes leading to the bargaining sets. These dynamic interpretations of the bargaining set models can be tested by a proper analysis of the bargaining process. No such analysis seems feasible for the static theory of von Neumann and Morgenstern.

EFFECTS OF INDEPENDENT VARIABLES

From the four factors that were manipulated in the experiment, the group size and order of communication emerged as the most prominent factors. Run effects were only noted when Apex's initial offers were analyzed, whereas the value of the Apex coalition significantly affected behavior in none of the analyses we have conducted. Factors $N$ and $O$, besides significantly affecting the final outcomes, also affected the Base's bargaining behavior at the outset of the game. Since only two group size conditions were run, the results are presently not generalizable beyond $n = 5$. They suggest, however, that the larger the $n$ the less cohesive are the Base players on the first round of negotiations in Apex games. This hypothesis is testable in other experiments in which $n > 5$. The results also suggest that when $n$ is small, cohesion among the Base players increases if, rather than letting the Apex player attempt to form an Apex coalition, the communication rules present the Base players with the opportunity to briefly negotiate with one another before the Apex's intervention.

The importance of group size and order of communication is supported by two additional statistical tests, not reported above and unrelated to the final outcomes. Two 2×2×2×2 analyses of variance, employing a multivariate approach as before, were conducted on (i) the total number of messages sent during each game, and (ii) the number of tentative coalitions formed in each game. The only significant effects in both tests were again attributable to $N$, $O$, or their interaction.

The following picture emerges, then, regarding the bargaining behavior of the players. If the Apex player communicates first when $n = 4$, he controls the game during the first phase of the experiment, making negotiations among the Base players very unlikely. But if the Apex communicates last, after the Base players, the latter are more likely to communicate with one another, thus exerting moderate pressure on the Apex, who, in turn, responds by initiating or accepting a less favorable share to insure the formation of the Apex coalition. Since almost all the first tentative coalitions were formed on the first two rounds of negotiations, and more than half of them were later ratified, presumably because the penalty for dissolving a tentative coalition was high, Apex's mean final outcome did not differ significantly from his mean demand in condition $O_1$, but was significantly smaller in condition $O_2$. Increasing the number of Base players from three to four almost completely prevented cooperation among the Base players, thus decreasing the likelihood of the formation of the Base coalition. Hence, when $n = 5$, the order of communication did not affect the initial orientation of the players and, consequently, the final outcomes.

With respect to Base's behavior, the following very simple policy seems to enhance his chances to win. When Apex's initial offer to him is high relative to what he could obtain from a symmetric apportionment of the value of the Base coalition, the Base should counter-offer demanding less for himself. Otherwise, he should accept Apex's offer immediately, and remain in coalition with the Apex until ratification. The analysis of the bargaining process showed that most of the Base players who dissolved a tentative coalition with an unjustified objection ended as losers. Hence, Base's best policy is to adhere to the prescriptions of the two bargaining process models, which are the same for his bargaining behavior.

THE BARGAINING PROCESS

The only data directly reflecting the bargaining process consisted of the messages typed and transmitted by the subjects. Such data provide only occasional glimpses of the bargaining process, partly because the experimental design allowed the players to communicate with only a small set of legal messages, and, more importantly, because the threats, counter-threats, promises, and other, more subtle, negotiation moves that the players might have considered, could not be reflected in the messages they sent. Additional information about the bargaining process may, perhaps, be obtained by requiring the players during the game to state the reasons for their moves and explain in as much detail as possible their thought processes. The talking aloud procedure, which has been proved useful in some problem solving studies, may provide equally fruitful information in bargaining studies.

Notwithstanding the limitations of the analysis, the results supported the two bargaining process models. In particular, the analysis showed that whether a tentative coalition was dissolved by an objection depended on whether the objection was justified. Additionally, this dependence was affected by the type of the objection. Both models were supported when the objector possessed only unjustified objections, unless the objection was of the type "Base against Base". The support given to the bargaining process leading to $H_1$ is particularly impressive since, it may be recalled, $H_1$ consists of only a single $p.c.$.

Both models of the bargaining process suffer from several deficiencies. The first weakness concerns the proposed test, which, if answered negatively, leads to ratification (see Figure 1). To perform this test, the players are supposed to search for justified objections against $X$. Although the set of objections they are assumed to consider is finite, it may be very large, making an effective search unfeasible. To allow for an effective search, the set of objections considered by each player should be restricted. A second, more serious weakness, is that the *'distance'* of $(x; X)$ from $M_1$ (or $H_1$) does not affect its dissolution by a justified objection. A more reasonable model would require the dissolution of the tentative coalition $X$ by a justified objection $Y$ to be probabilistically rather than deterministically determined, with the probability of dissolution increasing monotonically as the '*distance*' of $(x; X)$ from $M_1$ (or $H_1$) increases.

## COMPARISONS WITH PREVIOUS STUDIES

The results of the present experiment may be compared to results obtained in two other experiments that employed Apex games. Maschler (1965) employed two Apex games among several three- and four-person games in characteristic function form played by Israeli high school students. The first, Game I, was defined by the characteristic function $v(AB) = v(AC) = v(AD) = v(BC) = v(BD) = v(CD) = 50,$ $v(BCD) = 111,$ and $v(X) = 0$ for any other coalition $X$. The second, Game II, was like Game I, with the only difference being that $v(BCD) = 120$. Each of the two games was played once by each of five different quartets of players. As in the present study, the Base coalition, $BCD$, was formed in only one of 10 cases. In eight of the nine cases that the Apex coalition was formed, the final outcome was included in $M_1$ but never in $K$ or $H_1$. The predicted payoffs for Game I in $M_1$, $K$, and $H_1$ for the Base winner were $37 \leq x_\beta \leq 43$, $x_\beta = 43$, and $x_\beta = 37$, respectively. The respective predictions for Game II are $40 \leq x_\beta \leq 47.5$, $x_\beta = 47.5$, and $x_\beta = 40$. The final outcomes for the Base winner were 38, 40, 40, 40, and 45 for Game *I*, and 41, 41, 45, and 45 for Game II.

In an experiment conducted by Selten and Schuster (1968), 12 groups of five subjects each played a five-person game with the characteristic function $v(AB) = v(AC) = v(AD) = v(AE) = v(ABC) = v(ABD) = v(ABE) = v(ACD) = v(ACE) = v(ADE) = v(ABCD) = v(ABCE) = v(ABDE) = v(ACDE) = v(ABCDE) = v(BCDE) =$ DM 40, where DM 40 equals approximately \$10. The Base coalition was formed in two of 12 cases. A two-person Apex coalition was formed in eight of 12 cases, yielding the Base winner the payoffs 12, 15, 15, 15, 15, 15, 20, and 22. The predictions of $M_1$, $K$, and $H_1$ are $10 \leq x_\beta \leq 20$, $x_\beta = 20$, and $x_\beta = 10$, respectively. The median payoff, 15, fell in the middle of $M_1$. In one game a coalition among the Apex and three Base players was formed, and in another game coalition $ABCDE$ was formed for an equal split of its value.

All three experiments were designed to test the bargaining set and kernel models. The final outcomes clearly support the former model and reject the latter. Another common finding is the rarity of the Base coalition. This finding is of interest, because it seems to refute the widespread conviction, as well as the predictions of some social psychological theories, that the weak Base players are likely to unite against the strong Apex player instead of the other way around.

With regard to a comparison between $M_1$ and its extreme point $H_1$, the results of the three studies are less consistent. Whereas most of the final outcomes in the present study were distributed in one half of $M_1$, with an average very close to $H_1$, the final outcomes of the quartet games in condition $O_2$ and those of the experiments by Maschler (1965) and Selten and Schuster (1968) were distributed over the entire set of solutions comprising $M_1$, with an average very close to its middle. Because of the differences among the studies in the values of the characteristic functions, the experimental designs, and the nationality and the age of the subjects, the discrepancy between the final outcomes may be attributed to a variety of factors. In particular, and as suggested before, the discrepancy between the central tendencies of the final outcomes of the three studies in comparison to $M_1$ may be attributed to the difference among the studies in the form of communication. Whereas Maschler as well as Selten and Schuster allowed free, face to face negotiations, the present experiment limited the communication to a small preselected set of formal messages without allowing the players to see or hear one another or even know the identity of the other players. Face to face contact allows the communication of intentions, gestures, and emotions, thus probably enhancing the salience of social norms of equity, decreasing competitiveness, and increasing the determinateness to form a coalition. The lack of personal contact, on the other hand, might have facilitated competitive tendencies and strengthened the desire for a stronger stability.

This research was supported in part by a PHS Grant No. MH-10006 from the National Institute of mental Health and in part by a University Science Development Program Grant No. GU-2059 from the National Science Foundation given to the L. L. Thurstone Psychometric Laboratory at the University of North Carolina. The authors wish to thank James P. Kahan for developing the *Coalitions* computer program and for many valuable discussions, and Thomas S. Wallsten and Michael Maschler for many helpful suggestions.

## Bibliography

Aumann, R. J. and Maschler, M., "The Bargaining Set for Cooperative Games," in M. Dresher, L. S. Shapley, and A. W. Tucker (eds.), *Advances in Game Theory*, Princeton University Press, Princeton, N. J., 1964.

Davis, M. and Maschler, M., "The Kernel of a Cooperative Game," *Naval Research Logistics Quarterly* 12 (1965) 223-259.

Davis, M. and Maschler, M., "Existence of Stable Payoff Configurations for Cooperative Games," in M. Shubik (*ed.*), *Essays in Mathematical Economics in Honor of O. Morgenstern*, Princeton University Press, Princeton, N. J., 1967.

Horowitz, A. D., *The Competitive Bargaining Set: Development, a Test, and Comparison with the Bargaining Set and Kernel in n-Person Games,* Research Memorandum No. 36, The L. L. Thurstone Psychometric Laboratory, University of North Carolina, 1971.

Horowitz, A. D., "The Competitive Bargaining Set for Cooperative n-Person Games," *Journal of Mathematical Psychology* 10 (1973) 265-289.

Kahan, J. P. and Helwig, R. A., "*A* System of Programs for Computer-Controlled Bargaining Games," *General Systems* 16 (1971) 31-41.

Kahan, J. P. and Rapoport, A., "Test of the Bargaining Set and Kernel Models in Three-person Games," in A. Rapoport (*ed.*), *Game Theory as a Theory of Conflict Resolution*, Reidel, Dordrecht, Holland, 1974.

Luce, R. D. and Raiffa, H., *Games and Decisions: Introduction and Critical Survey*, Wiley, N. Y. 1957.

Maschler, M., *Playing an n-Person Game, an Experiment*, Econometric Research Program. Research Memorandum No. 73, Princeton University, 1965.

Maschler, M., Peleg, B., and Shapley, L. S., *The Kernel and the Nucleolus of a Cooperative Game as Locuses in the Strong &-Core*. RPGTME RM 60, Department of Mathematics, Hebrew University of Jerusalem, May 1970.

von Neumann, J. and Morgenstern, O., *Theory of Games and Economic Behavior*, 2nd ed., Princeton University Press, Princeton, N. J., 1947.

Rapoport, A., *Two-Person Game Theory: The Essential Ideas*, The University of Michigan Press, Ann Arbor, 1966.

Rapoport, A. *n-Person Game Theory: Concepts and Applications*, The University of Michigan Press, Ann Arbor, 1970.

Rapoport, A. "Three- and Four-Person Games," *Comparative Group Studies* 2 (1971) 191-226.

Schelling, T. C., *The Strategy of Conflict*, Harvard University Press, Cambridge, 1960.

Selten, R., and Schuster, K. G., "Psychological Variables and Coalition-Forming Behavior," in K. Borch and J. Mossin (eds.), *Risk and Uncertainty*, Macmillan, London, 1968.

Shapley, L. S., "*A* Value for *n*-Person Games," in H. W. Kuhn and A. W. Tucker (eds.), *Contributions to the Theory of Games*, Vol. II. Princeton University Press, Princeton, N. J., 1953.

Stearns, R. E., *Convergent Transfer Schemes for n-Person games*, General Electric Report No. 67-C-311, Schenectady, N. Y., 1967.

# STANDARDS OF FAIRNESS
# IN 4-PERSON MONOPOLISTIC COOPERATIVE GAMES

**ABSTRACT**: Six quartets of players participated in a sequence of 16 4-person nonconstant-sum characteristic function games in which one player (the monopolist) was necessarily a member of any coalition that could form. The sixteen games were four repetitions each of four game types, arranged in a 2 × 2 design depending on (*i*) whether or not the grand coalition of all four players was allowed to form, and (*ii*) whether or not the monopolist players were symmetric. The outcomes of these games were compared to predictions derived from the $M_1^{(i)}$ bargaining set [Maschler, 1963b], and from a modification of Maschler's [1963a] power model. The results indicated that each quartet established a standard for the range of the monopolist's payoff early in the sequence, and that this standard took on the function of a norm in defining the legitimate bargaining ground for that quartet for the remainder of the sequence. Two quartets' standards were well within the prediction of the bargaining set; one quartet supported the power model. Analysis of the patterns of coalition structure and rudimentary analyses of the bargaining processes indicate that the central concept of standards of fairness underlying the power model is appropriate and timely.

Coalition formation situations presented as games in characteristic function form have attracted the attention of game theorists, resulting in a proliferation of proposed solution concepts. Although no single volume contains a summary of all of these solution concepts, major summaries may be found in e.g. Davis [1970], Luce/Raiffa [1957], Owen [1968], and Rapoport [1970]. Social scientists have received these solution concepts with varying degrees of interest. On the one hand, some social scientists have been content to relegate these theories to the arcane realm of mathematics and to dismiss them as irrelevant to their own experimental research. In contrast to this group is a growing number of scientists who argue that it is the interpretability of an abstract mathematical model or the applicability of the interpreted theory rather than the formal structure that is important, and who have produced a sizeable corpus of coalition formation experiments that attempt to test the predictive power of the mathematical solution concepts.

The bargaining set [Aumann/Maschler] and its variants have enjoyed the focus of attention of social scientists, because they are founded on assumptions that are psychologically meaningful [Kahan/Rapoport, 1974], and because they are applicable to both superadditive and nonsuperadditive characteristic function games. An impressive array of studies can be summoned to examine coalition formation and bargaining from the bargaining set orientation [Albers; Funk; Horowitz; Horowitz/Rapoport; Kahan/Rapoport, 1974, 1977, 1979; Levinsohn/Rapoport; Maschler, 1978; Medlin; Michener/Sakurai/Yuen/Kasen; Michener/Yuen/Ginsberg; Murnighan/Roth; Rapoport/ Kahan, 1976; Rapoport/Kahan/Wallsten; Riker, 1967, 1972; Riker/Zavoina; Selten/ Schuster]. The consensus judgment of these studies is mixed; whereas most of them have supported the bargaining set predictions of payoff disbursements as a good first order approximation, others have shown systematic discrepancies as a function of the structure of relationships among the players and as a function of the communication conditions of the particular experiment.

Maschler[1] [1978] introduced a 3-person game with a very simple structure that provides perhaps the strongest evidence against the uniform validity of the bargaining set. In this game, there is one monopolistic player who may join in coalition with either of two players; they, in turn, must either join with the monopolist or remain out of any coalition. Maschler's data caused him to question whether the value of a coalition is an adequate measure of its power, and led him to propose a new measure of power for coalitions [Maschler, 1963a] based not only on the values to the particular coalitions, but also on the ability of the members of a coalition to block other players from realizing gains. Maschler [1963a] termed this new solution concept the *power model*.

In the present paper, we shall compare the $M_1^{(i)}$ bargaining set with a revision of the power model that ameliorates some of the problems inherent in it. We shall then present an experiment that serves as a prototype of certain monopolistic conflict situations that are of interest to both economists and psychologists. This experiment will provide data for a comparative test of the two models that overcomes some problems inherent in previous comparisons [Maschler, 1978; Michener et al., 1977, 1978]. Editorial limitations on space force us to presume that the reader is generally familiar with game theoretical terminology and the notion of bargaining sets; the references cited in the first paragraph can serve to remedy such a lack of familiarity.

The following games in characteristic function form will serve as useful examples in the argument presenting the power model.

$G1$: $v(12) = 95$, $v(13) = 90$, $v(23) = 65$, $v(1) = v(2) = v(3) = v(123) = 0$.

$G2$: $v(12) = v(13) = 50$, $v(23) = v(1) = v(2) = v(3) = v(123) = 0$.

$G3$: $v(14) = v(24) = v(34) = 62$, $v(124) = v(134) = v(234) = 80$,

$\quad\quad v(1234) = 95$,

$\quad v(1) = v(2) = v(3) = v(4) = v(12) = v(13) = v(23) = v(123) = 0$.

## Maschler's Critical Experiment and the Bargaining Set

The bargaining set $M_1^{(i)}$ [Maschler, 1963b; Peleg] achieves a stability in the allocation of payoffs such that for any two members of a given coalition, every threat by one member against another can be met by a counterthreat by the latter against the former. For example game G1, the bargaining set solution is given by

---

[1]Maschler's paper, although published in 1978, is the first appearance in print of an experiment performed in the early 1960s [Maschler, 1965].

$$
M_1^{(i)} = \left\{ \begin{array}{l} (60,35,\ 0;\ 12,3) \\ (60,\ 0,30;\ 13,2) \\ (\ 0,35,30;\ 1,23) \\ (\ 0,\ 0,\ 0;\ 123) \\ (\ 0,\ 0,\ 0;\ 1,2,3)\ . \end{array} \right.
$$

This solution is arguably and empirically [Kahan/Rapoport, 1974] reasonable. But consider the solution to G2, given by,

$$
M_1^{(i)} = \left\{ \begin{array}{l} (50,\ 0,\ 0;\ 12,3) \\ (50,\ 0,\ 0;\ 13,2) \\ (\ 0,\ 0,\ 0;\ 1,23) \\ (\ 0,\ 0,\ 0;\ 123) \\ (\ 0,\ 0,\ 0;\ 1,2,3)\ . \end{array} \right.
$$

Here, players 2 and 3 are unlikely to be satisfied with zero points, and $M_1^{(i)}$ is neither arguably nor empirically [Maschler, 1978] reasonable.

Maschler [1978] employed game G2 in 13 instances involving different subsets of 38 Israeli high school students as subjects. Players bargained face-to-face, with minimal control over their interaction. Twice, no agreement was formed, and in the remaining 11 plays, player 1's mean payoff was 37.82, as opposed to the $M_1^{(i)}$ prescription of 50. Maschler's informal observations are quite enlightening and merit direct quotation:

> "At first, the games indeed ended in such a way that player 1 received almost 50, giving another player a very small amount....However, as more games were played, some of the weak players realized that it is worthwhile to flip a coin under the condition that the loser would 'go out of the game,' thus 'forcing' a split 25:25 between the winner and player 1. Eventually, player 1 realized that he ought to offer player 2 or player 3 some amount around 12 1/2, in order that the 'coalition' 23 will not form, because 12 1/2 was the expectation for each of the weak players....it appears from the accounts of the players that many were guided by some 'justice' feelings, that the 'right thing to do' in a 2-person game $v(1) = v(2) = 0$, $v(12) = 50$, is to split equally, and on the basis of this knowledge they acted as if the value of the coalition {23} was 25 and not 0 [Maschler, 1963a, p. 9]."

It is easy to verify that if $v(23) = 25$, $v(1) = 25$, and the other values remain as stated in G2, $M_1^{(i)}$ prescribes 37 1/2 points for player 1 in either of his 2-person coalitions.

**The Power Model**

Maschler [1963a] argued that the "power" of a coalition  resides not only in the gains that accrue jointly to the members of the coalition but also in the losses it may inflict on other players by not cooperating with them.   He attempted to capture some of the various notions of the power of a coalition by proposing a power function that would serve as a more adequate representation of the game than would the original characteristic function.   A solution could be derived by translating the characteristic function into the power function, solving the derived game thus determined, and then inverting the solution back to the original characteristic function.   The determination of the power function was embodied in Maschler's term "standards of fairness," which, like the "standards of behavior" of von Neumann/Morgenstern [1947], refers to moral or conventional rules imposed by society or to social norms by which individual players determine or evaluate a particular disbursement of payoffs.

The formidable task of empirically determining standards of fairness and the conditions that affect them has been graciously relegated to the social sciences by both Maschler and von Neumann/Morgenstern.   Previous research has employed two examples of such standards, a "cooperative standard of fairness" based on the principle of equal sharing among negotiating bodies [Maschler, 1978; Michener et al., [1978], and a "Shapley value standard of fairness" in which the Shapley values of the negotiating bodies represent the principle of sharing [Michener et al., 1977].   In the modification of Maschler's [1963a] model presented below, we adopt the cooperative standard for the basis of our calculation, although the Shapley value standard yields identical results.

Generally, a standard of fairness for a game $(N; v)$ may be expressed as a vector valued function

$$\phi([P]) = \{\phi_1([P]), \phi_2([P]),...,\phi_t([P])\},$$

defined for each partition $P = (P_1, P_2,...,P_t)$ of $N$ into $t$ negotiation groups $(t \leq n)$.  $P_j$ denotes a negotiation group in the partition $[P]$, and $\phi_j([P])$ designates the payoff to negotiation group $P_j$ in the partition $[P]$ based on a given standard of fairness.   The function $\phi([P])$ is assumed to satisfy two conditions:

$$\phi_j([P]) \geq v(P_j), \; j = 1, \, ..., \, t,$$

$$\phi_1([P]) + \phi_2([P]) + ... + \phi_t([P]) = v(N).$$

The first condition simply states that a negotiation group will refuse to obtain less than its value if the negotiation group is a coalition in G.   The second condition claims that the maximum joint reward $v(N)$ is the amount to be shared by all the t negotiation groups that form.   Finally, the pair $(N; \phi([P]))$, where $N$ is the set of players as before and $\phi([P])$ is a standard of fairness, is called the *game space*.

The implicit requirement that the grand coalition's value $v(N)$ be the largest in the game deserves comment.   It is often the case in experimental games that the grand coalition technically cannot form, in that the experimenter does not permit an explicit agreement among all of the players on how to divide their joint winnings.   In such cases, for all purposes of calculation of the game space, $v(N)$ is taken as the maximum of the various other coalitions.   We note here that even when the grand coalition is explicitly prohibited by the experimenter's rules of the game, researchers [e.g., Maschler, 1978; Riker, 1972] have recorded striking examples of how subjects transform the situation in which they find themselves into a game permitting the grand coalition.

Although Maschler [1963a] permitted all possible partitions of players to be considered in constructing the game space, we have simplified the procedure by specifying that, for any negotiation group $S$ that forms, its complement will form to negotiate against it.   This modification greatly reduces the number of partitions that may be considered, and makes the power model more reasonable from the point of view of cognitive constraints about information processing on the part of human players.   The modification also alleviates a conceptual problem arising in the original formulation as to the nature of side payments both within and across coalitional boundaries.   Table 1 presents the game space and the cooperative standard of fairness for game G3, which is employed in the present experiment.   Instead of the 15 partitions that a full partition function would require, we need only consider eight possible breakdowns into coalition structures.   Note that the cooperative standard of fairness assumes that the grand coalition will form, and that the two negotiation groups split the surplus over their individual coalition values equally.

Table 1.   Characteristic function, game space, and power function for game G3.

---

$v(14) = v(24) = v(34) = 62,\ v(124) = v(134) = v(234) = 80,\ v(1234) = 95,$
$v(1) = v(2) = v(3) = v(4) = v(12) = v(13) = v(23) = v(123) = 0$

| Game space | Cooperative standard of fairness | |
|---|---|---|
| {12, 34} | $\phi_{12} = 16.5,$ | $\phi_{34} = 78.5$ |
| {13, 24} | $\phi_{13} = 16.5,$ | $\phi_{24} = 78.5$ |
| {14, 23} | $\phi_{14} = 78.5,$ | $\phi_{23} = 16.5$ |
| {1, 234} | $\phi_1 = 7.5,$ | $\phi_{234} = 87.5$ |
| {2, 134} | $\phi_2 = 7.5,$ | $\phi_{134} = 87.5$ |
| {3, 124} | $\phi_3 = 7.5,$ | $\phi_{124} = 87.5$ |
| {4, 123} | $\phi_4 = 47.5$ | $\phi_{123} = 47.5$ |
| {1234} | $\phi_{1234} = 95$ | |

$u(1) = u(2) = u(3) = 7.5,\ u(4) = 47.5,\ u(12) = u(13) = u(23) = 16.5,$
$u(14) = u(24) = u(34) = 78.5,\ u(123) = 47.5,\ u(124) = u(134) = u(234) = 87.5,$
$u(1234) = 95$

---

The results of the cooperative standard of fairness may be read directly to produce a power function for game G3, which we denote by $u$, and show in the bottom of Table 1. Directly following Maschler [1963a], we would now find the bargaining set for the derived game expressed by $(N;u)$. But Maschler's model implicitly assumes that the grand coalition will always form, while experimental studies of coalition formation have clearly demonstrated that subjects do not always maximize joint reward; systematic differences in the propensity to maximize joint payoff as a function of the characteristic function $v$ have been shown in 3-person games both with [Medlin], and without [Levinsohn/Rapoport] grand coalitions. Even in Maschler's [1978] experiment, where the communication conditions strongly favored joint reward maximization, 19% of the games that could terminate with a single $(n - 1)$-person coalition did not maximize joint reward.

There are various tactics available to accommodate this difficulty. For example, the difference between the sum of the payoffs to the members of a coalition $S$ prescribed by the solution, given by $u(S)$, and its actual value, $v(S)$, could be considered as a loss shared equally among the members of the coalition. However, Maschler[2] has proposed a more elegant resolution to this difficulty, developing a modification of the power model that maintains its central idea that the game is played in terms of the power function while acknowledging that the players within any coalition structure are rewarded according to the original characteristic function of the game. Like $M_1^{(i)}$, this modification retains solutions for coalition structures and no longer requires group rationality. We present this model immediately below.

Assume that the outcome of a game is an individually rational payoff configuration (PC) that satisfies the two requirements of $M_1^{(i)}$,

$$x_i \geq v(i), \quad \text{for all } i \in N,$$

$$\sum_{i \in B_j} x_i = v(B_j) \quad \text{for every } B_j \in B, \quad j = 1, 2, \ldots, m.$$

The *power bargaining set* $M^P$ is then defined as the set of all PCs satisfying these requirements, such that for all $B_j \in B$, and all distinct players $k, l \in B_j$, for every objection of $k$ against $l$ in $(N;u)$, there is a counterobjection of $l$ against $k$ in $(N;u)$. Objections and counterobjections are defined as in $M_1^{(i)}$ in Aumann/Maschler [1964]. That is, although the original PC is in $(N;v)$, the objections and counterobjections are in $(N;u)$.

The power bargaining set $M^P$ is based on the idea that players negotiate as if the value of each coalition $S$ is $u(S)$. However, if a coalition structure $B$ is formed, there is a reality barrier in the form of $v(B_j)$, which constrains the members of the coalition $B_j$

---

[2]Maschler, in a careful, lengthy review of an earlier draft of this paper, provided the $M^P$ model as his resolution of the difficulty presented above. To our knowledge, he has not yet formally published this variation on the power bargaining set.

from jointly gaining more than this value while in this coalition structure. Thus, $M^P$ may be interpreted as a procedure for reaching stability in dividing the real values $v(B_j)$ for each $B_j \in \underline{B}$ by basing objections and counterobjections, but not payoffs, on the players' perceived game $(N;u)$.

Assuming that $u(123) = \max \{v(12), v(13), v(23)\}$, the reduced power function for game G1 is given by $u(1) = 15$, $u(2) = 2\ 1/2$, $u(3) = 0$, $u(12) = 95$, $u(13) = 92\ 1/2$, $u(23) = 80$, and $u(123) = 95$.

The power bargaining set for this game is:

$$
M^P = \left\{
\begin{array}{lccl}
53\frac{3}{4}, & 41\frac{1}{4}, & 0\ ; & 12,3 \\[4pt]
52\frac{1}{2}, & 0\ , & 37\frac{1}{2}; & 13,2 \\[4pt]
0\ , & 33\frac{3}{4}, & 31\frac{1}{4}; & 23,1 \\[4pt]
0\ , & 0\ , & 0\ ; & 1,2,3 \\[4pt]
0\ , & 0\ , & 0\ ; & 123\ .
\end{array}
\right\}
$$

The corresponding operations for game G2 yield the reduced power function: $u(1) = 25$, $u(2) = u(3) = 0$, $u(12) = u(13) = 50$, $u(23) = 25$, and $u(123) = 50$.

This produces the power bargaining set

$$
M^P = \left\{
\begin{array}{lccl}
37\frac{1}{2}, & 12\frac{1}{2}, & 0\ ; & 12,3 \\[4pt]
37\frac{1}{2}, & 0\ , & 12\frac{1}{2}; & 13,2 \\[4pt]
0\ , & 0\ , & 0\ ; & 23,1 \\[4pt]
0\ , & 0\ , & 0\ ; & 1,2,3 \\[4pt]
0\ , & 0\ , & 0\ ; & 123.
\end{array}
\right\}
$$

It is interesting to note that $M^P$ agrees better with Maschler's [1978] informal analysis of G2, which motivated the power model, than his original proposal [Maschler, 1963a], and even is in better agreement with his data.

## Method

### SUBJECTS

Subjects were 24 male volunteers, mostly undergraduate students at the University of North Carolina at Chapel Hill, who were recruited via posters placed around campus advertising cash to be earned by participation in a multi-session coalition formation and bargaining experiment.   Subjects were sorted randomly (within the constraints of time of volunteering) into six quartets; close friends were not allowed to participate in the same quartet.   Volunteers with previous experience in computer-controlled coalition formation experiments were not allowed to participate, although those who had been in other computer-controlled experiments for monetary gain were accepted.

## PROCEDURE

Subjects played 16 successive characteristic function games in a computer-controlled experimental procedure called *Coalitions*.   As *Coalitions* has been repeatedly described in a variety of publications [Kahan/Helwig; Kahan/Rapoport, 1974; Rapoport/Kahan, 1974], we shall not repeat it here.   Very briefly, the game consists of a three-stage process: a negotiation stage, in which the potentials of various coalitions may be explored, an acceptance stage, in which a particular PC is seriously considered, and a ratification stage, in which the agreement on a division of coalitions' values within a given coalitional structure becomes binding.   Messages are typed and the game protocols remain available throughout the game.   Communication among the players takes place through the use of the following keywords: *offer, accept, reject, pass, solo,* and *ratify*.   All communications are transmitted to all players except *offers,* which may instead be sent secretly to selected players involved in a proposed coalition, at the option of their authors.   Ratification of a PC cannot occur until two rounds of communication, which amount to eight messages, have taken place in its acceptance stage.

At the beginning of the experiment, subjects in each quartet were gathered together for a three hour practice session of written and verbal instructions of how to play the *Coalitions* game.   Following the instructions and a question and answer period, subjects participated in three or four characteristic function practice games to acquaint them with the teletypewriters, the nature of the messages and keywords, and various tactics of bargaining.   For this experimenter-supervised training session, subjects were paid $4.50 each.

Several days later, quartets returned individually for three experimental sessions, each lasting approximately three hours, spaced from two to seven days apart.   Within this period, each quartet played each of four different games four times, for a total of 16 games per quartet.   Although players participated as a unified quartet for all 16 games, the actual identity of the other players within any game was not known, as role identification letters $(A, B, C, D)$ were shifted between successive games within and between sessions.

## EXPERIMENTAL GAMES

Four different 4-person games were played in a $2 \times 2$ design.   The characteristic functions of these four games are presented in Table 2.   All four games share an important property, namely, that any coalition of two or more players must include player $D$.   Player $D$ assumes, therefore, the role of a monopolist; he may veto any PC offered by $A$, $B$, or $C$ except the trivial case of all players in their 1-person coalitions. The two factors of the design are symmetry of the weak players' $(A, B, C)$ payoffs and superadditivity vs. non superadditivity.   Thus, games I and II are symmetric and III and

*Table 2.  Characteristic functions for four games**

| Game | v(DA) | v(DB) | v(DC) | v(DAB) | v(DAC) | v(DBC) | v(DABC) |
|------|-------|-------|-------|--------|--------|--------|---------|
| I    | 62    | 62    | 62    | 80     | 80     | 80     | 0       |
| II   | 62    | 62    | 62    | 80     | 80     | 80     | 95      |
| III  | 54    | 62    | 70    | 69     | 77     | 85     | 0       |
| IV   | 54    | 62    | 70    | 69     | 77     | 85     | 90      |

*$v(A) = v(B) = v(C) = v(D) = v(AB) = v(AC) = v(BC) = v(ABC) = 0$ for each game.

IV are not; games II and IV are superadditive, whereas I and III are not.

The 16 games were played in the following order by each quartet: II, I, IV, III, I, II, III, IV, III, IV, I, II, IV, III, II, I.  Five to seven games were played within a session, depending on the time spent per game.  In all cases, the monopolist communicated in each round after all three weak players (i.e., A, B, C, D, A,...).

In addition to the \$4.50 earned at the practice session, subjects were paid according to the number of points they accumulated, at the rate of 5 cents per point.  No other payment was provided.  In accordance with agreements made with the subjects at the beginning of the experiment, no earnings were paid until the entire experiment terminated.  The mean and standard deviation of payoff per subject for the experimental games were \$16.87 and \$1.41, respectively.

## Results

Presentation of the results of the experiment will first be oriented directly at the different predictions of the $M_1^{(i)}$ and $M^P$ models, and then shall turn to such features as coalition frequencies and bargaining processes in an attempt to cast light on the paths by which various outcomes might be obtained.

A COMPARISON OF MODELS

Table 3 presents the $M_1^{(i)}$ prescriptions for the experimental games.  The prescriptions for 2- and 3-person coalition outcomes are not affected by the presence of non-zero 4-person coalition values, so games types I and II, and III and IV are collapsed for economy of space.  Note that the addition of the grand coalition creates a wide span in the $M_1^{(i)}$ prescribed range for player D's payoffs, if this coalition is the outcome; the payoff range corresponds exactly with the core, and its low boundary (from player D's point of view) coincides with the kernel [Davis/Maschler] solution.

Table 4 presents the $M^P$ solutions for the reduced power function for all four game types separately. A comparison of Tables 3 and 4 shows that the range of outcomes in the solution $M^P$ is small for each coalition structure, while the corresponding ranges for $M_1^{(i)}$ are either point predictions or rather large spans. The reduced power model generally produces, as expected, a more egalitarian prediction than the bargaining set model.

*Table 3. $M_1^i$ payoff configurations for all four game types*

### Game Types I and II

| | | | | |
|---|---|---|---|---|
| 0, | 0, | 0, | 62; | AD,B,C |
| 0, | 0, | 0, | 62; | BD,A,C |
| 0, | 0, | 0, | 62; | CD,A,B |
| 0, | 0, | 0, | 80; | ABD,C |
| 0, | 0, | 0, | 80; | ACD,B |
| 0, | 0, | 0, | 80; | BCD,A |
| $0 \leq x \leq 15,$ | $0 \leq y \leq 15,$ | $0 \leq z \leq 15,$ | $50 \leq w \leq 95;$ | ABCD[1] |
| 0, | 0, | 0, | 0; | A,B,C,D |

### Game Types III and IV

| | | | | |
|---|---|---|---|---|
| 0, | 0, | 0, | 54; | AD,B,C |
| 0, | 0. | 0, | 62; | BD,A,C |
| 0, | 0, | 70 – w, | $69 \leq w \leq 70;$ | CD,A,B |
| 0, | 0, | 0, | 69 | ABD,C |
| 0, | 0, | 77 – w, | $69 \leq w \leq 77;$ | ACD, B |
| 0, | $0 \leq y \leq 8,$ | $0 \leq z \leq 16,$ | $61 \leq w \leq 85;$ | BCD, A[2] |
| $0 \leq x \leq 5,$ | $0 \leq y \leq 13,$ | $0 \leq z \leq 21,$ | $51 \leq w \leq 90;$ | ABCD[3] |
| 0, | 0, | 0, | 0; | A,B,C,D |

[1]For game type II only; we require that x + y + z + w = 95.
[2]Such that y + z + w = 85.
[3]For game type IV only; we require that x + y + z + w = 90.

In moving from predicted to actual outcomes, some difficulties present themselves. First, for the $M_1^{(i)}$ solution, some players are assigned zero points while in coalition, an outcome that appears realistically infeasible. The point of the bargaining set argument is that players can be forced to the limit of zero; in any play of the game, the "costs" of entering into the coalition would certainly be taken into consideration. Second, the predictions of the models are typically small ranges in the real numbers, whereas the players actually bargained in integer values, and showed a pronounced tendency to think in units of five points. Third, if a player withdrew from the game via a *solo* move, the prescriptions of the models for the remaining players were changed from those presented in Tables 3 and 4.

Each of these difficulties was accommodated in considering the accuracy of the $M_1^{(i)}$ and $M^P$ models. First, if a player's prescribed outcome for a given game was zero, any outcome to him of five or fewer points was regarded as supporting the model. In this instance, even if such a five point payoff reduced another player's outcome below prescription, the model was counted as supported. Second, the prescribed ranges for all players were extended both downwards and upwards to the nearest integer evenly divisible by five, and any outcome giving all of the players in the coalition outcomes within their extended ranges was counted as supporting the model. It is important to note with respect to this adjustment that we are not extending the ranges in the service of a theoretical adjustment such as Riker's [1967] point-shaving, but rather as an accommodation to a consistent and easily understood cognitive simplification in arithmetic that virtually all experimentally played games have shown. This is why all players must be within their prescribed ranges, instead of all but one of them. Third, if a player chose *solo* and there was subsequent bargaining among the remaining players (as occurred 16 times out of 96 games), the revised prescriptions of the models were calculated, and judgments of support or nonsupport were made on these additional calculations; space precludes their presentation here. With these three adjustments, then, the outcomes of all 96 games could be compared with the prescriptions of the $M_1^{(i)}$ and $M^P$ models.

Table 5 presents the outcomes of the 96 plays of the four game types, classified by iteration and by quartet. The 16 games in which a player departed the game before a coalition was affirmed are indicated by footnotes. The most striking feature of Table 5 is the non-independence of the games; the within-quartet variance for the outcome to the monopolist player $D$ is quite small, whereas the between-quartet variance for that value is quite large. Thus, the consistent finding of previous work with *Coalitions* [Kahan/Rapoport, 1974, 1977; Rapoport/Kahan, 1976; Rapoport et al., 1978] that players encounter each game as a separate task independent of its predecessors is clearly contradicted in the present case. Moreover, the actual game type appears to have little effect on the payoff to the monopolist. This is not to say that game type was completely ignored. In the two superadditive games II and IV, the 4-person outcome was frequently chosen. More importantly, in the two symmetric games I and II, out of 46 outcomes with payoffs to two or more nonmonopolist players, 37 were equal divisions. For the two nonsymmetric games III and IV, the corresponding figures are 11 equal divisions in 39 games. In all 28 cases of unequal payoffs, the player with the stronger position vis à vis the characteristic function received the higher payoff.

*Table 4.* $M^P$ payoff configurations for the derived games $(N; u)$.

**Game Type I**

| | | | | |
|---|---|---|---|---|
| $7\frac{1}{3} \leq x \leq 11$, | 0, | 0, | $62 - x$; | AD,B,C |
| 0, | $7\frac{1}{3} \leq x \leq 11$, | 0, | $62 - x$; | BD,A,C |
| 0, | 0, | $7\frac{1}{3} \leq x \leq 11$, | $62 - x$; | CD,A,B |
| $11.6 \leq x \leq 12\frac{1}{4}$, | $x$, | 0, | $80 - 2x$; | ABD,C |
| $11.6 \leq x \leq 12\frac{1}{4}$, | 0, | $x$, | $80 - 2x$; | ACD,B |
| 0, | $11.6 \leq x \leq 12\frac{1}{4}$, | $x$, | $80 - 2x$; | BCD,A |
| 0, | 0, | 0, | 0; | A,B,C,D |

**Game Type II**

| | | | | |
|---|---|---|---|---|
| $4\frac{5}{6} \leq x \leq 11$, | 0, | 0, | $62 - x$; | AD,B,C |
| 0, | $4\frac{5}{6} \leq x \leq 11$, | 0, | $62 - x$; | BD,A,C |
| 0, | 0, | $7\frac{5}{6} \leq x \leq 11$, | $62 - x$; | CD,A,B |
| $10.1 \leq x \leq 12\frac{1}{4}$, | $x$, | 0, | $80 - 2x$; | ABD,C |
| $10.1 \leq x \leq 12\frac{1}{4}$, | 0, | $x$, | $80 - 2x$; | ACD,B |
| 0, | $10.1 \leq x \leq 12\frac{1}{4}$, | $x$, | $80 - 2x$; | BCD,A |
| $11.5 \leq x \leq 12.8$, | $x$, | $x$, | $95 - 3x$; | ABCD |
| 0, | 0, | 0, | 0; | A,B,C,D |

**Game Type III**

| | | | | |
|---|---|---|---|---|
| $0 \leq x \leq 5\frac{3}{4}$, | 0, | 0, | $54 - x$; | AD,B,C |
| 0, | $6\frac{1}{2} \leq x \leq 11\frac{3}{4}$, | 0, | $62 - x$; | BD,A,C |
| 0, | 0, | $13\frac{1}{6} \leq x \leq 17\frac{3}{4}$, | $70 - x$; | CD,A,B |
| $4.3 \leq x \leq 6.5$, | $x + 4$, | 0, | $65 - 2x$; | ABD,C |
| $5.9 \leq x \leq 7.5$, | 0, | $x + 8$, | $69 - 2x$; | ACD,B |
| 0, | $11.5 \leq x \leq 12.5$, | $x + 4$, | $81 - 2x$; | BCD,A |
| 0, | 0, | 0, | 0; | A,B,C,D |

**Game Type IV**

| | | | | |
|---|---|---|---|---|
| $0 \leq x \leq 5\frac{3}{4}$, | 0, | 0, | $54 - x$; | AD,B,C |
| 0, | $5\frac{2}{3} \leq x \leq 11\frac{3}{4}$, | 0, | $62 - x$; | BD,A,C |
| 0, | 0, | $12\frac{1}{3} \leq x \leq 17\frac{3}{4}$, | $70 - x$; | CD,A,B |
| $3.8 \leq x \leq 6.5$, | $x + 4$, | 0, | $65 - 2x$; | ABD,C |
| $5.4 \leq x \leq 7.5$, | 0, | $x + 8$, | $69 - 2x$; | ACD,B |
| 0, | $12.5 \leq x \leq 15$, | $x + 4$, | $81 - 2x$; | BCD,A |
| $6\frac{3}{7} \leq x \leq 7.8$, | $x + 4$, | $x + 8$, | $78 - 3x$; | ABCD |
| 0, | 0, | 0, | 0; | A,B,C,D |

Table 5. Outcomes by game type, iteration, and quartet

| Game/Iteration | Quartet 1 A | B | C | D | Quartet 2 A | B | C | D | Quartet 3 A | B | C | D | Quartet 4 A | B | C | D | Quartet 5 A | B | C | D | Quartet 6 A | B | C | D |
|---|---|---|---|---|---|---|---|---|---|---|---|---|---|---|---|---|---|---|---|---|---|---|---|---|
| I 1 | | 25 | | 37 | 5 | | 11 | 64 | 6 | | 9 | 65 | 15 | 15 | 15 | 50[3] | 12 | | 12 | 56[2] | | 8 | 8 | 64 |
| 2 | 18 | 18 | | 44 | 8 | 8 | | 64 | 10 | | 10 | 60 | | 17 | 15 | 48 | 5 | | 4 | 72 | 1 | 1 | | 78 |
| 3 | 11 | 12 | | 57 | 8 | 8 | 8 | 64 | 7 | 7 | 5 | 68 | 18 | 18 | 20 | 44[3] | | 5 | 5 | 70[3] | | 4 | 4 | 72[1] |
| 4 | 15 | | 10 | 55 | 5 | 5 | 5 | 70 | 6 | | | 67 | 20 | 20 | | 40[2] | | 5 | 5 | 70 | | 1 | 1 | 78 |
| II 1 | 22 | 22 | 22 | 29 | 9 | | 9 | 62 | 10 | 10 | 10 | 65 | 17 | 17 | 17 | 44 | 16 | 16 | 16 | 47 | 5 | 10 | 10 | 60 |
| 2 | | | 15 | 47 | | 11 | 11 | 58 | 10 | 10 | 10 | 65 | 15 | 15 | 15 | 50 | 7 | 7 | 7 | 74 | 6 | 5 | 5 | 80 |
| 3 | 15 | 15 | 15 | 50 | 11 | 11 | 13 | 60 | 10 | 10 | 10 | 65 | 15 | 15 | 15 | 50 | 6 | 6 | 6 | 77 | 5 | 6 | 6 | 77 |
| 4 | 15 | 15 | 15 | 50 | 10 | 10 | 10 | 65 | 10 | 10 | 10 | 65 | 15 | 15 | 15 | 50 | 8 | 8 | 8 | 71 | 5 | 6 | 4 | 80 |
| III 1 | | | 25 | 45 | | 10 | 10 | 65 | 5 | 5 | 15 | 65 | 15 | 15 | 25 | 45[1] | | 8 | 8 | 69[1] | | 9 | 9 | 67[1] |
| 2 | | | 20 | 50 | | 10 | 15 | 55 | 5 | 5 | 15 | 65 | | | 25 | 45[3] | | 4 | 8 | 73 | | 4 | 5 | 77 |
| 3 | | | 15 | 55 | | 12 | 14 | 59 | 5 | 5 | 15 | 65 | | 20 | 25 | 40[1] | | 4 | 8 | 73 | | 5 | 5 | 75 |
| 4 | | 15 | 18 | 52 | 8 | 8 | 12 | 65 | 10 | 10 | 10 | 65 | 4 | | | 50 | 27 | | 8 | 27[4] | | 4 | 7 | 74[1] |
| IV 1 | | | 30 | 40 | 5 | 15 | 15 | 55 | 5 | | 11 | 59 | 10 | 25 | 25 | 35[1] | 7 | 7 | 7 | 69 | 5 | 11 | 11 | 63[1] |
| 2 | 7 | | 18 | 52 | 8 | 10 | 10 | 62 | 5 | 10 | 10 | 65 | 10 | 12 | 18 | 50 | 4 | 4 | 6 | 76 | | 5 | 5 | 75 |
| 3 | | | 20 | 50 | 8 | 12 | 12 | 60 | 5 | 10 | 10 | 65 | 10 | 12 | 18 | 50 | 4 | 5 | 7 | 74 | | 5 | 6 | 74[1] |
| 4 | 10 | 15 | 15 | 50 | 5 | 7 | 13 | 65 | 5 | 10 | 10 | 65 | 10 | 14 | 18 | 48 | 3 | 5 | 8 | 74 | 2 | 5 | 5 | 78 |

[1] Following a solo by player A
[2] Following a solo by player B
[3] Following a solo by player C
[4] Following a solo by players B and C

The high incidence of identical solutions for a game, particularly in quartets 3 and 4, indicates that each quartet separately arrived at a standard range for an allocation to the monopolist, and then played the game within that standard. Results presented later will attempt to investigate the nature of those standards. But first, a comparison of $M_1^{(i)}$ and $M^P$ is in order. Table 6 presents a breakdown of the outcomes for each game and quartet separately according to whether either or both of the models were supported by the outcomes. Overall, 58% of the outcomes supported $M_1^{(i)}$, while 38% supported $M^P$. More than twice as many outcomes supported $M_1^{(i)}$ but not $M^P$ than vice-versa, but because of the nonindependence of games, such results cannot be accepted on face value. A look at the results by game type in Table 6 reveals that for type I and II, without grand coalitions, the power model suffered with respect to the bargaining set model, but for the superadditive games type II and IV, the two models fare about equally well.

*Table 6. A comparison of the $M_1^{(i)}$ and $M^P$ predictions, by game type and by quartet*

| | Neither model supported | Both models supported | $M_1^{(i)}$ alone supported | $M^P$ alone supported | $M_1^{(i)}$ supported | $M^P$ supported |
|---|---|---|---|---|---|---|
| All games | 22 | 18 | 38 | 18 | 56 | 36 |
| Game type I | 10 | 1 | 10 | 3 | 11 | 4 |
| Game type II | 4 | 11 | 6 | 3 | 17 | 14 |
| Game type III | 4 | 2 | 14 | 4 | 16 | 6 |
| Game type IV | 4 | 4 | 8 | 8 | 12 | 12 |
| Quartet 1 | 6 | 2 | 0 | 8 | 2 | 10 |
| Quartet 2 | 5 | 3 | 4 | 4 | 7 | 7 |
| Quartet 3 | 3 | 7 | 4 | 2 | 11 | 9 |
| Quartet 4 | 5 | 5 | 3 | 3 | 8 | 8 |
| Quartet 5 | 2 | 1 | 13 | 0 | 14 | 1 |
| Quartet 6 | 1 | 0 | 14 | 1 | 14 | 1 |

Two of the six quartets (numbers 5 and 6) showed substantial support for $M_1^{(i)}$. In these two quartets, the monopolist was able to extract his full value (according to the bargaining set) on nearly every trial. Additionally, quartet 3 supported $M_1^{(i)}$, but the range of payoff was such that it also supported $M^P$: in seven of the 16 games, the outcome was in the supporting range of both models. Quartet 4 also supported each model equally often, although less frequently than quartet 3. Quartet 2 similarly supported both models equally, but an examination of Table 5 for this quartet shows that $M_1^{(i)}$ would have been more supported except that when the grand coalition formed, the weakest player received about 8 points rather than the model's limit of 5. Finally, quartet 1 provides the strongest support for $M^P$ to the exclusion of $M_1^{(i)}$; the outcomes to the monopolist were the lowest in this quartet.

These results mildly but certainly not conclusively favor $M_1^{(i)}$ over $M^P$. Most of the outcomes for the superadditive games type II and IV were 4-person coalitions, in which the range of the bargaining set is four to five times the range of the power model; just by chance more outcomes favorable to the bargaining set will occur in these instances. But the effect of this large range should not necessarily discount the favorability of the bargaining set. The characteristic functions for all four game types produced about the same range for the monopolist payoffs for the power model, and defined a similar interval for non-4-person coalitions in the bargaining set into which fell almost all the outcomes of quartets 3, 5, and 6. In a sense, then, the part of the monopolist's predicted range that was appropriate for nonsuperadditive games was the useful range for the superadditive games as well, and this part of the range was not larger than the range prescribed by the power model.

Finally, we note that other power models [Maschler, 1963a] were also tested, but none fared better than $M^P$.

COALITION FREQUENCIES

The principal question in examining coalition structures is how often a Pareto optimal coalition structure obtained. Pareto optimality required the formation of the grand coalition in game types II and IV, coalition BCD in game type III, and any of the possible 3-person coalitions in game type I. Over all 96 games, the Pareto optimal coalition structure occurred 78 times. The 18 counterinstances were distributed evenly over quartets except for quartet 1, who formed 8 of them. For the remaining five quartets, there were from one to three non-Pareto optimal coalitions. If we exclude the 16 games with *solo*, then 67 of the 80 games ended in a Pareto optimal coalition structure, with 8 of the 13 deviants in quartet 1. Thus, overall, Pareto optimality was achieved.

DIFFERENCES AMONG QUARTETS

In the present experiment, as well as in previous experiments employing the *Coalitions* program, deliberate and elaborate attempts were made to achieve independence between successive games. The entire sequence of 16 games was broken into three separate sessions, the identity of the players was kept secret, and role assignment changed according to a balanced experimental design over games. Moreover, players were specifically instructed to play each game independently of the results of previous games. Whereas this experimental manipulation achieved its goal in the previous experiments, Table 5 clearly shows its failure in the present instance. Further light on this difference among quartets is shown in Figure 1, where the outcomes to the monopolist player D are displayed in order of the 16 games played, ignoring game type and iteration categorizations.

Inspection of Figure 1 shows three classes of quartets, one consisting of quartets 1 and 4, a second of quartets 2 and 3, and the third of quartets 5 and 6. After the third game played by the quartets, there is only one overlap in player D's payoff among these

three classes, and that is the single instance of two players choosing *solo*, leaving players
A and D to divide 54 points equally.   Overall, there was an increase for all six quartets
in the payoff to player D over the first four games, after which a norm was established
which, within a range of only a few points, contained player D's payoff for the
remaining 12 games.

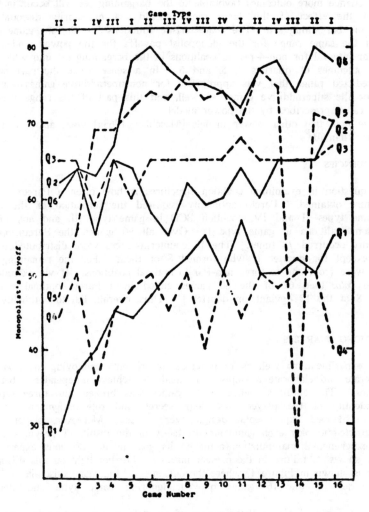

*Figure 1.*

BARGAINING ANALYSES

The observation of striking quartet differences, where each quartet achieved its own consistent mode of solving the game, indicates the need for analysis of the path by which the outcomes were achieved. To this end, the individual protocols of each game, as recorded by the computer, were examined in an *ad hoc* fashion, using constructed indicators suggested by the quartet differences in outcomes.

Although there were a considerable number of times that a quartet would come to an outcome identical to a previous one for a given game this did not mean that all of the negotiations were done in the first iteration through the four game types. Indeed, as is typically the case, later games did proceed more quickly, with means of 41.58, 35.38, 30.38, and 27.88 messages per game for iterations one through four, respectively. However, even this last value is more than twice the minimum of 12 messages needed for the play of a game. Only in quartet 3 could it be legitimately said that the outcome was virtually determined at the beginning of a game. The range of outcomes that each quartet considered legitimate for the monopolist player $D$ was typically not just one point; furthermore, particularly in the nonsuperadditive game types I and III, the outcomes to the nonmonopolist players could be heavily contested.

One very useful bargaining indicator was how Pareto optimality was achieved, when it did occur. For this analysis, each game was assigned to one of four mutually exclusive categories based on how or if Pareto optimality was arrived at. The four categories were: $N$ (Not Pareto): Pareto optimality not achieved; $I$ (Immediate): Pareto optimal coalition formed by ratification of an offer made on the first round of bargaining; $P$ (Pareto only): Only the Pareto optimal coalition that was formed was considered by those players that did eventually form it; and $B$ (Bargained): Other coalitions than the one that eventually formed were offered and accepted during the course of the game.

Table 7 presents the incidence of these four categories collapsed over the 16 games, for each quartet separately. From the incidence data, a bargaining index of the proportion of pareto optimal coalitions in category $B$ is shown, and is compared to the mean payoff for player $D$ in Pareto optimal games (last row of Table 7). The coefficient of correlation between this index and this mean is $r = -0.99$, indicating that the more coalitions other than the Pareto optimal one were considered, the lower was the payoff to player $D$. It is particularly interesting to note that the most active bargaining, in the sense of different coalition structures considered, occurred in the two quartets 1 and 4, which least supported the bargaining set model; only in more egalitarian PCs is there room for players to make offers and counteroffers against each other. For game type I, about two-thirds of the Pareto optimal coalitions were bargained; this ratio was reversed for the other three game types. This finding is not surprising in view of the fact that in game type I, three coalitions were equivalently Pareto optimal, as compared to a single coalition in the remaining game types.

The second bargaining analysis attempts to examine the first games played in order to trace the development of the norms demonstrated in Figure 1. Because there were only six quartets, a formal analysis of bargaining style is impossible. This section should be regarded as suggestive of both what occurred in the present experiment and of what could grow to be an analytical method of studying bargaining processes. Quartets will be considered individually with respect to their bargaining on the first four games.

*Table 7. Paths of Pareto optimal outcomes, by quartet.*

|                        |       |       | Quartet |       |       |       | over    |
| Category               | 1     | 2     | 3       | 4     | 5     | 6     | quartet |
| --- | --- | --- | --- | --- | --- | --- | --- |
| Not Pareto             | 8     | 2     | 1       | 3     | 1     | 1     | 18      |
| Immediate              | 2     | 4     | 5       | 2     | 2     | 2     | 17      |
| Pareto only            | 1     | 4     | 4       | 3     | 9     | 8     | 29      |
| Bargained              | 5     | 6     | 6       | 8     | 4     | 3     | 32      |
| $B/(B + I + P)$        | 0.62  | 0.43  | 0.40    | 0.62  | 0.27  | 0.23  | 0.41    |
| Mean payoff to         |       |       |         |       |       |       |         |
| $D$ in Pareto          |       |       |         |       |       |       |         |
| optimal Coalitions     | 48.38 | 62.36 | 65.00   | 46.85 | 69.97 | 75.00 | 62.36   |

Quartet 1 provides the only clear example of a coalition of the three nonmonopolist players against player $D$.   The first game started out with a sequence of accepted 2-person offers, each one giving player $D$ a few points more than the previous one. However, first player $A$, then $B$ and $C$, came to insist on the PC (22, 22, 22, 29; $ABCD$), and player $D$ bowed to their pressure.   Player $D$ only tried once more for a high payoff on game 3, when again reference by player $C$ to a coalition of the whole against him forced him down.   Thus, in this quartet, there appears to have developed a low payoff for the monopolist because of the union of the other players against him.   Maschler's [1978] argument is clearly manifest for this quartet.

Quartet 4, the other quartet with low payoffs for player $D$, arrived at this outcome by a different method.   In the first round, player $D$ was very passive, and eventually settled for 47 points.   In the second round, a new player $D$ was about to ratify a 3-person PC giving him 63 points when the player not in the coalition played *solo*.   The other two players immediately re-negotiated the coalition to 50 points for player $D$.   A nearly identical sequential process occurred in the next two rounds, and by then the low norm of 45–50 for player $D$ had been accepted.   In any future game, if a player $D$ tried to get more points, one of the other players chose *solo*, causing a re-negotiation.   Thus, the monopolist was held in line by the emphatic refusal of one of the other players to participate further in the escalation of the monopolist's payoffs.   Whether this move was seen as a warning of other *solo* moves in the game or not can only be conjectured; what is known is that for this quartet, the *solo* did reduce player $D$'s payoff every time.

Quartets 2 and 3 were characterized by smooth bargaining among the parties resulting in a compromise in the range of 60 (for quartet 2) or 65 (for quartet 3).   For quartet 3, the point solution of 65 for player $D$ was established on the first round of the game, and held for 11 of the remaining rounds.   Attempts at deviation from this norm were met by solid opposition from the remaining players; player $D$ only got fewer points if he did not seek his 65 points (the same player twice), or more when the other three could not agree on how to split the remainder (two games). Quartet 2, unlike all the others, showed a suggestion of an overall increase in player $D$'s gains over all 16 rounds; the other players did not unite against him at any time, and his payoff limit was apparently only set by his own interpretation of an appropriate payoff.

Quartets 5 and 6 were characterized by player $D$ setting a high value for himself, and then holding to it, insisting that the other players do more towards meeting his requests than he to meeting theirs. Although *solo* moves did occur in these games, they did not have the effect they had for quartet 4. Both these quartets were characterized by a round of repeated identical offers with no concessions, until one and then more players gave in to most of the demand of player $D$. When the nonmonopolist objected to the monopolist, he apparently did not feel the complaints to be justified.

Thus, through this decidedly informally scrutiny of the bargaining, there appears to be a breakdown of types of bargaining process that corresponds to the low, middle, and high payoffs to player $D$ demonstrated in Figure 1. Quartets adopting low norms were characterized in the early bargaining by the nonmonopolist not conceding to the demands of the monopolist, albeit by various methods. Quartets adopting the middle norms were characterized by a traditional pattern of bargaining, where all parties gave reciprocal concessions. Finally, quartets adopting high norms were characterized by the monopolist insisting on, and eventually gaining, the amounts he wanted. Again, this analysis is based on the first four rounds played; typically later rounds had incorporated the norms, and bargaining proceeded more quickly to a solution in what the particular quartet had defined as its appropriate range of payoffs; players would steadfastly hold against encroachments of this range, whether by the monopolist or a nonmonopolist.

## Discussion

The major finding of the present study is that the variations in game type took second place to the search for a norm for the monopolist's payoff that was idiosyncratic to the individual quartets who participated in the game. That is, early in the sequence of games, the players established a standard range of payoff for the monopolist, and this standard, plus the game type, served as the framework for their negotiations in the remaining games. Characteristics of the performance of the players that give clues as to the genesis of the monopolist's standard range come form the relationship of the outcomes (expressed as PCs) to the $M_1^{(i)}$ and $M^P$ prescriptions, the incidence of Pareto optimal coalitions, and the characteristics of the bargaining leading to the outcomes of the earlier games in the sequence. The discussion will elaborate on each of these characteristics.

The bargaining set $M_1^{(i)}$ was supported by 56 of the 96 games played; more importantly, two of the quartets had 14 of 16 games in the bargaining set, while a third had 11 of 16 games in the prescribed range. Moreover, the support for the bargaining set comes form the upper range of monopolist payoffs in its solution space. Although this support corresponds to previous findings [Kahan/Rapoport, 1977, 1978; Rapoport/Kahan, 1967; Rapoport et. al, 1978], the fact that only half of the groups supported $M_1^{(i)}$ must be taken into consideration. These nonconfirmatory quartets should not be cause to reject the bargaining set, however. They were characterized by normative ranges for the monopolist that gave the nonmonopolists some "bargaining room" in which to negotiate among each other and with the monopolist. In other words, for these quartets, there was room for the use of coalitions other than a single Pareto optimal one to make claims and counter-claims in the sense of objection and counter-objection used in the bargaining set. The result that the lower the payoff to the monopolist, the more games ended in a Pareto optimal outcome bargained from many alternative outcomes (Table 7) supports this argument. In other words, for quartets with norms that accord the monopolist a high outcome, there are no coalitions available for use as objections, while for quartets assigning the monopolist a lower outcome norm, objecting coalitions may be found.

This line of reasoning supports the sense, if not the substance, of Maschler's [1963a] reasoning leading to $M^P$. The central idea of the establishment of "standards of fairness" is correct, but in the absence of compelling extraneous conditions, a consistent standard over groups does not materialize. Each quartet rapidly generated its own "standard of fairness," which for some was the objective standard leading to $M_1^{(i)}$, but for others was different.

Still, there is the difference between Maschler's [1978] and the present findings to reconcile. An obvious conjecture as to a source of this difference is the difference between Maschler's communication conditions and those of the present experiment. Here, yet a third experiment with monopolists in which communication was specifically manipulated can be of assistance. Murnighan/Roth [1977] used a 3-person monopolist game in which $v(12) = v(13) = 100$, $v(S) = 0$, otherwise, in which the payoffs were either public or secret, offers were either public or secret, and messages were either forbidden, secret, or public. As they used no monetary or other extrinsic incentive to maximize points, a direct comparison to either Maschler or the present experiment is impossible. Murnighan/Roth did find that there was a relationship between openness and flexibility of communication and payoff that in general was in the direction of more equitable payoffs with more open communication, but this relationship was not monotonic for their six communication conditions. The most striking result they bring to bear on this issue is that, in their terminal three trials, games with messages allowed (whether secret or public) ended with the monopolist receiving an average of 56 points, while games without messages yielded the monopolist an average of 76 points. Here, the more restrictive communications support the power model, but, again, the incentives are not clear. The larger point, that the presence or absence of open communications does make a difference, however, is clearly established, and calls for further study of this factor in bargaining.

With only six quartets to examine, a true analysis of how different norms for the monopolist's payoffs arise cannot be ascertained; there is an indication that, however they are obtained, they rapidly take on the status of group norms, and define the reasonable bargaining range within which each game would be separately negotiated. It is both true and trivial to say that individual personality differences determine a large part of the establishment of such norms; our scrutiny of the bargaining protocols indicates that, for example, the quality of stubbornness might well be advantageous to a monopolist. When the nonmonopolists were united and steadfast, they could win their case against all but the most stubborn of monopolists.

That the standard of fairness for the present quartets was largely centered on the payoff of the monopolist can be attributed to two causes, one structural, and one artifactual. In the construction of the four game types, one basic game was used, and so the actual characteristic functions of the games were so similar that a common point value to the monopolist serves as a very convenient orientation that will facilitate bargaining in all four game types. In retrospect, modifying the characteristic functions of the individual game types slightly would have made interpretation of the norms easier. Even given this artifact, though, the necessity of the monopolist makes it logical that his payoff should be central to the negotiations, and the other allocations secondary. In apex games, where the weak players may form a coalition in the absence of the strong player, the structure dictates a central role to their payoffs in that weak coalition, against which the strong player must focus his attention. Experimental results from apex games [Horowitz/Rapoport; Kahan/Rapoport, 1979; Rapoport et al., 1978] show that this structural logic is followed by bargainers.

The conclusions that may be drawn form the present results are of course limited. Future experiments that employ more groups and investigate a wider range of payoffs will cast more light on the types of solutions and paths of bargaining that are mandated by negotiation situations where one party holds the lion's share of the power. But our results are strongly supportive of Maschler's [1963a] conclusion that the power of a coalition lies not only in its characteristic function, but also in what the members of the coalition can do by *not* entering into coalitions. We have evidence that the definition of that true power will vary as a function of features other than the characteristic function itself; future experiments must therefore scrutinize bargaining processes as well as outcomes.

Research reported in this paper was supported by National Science Foundation Grant BNS76-84285. This paper was written while both authors were Fellows-in-Residence at the Netherlands Institute for Advanced Study in the Humanities and Social Sciences. We wish to thank S. G. Funk and A. D. Horowitz for their assistance in data collection and analysis. We wish to particularly thank Michael Maschler, with whom we have had a long and lively interaction on the power model, for his many helpful comments and suggestions for improving the paper.

## References

Albers, W.: Bloc forming tendencies as characteristics of the bargaining behavior in different versions of apex games. Beiträge zür experimentellen Wirtschaftsforschung. Ed. by H. Sauermann. Vol. VII, Tübingen 1978.

Aumann, R. J., and M. Maschler: The bargaining set for cooperative games. Advances in game theory. Ed. by M. Dresher, L. S. Shapley and A. W. Tucker. Princeton 1964.

Davis, M.: Game theory: A nontechnical introduction. New York 1970.

Davis, M., and M. Maschler: The kernel of a cooperative game. Naval Research Logistics Quarterly 12, 1965, 223-259.

Funk, S. G.: Value power and positional power in n-person games. L.L. Thurstone Psychometric Laboratory Report No. 152, Chapel Hill, 1970.

Horowitz, A. D.:   A test of the core, bargaining set, kernel, and Shapley models in n-person quota games with one weak player.   Theory and decision **8**, 1977, 49-65.

Horowitz, A. D., and Am. Rapoport:   Test of the kernel and two bargaining set models in four- and five-person games.   Game theory as a theory of conflict resolution. Ed. by An. Rapoport. Dordrecht, 1974.

Kahan, J. P., and R. A. Helwig:   Coalitions:   A system of programs for computer-controlled bargaining games.   General Systems **16**, 1971, 31-41.

Kahan, J. P., and Am. Rapoport:   Test of the bargaining set and kernel models in three-person games.   Game theory as a theory of conflict resolution.   Ed. by An. Rapoport. Dordrecht, 1974.

:When you don't need to join:   The effects of guaranteed payoffs on bargaining in three person cooperative games.   Theory and Decision **8**, 1977, 97-126.

:The influence of structural relationships on bargaining in 4-person apex games. European Journal of Social Psychology **9**, 1979, 339-361.

Levinsohn, J. R., and Am. Rapoport:   Coalition formation in multistage three-person cooperative games.   Beiträge zür experimentellen Wirtschaftsforschung. Ed. by H. Sauermann. Vol. VII, Tübingen 1978.

Luce, R. D., and H. Raiffa:   Games and decisions:   Introduction and critical survey. New York 1957.

Maschler, M.:   The power of a coalition.   Management Science **10**, 1963a, 8-29.

:n-Person games with only 1, n - 1, and n-person permissible coalitions.   Journal of Mathematical Analysis and Applications, **6**, 1963b, 230-256.

:Playing an n-person game:   An experiment.   Princeton:   Economic Research Program, Research Memorandum No. 73, Princeton 1965.

:Playing an N-person game:   An experiment.   Beiträge zur experimentellen Wirtschaftsforschung. Ed. by H. Sauermann. Vol. VII, Tübingen 1978.

Medlin, S. M.:   Effects on grand coalition payoffs on coalition formation in 3-person games.   Behavioral Science **21**, 1976, 48-61.

Michener, H. A., M. M. Sakurai, K. Yuen, and T. J. Kasen:   A competitive test of the $M_1^{(i)}$ and $M_1^{(im)}$ bargaining set solutions in three-person conflicts.   Journal of Conflict Resolution **23**, 1979, 102-119.

Michener, H. A. K. Yuen, and I. J. Ginsberg:   A competitive test of the $M_1^{(im)}$ bargaining set, kernel, and equal share models.   Behavioral Science **22**, 1977, 341-355.

Murnighan, J. K, and A. E. Roth:   The effects of communication and information availability in an experimental study of a three-person game.   Management Science **23**, 1977, 1336-1348.

Owen, G.:   Game theory.   Philadelphia, 1968.

Peleg. B.:   Existence theorem for the bargaining set $M_1^{(i)}$.   Essays in mathematical economics in honor of Oskar Morgenstern.   Princeton, 1967.

Rapoport, Am., and J. P. Kahan:   Computer controlled research on bargaining and coalition formation.   Behavior Research Methods and Instrumentation **6**, 1974, 87-93.

:When three isn't always two against one:   Coalitions in experimental three-person games.   Journal of Experimental Social Psychology **12**, 1976, 253-273.

Rapoport, Am., J. P. Kahan, and T. S. Wallsten: Sources of power in 4-person apex games. Beiträge zür experimentellen Wirtschaftsforschung. Ed. by H. Sauermann. Vol. VIII. Tübingen, 1978.

Rapoport, An.: n-person game theory: Concepts and applications. Ann Arbor, Michigan, 1970.

Riker, W. H.: Bargaining in a three-person game. American Political Science Review 61, 1967, 642-656.

:Three-person coalitions in three-person games: Experimental verification of the theory of games. Mathematical Applications in Political Science VI. Ed. by J. F. Herndon and J. L. Bernd. Charlottesville 1972.

Riker, W. H., and W. J. Zavoina: Rational behavior in politics: Evidence from a three-person game. American Political Science Review 64, 1970, 48-60.

Schelling. T. C.: The strategy of conflict. Cambridge, 1960.

Selten. R., and K. G. Schuster: Psychological variables and coalition forming behavior. Risk and Uncertainty.. Ed. by K. Borch and D. Mossin. London, 1968.

von Neumann J., and O. Morgenstern: Theory of games and economic behavior, 2nd. ed. Princeton, N.J., 1947.

# CHAPTER 11

# COALITION FORMATION IN THE TRIAD
# WHEN TWO ARE WEAK AND ONE IS STRONG

**ABSTRACT**: Eighteen groups of subjects each participated in five different computer-controlled superadditive 3-person characteristic function games with sidepayments, that modeled negotiable conflicts in which two of the players are weak and one is considerably stronger. Both the degree to which the strong player was powerful and the type of communication were experimentally manipulated. The 90 game outcomes rejected any solution concept that predicts a single payoff vector for a given coalition structure, but supported the recently developed single-parameter α-power model that allows range predictions. Both the degree of power and type of communication were found to affect game outcomes and to determine the predictive power of models that make point predictions in 3-person games.

## Introduction

One of the most interesting cases of coalition formation in the triad, that motivated the early theory and experimentation within social psychology (Caplow, 1968), is when two players are weak and one is considerably stronger. The tasks of the two players is to prevent exploitation by finding a means of achieving solidarity between themselves. Within the "resource weight" experimental paradigm of social psychology, solidarity is easily achieved by merely forming the coalition of the two weak players. However, in the characteristic function representation of a game (e.g., Luce and Raiffa (1957); Rapoport (1970)), the weakness of the two players is reflected in their coalition being of little or zero value, and so other paths to solidarity must be found.

The bargaining set theory (Aumann and Maschler (1964); Maschler (1963b)), which has been central to much of the experimental research on characteristic function games, predicts exploitation of the two weak players. Perhaps because that theory showed early promise in accounting for experimental outcomes, the two weak and one strong case has been largely neglected in 3-person characteristic function game experiments (Kahan and Rapoport (1974, 1977); Medlin (1976); Rapoport and Kahan (1976); Riker (1967, 1971)). However, theoretical advances (Maschler (1963a); Rapoport and Kahan (1979: Note 1)) and preliminary experimental results (Maschler (1978)) have challenged the necessity of low payoffs to the weak players, and therefore systematic investigation of the case of two weak and one strong player in characteristic function games is mandated. The present study explores this case in light of the recently developed α-power model (Rapoport and Kahan (1979; Note 1)) and under two communication conditions that might differentially enhance the ability of the two weak players to manifest their solidarity. But, before proceeding to the experiment, brief expositions of the characteristic function representation as an experimental paradigm and of the α-power model are necessary.

## Games in Characteristic Function Form

The characteristic function is the cornerstone of the mathematical theory of cooperative $n$-person games with sidepayments (Luce and Raiffa (1957); Rapoport (1970); von Neumann and Morgenstern (1947)). About two dozen recent studies have established that it also constitutes a viable experimental paradigm for examining coalition formation bargaining behavior in $n$-person conflicts (Murnighan (1978)). The ideal of the characteristic function is to capture in a single real number the worth of each coalition of players, including 1-person coalitions. Emphasis is placed on coalition payoffs; all questions pertaining to bargaining tactics, information structures, or physical transactions of valuable commodities among coalition members are left aside. In particular, the two related social psychological questions of resource weight allocation and players' abilities to be in different numbers of coalitions become moot, subsumed in the body of the characteristic function.

For a 3-person game, with players labeled $A$, $B$, and $C$, the characteristic function is defined by a real-valued function $v$ on all nonempty subsets $S$ ('coalitions') of the set of players $N = \{A, B, C\}$. $v(S)$ can be interpreted as a measure of a coalitions's worth in terms of the payoff jointly commanded by that coalition against all of the other players in the game. The specification of a 3-person characteristic function game thus resolves itself to the enumeration of seven values:

$v(ABC)$, $v(AB)$, $v(AC)$, $v(BC)$, $v(A)$, $v(B)$, $v(C)$ .

Without loss of generalization, we may assume in the remainder of this discussion that $v(A) = v(B) = v(C) = 0$; i.e., players not in a coalition with other players obtain zero payoffs.

For example, consider a 3-person game given by:

$$G1: \quad v(ABC) = 198, \ v(AB) = 186, \ v(AC) = 18, \ v(BC) = 192 . \tag{1}$$

In this game (henceforth called game G1), if players A and B form a coalition, they have 186 units of reward ('points') to partition between them, while if players $A$ and $C$ form a coalition, they have but 18 points. Players $B$ and $C$ have 192 points to share, and if all three players join together, they have 198 points to allocate amongst themselves.

It is convenient to notate proposed or actual outcomes of 3-person characteristic function games by a *payoff configuration* (PC):

$$(x; \delta) = (x_A, x_B, x_C; S_1, ..., S_m) ,$$

where $x = (x_A, x_B, x_C)$ is a 3-dimensional real vector, called the *payoff vector*, which represents a realizable disbursement of points among the three players, and $\delta$, called the *coalition structure*, is a partition of the three players into $m$ mutually disjoint coalitions ($1 \leq m \leq 3$). For example, if in game G1 players $A$ and $B$ were to consider a 116-70 split of their 186 points (leaving player $C$ with zero), this would be represented by the PC (116, 70, 0; AB, C). Players $A$ and $C$ splitting their 18 points equally is shown by (9, 0, 9; $AC$, $B$), and if all three players split their joint 198 points giving player $B$ 60 points more than each of the others, this is the PC (46, 106, 46; $ABC$). Finally, if no two players can agree on a coalition, this is expressed by the PC (0, 0, 0; $A$, $B$, $C$).

## The Rise and Fall of the Bargaining Sets

Despite the simplicity of the characteristic function representation of $n$-person conflicts, many distinct theories have been built on the same foundation (Luce and Raiffa (1957); Murnighan (1978); Rapoport (1970)). Social scientists using 3-person characteristic function games to experimentally test these theories have concentrated on a particular family of theories called the bargaining sets (Aumann and Maschler (1964)). Each of the various bargaining sets in this family specifies as a solution to payoff allocation in the $n$-person conflict a set of PCs, each element of which is 'stable' in a psychologically interpretable sense of any threat by one player against another within the same coalition being able to be met by a legitimate counterthreat. Since the theoretical foundation and psychological interpretations of the bargaining set theory for 3-person games have been repeatedly set forth, both in mathematically oriented (Aumann and Drèze (1974); Aumann and Maschler (1964); Maschler (1963b)) and social scientifically oriented (Davis (1970); Hamburger (1979); Kahan and Rapoport (1974); Michener, Sakurai, Yuen and Kasen (1979); Rapoport and Kahan (1976); Rapoport (1970); Riker (1967)) publications, we eschew an elaborate presentation.

For he experimental 3-person games employed below, all the various bargaining sets coincide to prescribe the following unique PCs:

$$(q_A, q_B, 0; AB, C), (q_A, 0, q_C; AC, B), (0, q_B, q_C; A, BC),$$

$$(q_A, q_B, q_C; ABC), (0, 0, 0; A, B, C).$$ 
(2)

The values $q_i$ in (2), $i = A, B, C$, are referred to as the *quotas* of the respective players (Maschler (1963b)), and are calculated by solving the following three equation in three unknowns: $q_A + q_B = v(AB)$, $q_A + q_C = v(AC)$, and $q_B + q_C = v(BC)$.

A series of experiments have shown the bargaining sets to have been largely successful in predicting payoff allocations in 3-person games (Kahan and Rapoport (1974); Levinsohn and Rapoport (1978); Medlin (1976); Murnighan and Roth (1977); Rapoport and Kahan (1976); Riker (1967, 1971)). However, other studies have shown that relaxing the requirement that players excluded from coalitions receive zero points (Kahan and Rapoport (1977); Kaufmann and Tack (1975)), altering the nature of the game so that there exist sequential dependencies among the different games played by the same players (Laing and Morrison (1974); Levinsohn and Rapoport (1978)), or employing normal form representations of a game instead of the characteristic function representation (Michener et al. (1979)) result in payoff vectors not conforming to the predictions of the bargaining sets. Nonetheless, the current state of the art has been well summarized by Murnighan (1978, p. 1144), "results from experiments using characteristic function games generally support the predictions of the bargaining set, although this support has not been universal."

One prominent exception to this support for the bargaining set is an early study by Maschler (1978),[1] which concentrated on two games in which one of the three players is an actual or virtual monopolist. These two games, referred to as M1 and M2, respectively, are given by the characteristic functions:

M1:         $v(A) = v(B) = v(C) = v(ABC) = 0$ ,

            $v(AB) = 50, v(BC) = 50, v(AC) = 0$ ;                              (3)

M2:         $v(A) = v(B) = v(C) = v(ABC) = 0$ ,

            $v(AB) = 60, v(BC) = 60, v(AC) = 10$ .                             (4)

It can easily be shown that the bargaining set prediction allocates all 50 points to player $B$ in game M1, and 55 of the 60 points to him in game M2, given that he is in a coalition. However, it seems unlikely that players $A$ and $C$ would be satisfied with their zero payoffs in game M1. Maschler's (1978) study supports this skepticism. In the 13 plays of M1 reported in Maschler (1978), the PC (0, 0, 0; A, B. C) occurred twice, player $B$ obtained 49 of the 50 points on four occasions, equal splits occurred three times, and the remainder of the games were in the range of 30 to 40 points for player $B$. Similar results were obtained in game M2.

Maschler's informal description of the evolution of his players' thought as they played game M1 is instructive:

> "At first, the games indeed ended in such a way that player [$B$] received almost 50, giving another player a very small amount. ...However, as more games were played, some of the weak players realized that it is worthwhile to flip a coin under the condition that the loser would "go out of the game," thus "forcing" a split 25:25 between the winner and player [$B$]. Eventually, player [$B$] realized that he ought to offer player [$A$] or player [$C$] some amount around 12 1/2, in order that the 'coalition' [$AC$] will not form, because 12 1/2 was the expectation for each of the weak players. It appears from the accounts of the players that many were guided by some "justice" feelings, that the "right thing to do" in a 2-person game $v([B]) = v([A]) = 0$, $v([AB]) = 50$, is to split equally, and on the basis of this knowledge they acted as if the value of the coalition [$AC$] was 25 and not 0." (Maschler (1963a, p. 9)).

Maschler (1963a) used these data to develop a generalization of the bargaining set theory in which the power of a coalition $S$ is not simply based on $v(S)$, but is also a function of the ability of its members, by not joining into coalitions with other players, to limit the opportunities of these other players to obtain rewards. He posited that a group playing an $n$-person game develops what he termed a *standard of fairness*, or social norm, based on the relative contribution of the values of coalitions to the power of players, and exhibited two examples of standards of fairness which led to solution concepts whose predictions for games M1 and M2 were near the mean payoffs for those games.

---

[1]Although Maschler (1978) is a recent publication, the data were originally collected in the early 1960's and have been available in prepublication form for about 15 years. In particular, Maschler (1963a) made excellent use of these data in the early development of the theory of bargaining sets.

But an examination of Maschler's (1978) data indicates that no single standard of fairness can account for even a substantial fraction of the individual outcomes; these and other similar games (Rapoport and Kahan (1979)) manifest wide ranges of outcomes, so that no single point prediction is satisfactory.   These findings led Rapoport and Kahan (Note 1) to construct a single-parameter solution concept that predicts a range of payoff vectors for a given coalition structure.   This model, which is sketched below, has the advantage that specific points in its range of prediction may be identified as the point prediction of earlier solution concepts.

## The α-Power Model

Applied to the general 3-person characteristic function game, the α-power model constructs a standard of fairness function $u$ which is defined for all coalitions $S$ as a function of the value of the grand coalition, $v(ABC)$, the coalition value $v(S)$, and the value of the complement of $S$, $v(\bar{S})$, in conjunction with the free parameter $\alpha$.   It is assumed that any coalition's assessment of its own power will not be less than the value it can command by itself, and that the total power in the group equals the value that the grand coalition can command.   In other words,

$$u(S) \geq v(S) , \qquad u(ABC) = v(ABC) ,$$

and

$$u(S) + u(\bar{S}) = v(ABC) , \qquad \text{for all } S \subseteq N .$$

The free parameter $\alpha$ $(0 \leq \alpha \leq 1)$ defines how the two complementary groups will partition their excess of $v(ABC) - v(S) - v(\bar{S})$ in assessing their power. If it is further assumed (Rapoport and Kahan (Note 1)) that the parameter $\alpha$ is independent of which coalition forms, then a standard of fairness function $u$ may be derived as

$$u(AB) = v(AB) + \alpha[v(ABC) - v(AB) - v(C)]; \qquad u(C) = u(ABC) - u(AB);$$

$$u(AC) = v(AC) + \alpha[v(ABC) - v(AC) - v(B)]; \qquad u(B) = u(ABC) - u(AC);$$

$$u(BC) = v(BC) + \alpha[v(ABC) - v(BC) - v(A)]; \qquad u(A) = u(ABC) - u(BC);$$

$$u(ABC) = v(ABC) .$$

$$(5)$$

This standard of fairness function has been proposed as a more adequate representation of the perceived power of the various coalitions than the characteristic function.

Rapoport and Kahan (Note 1) then defined stability in payoff disbursement as a set of PCs in which the differences between a player's payoff $x_i$ and his power $u(i)$ (5) are equal for all members within each coalition $S_j$, $S_j \in \delta$. For the 3-person game, the set of all stable PCs, $P_\alpha$, depends an $\alpha$ and is given by:

$$
\mathbf{P}_\alpha = \begin{cases}
\left[ \dfrac{v(AB) + (1 - \alpha)[v(AC) - v(BC)]}{2} , \dfrac{v(AB) + (1 - \alpha)[v(BC) - v(AC)]}{2} , 0;\ AB,\ C \right] \\[2em]
\left[ \dfrac{v(AC) + (1 - \alpha)[v(AB) - v(BC)]}{2} , 0, \dfrac{v(AC) + (1 - \alpha)[v(BC) - v(AB)]}{2} ;\ AC,\ B \right] \\[2em]
\left[ 0, \dfrac{v(BC) + (1 - \alpha)[v(AB) - v(AC)]}{2} , \dfrac{v(BC) + (1 - \alpha)[v(AC) - v(AB)]}{2} ;\ A,\ BC \right] \\[2em]
\left[ \dfrac{v(ABC) + (1 - \alpha)[v(AB) + v(AC) - 2v(BC)]}{3} , \right. \\[1.5em]
\quad \dfrac{v(ABC) + (1 - \alpha)[v(AB) + v(BC) - 2v(AC)]}{3} , \\[1.5em]
\quad \left. \dfrac{v(ABC) + (1 - \alpha)[v(AC) + v(BC) - 2v(AB)]}{3} ;\ ABC \right] \\[2em]
(0,\ 0,\ 0;\ A,\ B,\ C) .
\end{cases}
\tag{6}
$$

If equation (6) is applied to game G1, some properties of the $\alpha$-power model become manifest.   First, if $\alpha = 0$; then (6) reduces to (2) and is identical to the bargaining sets.   Second, if $\alpha = 1$, then the second term in all the payoffs in (6) reduces to zero, and equal splits are predicted for all coalition structures.   Intermediate values of $\alpha$ result in intermediate locations on a line between the two bargaining set and equality point predictions for each given coalition structure.   For example, $\alpha = 1/2$ results in

$$
P_{0.5}(G1) = \begin{cases}
(49.5,\ 136.5,\ 0;\ AB,\ C) \\
(7.5,\ 0,\ 11.5;\ AC,\ B) \\
(0,\ 139.5,\ 52.5;\ A,\ BC) \\
(36.0,\ 123.0\ 39.0;\ ABC) \\
(0,\ 0,\ 0;\ A,\ B,\ C) .
\end{cases}
$$

The least squares estimates of $\alpha$ for any given PC are given by (Rapoport and Kahan (Note 1)):

$$\hat{\alpha} = \begin{cases} [v(AC) - v(BC) + v(AB) - 2x_A]/[v(AC) - v(BC)], & \text{if coalition } \{AB, C\} \text{ forms,} \\[2mm] [v(AB) - v(BC) + v(AC) - 2x_A]/[v(AB) - v(BC)], & \text{if coalition } \{AC, B\} \text{ forms,} \\[2mm] [v(AB) - v(AC) + v(BC) - 2x_B]/[v(AB) - v(AC)], & \text{if coalition } \{BC, A\} \text{ forms,} \\[2mm] 1 - \displaystyle\sum_{i \in N} x_i K_i / 2K , & \text{if coalition structure } \{ABC\} \text{ forms,} \end{cases} \tag{7}$$

where

and

$$K_i = v(ij) + v(ik) - 2v(jk), \qquad i, j, k \in \{A, B, C\}, i \ne j \ne k,$$

$$K = v(AB) + v(AC) + v(BC) - v(AB)v(AC) - v(AB)v(BC) - v(AC)v(BC).$$

Returning to game G1 as an example, the PC (0, 117, 75; *BC, A*) has a best-fit $\hat{\alpha} = 0.52$. And the grand coalition PC (55, 86, 57; *ABC*) yields $\hat{\alpha} = 0.82$.

## Weak and Strong Players

A convenient index that expresses the power structure within a 3-person characteristic function game is the ratio of the sum of the quotas of the two weak players to the quota of the powerful one. If player *B* is signaled to be the powerful individual, as we have implicitly assumed in all of our examples above, this index is defined as

$$Q = (q_A + q_C)/q_B . \tag{8}$$

The index $Q$ takes on its minimum value if player *B* is a pure monopolist, as in Maschler's game M1, where $Q = 0$. It takes on its maximum value if all three players are equal, i.e, $v(AB) = v(AC) = v(BC)$, in which case $Q = 2$. Between these two extremes, the larger the value of $Q$, the less dominant is the powerful player *B*.

There exists some rudimentary evidence that the accuracy of the bargaining set predictions (2) of the quotas $q_i$ depends on the index $Q$. As mentioned before, the bargaining set was a poor predictor for Maschler's (1978) games, which had indices of $Q = 0$ for game M1 and $Q = 0.18$ for game M2. Additional evidence comes from a 3-person game experiment of Kahan and Rapoport (1974), where overall support was found for the bargaining set. However, in that study, significant game differences were found such that two games with $Q$ values of 1.59 and 1.42 had mean outcomes giving the powerful player more than his quota, while the remaining three games, with $Q$ values of 1.08, 1.05, and 0.66, had mean outcomes giving the powerful player less than his quota. Levinsohn and Rapoport (1978) employed 25 different 3-person characteristic functions in 90 plays, with $Q$ indices ranging from 0.55 to 1.69. For these games, the higher the value of $Q$, the more the most powerful player received relative to his quota ($r$ = +0.50, $p$ < 0.0001). The present study fills the gap in the continuum of $Q$ by systematically examining the outcomes of 3-person games with values of $Q$ of 0.1, 0.2, 0.3, 0.4, and 0.5.

When a game features one powerful player against two considerably weaker ones, the only way that the two weaker players can hope to obtain good outcomes is to indicate to the strong player their solidarity.   As, by definition, $v(AC)$ is low, and forming that coalition is unsatisfactory to players $A$ and $C$ (just as the 1-person coalition $v(B)$ = 0 is unsatisfactory to player $B$), it is likely that the more flexible the communication opportunities, the more easily players $A$ and $C$ will find their common power base that exists outside of the value of their coalition.   Although Kahan and Rapoport (1974) and Rapoport and Kahan (1976) found no evidence of any influence of varying communication conditions, and although Levinsohn and Rapoport's (1978) freer communication conditions still replicated Kahan and Rapoport's (1974) findings for games the two studies had in common, it is quite possible that for games with low values of $Q$, communications make a difference.   Support for this supposition comes from Murnighan and Roth (1977), who played a 3-person game with $Q$ = 0 under varying communications conditions, one allowing and one not mentioning the possibility of informal, unstructured messages.

## Method

### SUBJECTS

Subjects were 72 male and female volunteers, mostly undergraduate students at the university of North Carolina at Chapel Hill, who were recruited via posters placed around campus advertising cash to be earned by participation in multi-session bargaining experiments.   Subjects were gathered randomly (within the constraints of time of volunteering) into 18 quartets, of which half were assigned to one communication condition and half to the other.   The only remaining constraints on participation were that friends could not be in the same quartet and that volunteers having previously participated in coalition formation experiments were refused.

### COALITIONS

The present experiment employed *Coalitions-II*, a successor to our earlier computer-controlled *Coalitions* system, which possesses a wider game vocabulary than its predecessor and is programmed for a PDP-11, a newer and faster computer.   A full description of the new computer program and a comparison of it with the earlier version can be found in Kahan, Coston, Helwig, Rapoport and Wallsten (1976); only a brief description will be presented here.

*Coalitions* defines bargaining as passing through three stages, which loosely correspond to the four stages of bargaining of Thibaut and Kelley (1959).   Our first stage, called the *negotiation stage*, corresponds to Thibaut and kelley's sampling and bargaining phases of the process, where players first learn of the available outcomes and then establish bargaining positions through negotiations and proposals to each other.   The second, or *acceptance stage*, corresponds to Thibaut and Kelley's commitment phase. Players comprising a coalition have agreed in principle upon a particular division (PC) of their joint payoff. Although this agreement is not yet binding, it is sufficiently strong to restrict players' bargaining mobility. Players not in the agreement attempt to disrupt it in favor of a PC more favorable to themselves, while those in the coalition must decide on maintenance of the present agreement versus gambling for a better outcome within or outside of that coalition.. The game passes to the final or *ratification stage*, which corresponds to Thibaut and Kelley's institutionalization phase, when an accepted PC, having survived for a certain length of time, is voted into ratification by its members, and becomes the outcome of the game. If all members of the coalition vote in favor of ratification, the game terminates and each player is given his payoff as prescribed by the ratified PC.

Subjects communicate to each other by transmitting messages coded in keywords via teletypewriters connected to a PDP-11/45. The computer checks the legality of the messages, reformats them to be easily readable, adds messages informing players of the effects of the present move on previous moves in the game, and transmits the entire package to its intended recipients. The keywords used by *Coalitions-II* and their effects, as well as the implications of being in the acceptance stage (called "All-accepted" in the figure) are presented in Fig. 1. With only minor alterations, this figure comprised the chart of keywords which is always available to the subjects.

PROCEDURE

Each of the 18 quartets was introduced to the experimental apparatus and rules of the game in a 3-hour training session consisting of written instruction, verbal elaborations, and three separate experimenter-guided practice games. For this familiarization session, players were paid $4.50 each. In two or three subsequent sessions, spaced from two to seven days apart, players participated in eight 4-person and five 3-person games. The 4-person games were of a different game structure than the 3-person games reported here, and address different, albeit similar, theoretical issues. The five 3-person games reported here were the third, fifth, seventh, tenth, and twelfth in the series of 13. Although players participated as unified quartets, role assignments were randomly varied from game to game so that individual identification of co-players was impossible. For the five 3-person games, one of the four players of the quartet had the role of "observer," which means that he observed the play of the game, but could not participate himself. Each member of the quartet was observer once, with one member observing twice. The technique of randomly shifting roles and employing observers has repeatedly (Kahan and Rapoport (1974, 1977); Rapoport and Kahan (1976)) resulted in experimental series whose individual games within groups are independently and separately negotiated.

COMMUNICATIONS

Each quartet employed one of two communication conditions throughout all of its games. In group R (remarks), the keyword *remark* (see Figs. 1 and 2) was permitted, and subjects could send messages to each other in place of keywords. Although the computer does not edit these remarks in any way, subjects were instructed to only use remarks where a keyword could not communicate what they wished to say, to only refer to the present game (as opposed to past or future games), and not to identify themselves. Analysis of the protocols shows that, with only one or two minor exceptions throughout the entire experiment, these instructions were obeyed. Figure 2 presents game G2 of quartet R2 as an example of the use of remarks.

In group N (no remarks), the keyword *remark* was deactivated and the instructions and charts (Fig. 1) were modified so that no mention of that keyword was made. Thus, players in group N not only could not use remarks, but were unaware that they had been denied the option.

With the exception of *remark* and the two keywords *solo* and *message*, which were irrelevant to this study and therefore deactivated and deleted from the instructions, all of the keywords in Fig. 1 were available to the subjects.

EXPERIMENTAL GAMES

The five 3-person games reported in the present study are shown in characteristic function form in Table 1. This table also gives the quotas that were used to generate these five games. Note that the values of all 2-person coalitions equal the sum of the quotas of the included players, while the value of each 3-person coalition is the sum of the quotas of all three players. In all cases, all 1-person coalitions had zero value. Each of the games was designed so that the quota of the powerful player $B$ was of roughly the same magnitude, while the ratio $Q$ (equation (8)) was systematically set at 0.1, 0.2, 0.3, 0.4, and 0.5 for game G1 through G5, respectively. The five games were played in the single order G5, G1, G3, G2, G4 by all quartets.

INCENTIVES

The incentive to maximize gain was established by paying each subject three cents for each point earned. No other payment was provided. In accordance with agreements made before the beginning of the training session, subjects were paid their entire earnings at the completion of the entire experiment.

## Results

The data of a game consist of the communications (keywords, parameters of keywords, contents of remarks) transmitted by players during the game, beginning with the first communication from player $A$ and ending with a ratification of a PC. Following established practice, we shall first concern ourselves with the outcomes of the games, as expressed separately by the coalition structures and payoff allocations, and then with selected facets of the paths that lead to the outcomes.

*Table 1.  Quota values and characteristic functions for five 3-person games.*

| Game type | Quota | | | $v(i)^a$ | $v(AB)$ | Characteristic function | | |
| | $q_A$ | $q_B$ | $q_C$ | | | $v(AC)$ | $v(BC)$ | $v(ABC)$ |
|---|---|---|---|---|---|---|---|---|
| G1 | 6 | 180 | 12 | 0 | 186 | 18 | 192 | 198 |
| G2 | 17 | 210 | 25 | 0 | 227 | 42 | 235 | 252 |
| G3 | 28 | 200 | 32 | 0 | 228 | 60 | 232 | 260 |
| G4 | 25 | 155 | 37 | 0 | 180 | 62 | 192 | 217 |
| G5 | 40 | 172 | 46 | 0 | 212 | 86 | 218 | 258 |

$a_i = A, B, C.$

COALITION STRUCTURES

Table 2 presents the frequencies of ratified coalitions by game type and communication condition.  The powerful player $B$ was in 86 of the 90 coalitions formed; each of the four $AC$ coalitions was an equal split of their small coalition value.  It is interesting to note that three of these four occurrences of coalition $AC$ were in game G5. Unfortunately, game G5 was both the first 3-person game played (due to random ordering) and the game with the largest $Q$ ratio, so which of these features might cause such self-immolative behavior cannot be ascertained.  The remaining 36 2-person coalitions were split evenly between the $AB$ and $BC$ coalitions.

There were no differences in coalition structure frequency with respect to communication condition.  In each of the two conditions, exactly 25 of the 45 games ended in a 3-person coalition; moreover, no differences between the incidences of the 2-person coalition were observed.  There is a possible effect of game played on coalition structure, as the frequencies of 3-person coalitions approach statistical significance $\chi_4^2 = 8.55$, $0.05 < p < 0.10$).  Examining Table 2, though, shows that this possible effect is not one of game type as much as a tendency for 3-person coalitions to occur later in the sequence of games.  Recall that the order of games was G5, G1, G3, G2, G4, which corresponds exactly to the increasing incidence of 3-person coalitions.  Thus, while these data do not support the existence of any structural influence of game type on coalition, they suggest that increasing experience may lead to greater tendencies to form grand coalitions.

| Keyword | E.g. of parameter | Primary effect | Other effect on this coalition | Effects outside named coalition |
|---|---|---|---|---|
| PASS | (none) | Send null message | (none) | (none) |
| SOLO | (none) | Immediate ratification of player's one-person coalition | (none) | Player is removed from further play in this game |
| OFFER | A = 20, B = 18, C = 17 | Make a proposal | Supersedes player's previous OFFER, AGREE and ACCEPT | (none) |
| SUGGEST | A = 20, C = 15 to ACD | Make informal, secret proposal | (none) | (none) |
| REJECT | ACD BY C | Erase an offer | (none) | (none) |
| AGREE | ACD BY C | Show liking for an offer | Same as for OFFER | Erases any ACCEPT made by this player |
| ACCEPT | ACD BY C | Tentative commitment to an offer | Same as for OFFER | Erases any AGREE or ACCEPT made by this player |
| (when all players have accepted an offer) | | Game moves to acceptance stage | (none) | Erases all other positions taken by included players. They may make no new OFFER except to subsets or supersets of the accepted coalition |
| AFFIRM | ACD | Stand by previous action | (none) | (none) |
| RATIFY | (none) | Propose move to ratification | Form coalition if all members agree to ratification. Coalition is dissolved otherwise | Concludes game for players in ratified coalitions |

| | | |
|---|---|---|
| REMARK | AC (text) | Send (text) to named player(s). Counts as a communication |
| MESSAGE | A = 1, C = 3 | Send numbered message(s) to named player(s). Counts as a communication |
| VALUE | (none) | Information: Give all values in the game except those involving removed players. Does not count as a communication |
| VALUE | ACD | Information: Give value of that named coalition. Does not count as a communication |
| STATUS | (none) | Information: Give current statements involving every coalition in the game. Does not count as a communication |
| STATUS | ABC | Information: Give current statements regarding named coalition. Does not count as a communication |
| STATUS | ABOUT AC | Information: Give current statements involving coalitions including named player(s). Does not count as a communication |
| STATUS | BY AC | Information: Give current positions taken by named player(s). Does not count as a communication |

Figure 1. Keywords and their effects in the computer program Coalition 11 for characteristic function games.

Quartet R2; Game 2.

COALITIONS HAVE THE FOLLOWING VALUES: $\underline{v}$(AB)=227  $\underline{v}$(AC)=42  $\underline{v}$(BC)=235  $\underline{v}$(ABC)=252

```
MOVE              ACTION
  1    A OFFERS ABC:  A=90; B=90; C=72
  2    B OFFERS BC:  B=135; C=100
  3    C AGREES BC BY B:  B=135; C=100
  4    A OFFERS ABC:  A=80; B=100; C=72
  5    B REMARKS TO AC:  EACH OF YOU MAKE 1, REPEAT 1, OFFER. I'LL TAKE THE
                         BEST ONE
  6    C REMARKS TO A:  LET'S GET TOGETHER & WE WONT GET HURT BY B
  7    A REMARKS TO C:  RIGHT!! ACCEPT MY OFFER ITS FAIR
  8    B REMARKS TO AC:  I'M WAITING FOR YOUR SUGGESTIONS
  9    C OFFERS ABC:  A=81; B=90; C=81
 10    A ACCEPTS ABC BY C:  A=81; B=90; C=81
 11    B REMARKS TO AC:  NO DICE!!!!!!!!!!!!!!!!!!
 12    C REMARKS TO AB:  A AND I ARE A TEAM!  TAKE IT OR LEAVE IT
 13    A AFFIRMS HIS OFFER TO ABC:  A=81; B=90; C=81
 14    B OFFERS ABC:  A=76; B=100; C=76
 15    C ACCEPTS ABC BY C:  A=81; B=90; C=81
 16    A REJECTS ABC BY B:  A=76; B=100; C=76
 17    B OFFERS ABC:  A=76; B=100; C=76
 18    C AFFIRMS HIS OFFER TO ABC:  A=81; B=90; C=81
 19    A REMARKS TO BC:  FORGET IT B, ACCEPT OUR OFFER!
 20    B PASSES
 21    C REMARKS TO AB:  ACCEPT THE OFFER B, OR WE WILL SUGGEST AN EVEN SPLIT
 22    A REMARKS TO C:  IF HE DOESN'T ACCEPT LETS LEAVE HIM OUT
 23    B OFFERS BC:  B=117; C=118
 24    C PASSES
 25    A OFFERS AC:  A=21; C=21
 26    B REMARKS TO C:  I STAND BY ME OFFER!!  LETS RATIFY & END THIS GAME!
 27    C REMARKS TO AB:  NO WAY B!  ACCEPT & THEN WE ALL RATIFY
 28    A REMARKS TO BC:  C'S RIGHT WE'LL LEAVE YOU OUT IF YOU DONT ACCEPT
 29    B REMARKS TO C:  YOU'RE CRAZY C.  ALL THOSE POINTS!  OK YOU WIN
 30    C AFFIRMS HIS OFFER TO ABC:  A=81; B=90; C=81
 31    A PASSES
 32    B ACCEPTS ABC BY C:  A=81; B=90; C=81
 33    C PASSES
 34    A REMARKS TO BC:  YAY!!
 35    B REMARKS TO A:  SHUT UP & RATIFY
 36    C PASSES
 37    A PASSES
 38    B PASSES
 39    C CALLED FOR RATIFICATION
 39        ABC VOTED TO RATIFY
 39        ABC ARE NOW IN RATIFIED COALITIONS AND REMOVED FROM PLAY
!!GAME OVER!!

A=81; B=90; C=81
```

Fig. 2. A game protocol for a 3-person game with remarks.


*Figure 2.  A game protocol for a 3-person game with remarks.*

*Table 2.  Coalition frequencies by communication condition and game type.*

| Game type | Condition $R$ | | | | Condition $N$ | | | | Over Condition | | | |
|---|---|---|---|---|---|---|---|---|---|---|---|---|
| | AC | AB | BC | ABC | AC | AB | BC | ABC | AC | AB | BC | ABC |
| G1 | 0 | 3 | 2 | 4 | 0 | 2 | 2 | 5 | 0 | 5 | 4 | 9 |
| G2 | 0 | 1 | 1 | 7 | 0 | 1 | 3 | 5 | 0 | 2 | 4 | 12 |
| G3 | 0 | 4 | 0 | 5 | 1 | 1 | 3 | 4 | 1 | 5 | 3 | 9 |
| G4 | 0 | 1 | 2 | 6 | 0 | 0 | 1 | 8 | 0 | 1 | 3 | 14 |
| G5 | 3 | 0 | 3 | 3 | 0 | 5 | 1 | 3 | 3 | 5 | 4 | 6 |
| Over game | 3 | 9 | 8 | 25 | 1 | 9 | 10 | 25 | 4 | 18 | 18 | 50 |

PAYOFF DISBURSEMENTS

Table 3 presents the outcomes of all 90 games played, organized by game type, communication condition, and quartet.  If payoffs are entered for all three players, then the 3-person coalitions formed; otherwise the zero payoff to the player excluded from a 2-person coalition is deleted.  In addition, the best-fit value of $\hat{\alpha}$, calculated from (7), is provided.  Since the five game types vary from one to another in their coalition values, the actual payoffs in Table 3 may not be  employed to test the effects of the experimental variables.  Instead, we may take advantage of the fact that the value of a coalition equals the sum of the quotas of the included players (see Table 1) to define a discrepancy score $d(q)$ which is the mean absolute deviation of each player's payoff in a winning coalition from his quota.  This index, first introduced by Rapoport and Kahan (1976), is becoming more generally adopted (e.g, Komorita (1978)) as a discrepancy measure of payoff disbursement.  Since $d(q)$ is defined for any coalition structure, it can be calculated for each ratified PC as:

$$d(q) = \sum_{i \in S} |x_i - q_i| / s ,\tag{9}$$

where $x_i$ and $q_i$ are, respectively, the payoff and quota of player $i$ in a ratified coalition $S$, and $s = |S|$ is the size of that coalition.  For example, employing the quotas given in Table 1 and the observed payoffs in Table 3, the $d(q)$ scores for quartet R1 in games G1 and G2 are 84.00 and 56.00, respectively.

A 5×2 game type by communication condition analysis of variance (ANOVA) with repeated measures on game type was conducted on the discrepancy scores, with the four degrees of freedom for game type subdivided by planned comparisons into a linear component (1 $df$) and a residual (3 $df$). Additionally, as there was some indication (Table 2) that different game types might have different frequencies of coalition structures, the analysis was conducted with a covariate, whose value was defined as 1 if the $AC$ coalition between the two weak players formed, 2 if another 2-person coalition formed, and 3 if the grand coalition of all three players formed. As the mean of $d(q)$ was 3.00, 46.94, or 54.69 for the covariate taking on the values 1, 2, and 3, respectively, the covariance analysis was necessary to avoid confounding the possible effects of coalition structure and experimental manipulations.

As might be anticipated, the regression of the coalition structure covariate on $d(q)$ was significant, both for the quartet within condition error term ($F_{1,15} = 5.36$, $p < 0.035$) and the game by quartet within condition error term ($F_{1,63} = 12.93$, $p < 0.001$). The only other tests to reach significance (Type $I = 0.10$) were the linear contrast over games main effect ($F_{1,63} = 20.04$, $p < 0.001$) and the linear contrast by communication condition interaction ($F_{1,63} = 5.98$, $p < 0.017$). In an uncovaried ANOVA, the identical pattern of significances obtained.

Figure 3 depicts the mean $d(q)$ scores, by game type and communication condition. The linear trend for game type is immediately evident in the over condition means; $d(q)$ drops sharply as the ratio $Q$ increases. Moreover, the communication condition by game type interaction is equally evident; the linear trend is strongly established in the remarks condition, but only weakly if at all present when remarks were not permitted. Although the very low mean for game G5 in condition R is strongly affected by one-third of the entries being $AC$ coalitions, the covariance analysis assures us that the presence of the linear trend is independent of coalition structure effects.

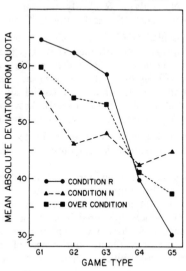

*Figure 3.  Mean discrepancy scores as a function of game type and communication condition.*

## TESTS OF THE α-POWER MODEL

Table 3 shows the best-fit values of the single parameter of the α-power model. All 90 games satisfy a derived prediction of the model that $0 \leq \alpha \leq 1$, a comfortable but not definitive finding, as the range of $A$ spans a large part of the payoff space for games with low Q indices. Figure 4 recaptures the information form Table 3, depicting the frequency of occurrence of $\hat{\alpha}$ in steps of width 0.1 from zero to one. The instances in Fig. 4 are identified by communication condition. Although the entire range of $A$ is spanned, there is concentration at the higher end of the range.

A 5×2 repeated measures ANOVA on the $\hat{\alpha}$ scores showed no significant differences due to either game type or communication condition, in spite of the fact that all eight instances of $\hat{\alpha} \leq 0.40$ occurred in condition $N$ (Fig. 4). However, there were differences in $\hat{\alpha}$ due to coalition type. The mean $\hat{\alpha}$ for grand coalitions was $\hat{\alpha} = 0.78$, compared to $\hat{\alpha} = 0.60$ for the 2-person coalitions $AB$ and $BC$. (When the two weak players joined in their 2-person coalition, they always split their proceeds equally or $\hat{\alpha} = 1$.) The difference in rank order of the $\hat{\alpha}$ values between the $AB$ and $BC$ coalitions on the one hand and the grand coalition on the other is significant by Mann–Whitney $U$ ($z = 3.49$, $p < 0.001$). Put another way, the tendency towards equality of payoff increases as the number of players in the coalition increases from two to three, given that the most powerful player is included in the coalition.

The parameter $\alpha$ may be briefly used to show that solution concepts previously tested in experimental coalition formation games do not fare well in the present study. For 3-person games such as the present ones, the various bargaining sets (Aumann and Maschler (1964); Maschler (1963b)) and the kernel (Davis and Maschler (1965)), which are defined for all possible coalition structures, as well as the core (Gillies (1959)) and the nucleolus (Schmeidler (1969)), which make predictions only for the grand coalition, all coincide at the point $\alpha = 0$. Not only is $\hat{\alpha}$ clearly not zero, but only three of the 90 outcomes are within 0.20 of that value. Similarly, the $M_1^{lin}$ model based on the Shapley value standard of fairness (Maschler (1963a)), the $M^P$ power bargaining set (Rapoport and Kahan, 1979), and the Shapley value (Shapley (1953)), which latter is only defined for the grand coalition, all coincide at $\alpha = 1/2$, which is also disconfirmed by the data. An egalitarian model (Gamson (1964)) explicitly, as well as, *faute de mieux*, all extant social psychological theories, posit $\alpha = 1$, which has partial support in that 28% of the outcomes are within 0.10 of that point. These models, however, are also deficient in light of the data. Finally, the $M_1^{lin}$ model based on the cooperative standard of fairness (Maschler (1963a)) moves monotonically from $\alpha = 0.360$ to $\alpha = 0.500$ in games G1 through G5, and thus can account neither in magnitude nor direction for the observed data.

Although the $\hat{\alpha}$ estimates are between zero and one for all 90 games, only in 2-person coalition outcomes does this imply that the observed payoff vectors fit the α-power model prediction exactly. For 2-person coalition outcomes, the space of all payoff allocations is a line, of which the prediction is a segment. In the present experiment, all 40 2-person payoff vectors were on the predicted segments of their respective lines. But for 3-person coalitions, the space of all payoff vectors is a 2-dimensional simplex (Rapoport (1970)), within which the α-power model prediction is a

Table 3. Payoff configurations and â values for all games, by game type, communication condition, and quartet.

| Quartet | Game 1 A | B | C | â | Game 2 A | B | C | â | Game 3 A | B | C | â | Game 4 A | B | C | â | Game 5 A | B | C | â |
|---|---|---|---|---|---|---|---|---|---|---|---|---|---|---|---|---|---|---|---|---|
| R1 | 65 | 96 | 96 | 1.00 | 63 | 126 | 63 | 0.67 | 88 | 140 |    | 0.70 |    | 96 | 96 | 1.00 |    | 113 | 105 | 0.94 |
| R2 | 46 | 121 |    | 0.68 | 81 | 90 | 81 | 0.95 | 85 | 90 | 85 | 0.97 | 70 | 77 | 70 | 0.94 |    | 145 | 73 | 0.43 |
| R3 | 66 | 140 | 66 | 0.46 | 57 | 170 |    | 0.41 | 88 | 140 |    | 0.70 | 43 | 120 | 54 | 0.42 | 43 |    | 43 | 1.00 |
| R4 | 51 | 66 |    | 1.00 | 61 | 130 | 61 | 0.64 | 70 | 120 | 70 | 0.71 | 55 | 102 | 60 | 0.64 | 86 | 86 | 86 | 1.00 |
| R5 | 55 | 135 | 57 | 0.52 | 63 | 125 | 64 | 0.68 | 73 | 155 |    | 0.52 |    | 120 | 72 | 0.59 | 43 |    | 43 | 1.00 |
| R6 | 66 | 86 | 66 | 0.82 | 75 | 100 | 77 | 0.87 | 70 | 120 | 75 | 0.71 | 58 | 100 | 59 | 0.67 | 43 |    | 43 | 1.00 |
| R7 | 66 | 66 | 66 | 1.00 | 71 | 110 | 71 | 0.79 | 75 | 110 | 75 | 0.79 | 58 | 101 | 58 | 0.66 | 40 | 110 | 108 | 0.70 |
| R8 |    | 66 |    | 1.00 | 76 | 100 | 76 | 0.87 | 80 | 100 | 80 | 0.88 | 69 | 79 | 69 | 0.92 | 84 | 132 | 42 | 0.48 |
| R9 |    | 117 | 75 | 0.75 | 76 | 148 | 87 | 0.67 | 83 | 145 |    | 0.64 | 55 | 125 |    | 0.46 |    | 124 | 94 | 0.76 |
| N1 | 52 | 117 | 75 | 0.75 | 40 | 187 | 25 | 0.19 | 80 | 160 | 72 | 0.48 | 40 | 130 | 47 | 0.30 | 98 | 114 |    | 0.88 |
| N2 | 36 | 145 | 47 | 0.42 | 26 | 200 | 26 | 0.08 | 30 | 180 | 52 | 0.24 | 72 | 73 | 72 | 0.99 | 82 | 130 |    | 0.64 |
| N3 | 54 | 80 | 66 | 0.88 | 62 | 165 | 80 | 0.47 | 70 | 100 | 80 | 0.88 | 63 | 91 | 63 | 0.78 |    | 160 | 58 | 0.19 |
| N4 | 52 | 150 |    | 0.34 | 80 | 92 | 65 | 0.94 | 80 | 140 | 30 | 1.00 | 65 | 87 | 65 | 0.82 | 62 | 150 |    | 0.33 |
| N5 | 60 | 90 | 54 | 0.79 | 82 | 170 | 82 | 0.43 | 68 | 91 | 50 | 0.53 | 25 | 96 | 96 | 0.67 | 38 | 110 | 110 | 0.70 |
| N6 | 66 | 94 | 52 | 0.76 | 52 | 88 | 100 | 0.97 | 78 | 116 | 89 | 0.96 | 69 | 79 | 69 | 0.92 | 86 | 86 | 86 | 1.00 |
| N7 | 49 | 72 | 66 | 0.95 |    | 100 | 50 | 0.86 |    | 160 | 116 | 1.00 | 72 | 120 | 72 | 0.59 | 92 | 120 |    | 0.79 |
| N8 |    | 120 |    | 0.69 |    | 185 | 75 | 0.27 |    | 100 | 82 | 0.46 | 58 | 73 | 72 | 0.99 | 106 | 106 | 85 | 1.00 |
| N9 |    | 99 | 50 | 0.71 |    | 160 |    | 0.54 |    |    |    | 0.88 |    | 95 | 64 | 0.72 | 73 | 100 |    | 0.83 |

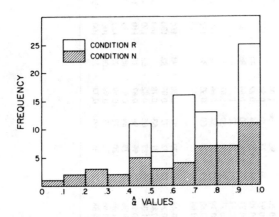

*Figure 4.   Frequency distribution of $\hat{\alpha}$ by communication condition.*

line segment (Rapoport and Kahn (Note 1)).   The outcome is a point in the simplex, and need not fall on the line to yield an estimate $0 \leq \hat{\alpha} \leq 1$, and so a goodness-of-fit test is necessary.    Following  a  procedure  developed  by  Rapoport  and  Kahan  (Note 1),  the 2-dimensional Euclidean distance between each payoff vector (a point in the simplex) for the grand coalition and its least-squares estimate $\hat{\alpha}$ on the prediction line segment was calculated  as  a  measure  of  error  $e$.    This  measure  was  then  used  to  calculate  a 2-dimensional  space  bounded  by  $e$  units  from  the  predicted  line.    (This  space  is  a rectangle  of  width  $2e$  centered  on  the  prediction  line  segment,  to  which  are  added semicircles of radius $e$ at the endpoints of the prediction line segment.)   Finally, the proportion  of  this  2-dimensional  error  space  to  the  entire  payoff  simplex  provides  a measure of the efficiency of the model for the grand coalition.

Figures 5 through 9 show the locations of all 50 observed 3-person payoff vectors, for each game separately.   As can be seen, with the exception of game G5, the data points  fall  close  to  the  prediction  line.    A  proportion  of  0.05  of  the  payoff  simplex contains 42 of the 50 grand coalition payoff vectors, with three of the remaining eight being  between  0.05  and  0.10  of  the  area.    Although  three  of  the  five  "worst"  cases  are from game G5, the low frequency of 3-person coalitions in that game renders a test of game type inadvisable.    On  the  other  hand,  comparing  the  rank  orders  of  these proportions  yielded  a  difference  between  the  two  communication  conditions,  with  games in condition $R$ having smaller discrepancies from the prediction line segment than games in condition $N$ (Mann–Whitney $U$ test $z = 2.00$, $p < 0.05$). In other words, for 3-person coalitions, the ability to send informal, unstructured messages resulted in payoff vectors closer to the predictions of the $\alpha$-power model.

BARGAINING ANALYSIS

We turn next to selected aspects of the bargaining protocols (Fig. 2), to attempt to ascertain the origins of the differences among outcomes noted above. First, although it might have been expected that subjects in condition R would send more messages than subjects in condition N, this was not the case; the two conditions averaged 35.0 and 37.9 messages per game, respectively. The range of messages per game ran from 32.6 to 40.3 for the five game types, which was again well within confidence limits of an hypothesis of no differences. However, the four games ending in an $AC$ coalition averaged 71.0 messages, while the remaining 36 2-person coalitions averaged 35.0 messages and grand coalitions took 34.9 messages per game. This indicates that these $AC$ game outcomes arose only after prolonged negotiations, and justifies our separation of these games from the main body of the data in previous analyses.

The *remark* keyword was used in 37 of the 45 games in which it was enabled, and in at least three of the five games by all quartets in condition R. The content of remarks varied from correcting erroneous plays to statements elaborating strategy to making fun of oneself or other players. The two most common uses of *remark* (16 games and 14 games, respectively) both concerned attempts to form the 3-person coalition, but were of two very different types. In the first, players $A$ and $C$ established and/or maintained their solidarity and tried to establish a power base that would force player $B$ to give them more points. This of course meant the formation of the 3-person coalition, but more as a 2-party grouping with player $B$ joining the protocoalition $AC$. The second type of 3-person coalitions was simply a coalition of the whole, with no mention of factions. An example of the former type is a remark by player $C$ to player $B$ in quartet R2 in game G2:

"$A$ and I are a team!  Take it or leave it."

This can be distinguished from player $C$'s remark to player $B$ in quartet R6, game G5:

"If you accept your $ABC$ suggest, I'll accept."

Many of the remaining types of remarks dealt with a player's faithfulness to a contract, of his inability to ratify because time was not yet ready, or of his need to pay bills. All in all, the players in the remarks condition can fairly be considered a chatty bunch; rather than pass, they would send some sort of message.

A broader look at bargaining as a whole is enlightening. Two prominent patterns of bargaining might be termed "escalation," where player $B$ would let players $A$ and $C$ take turns offering him successively more points, until he finally got an offer that he stayed with, and "weak coalition," where players $A$ and $C$, either through remarks or through agreeing with each others' offers, would either attempt to keep player $B$'s payoff near theirs, or force a 3-person coalition. Thirty-two of the 90 games may be classified

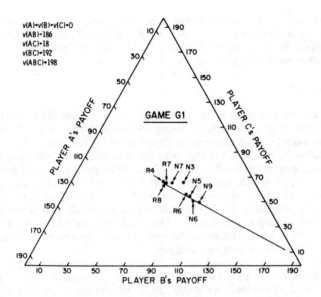

*Figure 5.   Predicted and observed payoff vectors for the grand coalition in game G1.*

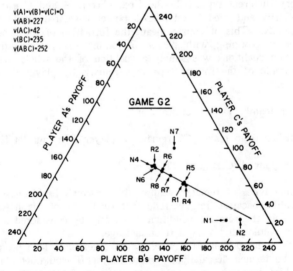

*Figure 6.   Predicted and observed payoff vectors for the grand coalition in game G2.*

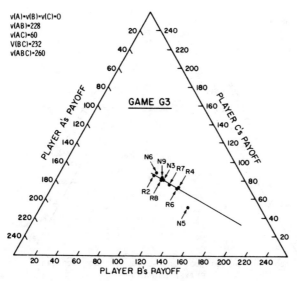

*Figure 7. Predicted and observed payoff vectors for the grand coalition in game G3.*

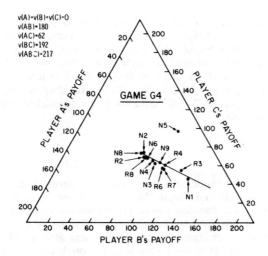

*Figure 8. Predicted and observed payoff vectors for the grand coalition in game G4.*

*Figure 9.  Predicted and observed payoff vectors for the grand coalition in game G5.*

as having escalation, while players in 35 games attempted to form weak coalitions.  In condition N, player *B* was successful on 17 out of 19 escalation attempts, while in condition R, he only succeeds 6 out of  13 times ($\chi_1^2$ = 7.167, *p* < 0.01).   Contrariwise, when players *A* and *C* attempted to hold *B*'s gain down, they were successful 7 out of 14 times in condition N and 17 of 21 times (with 3 of the 4 failures being *AC* coalition outcomes) in condition R  ($\chi_1^2$ = 3.734, 0.05 < *p* < 0.01).   In other words, the presence of remarks permitted the solidarity of the *AC* coalition to be established, and player B was forced to accede to its demands.

## Discussion

It is instructive to compare the results of the present experiment to the previous tests of the $\alpha$-power model by Rapoport and Kahan (Note 1), who examined the results of 1445 plays of 3-person characteristic function games from nine different experiments.   That survey reported that 62% of all outcomes had estimates of $\hat{\alpha}$ between zero and one, 62% of all 2-person outcomes were predicted by the model, and 80% of all grand coalitions were in the 5% area of the payoff simplex closest to the prediction line segment.   In the present experiment, 100% of all outcomes satisfied the prediction of $0 \leq \hat{\alpha} \leq 1$, 100% of all 2-person outcomes were as predicted by the model, and 84% of the 3-person outcomes

were in the 5% area of the payoff simplex.   Not only do the present results provide
unequivocal support for the $\alpha$-power model, but they also suggest that $Q$ may affect the
predictability of the model so that the smaller is $Q$, the more adequate is the model.
The two studies with smallest $Q$ values, namely Maschler (1978) and the present study,
had 94% and 100% of the outcomes within $0 \leq \hat{\alpha} \leq 1$, while the corresponding
percentage for eight other studies with higher $Q$ values ranged from 55% to 68%
(Rapoport and Kahan (Note 1)).

The bargaining protocols not only illuminated the origins of differences among
outcomes and how *remarks* better enabled players $A$ and $C$ to establish their
protocoalition, but they also can help explain most of the failures of the $\alpha$-power model.
Recall that only eight out of 50 grand coalition outcomes were outside of the 5% of the
payoff simplex closest to the prediction line segment.   Five of these eight outcomes were
the *only* five instances of a bargaining pattern termed by Rapoport and Kahan (1976)
*insertion*.   Insertion occurs when a 2-person coalition has reached the agreement stage,
and then yielding to the often desperate pleas of the excluded third player, its two
members agree to expand their accepted coalition to include the third player, adding few
or no additional points to their own payoffs, but giving the third player virtually all of
the difference between the value of the grand coalition and the value of their own
accepted 2-person coalition.   The five cases of insertion are quite prominent in Figs. 5
through 9:   Quartet N1 in game G2, quartet N5 in game G4, and quartets N5, R7, and
R8 in game G5.   The $\alpha$-power model assumes that players cannot be bound to any
coalition other than the final one; indeed, Selten (1972) regards this assumption to be a
necessary ingredient of any coalition formation experiment (contra Gamson (1961)).   But
the present data suggest that players may voluntarily regard themselves as bound to an
agreement, and when this occurs, the model is unable to account for the outcome.

The linear contrast of $Q$ with the discrepancy from quota score $d(q)$ suggests that
the ratio $Q$ may determine the predictive power of the bargaining sets which, for all
coalitions in the present study, prescribe the quotas.   It is instructive to ascertain
whether this linear trend can be extrapolated beyond the experimental range $0.10 \leq Q \leq$
$0.50$.   To this end, we have examined the outcomes of the previous 3-person
characteristic function games (Rapoport and Kahan (Note 1)) that share with the present
set of games three criteria:
  (i) $v(i) = 0$ for all three players, $i = A, B, C$;
  (ii) the game ends in a 2- or 3-person coalition (i.e., coalition structure $\{A, B, C\}$ is
excluded);
  (iii) either $v(ABC) = 0$ or $v(ABC) = q_A + q_B + q_C$.
These criteria are sufficient for the bargaining sets to predict the quotas for any coalition
that forms.

We have found six other 3-person game experiments that satisfy these criteria.
Three of these experiments (Kahan and Rapoport (1974); Levinsohn and Rapoport (1978);
Medlin (1976)) employed an earlier version of the *Coalitions* program, while the other
three studies (Maschler (1978); Riker (1967, 1971)) used different varieties of direct face-
to-face bargaining.   Since the characteristic functions of these games differed widely, and
since the discrepancy scores $d(q)$, as defined in equation (9), depend on the coalition
values, we normalized the discrepancy scores by dividing each $d(q)$ by the value of the
coalition for which it was computed.

Figure 10 presents the means of the normalized discrepancy scores over all seven studies combined as a function of $Q$. The number of cases contributing to each point is also given. The regularity of the line connecting the 16 points is impressive, given the large methodological differences among the studies (Komorita and meek (1978)). Monotonicity is violated only twice, once at $Q = 0$ (Maschler's game M1), and once at $Q = 1.14$ (all of Riker's games). Although these aberrations might be indicative of a difference in experimental method (face-to-face vs. restricted bargaining), the sample of studies is too small for a firm statement to be made. Figure 10 justifies the experimental design of the present study, as the relationship of $Q$ to normalized discrepancy from quota scores would not be unified without the values of $Q$ unique to this experiment.

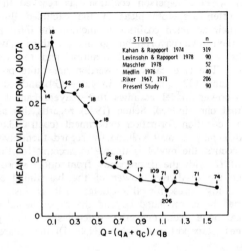

*Figure 10. Mean deviation from quotas as a function of the $Q$ ratio for six different studies.*

The outcomes of all the 3-person characteristic function game experiments taken together point to an elaboration of Murnighan's (1978) comment on the adequacy of the bargaining set quoted earlier. We can now ascertain three features that influence the predictive power of the bargaining set, of which two are structural properties of the characteristic function and one is a non-structural property of the bargaining environment. The two structural properties of the characteristic function are whether or not 1-person coalitions values are positive and the index $Q$. When 1-person coalition values are positive, and particularly when these values have the same ordinal relationship among the three players as the quotas, the bargaining set performs poorly (Kahan and Rapoport (1977); Rapoport and Kahan (Note 1)). When the index $Q$ is low, again the bargaining set does poorly, but in the upper half of the range of $Q$ the bargaining set is a good predictor of payoff disbursements (Fig. 10).

The non-structural property of the bargaining environment is the latitude of communications permitted, which appears to interact with the index $Q$. The present experiment showed a communication condition by linear contrast of $Q$, such that when *remarks* were permitted, the index $Q$ more strongly influenced the $d(q)$ scores than when they were not. Additionally, at the upper range of $Q$, unrestricted communications (Riker (1967, 1971)) did not appreciably yield different $d(q)$ scores than a variety of communication conditions (Kahan and Rapoport (1974)). Recall that $Q$ is a measure of the strength of the stronger player, such that when $Q$ is low, he is in a very strong position, but when $Q$ is high, all three players are about equal in power. This interaction indicates that the two weaker players require the ability to establish their solidarity against the strong player by means other than proposals addressing the disbursement of coalition values, and that when these communication possibilities exist, then standards of fairness may be established that are more in the direction of equality and less in the direction of the quotas. However, when $Q$ is high, the bargaining among the three players is on the level of a battle among equals, and the need for extensive communications is reduced, as the power of each player can be effectively manifested through proposals to different coalitions. This standard of fairness argument is buttressed by the finding that, irrespective of the value of $\hat{\alpha}$, grand coalition outcomes in condition R were closer to the prediction of the $\alpha$-power model than those in condition N.

We close with a comment on the relationship of the $\alpha$-power model to social psychology. Although the $\alpha$-power model may seem to be entirely dissociated from social psychological theories of coalition formation, it shares some interesting features with the bargaining theory of Komorita and Chertkoff (1973) that warrant brief discussion. Both theories recognize, albeit in different ways, the salience of social norms as anchor points for bargaining. Thus, assumption 2 of Komorita and Chertkoff (1973) establishes parity and equality as the two norms advocated by the strong and weak players respectively. The $\alpha$-power model's endpoints of $\alpha = 0$ and $\alpha = 1$ correspond to these parity and equity norms, if a player's quota is defined as his parity point. But, rather than merely postulating these norms, as does bargaining theory, the $\alpha$-power model (Rapoport and Kahan (Note 1)) derives the endpoints as a consequence of more fundamental assumptions about stability in disbursing payoffs. Given the parity and equality norms, both theories (Assumption 3 in bargaining theory, equation (6) of the $\alpha$-power model) tentatively accept the entire range as a feasible bargaining space. But, whereas the $\alpha$-power model admits the entire range of outcomes, and leaves the particular social norm set by the group as a psychologically interpretable free parameter, the bargaining theory (Assumption 5), with admitted trepidation, forces a point prediction by postulating a compromise of two norms.

## Acknowledgment

The research reported here was supported by National Science Foundation grant BNS76-84285. We wish to thank Richard A. Helwig for his assistance in computer program development and experimental laboratory supervision, and Michele Fogelson and Tim Byerly for their assistance in data collection.

## Reference Notes

A. Rapoport and J. P. Kahan, Coalitional power and payoff disbursement in three-person cooperative games. Chapell Hill, NC: L. L. Thurstone, Psychometric Laboratory Report No. 159 (1979).

## References

Aumann R. J., and Drèze, J. H., Cooperative games with coalition structures, Internat. J. Game Theory 3 (1974) 217-237.

Aumann R. J., and Maschler, M., The bargaining set for cooperative games, in: M. Dresher, L. S. Shapley, and A. W. Tucker (Eds.), Advances in Game Theory (Princeton University Press, Princeton, 1964).

Caplow, T., Two against One: Coalitions in Triads (Prentice-Hall, Englewood Cliffs, NJ, 1968).

Davis, M., Game Theory: A Nontechnical Introduction (Basic Books, New York, 1970).

Davis, M. A., and Maschler, M., The kernel of a cooperative game, Naval Res. Logist. Quart. 12 (1965) 223-259.

Gamson, W. A., An experimental test of a theory of coalition formation, Amer. Soc. Rev. 26 (1961) 565-573.

Gamson, W. A., Experimental studies of coalition formation, in: L. Berkowitz (Ed.), Advances in Experimental Social Psychology, Vol. 1 (Academic Press, New York, 1964).

Gillies, D. B., Solutions to general non-zero-sum games, in: A. W. Tucker and R. D. Luce (Eds.), Contributions to the Theory of Games, IV (Princeton University Press, Princeton, 1959).

Hamburger, H., Games as Models of Social Phenomena (W. H. Freeman, San Francisco, 1979).

Kahan, J. P., Coston, A. W., Helwig, R. A., Rapoport, A. and Wallsten, T. S., A PDP-11/45 program for playing n-person characteristic function games, Behavior Res. Meth. Instrumentation 8 (1976) 165-169.

Kahan, J. P. and Rapoport, A., Test of the bargaining set and kernel models in three-person games, in: A. Rapoport (Ed.), Game Theory as a Theory of Conflict Resolution (D. Reidel, Dordrect, 1974).

Kahan, J. P., and Rapoport, A., When you don't need to join: The effects of guaranteed payoffs on bargaining in three-person cooperative games, Theory and Decision 8 (1977) 97-126.

Kaufmann, M. and Tack, W. H., Koalitionsbildung und Gewinnaufteilung bei strategisch aequivalenten 3-Personen-Spielen, Z. Socialpsychologie 6 (1975) 227-245.

Komorita, S. S., Evaluating coalitions theories: Some indices, J. Conflict Resolution 22 (1978) 691-706.

Komorita, S. S., and Chertkoff, J. M., A bargaining theory of coalition formation, Psychological Rev. 80 (1973) 149-162.

Komorita, S. S., and Meek, D. Generality and validity of some theories of coalition formation, J. Personality Soc. Psychology 36 (1978) 392-404.

Laing, J. D., and Morrison, R. J., Coalitions and payoffs in three-person supergames under multiple-trial agreements, in: A. Rapoport (Ed.), Game Theory as a Theory of Conflict Resolution (D. Reidel, Dordrecht, 1974).

Levinsohn, J. R., and Rapoport, Am., Coalition formation in multistage three-person cooperative games, in: H. Sauermann (Ed.), Coalition Forming Behavior (J. C. B. Mohr, Tübingen, 1978).

Luce, R. D, and Raiffa, H., Games and Decisions: Introduction and Critical Survey (Wiley, New York, 1957).

Maschler, M., The power of a coalition, Management Sci. 10 (1963a) 8–29.

Maschler, M., n-person games with only 1, n - 1, and n-person permissible coalitions, J. Math. Anal. Appl. 6 (1963b) 230–256.

Maschler, M., Playing an n-person game--an experiment, in: H. Sauermann (Ed.), Coalition Forming Behavior (J. C. B. Mohr, Tübingen, 1978).

Medlin, S. M., Effects of grand coalition payoffs on coalition formation in three-person games, Behavioral Sci. 21 (1976) 48–61.

Michener, H. A., Sakurai, M. M. Yuen, K., and Kasen, T. J., A competitive test of the $M_1^{(i)}$ and $M_1^{(im)}$ bargaining set solutions in three-person conflicts, J. Conflict Resolution 23 (1979) 102–119.

Murnighan, J. K., Models of coalition behavior: Game theoretic, social psychological, and political perspectives, Psychological Bull. 85 (1978) 1130–1153.

Murnighan, J. K., and Roth, A. E., The effects of communication and information availability in an experimental study of a three-person game, Management Sci. 23 (1977) 1336–1348.

Rapoport, A., and Kahan, J. P., When three isn't always two against one: Coalitions in experimental three-person games, J. Experimental Soc. Psychology 12 (1976) 253–273.

Rapoport, A., and Kahan, J. P., Standards of fairness in 4-person monopolistic cooperative games, in: S. Brams, A. Schotter, and G. Schwödiauer (Eds.), Advances in Applied Game Theory (Springer-Verlag, Heidelberg, 1979).

Rapoport, A., N-Person Game Theory: Concepts and Applications (The University of Michigan Press, Ann Arbor, MI, 1970).

Riker, W. H., Bargaining in a three-person game, Amer. Polit. Sci. Rev. 41 (1967) 642–656.

Riker, W. H., An experimental examination of formal and informal rules of a three-person game, in: B. Lieberman (Ed.), Social Choice (Gordon and Breach, New York, 1971).

Schmeidler, The nucleolus of a characteristic function game, SIAM J. Appl. Math. 17 (1969) 1163–1170.

Selten, R., Equal share analysis of characteristic function experiments in: H. Sauermann (Ed.), Contributions to Experimental Economics, Vol. 3 (J. C. B. Mohr, Tübingen, 1972).

Shapley, L. S., A value for n-person games, in: H. W. Kuhn and A. W. Tucker (Eds.), Contributions to the Theory of Games, Vol. 2 (Princeton University Press, Princeton, 1953).

Thibaut, J. W., and Kelley, H. H., The Social Psychology of Groups (Wiley, New York, 1959).

Von Neumann, J., and Morgenstern, O., Theory of Games and Economic Behavior (Princeton University Press, Princeton, 1947). Second edition.

# CHAPTER 12

# THE POWER OF A COALITION AND PAYOFF DISBURSEMENT IN THREE-PERSON NEGOTIABLE CONFLICTS

**ABSTRACT:** A descriptive model is presented for $n$-person negotiable conflicts represented by games in characteristic function form. It measures the power of a coalition by a generalized cooperative standard of fairness (Maschler, 1963a), which requires the independent estimation of a single parameter. Stability in allocating payoff within a coalition is achieved by equalizing the differences between a player's payoff and his power for all members of the coalition. Estimation procedures for $\alpha$ and measures of goodness of fit of the model are provided, and the relationships between the model and previously advocated solution concepts are explored. The model is then examined in a review of the outcomes of nine previously published experiments using 3-person games in characteristic function form.

The characteristic function is a simple mathematical entity that for the last 30 years or so has underlain most of the theoretical research on negotiable conflicts modeled by cooperative $n$-person games (Luce & Raiffa, 1957; Rapoport, 1970). The idea of a characteristic function is to capture in a single real number the worth of each coalition of players, where a coalition is a group whose members agree to coordinate in a common strategy to utilize joint resources so as to maximize joint reward. Therefore, the characteristic function places its emphasis on coalition payoffs, leaving aside all questions pertaining to bargaining tactics, information structures, or physical transactions of valuable commodities among its members. It is primarily a theoretically useful device for eliminating as many distractions as possible in preparation for the confrontation with the indeterminacy that permeates most $n$-person conflicts (Shapley & Shubik, 1973).

Recently, the characteristic function has come to be employed in various social sciences as an experimental paradigm for investigating coalition formation and bargaining behavior in small groups (Murnighan, 1978), thereby fulfilling a prophecy by Luce (1955, p. 32):

> Those aspects of game theory which are probably of most interest to the social scientist are the theories of coalition formation for games with a transferable utility which are based on the notion of a characteristic function of a game.

This recent research effort has been instigated by mathematical theories, also referred to as *solution concepts*, erected on the characteristic function representation of $n$-person negotiable conflicts. Among these, several have been tested experimentally, including the stable set (von Neumann & Morgenstern, 1947), the core (Gillies, 1953), the Shapley value (Shapley, 1953), the bargaining set $M_1^{(i)}$ (Maschler, 1963b), other bargaining sets (Aumann & Maschler, 1964; Horowitz, 1973; Maschler, 1963a), the kernel (Davis & Maschler, 1965), the nucleolus (Schmeidler, 1969), and equal share analysis (Selten, 1972).

This state of affairs is not unique; analogous situations, where theories erected on a common foundation differ from one another in their assumptions about the subjective representation of the task or the subjects' motivations, may be found in the areas of probability learning (Neimark & Estes, 1967), paired associate learning (Atkinson, Bower, & Crothers, 1965), individual binary choice (Luce & Suppes, 1965), and the Prisoner's Dilemma game (Rapoport & Chammah, 1965). In the case of characteristic function games, the lack of a compelling principle of societal rationality, the existence of various norms of fairness, justice, equity, or parity that players may invoke when allocating their joint reward, and the difficulty of capturing within a single definition all of the nuances of the concept of stability have jointly contributed to this proliferation of theories.

All of these solution concepts for games in characteristic function form with sidepayments require (Aumann, 1967) that the utility of money to each player be fixed for any given game with all players preferring more money to less money. The solution concepts are then limited to non-zero-sum games played for money or its equivalent. This restriction has a liberating quality, though, since Aumann proved that,

> To represent preferences between actual sums of money, ... utilities are not needed, as the dollar amount is a perfectly good measure for this purpose. Therefore we may calculate [any solution] and the intuitive validity of the result is not based on any consideration of "linear utility," "transferable utility," "comparable utility," or indeed any utility whatsoever (Aumann, 1967, pp. 14-15).

Criticisms of these solution concepts by social scientists have been largely based on the grounds that they are normative rather than descriptive, that they fail to incorporate some very important psychological, sociological, or economic variables, or that they do not attempt to predict which coalition will form, but only address payoff allocations. Although we have repeatedly argued (Kahan & Rapoport, 1979; Rapoport & Kahan, 1974; Rapoport, Kahan, Funk & Horowitz, 1979) that many of these criticisms are based on misconceptions about the nature of solution concepts, and that a sharp boundary between normative and descriptive theories of coalition formation is untenable, it is nonetheless true that most solution concepts adopt a monolithic stance with regard to the underlying dispositions of the players, to social norms of fairness and justice, to individual differences in bargaining ability, and to other features inherent in either the individual players or specific experimental games that collectively affect the players' behavior. Moreover, published evidence against any single solution concept may be easily found (Kahan & Rapoport 1980).

In the present paper, we construct and then test a model which is within the tradition of previous solution concepts, yet specifies a free parameter which may be interpreted as a group social norm of fairness. Although this theory, which extends earlier work by Maschler (1963a) and ourselves (Rapoport & Kahan, 1979), is more descriptive than its predecessors, it does not explicitly consider structural and psychological variables (Vinacke, 1969) that have been shown to influence coalition forming behavior. However, the theory could incorporate such variables, once adequate methods of measuring them develop.

## Terminology

Before presenting the theory and examining extant data in its light, it is useful to define terms that will be needed later.   Consider a finite set $N$ of $n$ players who are labeled by the numbers $1,2,...,n$.   The characteristic function, denoted by the letter $v$, is a function from the $2^n$ subsets of $N$ to the real numbers.   Calling any subset $S \subseteq N$ a *coalition*, the value of coalition $S$, $v(S)$, is a measure of coalition worth in terms of the payoff jointly commanded by that coalition against all of the other players in the game. It is natural to require that this real-valued set function defined over all subsets of $N$ satisfy the condition

$$v(\phi) = 0,$$

which represents the strategic inconsequence of the null set.   Occasionally, we shall make use of another condition called *superadditivity*, which states that any two coalitions $S$ and $R$ with no members in common do at least as well by joint effort as they can do separately.[1]   Formally, superadditivity is expressed by the inequality

$$v(R \cup S) \geq v(R) + v(S) \quad \text{for all } R, S \subseteq N, \text{ such that } R \cap S = \phi .$$

In the development of the theory, it will be convenient to assume, unless otherwise stated, that the characteristic function satisfies the condition[2]

$$v(i) = 0, \quad \text{for all } i \in N \ . \tag{1}$$

Equation (1) implies no loss of generality, as we shall demonstrate in Theorem 1 below. Together with (1), superadditivity implies

$$v(S) \geq 0 \quad \text{for all } S \subseteq N \ ,$$

which restricts all discussion to the non–negative real numbers.

The assigned real-valued set function $v$ and the identification of the $n$ players determine a *cooperative n-person game in characteristic function form*, which is denoted by $(N;v)$.   Proposed or actual outcomes of the game will be represented by a *payoff configuration* (PC)

$$(\mathbf{x};S) = (x_1, x_2, \ ..., \ x_n; \ S_1, S_2, \ ..., \ S_m) \quad ,$$

where $\mathbf{x} = (x_1, x_2, \ ..., \ x_n)$ is an $n$-dimensional real vector called the *payoff vector*,

representing a realizable allocation of payoff ($\sum_{i \epsilon S_j} x_i = v(S_j)$, for $j = 1, \ ..., \ m$) to each

player (arranged in a lexicographic order), and $S = \{S_1, S_2, \ ..., \ S_m\}$, called a *coalition structure*, is a partition of the set of players $N$ into $m$ ($1 \leq m \leq n$) coalitions (i.e.,

$S_j \cap S_k = \phi$ if $j \neq k$, and $\displaystyle\bigcup_{j=1}^{m} S_j = N$). The assumption of *individual rationality* states that no player will accept a final payment less than he can insure for himself:

$$x_i \geq v(i) \quad , \quad i \in N \quad .$$

A PC that satisfies this condition is called an *individually rational payoff configuration* (IRPC).

To exemplify these concepts, consider a 3-person superadditive game with a set of players $N = \{A,B,C\}$, where, in accordance with standard experimental notation, players are identified by upper case letters rather than numbers. The characteristic function of this game:

$$v(AB) = 95, \quad v(AC) = 90, \quad v(BC) = 65, \quad v(N) = 120,$$

states that players $A$ and $B$ can jointly gain 95 units of payoff (called "points" for convenience), players $A$ and $C$ can gain 90 points between them, players $B$ and $C$ can realize 65 points, and all three players together can gain 120 points. If $A$ and $C$ were to consider a 58-32 split of $v(AC)$ (leaving $B$ with zero points), this consideration would be denoted by the PC

$$(58, 0, 32; \quad AC, B) \quad .$$

The grand coalition of all three players, with an equal division of payoff, would be indicated by the PC

$$(40, 40, 40; \quad ABC) \quad ,$$

while if no agreement were reached, leaving each player in his 1-person coalition, this outcome would be expressed by the PC

$$(0, 0, 0; \quad A, B, C) \quad .$$

Without loss of generality, and for ease of presentation, we shall assume that $v(AB) \geq v(AC) \geq v(BC)$ throughout; this provides a lexicographic "ranking" of the players in terms of the value of the coalitions they belong to.


## The α-Power Model

The two major and largely independent components of most theories of characteristic function games are (i) a measure of the power of a coalition, and (ii) a definition of stability. With only a few exceptions, the solution concepts all accept the characteristic function as an adequate measure of power, but differ from one another in their

approach to stability.   Following Maschler (1963a), the present model proposes that the
value of a coalition may not be an adequate measure of its power.   Rather, the power
of a coalition is determined not only by the gains that accrue jointly to the coalition
members, but also by the losses they may inflict on the remaining players by deciding
*not* to coalesce with them.   Moreover, a specification of a set of social norms of fairness
or justice is necessary in order to know how to integrate the joint effects of both
potential gains and losses.

DEFINING THE POWER FUNCTION

Having recognized this distinction between the value of a coalition and its power, the
next step is to construct a more adequate representation of the power structure.   To do
so, assume a superadditive $n$-person game in characteristic function form and let a
*standard of fairness* (SOF) be a function $u$ defined on all subsets $P$ of $N$.   This function
is constructed by partitioning $N$ into two sets called *negotiation groups*.[3]   $P$ thus denotes
a negotiation group in the partition $[P, \bar{P}]$, where $\bar{P} = N - P$, and $u(P)$ is assumed to
designate the power of that negotiation group.   The terms "negotiation group" refers to
the reason for partitioning $N$, namely to gain strategic advantage, and the term "standard
of fairness" refers to those psychological and sociological principles determining the
players' behavior when negotiating for the disbursement of their coalition value
(Maschler, 1963a) that are captured by the function $u$.   In particular, note that we do not
label $P$ a "coalition" because the members of $P$ have (conceptually) not yet decided
whether or not to coalesce.

Any SOF function $u$ will be assumed to satisfy two conditions:

$$u(P) \geq v(P) \quad , \quad \text{for all } P \subseteq N \quad ; \tag{3}$$

$$u(P) + u(\bar{P}) = v(N) \quad . \tag{4}$$

Condition (3) is straightforward; the power of a negotiation group by definition cannot be
smaller than its value, which is guaranteed to it.   Condition (4), which serves as a
"reality barrier," states that the sum of the powers of the complementary negotiation
groups equals the maximum (because of superadditivity) payoff.   This implies that the
power function is constant-sum, even if the original characteristic function is not.   It
may be noted that $N$ may be trivially partitioned into itself and the null set, and that
conditions (3) and (4) therefore jointly imply the natural finding that the power of the
grand coalition equals its value, i.e., $u(N) = v(N)$.

The specification of $u(P)$ then is a resolution of the issue of allocation of the
"excess" of power

$$u(N) - [v(P) + v(\bar{P})] \quad ,$$

after each negotiation group's minimum power is taken from the group's constant-sum
total.   Although there are an infinity of functions that could resolve this issue, a
simplifying and reasonable restriction is that the partition of power should be expressed
as a simple proportion of the excess, and that this linear proportion be expressed as a

free parameter, which can depend on the structure of the game or a social norm inherent in the group playing the game that dictates the allocation of rewards. Denoting this free parameter by $\alpha(P)$, we define the power of a negotiation group as

$$u(P) = v(P) + \alpha(P) [u(N) - v(P) - v(\bar{P})], \quad P \subseteq N \ . \tag{5}$$

As the SOF function $u$ generalizes Maschler's (1963a) "cooperative SOF," we term it the *generalized cooperative standard of fairness* (GCSOF).

The parameter $\alpha(P)$ in (5) serves as a normalizing weight that satisfies two conditions for any $P \subseteq N$:

$$\alpha(P) \geq 0 \quad ; \tag{6}$$

$$\alpha(P) + \alpha(\bar{P}) = 1 \ . \tag{7}$$

It is easy to verify that if conditions (6) and (7) on $\alpha(P)$ are met, the GCSOF in (5) satisfies conditions (3) and (4). Because of condition (7), which is again a reflection of the constant-sum nature of the function $u$, we may write $\alpha(\bar{P}) = 1 - \alpha(P)$, which shows that there is only one free parameter for each partition of $N$ into two complementary negotiation groups. Moreover, conditions (6) and (7) together imply that

$$0 \leq \alpha(P) \leq 1 \ , \tag{8}$$

a meaningful property that will prove useful later. The pair $(N;u)$, where $N$ is the set of players in the characteristic function game $(N;v)$, and $u$ is the GCSOF function (5), will be called an $\alpha$-*power game*.

The parameter $\alpha(P)$ thus determines for each partition of $N$ into two complementary negotiation groups $P$ and $\bar{P}$ the portion of the excess between the value of the grand coalition $v(N)$ and the sum of the values of the two negotiation groups $v(P) + v(\bar{P})$, which is added to the value of the negotiation group $P$ in accessing its power. The excess $v(N) - [v(P) + v(\bar{P})]$ is non-negative if the game $(N;v)$ is superadditive. The value of $\alpha(P)$ cannot be specified a priority unless the effects of social norms, moral conventions, and varieties of characteristic function games can be numerically measured. The social psychological research invoking such norms as equity or parity for coalition formation (e.g., Gamson, 1961; Komorita & Chertkoff, 1973) has typically merely postulated the particular norm; in this sense, that line of research goes no further than Maschler (1963a) in determining a SOF.

At this time, we are not prepared to translate social norms into parametric values; such a Herculean task awaits better measurement of such norms and individual's adoption of them. Contrarily, neither are we content with a priori fixing of the parameter at any set value. Instead, we shall explore here the consequences of a reasonable constraint (Albers, 1978; Komorita, 1974) on $\alpha(P)$ that, for any particular game and set of individuals playing it, requires that

$$\alpha(P_1) = \alpha(P_2), \quad \text{if } |P_1| = |P_2| \ , \tag{9}$$

where $P_1$ and $P_2$ are two (not necessarily disjoint) negotiation groups of $N$, and $|P_j|$ is the cardinality of negotiation group $P_j$. This simplifying assumption drastically reduces the number of parameters in the model. For the general 3-person characteristic function game, there are three different non-trivial partitions of $N$ into two negotiation groups, namely $[AB,C]$, $[AC,B]$, and $[A,BC]$. For each of these partitions, the numbers of players in the two negotiation groups are two and one, so equation (9) implies that

$$\alpha(AB) = \alpha(AC) = \alpha(BC) \equiv \alpha \ .$$

Similarly, in a 4-person game, there will again be only _one free parameter, as in each partition of $N$ into two negotiation groups, either $|P| = |P| = 2$ or $|P| = 3$ and $|P| = 1$. But when $|P| = 2$, it is necessarily true that $\alpha(P) = 1/2$, so the only free parameter is $\alpha(ABC) = \alpha(ABD) = \alpha(ACD) = \alpha(BCD) \equiv \alpha$.

To exemplify the computation of the $\alpha$-power function, consider game (2) and arbitrarily let $\alpha = 1/3$. Then the GCSOF in (5) yields the $\alpha$-power game:

$$(N; u) = \begin{cases} u(A) = 36 \ 2/3, \ u(B) = 20, \ u(C) = 16 \ 2/3, \\ u(AB) = 103 \ 1/3, \ u(AC) = 100, \ u(BC) = 83 \ 1/3, \\ u(N) = 120. \end{cases}$$

STABILITY

Our approach to stability follows Aumann and Dréze (1974) in seeking stable IRPCs for each possible coalition structure rather than determining which coalition structures are stable. We choose here to adopt a notion of stability consonant with the analysis of excesses in the determination of power, and follow the kernel (Davis & Maschler, 1965; see Komorita, 1979, for a similar approach from a very different starting point) in positing that stability is reached when there is equality of excess gain over a status quo point. That is, in disbursing their coalition value $v(S)$, each member $k$ of coalition $S$ in a given coalition structure will reject an outcome $x_k$ if the difference between his outcome and his individual power $u(k)$ is smaller than the corresponding difference for one or more of his coalition partners. A coalition will achieve stability in payoff allocation, then, only if the differences $x_k - u(k)$ are equal for all members of that coalition. Since stability depends on the function $u$, which is in turn dependent on the parameter $\alpha$, we call the set of all stable payoff configurations the $\alpha$-*power set*, and denote it by $P_\alpha$. Formally, let $(x;S)$ be an IRPC for a game $(N;v)$. An IRPC is said to belong to the $\alpha$-power set $P_\alpha$ if for any coalition $S_j \in S$ $(j=1,...,m)$ with two or more members,

$$x_k - u(k) = x_\ell - u(\ell)$$

for every two distinct players $k, \ell \in S_j$. Single-person coalitions in which each player receives his 1-person coalition value are assumed stable.[4]

THE 3-PERSON GAME

The GCSOF (5) for the general superadditive 3-person game is given by:

$$(N; u) = \begin{cases} u(AB) = v(AB) + \alpha[v(N) - v(AB) - v(C)]; & u(C) = v(N) - u(AB); \\ u(AC) = v(AC) + \alpha[v(N) - v(AC) - v(B)]; & u(B) = v(N) - u(AC); \\ u(BC) = v(BC) + \alpha[v(N) - v(BC) - v(A)]; & u(A) = v(N) - u(BC); \\ u(N) = v(N). \end{cases} \qquad (10)$$

It can be shown that $P_\alpha$ may not always be non-empty for all coalition structures, depending on the function $v$ and the value of the parameter $\alpha$. Although the strict mathematical interpretation of such an empty case is that the model makes no prediction in that instance, another equally plausible interpretation is that no payoff vector is stable for that coalition structure. Hence the $\alpha$-power model not only prescribes payoff allocation for a given coalition structure, but also can predict which coalition structures might or might not form for a given GCSOF. For example, let $N = \{A,B,C\}$ and

$$\begin{aligned} v(AB) &= v(N) = 100, \ v(AC) = 10, \\ v(A) &= v(B) = v(C) = v(BC) = 0. \end{aligned} \qquad (11)$$

Assume $\alpha = 0$. Then $(0, 0, 0; \ A, B, C)$ and $(55, 45, 0; \ AB, C)$ are the only IRPCs in $P_0$. The $\alpha$-power model thus says that for $\alpha = 0$, there are no stable ways to allocate rewards if the coalition structures $(AC, B)$, $(A, BC)$, or $(ABC)$ attempt to form. We can by inference consider their formation unlikely. In the range $0 \leq \alpha \leq 1$, increasing $\alpha$ will increase the number of coalition structures in game (11) for which $P_\alpha$ exists. For example, if we set $\alpha = 0.8$, then the solution for game (11) is

$$P_{0.8} = \begin{cases} 51, 49, 0; \ AB, C \\ 40 \ 2/3, 38 \ 2/3, 20 \ 2/3; \ ABC \\ 0, 0, 0; \ A, B, C \end{cases}$$

And if $\alpha = 1$, the model predicts equal splits:

$$P_{1.0} = \begin{cases} 50, 50, 0; \ AB, C \\ 5, 0, 5; \ AC, B \\ 0, 0, 0; \ BC, A \\ 33 \ 1/3, 33 \ 1/3, 33 \ 1/3; \ ABC \\ 0, 0, 0; \ A, B, C \end{cases}$$

Before stating necessary and sufficient conditions for the non-emptiness of $P_\alpha$, we show that the $\alpha$-power model shares the following property, expressed as Theorem 1, with all major solution concepts.

**THEOREM 1.** *The $\alpha$-power set is relatively invariant under strategic equivalence.*

The proof is presented in the Appendix.

Strategic equivalence has to do with linear transformations of $v(S)$. Two games $(N;v)$ and $(N;w)$ defined over the same set of players $N$ are said to be strategically equivalent (Luce & Raiffa, 1957; Rapoport, 1970) if there exist $n+1$ real constants $\gamma > 0$ and $\beta_k$ $(k=1,2,...,n)$, such that

$$w(S) = \gamma \left[ v(S) + \sum_{k \in S} \beta_k \right], \quad \text{for all } S \subseteq N.$$

If two games are strategically equivalent, then a solution is said to be *relatively invariant under strategic equivalence* if the IRPC $(\mathbf{x}';S)$ belongs to the solution of $(N;w)$ whenever the IRPC $(\mathbf{x};S)$ belongs to the solution of $(N;v)$, where $\mathbf{x}' = \gamma(\mathbf{x}+\beta)$ and $\beta = (\beta_1, \beta_2, ...,$ $\beta_n)$. Relative invariance under strategic equivalence thus means that linear transformations of coalition values, which only change the unit of measurement and origin, do not affect the solution. The generality of the $\alpha$-power set is therefore not restricted to the constraint $v(i) = 0$.

Necessary and sufficient conditions for the existence of $P_\alpha$ for different coalition structures may now be specified. Recall in the arguments below that $v(AB) \geq v(AC) \geq v(BC)$.

**THEOREM 2:** *In a superadditive 3-person game $P_\alpha$ is nonempty for the coalition structure*

(1)    $\{AB,C\}$,    always;
(2)    $\{AC,B\}$,    iff $v(AC)/[v(AB) - v(BC)] \geq 1-\alpha$;
(3)    $\{A,BC\}$,    iff $v(BC)/[v(AB) - v(AC)] \geq 1-\alpha$;
(4)    $(ABC)$,    iff $v(N)/[2v(AB) - v(AC) - v(BC)] \geq 1-\alpha$.

The proof is given in the Appendix.

Two corollaries implied by Theorem 2 state conditions on the characteristic function that imply the nonemptiness of $P_\alpha$ for all $\alpha$. The condition for the first corollary is known as the "triangle inequality" (Aumann & Maschler, 1964):

$$v(AC) + v(BC) \geq v(AB). \tag{12}$$

**Corollary 2a:**   *If a superadditive 3-person game satisfies (12),* $P_\alpha$ *is given (for* $0 \le \alpha \le 1$ *) by*

$$
P_\alpha = \begin{cases}
\left[ \dfrac{v(AB)+(1-\alpha)[v(AC)-v(BC)]+\alpha[v(A)-v(B)]}{2}, \ \dfrac{v(AB)+(1-\alpha)[v(BC)-v(AC)]+\alpha[v(B)-v(A)]}{2}, \ v(c); \ AB,C \right] \\[12pt]
\left[ \dfrac{v(AC)+(1+\alpha)[v(AB)-v(BC)]+\alpha[v(A)-v(C)]}{2}, \ v(B), \ \dfrac{v(AC)+(1+\alpha)[v(BC)-v(AB)]+\alpha[v(C)-v(A)]}{2}; \ AC,B \right] \\[12pt]
\left[ v(A), \ \dfrac{v(BC)+(1-\alpha)[v(AB)-v(AC)]+\alpha[v(B)-v(C)]}{2}, \ \dfrac{v(BC)+(1-\alpha)[v(AC)-v(AB)]+\alpha[v(C)-v(B)]}{2}; \ BC,A \right] \\[12pt]
(\{v(N) + (1-\alpha)[v(AB) + v(AC) - 2v(BC)] + \alpha[2v(A) - v(B) - v(C)]\}/3, \\
\quad \{v(N) + (1-\alpha)[v(AB) - v(BC) - 2v(AC)] + \alpha[2v(B) - v(A) - v(C)]\}/3, \\
\quad \{v(N) + (1-\alpha)[v(AC) + v(BC) - 2v(AB)] + \alpha[2v(C) - v(A) - v(B)]\}/3; \ ABC) \\[6pt]
(0,0,0; \ A,B,C)
\end{cases}
\tag{13}
$$

The proof of Corollary 2a is presented in the Appendix. This corollary states that if the triangle inequality is satisfied, the $\alpha$-power set $P_\alpha$ is nonempty for all coalition structures, the payoff to each player is a linear function of $\alpha$, $0 \le \alpha \le 1$, and the solution for each coalition structure is unique.

**Corollary 2b:**   *In a superadditive 3-person game, if* $1/2 \le \alpha \le 1$, $P_\alpha$ *for the grand coalition exists and is given in (13).*

The proof of this corollary is also presented in the Appendix; it does not depend on the triangle inequality.

Corollaries 2a and 2b show that fairly mild conditions imposed on either the characteristic function or the value of $\alpha$ insure the existence of a unique solution in $P_\alpha$ for every coalition structure of a 3-person game. Note in (13) that $v(N)$ does not enter into the determination of any of the coalition structures except the grand coalition. It can be shown that the unique solution to the 2-person coalition structures is independent of the value of $v(N)$ and whether or not $P_\alpha$ for $v(N)$ is nonempty. Consequently, superadditivity is not required to predict 2-person coalition outcomes. Only when the game is not superadditive and the inequality (12) is violated does the solution (13) require modification for 2-person coalitions.[5]

THE $\alpha$-POWER MODEL AND OTHER CONCEPTUALIZATIONS

Several properties of the solution (13) enhance the attractiveness of the $\alpha$-power model for 3-person games. If $\alpha = 0$ and the triangle inequality (12) is satisfied, then $P_0$ coincides with both the kernel $K$ (Davis & Maschler, 1964; Maschler, 1963b) for all coalition structures except the grand coalition. For that latter, it is always true that $P_0 \subseteq M_1^{(i)}$, while when $2v(AC) + 2v(BC) - v(AB) \ge v(N) \ge 2v(AB) - v(AC) - v(BC)$, a condition met by the majority of games actually played experimentally, $P_0 = K$. Since the kernel and bargaining set, like other mathematical solution concepts, employ the characteristic function as a measure of a coalition's power, this means that when $\alpha = 0$, the power of a coalition is the same as its value. On the other hand, when $\alpha = 1$, it can easily be shown that $P_{1.0}$ yields equal sharing. That is, when $v(i) = 0$ as in condition (1), any coalition that forms will split its reward equally, and differences among players' coalitional opportunities are entirely ignored.

Some intermediate values of $\alpha$ also have interpretations as solution concepts. If $\alpha = 1/2$, then the $\alpha$-power solution for the 3-person game coincides with the $M_1^{(im)}$ modified bargaining set based on the Shapley value SOF (Maschler, 1963a) and the $M^P$ power bargaining set (Rapoport & Kahan, 1979). If, in addition, the game is superadditive, then $P_{0.5}$ for the grand coalition equals the Shapley value of the game (see Corollary 2b in the Appendix). If $\alpha = 2/3$, the solution $P_{.67}$ for the grand coalition coincides with the equal propensity to disrupt solution (Charnes, Rousseau & Seiford, 1978), which latter equalizes players' "average" capability to reduce others' payoffs by retreating to their 1-person coalitions. These connections between $P_\alpha$ and other solution concepts enhance the appeal of the $\alpha$-power model for 3-person games.

Two useful dimensions on which to classify 3-person characteristic function games are (i) whether or not $v(N) = 0$ and (ii) whether or not all of the $v(i) = 0$. When $v(N) = 0$, the grand coalition is in effect not permitted to form, while when $v(i) > 0$, players in 1-person coalitions (playing "solo") have positive gains (Kahan & Rapoport, 1977). The parameter $\alpha$ has an interpretation for 2-person coalition structures in non-solo games that parallels Komorita and Chertkoff's (1973) bargaining theory. When $\alpha = 0$, $P_\alpha$ prescribes the "quota" (Maschler, 1963a) of the kernel if the triangle inequality (12) is satisfied. To the extent that the quotas represent player's power, this corresponds to a parity-based division of points. As $\alpha$ moves from 0 to 1, the payoff to the more powerful player in the coalition proportionally decreases until at $\alpha = 1$ the two players share the proceeds equally. This equality is the other anchor point of the bargaining theory. While bargaining theory's (first round) prediction could then be taken at $\alpha = 1/2$; instead, we here accept the full range of $0 \leq \alpha \leq 1$.

This simple interpretation of $\alpha$ requires a slight modification to incorporate grand coalitions. If a grand coalition forms, then the space of possible payoff disbursements of $v(N)$ is a 2-dimensional simplex of the 3-dimensional space of payoff vectors which satisfy the condition $x_A + x_B + x_C = v(N)$. Within this simplex, the prediction of the $\alpha$-power model is a line segment. Figure 1 provides an example of such a simplex for the 3-person game given by the characteristic function

$$v(AB) = 106, \ v(AC) = 86, \ v(BC) = 66, \ v(ABC) = 124,$$
$$v(i) = 0, \ i = A,B,C. \tag{14}$$

$P_\alpha$ for the grand coalition of game (14) is the line segment connecting the two endpoints (41 1/3, 41 1/3, 41 1/3) and (61 1/3, 41 1/3, 21 1/3). The proportion between equality and the quota holds only if the outcome is exactly on the prediction line. Otherwise, the interpretation loses meaning. For example, if the outcome to game (14) were the IRPC (55, 49, 20; $ABC$), as shown in Figure 1, then the least-squares distance to the prediction line yields a parameter value of $\hat{\alpha} = 0.125$, even though the weakest player $C$ receives less than his quota of 21 1/3. The point solution $P_{.125}$ does have the desired property, being the IRPC (58 5/6, 41 1/3, 23 5/6; $ABC$). In Figure 1, all points having a best estimate of $\hat{\alpha} = .125$ are shown by the line intersecting $P_\alpha$.

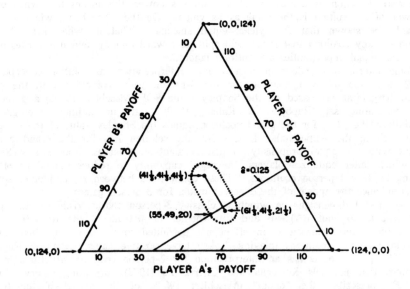

*Figure 1.   A 2-dimensional simplex for the 3-person characteristic function game:* $v(AB)$ = *106,* $v(AC)$ = *86,* $v(BC)$ = *66,* $v(ABC)$ = *124,* $v(A)$ = $v(B)$ = $v(C)$ = *0.*

When solo games are considered, on the other hand, the simple interpretation of α as a proportion between parity and equality falls apart.    This is because the α-power model assesses payoffs on the basis of relative gains above guaranteed earnings rather than absolute outcomes, a feature shared by most game theoretical solutions to *n*-person games and one strongly advocated as descriptive of utility evaluation by human decision makers (Kahneman & Tversky, 1979).    Put another way, players are assumed to negotiate from status quo positions based not at zero, but at their guaranteed payoffs $v(i)$.

## Tests of the α-Power Model

A formal test of the α-power model would require an a priori assessment of the parameter α for each game or group, after which a statistical analysis of the goodness of fit of the model could proceed straightforwardly.    Unfortunately, only a very few coalition formation experiments have included data on the personality of the players and their expectations regarding outcomes of the game (e.g., Albers, 1978; Selten & Schuster, 1968), and even if such data were available, an algorithm transforming this information into a value of α remains entirely unknown.

The alternative, less preferred, strategy is to estimate a value of $\alpha$ a posteriori from the outcome of a game, and then to examine the behavior of this estimate over types of games to examine (i) the extent to which the theoretically necessary restriction $0 \leq \alpha \leq 1$ is empirically obtained, and (ii) if there are any systematic differences in the distribution of $\hat{\alpha}$ depending on the structure of the game. To this end, we will examine the outcomes of 1445 plays of 3-person characteristic function games gathered from nine published studies of coalition formation. But before turning to these data, we must first discuss the problem of estimating $\alpha$.

PARAMETER ESTIMATION

For 3-person games, the uniqueness of the solutions in (13) allows an estimation of $\alpha$ when a coalition with two or more players forms. The traditional least squares procedure yields an estimate $\hat{\alpha}$ as the unique value of $\alpha$ that minimizes the sum

$$\sum_{k \in S_j} (y_k - x_k)^2, \ S_j \ \epsilon \ \mathbf{S}$$

where $x_k$ is the prescribed payoff in (13) for player $k$ in coalitions $S_j$, $y_k$ is the corresponding observed payoff of player $k$, and $|S_j| \geq 2$. differentiating this sum with respect to $\alpha$, and solving for $\hat{\alpha}$, yields the estimates

$$\hat{\alpha} = \begin{cases} \dfrac{v(AC) - v(BC) + v(AB) - 2y_A}{v(AC) - v(BC) - v(A) + v(B)}, & \text{if coalition } AB \text{ forms,} \\[2ex] \dfrac{v(AB) - v(BC) + v(AC) - 2y_A}{v(AB) - v(BC) - v(A) + v(C)}, & \text{if coalition } AC \text{ forms,} \\[2ex] \dfrac{v(AB) - v(AC) + v(BC) - 2y_B}{v(AB) - v(AC) - v(B) + v(C)}, & \text{if coalition } BC \text{ forms,} \\[2ex] \dfrac{[y_A + v(BC)] K_A + [y_B + v(AC)] K_B + [y_C + v(AB)] K_C}{2[v(AB) K_C + v(AC) K_B + v(BC) K_A + K - Q]}, & \text{if coalition } ABC \text{ forms,} \\[2ex] \text{where} \\[1ex] K_i = v(ij) + v(ik) - 2v(jk) - 2v(i) + v(j) + v(k), \ i, j, k \ \epsilon \ N, \ i \neq j \neq k, \\[1ex] K = v(AB)^2 + v(AC)^2 + v(BC)^2 - v(AB)v(AC) - v(AB)v(BC) - v(AC)v(BC), \\[1ex] Q = v(A)^2 + v(B)^2 + v(C)^2 - v(A)v(B) - v(A)v(C) - v(B)v(C) . \end{cases}$$

(15)

If $v(A) = v(B) = v(C)$, then these equations simplify considerably; the estimate for the grand coalition becomes:

$$\hat{\alpha} = 1 - \sum_{i=A,B,C} y_i K_i /2K \quad ,$$

where $K_i$ and $K$ are defined in (15).

DATA BASE

The predictions of the $\alpha$-power model will now be compared to the outcomes of 1445 plays of 3-person characteristic function games played in experimental laboratories, for which Aumann's (1967) requirement that players regard gains in terms of money is tenable.  This collection includes all (to the best of our knowledge) published reports of experimental 3-person games that meet the following weakened version of Selten's (1972) stringent criteria for the validity of an experimental game as a test of theory:   (1) The games are presented to players in characteristic function form, with the rules of the game fully explained to the players.   (2) Players are strongly motivated to maximize their gain in the experimental units given, as these units are equivalent to money.   (3) There are no explicit sequential dependencies of either payoffs or games if players participate in multiple games.   (4) Communications are sufficiently open and flexible so that players may send intricate or subtle messages to each other.   (5) Precoalitions are not allowed in the sense that players are only committed to a coalition at the termination of a game. Indeed, the rules of most of the experimental games define this commitment as the termination of a game.

　　　Nine published studies, enumerated in Table 1, form the body from which the 1445 plays were drawn.  As can be seen from that table, these games differed in the total number of characteristic functions, the total number of plays reported, whether or not the grand coalition could form, whether or not 1-person coalitions had zero value, and the experimental method employed.  In the Riker (1967, 1971) and Kaufmann and Tack (1975) studies, subjects played one game apiece, while in the remainder, the same subjects might play multiple games, albeit sometimes with different co-players.

　　　In the analyses reported below, we shall first begin with some overall considerations of the 1445 games, and then break down games by certain structural properties of the characteristic functions.  Then, we will examine some ways in which the efficacy of the $\alpha$-power model is affected by which of the coalition structures formed.

*Table 1. Sources of data for 3-person game experiments*

| Source | | Number of Games | Number of Different Characteristic Functions | $v(N) > 0$? | $v(i) = 0$? | Experimental Methods |
|---|---|---|---|---|---|---|
| Kahan & Rapoport | (1974) | 320 | 5 | no | yes | *Coalitions* |
| Rapoport & Kahan | (1976) | 160 | 5 | yes | yes | *Coalitions* |
| Medlin | (1976) | 160 | 20 | yes | yes | *Coalitions* |
| Kahan & Rapoport | (1977) | 320 | 20 | half | no | *Coalitions* |
| Levinsohn & Rapoport | (1978) | 90 | 25 | no | yes | *Coalitions* |
| Riker | (1967, 1971) | 227 | 1 | no[a] | yes | sequential 2-person negotiations |
| Kaufmann & Tack | (1975) | 90 | 9 | yes | no | 3-person face-to-face |
| Maschler | (1978) | 78 | 43 | some | yes | 3-person face-to-face |

[a] Although Riker's single game had $v(N) = 0$, he (Riker, 1972) reports six instances where the players spontaneously modified their rules to create a superadditive game with $v(N) = v(AB)$.


FREQUENCY OF CORRECT RANGE OF $\hat{\alpha}$

The first question asked of this data base is how often the constraint of equation (8) that $0 \leq \alpha \leq 1$ was satisfied. Table 2 presents the frequencies of outcomes by study further broken down into percentages of model violations of $\hat{\alpha} < 0$ and $\hat{\alpha} > 1$. An important caveat regarding Table 2 is that the [0,1] range of $\hat{\alpha}$ shrinks to a single point for coalitions exclusively among symmetric (identical save for name) players. For 11 plays, such a coalition between symmetric players occurred; these were dropped from analysis. Another 24 games were excluded because they ended with the IRPC $(v(A), v(B), v(C); A,B,C)$. Thus the percentages given in Table 2 are based on exclusion of these 35 undefined cases.

*Table 2.   Values of the parameter* $\hat{\alpha}$ *by study*

| Study | | Total N | N Undefined | $\hat{\alpha}<0$ | $\hat{\alpha}>1$ | $0\leq\hat{\alpha}\leq1$ |
|---|---|---|---|---|---|---|
| Kahan & Rapoport | (1974) | 320 | 1 | 123 (38.6) | 20 (6.3) | 176 (55.2) |
| Rapoport & Kahan | (1976) | 160 | 0 | 69 (43.1) | 3 (1.9) | 88 (55.0) |
| Medlin | (1976) | 160 | 0 | 50 (31.2) | 1 (0.6) | 109 (68.1) |
| Kahan & Rapoport | (1977) | 320 | 5 | 67 (21.3) | 55 (17.5) | 193 (61.3) |
| Levinsohn & Rapoport | (1978) | 90 | 0 | 33 (36.7) | 3 (3.3) | 54 (60.0) |
| Riker | (1967, 1971) | 227 | 16 | 69 (32.7) | 5 (2.4) | 137 (64.9) |
| Kaufmann & Tack | (1975) | 90 | 2 | 7 (8.0) | 29 (33.0) | 52 (59.1) |
| Maschler | (1978) | 78 | 11 | 2 (3.0) | 2 (3.0) | 63 (94.0) |
| Over study | | 1445 | 35 | 420 (29.8) | 118 (8.4) | 872 (61.8) |

Inspection of the bottom row of Table 2 shows that overall, 61.8% of 1410 games were within the limits $0 \leq \hat{\alpha} \leq 1$. Moreover, the range of this percentage is remarkably stable over studies, considering the variety of characteristic functions and experimental conditions employed. With the exception of one study (Maschler, 1978), the range is from 55.0% to 68.1%. And this singular experiment had the special property that many of the games played featured one virtual monopolist against two players in very weak positions. Such games resulted in ranges of $\hat{\alpha}$ encompassing almost all of the reasonable bargaining space.

When a game did not satisfy equation (8), it was more likely to be with a negative $\hat{\alpha}$ (29.8% of the time) than $\hat{\alpha} > 1$ (8.4%). Again, this finding was by and large constant over the studies, but again with two exceptions: Kahan and Rapoport (1977) and Kaufmann and Tack (1975). Inspection of Table 1 shows that these two studies were the only ones that employed solo games.

DIFFERENCES AMONG CHARACTERISTIC FUNCTIONS

Table 3 presents a tabulation of outcomes satisfying $0 \leq \hat{\alpha} \leq 1$ by the 2-dimensional classification of games based on $v(N)$ and $v(i)$, while Figure 2 graphically shows the distribution of $\hat{\alpha}$ for games meeting that requirement. Examination of Table 3 shows that there was not a great difference in the predictive accuracy of $P_\alpha$ as a function of either classification variable, but that the type of violation of equation (8) depended on whether or not $v(i) = 0$. This observed difference is interpretable in terms of the reversal of power positions in the strategic equivalents to about half of the solo games played; the violations indicate that, contrary to Kahneman and Tversky's (1979) heuristic of taking the status quo as the guaranteed position, players in our games bargained from a zero-oriented status quo point. The implications of this finding for differences between individual and game decision making behavior are important, but beyond the scope of the present paper.

Figure 2 displays the distribution of $\hat{\alpha}$, given $0 \leq \hat{\alpha} \leq 1$, in terms of $v(N)$ and $v(i)$. For three of the four graphs, the intervals at the extremes are the most frequent; the only exception is $v(N) = 0$ and $v(i) > 0$, for which $\alpha = 1$ does not imply an equal split. All games show a mode near the $\hat{\alpha} = 0$ end of $P_\alpha$. However, when neither the quota nor equality SOF predominates, there is no apparent pattern as to the location of a compromise.

Although characteristic functions may differ in the relationships among the various 2-person coalitions, and in how the value of the 3-person coalition relates to the 2-person coalition values, there is no well-established index to identify these relationships. Levinsohn and Rapoport (1978) proposed one measure of the relationships among the 2-person coalition values, and several authors have tied the 3-person coalitional value to the three 2-person coalition values of a 3-person game via the size of the core, if it is nonempty (Kaufmann & Tack, 1975; Michener, Ginsberg, & Yuen, 1979; Shapley & Shubik, 1966). However, none of these measures had a correlation with $\hat{\alpha}$ greater than 0.26 in absolute value. Although, with over 1000 outcomes, such a correlation is confidently not zero, it explains so little of the variance of $\hat{\alpha}$ as to be of minor importance.

GLOBAL GOODNESS OF FIT

The problem of goodness of fit may be addressed by constructing a measure that assesses the improvement of a solution concept over a null hypothesis that any IRPC is as likely as any other. This necessitates separate treatments for 2- and 3-person coalitions. If a 2-person coalition forms, then the payoff for one of its members ranges from zero to

*Table 3.*        *Percentage of games satisfying* $0 \leq \hat{\alpha} \leq 1$, *by game*
                 *category and coalition structure.*

| Classification[a] | Number of Games | $\hat{\alpha}<0$ | $\hat{\alpha}>1$ | $0\leq\hat{\alpha}\leq1$ |
|---|---|---|---|---|
| $v(N) = 0,\ v(i) = 0$ | 653 | 34.6% | 4.3% | 61.1% |
| $v(N) = 0,\ v(i) > 0$ | 159 | 20.1% | 20.8% | 59.1% |
| $v(N) > 0,\ v(i) = 0$ | 354 | 33.8% | 1.7% | 64.4% |
| $v(N) > 0,\ v(i) > 0$ | 244 | 17.2% | 20.9% | 61.9% |
| $v(N) = 0$ | 812 | 31.8% | 7.5% | 60.7% |
| $v(N) > 0$ | 598 | 27.1% | 9.5% | 63.4% |
| $v(i) = 0$ | 1007 | 34.4% | 3.4% | 62.3% |
| $v(i) > 0$ | 403 | 18.4% | 20.8% | 60.8% |
| $CS = \{AB,C\}$ | 627 | 25.5% | 6.1% | 68.4% |
| $CS = \{AC,B\}$ | 264 | 36.0% | 5.7% | 58.3% |
| $CS = \{A,BC\}$ | 189 | 37.0% | 15.9% | 47.1% |
| $CS = \{ABC\}$ | 330 | 28.8% | 10.6% | 60.6% |
| All games | 1410 | 29.8% | 8.4% | 61.8% |

[a] $i = A,B,C$.

$v(S)$.  This range of payoff may be thought of as a line segment, of which the prediction of the $\alpha$-power model is a part.   If the model is of no value, then we would expect a proportion of outcomes within the model's prediction equal to the proportion of the line segment $v(S)$ in the model.   As both the value $v(S)$ and the proportion of $v(S)$ in the model vary from game to game, we adjust each outcome by defining a variable

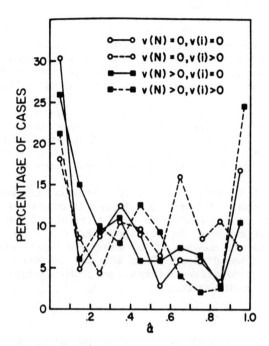

*Figure 2. Distribution of α̂ for a 2 × 2 classification of the 3-person games in terms of v(N) and v(i).*

$$H = \begin{cases} 0 \text{ if } (y;S) \in P_\alpha \\ 1/(1 - p), \text{ otherwise,} \end{cases}$$

where $p$ is the proportion of $v(S)$ in the solution. For the coalition structure $(ij,k)$, $p$ is given by

$$p = \left| \frac{v(ik) - v(jk) - v(i) + v(j)}{2v(ij)} \right| .$$

The statistic $H$ has the property that if the model successfully accounts for all games, the mean value of $H$ will be zero; if, on the other hand, the $\alpha$-power solution is no improvement over chance, then the mean value of $H$ will be one.

For 3-person coalitions, where the outcome is a simplex and the prediction is a line segment in that simplex, the distance between any outcome and the nearest (best-fit) point on the line segment forms the basis of the goodness-of-fit measure. We construct the area within the simplex of outcomes that is the locus of all points as close or closer to the prediction line segment than the outcome. Such an area, in dotted lines in Figure 1, has the shape of a rectangle along the length of $P_\alpha$, to which are attached semicircles about each endpoint. We define $A$ as the proportion of this area to the whole area of the simplex. This proportion $A$, like $H$ for the 2-person coalition case, provides a measure of accuracy, such that if all outcomes are precisely as predicted, $A = 0$, while if the model offers no improvement over the null hypothesis of uniform distribution of outcomes, $A = 1$.

The two goodness-of-fit measures $H$ and $A$ cannot be strictly used to test the model as a whole, as the algebraic model strictly posits the easily refutable $H = A = 0$, and offers no theory of error variance for either. Nevertheless, employing the reduction of uncertainty interpretation of these measures, they may be cursorily examined over the data as a whole, and employed to compare different games or different coalition structures.

The mean value of $H$, aggregated over 1091 2-person coalition outcomes, was 0.42, indicating that the uncertainty of location of outcome was reduced by over half by the $\alpha$-power model. For grand coalitions, the statistic $A$ provided even better support. Over all 330 observed grand coalitions, the mean proportion was 0.034, with a standard deviation of 0.056. But the skewness of the distribution biases even these favorable statistics. The median $A$ was 0.015 and 80% of all games had values of $A \leq 0.050$. In other words, 80% of all grand coalition outcomes were clustered around the prediction $P_\alpha$ in 1/20 the area of the payoff simplex.

COALITION STRUCTURES

We conclude this section with an examination of the effects of different obtained coalition structures on the predictions of $P_\alpha$. Table 3 shows the proportion of times outcomes satisfied the requirement $0 \leq \alpha \leq 1$ by coalition structure. There is a definite drop in the predictive accuracy of the model as the obtained coalition structure moves from $\{AB,C\}$ through $\{AC,B\}$ to $\{A,BC\}$. This corresponds directly to decreasing values of the 2-person coalitions, so an interpretation of this finding is, the lower the value of a 2-person coalition, within a given characteristic function game, the less likely an outcome in that coalition structure will be predicted by the $\alpha$-power model. The grand coalition does slightly less well than the weighted mean of 2-person coalitions. The difference among 2-person coalition structures is reinforced by the mean values of the goodness of fit index $H$, which were 0.34, 0.52, and 0.56 for coalition structures $\{AB,C\}$, $\{AC,B\}$, and $\{A,BC\}$, respectively.

The differences in proportion of outcomes with $\hat{\alpha} < 0$ and $\hat{\alpha} > 1$ from a "baseline" of the modal $\{AB,C\}$ coalition structure have relatively straightforward explanations. Player $C$ perceived himself as being in a position of weakness; the most likely coalition structure was one that excluded him. Therefore, to attempt to be included, he was likely to "shave" (Riker, 1967) his perceived fair share in order to entice one of the other players away from coalition $AB$. If he dropped below his quota, then the outcome of the game had $\hat{\alpha} < 0$.

In the instance of grand coalitions, a frequent course of bargaining leading to a grand coalition was for a 2-person coalition to form, and then for the third player to be inserted (Rapoport & Kahan, 1976), taking most of the difference between $v(N)$ and the value of the tentatively-formed 2-person coalition. Typically, this included third player received the lowest payoff of the triad; he always obtained less than his quota. When the earlier 2-person coalition was $AC$ or $BC$, then a reversal of payoff order was likely, resulting in an estimated $\hat{\alpha} > 1$. Thus, the way in which a 3-person coalition formed partly determined the outcome, and the $\alpha$-power model shares the weakness with all other mathematical theories of $n$-person games of ignoring this important phenomenon.

Figure 3 shows the percentage of values of $\hat{\alpha}$, given that the constraint $0 \leq \hat{\alpha} \leq 1$ was satisfied, by formed coalition structure. For all four coalition structures, the modal range is in $0 \leq \hat{\alpha} \leq 0.1$, near the prediction $\alpha = 0$ of the $M_1^{(i)}$ bargaining set. Additionally, except for coalition $AC$, there is a secondary mode at equality ($\alpha = 1$). This exception is easily explained; an equal split between players of adjacent power, as $A$ and $B$, or $B$ and $C$, is somewhat natural. Similarly, if all three players are together, they might split equally. But if the 2-person coalition $AC$ forms, the presence of player $B$ in the game remains salient, and acts as a buffer between $A$ and $C$, enforcing their relative payoff differences.

## Discussion

We close with several comments regarding the nature of the $\alpha$-power model, and its relationship to previous psychological research on coalition formation. As with any algebraic model, ours allows no "errors" and hence technically fails with the first case of a parameter estimate outside of the range $0 \leq \alpha \leq 1$, or a 3-person coalition outcome not on the prediction line. However, instead of employing this too-stringent criterion, we have tested the model by comparing it to other algebraic models and by presenting results in terms of the reduction of information in the data that is provided by the model (Estes, 1975). By the latter criterion, the $\alpha$-power model does moderately well for 2-person coalition structures and very well for grand coalitions. For the former criterion, we must consider that previous models were parameter-free and made point predictions.

Although both mathematicians (Maschler, 1963a) and psychologists (Komorita & Chertkoff, 1973) have recognized the need for theories that posit ranges instead of point predictions, rather than accept a parameterization which provides a range, they have instead invoked assumptions of psychological norms or standards of fairness, albeit with expressed trepidation, to construct the point solution. However, the combined data from nine 3-person games studies clearly refute any point solution. If we were to calculate a mean value for $\hat{\alpha}$ over all studies, it would be about 0.42, which is within shouting distance of .50. Thus, if we had postulated that there are opposing forces of equality and parity (quota power) that are resolved in bargaining to a compromise between the two, and thereby constructed a theory specifying $\alpha = .50$, our aggregate statistics would support such a theory. But, as we have seen (Figures 2 and 3), the two opposing forces typically do not balance; instead one or the other predominates for most given plays of the games. For *any* point solution concept, whether mathematical or social psychological in origin, the majority of outcomes refute it. It is an open and interesting question the

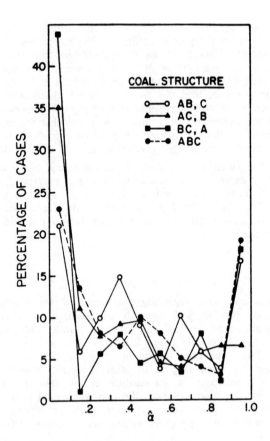

*Figure 3. Distribution of $\hat{\alpha}$ for the coalition structure that formed.*

extent to which support for "compromise" theories (e.g., Chertkoff, 1970) arise from statistical aggregations of outcomes.

It should be noted that the $\alpha$-power model is useful only for nonconstant-sum games.  If the characteristic function is such that the game may be represented as constant-sum, as in the weighted majority games which constitute the bulk of social psychological empirical data on coalition formation, then the model degenerates to posit equal splits among members of a coalition, no matter what the value of $\alpha$ and no matter which coalition structure forms.  For this reason, in our survey of 3-person games, we have ignored games played in weighted-majority form.

The $\alpha$-power model, as it stands, is not a complete answer to the question of payoff disbursement in coalition formation games, but even its more obvious problems have the benefit of indicating directly the path future efforts must take.  The systematic differences in predictability, depending on which of the various 2-person coalitions forms, indicate that these outcomes may be functions of different paths of bargaining; detailed analysis of the process as well as the outcome of a negotiated game is mandated if we are to understand this difference.    Different experimental methods may well induce different outcomes (Komorita & Meek, 1978).   Similarly, the outcomes of 3-person games appear to be the result of multiple strategies of bargaining, including instances where the grand coalition forms from the addition of the third player to a 2-person coalition as well as its formation from the three players acting in concert.    That these two general methods of growth might yield different payoff configurations is a problem that no theory has yet effectively addressed.   The differences between solo and non-solo games indicate that players regard their status quo as where they begin the game rather than the payoff they are guaranteed.   This implies that there may be differences in individual and interactive approaches to rationality (Kahan, 1974) which require specification.

Finally, the present solution concept shares with its direct antecedents (Maschler, 1963a; Rapoport & Kahan, 1979) the intriguing and potentially fruitful notion that bargaining in a coalition situation takes place not in the outcome space, as specified by the characteristic function, but rather in a subjective constant-sum power space, which is constructed from both the characteristic function and the standard of fairness.   Maschler (1963a) assumed superadditive games and group rationality, such that the resolution of the game would be some disbursement of the maximum value obtainable, $v(N)$.   Rapoport and Kahan (1979) and this paper instead maintain the characteristic function as a "reality constraint" on coalitions, such that if coalition $S$ forms, although its allocation to its members is determined by the function $u$, the payoff must sum to $v(S)$.   This separation of the payoff space and the bargaining space could prove the means by which considerations such as trustworthiness, equity, altruism, etc., which have often been cited as bases for behavior, can be formally introduced into theories of coalition formation without having to first transform these social motives into utility measures on the same scale as the game payoffs.

## Acknowledgments

Data analyses and preparation of this paper were supported by National Science Foundation Grant No. BNS76-84285.   We wish to thank Richard A. Helwig for his assistance in data analysis and Jim Laing and Gina Shimburski for helpful suggestions. We also wish to especially thank Michael Maschler for many letters and conversations which clarified and focused our understanding of models of $n$-person games.

## Notes:

1.   Although the earliest solution concepts such as the stable set, core, and Shapley value were only defined for superadditive games, later work obviated that constraint.    More recently, Aumann and Dréze (1974) have shown that any solution concept can be expressed for non-superadditive games.

2.   We shall employ $v(k)$ and later $u(k)$ and $w(k)$ as simplifications of the more technically correct $v(\{k\})$, $u(\{k\})$, and $w(\{k\})$, respectively.

3.  The following development closely follows Maschler (1963a). However, whereas Maschler allowed all possible partitions of the $n$ players to form as negotiation groups, we restrict the game space to only complementary pairs of negotiation parties (see Rapoport & Kahan, 1979). This restriction affords us considerable simplification, as any subset $P$ of $N$ has only one value under the SOF.

4.  Our definition of stability in characteristic function games might be rephrased as payoff vectors that give coalition members equal excesses over their respective 1-person power function values. In this way, this definition is akin to that of the kernel (Davis & Maschler, 1965), a solution concept that has been extensively tested and that provides solutions identical to the $M_1^{(i)}$ bargaining set for all 2-person coalition outcomes and almost all grand coalition outcomes of the 3-person games we shall examine below. Social scientific expositions of the kernel may be found in Davis (1970), Horowitz and Rapoport (1974), Michener and Sakurai (1976), Rapoport, Kahan and Wallsten (1978), and Rapoport (1970).

5.  The violation of the "triangle inequality" results in one player being "weak" (Maschler, 1963b), who can make no contributions to the power of other players. In all experimental games examined below, the triangle inequality condition (12) is met and the games are either superadditive or formally interdict the grand coalition.

## References

Albers, W. (1978) Block forming tendencies as characteristics of the bargaining behavior in different versions of apex games. In H. Sauermann (Ed.), *Beiträge zur Experimentellen Wirtschaftsforschung, Vol. VIII: Coalition forming behavior.* Tübingen: J. C. B. Mohr.

Atkinson, R. C., Bower, G. H. and Crothers, C. J. (1965) *Introduction to Mathematical Learning Theory.* New York: Wiley.

Aumann, R. J. (1967) A survey of cooperative games with side payments. In M. Shubik (Ed.), *Essays in Mathematical Economics in Honor of Oskar Morgenstern.* Princeton: Princeton University Press.

Aumann, R. J. and Dréze, J. H. (1974) Cooperative games with coalition structures. *International Journal of Game Theory* 3: 217-237.

Aumann, R. J. and Maschler, M. (1964) The bargaining set for cooperative games. In M. Dresher, L. S. Shapley and A. W. Tucker (Eds.), *Advances in Game Theory.* Princeton: Princeton University Press.

Buckley, J. J. and Westen, R. E. (1973) The symmetric solution to a five-person constant-sum game as a description of experimental game outcomes. *Journal of Conflict Resolution* 17: 703-718.

Charnes, A., Rousseau, J. and Seiford, L. (1978) Complements, mollifiers, and the propensity to disrupt. *International Journal of Game Theory* 7: 37-50.

Chertkoff, J. M. (1970) Sociopsychological theories and research on coalition formation. In S. Groennings, E. W. Kelley and M. Leiserson (Eds.), *The Study of Coalition Behavior.* New York: Holt, Rinehart & Winston.

Davis, M. (1970) *Game Theory: A Nontechnical Introduction.* New York: Basic Books.
Davis, M. and Maschler, M. (1965) The kernel of a cooperative game. *Naval Research Logistics Quarterly* 12: 223-259.
Estes, W. K. (1975) Some targets for mathematical psychology. *Journal of Mathematical Psychology* 12: 263-282.
Gamson, W. A. (1961) A theory of coalition formation, *American Sociological Review* 26: 373-382.
Gillies, D. B. (1953) Discriminatory and bargaining solutions to a class of symmetric N-person games. In H. W. Kuhn and A. W. Tucker (Eds.), *Contributions to the Theory of Games,* III. Princeton: Princeton University Press.
Horowitz, A. D. (1973) The competitive bargaining set for cooperative n-person games. *Journal of Mathematical psychology* 10: 265-289.
Horowitz, A. D. and Rapoport, Am. (1974) Test of the kernel and two bargaining set models in four- and five-person games. In An. Rapoport (Ed.), *Game Theory as a Theory of Conflict Resolution.* Dordrecht, Holland: D. Reidel.
Kahan, J. P. (1974) Rationality, the Prisoner's Dilemma, and population. *Journal of Social Issues* 30: 189-210.
Kahan, J. P. and Helwig, R. A. (1971) Coalitions: A system of programs for computer-controlled bargaining games. *General Systems* 16: 31-41.
Kahan, J. P. and Rapoport, Am. (1974) Test of the bargaining set and kernel models in three-person games. In An. Rapoport (Ed.), *Game Theory as a Theory of Conflict Resolution.* Dordrecht, Holland: D. Reidel.
Kahan, J. P. and Rapoport, Am. (1977) When you don't need to join: The effects of guaranteed payoffs on bargaining in three-person cooperative games. *Theory and Decision* 8: 97-126.
Kahan, J. P. and Rapoport, Am. (1979) The influence of structural relationships on coalition formation in 4-person apex games. *European Journal of Social Psychology* 9: 339-362.
Kahan, J. P. and Rapoport, Am. (1980) Coalition formation in the triad when two are weak and one is strong. *Mathematical Social Sciences* 1: 11-38.
Kahneman, D. and Tversky, A. (1979) Prospect theory: An analysis of decision under risk. *Econometrica* 47: 263-291.
Kaufmann, M. and Tack, W. H. (1975) Koalitionsbildung und gewinnaufteilung bei strategisch aquivalenten 3-Personen-Spielen. *Zeitschrift für Sozialpsychologie* 6: 227-245.
Komorita, S. S. (1974) A weighted probability model of coalition formation. *Psychological Review* 81: 242-256.
Komorita, S. S. (1979) An equal excess model of coalition formation. *Behavioral Science* 24: 369-381.
Komorita, S. S. and Chertkoff, J. M. (1973) A bargaining theory of coalition formation. *Psychological Review* 80: 149-162.
Komorita, S. S. and Meek, D. (1978) Generality and validity of some theories of coalition formation. *Journal of Personality and Social Psychology* 36: 392-404.

Levinsohn, J. R. and Rapoport, Am. (1978) Coalition formation in multistage three-person cooperative games. In H. Sauermann (Ed.), *Beiträge zur Experimentellen Wirtschaftsforschung, Vol. VII: Coalition Forming Behavior*. Tübingen: J. C. B. Mohr.

Luce, R. D. (1955) Psychological stability: A new equilibrium concept for n-person game-theory. In P. Lazarfeld (Ed.), *Mathematical Models of Human Behavior*. Stamford, CT: Dunlap and Associates.

Luce, R. D. and Raiffa, H. (1957) *Games and Decisions: Introduction and Critical Survey*. New York: Wiley.

Luce, R. D. and Suppes, P. (1965) Preference, utility, and subjective probability. In R. D. Luce, R. R. Bush, and E. Galanter (Eds.), *Handbook of Mathematical Psychology, Vol. III*. New York: Wiley.

Maschler, M. (1963a) The power of a coalition. *Management Science* 10: 8-29.

Maschler, M. (1963b) n-Person games with only 1, n-1, and n-person permissible coalitions. *Journal of Mathematical Analysis and Applications* 6: 230-256.

Maschler, M. (1978) Playing an n-person game: An experiment. In H. Sauermann (Ed.), *Beiträge zur experimentellen Wirtschaftsforschung, Volume III: Coalition Forming Behavior*. Tübingen: J. C. B. Mohr.

Medlin, S. M. (1976) Effects of grand coalition payoffs on coalition formation in 3-person games. *Behavioral Science* 21: 48-61.

Michener, H. A., Ginsberg, I. J., and Yuen, K. (1979) Effects of core properties in four-person games with sidepayments. *Behavioral Science* 24: 263-280.

Michener, H. A. and Sakurai, M. M. (1976) A research note on the predictive adequacy of the kernel. *Journal of Conflict Resolution* 20: 129-142.

Murnighan, J. K. (1978) Models of coalition behavior: Game theoretic, social psychological, and political perspectives. *Psychological Bulletin*, 85: 1130-1153.

Neimark, E. D. and Estes, W. K. (1967) *Stimulus Sampling Theory*. San Francisco: Holden-Day.

Rapoport, Am. and Kahan, J. P. (1974) Computer controlled research on bargaining and coalition formation. *Behavior Research Methods & Instrumentation* 6: 87-93.

Rapoport, Am. and Kahan, J. P. (1976) When three isn't always two against one: Coalitions in experimental three-person games. *Journal of Experimental Social Psychology* 12: 253-273.

Rapoport, Am. and Kahan, J. P. (1979) Standards of fairness in 4-person monopolistic cooperative games. In S. Brams, A. Schotter, and G. Schwödiauer (Eds.), *Applied Game Theory*. Vienna: Physica-Verlag.

Rapoport, Am., Kahan, J. P., Funk, S. G. and Horowitz, A. D. (1979) *Coalition Formation Games with Sophisticated Players*. Heidelberg Springer-Verlag.

Rapoport, Am., Kahan, J. P. and Wallsten, T. S. (1978) Sources of power in 4-person apex games. In H. Sauermann (Ed.), *Beiträge zur Experimentellen Wirtschaftsforschung, Vol. VIII: Coalition Forming Behavior*. Tübingen: J. C. B. Mohr.

Rapoport, An. (1970) *n-person Game Theory: Concepts and Applications*. Ann Arbor: University of Michigan Press.

Rapoport, An. and Chammah, A. (1965) *Prisoner's Dilemma*. Ann Arbor: University of Michigan Press.

Riker, W. H. (1967) Bargaining in a three-person game. *American Political Science Review* **61**: 642-656.

Riker, W. H. (1971) An experimental examination of formal and informal rules of a three-person game. In B. Lieberman (Ed.), *Social Choice*. New York: Gordon and Breach.

Riker, W. H. (1972) Three-person coalitions in three-person games: Experimental verification of the theory of games. In J. F. Herndon and J. L. Bernd (Eds.), *Mathematical Applications in Political Science VI*. Charlottesville: University of Virginia Press.

Schmeidler, D. (1969) The nucleolus of a characteristic function game. *SIAM Journal of Applied Mathematics* **17**: 1163-1170.

Selten, R. (1972) Equal share analysis of characteristic function experiments. In H. Sauermann (Ed.), *Beiträge zur Experimentellen Wirtschaftsforschung, Vol. III (Contributions to experimental economics)* Tübingen: J. C. B. Mohr.

Selten, R. and Schuster, K. G. (1968) Psychological variables and coalition forming behavior. In K. Borch and J. Mossin (Eds.), *Risk and Uncertainty*. London: Macmillan.

Shapley, L. S. (1953) A value for n-person games. In H. Kuhn and A. W. Tucker (Eds), *Contributions to the Theory of Games II*. Annals of Mathematical Studies 28. Princeton: Princeton University Press.

Shapley, L. S. and Shubik, M. (1973) Game theory in economics - Chapter 6: Characteristic function, core, and stable set. The RAND Corporation Report No. R-904-NSF/6. Santa Monica, California.

Vinacke, W. E. (1969) Variables in experimental games: Toward a field theory. *Psychological Bulletin* **71**: 293-318.

von Neumann, J. and Morgenstern, O. (1947) *Theory of Games and Economic Behavior*, 2nd Edition. Princeton: Princeton University Press.

## Appendix

PROOF OF THEOREM 1

Let

$$w(S) = \gamma \left[ v(S) + \sum_{i \in S} \beta_i \right], \text{ for all } S \subseteq N ,$$

where $\beta_i$ is a real constant and $\gamma > 0$. Then denoting the power for game $(N;w)$ by $u'$, we obtain

$$u'(A) = (1 - \alpha) \, \gamma \, [v(N) + \beta_A + \beta_B + \beta_C] - (1 - \alpha) \, \gamma \, [v(BC) + \beta_B$$
$$+ \, \beta_C] + \alpha\gamma \, [v(A) + \beta_A)]$$

$$= \gamma \, \{(1 - \alpha) \, [v(N) - v(BC)] + \alpha v(A) + \beta_A\} \quad .$$

Similarly,

$$u'(B) = \gamma\{(1 - \alpha) \, [v(N) - v(AC)] + \alpha v(B) + \beta_B\}$$

$$u'(C) = \gamma\{(1 - \alpha) \, [v(N) - v(AB)] + \alpha v(C) + \beta_C\} \quad .$$

To achieve stability, the payoffs for the grand coalition of game $(N;w)$, $x_A'$, $x_B'$, and $x_C'$, must satisfy the equalities

$$x_A' - u'(A) = x_B' - u'(B),$$

$$x_A' - u'(A) = x_C' - u'(C),$$

$$x_B' - u'(B) = x_C' - u'(C),$$

$$x_A' + x_B' + x_C' = \gamma[v(N) + \beta_A + \beta_B + \beta_C] \quad .$$

Solving these equations yields

$$x_i' = \gamma[x_i + \beta_i] \quad , \quad i = A,B,C \quad ,$$

which completes the proof for coalition structure $(ABC)$. The proofs for the other coalition structures are similar and not given here.

PROOF OF THEOREM 2

Because of Theorem 1, we can assume without loss of generality that $v(i) = 0$, $i \in N$. From (5) it follows that

$$u(A) = (1 - \alpha) \, [v(N) - v(BC)] \tag{1'}$$

$$u(B) = (1 - \alpha) \, [v(N) - v(AC)] \tag{2'}$$

$$u(C) = (1 - \alpha) \, [v(N) - v(AB)] \tag{3'}$$

Consider first the coalition structure $\{AB,C\}$. $P_\alpha$ is non-empty if there exist $x_A$ and $x_B$ such that

$$x_A - u(A) = x_B - u(B),$$                                              (4')

$$x_A + x_B = v(AB), \quad x_A \geq 0, \; x_B \geq 0.$$                    (5')

Substituting (4') for $x_A$ in (5') yields

$$v(AB) = x_B + x_B - u(B) + u(A).$$                                      (6')

subtracting (2') from (1') and substituting for $u(A) - u(B)$ in (6') yields

$$v(AB) = 2x_B + (1 - \alpha) \, [v(AC) - v(BC)].$$                       (7')

In a similar way, it can be shown that

$$v(AB) = 2x_A + (1 - \alpha) \, [v(BC) - v(AC)].$$                       (8')

Equations (7') and (8') imply that

$$x_B \geq 0 \text{ iff } v(AB) \geq (1 - \alpha) \, [v(AC) - v(BC)],$$

$$x_A \geq 0 \text{ iff } v(AB) \geq (1 - \alpha) \, [v(BC) - v(AC)],$$

which, in turn, imply that $P_\alpha$ is non-empty for the coalition structure $\{AB,C\}$ if and only if

$$v(AB)/[v(AC) - v(BC)] \geq 1 - \alpha \quad .$$

Given the convention $v(AB) \geq v(AC) \geq v(BC) \geq 0$, it can easily be seen that it is always true that $v(AB)/[v(AC) - v(BC)] \geq 1 \geq 1 - \alpha$, so $P_\alpha$ will always be non-empty for the largest 2-person coalition.

It can similarly be shown that the steps (4') through (8') hold for coalition structures $\{AC,B\}$ and $\{BC,A\}$ through the permutation of players. Hence, we obtain nonemptiness conditions for these two coalition structures as:

$$v(AC)/[v(AB) - v(BC)] \geq 1 - \alpha \quad ,$$

and

$$v(BC)/[v(AB) - v(AC)] \geq 1 - \alpha \quad ,$$

respectively.

Consider next the grand coalition $\{ABC\}$. $P_\alpha$ is nonempty if there exist non-negative numbers $x_A$, $x_B$, and $x_C$ such that

$$x_A - u(A) = x_B - u(B) = x_C - u(C);$$

$$x_A + x_B + x_C = v(N) .$$

Again using equations (1'), (2'), and (3'), we obtain

$$v(N) = x_A + x_B + x_C = x_C - v(C) + u(A) + x_C + x_C - v(C) + u(B)$$

$$= 3x_C + u(A) + u(B) - 2u(C)$$

$$= 3x_C + (1 - \alpha) [v(N) - v(BC) + v(N) - v(AC) - 2v(N) + 2v(AB)]$$

$$= 3x_C + (1 - \alpha) [2v(AB) - v(AC) - v(BC)].$$

This implies that

$$x_C \geq 0 \text{ iff } v(N) \geq (1 - \alpha) [2v(AB) - v(AC) - v(BC)]. \tag{9'}$$

Similarly, it can be shown that

$$x_A \geq 0 \text{ iff } v(N) \geq (1 - \alpha) [2v(BC) - v(AB) - v(AC)];$$

$$x_B \geq 0 \text{ iff } v(N) \geq (1 - \alpha) [2v(AC) - v(AB) - v(BC)].$$

These latter two conditions are implied by (9'), given $v(AB) \geq v(AC) \geq v(BC)$, so all three conditions are satisfied if it can be assumed that $x_C \geq 0$. This completes the proof.

PROOF OF COROLLARY 2a

The triangle inequality can be rewritten as

$$v(BC)/[v(AB) - v(AC)] \geq 1,$$

which proves its sufficiency for the nonemptiness of $P_\alpha$ for the coalition structure $\{A,BC\}$ for any $0 \leq \alpha \leq 1$. Similarly, whenever $P_\alpha$ is nonempty for $\{A,BC\}$, it will also be nonempty for $\{AC,B\}$, because $v(AC) \geq v(BC)$.

To verify $P_\alpha$ for coalition structure $\{AB,C\}$, note that $x_C = v(C) \geq 0$ as required. To achieve stability, $x_A$ and $x_B$ must satisfy (4') and (5'). Rewriting (4') in terms of the powers $u(A)$ and $u(B)$ in (10), we obtain

$$x_A - v(N) + u(BC) = x_B - v(N) + u(AC). \tag{10'}$$

Using again (10) to express $u(BC)$ and $u(AC)$ in terms of the coalition values yields

$$x_A + v(BC) + \alpha[v(N) - v(BC) - v(A)] = x_B + v(AC)$$

$$+ \alpha[v(N) - v(AC) - v(B)]. \tag{11'}$$

Solving (5') and (11') for $x_A$ and $x_B$ yields the result in (13) for coalition structure $\{AB,C\}$.

To prove that $x_A \geq 0$, write

$$x_A = \{v(AB) + (1 - \alpha)\ [v(AC) - v(BC)] + \alpha[v(A) - v(B)]\}/2$$

$$= \{v(AB) + v(AC) + v(BC) + \alpha[v(BC) - v(AC) + v(A) - v(B)]\}/2 \ . \tag{12'}$$

Since $x_A$ is a linear function of $\alpha$, it is sufficient to consider only the extreme values of $\alpha = 0$ and $\alpha = 1$. If $\alpha = 0$, (11') reduces to

$$x_A = [v(AB) + v(AC) - v(BC)]/2 \ .$$

Here $x_A \geq 0$ because of (12). If $\alpha = 1$, (12') reduces to

$$x_A = [v(AB) + v(A) - v(B)]/2 \ .$$

Here $x_A \geq 0$ because of superadditivity. The proof that $x_B \geq 0$ is similar.

The stability of the payoff configurations in (13) for coalition structures $\{AC,B\}$ and $\{BC,A\}$ is proved as for coalition structure $\{AB,C\}$.

Consider next the coalition structure $\{ABC\}$. To achieve stability, $x_A$, $x_B$, and $x_C$ must satisfy the conditions

$$x_A - u(A) = x_B - u(B) = x_C - u(C)$$

$$x_A + x_B + x_C = v(N),$$

$$x_A \geq 0,\ x_B \geq 0,\ x_C \geq 0.$$

Using (10) for expressing $u(i)$ in the expressions above in terms of the coalition values, and then solving these equations for the payoffs $x_A$, $x_B$, and $x_C$, yields the payoff configuration in (13) for coalition structure $\{ABC\}$. To show that $x_A \geq 0$, write

$$x_A = \{v(N) + (1 - \alpha)\ [v(AB) + v(AC) - 2v(BC)]$$

$$+ \alpha[2v(A) - v(B) - v(C)]\}/3$$

$$= \{v(N) + v(AB) + v(AC) - 2v(BC) + \alpha[2v(BC) - v(AB)$$

$$- v(AC) - v(B) - v(C) + 2v(A)]\}/3. \tag{13'}$$

It is again sufficient to consider only $\alpha = 0$ and $\alpha = 1$ because of the linearity of $x_A$ in $\alpha$. If $\alpha = 0$, (13') reduces to

$$x_A = \{[v(N) - v(BC)] + [v(AB) + v(AC) - v(BC)]\}/3.$$

Both terms in the brackets are nonnegative, the first because of superadditivity and the second because of the "traingle inequality." Hence $x_A \geq 0$, if $\alpha = 0$. If $\alpha = 1$, (13') reduces to

$$x_A = \{v(N) - [v(B) + v(C)] + 2v(A)\}/3 \quad,$$

which is nonnegative because of superadditivity. The proofs that $x_B \geq 0$ and $x_C \geq 0$ are similar and not repeated here.

PROOF OF COROLLARY 2b

We have already shown, without invoking the "triangle inequality," that the solution in (13) for the grand coalition belongs to $P_\alpha$. We only have to show that $x_i \geq 0$, $i \in N$, if $1/2 \leq \alpha \leq 1$. Because of the linearity of $x_i$ in $\alpha$, it is sufficient to consider $\alpha = 1/2$ and $\alpha = 1$. If $\alpha = 1/2$, (13') reduces to

$$x_A = \frac{v(N) - v(BC)}{3} + \frac{v(AB) - v(B)}{6} + \frac{v(AC) - v(C)}{6} + \frac{v(A)}{3} \quad.$$

Each of the four terms is nonnegative because of superadditivity. Hence $x_A \geq 0$, if $\alpha = 1/2$. If $\alpha = 1$, then we have already shown, without invoking the "triangle inequality," that $x_A \geq 0$. The proof that $x_B \geq 0$ and $x_C \geq 0$ are similar.

# CHAPTER 13

# COALITION FORMATION IN A FIVE-PERSON MARKET GAME

ABSTRACT. Market games constitute a class of cooperative $n$-person games with sidepayments in which several coalitions may form simultaneously. In order to study coalition forming behavior in such games and to test the descriptive power of four major solution concepts that yield differing prescriptions for market games, 11 pentads of students each played 6 different market games presented in characteristic function form through a computer-controlled experimental procedure. The outcomes showed strong consistencies over pentads and sharp differences among games. None of the models fully accounted for these data. Instead, considerations of sequential formation of coalitions within a coalition structure, the concept of maximal share structure suggested in the equal share solution, and a recently developed model, that encompasses the predictions of the bargaining set and equal shares, served jointly as the first-order determinants of both the decision of which coalition to form and the allocation of payoff to coalition members.

## 1. Introduction

Market games constitute a class of cooperative $n$-person games in characteristic function form that were originally introduced and studied by Shapley and Shubik (1969a, b, 1975). These abstract games arise from trading economies in which the players are initially supplied with a number of idealized commodities which they can trade among themselves without any restriction. Money, too, may be transferred in any amount. When the game terminates, possibly with several multi-person trades concluded, the payoff to each player is just his utility for his final holding of money and goods, where the utility is assumed to be continuous and concave, and expressed in monetary units. The payoff is determined without regard for the particular sequence of trades that took place during the game and without regard for the final holdings of the other players (Shapley and Shubik, 1973).

Our interest in market games, and in particular our motivation to experimentally study coalition forming behavior in them, was instigated by a recent paper by Maschler (1976), in which he presented a 5-person market game and argued that for the grand coalition the core does not reflect the economic forces at work in that game. Instead, the $M_1^{(i)}$ bargaining set, which for Maschler's example game contains both the core and outcomes not in the core, "reflects the economics of that situation better and may yield new insights on the nature of the competition between traders" (Maschler, 1976, p. 185). In the present paper, we shall pursue Maschler's analysis further and argue that although the $M_1^{(i)}$ bargaining set for the grand coalition may indeed be intuitively more acceptable than the core for that same coalition structure, its intuitive appeal diminishes when other coalition structures that might more easily form are considered. In addition to the core and bargaining set, two other solution concepts, the Shapley (1953) value and equal share analysis (Selten, 1972), which provide prescriptions different from either of the former pair, will be examined. To buttress the heuristic arguments that arise, explain

295

regularities in the outcomes, and test the descriptive power of the four solution concepts, we shall report and analyze, both in terms of the coalition structures that formed and the disbursement of payoff to coalition members, experimental outcomes of six variations of a 5-person market game.

## 2. The 5-Person Symmetric Market Game

The economy considered by Maschler (1976) consists of five traders.  Traders 1 and 5 each initially hold one unit of commodity A, and traders 2, 3, and 4 each initially hold $a$ units of commodity B, $a > 0$.  It is assumed that the commodities are completely complementary goods that are useful only in equal quantities.  It is also assumed that from one unit of commodity A and one unit of commodity B, one unit of finished product is produced that can be sold at a net profit of one unit of money.

This market can be represented as a cooperative game with sidepayments $(N;v)$, whose characteristic function is

$$v(S) = \text{Min}[\, |S \cap P| \,, a\, |S \cap Q| \,] \text{ for all } S \subseteq N, \tag{1}$$

where $P = \{1,5\}$, $Q = \{2,3,4\}$, $N = P \cup Q$, and $|T|$ denotes the number of traders in the set $T$.

Game (1) is a particular case of the market games considered by Shapley and Shubik (1969a).  Postlewaite and Rosenthal (1974) treated this game with $a = 1/2$, Shapley and Shubik (1969b) discussed the case $a = 1$, whereas Maschler (1976) considered the general case $0 \leq a$.

Maschler used an example with $a = 1/2$ to motivate game (1).  Each of two manufacturers (players 1 and 5) owns a factory with two machines, where each machine must be operated by a skilled worker.  There are three available skilled workers (players 2, 3, and 4), each willing to work at most one shift per day.  When a worker operates one machine for one shift, he produces goods that can be sold at a profit of 1/2 unit of money, where profit is computed before paying wages to the workers.  The central question is to determine the workers' wages.  This question may be further broken down depending on how workers and manufacturers sign labor contracts (i.e., which coalition structure forms).

For another interpretation (Shapley, 1959; Shapley and Shubik, 1969b), suppose that when the game commences each player $p$ $(p \in P)$ possesses a given number of right-handed gloves and each player $q$ $(q \in Q)$ possesses $a$ times as many left-handed gloves. The players may trade gloves freely, or buy and sell them for money without restriction. When the game terminates, each assembled pair of gloves is worth a fixed amount of money to its holder.  This example, like its predecessor, demonstrates the complementarity between economic units of different types abstractly expressed by game (1); traders on the same side of the market stand in the position of perfect substitutes, whereas traders on opposite sides are perfect complements (Shapley and Shubik, 1969b).

## 3. Solution Concepts for Market Games

Four major solution concepts for the 5-person symmetric market game are considered below, namely the core, the $M_1^{(i)}$ bargaining set (henceforth referred to merely as the bargaining set), the Shapley value, and the equal share solution. In presenting these solution concepts, an outcome, whether predicted or observed, will be represented by a *payoff configuration* (PC).

$$(\mathbf{x};\rho)=(x_1,...,x_n;S_1,...,S_m),$$

where $\rho = \{S_1,...,S_m\}$, called a *coalition structure*, is a partition of $N$ into $m$ coalitions $(1 \leq m \leq n)$, and $\mathbf{x} = (x_1,...,x_n)$ is an $n$-dimensional *payoff vector* that satisfies individual rationality $(x_i \geq 0$ for all $i \in N)$ and guarantees each coalition in the coalition structure its full value, i.e.,

$$\sum_{i \in S_j} x_i = v(S_j) \text{ for all } j = 1,...,m . \tag{2}$$

### 3.1. THE CORE

Because outcomes in the core are required to be Pareto optimal, only a coalition structure for which $\sum_{S \in \rho} v(S) = v(N)$ can be part of a PC in the core. For any payoff vector that meets the eligibility requirements of the core, any coalition structure for which the payoff vector can satisfy (2) joints with the payoff vector to place a PC in the core. We may therefore consider the core's prescriptions in terms of $v(N)$. When $a \leq 1/2$ in game (1), $v(N) = 3a$, and the core gives all the reward to the player of class Q, i.e., $(0,a,a,a,0; \rho)$, where $\rho \in \{\{N\}, \{pqqq,p\},\{pq,pq,q\}\}$. For $1/2 < a \leq 2/3$, the core encompasses a range which includes giving the members of $P$ payoffs of zero, while for $2/3 < a < 1$, the range of the core includes giving the members of $Q$ zero payoffs. Throughout, unequal allocations of payoff within either trader class are admissible in the core.

In particular, when $a = 1/2$, the core of game (1) for the grand coalition consists of the single PC $(0,1/2,1/2,1/2,0; 12345)$. Such an outcome can result from the oversupply of commodity A, which serves to drive down the payoffs of 1 and 5 to zero, since any attempt by either trader to get more will lead the other one forming a 3-person coalition with two of the three members of $Q$ and "underselling" him.

However, Maschler (1976) pointed out that the $P$ traders are not helpless; to reach the Pareto optimal total income of $3a = 3/2$ the other four traders must obtain the cooperation of every $P$ trader. Moreover, argues Maschler, the process of underselling may work both ways, and the arguments in support of the core can be employed just as well among the members of $Q$ to drive their payments down.

## 3.2.  THE $M_1^{(i)}$  BARGAINING SET

The considerations which question the intuitive justification of the core for the grand coalition in 5-person market games suggest that it is not sufficient to consider only threat capabilities.  Rather, in the spirit of the theory of bargaining sets (Aumann and Maschler 1964), one must study how traders can react when faced with such threats.   The bargaining set defines PCs as stable if every "objection" by one coalition member against another can be met with a "counterobjection."   When applied to game (1), the intuitive rationale of these notions means that cutting down profits is not justified if a trader can protect his payoff when faced with various threats.

Maschler showed that when $a = 1/2$, the bargaining set for the grand coalition "consists of every outcome that can be determined by assigning properly normalized prices to the commodities" (Maschler 1976, p. 188); namely, it consists of the straight line segment $(\alpha,\beta,\beta,\beta,\alpha; 12345)$, such that $0 \leq \alpha \leq 3/4$ and $2\alpha + 3\beta = 1/2$.  More generally, Maschler showed that although for $a \leq 1/3$, and for $a > 1$, the bargaining set for the grand coalition coincides with the core, when $1/3 < a \leq 1$, the bargaining set for the grand coalition admits many more allocations than the core (see Table 1), as the example of $a = 1/2$ shows.

But the bargaining set contains at least one payoff vector for every possible coalition structure and, unlike the core, a payoff vector in the bargaining set with one coalition structure may not be admissible with a different coalition structure.  Consider again the example of $a = 1/2$, with the Pareto optimal coalition structure $\{12,345\}$.  The bargaining set for this coalition structure consists of the singleton $(0,1/2,1/2,1/2,0;12,345)$, while Maschler (1976) showed that the bargaining set for the grand coalition, disbursing the identical amount, admits many other payoff vectors.  As the bargaining set theory is moot with regard to the question of coalition formation, there is no inherent reason for the grand coalition to form rather than another Pareto optimal coalition structure; indeed, a strong psychological argument might be made in favor of a $\{pq,qqp\}$ structure over $\{12345\}$, as smaller coalitions are easier to form and maintain than larger ones (Komorita 1974).   But the bargaining set for the coalition structure $\{pq,qqp\}$ consists of but the single point that is in the core for this coalition structure.   And we, like Maschler, believe that players "act stupidly if they [enter into coalitions] at no profit" (1976, p. 187), regardless of which coalition structure forms.   Therefore, on both common sense and perhaps also real life experience, it seems to us that the criticism leveled by Maschler against the reasonableness of the core in the case of the grand coalition holds for both core and bargaining set in the case of other coalition structure.[1]

The above argument is not peculiar to the case $a = 1/2$.  Table 1 presents the bargaining set for all coalition structures of game (1) that are Pareto optimal, sorted by the classes of the parameter $a$; the results for the grand coalition are taken from Maschler (1976), while those for other coalition structures are original derivations.  The proofs for the latter closely follow that provided by Maschler for the former and are not given here.

Table 1 shows that for $1/2 < a < 1$, only the grand coalition is Pareto optimal, so the issue raised above is moot.  However, in the interval $1/3 < a \leq 1/2$, although the bargaining set for the grand coalition admits a range of possible outcomes, the prescription for the $\{pqq,qp\}$ coalition structure is the singleton in the core, and therefore is susceptible to the criticism laid against that latter solution concept.   In the outside ranges of $a \leq 1/3$ and $a > 1$, the prescriptions of the bargaining set do not differ among the several Pareto optimal coalition structures, and all of these coincide with the core.

*Table 1.*   $M_1^i$ solutions* for Pareto optimal coalitions of the 5-person market game $v(S) = Min[|S \cap P|, a|S \cap Q|]$, by class of $a$.

| Class of $a$ | Payoff Configurations |
|---|---|
| $0 \leq a \leq 1/3$ | $(0,a,a,a,0;12345)$<br>$(0,a,a,a,0;pq,qqp)$<br>$(0,a,a,a,0;pqqq,p)$ |
| $1/3 < a \leq 1/2$ | $(\alpha,\beta,\beta,\beta,\alpha;12345)$: $0 \leq \alpha \leq (9a-3)/2,\ 2\alpha+3\beta=3a$.<br>$(0,a,a,a,0;pq,qqp)$ |
| $1/2 < a \leq 2/3$ | $\{(\alpha_1,\beta_2,\beta_3,\beta_4,\alpha_5;12345): a \leq \alpha_p+\beta_q \leq 3a-1,\ 0 \leq \alpha_p,\ 0 \leq \beta_q,\ \alpha_1+\beta_2+\beta_3+\beta_4+\alpha_5=3a\}$<br>$\cup \{(\alpha,\beta,\beta,\beta,\alpha;12345): 0 \leq \alpha \leq 3a/2,\ 2\alpha+3\beta=3a\}$ |
| $2/3 \leq a < 1$ | $\{(\alpha_1,\beta_2,\beta_3,\beta_4,\alpha_5;12345): a \leq \alpha_p+\beta_q \leq 1,\ 0 \leq \alpha_p,\ 0 \leq \beta_q,\ \alpha_1+\beta_2+\beta_3+\beta_4+\alpha_5=2\}$ |
| $1 \leq a < 2$ | $(1,0,0,0,1;12345)$<br>$(1,0,0,0,1;pq,q,qp)$<br>$(1,0,0,0,1;pq,qqp)$<br>$(1,0,0,0,1;pqqp,q)$ |
| $2 \leq a \leq \infty$ | $(1,0,0,0,1;12345)$<br>$(1,0,0,0,1;pq,q,qp)$<br>$(1,0,0,0,1;pq,qqp)$<br>$(1,0,0,0,1;pqp,q,q)$<br>$(1,0,0,0,1;pqqp,q)$ |

*$p \in P = \{1,5\}$; $q \in Q = \{2,3,4\}$

3.3.  THE SHAPLEY VALUE

In addition to the core and bargaining set, a third solution concept has been proposed as a representation of power in market games.  This is the Shapley value (Shapley 1953), which "seeks to evaluate each player's position in the game a priori, taking into account both his own strategic opportunities and his bargaining position with respect to gains attainable through collaboration" (Shapley and Shubik 1969b, p. 340).  Like the core and bargaining set, the Shapley value presupposes that the market is a collusive multi-person game.  Unlike the other solution concepts, it looks for a unique, equitable compromise among all opposing interests by disbursing the proceeds of total cooperation among the $n$ players in a way that takes fair account of each player's contribution to each possible cooperative venture (Shapley and Shubik 1969b).  In its original form, the Shapley value prescribed a payoff vector only for the grand coalition of market games, but, following Aumann and Dréze (1974), a Shapley value may be provided for each coalition structure that might form.  As with the bargaining set, these different solutions will not necessarily contain the same payoff vector.

It was argued by Shapley and Shubik (1969b) that, for certain values of $a$ in game (1), the Shapley value provides an intuitively more satisfactory measure of the "equities" inherent in the market than does the core (or the bargaining set).  For example, consider again game (1) with $a = 1$.  The core and the bargaining set (for any Pareto optimal coalition structure) contain the unique payoff vector $(1,0,0,0,1)$, whereas the Shapley value for the grand coalition is the single point $(13/20, 7/30, 7/30, 7/30, 13/20; 12345)$.  A negotiation procedure that might lead the members of $Q$ to get positive rather than zero wages is as follows.  Facing a total defeat under pure competition among themselves, the members of $Q$ may decide to join forces, select two of their number to "withdraw from the market," and thus turn the tables on $P$.  Although this behavior would not be Pareto optimal, the threat is credible and might well raise the wages of the remaining single player of $Q$ from zero to some quantity between $1/3$ and $1$, and, consequently, the expectation of each player $q$ from zero to some quantity between $1/9$ and $1/3$.[2] Interestingly, it is the same argument that led Maschler (1963) to question whether a coalition's value is an adequate measure of the coalition's "power" for any game given in characteristic function form.  Experimental evidence provided by Maschler (1978) and Kahan and Rapoport (1980) shows that bargaining behavior of the type described above does occur in 3-person characteristic function games.

For game (1) with $a = 1/2$, the Shapley value for Pareto optimal coalition structures consists of two PCs: $(39/120, 34/120, 34/120, 34/120, 39/120; 12345)$ and $(1/2, 1/4, 1/4, 1/4, 1/4; pqq,qp)$.  While these PCs do not follow the intuitive argument supplied for $a = 1$ above, they do provide payoff allocations which have the properties of being point prescriptions and not assigning all of the outcome to members of one trader class.

3.4.  EQUAL SHARE ANALYSIS

This final solution concept to be considered was developed by Selten (1972) as an alternative to the core and bargaining set for predicting the outcomes of experimental characteristic function games.  Its underlying theory may be summarized in three hypotheses about the outcome of the game.  The first hypothesis states that the coalition structure that emerges will not allow any profitable merger of several coalitions.  For market games, it directly implies a Pareto optimal outcome. The second hypothesis asserts that any payoff vector in the solution will be in the equal division core. A payoff vector **x** is in the equal division core if there is no coalition S such that its equal share $v(S)/s$ is greater than $x_i$ for all $i \in S$. The third hypothesis claims that "stronger" players will not receive higher payoffs than their "weaker" coalition partners. Strength is concretely defined in Selten (1972); for the 5-person market games under present consideration, a P trader is stronger than a Q trader when $a > 2/3$, and the reverse is true when $a \leq 1/3$. Between these two values, there are no strength distinctions between trader classes.

The equal share solution, then, is the set of PCs that satisfy all three hypotheses. The first hypothesis limits the coalition structures of PC in the solution to Pareto optimal ones, just as the core. Also like the core, if a payoff vector meets the admissibility requirements for being an element of the solution, then any feasible coalition structure may carry that payoff vector.

For the example case $a = 1/2$, all of the following PCs are elements of the equal share solution:

$$(3/4,0,0,0,3/4;12345) \quad (0,1/2,1/2,1/2,0;12345) \quad (0,1/4,1/3,11/12,0;12345),$$

$$(1/3,0,0,0,7/6;12345), \quad (3/10,3/10,3/10,3/10,3/10;12345).$$

As can be seen, the equal share solution encompasses a considerable portion of the possible payoffs that can occur in the game. If there are differences in strength according to trader class, then restrictions on the solution alleviate the problem somewhat, but still the solution space remains large.

## 4. From Theory to Experiment

Heuristic arguments, though no substitute for mathematical statements, are indispensable in discussing the plausibility and acceptability of solution concepts for selected classes of characteristic function games. Yet any appeal to intuition should be approached with caution because intuition changes with experience or practice, and what is intuitively acceptable to one may be intuitively unacceptable to another (see Davis and Maschler 1965). Systematic observations of empirical outcomes may augment or revise intuition about coalition forming behavior in characteristic function games, and possibly provide regularities that may be reflected by or incorporated in new solution concepts. Experimental studies of coalition forming behavior may also determine the descriptive power of present solution concepts. To this end, we conducted a series of experimental 5-person market games in which the value of $a$ in game (1) was systematically varied. The experimental design and results of this study are described below.

## 5. Method

### 5.1. SUBJECTS

Subjects were 55 male and female volunteers, students at the University of North Carolina at Chapel Hill, who were recruited via posters placed around campus advertising cash to be earned by participation in a multi-session coalition formation experiment. Subjects were grouped within the constraints of time of volunteering into 11 pentads, except that candidates indicating that they were friends could not be in the same pentad.

### 5.2. COALITIONS

The present experiment employed Coalitions II (Kahan, Coston, Helwig, Rapoport, and Wallsten 1976), a PDP-11/45 computer-controlled system designed to govern the play of n-person games in characteristic function form with sidepayments. The Coalitions game explicitly defines three stages in the bargaining that follows the presentation of the characteristic function to the players. The first, the *negotiation stage*, is that time when players explore the potential of various coalitions. Different offers are made to different coalitions as players gain awareness of their relative strengths and weaknesses, acquire information about expectations of other players, and learn about their intentions and tactics.

The second stage, termed the *acceptance stage*, begins when a subset of players indicates a general agreement on a division of their coalition value. Although this agreement is not binding, it indicates serious consideration. During the acceptance stage the members of a tentative coalition may be interested in modification of the agreement for that coalition in addition to what other coalitions might have in store for them. It is in this stage that various strategies and counter-strategies may become their most complex.

The third stage, or *ratification stage*, terminates the bargaining process for payoff disbursement. The members of a coalition, having considered an offer for payoff disbursement and seen it through acceptance, are now willing to make it a binding agreement. Satisfaction with the proposed coalition and its division of the coalition value is therefore indicated and, by passing into ratification, each party receives its payoff and the bargaining (and game playing) process for that coalition is terminated.

Subjects communicate to each other by transmitting messages coded in keywords via teletypewriters connected to a PDP-11/45 computer. The computer checks the legality of the messages, reformats them to be easily readable, informs subjects of their errors, adds messages informing subjects of the effect of the present move on the outcomes of previous moves in the game, and transmits the entire package to its intended recipients. The complete list of keywords used by *Coalitions*-11 and their effects, as well as the implications of being in the acceptance stage (called "All-accepted" in the figure), is presented in Figure 1. With Figure 1 in hand (which is a version of one available at all times to players), the use and effects of keywords are self-explanatory. In the present experiment all keywords were enabled with the exception of SOLO, REMARK, and MESSAGE; these latter were deleted from the list of keywords given to the subjects.

| Key Word | E.g. of Parameters | Primary Effect | Other effects on this coalition | Effects outside named coalition |
|---|---|---|---|---|
| PASS | (none) | Send null messages. | (none) | (none) |
| SOLO | (none) | Immediate ratification of player's one-person coalition. | (none) | Player is removed from further play in this game. |
| OFFER | A-20; B-18; C-17 | Make a proposal. | Supersedes player's previous OFFER, AGREE, & ACCEPT. | (none) |
| SUGGEST | A-20;C-15 to ACD | | Make informal, secret proposal. | (none) |
| REJECT | ACD by C | Erase an offer. | (none) | (none) |
| AGREE | ACD by C | Show liking for an offer. | Same as for OFFER. | Erases any ACCEPT made by this player. |
| ACCEPT | ACD BY C | Tentative commitment to an offer | Same as for OFFER. | Erases any AGREE or ACCEPT made by this player. |
| AFFIRM | ACD | Stand by previous action. | (none) | (none) |
| RATIFY | (none) | Propose move to ratification | Form coalition if all members agree to ratification. Coalition is dissolved otherwise. | Concludes game for players in ratified coalition. |
| REMARK | AC(text) | Send (text) to named player(s). Counts as a communication. | | |
| MESSAGE | A-1,C-3 | Send numbered message(s) to named player(s). Counts as a communication. | | |
| VALUE | (none) | Information: Give all values in the game except those involving removed players. Does not count as a communication. | | |
| VALUE | ACD | Information: Give value of that named coalition. Does not count as a communication. | | |
| STATUS | (none) | Information: Give current statements involving every coalition in the game. Does not count as a communication. | | |
| STATUS | ABC | Information: Give current statements regarding named coalition. Does not count as a communication. | | |
| STATUS | ABOUT AC | Information: Give current statements involving coalitions including named player(s). Does not count as a communication. | | |
| STATUS | BY AC | Information: Give current positions taken by named player(s). Does not count as a communication. | | |

Figure 1. Key Words and Their Effects.

5.3.  PROCEDURE

Each of the 11 pentads was introduced to the experimental apparatus and rules of the game in a 3-hour training session consisting of written instructions, verbal elaborations, and two to three separate experiment-guided 5-person practice games that were not market games.  The purpose of the practice games was to acquaint the subjects with the teletypewriters, the nature of the keywords, and the experimental procedure.  For this training session subjects were paid $7.50 each.

Pentads then returned for several experimental sessions, each lasting approximately three hours, spaced from two to seven days apart.  Each pentad played a series of six 5-person market games that required two to four sessions to complete.  Although players participated as unified pentads, role assignments (letters) were randomly varied from game to game so that individual players could not identify their co-players.  The players were also requested not to talk with one another between sessions until the experiment was over.  This technique of randomly shifting roles has repeatedly (Kahan and Rapoport 1974, 1977; Rapoport and Kahan 1976) resulted in experimental series whose individual games are independently and separately negotiated.

Procedures for ratification differed depending on the type of coalition in the acceptance stage.  For any single accepted coalition including both members of $P$ or all three members of $Q$, or for any two independently accepted coalitions within a coalition structure, at least two complete rounds of communication (i.e., 10 messages) had to occur before the coalition(s) might enter the ratification stage (which occurred if a member of *any* accepted coalition sent the keyword RATIFY).  Once RATIFY was transmitted, each of the remaining members of the accepted coalition(s) was immediately required to concur with ratification or veto ratification.  If all members of any accepted coalition concurred, the coalition was considered in force; if any member of a coalition vetoed, that tentative coalition was dissolved.  When all of the players in the game were in ratified coalitions, or if all players but one were in ratified coalitions, then the game terminated, and the players received points according to their coalitional agreements.  This ratification procedure was termed *simultaneous* ratification.

By contrast, *sequential* ratification was the prescribed procedure if either a 2-person or 3-person coalition was accepted by all its members, but the remaining players were still in the negotiation stage.  Here, the accepted coalition of either two or three members could ratify an agreement after eight rounds of communication (i.e., 40 messages).  Upon ratification, the members of the ratified coalition were removed from the game, leaving the remaining (either three or two) players to bargain among themselves.

5.4.  EXPERIMENTAL GAMES

Six different values of the parameter $a$ in game (1) were used, namely, $a = 2/12, 5/12, 6/12, 7/12, 10/12$, and $14/12$, to construct the games labeled G1 through G6, respectively.  The value of each coalition of a game was multiplied by an arbitrary constant $k$ so that all values would be integers and $v(N)$ would be between 48 and 64.  Table 2 presents the characteristic functions of the six games together with the values of $a$ and $k$.  The games were played by all pentads in the (randomly determined) order G5,G3,G1,G4,G6, and G2.

Table 2.  5-Person  Market  Games:  Six  Characteristic  Functions.*

| Game | v(pq) | v(ppq) | v(pqq) | v(ppqq) | v(pqqq) | v(N) | a | k |
|------|-------|--------|--------|---------|---------|------|-----|-----|
| G1 | 20 | 20 | 40 | 40 | 60 | 60 | 2/12 | 120 |
| G2 | 20 | 20 | 40 | 40 | 48 | 60 | 5/12 | 48 |
| G3 | 18 | 18 | 36 | 36 | 36 | 54 | 6/12 | 36 |
| G4 | 21 | 21 | 36 | 42 | 36 | 63 | 7/12 | 36 |
| G5 | 20 | 20 | 24 | 40 | 24 | 48 | 10/12 | 24 |
| G6 | 24 | 28 | 24 | 48 | 24 | 48 | 14/12 | 24 |

\* $p \in \{P,Q\} = \{1,5\}$, $q \in \{X,Y,Z\}=\{2,3,4\}$, and $v(S) = 0$ for all $S \subseteq N$ not
specified in the table.

## 5.5.  INCENTIVE

The incentive to maximize gain was established by paying each player ten cents for each
unit of money (called a point) earned during the experimental sessions, in addition to a
flat rate of $1.50 per hour of play (for up to six hours of play).  When the experiment
was over, one of the games played was randomly chosen and each player was paid a
bonus of 30 cents for each point earned in this game.  In accordance with agreements
made before the beginning of the experiment, subjects were paid their entire earnings,
including the $7.50 for the practice session, at the completion of the final session.

## 6.  Results

The data of major interest are the coalition structures that formed and the payoff
allocations made by players within these coalition structures.  However, before turning to
these principal data analyses, we should first reassure ourselves that the subjects took the
task seriously, and bargained in good faith.

The best evidence of this reassurance comes from the time and number of messages
players took to complete games.  If the subjects perceived themselves to be in a 6-person
zero-sum game against the experimenter, where the objective was to take her money as
quickly as possible, an obvious strategy would be to form the grand coalition with equal
splits in as few messages as possible, and then go on to the next game.[3]   Because
player roles were randomly shifted from game to game, any other strategy would be
difficult to implement; additionally, delaying the game with needless and useless
bargaining defeated the purpose of maximizing income while minimizing time invested.

Table 3, which shows the mean time and number of messages taken to complete each game, demonstrates that subjects fully adopted their roles as players. The two variables of time and number of messages are obviously closely related, with the major part of their difference due to a lower frequency of erroneous inputs and smoother typing as players became familiar with the game. On the average, players spent nearly one hour negotiating each of the six games played, and even in game G4, the mean number of messages needed was twice the minimum for completion of a game. The between-game differences in number of messages are statistically significant by repeated-measures analysis of variance ($F_{5,50}$ = 5.86, p < 0.001); similar results obtain for time. However, neither the value of the parameter $a$ nor the order of games played was a good predictor of the length of negotiations. Below, in our discussion of maximal share structures, we shall return to these results.

*Table 3. Summary Statistics for Time and Number of Messages per Play.*

| Game | Order of Play | Time (in Minutes) Mean | Time (in Minutes) S.D. | Number of Messages Mean | Number of Messages S.D. |
|------|---------------|------|------|------|------|
| G1 | 3 | 46.2 | 29.7 | 53.6 | 28.1 |
| G2 | 6 | 49.5 | 23.1 | 73.5 | 25.5 |
| G3 | 2 | 89.5 | 55.2 | 108.2 | 56.3 |
| G4 | 4 | 19.9 | 10.9 | 32.1 | 15.2 |
| G5 | 1 | 70.4 | 33.5 | 73.2 | 34.6 |
| G6 | 5 | 67.6 | 33.2 | 105.8 | 68.2 |

Table 4 presents the PCs for all 66 plays, by game and by pentad. Because preliminary inspections of the data indicated a complete absence of effects due to letter assignment (i.e., order of speaking) within trader class, the coalition structures in Table 4 have been permuted to reflect the order[4] in which the coalitions formed. In all cases, outcomes to the P traders (players 1 and 5) are the first and last elements of the payoff vector, but the association of players and coalitions is given by the coalition structure. Thus, for example, in game G2 of pentad 1 coalition (*pqq*) formed first, with the *p* trader receiving 13 points, one of the *q* traders receiving 13 points, and the second *q* trader receiving 14 points. In the complementary 2-person (*qp*) coalition, the two players split their 20 points evenly. For all of the PCs in Table 4, the order of players in the coalition structure corresponds to the order of players in the payoff vector. In the instances where ratification was sequential, i.e., where one coalition ratified before the remaining players were in an accepted coalition, that first coalition within the structure is underscored in Table 4.

Table 4. Ratified Outcomes of 5-Person Market Games

| Pentad | Game G1 | Game G2 | Game G3 |
|---|---|---|---|
| 1 | $(13,13,14,10,10,pqq,qp)$ | $(13,13,14,10,10;pqq,qp)$ | $(12,12,12,9,9;pqq,qp)$ |
| 2 | $(10,16,17,17,0,pqqq,p)$ | $(13,12,15,10,10,pqq,qp)$ | $(11,11,14,9,9;pqq,qp)$ |
| 3 | $(10,10,20,20,0;pqqq,p)$ | $(14,13,13,10,10;pqq,qp)$ | $(12,12,12,18,0;pqq,qp)$ |
| 4 | $(15,15,15,15,0;pqqq,p)$ | $(14,12,14,10,10;pqq,qp)$ | $(12,12,12,9,9;pqq,qp)$ |
| 5 | $(15,15,15,15,0;pqqq,p)$ | $(12,12,12,12,12;pqqqp)$ | $(11,12,13,9,9,pqq,qp)$ |
| 6 | $(2,19,19,19,1;pqqqp)$ | $(13,13,14,10,10;pqq,qp)$ | $(12,12,12,9,9;pqq,qp)$ |
| 7 | $(15,15,15,15,0;pqqq,p)$ | $(14,12,14,10,10;pqq,qp)$ | $(11,11,14,9,9;pqq,qp)$ |
| 8 | $(12,12,12,12,12;pqqqp)$ | $12,14,14,10,10;pqq,qp)$ | $(12,12,12,9,9;pqq,qp)$ |
| 9 | $(15,15,15,15,0;pqqq,p)$ | $(12,13,15,10,10;pqq,qp)$ | $(10,11,15,9,9;pqq,qp)$ |
| 10 | $(3,19,19,19,0;pqqq,p)$ | $(12,12,12,12,12;pqqqp)$ | $(12,12,12,9,9;pqq,qp)$ |
| 11 | $(5,17,17,17,4;pqqqp)$ | $(12,12,12,12,12;pqqqp)$ | $(12,12,12,9,9;pqq,qp)$ |

| Pentad | Game G4 | Game G5 | Game G6 |
|---|---|---|---|
| 1 | $(13,12,13,13,12;pqqqp)$ | $(14,6,0,6,14;pq,q,qp)$ | $(13,11,0,10,14;pq,q,qp)$ |
| 2 | $(13,12,13,13,12;pqqqp)$ | $(14,6,0,5,15;pq,q,qp)$ | $(18,6,0,8,16;pq,q,qp)$ |
| 3 | $(14,10,11,14,14;pqqqp)$ | $(12,8,0,7,13;pq,q,qp)$ | $(16,8,0,3,21;pq,q,qp)$ |
| 4 | $(13,12,13,13,12;pqqqp)$ | $(10,8,10,10,10;pqqqp)$ | $(13,11,0,11,13,pq,q,qp)$ |
| 5 | $(13,12,13,13,12;pqqqp)$ | $(12,8,0,2,18;pq,q,qp)$ | $(23,1,0,1,23;pq,q,qp)$ |
| 6 | $(12,13,13,13,12;pqqqp)$ | $(10,10,0,8,12;pq,q,qp)$ | $(14,6,7,7,14;pqqqp)$ |
| 7 | $(13,12,12,13,12;pqqqp)$ | $(16,5,6,6,15;pqqqp)$ | $(14,10,5,5,14;pq,qqp)$ |
| 8 | $(12,13,13,13,12;pqqqp)$ | $(13,7,8,8,12;pqqqp)$ | $(13,11,0,11,13;pq,q,qp)$ |
| 9 | $(13,12,13,13,12;pqqqp)$ | $(12,8,3,10,11;pq,qqp)$ | $(17,7,0,2,22;pq,q,qp)$ |
| 10 | $(12,13,13,13,12;pqqqp)$ | $(15,5,2,2,20;pq,qqp)$ | $(15,9,0,10,14;pq,q,qp)$ |
| 11 | $(13,12,13,13,12;pqqqp)$ | $(10,10,8,8,8,;pq,qqp)$ | $(12,12,0,12,12;pq,q,qp)$ |

## 6.1. COALITION STRUCTURE

Examination of Table 4 in conjunction with Table 1, which lists Pareto optimal outcomes by class of market games, shows that 58 of the 66 plays resulted in Pareto optimal outcomes, and that, moreover, all eight of the exceptions occurred in game G5, the first game to be played in the sequence of six. This result strongly supports the contention that players were motivated to maximize their collective gain; players quickly learned which were the most lucrative coalition structures.

However, as Table 4 also shows, the grand coalition, which is always Pareto optimal, was predominant only in game G4, where it was the sole Pareto optimal coalition structure. In games G2 and G3, the $(pqq,qp)$ coalition structure was preferred, with 19 out of 22 plays ending in that configuration. In games G1 and G6, where all five players were not required to be in multi-person coalitions in order for a Pareto optimal outcome to result, in only 6 out of 22 plays did all five players obtain nonzero payoffs. In game G1, the predominant coalition structure was $(pqqq,p)$, excluding a $P$

trader, while in game G6, the predominant coalition structure was $(pq,q,qp)$, which excluded a $Q$ trader.

## 6.2. PAYOFF ALLOCATIONS

Because the games differed from one another in both the values of $a$ and $k$, as well as in the observed coalition structure frequency distributions, they may not be directly compared one to another. Instead, relative patterns of payoff distributions are of interest. The most apparent difference is between games G2, G3, and G4 on the one hand and G1, G5, and G6 on the other. In the former set of three games, for which the $a$ values are moderate ($5/12 \leq a \leq 7/12$), there is a remarkable uniformity over pentads in favor of an even split among coalition partners. In all three games, there is but one coalition ($pq$ of pentad 3 in game G3) that is more than three points away from an equal split (within the constraint of integer payoffs), and this single exception, by its absurdity, underscores the point about the dominance of equality within coalitions.

By contrast, the latter set of games G1, G5, and G6, for which the $a$ values are "extreme," exhibits no consistency of payoff allocation over pentads; neither is there any tendency for individual pentads to be consistently egalitarian or exploitative over games. This is not to say that there are no systematic observations to make for these games. It can be seen that symmetric players (from the same trader class) in a common coalition tended to obtain the same payoffs. Moreover, in coalition structures $(pq,qqp)$ and $(pq,q,qp)$ of games G5 and G6, the payoffs of the two class $P$ traders were highly correlated ($r = +0.79$, $p < 0.001$), even though their payoffs were the result of independently agreed-upon coalitions. This statistically significant correlation does not imply that the $P$ traders obtained equal payoffs though; in general the $P$ trader in the first coalition to be formed received on the average 1.1 points fewer than the player in the second coalition ($t_{17} = 1.89$, $p < 0.04$).

## 6.3. MODEL TESTING

The comparison of the obtained payoff vectors to the four theoretical models was achieved by taking each PC and checking whether or not it fell into or near (within integer rounding error) the prescription of the particular model. Table 5 presents model prescriptions for the core, bargaining set, Shapley value, and part of the equal share solution; a full specification of that latter is impossible within the confines of any readable table. Note in Table 5 that the Shapley value always consists of a single vector for any given coalition, while the remaining solution concepts may encompass ranges. The bargaining set and Shapley value are nonempty for each coalition, while the core and equal share solution are empty for the non-Pareto outcomes of game G5. Finally, note the well-established finding that the core, when nonempty, is contained within the bargaining set and for the present games, within the equal share solution as well.

Our first observation is that Maschler's (1976) criticism of the core is empirically sustained; when the core posited a point prediction giving the members of one or the other trader class an outcome of zero, only in five plays were the "discriminated against" traders held to as few as three points (plays G1,6; G1,10; G6,3; G6,5; and G6,9). When the core prescribed a range, it was more useful. All of the plays in G4 and two of the three Pareto optimal outcomes in game G5 fell within the core. The usefulness of the core is qualified, however, by the fact that the predicted range is very wide. In game G4, the range for a *P* player includes 18 points out of a total of 63 points for all five players.

*Table 5. Predictions\* of Four Theoretical Models for Six Market Games, by Coalitions.\*\**

| Game | Coalition | Core | | Bargaining Set | | Shapley Value | | Equal Share Solution | |
|------|-----------|------|------|------|------|------|------|------|------|
| | | *p* | *q* | *p* | *q* | *p* | *q* | *p* | *q* |
| G1 | *pqqqp* | 0.0 | 20.0 | 0.0 | 20.0 | 10.0 | 13.3 | 0.0-7.5 | 20.0-15.0 |
| | *pqqq* | 0.0 | 20.0 | 0.0 | 20.0 | 30.0 | 10.0 | 0.0-15.0 | 20.0-15.0 |
| | *pqq* | 0.0 | 20.0 | 0.0 | 20.0 | 20.0 | 10.0 | see note a | |
| | *pq* | 0.0 | 20.0 | 0.0 | 20.0 | 10.0 | 10.0 | see note a | |
| G2 | *pqqqp* | 0.0 | 20.0 | 0-18 | 20-8 | 11.8 | 12.1 | 0.00-10.0 | 20.0-13.3 |
| | | | | | | | | 13.3-30.0 | 11.1-0.0 |
| | *pqq* | 0.0 | 20.0 | 0.0 | 20.0 | 20.0 | 10.0 | see note a | |
| | *pq* | 0.0 | 20.0 | 0.0 | 20.0 | 10.0 | 10.0 | see note a | |
| G3 | *pqq* | 0.0 | 18.0 | 0.0 | 18.0 | 18.0 | 9.0 | see note a | |
| | *pq* | 0.0 | 18.0 | 0.0 | 18.0 | 9.0 | 9.0 | see note a | |
| G4 | *pqqqp* | 0-18 | 21-9 | any symmetric payoff | | 14.9 | 11.1 | any symmetric payoff | |
| G5 | *pqqqp* | 12-24 | 8-0 | 12-24 | 8-0 | 13.8 | 6.8 | 10.0-24.0 | 9.3-0.0 |
| | *pqq* | empty | | 16.0 | 4.0 | 14.7 | 4.7 | empty | |
| | *pq* | empty | | 16.0 | 4.0 | 10.0 | 10.0 | empty | |
| G6 | *pqqqp* | 24.0 | 0.0 | 24.0 | 0.0 | 16.0 | 5.3 | 12.0-24.0 | 8.0-0.0 |
| | *pqq* | 24.0 | 0.0 | 24.0 | 0.0 | 16.0 | 4.0 | see note a | |
| | *pq* | 24.0 | 0.0 | 24.0 | 0.0 | 12.0 | 12.0 | see note a | |

\*     Only solutions for equal payoffs within trader class are reported.
\*\*    Only coalitions that formed are reported. It is assumed that (*pqq,qp*), (*pq,qqp*) and (*pq,q,qp*) coalition structures were ratified simultaneously.
a.    Under appropriate payoffs for the complementary coalition, any symmetric payoff may be in the solution.

The bargaining set fares little better than the core. Given the coalition structures that obtained, the core and bargaining set coincide for games G1, G3, and G6, so the bargaining set cannot improve on the poor showing of the core. For game G4, the bargaining set in effect remains silent, as it admits any symmetric outcome in addition to outcomes in the core. For game G2, the bargaining set predictions were quite distant from the payoffs obtained in the modal coalition structure ($pqq,qp$), and specified a wide range $0 \leq x_p \leq 18$) for the $P$ players in the coalition structure ($pqqqp$), whereas all three outcomes with that coalition structure were equal splits. Finally, in game G5, the bargaining set did well in predicting ($pq,qqp$) and ($pq,q,qp$) payoff vectors, but systematically underpredicted the payoffs of the class $Q$ traders.

The Shapley value is an inconsistent predictor, being quite accurate for some games and some coalitions, but being considerably far from the data for others. In particular, it fails to predict any ($pqq$) coalition outcomes, but does reasonably well for grand coalition ($pqqqp$) outcomes. For ($pq$) coalitions in a ($pqq,qp$) coalition structure, the Shapely value prediction of equal division is accurate, but the same prediction fails for that same coalition in ($pq,qqp$) or ($pq,q,qp$) coalition structures. Systematic, though small, discrepancies between observed payoffs and Shapley value predictions were related to the game parameter $a$. In 39 of the 44 plays of games G1 through G4, where $a < 2/3$, the traders in class $Q$ received more than their Shapley value prescriptions. The direction of this discrepancy was reversed in games G5 and G6, whereas $a > 2/3$, and all three traders in class $Q$ received less than their prescribed share in 14 out of 22 plays.

Finally, we turn to equal share analysis. On first glance, support for that theory looks impressive as 54 out of the 66 payoff vectors are in the equal division core and 47 of the 66 plays meet the criteria set by all the three hypotheses of the theory. Eight plays of game G5 were not Pareto optimal, while 11 (two in G1, six in G2, and three in G3) fall outside the equal division core. These impressive results must be qualified by the fact that the equal share solution is large by ($n$-dimensional) volume, and consequently its predictive power is weak. In game G3, for example, both the PCs (12, 12, 12, 18, 0; $pqq,qp$) and (12, 12, 12, 9, 9,; $pqq,qp$) fall in the solution, and in game G4, as with the bargaining set, any symmetric solution is in the solution space. Perhaps more disturbing, though, is where the equal division core failed. In game G2, three of the plays falling outside the equal division core were the equal division (12, 12, 12, 12, 12; $pqqqp$). Here, the equal division core admits virtually all symmetrical payoff vectors except those in a small window around equal payments between trader class, a finding that is counterintuitive to the importance placed on equal divisions by the theory.

The tests of the four models reported above lumped together games ending in either simultaneous or sequential ratifications. Strictly speaking, these tests are inappropriate as the models are only applicable to simultaneous ratification games. Reanalyses of the models applied only to the 46 games that ended in simultaneous ratifications (see Table 4) yielded essentially the same results.

## 7. Discussion

None of the four solution concepts that were examined was entirely successful. The predictions of the core and bargaining set for the coalition structures that formed were mostly "extreme," providing that one class of traders receive all of the gain from the coalition; such outcomes only rarely obtained. Although the Shapley value was superior to these first two solution concepts for some games, it did poorly in others. Furthermore, when individual plays were considered, systematic discrepancies from the Shapley value depending on the value of $a$ were found. Finally, equal share analysis provided empirically satisfying results for most games, but its large solution space made it predictively weak. Moreover, this solution concept failed to predict outcomes that it should be most strong on.

These negative results should not be construed as conclusive evidence against the descriptive power of these models for characteristic function games. There is a growing body of experimental data (Kahan and Rapoport 1974, 1980, Maschler 1978, Rapoport and Kahan 1976, 1982, Selten 1972) showing that the descriptive power of solution concepts strongly depends on selected features of the characteristic function that are yet to be fully specified; solution concepts that do well in one class of games fare poorly in others. Moreover, examination of the bargaining protocols of the 66 plays suggests that, in one important way, the present experiment may not be considered a fair test of the four solution concepts. These solution concepts assume the simultaneous ratification of all coalitions in a PC; before that time, any tentative agreement is subject to disruption. But when two multi-person coalitions formed within a coalition structure, they often formed sequentially rather than simultaneously. That is, at some point in the game an accepted coalition was regarded as firm, although it had not yet been ratified. From that point on, the remaining players bargained exclusively among themselves, and the players in the all-accepted coalition did not communicate with players outside the coalition. Thus, although most of our games arrived at simultaneous ratification when formal moves were considered, from the point of view of the players, ratification of multiple coalitions was typically sequential.

Analyses of the bargaining protocols indicate, then, that most games were played in two stages. First, a 5-person game was played until one coalition was formed. If the first formed coalition was 4- or 5-person, the game terminated. But if it was 2- or 3-person, the remaining (3 or 2) players participated in a *reduced game*. We note that the effect of sequential ratification on the four solution concepts is drastic. Only the first coalition may be analyzed as a 5-person market game; the remaining coalitions that form must be analyzed as a reduced game (Maschler 1978), for which the solutions are different from the market game (except for the Aumann-Dréze extension of the Shapley value we have employed).

To account for the observed PCs, we invoke two concepts and treat separately the two central issues of coalition formation and payoff disbursement. With regard to the former issue, the notion of a *maximal share structure* (Selten 1972) can explain the pattern of coalition structures in all six games. A maximal share structure may be interpreted as a coalition structure arising from a process where coalitions form sequentially, and, at each stage in the sequence, players attempt to form a coalition with the highest possible equal share within that coalition. That is, the first coalition to form is any coalition $S \subseteq N$ that maximizes $v(S)/s$, where $s = |S|$. Then, given that coalition $S$ has formed, the second coalition is one $T \subseteq (N-S)$ that maximizes $v(T)/t$, and so on until the coalition structure is completed.

Table 6 presents all possible orderings[5] in which a coalition structure could be formed in the present experiment, along with the mean payoff per coalition member and the frequency of occurrence of that ordered coalition structure. Table 6 shows that fully 51 of the 66 plays ended in maximal share coalition structures, and such a structure was the modal outcome for all six games. Indeed, all but 5 of the 66 outcomes were either grand coalitions or maximal share coalition structures, and for 4 of these exceptional outcomes, the first coalition to form in the game was one that maximized equal share, while the second eschewed a maximal share in favor of including all of the remaining players in the coalition. Thus, the two notions of maximal share structure and forming grand coalitions together account for all but one of the 66 coalition structures that formed.

The between game differences in coalition structure also provide an explanation for the differences in length of negotiations noted earlier. In games G1 and G4, the maximal share structure is one with only one multi-person coalition, while in games G2, G3, G5, and G6, the maximal share structure is one with two multi-person coalitions.[6] When the contrast of games G1 and G4 against the other four is tested using Scheffe's (1959) post-hoc comparison technique, the difference in number of messages is significant. Not surprisingly, it would therefore appear that it takes longer to conclude two coalition agreements than one.

With regard to the second issue of payoff disbursement, we invoke a combination of the bargaining set and the norm of equal share, and apply them to the first formed and second formed coalitions separately. This is done by considering the $\alpha$-power model, a model recently proposed to account for payoff allocation in characteristic function games (Kahan and Rapoport 1980; Rapoport and Kahan 1982). Following Maschler (1963), the $\alpha$-power model proposes that the value of a coalition may not be an adequate measure of its power. Rather, it represents the power of a coalition by a function, which is a linear combination of the values of that coalition, its complement, and the maximal value that any coalition structure may receive. This function depends on a parameter $\alpha$ ($0 \leq \alpha \leq 1$), which is interpretable as a standard of fairness based on social norms and moral conventions. In its present form, the model is restricted to $n \leq 3$; computational schemes have not been extended beyond $n = 3$. For 3-person reduced games arising from the present market games, the $\alpha$-power model prescribes (for a given value of $\alpha$) a single payoff vector for each coalition structure. If $\alpha = 0$, this solution coincides with the bargaining set, whereas if $\alpha = 1$, it prescribes equal division of the value of each coalition among its members.

Inspection of Table 4 shows that 54 of the 66 first formed coalitions either divided their value equally among their members, or were in the bargaining set. The discrepancies from the predicted payoff vectors never exceed three points (which we consider as "errors" due to the costs of breaking up or joining coalitions). The 12 exceptions are plays G1,2; G1,3; G1,11; G3,9; G5,3; G5,5; G5,7; G6,2; G6,3; G6,6; G6,9; and G6,10. Most of the exceptions in games G5 and G6 fall between the two "extreme" point solutions of the bargaining set and equal division.

The $\alpha$-power model is most applicable to the reduced games that were played by the (either two or three) members of the second formed coalitions. As shown in Table 4, reduced games were played in 38 instances (1,8,11,0,8, and 10 plays in games G1

*Table 6. Mean Payoff per Member of a Coalition and Frequencies of Ratified Coalition Structures\**

| Ordered Coalition Structure | Game G1 Means | Freq. | Game G2 Means | Freq. | Game G3 Means | Freq. | Game G4 Means | Freq. | Game G5 Means | Freq. | Game G6 Means | Freq. |
|---|---|---|---|---|---|---|---|---|---|---|---|---|
| (pqqqp) | 12.0 | 3[a] | 12.0 | 3[a] | 10.8 | 0[a] | 12.6 | 11[ab] | 9.6 | 3[a] | 9.6 | 1[a] |
| (pqqq,p) | 15.0 | 7[ab] | 12.0 | 0 | 9.0 | 0 | 9.0 | 0 | 6.0 | 0 | 6.0 | 0 |
| (pqqp,q) | 10.0 | 0 | 10.0 | 0 | 9.0 | 0 | 10.5 | 0 | 10.0 | 6 | 12.0 | 0[ab] |
| (pqq-qp) | 13.3, 10.0 | 1[a] | 13.3, 10.0 | 8[ab] | 12.0, 9.0 | 11[ab] | 12.0, 10.5 | 0 | 8.0, 10.0 | 0 | 8.0, 12.0 | 0 |
| (ppq,q,q) | 6.7 | 0 | 6.7 | 0 | 6.0 | 0 | 7.0 | 0 | 6.7 | 0 | 9.3 | 0 |
| (pq,qqp) | 10.0, 13.3 | 0[a] | 10.0, 13.3 | 0[a] | 9.0, 12.0 | 0[a] | 10.5, 12.0 | 0 | 10.0, 8.0 | 3 | 12.0, 8.0 | 1[a] |
| (pq,pq,q) | 10.0, 10.0 | 0 | 10.0, 10.0 | 0 | 9.0, 9.0 | 0 | 10.5, 10.5 | 0 | 10.0, 10.0 | 5[b] | 12.0, 12.0 | 9[ab] |
| Pareto Optimal | | 11 | | 11 | | 11 | | 11 | | 3 | | 11 |
| Maximal Share | | 7 | | 8 | | 11 | | 11 | | 5 | | 9 |

\* 1-person coalitions, having a value of zero, are not entered in the table.
[a] Pareto optimal coalition structure.
[b] Maximal share coalition structure.

through G6, respectively). Thirty-six of these 38 plays ended up in the $\alpha$-power set without error. The only two exceptions where deviations between observed and predicted payoff vectors were noted are plays G3,3 and G5,9. Of special interest are games G5 and G6, in which reduced games were played in 18 instances following the formation of a 2-person coalition. Having estimated $\alpha$ by a least squares procedure, the prediction of the model that $0 \leq \alpha \leq 1$ was sustained in all 18 cases. For 17 of the 18 2- or 3-person coalitions that were formed, the singly predicted payoff vectors corresponded to the observed payoff vectors without any error. And the U-shaped distribution of the estimated $\alpha$ values correspond closely to the distribution of $\alpha$ in the combined outcomess over a thousand games in nine 3-person game studies analyzed by Rapoport and Kahan (1982).[7]

## Notes

[1]Maschler writes to us that (i) he feels that the arguments against the core are valid for the grand coalition and not necessarily for other coalition structures; (ii) he feels that, say, for $\{pq,qqp\}$, the payoff vector $(0,1/2,1/2,1/2,0)$ is sound if both coalitions form simultaneously and standard of fairness considerations do not occur; (iii) he feels that, nevertheless, this will not be the real outcome in most cases, because coalitions do not form simultaneously and because standards of fairness considerations do take place.

[2]When two $q$ traders withdraw, there remain two $P$ and one $Q$ traders. Hence $v(pq)=v(pqp)=1$ and $v(S)=0$ otherwise in the reduced game. Player $q$ may get at most one (as predicted by the bargaining set and the core). Taking the other extreme of an equal split of $v(pqp)$, he will get $1/3$.

[3]The players could not publicly communicate with each other to adopt the straightforward and normatively appealing strategy of equal split if, indeed, they were perceiving themselves in a 6-person zero-sum game. However, a tacit agreement could be easily reached by all five players sequentially accepting the first equal split offer. Such offers appeared in all six games, but were accorded serious consideration only in some.

[4]Consequently, we shall henceforth write $(pq,pqq)$ rather than $\{pq,pqq\}$ as order does count, and we shall distinguish between $(pq,pqq)$ and $(pqq,pq)$ as two different ordered coalition structures.

[5]Excluding coalition structures in which a 1-person coalition was the first to form or ones with two 1-person coalitions.

[6]It is true that the coalition structure $(pqqp,q)$ is maximal for games G5 and G6. But the 4-person coalition $(pqqp)$ provides absolutely no advantage to any player over the $(pq,pq)$ pair of coalitions, and has the distinct disadvantages (Komorita 1974) of being harder to coordinate and less stable. Our subjects by and large ignored the $(pqqp)$ coalition in all of their negotiations.

[7]The study reported here was supported by the National Science Foundation Grant BNS76-84285. We wish to thank Michele Fogelson for assistance in data collection, Richard A. Helwig for his assistance in all phases of data collection and analysis, and Joseph Greenberg, Michael Maschler, and an anonymous reviewer for critical readings of earlier drafts of the manuscript.

## References

Aumann, R. J. and J. H. Dréze. "Cooperative Games with Coalition Structures," *Internat. J. Game Theory*, **3** (1974), 217-237.

———— and M. Maschler. "The Bargaining Set for Cooperative Games," in M. Dresher, L. S. Shapley and A. W. Tucker (Eds.). *Advances in Game Theory*, Princeton University Press, Princeton, N.J., 1964.

Davis, M. and M. Maschler. "The Kernel of a Cooperative Game," *Naval Res. Logist. Quart.*, **12** (1965), 223-259.

Kahan, J. P., A. W. Coston, R. A. Helwig, Am. Rapoport and T. S. Wallsten. "A PDP-11/45 Program for Playing n-Person Characteristic Function Games," *Behavior Research Methods and Instrumentation*, **8** (1976), 165-169.

———— and Am. Rapoport. "Test of the Bargaining Set and Kernel Models in Three-Person Games," in An. Rapoport (Ed.) *Game theory as a Theory of Conflict Resolution*, Reidel, Dordrecht, Holland, 1974.

———— and ————. "When You Don't Need to Join: The Effects of Guaranteed Payoffs on Bargaining in Three-Person Cooperative Games," *Theory and Decision*, **8** (1977), 97-126.

———— and ————, "Coalition Formation in the Triad When Two Are Weak and One is Strong," *Math. Social Sci.*, **1** (1980), 11-38.

Komorita, S. S. "A Weighted Probability Model of Coalition Formation," *Psychological Rev.*, **81** (1974), 242-256.

Maschler, M. "The Power of a Coalition," *Management Sci.*, **10** (1963), 8-29.

————. "An Advantage of the Bargaining Set over the Core," *J. Econom. Theory*, **13** (1976), 184-192.

————. "Playing an n-Person Game: An Experiment," in H. Sauermann (Ed.), *Beiträge zur experimentellen Wirtschaftsforschung*, Vol. VIII: *Coalition Forming Behavior*, J. C. B. Mohr, Tubingen, 1978.

Postlewaite, A. and R. W. Rosenthal. "Disadvantageous Syndicates," *J. Econom. Theory*, **9** (1974), 324-326.

Rapoport, Am. and J. P. Kahan. "When Three Isn't Always Two Against One: Coalitions in Experimental Three-Person Games," *J. Experimental Social Psych.*, **12** (1976), 253-273.

———— and ————. "The Power of a Coalition and Payoff Disbursement in Three-Person Negotiable Conflicts," *J. Math. Sociol.*, **8** (1982), 193-225.

Scheffé, H. *The Analysis of Variance*. Wiley, New York, 1959.

Selten, R. "Equal Share Analysis of Characteristic Function Experiments," in H. Sauermann (Ed.). *Beiträge zur experimentellen Wirtschaftsforschung*. Vol. III, J. C. B. Mohr, Tubingen, Germany, 1972.

Shapley, L. S.   "A Value for n-Person Games," in H. Kuhn and A. W. Tucker (Eds.)
   *Contributions to the Theory of Games.*   II. *Ann. of Math. Studies,* **28,** Princeton
   University Press, Princeton, N.J., 1953.

_____.   "The Solutions of a Symmetric Market Game."   *Ann. of Math Studies,* **40**
   (1959),   145-162.

_____ and M. Shubik.   "On Market Games."   *J. Econom. Theory,* **1,** (1969a), 9-25.

_____ and _____.   "Pure Competition, Coalitional Power and Fair Division."
   *Internat. Econom. Rev.,* **10** (1969), 337-363.

_____ and _____.   "Game Theory in Economics.   Chapter 6. Characteristic Function,
   Core and Stable Set,"   RAND Report R-904-NSF/6, July 1973.

_____ and _____.   "Competitive Outcomes in the Cores of Market Games."   *Internat.*
   *J. Game Theory,* **4** (1975), 229-327.

# CHAPTER 14

# RELATIVE GAIN MAXIMIZATION IN SEQUENTIAL 3-PERSON CHARACTERISTIC FUNCTION GAMES

**ABSTRACT:** The present study tested competitively three descriptive models of coalition formation and payoff disbursement in sequential 3-person games in which each player seeks to maximize the rank of his or her total score in a sequence of interdependent characteristic function games with sidepayments. Two of the models were originally proposed and tested by J. D. Laing and R. J. Morrison. A third mixed-signal model is proposed, postulating that the starting rank position and the values of the characteristic function, which operate as two independent signals, are combined to determine both coalition frequencies and payoff division. To test these models, 25 subjects played 46 different sequences for a total of 236 games in a new experimental paradigm, which generalizes previous research by assigning different values to the three 2-person coalitions, introducing dependency between successive characteristic functions, and eliminating face-to-face bargaining. The results support the mixed-signal model over its competitors.

In experimental studies of mixed-motive conflicts, subjects are typically instructed to maximize their own individual gain and are subsequentially paid proportionally to their total score. There is strong evidence that subjects do not always adhere to these unambiguous instructions. The results of experiments conducted by McClintock and McNeel (1966, 1967) suggest that in mixed-motive contexts represented by 2-person nonnegotiable nonzero-sum games, players do not only try to maximize their payoffs, but are, in fact, more concerned with their scores relative to the other player than with the magnitude of their own individual scores (Messick & McClintock, 1968). In such situations, therefore, it may be adequate to describe person $i$'s payoff, $T_i$, as $T_i = f(P_i, D_i)$, where $P_i$ denotes $i$'s absolute gain, $D_i$ denotes $i$'s relative gain ($D_i = P_i - P_j$), and the function $f$ is monotonically increasing in each of its two arguments. In a series of experiments, Messick and Thorngate (1967) demonstrated that subjects do, in fact, tend to maximize relative gain when knowledge of the other person's payoffs is available.

Although the experimental evidence referred to above has been gathered in 2-person interactions, relative gain maximization may also be a major source of motivation in groups with three or more persons. In social situations such as class examinations, various sport competitions, and many group experiments, some individuals strive to be good at that which they do, others attempt to be better than their peers, and yet others try to be best (Shubik, 1971). Indeed, many social situations are designed to render relative gain maximization or, equivalently, rank position maximization of paramount importance to the participants. For example, at military academies such as West Point and at many schools in France, performance traditionally has been publicly recorded in terms of final class standing at graduation. The presidential primary system in the United States is another instance in which maximization of final rank position is the ultimate goal (Chertkoff, Skov, & Catt, 1980). And in the Olympic games, the gold, silver, and bronze medals are awarded to individual athletes or teams (e.g., basketball) ranked first, second, and third, respectively.

Realizing that status or social position is often more important in a society than wealth or other physical goods, Shubik (1971) introduced a class of games of status, which are characteristic function (CF) games with sidepayments (Kahan & Rapoport, 1984; Luce & Raiffa, 1957; Rapoport, 1970; Shubik, 1982) in which the true payoff of the game is not the score an individual player obtains but, rather, the player's status, which is determined by the rank order of the amount he or she obtains. Whereas Shubik focused on single-trial games of status, Laing and Morrison (1973, 1974a, 1974b) introduced a special class of multi-trial or sequential 3-person games of status in which the three players participate in a sequence of interdependent CF games (trials) and get paid according to their final rank. Laing and Morrison extended several game-theoretic solution concepts to their sequential 3-person game of status and, as an alternative, proposed two heuristic models to predict coalition frequencies and payoff allocation among status striving players. The two models, called *myopic* and *hyperopic*, are based on the assumption that players are unable to represent the overall structure of the sequential 3-person game of status in all its complexity. Rather, in accordance with current trends in behavioral decision theory, the players are assumed to act as if they form simplified representations of the game, adopting short-term, surrogate objectives and simple heuristics in choosing strategies intended to attain the long-term objective of highest final rank.

Subsequent to the myopic and hyperopic models, which should be regarded as complementary rather than antithetical (Laing & Morrision, 1974b), Friend, Laing, and Morrison (1978) proposed and tested a two-signal model, which combines Gamson's minimum resource theory (1961) and the hyperopic model to yield predictions concerning both coalition frequencies and payoff disbursement. Gamson's theory postulates that players entering into a coalition agreement divide their joint payoff according to a parity norm specifying that payoffs should be disbursed in proportion to the resources the players contribute to the coalition. In some experimental paradigms there is a natural way to assess the players' "resources" or "power," such as in Vinacke's experiment (1959) in which each player's power is determined by the "weight" assigned to him or her by the experiment. But in CF games there is no natural way to determine the player's power. Consequently, in its present form the two-signal model of Friend et al. (1978) is not directly applicable to our CF game experiment. However, the idea of combining two different signals in the same model is taken up in the mixed-signal model we propose below.

In a more recent study Chertkoff, Skov, and Catt (1980) tested the myopic and hyperopic models by introducing a new experimental paradigm differing from the one employed by Laing and Morrison in three major respects: (a) a sequence length that is prespecified and known to the subjects; (b) a different procedure for conducting the bargaining, which is supposed to reduce the effects of variables not included in the myopic and hyperopic models; and (c) unequal rank positions assigned to the three players when the sequence of games of status starts.

Following and extending these recent developments by Friend et al. (1978) and Chertkoff et al. (1980), the present study has two major purposes. The first is to generalize the experimental procedure without detracting from the applicability of the myopic and hyperopic models. This generalization is achieved by (a) assigning different values to the three permissible 2-person coalitions, (b) introducing dependency between trials by making the characteristic function presented on trial $t$ dependent on the outcome of trials $1,...,t-1$, and (c) employing a computer-controlled bargaining procedure which completely eliminates face-to-face negotiations. The second major purpose is to develop and test a new heuristic model, called the *mixed-signal* (MS) model, which predicts both coalition frequencies and payoff allocation.

## Basic Concepts

### CHARACTERISTIC FUNCTION GAMES

Negotiable coalition formation situations are frequently abstracted as games in CF form with sidepayments (Luce & Raiffa, 1957). Let $N$ denote the set of players in the game. A *characteristic function* is a rule that assigns a real number value $v(S)$ to any $S \subseteq N$. $S$ is called the *coalition*, and its *value*, $v(S)$, represents the reward jointly commanded by the members of coalition $S$ against the remaining players in the game. A coalition is formed when its members agree on how to allocate its value among the members. The assigned real value function $v$ and the rules governing communication among the players completely specify the game. It is assumed in the following that $v(\phi) = v(i) = v(N) = 0$.

To exemplify the notion of a CF, consider one of the 3-person games employed in the present study:

$G1$:  $v(AB) = 300$,  $v(AC) = 200$,  $v(BC) = 270$.

In game $G1$, $N = \{A, B, C\}$ and $n = |N| = 3$. If players $A$ and $B$ form a coalition, they jointly have 300 units of reward to disburse between themselves, leaving $C$ with zero reward. Similarly, players $A$ and $C$ have 200 units to share between themselves, whereas $B$ and $C$ jointly command 270 units.

The outcome of a CF game is represented by a *payoff configuration* (PC), which has the form

$$(\mathbf{x};\mathbf{S}) = (x_1, x_2,...,x_n ; S_1, S_2,...,S_r).$$

A PC consists of two parts, separated from each other by a semicolon. The first part pertains to the allocation of reward among the $n$ players, and the second to the various coalitions formed. $\mathbf{x} = (x_1,...,x_n)$ is an $n$-dimensional row vector of real numbers, called the *payoff vector*, representing a realizable allocation of payoff among the $n$ members, who appear in alphabetical order. Thus, $x_i$ is the payoff of player $i$ in the allocation $\mathbf{x}$. $\mathbf{S} = \{S_1,...,S_r\}$ is a set of $r$ mutually exclusive and collectively exhaustive coalitions $(1 \leq r \leq n)$, called a *coalition structure*. Players are assumed to obtain their joint reward as specified by the CF. Thus

$$\sum_{i \in S_j} x_i = v(S_j), \quad \text{if} \quad S_j \in S.$$

To illustrate these terms, consider game $G1$. If at some stage players $A$ and $C$ were to consider the coalition $AC$ with $A$ receiving $x_A = 120$ and $C$ receiving $x_C = 80$, leaving $B$ with zero reward, this consideration would be denoted as the PC (120, 0, 80; $AC$, $B$).

## SEQUENTIAL GAMES OF STATUS

Suppose that the same three players participate in a sequence of temporally disjoint CF games, and denote by $x_{i,t}$ the payoff obtained by player $i$ in the game played on trial $t$ ($t = 1, 2,...$). Before the sequence starts, at trial 0, each player $i$ gets an endowment of $x_{i,0}$. Then the total score accumulated by player $i$ across the first $t$ trials of the sequence is $\delta_{i,t} = \sum_{h=0}^{t} x_{i,h}$. Knowing the total scores of all three players at the end of any trial $t$, we can compute $r_{i,t}$ — the *rank* of player $i$'s total score relative to the scores of the other two players. Player $i$ is said to have a higher rank than player $j$ at the end of $t$ trials, written as $r_{i,t} > r_{j,t}$, if and only if $\delta_{i,t} > \delta_{j,t}$. Following Laing and Morrison (1974a), the two-way tie between the two players with the highest rank is denoted by $r = 1.5$ and the two-way tie between the two players with lowest rank by $r = 2.5$. The three-way tie is denoted by $r = 2$. There are altogether five possible ranks: 1, 1.5, 2, 2.5, 3.

A social situation falling within the domain analyzed by Laing and Morrison's models (1973) must satisfy three conditions:

(1) The same three players participate in a sequence of one or more temporally disjoint 3-person CF games with side payments (in which $v(ABC) = 0$).

(2) Each of the three players seeks to maximize the rank (status) he or she holds at the end of the sequence.

(3) Each of the three players is uncertain about the number of trials in the sequence.

At the end of trial $t$, the attainable ranks for each subject depend both on the distribution of total scores at the end of trial $t - 1$ and the CF values, $v(S)_t$, at trial $t$. For example, suppose $\delta_{A,t-1} = 30$, $\delta_{B,t-1} = 20$, $\delta_{C,t-1} = 5$. Let the CF on trial $t$ be given by

$$G2: \quad v(AB)_t = 12, \quad v(AC)_t = 14, \quad v(BC)_t = 10.$$

Clearly, $r_{A,t-1} = 1$, $r_{B,t-1} = 2$, and $r_{C,t-1} = 3$. At the end of trial $t$, player $B$ may improve her rank through coalitions $AB$ or $BC$, but player $B$'s rank will not deteriorate if coalition $AC$ forms. There is no way for player $C$ to improve her rank position (even if $x_{C,t} = 14$ in coalition $AC$ or $x_{C,t} = 10$ in coalition $BC$, player $C$ is left with the third rank). Suppose, however, that the distribution of total scores at the end of trial $t - 1$ is as above, but that the CF on trial $t$ is given by

$$G3: \quad v(AB)_t = v(AC)_t = v(BC)_t = 50.$$

Then player $C$ may attain each of the five possible ranks. The two examples above show that to achieve a wide range of sequential 3-person games of status, where various combinations of ranks on successive trials are possible, the CF values $v(S)_t$ must be chosen judiciously.

## Models For Sequential 3-Person Games of Status: Bargaining Heuristics

In line with recent theoretical developments in behavioral decision theory, which postulate simplified representations of the task by the subject (Slovic, Fischhoff, & Lichtenstein, 1977), the approach proposed by Laing and Morrision for sequential games of status assumes

> that players are unable to represent the overall structure of our sequential three-person game in all its complexity. In particular, we depart from game-theoretic approaches by assuming that players, lacking omniscience, act as if they form simplified representations of the game, adopting short-term, surrogate objectives and simple rules of thumb in choosing strategies intended to attain the long-run objective of highest final rank. (Laing & Morrison, 1973, p. 5).

To describe these rules of thumb, or heuristics, several terms are necessary. Define the *interval position* of player $i$ at the end of stage $t$ to be the sum of differences between his or her total score and those of the other two players:

$$d_{i,t} = (\delta_{i,t} - \delta_{j,t}) + (\delta_{i,t} - \delta_{k,t}),$$

for distinct players $i$, $j$, and $k$. Player $i$'s *position* at the end of trial $t$ is defined in terms of both the rank and interval position:

$$p_{i,t} = (r_{i,t}, d_{i,t}).$$

Bargaining heuristics or decision rules delimiting the payoff divisions between coalition partners are incorporated into three behavioral assumptions that all three players are expected to obey.

*Assumption 1.* A member of the winning coalition would not agree to a payoff vector that causes his or her coalition partner to overtake or pass this member in rank.

*Assumption 2.* A member of the winning coalition would not agree to a payoff vector that not only fails to grant him or her an improved rank but also causes the member to lose interval position.

*Assumption 3.* A member of the winning coalition who holds a rank-based preference for his or her partner would not accept a payoff smaller than that necessary to achieve the rank upon which this preference is based.

The first two assumptions state a version of the principle of individual rationality (Kahan & Rapoport, 1984; Rapoport, 1970); players will not enter into coalitions in such a manner as to deteriorate their overall positions. The meaning of Assumption 3 becomes clear after defining "rank-based preference" below.

Using these three assumptions, the myopic, hyperopic, and mixed-signal models described below identify a *negotiation range* -- the set of all alternative agreements consistent with the three bargaining heuristics. They all predict that the actual payoff vector will lie in this range. The three assumptions above are sufficient to predict uniquely for each 2-person coalition the rank each player will attain if that coalition forms; all agreements within a negotiation range yield the same rank outcomes (Friend et al., 1978).

## THE MYOPIC MODEL

All the models described below assume that players forget or ignore all history of the play except as summarized by the current distribution of accumulated scores. Adhering to this assumption, as well as to Assumptions 1 through 3 above, the myopic and hyperopic are two alternative models which differ from each other in the planning horizon players are assumed to use. The myopic model (termed model M) assumes that players adopt the surrogate objective of maximizing position on the present trial, ignoring all future trials. Based on Assumptions 1 through 3 above and on the assumption that the potential coalition partners will employ the same reasoning as he or she, each player finds the best rank that can be achieved from each coalition and the minimum payoff needed to achieve that rank.

The best ranks for each possible 2-person coalition serve as the basis for determining which coalition the player will choose ("rank-based preference"). These choices are not deterministic, but rather are governed by a probabilistic mechanism with a single parameter $\epsilon$. (The parameter $\epsilon$ is assumed to be fixed for all three players in the triad and for all the games in the sequences.) If player $i$ expects to attain a higher rank from a coalition with player $j$ rather than with $k$, then the myopic model assumes that $i$ will choose $j$ with probability $a_{ij} = 1 - \epsilon$ and $k$ with probability $a_{ik} = \epsilon$, where $0 < \epsilon < 1/2$. According to the myopic model, each player $i$ who is indifferent between $j$ and $k$ as alternative coalition partners on the basis of rank consideration, chooses $j$ and $k$ with probabilities in proportion to the probabilities that his or her choice is reciprocated: $a_{ij}/a_{ik} = a_{ji}/a_{ki}$. In later papers (Friend, Laing, & Morrision, 1977, 1978) the assumption is simply that a rank-indifferent player chooses each possible partner with probability 1/2. We adopted the earlier assumption because it better fits our data.

The probabilistic preferences constitute the *attraction structure* of the game, which is used, in turn to generate the probabilities of each coalition forming, such that a 2-person coalition will form with a (normalized) probability equal to the product of the players' preferences for each other. For example, if player $A$ prefers player $C$, $C$ prefers $B$, and $B$ is indifferent between $A$ and $C$ (based on rank consideration), then the attraction structure has player $A$ choosing $B$ and $C$ with probabilities $a_{AB} = \epsilon$ and $a_{AC} = 1 - \epsilon$, player $C$ choosing $A$ and $B$ with probabilities $a_{CA} = \epsilon$ and $a_{CB} = 1 - \epsilon$, and player $B$ choosing $A$ and $C$ with probabilities $a_{BA} = \epsilon$ and $a_{BC} = 1 - \epsilon$ (the reciprocity assumption). Therefore, the coalition probabilities $p'(ij)$ are

$$p'(AB) = \epsilon^2, \qquad p'(AC) = \epsilon(1 - \epsilon), \qquad p'(BC) = (1 - \epsilon)^2. \qquad (1)$$

The probability that no coalition is formed is $1 - p'(AB) - p'(AC) - p'(BC)$. In a manner similar to Chertkoff (1967), it is assumed that when no coalition is formed, negotiations begin afresh; therefore, the normalized coalition probabilities are obtained by dividing each of the unnormalized probabilities by their sum. In the example above, $p'(AB) + p'(AC) + p'(BC) = \epsilon^2 - \epsilon + 1$, so that each probability in Eq. (1) should be divided by that amount to obtain the normalized probabilities, $p(ij)$.

The myopic model predicts that the payoff vector will lie in the negotiation range identified on the basis of the three bargaining heuristics. It further asserts that any disagreement between coalition partners over alternative allocations within the negotiation range will be resolved in favor of the player who enjoys a bargaining advantage within the coalition. Within a coalition $ij$, player $i$ enjoys a *bargaining advantage* over $j$ if and only if $a_{ij}/a_{ki} < a_{ji}/a_{kj}$. The model "predicts that the payoff to the player enjoying a bargaining advantage over his partner will tend to lie toward the former's preferred end of the negotiation range" (Friend et al., 1978, p. 33). If no bargaining advantage is identified within the coalition, then the partners will tend to agree to that payoff allocation nearest the mid-point of the negotiation range.

To exemplify the predictions of the myopic model, consider a situation where the total scores at the end of trial $t - 1$ are

$$\delta_{A,t-1} = 160, \delta_{B,t-1} = 200, \delta_{C,t-1} = 130,$$

and the characteristic function on trial $t$ is

$$v(AB)_t = 90, \qquad v(AC)_t = 80, \qquad v(BC)_t = 70.$$

Clearly, $r_{A,t-1} = 2$, $r_{B,t-1} = 1$, and $r_{C,t-1} = 3$. Player $A$ expects to achieve sole possession of first place through coalition $AC$ but to remain in her current position if coalition $AB$ forms. Thus, she has rank-based preference for coalition $AC$, which means that she chooses $C$ with probability $a_{AC} = 1 - \epsilon$ and $B$ with $a_{AB} = \epsilon$. Player $C$ prefers coalition $BC$ over coalition $AC$ for a similar reason, choosing $B$ with probability $a_{CB} = 1 - \epsilon$ and $A$ with probability $a_{CA} = \epsilon$. Expecting to remain in her first position, player $B$ is indifferent between her prospective coalition partners (on rank consideration). Hence, in accordance with the reciprocity assumption $a_{BA} = \epsilon$ and $a_{BC} = 1 - \epsilon$.

The attraction structure is used next to determine bargaining advantages. Player $B$ enjoys a bargaining advantage over $A$ because $a_{BA}/a_{CB} < a_{AB}/a_{CA}$. Player $C$ has a bargaining advantage over $A$ because $a_{CA}/a_{BC} < a_{AC}/a_{BA}$. And player $C$ also enjoys a bargaining advantage over $B$ because $a_{CB}/a_{AC} < a_{BC}/a_{AB}$.

Consider first coalition $AB$. As player $B$ is first-ranked and $A$ is second-ranked, $B$ will not accept any payoff allocation that reverses their rank order, so a preliminary boundary on any agreement between them is $x_{A,t} - x_{B,t} < 40$ (Assumption 1). But this boundary is superceded for this coalition by Assumption 2, which states that if there is no improvement in rank order, then a player will not accept an offer that would lose her interval position. To maintain interval position, each player must receive at least an outcome of 30, so the negotiation range is between (30, 60; $AB$) and (60, 30; $AB$). Because player $B$ enjoys a bargaining advantage over $A$, it is predicted that the payoff to

$B$ will tend to lie toward her preferred end of the negotiation range ("tend to lie" has been interpreted to mean that the payoff will fall above the mid-point of the negotiation range), namely, $(90 - x_B, 45 < x_B < 60; AB)$.

Similar considerations applied to coalitions $AC$ and $BC$ result in the following set of PCs:

$(90 - x_B, 45 < x_B \leq 60, 0; AB, C)$

$(80 - x_C, 0, 33 \ 1/3 < x_C \leq 40; AC, B)$

$(0, 70 - x_C, 38 \ 1/3 < x_C \leq 46 \ 2/3; BC, A)$.

The coalition structure probabilities are, respectively,

$$\frac{\epsilon^2}{\epsilon^2 - \epsilon + 1}, \quad \frac{(1 - \epsilon) \epsilon}{\epsilon^2 - \epsilon + 1}, \quad \frac{(1 - \epsilon)^2}{\epsilon^2 - \epsilon + 1}.$$

They can be determined numerically once $\epsilon$ is estimated from the data.

THE HYPEROPIC MODEL

Under the assumptions of the hyperopic model, termed model $H$, players behave as if whatever coalition structure forms in the present trial will continue to form in subsequent trials. This viewpoint does not presume that the payoff disbursement within that coalition structure will not change, nor does it explicitly call for a multiple-game agreement. Rather, the actual coalition values $v(S)$ are ignored and, instead, the relative standings of the players are the focal points of negotiations.

The effect of looking indefinitely into the future is that if there exists a difference in ranks between two members of a coalition, it can never be overcome. However, any disadvantage in rank of a player inside the coalition to a player outside the coalition can always be overcome. This viewpoint determines the coalitional preferences, which are then transformed into the probabilities $a_{ij}$ as in the myopic model. In the limit, there are only four distinct rank-order structures among three players, each of which leads to a unique attraction structure (Table 1). The point disbursements for given coalition structures are determined exactly as in the myopic model; presumably the point allocation, if not the coalition structure, is renegotiated on subsequent trials.

THE MIXED-SIGNAL MODEL

In reflecting on the results of experiments on weighted majority games (Shapley, 1962), Friend et al. (1978) noted that both relative status and the players' resources (weights) were attended to by the subjects. To account for these data, they proposed a two-signal model based on the assumption that " players in complex coalition situations do attend to more than one relevant signal in their decision environment, and these signals do act jointly to influence alliances and negotiated payoffs within those alliances" (1978, p. 23). The term "signal" in their theory denotes any cue which may be used by players in their decisions. Friend at el. (1978) provided evidence in support of the model

*Table 1.  Hyperopic  limiting  attraction  structure  probabilities*

| | Rank-order structure | | | |
| Condition | $A = B = C$ | $A = B > C$ | $A > B = C$ | $A > B > C$ |
|---|---|---|---|---|
| $p(A$ chooses $B)$ | .50 | $\epsilon$ | .50 | .50 |
| $p(A$ chooses $C)$ | .50 | $1 - \epsilon$ | .50 | .50 |
| $p(B$ chooses $A)$ | .50 | $\epsilon$ | $\epsilon$ | $\epsilon$ |
| $p(B$ chooses $C)$ | .50 | $1 - \epsilon$ | $1 - \epsilon$ | $1 - \epsilon$ |
| $p(C$ chooses $A)$ | .50 | .50 | $\epsilon$ | .50 |
| $p(C$ chooses $B)$ | .50 | .50 | $1 - \epsilon$ | .50 |
| $p(AB)$ | 1/3 | $\epsilon^2/(1 - \epsilon + \epsilon)^2$ | $(\epsilon/2)/(1 - \epsilon + \epsilon^2)$ | $2\epsilon/3$ |
| $p(AC)$ | 1/3 | $[(1 - \epsilon)/2]/(1 - \epsilon + \epsilon^2)$ | $(\epsilon/2)/(1 - \epsilon + \epsilon^2)$ | 1/3 |
| $p(BC)$ | 1/3 | $[(1 - \epsilon)/2]/(1 - \epsilon + \epsilon^2)$ | $(1-\epsilon)^2/(1 - \epsilon + \epsilon^2)$ | $2(1 - \epsilon)/3$ |

suggesting that subjects may adopt the logical combination of two one-signal models as a simplifying heuristic to cope with the complexity of the bargaining situation.

In a similar manner the MS model assumes that the sequential 3-person CF game of status in which the restriction $v(AB)_t = v(AC)_t = v(BC)_t$ no longer holds generates two prominent and distinct signals, each of which determines a different attraction structure. The first is the status signal as identified by the myopic model; the second signal is the CF values. One main assumption (based on experiments on ordinary CF games) concerns the second signal: each player prefers to join the coalition with the highest value. Just as subjects who are asked to maximize their absolute gain are, nevertheless, concerned with relative gain, so subjects who are asked to maximize relative gain are concerned with their absolute gain.

Before applying the MS model to data obtained from status games, we first test the effectiveness of the second signal in a class of games in which it should be most important, namely, the single-stage CF game with sidepayments in which subjects are paid in proportion to their absolute scores. The CF values should be the sole signal in this class of games.

*Parameter estimation.*  Assuming that the preferred partner is chosen with probability $1 - \epsilon$ and the other partner with probability $\epsilon$ $(0 \leq \epsilon < 1/2)$, Table 2 presents the four distinct attraction structures based on the four ordinal relations between the three coalition values $v(AB)$, $v(AC)$, and $v(BC)$.

The parameter $\epsilon$ in Table 2 may be estimated and then used to generate numerical predictions for $p(ij)$. When $v(AB) > v(AC) > v(BC)$, as is the case in all of the four studies that we examined below, the likelihood function is given by

*Table 2.  Attraction structure probabilities for 3-person characteristic function games*

| | Rank-order structure | | | |
|---|---|---|---|---|
| Condition | $v(AB) = v(AC)$ $= v(BC)$ | $v(AB) > v(AC)$ $= v(BC)$ | $v(AB) = v(AC)$ $> v(BC)$ | $v(AB) > v(AC)$ $> v(BC)$ |
| $p(A$ chooses $B)$ | .50 | $1 - \epsilon$ | .50 | $1 - \epsilon$ |
| $p(A$ chooses $C)$ | .50 | $\epsilon$ | .50 | $\epsilon$ |
| $p(B$ chooses $A)$ | .50 | $1 - \epsilon$ | $1 - \epsilon$ | $1 - \epsilon$ |
| $p(B$ chooses $C)$ | .50 | $\epsilon$ | $\epsilon$ | $\epsilon$ |
| $p(C$ chooses $A)$ | .50 | .50 | $1 - \epsilon$ | $1 - \epsilon$ |
| $p(C$ chooses $B)$ | .50 | .50 | $\epsilon$ | $\epsilon$ |
| $p(AB)$ | 1/3 | $(1-\epsilon)^2/(1-\epsilon+\epsilon^2)$ | $[(1-\epsilon/2)]/(1-\epsilon+\epsilon^2)$ | $(1-\epsilon)^2/(1-\epsilon+\epsilon^2)$ |
| $p(AC)$ | 1/3 | $(\epsilon/2)/(1-\epsilon+\epsilon^2)$ | $[(1-\epsilon/2)]/(1-\epsilon+\epsilon^2)$ | $(1-\epsilon)^2/(1-\epsilon+\epsilon^2)$ |
| $p(BC)$ | 1/3 | $(\epsilon/2)/(1-\epsilon+\epsilon^2)$ | $\epsilon^2/(1-\epsilon+\epsilon^2)$ | $\epsilon^2/(1-\epsilon+\epsilon^2)$ |

$$L = \frac{(f_{AB} + f_{AC} + f_{BC})!}{(f_{AB})! \, (f_{AC})! \, (f_{BC})!} \cdot \left[\frac{(1-\epsilon)^2}{1-\epsilon+\epsilon^2}\right]^{f_{AB}} \cdot \left[\frac{\epsilon(1-\epsilon)}{1-\epsilon+\epsilon^2}\right]^{f_{AC}} \cdot \left[\frac{\epsilon^2}{1-\epsilon+\epsilon^2}\right]^{f_{BC}},$$

where $f_{ij}$ is the observed frequency of coalition $ij$.  Taking the logarithm of $L$, differentiating $\log L$ with respect to $\epsilon$, setting the result equal to zero, and solving for $\epsilon$, yields the maximum likelihood estimate

$$\hat{\epsilon}_{1,2} = \frac{(f_{AB} + 2 f_{AC} + 3 f_{BC}) \pm \sqrt{(f_{AB} + 2 f_{AC} + 3 f_{BC})^2 + 4(f_{AB} - f_{BC})(f_{AC} + 2 f_{BC})}}{2(f_{BC} - f_{AB})}. \tag{2}$$

Maximum likelihood estimates may also be obtained for the two other nontrivial cases: $v(AB) > v(AC) = v(BC)$ and $v(AB) = v(AC) > v(BC)$.

*An experimental test.*  Table 3 presents observed and predicted coalition frequencies for four different 3-person game experiments in which the coalition values were rearranged so that $v(AB) > v(AC) > v(BC)$.  The first study is due to Riker (1967), who had three different groups of subjects, consisting of businessmen and undergraduate students, play the following 3-person CF game once:

$$v(AB) = \$6.00, \quad v(AC) = \$5.00, \quad v(BC) = \$4.00.$$

Of the 93 plays, 2-person coalitions were formed in 90 cases, whereas in 3 cases no agreement was reached. The second study is due to Kahan and Rapoport (1974), who had three groups of subjects under three different communication conditions. There were four triads in each group: each triad played five different CF games that were repeated four times. Table 3 summarizes the coalition frequencies over the three communication conditions and the five games. Medlin (1976) also presented his subjects with five different 3-person CF games. There were four experimental conditions in his study differing from one another in the value of $v(N)$. Of a total of 160 plays, the grand coalition formed on 71 plays. Table 3 reports only the frequencies of plays terminating with the formation of a 2-person coalition summed over games and conditions. The fourth study by Levinsohn and Rapoport (1978) included a variety of 3-person CF games with no grand coalition. One condition included 90 single-stage games, and a second condition consisted of 18 multi-stage games each of which played for five trials. Table 3 summarizes the coalition frequencies over games and both experimental conditions.

*Table 3. Observed and predicted coalition frequencies for four 3-person characteristic function game studies*

|  |  | Coalition | | | | | |
| --- | --- | --- | --- | --- | --- | --- | --- |
| Study |  | AB | AC | BC | Total | $\hat{\varepsilon}$ | $\chi^2$ |
| Riker (1967) | Observed | 44 | 28 | 10 | 90 | | |
|  | Predicted | 44.94 | 28.09 | 17.96 | 90 | 0.339 | 0.0005 |
| Kahan & Rapoport | Observed | 146 | 52 | 41 | 239 | | |
| (1974) | Predicted | 138.09 | 67.71 | 33.20 | 239 | 0.329 | 4.098 |
| Medlin (1976) | Observed | 49 | 23 | 17 | 89 | | |
|  | Predicted | 47.11 | 26.73 | 15.17 | 89 | 0.362 | 0.817 |
| Levinsohn & Rapoport | Observed | 112 | 45 | 23 | 180 | | |
| (1978) | Predicted | 110.33 | 48.42 | 21.25 | 180 | 0.305 | 0.411 |

Table 3 provides strong support for the probability model of coalition formation in 3-person CF games. In all four studies Eq. (2) yields $0 \leq \hat{\varepsilon} < 1/2$ as expected. Moreover, despite the wide variety of CF games and the procedural differences among the four studies, the range of $\hat{\varepsilon}$ is quite narrow, from 0.305 in the study by Levinsohn and Rapoport (1978) to 0.390 in the study by Riker (1967). As shown in Table 3, $\chi^2$ is nonsignificant for each of the four studies.

We have, then, two kinds of models, one focusing on status, and the other on coalition values. We have chosen the myopic model as one component of the MS model because of its relative success in previous experiments (Chertkoff et al., 1980). Each model predicts an attraction structure with a single parameter $\epsilon$ from which the coalition frequencies and the payoff disbursement can be derived. We must next consider how players' perceptions of the two signals interact with each other in influencing the overall pattern of outcomes. Model MS assumes that the two signals are combined with equal weights. This assumption breaks down into several cases. Let $a'_{ij}$ and $a''_{ij}$ denote the probability that player $i$ will choose $j$ according to the M and CF models, respectively. Denote by $a_{ij}$ the same probability according to the MS model. Then

$$a_{ij} = \epsilon, \quad \text{if} \quad a'_{ij} = \epsilon \text{ and } a''_{ij} = \epsilon,$$

$$\text{or } a'_{ij} = 1/2 \text{ and } a''_{ij} = \epsilon, \quad \text{or } a'_{ij} = \epsilon \text{ and } a''_{ij} = 1/2;$$

$$a'_{ij} = 1/2, \quad \text{if} \quad a'_{ij} = \epsilon \text{ and } a''_{ij} = 1 - \epsilon,$$

$$\text{or } a'_{ij} = 1 - \epsilon \text{ and } a''_{ij} = \epsilon, \quad \text{or } a'_{ij} = a''_{ij} = 1/2;$$

$$a_{ij} = 1 - \epsilon, \quad \text{if} \quad a'_{ij} = 1 - \epsilon \text{ and } a''_{ij} = 1 - \epsilon,$$

$$\text{or } a'_{ij} = 1/2 \text{ and } a''_{ij} = 1 - \epsilon, \quad \text{or } a'_{ij} = 1 - \epsilon \text{ and } a''_{ij} = 1/2.$$

Once the attraction structure is specified, the MS model determines who has the bargaining advantage and subsequently the payoff vector with the negotiation range in exactly the same way as do the myopic and hyperopic models.

## Previous and Current Experimental Procedures

In surveying experimental research on coalition forming behavior, Kahan and Rapoport noted that "creating an experimental game to study coalition formation behavior is no straightforward task, and virtually every investigator has his own idiosyncratic approach" (1984, p. 249). When several methodologies are employed, problems of comparison and integration arise, because the subjects' interpretations of the task, their motivations, their aspirations, and consequently the ensuing negotiations are affected by the experimental formulation of the task. Komorita and Meek (1978), for example, have demonstrated that the same experimental game supports differing social psychological theories, depending on the experimental conditions of information and communication. Similar procedural effects may take place in games of status. The present experiment differs from previous experimental studies of 3-person games of status in three important respects. The reasons for these changes are described in some detail below.

In the experiments of Laing and Morrison (1973, 1974a, 1974b), bargaining was face-to-face, completely informal, supervised, and public. In terms of generality, clarity of the task, integrity of the coalition formation process, and flexibility of negotiations, the unrestricted bargaining approach is an excellent technique. However, the control of motivation poses an obvious problem because face-to-face communication enhances the chances that the players' judgments will be altered by personality characteristics of their various opponents instead of the (for purposes of testing theory) structural variables imposed by the nature of the game. A vivid description of unrestricted negotiations has been provided by kalisch, Milnor, Nash, and Nering:

The tendency of a player to get into coalitions seemed to have a high correlation with talkativeness.... In many cases, aggressiveness played a role even in the first formation of a coalition; and who yelled first and loudest after the umpire said 'go' made a difference in the outcome. (1954, p. 307)

To resolve this problem, Chertkoff et al. had their subjects make initial choices concerning coalition partners in private. However, once two players chose each other, the negotiations of the terms of the agreement were conducted by the two coalition members face-to-face. Consequently, the procedure of Chertkoff et al. reduces, but certainly does not eliminate "the impact of variables not included in the Laing and Morrison theories" (Chertkoff et al., 1980, p. 254). In contrast, the present study employs the computer-controlled experimental paradigm NPER (Kahan & Helwig, 1971; Kahan & Rapoport, 1984; Rapoport & Kahan, 1974), which eliminates the effects of face-to-face bargaining. Details of the procedure are presented in the method section below.

In the Laing and Morrison experiments, the three players started the sequence with point totals $x_{A,0} = x_{B,0} = x_{C,0} = 0$, and then participated in a series of 3-person games of unknown length with

$$v(AB)_t = v(AC)_t = v(BC)_t = k, \quad k = 100, 300, 500.$$

As noted by Chertkoff et al., this procedure gives rise to a limited number of attraction structures the frequency of which cannot be controlled. It is, therefore, not always possible to reach conclusions about coalition forming behavior in prespecified attraction structures of special theoretical interest. In Chertkoff et al., players draw from a box three different cards with initial point $x_{A,0} \neq x_{B,0} \neq x_{C,0} > 0$, thus guaranteeing at least four different kinds of attraction structures on trial 1. However, the attraction structures are no longer manipulatable after the first trial because of the constraint $v(AB)_t = v(AC)_t = v(BC)_t = 100$. In contrast, the present study employs a procedure in which the CFs differ from one trial to another and the coalition values differ, in general, from one another. It was agreed above that this procedural change is of sufficient importance to introduce a new prominent signal into the coalition formation process and to control the attraction structures throughout the sequence.

The third major procedural difference between the present study and its predecessors concerns sequential dependencies in the CFs. In all previous studies of sequential games of status the CFs within a sequence were mutually independent. But if sequential games of status are intended to model or at least to reflect the major characteristics of continuing social interactions (Laing & Morrison, 1973), sequential dependencies between CFs may not be ignored. Rather, they ought to be incorporated into the experimental task (Levinsohn & Rapoport, 1978). In the present study, the coalition values $v(AB)_t$, $v(AC)_t$, and $v(BC)_t$ depend on the outcomes of the previous trials, as described in the method section below.

## A 3-Person Game Experiment

METHOD

   *Subjects.*   Subjects were 25 male and female volunteers, mostly undergraduate students at the University of Haifa, Israel, who were offered the opportunity to earn cash for their performance in a multi-session coalition formation experiment. To save time on instructions and training with the experimental procedure, only volunteers who had previously participated in a four session 12-hr coalition formation experiment employing the same computer-controlled *Coalitions* paradigm (see below) were recruited. This previous experiment had been designed to study coalition formation and payoff disbursement in 4-person CF games. Unlike the present study, the previous games had been sequentially independent with the identity of the subjects being rotated randomly from one game to another.

   *Coalitions.*   The present experiment employed the *Coalitions* package of programs. A full description of the computer program can be found in Kahan, Coston, Helwig, Rapoport, and Wallsten (1976), Kahan and Rapoport (1984), and numerous other publications; only a brief description is presented here.

   *Coalitions* defines bargaining as a passing through three stages, which loosely correspond to the four stages of bargaining of Thibaut and Kelley (1959). The first stage, called the *negotiation stage*, corresponds to Thibaut and Kelley's sampling and bargaining phases of the process, in which players first learn of the available outcomes and then establish bargaining positions through negotiations and proposals to each other. The second, or *acceptance stage*, corresponds to Thibaut and Keller's commitment phase. Players comprising a coalition have tentatively agreed upon a particular allocation (PC) of their joint payoff. Although this agreement is not yet binding, it is sufficiently strong to restrict players' bargaining mobility. Players not in the agreement attempt to disrupt it in favor of a PC more favorable to themselves, while those in the coalition must decide on maintenance of the present agreement versus gambling for a better outcome within or outside of that coalition. The game then passes to the third or *ratification stage*, which corresponds to Thibaut and Kelley's institutionalization phase. When an accepted PC, having survived for a certain length of time, is voted into ratification by its members, the game terminates and each player is given his or her payoff as prescribed by the ratified PC.

   Subjects never learn the personal identity of their co-players. They communicate with each other by transmitting messages coded in keywords via CRTs connected to a computer. The computer checks the legality of the messages, reformats them to be easily readable, adds messages informing players of the effects of the present move on previous moves in the game, and transmits the entire package to its intended recipients. The keywords used by *Coalitions* and their effects, as well as the implications of being in the acceptance stage (called "All-accepted" in the table), are explained in Table 4.

Table 4. Key words and their effects.

| Keyword | Example of parameter | Primary effect | Other effect on this coalition | Effects outside named coalition |
|---|---|---|---|---|
| PASS | None | Send null message | None | None |
| SOLO | None | Immediate ratification of player's 1-person coalition | None | Player is removed from further play in this game |
| OFFER | $A = 20$, $B = 18$ | Make a proposal | Supercedes player's previous OFFER, AGREE, and ACCEPT | None |
| SUGGEST | $A = 20$, $C = 15$ to AC | Make informal, secret proposal | None | None |
| REJECT | AC BY C | Erase an offer | None | None |
| AGREE | AC BY C | Show liking for an offer | Same as for OFFER | Erases any ACCEPT made by this player |
| ACCEPT | AC BY C | Tentative commitment to an offer | Same as for OFFER | Erases any AGREE or ACCEPT made by this player |
| When all players have accepted an offer | | Game moves to acceptance stage | None | Erases all other positions taken by included players (they may make no new OFFER except to subsets or supersets of the accepted coalition) |
| AFFIRM | AC | Stand by previous action | None | None |
| RATIFY | None | Propose move to ratification | Form coalition if all members agree to ratification (coalition is dissolved otherwise) | Concludes game for players in ratified coalitions |
| MESSAGE | $A = 1$, $C = 3$ | Send numbered message(s) to named player(s) (counts as communication) | | |
| VALUE | None | Information: Give all values in the game except those involving removed players (does not count as a communication) | | |

*Communication.* A chart of keywords that were always available to the subjects is shown in Table 4. The keyword MESSAGE, which counts as a communication, allows the subject to send a prespecified message by only typing its number. Based on extensive pretests, a list of 20 common messages was specifically prepared for the present study; it is presented in Table 5.

*Table 5. List of messages (translated from Hebrew) for games of status*

---

1. Believe me, for Pete's sake.
2. My next offer is serious.
3. If you accept my offer, you will improve your rank.
4. Join me to decrease your point discrepancy with the other player.
5. Join me now, as this may be the final game.
6. Join me in coalition for all the remaining games in the present sequence.
7. If you accept my offer, I'll join you in coalition for the remaining games.
8. I'll join you in coalition for all the remaining games.
9. If you don't accept my offer, you will never pass the other player.
10. My offer gives you more points.
11. Make a reasonable offer and we'll join together.
12. You are too greedy.
13. If we stick together, our situation will improve.
14. Don't trust the other player, stay with me.
15. I refuse to change my position.
16. Decide, and I'll follow suit.
17. Let us wait before ratification to see what happens.
18. Let us ratify as soon as possible.
19. I may terminate the game with a "solo."
20. I agree with your last message sent to me.

---

*Experimental procedure.* Twenty-three experimental sessions of approximately 3 hr each were conducted. In each session, 3 subjects were randomly selected from the group of 25 and assigned to the session under the constraint that no 2 players participated together in more than one session. Each session consisted of two sequences of 3-person games of status. Independence between sequences was achieved by randomly rotating the roles of the three players from one sequence to another. Within a sequence the three players maintained their roles. Forty-six sequences were generated, each including between 1 and 11 games. Altogether, 263 3-person CF games were played. The number of games per sequence varied considerably from one sequence to another; it was predetermined but not disclosed to the subjects.

Upon arrival in the laboratory, each subject was reacquainted with the experimental apparatus. The rules of the game of status were then introduced in a brief session consisting of written instructions and verbal elaborations. First, the *Coalitions* program was briefly reviewed. Then the specific features of games of status were emphasized. The subject was told that he or she would participate in several sequences of 3-person

CF games of different length, in which the same roles would be maintained over all games. When a sequence terminated after a prespecified but unknown number of trials, the members of the triad were paid $5.00, $3.00, $2.00, $1.00, and $0.50 for ranks 1, 1.5, 2, 2.5, and 3, respectively. Additionally, $0.50 was paid to each subject for each hour of play. Each subject had a full record of his or her position as well as the position of the other players during the entire sequence.

The three members of each triad were labeled $A$, $B$, or $C$. Communication on trial 1 proceed in the order $A$, $B$, $C$, $A$,.... Starting on trial 2, the order of communication was inversely related to rank, with the low player making the first move and the top player moving third. In case of a tie, the communication order was determined randomly.

*Experimental games.* The various CF games in each sequence were constructed to achieve two goals: (a) to reward players with a high rank on trial $t - 1$ by rendering the CF on trial $t$ more favorable to them, and (b) to maximize the discriminability among the three models. To achieve the former goal, three transformation rules were employed to determine the *ordinal* relations between the coalition values on trial $t$ as a function of the accumulated score at the end of trial $t - 1$:

(1)     If $\delta_{i,t-1} > \delta_{j,t-1} > \delta_{k,t-1}$, then $v(ij)_t > v(ik)_t > v(jk)_t$.

(2)     If $\delta_{i,t-1} = \delta_{j,t-1} > \delta_{k,t-1}$, then

(a)     $v(ij)_t > v(ik)_t > v(jk)_t$, if $x_{i,t-1} > 0$ and $x_{j,t-1} = 0$;

(b)     $v(ij)_t > v(jk)_t > v(ik)_t$, if $x_{j,t-1} > 0$ and $x_{i,t-1} = 0$;

(c)     either (a) or (b) above, if both $x_{i,t-1} > 0$ and $x_{j,t-1} > 0$ (determined randomly).

(3)     If $\delta_{i,t-1} > \delta_{j,t-1} = \delta_{k,t-1}$, then

(a)     $v(ij)_t > v(ik)_t > v(jk)_t$, if $x_{j,t-1} > 0$ and $x_{k,t-1} = 0$;

(b)     $v(ik)_t > v(ij)_t > v(jk)_t$, if $x_{k,t-1} > 0$ and $x_{j,t-1} = 0$;

(c)     either (a) or (b) above, if both $x_{j,t-1} > 0$ and $x_{k,t-1} > 0$ (determined randomly).

The transformation rules (1), (2), and (3) above place constraints on the CF values on trial $t$, but do not determine them uniquely. Because models $M$, $H$, and MS differ from one another in the attraction structures they predict, CF values for trial $t$ were chosen within the constraints imposed by the transformation rules to generate various CFs such that the predictions of the three models are maximally discriminable. Specifically, by solving sets of linear inequalities, CF values were determined for trial $t$, which generate one of the five classes of attraction structures (three classes according to the hyperopic model) presented in Table 6. All of the five (three) classes were represented in the experiment, though not with equal frequencies.

Table 6 shows the attraction structures predicted by the three models for the different classes we constructed. The predicted probabilities of coalitions $ij$, $ik$, and $jk$ are easily calculated from the information in Table 6.

*Table 6. Attraction structures for coalition partners by model*

| Class of attraction structure | Model | | | Example |
|---|---|---|---|---|
| | Myopic M | Hyperopic H | Mixed signal MS | |
| I | $i \rightarrow k$ | | $i \rightarrow$ equal | $\delta_{i,t-1} = 104$; $\delta_{j,t-1} = 72$; $\delta_{k,t-1} = 60$ |
| | $j \rightarrow$ equal | | $j \rightarrow i$ | $v(ij)_t = 54$; $v(ik)_t = 48$; $v(jk)_t = 30$ |
| | $k \rightarrow i$ | $i \rightarrow$ equal | $k \rightarrow i$ | |
| II | $i \rightarrow k$ | | $i \rightarrow$ equal | $\delta_{i,t-1} = 72$; $\delta_{j,t-1} = 56$; $\delta_{k,t-1} = 22$ |
| | $j \rightarrow k$ | $j \rightarrow k$ | $j \rightarrow$ equal | $v(ij)_t = 64$; $v(ik)_t = 54$; $v(jk)_t = 26$ |
| | $k \rightarrow i$ | | $k \rightarrow i$ | |
| III | $i \rightarrow$ equal | $k \rightarrow$ equal | $i \rightarrow j$ | $\delta_{i,t-1} = 74$; $\delta_{j,t-1} = 72$; $\delta_{k,t-1} = 24$ |
| | $j \rightarrow k$ | | $j \rightarrow$ equal | $v(ij)_t = 100$; $v(ik)_t = 60$; $v(jk)_t = 56$ |
| | $k \rightarrow j$ | | $k \rightarrow$ equal | |
| IV | $i \rightarrow k$ | $i \rightarrow k$ | $i \rightarrow$ equal | $\delta_{i,t-1} = 90$; $\delta_{j,t-1} = 90$; $\delta_{k,t-1} = 60$ |
| | $j \rightarrow k$ | $j \rightarrow k$ | $j \rightarrow$ equal | $v(ij)_t = 50$; $v(ik)_t = 40$; $v(jk)_t = 34$ |
| | $k \rightarrow$ equal | $k \rightarrow$ equal | $k \rightarrow i$ | |
| V | $i \rightarrow$ equal | $i \rightarrow$ equal | $i \rightarrow j$ | $\delta_{i,t-1} = 92$; $\delta_{j,t-1} = 56$; $\delta_{k,t-1} = 56$ |
| | $j \rightarrow i$ | $j \rightarrow k$ | $j \rightarrow i$ | $v(ij)_t = 66$; $v(ik)_t = 56$; $v(jk)_t = 33$ |
| | $k \rightarrow i$ | $k \rightarrow j$ | $k \rightarrow i$ | |

*Note.* $(i \rightarrow j)$ means that player $i$ prefers to form a coalition with player $j$ and will choose $j$ with probability $1 - \epsilon$ and $k$ with probability $\epsilon$; $(i \rightarrow$ equal) means that player $i$ is indifferent between players $j$ and $k$ as a possible coalition partner on pure rank considerations.

## Results

The myopic, hyperopic, and mixed-signal models provide alternative explanations of coalition behavior in 3-person games of status played in a sequence. Because each model attempts to account for the interdependence of games within a given sequence, we adopt the assumption that each game "is an 'independent event,' except for the interdependence identified by the model under investigation" (Laing & Morrison, 1973, p. 17). This assumption is not tenable if the same coalition that formed in $m$ ($m \geq 1$) consecutive games is dictated under the terms of a single agreement; the more appropriate and meaningful unit of analysis in this case is the composite event spanning $m$ games. As in Laing and Morrison (1973), only outcomes dictated under the terms of a single-trial agreement are, therefore, examined in the present study.

Two alternative criteria were employed to identify games falling under single-trial agreements. The first criterion (I) is based on analysis of formal communications, whereas the second criterion (II) is based on the analysis of outcomes of successive games. Under Criterion I, a sequence of games ($t$, $t + 1$,..., $t + m$) was classified as falling under a multiple-trial agreement if at least one of the messages 6, 7, or 8 in Table 5 (all pertaining to the remaining games in a sequence) was transmitted between the members of the winning coalition at trial $t$ (assume it is coalition $ij$), and in successive games (on trials $t + 1$, $t + 2$,..., $t + m$) players $i$ and $j$ formed a coalition while bargaining with each other with no further reference to player $k$. Forty-seven games were thus classified by Criterion I and removed from further analyses. Under Criterion II, a game was classified as falling under a multiple-trial agreement if it was included in a sequence of games in which (a) the same coalition was formed on each game and (b) no negotiation was conducted with the third player. One hundred twenty-four games were thus classified by Criterion II and removed from further analyses. Another game was omitted because of an error in the CF. In total, 188 and 111 games were analyzed under Criteria I and II, respectively. As the two criteria yielded very similar results, only the analyses of the games coded as single-trial agreements by Criterion I is presented below.

### TESTS OF BARGAINING HEURISTICS

Three bargaining heuristics, stated as Assumptions 1 through 3 above, are shared by the myopic, hyperopic, and mixed-signal models. Assumption 1 is the simplest and most straightforward, postulating that a member of a winning coalition will not accept a PC that allows his or her coalition partner to overtake or pass this member in rank. The first column in Table 7 shows the proportion of games in which this assumption was violated. The numerator shows the number of violations and the denominator the number of games in which the assumption was testable. Of the 19 games in which Assumption 1 was violated, in 2 games the two coalition members switched their ranks, in 3 games the two coalition members ended the game with equal ranks after they had started with different ranks, and in 14 games the two coalition members, having been tied for rank, ended the game with different ranks. Thus, most of the violations of Assumption 1 occurred because equality in rank was not maintained.

According to Assumption 2, a member of a winning coalition would not accept a PC that not only fails to grant him or her an improved rank but also worsens this

*Table 7. Proportion of violations of the three bargaining heuristics*

| | Assumption | | | |
|---|---|---|---|---|
| | 1 | 2 | 3 | 1-3 |
| Number | 19/163 | 37/137 | 24/89 | 74/188 |
| Proportion | .117 | .270 | .270 | .390 |

member's interval position.    Assumption 2 places stronger demands on the player than Assumption 1, because it concerns not only differences in rank, which are apparent and obvious, but also interval positions, which require nontrivial calculations.    In testing Assumption 2, we omitted games in which (i) both coalition members changed their ranks, (ii) a coalition was formed between players tied in rank, or (iii) Assumption 1 was violated.    The second column in Table 7 shows the proportion of games in which Assumption 2 was violated.

Assumption 3 concerns coalitions between players who hold rank-based preferences for each other.    It postulates that a member of such a coalition would not accept a payoff smaller than that necessary to achieve the rank upon which this preference is based.    Table 7 shows that this assumption was violated in 27% of the games in which it was tested.

The negotiation range is the set of PCs consistent with the three bargaining heuristics considered jointly.    All three models predict that the payoff vectors will fall within the negotiation range.    The right-hand column of Table 7 shows that this prediction was confirmed in 61% of all the games under single-trial agreements (67% under Criterion II).    These results are comparable to those of Laing and Morrison, who reported that "approximately two-thirds (51/76) of the payoff allocations observed under single-trial agreements conform to this prediction" (1973, p. 18).

COALITION FREQUENCIES

Models M, H, and MS differ from one another with respect to the predicted attraction structure.    To estimate $\epsilon$, a maximum likelihood procedure was employed.    Let $a$ denote a particular coalition structure, $c$ denote a permissible 2-person coalition ($ij$, $ik$, or $jk$), $f(a,c)$ denote the number of games in which coalition $c$ was formed under attraction structure $a$, and $P^*(a,c,\epsilon)$ denote the probability stated by the model under consideration as a function of $\epsilon$ that coalition $c$ forms under attraction structure $a$.    Then the likelihood function is given by (Laing & Morrison, 1973)

$$L = \prod_a C_a \left[ \prod_c P^*(a,c,\epsilon)^{f(a,c)} \right],$$ (3)

where $C_a = [\Sigma_c f(a,c)]!/\Pi_c [f(a,c)!]$.

Searching over the interval $[0,1]$, the value of $\epsilon$ that maximizes (3) was estimated separately for each of the three models. The result was 0.44, 0.66, and 0.22 for models M, H, MS, respectively. If the players always adhere to the model's assumptions, then $\hat{\epsilon}$ approaches zero. The estimated parameter value, $\hat{\epsilon}$ may be used, then as a measure of goodness of fit; the lower the value, the better the model describes the attraction structure. Using this criterion, the results support model MS over the other two models. In particular, they reject model H for which $1/2 < \hat{\epsilon}$, contrary to the assumption that $0 < \epsilon < 1/2$.

Using the estimated parameter values $\hat{\epsilon}$, the value of the likelihood function $L$, denoted by $L^*$, was computed separately for each model. The number in each cell of Table 8 shows the resulting likelihood ratio $L^*_{column}/L^*_{row}$ for the corresponding column and row models. The likelihood ratio $L^*_P/L^*_Q$ measures the goodness of fit of model P versus model Q.

*Table 8. Likelihood ratios for each pair of models*

| | Model | | |
|---|---|---|---|
| Model | M | H | MS |
| M | 1.000 | 0.117 | $2.11 \times 10^{23}$ |
| H | | 1.000 | $2.45 \times 10^{21}$ |
| MS | | | 1.000 |

Table 8 shows that model MS is the most successful of the three models in predicting coalition frequencies. Model M is the second best.

Having established the superiority of Model MS over its competitors, we move next to evaluate its success in predicting the frequencies of the observed coalitions. The observed coalitions formed under single-trial agreements are grouped by attraction structures. The five different attraction structure for model MS are shown and exemplified in Table 6. Note that the meanings of $i$, $j$, and $k$ are not the same for all five attraction structures. In Types I through III, $i$ is the top-ranked player whereas $j$ has rank two, and $k$ has the lowest rank. In type IV players $i$ and $j$ are tied for top rank and $k$ has the lowest rank, whereas in type V, $i$ is the top-ranked player whereas $j$ and $K$ are tied for the next rank. Of the two players in type IV who are tied for top rank we shall denote by $i$ the player who is a member of the highest value coalition and by $j$ the other player. Thus $v(ij)_t > v(ik)_t > v(jk)_t$. And of the two players who tie for the lowest rank, the one who is a member of a coalition with the highest value is denoted by $j$ and the other player by $k$. Thus, for all five types the players are named so that $v(ij)_t > v(ik)_t > v(jk)_t$.

The observed and predicted coalition frequencies by model MS are shown in Table 9 for the five different attraction structures. (The outcomes of the first trial in each sequence were omitted.) The estimated parameter value ($\hat{\epsilon} = 0.22$) was used to calculate the predicted coalition frequencies. Table 9 indicates generally good fit of the MS model; with one exception, the $\chi^2$ values for testing the difference between observed and predicted frequencies are not significant. These results should be interpreted with caution because of the low predicted frequencies in many of the cells and since the same set of three subjects contributed more than once to the data set.

*Table 9.    Observed and predicted coalition frequencies by model MS for five different attraction structures*

| Type of attraction Structure | | Coalition | | | | |
|---|---|---|---|---|---|---|
| | | $ij$ | $ik$ | $jk$ | Total | $\chi^2$ |
| I | Observed | 19 | 16 | 2 | 37 | 0.27 |
| | Predicted | 17.343 | 47.43 | 2.15 | | |
| II | Observed | 24 | 32 | 4 | 60 | 3.45 |
| | Predicted | 20 | 31.20 | 8.82 | | |
| III | Observed | 6 | 8 | 6 | 20 | 10.08* |
| | Predicted | 10.40 | 2.94 | 6.67 | | |
| IV | Observed | 7 | 14 | 5 | 26 | 0.70 |
| | Predicted | 8.66 | 13.52 | 3.82 | | |
| V | Observed | 4 | 4 | 0 | 8 | 4.37 |
| | Predicted | 5.87 | 1.66 | 0.46 | | |

* $p<.05$.

PAYOFF DIVISION

As the three models differ from one another in the attraction structures they predict, they also differ from one another in specifying who has the bargaining advantage. All three models share the prediction that the payoff to the member of a winning coalition who enjoys a bargaining advantage over his or her partner "will tend to lie toward the former's preferred end of the negotiation range" (Friend et al., 1978, p. 33). "Tend to lie" has been interpreted to mean that the payoff will fall above the mid-point of the negotiation range.

Morrison (1974) proposed to test this prediction by computing the difference between player $i$'s payoff and the lower bound of the negotiation range divided by the size of the negotiation range:

$$INS_i = (x_{ij} - x_{\underset{ij}{-}})/(x_{ij}^+ - x_{\underset{ij}{-}}).$$

In the above expression, $x_{ij}$ is player $i$'s payoff in coalition $ij$, and $X_{\underset{ij}{+}}$ and $x_{\underset{ij}{-}}$ are the upper and lower bounds, respectively, of his or her negotiation range. If either $INS_i < 0$ or $INS_i > 1$, then at least one of the three bargaining heuristics is violated. In terms of the numerical index $INS_i > 1/2$.

This prediction was tested in games played under single-trial agreements, which satisfy the following three conditions: (a) one of the two members of the winning coalition, say player $i$, enjoys a bargaining advantage over his or her partner; (b) the negotiation range includes at least two points; and (c) the payoff vector falls in the negotiation range (i.e., $0 \leq INS_i \leq 1$).  Table 10 presents the mean and variance of the INS measures for each model.  It also shows the number of games that satisfy conditions (a) through (c) above.  Table 10 shows that only for model MS is the mean INS significantly larger than $1/2$ ($t = 4.57$; $p < .05$).

Table 10.  Mean and variance of the INS measure by model

|  | | Model | |
| --- | --- | --- | --- |
| Model | M | H | MS |
| Mean | .468 | .373 | .648* |
| Variance | .099 | .071 | .082 |
| Frequency | 72 | 86 | 79 |

* $p<.05$.

## Discussion

METHODOLOGICAL ISSUES

Before evaluating the predictive success of the three models, several features of our experimental design merit discussion. First, we believe that by using NPER rather than some form of face-to-face bargaining the effects of personality variables, which are not accounted for by the models, have been significantly reduced. It is possible, however, that social norms of fairness and justice are not as strongly manifested under NPER as under face-to-face bargaining. Second, it may be contended that by employing subjects with previous experience in CF games, we might have biased the results in favor of the CF component of the MS model. Although this possibility can only be ruled out by additional experimentation, post-experimental interrogation of the subjects suggests that our subjects understood very well the difference between the two game situations and that carry-over effects, if any, disappeared after short experience with the status game. Third, it may also be argued that the order of communication, which interacts with the status of the players, and the list of messages (Table 5) might have affected the results. Only additional research on games of status using these factors as independent variables can settle this issue. Fourth, it may be recalled that coalition values were chosen on the basis of outcomes of the preceding trials such that players with a high rank on trial $t - 1$ were rewarded by rendering the CF on trial $t$ more favorable to them. Although this procedure better reflects the primary characteristics of continuing social interactions, it may be argued that it is biased against the hyperopic model because long-term agreements are easier to reach in a stationary environment. This argument, too, should be considered in future research on games of status.

Another methodological issue has to do with our choice of CFs so as to maximize the discriminability among the three models. Because the myopic and hyperopic models are regarded as complementary, not competing hypotheses, it has been argued by one of the reviewers that our attempt to discriminate among the models might have biased the results in favor of the MS model. To check this possibility, note that in class IV of attraction structures in Table 6 the myopic and hyperopic models make the same prediction which differs from the prediction of the mixed-signal model. The coalition frequencies in this class are 7, 14, and 5 for coalition $ij$, $ik$, and $jk$, respectively (Table 9). Analyzing this class separately yields $\hat{\varepsilon}$ values of .45 and .26 for the myopic/hyperopic and the mixed-signal models, respectively. Whether the superiority of the MS model will hold in other situations in which models M and H agree with each other but not with model MS is an open question.

It should also be noted that several aspects of the game environment, which may influence coalition behavior on trial $t$, are ignored by all three models. (a) The outcomes of trial 1 through $t - 1$ are presented to the subject at the end of trial $t - 1$ and may affect his or her behavior. (b) The history of bargaining from trial 1 through $t - 1$ may also provide important information about the bargaining heuristics that underlie the behavior of his or her co-players, their bargaining tactics, their toughness and trustworthiness, and the norms of fairness and justice to which they subscribe. (c) The actual value of $t$ may also be of significance. When the number of trials per sequence is not known, and even it if varies widely from one sequence to another, a player is likely to generate a fuzzy hypothesis about the sequence's duration. He or she may, therefore, behave differently when $t = 1$, believing that the sequence is likely to proceed for several more games, than when $t = 9$, believing that termination of the sequence is imminent.

MODEL EVALUATION

The prediction that the payoff vector lies in the negotiation range was supported by almost two-thirds of the games played under single-trial agreements. There was stronger support for Assumption 1 than for Assumptions 2 or 3, suggesting that subjects adhere more faithfully to simple rules of thumb that concern ranks than to cognitively more demanding rules that concern both ranks and interval positions.

The predictive success of the models cannot be evaluated, however, without knowledge of the size of the negotiation range. The prediction that the payoff vectors lie in the negotiation range is more powerful the smaller the size of the negotiation range is in relation to the CF values. To assess the predictive power of the models, the ratio $|x_{ij}^+ - x_{ij}^-|/v(ij)$ was computed separately for each single-trial agreement game. The resulting mean ratio was 0.253, showing that the negotiation range occupied on the average one-fourth of the corresponding CF value. The proportions of payoff vectors falling in the negotiation range were found previously to equal 0.61. This success rate is significantly higher than the one expected under the null hypothesis that any division of $v(ij)$ is equally likely ($z = 9.91$, $p < 0.01$).

Despite the statistical significance of the success rate reported immediately above, the failure of all the models to account for slightly more than one-third of the payoff vectors that fell outside of the negotiation range requires explanation. The models tested in this paper assumed that player $i$ who holds no rank-based preference for another player will choose $j$ and $k$ with probabilities in proportion to the probabilities that his or her choice is reciprocated. In a different two-parameter version of the myopic model, Laing and Morrison (1970) assumed that preferences for coalition partners also depend on interval position. If player $i$ is indifferent between two alternative coalition partners on the basis of rank consideration alone, then player $i$ would prefer to form a coalition with $j$ rather than $k$ if his or her expected interval position is larger when forming a coalition with $j$ rather than $k$. This version states that player $i$ will choose $j$ with probability $1 - \sigma$ and $k$ with probability $\sigma$, where $(1 - \epsilon) > (1 - \sigma) > 0.5$. This inequality assumes that probability of choice is highest when it is based on a rank preference and somewhat lower when based on interval position preference. Data from the original study (Laing & Morrison, 1970) yielded an estimate of $\sigma \cong 1/2$, indicating that interval position had no effect on coalition choices.

It is possible that the definition of interval position requires modification. The interval position, $d_{i,t}$, was originally defined as a linear function assigning equal weights to the point differences $(\delta_{i,t} - \delta_{j,t})$ and $(\delta_{i,t} - \delta_{k,t})$. But why should the two point differences be weighted equally? Suppose that players $A$, $B$, and $C$ are ranked first, second, and third, respectively, at the beginning of trial $t$. A reasonable assumption is that player $A$ will be more concerned with player $B$ than $C$ because $B$ is more likely to threaten his or her position in the future than $C$. Similarly, player

$C$ is more concerned with his or her point score relative to $B$ than to $A$, because it is easier for $C$ to overtake or pass in rank player $B$ than $A$. Player $B$ is probably equally concerned with player $C$, who may overtake or pass him or her in rank, and player $A$, whom $B$ wishes to overtake or pass in rank. All of these considerations suggest redefining the interval position by

$$d_{i,t} = \alpha_i(\delta_{i,t} - \delta_{j,t}) + (1 - \alpha_i)(\delta_{i,t} - \delta_{k,t}),$$

$$d_{j,t} = \alpha_j(\delta_{j,t} - \delta_{k,t}) + (1 - \alpha_j)(\delta_{j,t} - \delta_{i,t}),$$

$$d_{k,t} = \alpha_k(\delta_{k,t} - \delta_{i,t}) + (1 - \alpha_k)(\delta_{k,t} - \delta_{j,t}).$$

We would expect that $\alpha_i > 1/2$, $\alpha_k < 1/2$, and $a_j = 1/2$ in our previous example.

With regard to model-dependent predictions, the relative advantage of model MS over its competitors is well established in the present study. Four findings attest to the superiority of model MS; (a) the estimated parameter value $\hat{\epsilon}$, which is lower for model MS than for any of the other two models; (b) the results of the likelihood ratio (Table 8); (c) the relatively good fit of predicted to observed coalition frequencies for different attraction structures (Table 9); and (d) the significant effect that the bargaining advantage according to model MS has on the division of coalition values within the negotiation range (Table 10). Additional studies are required to test the generality of the mixed signal model, for example, of 3-person CF games of status in which each player's coalitional power, as reflected in the CF values on trial $t$, is negatively related to his or her ranking at the end of trial $t - 1$.

## Acknowledgment

The present research was conducted at the Institute for Information Processing and Decision Making, the University of Haifa, Israel. Thanks are due to Marcy Lansman for comments on a draft of this article and to two anonymous reviewers for very useful comments. Requests for reprints should be sent to Rami Zwick, who is now at the L. L. Thurstone Psychometric Laboratory, Department of Psychology, University of North Carolina, Davie Hall 013A, Chapel Hill, NC 27514.

## References

Chertkoff, J. M. (1967). A revision of Caplow's coalition theory. *Journal of Experimental Social Psychology*, 3, 172-177.

Chertkoff, J. M., Skov, R. B., & Catt, V. L. (1980). Tests of the Laing and Morrison coalition models under different planning horizons. *Journal of Mathematical Sociology*, 7, 241-260.

Friend, K. E., Laing, J. D., & Morrison, R. J. (1977). Game-theoretic analyses of coalition behavior. *Theory and decision*, 8, 127-157.

Friend, K. E., Laing, J. D., & Morrison, R. J. (1978). Contending "signals" in coalition choice. *Journal of Mathematical Sociology*, 6, 23-46.

Gamson, W. A. (1961). A theory of coalition formation. *American Sociological Review*, 26, 373-382.

Kahan, J. P., Coston, A. W., Helwig, R. A., Rapoport, Am., & Wallsten, T. S. (1976). A PDP-11/45 program for playing *n*-person characteristic function games. *Behavioral Research Methods and instrumentation*, 8, 165-169.

Kahan, J. P., & Helwig, R. A. (1961). Coalitions: A system of programs for computer-controlled bargaining games. *General Systems*, 16, 31-41.

Kahan, J. P., & Rapoport, Am. (1974). Test of the bargaining set and kernel models in three-person games. In An. Rapoport (Ed.), *Game theory as a theory of conflict resolution* (pp. 119-160). Dordrecht: Reidel.

Kahan, J.P., & Rapoport, Am. (1984). *Theories of coalition formation*. Hillsdale, NJ: Erlbaum.

Kalisch, G. K., Milnor, J. W., Nash, J. F., & Nering, E. D. (1954). Some experimental *n*-person games. In R. M. Thrall, C. H. Coombs, and R. L. Davis (Eds.), *Decision processes* (pp. 301-327). New York: Wiley.

Komorita, S. S., & Meek, D. (1978). Generality and validity of some theories of coalition formation. *Journal of Personality and Social Psychology*, 36, 192-404.

Laing, J. D., & Morrison, R. J. (1970). *Coalition formation in certain sequential three-person games. I. A myopic theory and results of a pilot study*. Working Paper No. 6-70-1, Pittsburgh, PA; Graduate School of Industrial Administration, Carnegie-Mellon University.

Laing, J. D. & Morrison, R. J. (1973). Coalitions and payoffs in three-person sequential games: Initial tests of two formal models. *Journal of Mathematical Sociology*, 3, 3-26.

Laing, J. D., & Morrison, R. J. (1974a). Sequential games of status. *Behavioral Science*, 19, 177-196.

Laing, J. D., & Morrison, R. J. (1974b). Coalitions and payoffs in three-person supergames under multiple-trial agreements. In An. Rapoport (Ed.), *Game theory as a theory of conflict resolution* (pp. 207-234). Dordrecht: Reidel.

Levinsohn, J. R., & Rapoport, Am. (1978). Coalition formation in multistage three-person cooperative games. In H. Sauermann (Ed.), *Coalition forming behanvior* (pp. 107-143). Tübingen: Mohr (Paul Siebeck).

Luce, R. D., & Raiffa, H. (1957). *Games and decisions*. New York: Wiley.

McClintock, C. G., & McNeel, S. P. (1966). Reward and score feedback as determinants of cooperative game behavior. *Journal of Personality and Social Psychology*, 4, 606-613.

McClintock, C. G., & McNeel, S. P. (1967). Prior dyadic experience and monetary reward as determinants of cooperative and competitive game behavior. *Journal of Personality and Social Psychology*, 5, 282-294.

Medlin, S. M. (1976). Effects of grand coalition payoffs on coalition formation in three-person games. *Behavioral Science*, 21, 48-61.

Messick, D. M., & McClintock, C. G. (1968). Motivational bases of choice in experimental games. *Journal of Experimental Social Psychology*, 4, 1-25.

Messick, D. M., & Thorngate, W. (1967). Relative gain maximization in experimental games. *Journal of Experimental Social Psychology*, 3, 85-101.

Morrison, R. J. (1974). *Rational models of coalition formation in the triad*. Unpublished doctoral dissertation, Carnegie-Mellon University.

Rapoport, Am., & Kahan, J. P. (1974). Computer controlled research on bargaining and coalition formation. *Behavioral Research Methods and Onstrumentation*, **6**, 87–93.

Rapoport, An. (1970). *N-person game theory: Concepts and applications.* Ann Arbor: Univ. of Michigan Press.

Riker, W. H. (1967). Bargaining in a three-person game. *The American Political Science Review*, **41**, 642–656.

Shapley, L. S. (1962). Simple games: An outline of the descriptive theory. *Behaviroal Science*, **7**, 59–66.

Shubik, M. (1971). Games of status. *Behavioral Science*, **16**, 117–129.

Shubik, M. (1982). *Game theory in the social sciences.* Cambridge, MA: MIT Press.

Slovic, P., Fischhoff, B., & Lichtenstein, S. (1977). Behavioral decision theory. *Annual Review of Psychology*, **28**, 1–39.

Thibaut, J. W., & Kelley, H. H. (1959). *The social psychology of groups.* New York: Wiley.

Vinacke, W. E. (1959). The effect of cumulative score on coalition formation in triads with various patterns of internal power (abstract). *American Psychologist*, **14**, 391.

# CHAPTER 15

# COMPARISON OF THEORIES FOR PAYOFF DISBURSEMENT OF COALITION VALUES

Experimental investigation of coalition forming behavior started with the pioneering studies on coalition formation in the triad by Vinacke and Arkoff (1957) and in the tetrad by Kalisch et al. (1954).  The former experiment was instigated by theoretical research in the social sciences and the latter was inspired by the mathematical theory of games.  Having witnesses much progress in the last three decades, these two disciplines have continued to serve as the main foci of research on coalition formation.  Although they differ sharply form each other in their orientation and main objects of focus, the approaches they have advocated are not necessarily antagonistic.  Social conflicts can and have provided mathematicians with insights necessary for abstract analyses, and experimental findings have stimulated the development of coalition formation models (Maschler, 1963).  From the other side, mathematical analyses of abstract conflicts have provided very powerful conceptual tools for the analysis of real conflicts and have stimulated much empirical and experimental research (Brams et al., 1979; Kahan and Rapoport, 1984; Ordeshook, 1978; Rapoport, 1974).  Even the design of experiments on coalition forming behavior has been strongly influenced by the language and abstract formulations of game theory.

Primarily because of this strong influence, recent experiments on coalition forming behavior have increasingly concentrated on a relative small number of experimental paradigms.  Research in the late 50s and early 60s mostly employed the Pachisi board paradigm, and several of its variations.  These experimental paradigms were later largely replaced by the more abstract weighted majority game, which focuses on the effects of "resources" or "weights" (e.g., delegations votes in a political convention, parliamentary seats, voting stock, etc.) on coalition formation and payoff allocation.  Realizing that the greater part of activity in forming economic or political coalitions is non-zero-sum in the sense that different coalitions win different amounts and "the loss to the loser may not equal the gain to the winner" (Riker, 1967, p. 643), more recent research on coalition forming behavior has been gradually replacing the above paradigms with negotiable conflicts modeled as characteristic function games with sidepayments (CF games).

These shifts in experimental paradigms have led to and been inspired by the construction of an unusually large number of coalition theories by mathematicians, psychologists, economists, and political scientists.  Several factors may account individually or collectively for this embarrassing richness.  (1) The bargaining process leading to the formation of coalitions and the division of rewards may vary considerably from one area of the social sciences to another, depending on the communication and information conditions and on whether individuals, groups, organizations, political parties, or nations are locked in the conflict.  (2) Serious problems are inherent in the extension of the notion of rational behavior from individual to group decision making.  (3) There are alternative ways of incorporating social norms of equality and parity, dictates of consciousness, standards of morality, and notions like trust, threat, and counterthreat into coalition theories (Aumann and Maschler, 1964; Maschler, 1963).  (4) There are alternative definitions of stability or equilibrium that may be proposed.  Whatever these factors are and regardless of how they interact, inspection of the experimental literature on CF games (which include weighted majority games as a special and important case) reveals a dozen or more theories of reward allocation which have been subjected to experimental scrutiny or tested competitively against each other.  Some of these theories also generate predictions about the likelihood of formation of different coalitions; these predictions are not discussed in the present paper.

The major psychological theories of reward allocation which have been subjected to experimental scrutiny include minimum resource theory (Gamson, 1961), minimum power theory (Gamson, 1964), the bargaining theory of Komorita and Chertkoff (1973), the weighted probability model (Komorita, 1974), the equal excess model (Komorita, 1979), and Caplow's model of control (1956, 1968).  Game theoretical models tested competitively against each other include the core (Gillies, 1953), the $M_1^{(i)}$ bargaining set (Aumann and Maschler, 1964) and its variants, the competitive bargaining set $H_1^{(i)}$ of Horowitz (1973) and the $M_1^{(im)}$ cooperative bargaining set of Maschler (1963), the kernel (Davis and Maschler, 1965), the nucleolus (Schmeidler, 1969), the Shapley value (Shapley, 1953), the equal share division model (Selten, 1972), and the equal division kernel (Crott and Albers, 1981).  The social psychological theories generally predict which coalitions are likely to form and the reward division but mostly limit themselves to simple games.  The game theoretical models predict reward allocation, some models make point predictions for some games, interval or area predictions for other games, or, for some games, no predictions at all.

There is now a large body of experimental research designed to test competitively the models mentioned above.  At least twenty experiments on coalition forming behavior in weighted majority games have been periodically reviewed by, among others, Davis et al. (1976) and Muringhan (1978).  Kahan and Rapoport (1984) recently summarized and critically evaluated the outcomes of more than 2200 plays from more than 21 separate studies of 3-, 4-, and 5-person CF games.  And Michener and his associated (Michener et al., 1980, 1983) have amassed more than 200 plays drawn from 12 different experiments of coalition formation in CF games.  Yet with all this extensive theory and all these numerous experiments, it is still the case (Chertkoff, 1967, 1971) that there are "surprisingly few accepted techniques for evaluating the accuracy of the sometimes markedly different predictions of the models" (Murnighan, 1983, p. 126).

When models of reward allocation make point predictions, a common and by now largely accepted technique of comparing these models to each other in terms of their predictive accuracy is (1) to compute for each model discrepancy scores, one for each outcome, which measure the numerical difference between observed and predicted payoffs for the member of each coalition while controlling for its size, and then (2) subject the resulting discrepancy scores for the different models to some statistical test (Komorita, 1978; Michener et al., 1976; Rapoport and Kahan, 1976).  When the predicted payoff vectors by at least one of the models are no longer unique, the comparison of models predicting larger or more dispersed set of payoff vectors is advantaged.  For example, if model $M_1$ predicts a unique allocation of payoffs to the members of a given coalition and model $M_2$ predicts several possible payoff allocations to the same coalition, model $M_2$ is obviously less refutable.  In the extreme case, when $M_2$ is the null model predicting the entire outcome space, it cannot be rejected at all.

Bonacich (1979) and Selten and Krischker (1983) attempted to resolve  this very important problem by introducing numerical measures for comparing to each other models making point, line, or area predictions of reward allocation.  I shall argue below that the numerical measures they proposed lead to paradoxical results which defy intuition or common practice.  The purpose of the present study is to introduce an alternative procedure which overcomes the deficiencies of its predecessors.  Because the basic ideas of the proposed procedure can be best explained and geometrically illustrated when the number of players does not exceed three, the presentation will be restricted to the 3-person CF game.  Extension to the general $n$-person CF games, which are considerably more technical, will be taken in a subsequent paper.

## Definitions and Notation

### CF GAMES

Before examining previous measures of predictive accuracy and proposing an alternative, it is warranted to define several terms that will be needed later.  An *n-person game in characteristic function form with sidepayments* (CF game) is a pair $(N; v)$, where $N = \{1, \ldots, n\}$ is a finite set of $n$ players and $v$, called a *characteristic function*, is a function from the $2^n$ subsets of $N$ to the real numbers.  Calling any subset $S \subseteq N$ a *coalition*, the *value* of coalition $S$, $v(S)$, is interpreted as a measure of coalition worth in terms of the payoff jointly commanded by the members of $S$ against all the other players.  It is natural to require that $v(\emptyset) = 0$, which represents the strategic inconsequence of the null set.  The game is *superadditive* if any two coalitions $S$ and $R$ with no members in common do at least as well by joint  effort as they can do separately.  Formally, superadditivity is expressed by the inequality

$$v(R \cup S) \geq v(R) + v(S) \text{ for all } R, S \subseteq N, \text{ such that } R \cap S = \emptyset.$$

Superadditivity implies that

$$v(S) \geq \sum_{i \in S} v(i) \text{ for all } S \subseteq N,$$

a condition satisfied by all the CF games which have been subjected to experimentation.

In a single play of a CF game a coalition $S$ is formed when its members reach a binding and enforceable agreement on how to divide $v(S)$ among themselves.  If several coalitions form simultaneously, they must be non-intersecting.  The resulting outcome of a CF game is expressed by a *payoff configuration*

$$(\mathbf{x};\ \mathbf{S}) = (x_1,\ ...,\ x_n;\ S_1,\ ...,\ S_m).$$

$\mathbf{S} = \{S_1,\ ...,\ S_m\}$ is called a *coalition structure*; it is a partition of $N$ into $m$ $(1 \le m \le n)$ coalitions. $\mathbf{x} = (x_1,\ ...,\ x_n)$, called the *payoff vector*, represents a realizable allocation of payoff to each of the $n$ players $(\Sigma_{i \epsilon S_h} x_i = v(S_h),\ h = 1,\ ...,\ m)$.

The assumption of *individual rationality*, which is shared by all the models above, states that a player will not accept a final payment less than she can insure for herself:

$$x_i \ge v(i),\ \text{for all } i \epsilon N.$$

A payoff configuration satisfying this assumption is called an *individually rational payoff configuration* (IRPC).

A CF game is called *integer valued* if $v(S)$ is an integer for all $S \subseteq N$. An *integer IRPC* is an IRPC where all payoffs $x_i$ are integers. Experimental games almost always employ integer valued characteristic functions and terminate with integer IRPCs.

To exemplify these concepts, consider a 3-person CF game with a set of players $N$ = $\{A, B, C\}$, where, in accordance with standard experimental notation, players are identified by upper Roman letters rather than integers. The characteristic function of this game is:

$$\begin{array}{lll} \text{G1:} & v(AB) = 99, & v(AC) = 93, \quad v(BC) = 30, \\ & v(ABC) = 120, & v(A) = v(B) = v(C) = 0. \end{array} \qquad (1)$$

Game G1 is superadditive. It states that player $A$ and $B$ can jointly gain 99 units of reward (called "points"), $A$ and $C$ can gain 93 points between them, $B$ and $C$ can realize together 30 points, each player alone can realize 0 points, and all three players together can gain 120 points. If $A$ and $C$ were to consider a 70-23 split of $v(AC)$ (leaving $B$ with zero points), this consideration would be denoted by the integer IRPC (70, 0, 23; $AC$, $B$). The grand coalition of all three players, with an equal division of payoff, would be indicated by the IRPC (40, 40, 40; $ABC$).

GEOMETRIC REPRESENTATION OF PAYOFF VECTORS

Consider a set of payoff vectors $(x_1,\ ...,\ x_n)$ satisfying the constraint $x_1 + ... + x_n = c$. If $n = 2$, the set of points represented by these vectors will constitute a straight line. If $n = 3$, the points will all lie on a plane. In general, the points of such a set will lie on a hyperplane in an $n$-dimensional space. Because the examples below concern 3-person games, the arguments for or against measures of predictive accuracy can be illustrated geometrically. We shall, therefore, have occasion to examine simplexes defined by the following conditions

$$x_i + ... + x_n = c, \qquad x_i \ge 0,\ i \epsilon N.$$

If $n = 3$, a simplex is an equilateral triangle formed by the intersection of the plane $x_A + x_B + x_C = c$, with the coordinate planes $x_A = 0$, $x_B = 0$, and $x_C = 0$. All the points on the sides of and inside the triangle constitute the simplex. Both predicted and observed payoff vectors may be represented within this simplex.

To illustrate this geometrical representation, consider the 3-person game G1 in (1) and assume the formation of the grand coalition. The Shapley value for the grand coalition is the unique IRPC (62.0, 30.5, 27.5; *ABC*). The kernel also prescribes a unique IRPC for the grand coalition: (84, 21, 15; *ABC*). The solution space prescribed by the core, which is the third model considered in the present example, is bounded by the three payoff vectors (72, 27, 21), (90, 9, 21), and (90, 27, 3). Geometrically, the core is the shaded inverted equilateral triangle in Figure 1. The predicted payoff vectors by the Shapley value and the kernel are represented by two points in Figure 1, one of which is seen to fall in the core and the other outside the core boundaries. Also depicted in Figure 1 are the outcomes of three hypothetical plays of game G1 all terminating in the formation of the grand coalition. The three observed payoff vectors (40, 40, 40), (90, 7, 23), and (80, 30, 10) are marked by small squares in Figure 1.

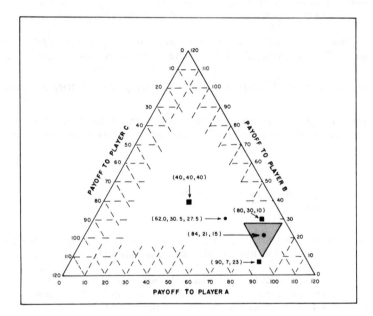

*Figure 1.   The solution space for the grand coalition in the 3-person game G1.*

## Two Previous Measures of Predictive Accuracy

BONACICH (1979)

For a given coalition structure $\{S_1, ..., S_m\}$ let $\hat{\mathbf{x}} = (\hat{x}_1, ..., \hat{x}_n)$ be a payoff vector predicted by some model $M$ and $H = \{\hat{\mathbf{x}}\}$ be the set of these vectors. $H$ could be a point, a set of isolated points, a line, or an area (Figure 1). Also, let $\mathbf{x} = (x_1, ..., x_x)$ be an observed payoff vector with the same coalition structure. To determine the relative accuracy of a model, thereby allowing for the comparison between models, Bonacich (1979) proposed a measure of error $E$, which is simply the mean squared 'distance' between $\mathbf{x}$ and the entire region $H$. When $H$ is a single point, $E$ is given by

$$E = \sum_{i=1}^{n} (x_i - \hat{x}_i)^2 \ . \tag{2}$$

If $H$ is not a single point, let $A(H)$ denote its size. (If $H$ is a line, $A(H)$ is its length; if $H$ is a plane, $A(H)$ is its area; if $H$ is a solid, $A(H)$ is its volume, etc.). $A(H)$ can be found by integrating over $H$: $A(H) = \int_H dH$. The reciprocal of $A(H)$ is proposed as the density function for the computation of the mean squared distance. The error measure $E$ is then the integral of the product of a function, the squared distance and its density $A(H)^{-1}$:

$$E = \int_H A(H)^{-1} \sum_{i=1}^{n} (x_i - \hat{x}_i)^2 \ dH. \tag{3}$$

The measure $E$ in (3) generalized $E$ in (2) to predictions involving an infinity of points rather than a single point: it has exactly the same meaning for point, line, and area predictions.

Because only integer IRPCs are realizable as experimental outcomes, there is no necessity to consider continuous areas and revert to calculus for computing their size. With only a small effect on precision, Eq. 3 may be replaced by

$$E = \sum_{\hat{x} \epsilon H} \sum_{i=1}^{n} (x_i - \hat{x}_i)^2 / N\{S_1, ..., S_m\} \ . \tag{4}$$

where $N\{S_1, ..., S_m\}$ is the number of integer payoff vectors in the predicted region $H$ with the coalition structure $\{S_1, ..., S_m\}$. Equation (4) is the discrete analog of (3); it, too, weighs each payoff vector in $H$ equally.

To illustrate equations (3) and (4), suppose that $H$ is the core of game G1 (for the grand coalition). The area of the core (a unilateral triangle) is 90.56, the area of the outcome space (for the grand coalition) is 4024.92, and the ratio of the area of the core to the area of the outcome space is 0.0225. When only integer payoff vectors are considered, the outcome space contains 7381 distinct payoff vectors and the core contains $N\{ABC\} = 190$ payoff vectors. The corresponding ratio is 0.0257. Calculation of the error measure $E$ in (4) yields 183.94 and 440.32 for the two observed payoff vectors (80, 30, 10) and (90, 7, 27), respectively (see Figure 1).

A major problem with Bonacich's error measure is that, unless $H$ is a point, $E$ is not monotonic with the *shortest distance* between $H$ and $x$. For example, the shortest distance between $x = (80, 30, 10)$ and the core of game G1 is 3 and the shortest distance between $x = (90, 7, 27)$ and the same core is 2. Yet, the $E$ value for the latter has been shown immediately above to be about 2.4 larger than for the former. Even more paradoxically, the $E$ value for a data point outside the predicted region $H$ may be smaller than the $E$ values for some data points in $H$, For example, consider the payoff vector $x = (90, 9, 21)$, which lies in the core of game G1. The $E$ value for this data point is 279; it is larger than the $E$ value for $x = (80, 30, 10)$, although the latter data point falls outside the core.

Noticing this paradoxical feature of $E$, Bonacich defended his error measure by arguing that "with $E$ a theory is evaluated not only on the basis of predictions close to the data, but also on the basis of its most incorrect predictions" (1979, p. 92). Michener et al. (1983) repeated essentially the same argument when they employed $E$ to test the core against five alternative models.

There are two major difficulties with Bonacich's argument. Coalition theories of reward allocation are algebraic. Their predictions have the following form: if a payoff vector with a given coalition structure satisfies certain requirements of stability, equilibrium, additivity, and the like, depending on the model under consideration, it is contained in $H$. If these requirements are not fully satisfied, the payoff vector is not in $H$. Consequently, if $x$ lies outside of $H$, all the predicted payoff vectors in $H$ are technically incorrect. The issue here is whether to allow for degree of error, and, if error is allowed for, whether the shortest distance between $x$ and $H$ or the mean squared distance is a more appropriate measure of the degree of the model's success. Although no formal argument is possible here, intuition suggests that error measures incorporating the shortest distance between $x$ and $H$ or the mean squared distance is a more appropriate measure of the degree of the model's success. Although no formal argument is possible here, intuition suggests that error measures incorporating the shortest distance between $x$ and $H$ are more satisfactory. Bonacich, too, considered the shortest distance. He writes: "A possible measure of the adequacy of a prediction would be the shortest distance between the set of distributions consistent with a prediction and the empirical distribution" (1979, p. 87). Presumably, he rejected this possibility because "this would give an advantage to less specific theories that implied a larger or more dispersed set of points" (1979, p. 87). It will be shown below that it is possible to develop error measures based on the shortest distance between $x$ and $H$, which do not provide the less specific theories this advantage.

Even if Bonacich's argument in favor of the mean squared distance is tenable, there is a second issue which has to do not with which predictions in $H$ to choose in order to test a coalition theory but with the weights assigned to them. In calculating $E$, equal weights are assigned to all the predicted payoff vectors in $H$. $E$ is the squared distance between a data point $x$ and the 'center of gravity' of $H$ based on the assumption that the payoff vectors in $H$ are distributed uniformly. But the assumption of uniform distribution is not a prediction of coalition theories. Nor can it be legitimized as a representation of 'very little information' or an expression of 'vague' opinions about $H$ (Raiffa and Schlaifer, 1961). For the coalition theories under consideration, the uniform distribution is as arbitrary as any other distribution over the predictions in $H$, and because of the paradoxical results it yields, the measure $E$ which incorporates it is untenable.

## SELTEN AND KRISCHKER (1983)

The measure introduced by Selten and Krischker (1983) and used later by Selten (1983) is also predicated on the assumption that the size of $H$ must be taken into account by any reasonable index of predictive accuracy. Unlike Bonacich, Selten and Krischker only consider integer IRPCs. Also unlike Bonacich, Selten and Krischker do not employ the mean squared distance between $x$ and $H$ or, indeed, any other continuous function to measure the *degree* of support that an observed payoff vector gives to a model. Rather, the continuous function advocated by Bonacich is replaced by a step function, where a model predicting the set $H$ is supported if and only if $x \in H$.

Let $K$ be the number of possible coalitions structures for some game $(N;v)$ and $N\{S_1, ..., S_m\}$ be defined as above. For every integer IRPC $\alpha = (\hat{x}_1, ..., \hat{x}_n; S_1, ..., S_m)$, define the *weight* $A(\alpha)$ of $\alpha$ by

$$A(\alpha) = \frac{1}{K} \cdot N\{S_1, ..., S_m\}.$$

The weight of an integer IRPC is the reciprocal of the product of the number of coalitions structures for a given game $(N; v)$ and the number of predicted IRPCs with the coalition structure specified by $\alpha$. Let $H$ be a set of predicted integer IRPCs. Then the *area* $A(H)$ is defined as the sum of the weights of the IRPCs contained in $H$:

$$A(H) = \sum_{\alpha \in H} A(\alpha).$$

Clearly, the set of all IRPCs with the same coalitions has the area $1/K$.

Suppose that we are given the observed outcomes of $k$ plays of games $(N; v)_1$, $(N; v)_2$, ..., $(N; v)_k$. The $k$ games may or may not differ from one another in the number of players or their characteristic functions. In particular, the same game may be iterated (with the same or different player sets) $k$ times. Also, the games may or may not terminate with the same coalition structure. Let $g$ be the number of plays terminating with observed outcomes supportive of model $M$, and define $R$ as the *gross rate of success*: $R = g/k$. Clearly, $0 \leq R \leq 1$.

Letting $a_r(H)$ be the area of a set of integer IRPCs predicted by model $M$ for game $(N; v)_r$ $(r = 1, ..., k)$, define the *average area* $A$ by

$$A = \frac{1}{k} \sum_{r=1}^{k} a_r(H) \quad .$$

Then the proposed measure of predictive accuracy of model $M$, called by Selten and Krischker the *net rate of success*, is defined as the difference between the gross rate of success and the average area: $SK = R - A$. Because both $R$ and $A$ are numbers between 0 and 1, $-1 \le SK \le 1$. The null theory which predicts the set of all integer IRPCs always has $SK = 0$ because $A = R = 1$ in this case.

To illustrate the SK measure, consider again game G1 and let the core be the model under scrutiny. Then for any integer IRPC $\alpha = (\hat{x}_1, ..., \hat{x}_n; ABC)$ in the core, $A$ $(\alpha) = 1/5 \cdot 190 = 1/950$. The area of the core is obtained by summing the weights of all 190 payoffs vectors in $H$: $A(H) = 190/950 = 1/5$. Suppose that we are given the outcomes of six plays of game G1, all terminating in the formation of the grand coalition. Suppose, further, that three of these six payoff vectors fall in the core. Then, $R = 3/6 = 1/2$, $A = 1/6 \cdot (6/5) = 1/5$, and $SK = 1/2 - 1/5 = 0.3$.

A major shortcoming of the SK measure may be illustrated with the above example. Note that the location of an observed payoff vector outside of $H$ has no effect on SK. In Figure 1, the two payoff vectors (80, 30, 10) and (40, 40, 40) are equally non supportive of the core. However, intuition suggests that the former payoff vector is more supportive of the core than the latter. Similarly, most researchers in the area of coalition forming behavior will accept the payoff vector $x$ = (85, 20, 15) as evidence supportive of the kernel of game G1 - (84, 21, 15) - but reject the payoff vector $x$ = (40, 40, 40) as disconfirming evidence. The SK measure treats both payoff vectors immediately above in exactly the same way. Although algebraic theories do not allow for human frailty and, consequently, make no account for error, experience gained in testing them in various areas of psychology strongly suggests that the magnitude of the discrepancy between observed and predicted results should not be ignored.

## Support Functions for Model Comparison

A procedure is developed in this section for testing competitively coalition theories making alternative and conflicting predictions about reward allocation in CF games. Dominance relations between theories will be proposed which are both asymmetric and transitive. Therefore, the procedure will only be concerned with two models, $M_1$ and $M_2$, without loss of generality.

Underlying the proposed test procedure is the following idea. The predictions of model $M_1$ will be compared to those of model $M_2$ with respect to the same coalition structure. But rather than taking the set of predicted payoff vectors by model $M_j$ ($j$ = 1, 2) as fixed, the prediction set will be allowed to gradually expand. It will be expanded at the same rate in all directions within the outcome space until it encompasses all the observed payoff vectors in this space. An observed payoff vector will be regarded as supportive evidence of a given model $M_j$ if, and only if, it falls within the expanded prediction set of model $M_j$. Consequently, a monotonically increasing step function relating the cumulative proportion of observed payoff vectors which support the model to the size of its expanded prediction set will be computed separately for each of the two models $M_1$ and $M_2$. To offset the advantage possessed by the less specific model, which initially (before the expansion) implies a larger or more dispersed set of predictions, the resulting two functions will be compared to each other at a continuum of points where the sizes of the two expanded sets are equal.

## SUPPORT FUNCTIONS

For a given coalition structure, let $O$ denote the set of all possible payoff vectors (*the outcome space*) and let $A(O)$ be its *size*. When $n = 3$ and the coalition structure is $\{i, j, k\}$, $O$ is a point and its size is zero. If the coalitions structure is of the form $\{ij, k\}$, $O$ is a line and $A(O) = v_{ij}$. And if the coalition structure is $\{ABC\}$, $O$ is an equilateral triangle whose size is equal to

$$A(O) = \sqrt{\frac{3}{4}} \cdot v(ABC)^2/2.$$

Let $H_j$ be the set of payoff vectors predicted by model $M_j$, and let $A(H_j)$ be its size. Assume that $H_j$ and $O$ are defined for the same coalition structure. The *relative size* of $H_j$ is given by

$$A(H_j)/A(O) = \delta_j, \ O \leq \delta_j \leq 1.$$

An *expanded set* $H_j(\delta)$ is defined as the set of all the payoff vectors contained in $H_j$ as well as all the payoff vectors within $O$ whose shortest distance from $H_j$ is equal to or smaller than some distance $d(\delta) \geq 0$. The distance $d(\delta)$ is determined so that

$$A(H_j(\delta))/A(O) = \delta, \ \delta_j \leq \delta \leq 1.$$

To illustrate $H_j(\delta)$, consider coalition $ABC$ in game G1 and suppose that $M_j$ is the Shapley value for this coalition. The outcome space for the grand coalition of game G1 is the equilateral triangle in each of the four panels of Figure 2. Figure 2(i) shows the predicted payoff vector by the Shapley value--(62.0, 30.5, 27.5). Figures. 2(ii), 2(iii), and 2(iv) portray $H_j(\delta)$ for three arbitrarily selected values of $\delta$, namely, 0.121, 0.406, and 0.852, respectively. The shaded area in each figure is the locus of all the payoff vectors in the outcome space $O$ whose distance from the single prediction is equal to or smaller than $d(\delta)$. Because $H_j$ consists of a single point, $H_j(\delta)$ is always an intersection of an equilateral triangle and a circle with an origin at (62.0, 30.5, 27.5) and radius $d(\delta)$.

Figure 3 also portrays the outcome space for game G1. But now model $M_j$ is the core. Figure 3(i) depicts the core of game G1 (see Figure 1). As shown before for game G1, $A(H_j)/A(O) = \delta_j = 0.0225$. Figures 3(ii), 3(iii), and 3(iv) portray $H_j(\delta)$ for $\delta = 0.162, 0.421$, and 0.774, respectively. Because $H_j$ is a triangle, $H_j(\delta)$ is the intersection of the triangle $O$ with an area consisting of three rectangles of length $d(\delta)$ erected on the three legs of the core connected by three equal sectors of a circle whose areas sum up to $d(\delta)^2\pi$.

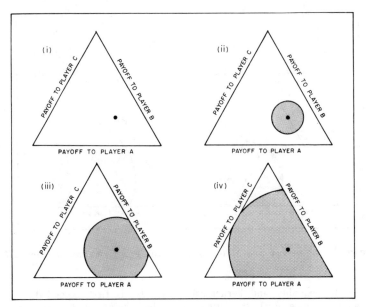

*Figure 2.   Expanded sets of the Shapley value for the grand coalition in game G1.*

Once $H_j$ is allowed to expand, the cumulative proportion of the observed payoff vectors contained in $H_j(\delta)$ can be computed as a function of $\delta$. This computation will yield a function with $k$ or fewer steps, where $k$ is the number of plays terminating with the formation of the coalition structure under consideration. We shall call this function the *support function* of model $M_j$.

EXAMPLES

Consider again game G1 in (1) and let $M_j$ be the $a$-power moel (Rapoport and Kahan, 1982). The $a$-power model predicts that if the grand coalition forms in game G1 the payoff vectors will all fall on a straight line connecting the equality solution (40, 40, 40) and the kernel (84, 21, 15). Figure 4 shows the prediction line as well as six hypothetical vectors (denoted by squares). One data point falls on the prediction line and two others lie within equal distance from it. $H_j(\delta)$ takes the form of two rectangles erected on both sides of the prediction line and two halves of a circle of radius $d(\delta)$

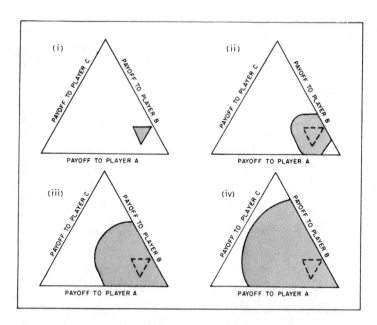

*Figure 3. Expanded sets of the core for the grand coalition in game G1.*

with origins at the equality and kernel solutions. $H_j$ is first expanded to include the data point with distance $d_1(\delta)$, then two more data points with distances $d_2(\delta)$, next another data point with distance $d_3(\delta)$, and finally the data point with distance $d_4(\delta)$. The resulting expanded sets have relative sizes of 0.026, 0.079, 0.363, and 0.419.

Figure 5 portrays the same six data points as in Figure 4. The model under consideration now is the Shapley value predicting the unique payoff vector (62.0, 30.5, 27.5). The expanded set takes the form of a circle, as in Figure 2. Because the six data points lie at different distances from the prediction point, $H_j$ has to be expanded six times to encompass all the data. The relative sizes of $H_j(\delta)$ are 0.008, 0.090. 0.129, 0.169, 0.340, and 0.479.

Figure 6 exhibits the support functions for the $\alpha$-power and Shapley value solutions. The two functions are computed for the six hypothetical data points in Figures 4 and 5. The support function for the $\alpha$-power model (left panel of Figure 6) has only four steps. Because one data point falls on the prediction line, the support function for the Shapley value (right panel of Figure 6) comprises six steps. Because none of the data points coincide with the prediction, the support function intersects the horizontal axis at 0.008.

When the coalition structure for a 3-person game has the form $\{ij, k\}$ rather than $\{ABC\}$ as before, the outcome space is a line of size $v(ij)$. A prediction may consist of a point, a set of isolated points, a segment of the outcome line, or a set of isolated

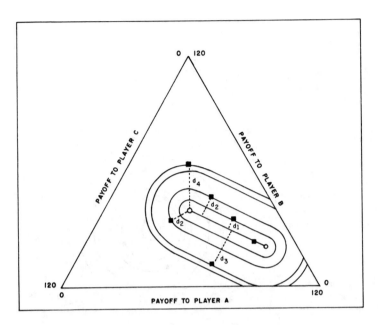

*Figure 4. Expanded sets of the α-power model (a straight line) for six hypothetical outcomes of game G1.*

segments. The computation of the support function in each case follows as above. For example, consider the 3-person CF game

$$\text{G2:} \quad v(AB) = 90, \ v(AC) = 40, \ v(BC) = 30, \ v(S) = 0, \text{ otherwise.} \tag{5}$$

Suppose that the coalition structure {*AB, C*} formed on ten plays of game G2 with player *A* getting 55, 50, 45, 30, 45, 40, 50, 40, 35, and 40. The bargaining set $M_1^{(i)}$ for the coalition structure {*AB, C*} prescribes that $40 \leq x_A \leq 60$ (and $x_B = 90 - x_A$). It may be compared to the equality solution prescribing $x_A = x_B = 45$.

Figure 7 shows the support functions for the bargaining set $M_1^{(i)}$ and the equality solutions. The support function for the bargaining set (left panel of Figure 7) has three steps: eight of the ten data points fall on the prediction line of relative size 2/9, nine data points fall on an expanded line (from 35 to 65) of relative size 3/9, and all the ten data points fall on yet a longer line whose relative size is 4/9. The support function for the equality solution (right panel of Figure 7) is seen to consist of four steps with δ assuming the values 0, 1/9, 2/9, and 3/9.

Although the presentation above concerned continuous expansions of the prediction set, it can be extended to integer IRPCs. In the 2-person example immediately above,

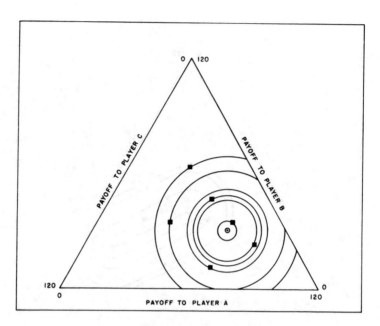

*Figure 5.   Expanded sets of the Shapley value (a point) for six hypothetical outcomes of game G1.*

$M_1^{(i)}$ will include 21 integer IRPCs ($x_A$ = 40, 41,...,60).   When expanded to include 60% and 100% of the data, it will comprise 31 and 41 integer IRPCs, respectively. Therefore, the relative size of the expanded set will assume the values 21/91, 31/91, and 41/91 rather than 2/9, 3/9, and 4/9 as before.

STRONG AND WEAK DOMINANCE

Whether integer or non-integer IRPCs are considered, let $F_1(\delta)$ and $F_2(\delta)$ denote the support functions of models $M_1$ and $M_2$, respectively, computed for a finite set of observed payoff vectors with the same coalition structure.   A criterion for choice between models relative to a set of data points is proposed as follows.

**Criterion SD.**   Given two support functions $F_1(\delta)$ and $F_2(\delta)$, model $M_1$ strongly dominates model $M_2$ if $F_1(\delta) \geq F_2(\delta)$ for all values of max($\delta_1$, $\delta_2$) $\leq \delta \leq$ 1, on the condition that for at least one value of $\delta$ the strong inequality $F_1(\delta) > F_2(\delta)$ holds.

The stipulation that the strong inequality must hold for at least one value of $\delta$ is tantamount to the requirement that the two support functions not be identical.   And the

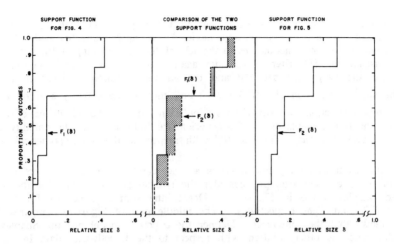

*Figure 6.* Support functions for the α-power model (left panel) and Shapley value (right panel) computed for the hypothetical data in Figures 4 and 5.

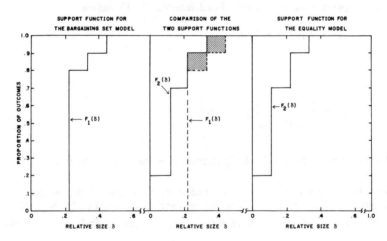

*Figure 7.* Support functions for the bargaining set $M_1^{(i)}$ (left panel) and equality solution (right panel) computed for ten hypothetical outcomes of game G1.

weak inequality $F_1(\delta) \geq F_2(\delta)$ is equivalent to the requirement that the two support functions do not intersect.  Geometrically, model $M_1$ strongly dominates model $M_2$ if, and only if, its entire support function lies to the left of the second support function.

To illustrate the SD criterion, consider again game G2 in (5) and the two support functions for the bargaining set $M_1^{(i)}$ and the equality solution depicted in Figure 7. Denote the support function of $M_1^{(i)}$ by $F_1(\delta)$ and that of the equality solution by $F_2(\delta)$. The two support functions are superimposed on each other in the middle panel of Figure 7.  Because the requirements of the SD criterion are fully satisfied, the equality solution strongly dominates the bargaining set $M_1^{(i)}$ with respect to the ten hypothetical 2-person outcomes.

Desirable as it is, strong dominance is a strict condition which may not be always satisfied in practice.  For example, consider the two support functions for the $\alpha$-power model and Shapley value in Figure 6.  Denote the support functions for these two models by $F_1(\delta)$ and $F_2(\delta)$, respectively.  The middle part of Figure 6 compares $F_1(\delta)$ to $F_2(\delta)$ and shows that they intersect.  Neither the $a$-power model nor the Shapley value strongly dominate the other solution with respect to the hypothetical data in Figures 4 and 5.  A conclusion might have been reached that neither model is to be preferred over the other.  However, an inspection of Figure 6 suggests that model $M_1$ has a slight advantage over model $M_2$; $F_1(\delta)$ lies to the left of $F_2(\delta)$ for most of the range [max $(\delta_1, \delta_2)$, 1].  Therefore, when the requirements for strong dominance are not satisfied, a weaker criterion for choice between models may be formulated.

For any support function on the closed interval [0, 1], define

$$F_j^1(\delta) = F_j(\delta), \; j = 1, \, 2,$$

and

$$F_{j(\delta)}^2 = \int_{\max(\delta_1, \, \delta_2)}^{\delta} F_j^1 (y) \; dy.$$

$F_j^2(\delta)$ is the area under the graph of $F_j^1(y)$ from $y = \max (\gamma_1, \gamma_2)$ to $y = \delta$.

**Criterion WD.**    Given two support functions $F_1(\delta)$ and $F_2(\delta)$, model $M_1$ weakly dominates model $M_2$ if $F_1^2(\delta) \geq F_2^2(\delta)$ for all values of $\max(\delta_1, \delta_2) \leq \delta \leq 1$, on the condition that for at least one value of $\delta$ the strong inequality $F_1^2(\delta) > F_2^2(\delta)$ holds.

According to the WD criterion, the support functions may intersect, but the *cumulative difference* between $F_1(\delta)$ and $F_2(\delta)$ must remain non-negative over the entire domain of $\delta$.

Inspection of the middle panel of Figure 6 shows that the cumulative area between the two support functions always remains positive.  Hence, criterion WD is fulfilled and the $\alpha$-power model weakly dominates the Shapley value for the hypothetical six data points in Figures 4 and 5.

Several properties of the strong and weak dominance relations follow directly from the theory of stochastic dominance (e.g., Fishburn and Vickson, 1978). It can be shown that strong dominance implies weak dominance. The converse, of course, is generally false. It can also be shown that either of the two dominance relations is both asymmetric and transitive. Consequently, either of the two dominance relations may be employed to compare to one another any finite number of models.

## Reanalysis of Outcomes from Two Previous Studies

The procedure proposed above is applied in the present section to test competitively several models for payoff division in two previous experiments by Rapoport and Kahan (1976) and Kahan and Rapoport (1980). I selected these two studies for reanalysis for three major reasons. The first reason is similarity in game structure. As shown below, the characteristic function of each of the 3-person games in both studies satisfies three conditions:

$$v(i) = 0, \quad i = A, B, C,$$
$$v(AC) + v(BC) \geq v(AB),$$
$$v(AB) \leq v(ABC) \leq [v(AB) + v(AC) + v(BC)]/2.$$

The first condition simply means that none of the three players had an 'outside alternative' with a positive payoff. Research by Kahan and Rapoport (1977, 1984) and Komorita et al. (1984) has shown that the availability of profitable alternatives to individual players outside of the coalition, which can be achieved without the consent of other players, significantly affects payoff division when a coalition is formed. The second condition, known as the 'triangle inequality' guarantees that the 3-person game has no player with a negative quota (see below), and the third condition states that the game is superadditive with an empty core or a single point core.

The second reason for selecting the two studies was that both allow the competitive testing of a relatively large number of models, which differ from one another in their predictions. And the third reason was that both studies used the same population of subjects and, more importantly, the same experimental procedure for conducting the bargaining, forming coalitions, and disbursing their values. To the extent that differences between the two studies are formed, with one model emerging victorious in the first study and another model having the advantage in the second study, they may not be attributed, as it is often done, to differences between experimental procedures.

RAPOPORT AND KAHAN (1976)

This study used the *Coalitions* sets of computer programs for playing characteristic function games. As the program structure and the rules by which $n$-person CF games are played in *Coalitions* have been extensively described elsewhere (Kahan and Rapoport, 1974, 1984; Rapoport and Kahan, 1974), they will not be repeated here. The study employed University of North Carolina community members, typically but not exclusively undergraduate students, recruited to play experimental games for cash reward. Games were played for points converted to cash at the rate of five cents per point. The subjects earned a mean of $29.90 for their actual participation. Eight tetrads of players played four iterations of the set of five games presented in Table I, for a total of 20 plays per group. In each play, three players within tetrads were rotated through positions (i.e., $A$, $B$, $C$) and the observer role from one play to another so that at any time, no one knew who was resting and who was in which game role. This technique of randomly shifting roles and employing observers has repeatedly (Kahan and Rapoport, 1974, 1977) resulted in experimental series whose individual games within groups are independently and separately negotiated.

*Table I. Games employed by Rapoport and Kahan (1976)*

| Game | Value of Coalition* | | | | Quota | | |
|------|--------|--------|--------|---------|-------|-------|-------|
|      | $v(AB)$ | $v(AC)$ | $v(BC)$ | $v(ABC)$ | $q_A$ | $q_B$ | $q_C$ |
| I    | 95     | 90     | 65     | 120     | 60    | 35    | 30    |
| II   | 115    | 90     | 85     | 140     | 60    | 55    | 30    |
| III  | 95     | 88     | 81     | 127     | 51    | 44    | 37    |
| IV   | 106    | 86     | 66     | 124     | 63    | 43    | 23    |
| V    | 118    | 84     | 50     | 121     | 76    | 42    | 8     |

* $v(A) = v(B) = v(C) = 0$ in all cases.

The five games in Table I, labeled I through V, were designed to represent different patterns of strength relationships among the players. The strength of player $i$ was defined by his or her *quota*, denoted by $q_i$ in Table I, and interpreted as the contribution of player $i$ to coalitional success. The three quotas $q_A$, $q_B$, and $q_C$ are the solutions of the following three equations in three unknowns:

$$v(AB) = q_A + q_B, \ v(AC) = q_A + q_C, \ v(BC) = q_B + q_C.$$

Table I shows that the quota differences among players increase from game III through IV to V with $q_A - q_B - q_C = 7$, 20, and 36 for games III, IV, and V, respectively. In game I, $q_A - q_B = 5(q_B - q_C)$ whereas in game II, $q_A - q_B = (q_B - q_C)/5$. And in all five games

$$v(ABC) = q_A + q_B + q_C - 5 = [v(AB) + v(AC) + v(BC)] /2-5.$$

Table II presents the frequencies of the coalition structures that actually formed by game and iteration. It is immediately apparent that the grand coalition was the dominant, though not exclusive, outcome for all games except game V, in which coalition $AB$ was predominant. Because the frequencies of the 2-person coalitions are too small to compute reliable support functions, the comparison of models below will be restricted to 3-person outcomes. Table II shows that with repeated exposure to a given game, the grand coalition was more likely to form; the percentage of grand coalitions increased monotonically from 55% to 80% over the four iterations. It seems that with increasing experience and practice with the games, the players realized that the more payoff they extracted jointly from the experimenter in each play, the larger might be their individual gains over a sequence of plays (Rapoport and Kahan, 1976).

*Table II. Frequency of coalition structures by game and iteration*

| | | Coalition Structure | | | | |
| --- | --- | --- | --- | --- | --- | --- |
| *Source* | | *{A,B,C}* | *{AB,C}* | *{AC,B}* | *{BC,A}* | *{ABC}* |
| Game | I | 0 | 4 | 3 | 2 | 23 |
| Game | II | 0 | 5 | 0 | 3 | 24 |
| Game | III | 0 | 2 | 1 | 1 | 28 |
| Game | IV | 0 | 5 | 2 | 0 | 25 |
| Game | V | 0 | 18 | 3 | 0 | 11 |
| Iteration 1 | | 0 | 13 | 4 | 1 | 22 |
| Iteration 2 | | 0 | 10 | 3 | 1 | 26 |
| Iteration 3 | | 0 | 7 | 1 | 1 | 31 |
| Iteration 4 | | 0 | 4 | 1 | 3 | 32 |
| Overall | | 0 | 34 | 9 | 6 | 111 |

Of the various game theoretic and social psychological models listed above, ten were selected for competitive testing. The equality model predicts that $x_i = v(ABC)/3$, $i\epsilon N$; the bargaining set $M_1^{(i)}$ prescribes that $x_i = q_i + \left[ v(ABC) - \sum_{i\epsilon N} q_i \right]/3$; and the Shapley value predicts that $x_i$ falls half-way between the two prescribed values above.

For the five games in Table I, Maschler's (1963) cooperative bargaining set $M_1^{(im)}$ (based on the cooperative standard of fairness) as well as the equal division kernel of Crott and Albers (1981) yield the same predictions as the Shapley value. Similarly, the kernel of Davis and Maschler (1965), the nucleolus of Schmeidler (1968), the competitive bargaining set $H_1^{(i)}$ of Horowitz (1973), and (asymptotically) the equal excess model of Komorita (1979) all coincide with the bargaining set $M_1^{(i)}$ for the five games in Table I. The tenth and last model to be tested is the $\alpha$-power model of Rapoport and Kahan (1982), which prescribes for each of the five games in Table I a prediction line, rather than a unique point solution, whose one end coincides with the equality solution and the other end with $M_1^{(i)}$. Thus, for each of the five games in the experiment of Rapoport and Kahan (1976), the $\alpha$-power model includes all the other nine models as special cases; $\alpha = 1$ yields the $M_1^{(i)}$ solution, $\alpha = 0$ yields the equality solution, and $\alpha = 1/2$ yields the Shapley value. Because the sum of quotas exceeds the value of the grand coalition for each of the five games, the core is empty in each case. Table III summarizes the different predictions.

*Table III.  Predicted payoff vectors for the grand coalition by three models*

| Model | | | | | | | | | |
|-------|---|---|---|---|---|---|---|---|---|
| | Equality | | | Shapley Value | | | Bargaining Set $M_1^{(i)}$ | | |
| Game | $A$ | $B$ | $C$ | $A$ | $B$ | $C$ | $A$ | $B$ | $C$ |
| I | 40 | 40 | 40 | 49.17 | 36.67 | 34.17 | 58.33 | 33.33 | 28.33 |
| II | 46.67 | 46.67 | 46.67 | 52.5 | 50 | 37.5 | 58.33 | 53.33 | 28.33 |
| III | 42.33 | 42.33 | 42.33 | 45.83 | 42.33 | 38.83 | 49.33 | 42.33 | 35.33 |
| IV | 41.33 | 41.33 | 41.33 | 51.33 | 41.33 | 31.33 | 61.33 | 41.33 | 21.33 |
| V | 40.33 | 40.33 | 40.33 | 57.33 | 40.33 | 23.33 | 74.33 | 40.33 | 6.33 |

The $\alpha$-power model prescribes a line between the two payoff vectors predicted by the equality and $M_1^{(i)}$ solutions.

For each game in Table I, support functions were computed separately for the equality, Shapley value, bargaining set $M_1^{(i)}$, and $\alpha$-power models. The game effect was significant, with all four models generating the steepest support functions in game III and the worst fit in game V. However, there was no evidence for game by model interaction. Consequently, the results were combined over all the 111 plays in games I through V to construct support functions for the four models. Figure 8 depicts the four support functions in steps of 0.02 on the horizontal axis. It shows that no two functions intersect. The bargaining set $M_1^{(i)}$ (and the models coinciding with it) strongly dominates all the other models. Next in goodness of fit is the $\alpha$-power model, which strongly dominates both the Shapley value and the equality solutions. Being strongly dominated by all the other models, the equality solution yields the worst fit.

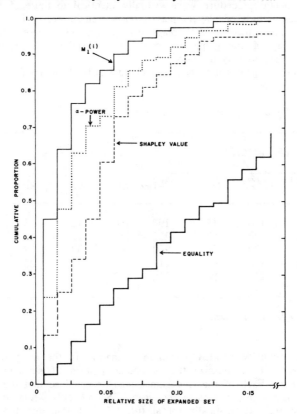

*Figure 8. Support functions for four different models tested competitively in the study by Rapoport and Kahan (1976).*

KAHAN AND RAPOPORT (1980)

This study, too, was conducted at the University of North Carolina. It employed *Coalitions - II* (Kahan et al., 1976), a successor to the computer-controlled *Coalitions* system, which possesses a wider game vocabulary than its predecessor. The subject population and experimental procedure were virtually identical to those of Rapoport and Kahan (1976). Eighteen tetrads of players played once a single set of five games (Table IV) for cash reward. As before, in each play only three players were active while the fourth observed the play of the game but could not participate. Player roles were randomly rotated from play to play as before.

The five experimental games are shown in characteristic function form in Table IV along with the player quotas.

*Table IV. Games employed by Rapoport and Kahan (1980)*

| Game | *Value of Coalition** | | | | *Quota* | | |
|------|-------|-------|-------|--------|-------|-------|-------|
|      | v(AB) | v(AC) | v(BC) | v(ABC) | $q_A$ | $q_B$ | $q_C$ |
| I    | 192   | 186   | 18    | 198    | 180   | 12    | 6     |
| II   | 235   | 227   | 42    | 252    | 210   | 25    | 17    |
| III  | 232   | 228   | 60    | 260    | 200   | 32    | 28    |
| IV   | 192   | 180   | 62    | 217    | 155   | 37    | 25    |
| V    | 218   | 212   | 86    | 258    | 172   | 46    | 40    |

* $v(A) = v(B) = v(C) = 0$ in all cases.

The study was originally entitled 'Coalition formation in the triad when two are weak and one is strong' to emphasize the particular pattern of strength relationships among the three players. Each of the five games was designed so that the quota of the powerful player A was roughly the same (between 155 and 210) while the ratio ($q_B$ + $q_C$)/$q_A$ was kept low and systematically set at 0.1, 0.2, 0.3, 0.4, and 0.5 for games I through V, respectively. It was anticipated that this pattern of strength relationships will lead the less powerful players B and C to join forces against A. Table IV shows that the value of the grand coalition in each game is equal to the sum of the three quotas.

Table V presents the frequencies of the coalition structures that actually formed. It shows that the powerful player A was included in 86 of the 90 coalitions formed. It further shows that the grand coalition formed in 50 of 90 plays and that the frequency of 2-person coalitions per game is too small to compute reliable support functions.

Concentrating again on 3-person outcomes, the same ten models as in the previous study were selected for competitive testing. The equality solution, the bargaining set

*Table V. Frequency of coalition structures by game*

| | Coalition Structure | | | | |
|---|---|---|---|---|---|
| Source | $\{A,B,C\}$ | $\{AB,C\}$ | $\{AC,B\}$ | $\{BC,A\}$ | $\{ABC\}$ |
| Game I | 0 | 4 | 5 | 0 | 9 |
| Game II | 0 | 4 | 2 | 0 | 12 |
| Game III | 0 | 3 | 5 | 1 | 9 |
| Game IV | 0 | 3 | 1 | 0 | 14 |
| Game V | 0 | 4 | 5 | 3 | 6 |
| Overall | 0 | 18 | 18 | 4 | 50 |

$M_1^{(i)}$, and the Shapley value make the same predictions of payoff disbursement as before (Table VI). Because $v(ABC) = q_A + q_B + q_C$, the core is no longer empty; for each of the five games in Table IV the core coincides with $M_1^{(l)}$. All the other models make the same predictions as before except the cooperative bargaining set $M_1^{(im)}$. The equations for computing $M_1^{(im)}$ (Maschler, 1963) vary depending on whether $3v(BC) > v(ABC)$. Table VI shows that, with the exception of game V for which $3v(BC) = v(ABC)$, the cooperative bargaining set $M_1^{(im)}$ does not coincide with the Shapley value and the equal division kernel. As before, the $\alpha$-power model includes all the other models as special cases except the cooperative bargaining set $M_1^{(im)}$ which does not fall on its prediction line. The predictions of the different models are summarized in Table VI.

For each game in Table IV, support functions were computed separately for the inequality, Shapley value, bargaining set $M_1^{(l)}$, cooperative bargaining set $M_1^{(im)}$, and the $\alpha$-power model. The cumulative proportions were combined over the 50 3-person outcomes in games I through V. The five support functions are displayed in Figure 9 in steps of 0.02 on the horizontal axis. The support function for the bargaining set $M_1^{(l)}$, which strongly dominated all other support functions in the previous study, is shown to be strongly dominated by all the other functions. The $\alpha$-power model, which provided the second best fit to the outcomes of the previous study, is seen to strongly dominate the equality solution, the Shapley value, and the $M_1^{(l)}$ bargaining set, but only weakly dominate the $M_1^{(im)}$ cooperative bargaining set. Comparison of Figures 8 and 9 further shows that all the models provide better fit to the 3-person outcomes in the previous than in the present study. This is evident from inspection of the horizontal axis in Figure 9 which, in comparison to Figure 8, had to be reduced by a factor of two to accommodate the various support functions for the present study.

*Table VI.   Predicted payoff vectors for the grand coalition by four models*

| Game | Equality | | | Shapley Value | | | $M_1^{(i)}$ | | | $M_1^{(im)}$ | | |
|------|-----|-----|-----|-------|-------|-------|-----|-----|-----|--------|-------|-------|
|      | *A* | *B* | *C* | *A*   | *B*   | *C*   | *A* | *B* | *C* | *A*    | *B*   | *C*   |
| I    | 66    | 66    | 66    | 123    | 39    | 36    | 180 | 12  | 6   | 107    | 47    | 44    |
| II   | 84    | 84    | 84    | 147    | 54.5  | 50.5  | 210 | 25  | 17  | 133    | 61.5  | 57.5  |
| III  | 86.67 | 86.67 | 86.67 | 143.33 | 59.33 | 57.33 | 200 | 32  | 28  | 134.44 | 63.78 | 61.78 |
| IV   | 72.33 | 72.33 | 72.33 | 113.67 | 54.67 | 48.67 | 155 | 37  | 25  | 110.22 | 56.39 | 50.39 |
| V    | 86    | 86    | 86    | 129    | 66    | 63    | 172 | 46  | 40  | 129    | 66    | 63    |

The $\alpha$-power model prescribes a line between the two payoff vectors predicted by the equality and $M_1^{(i)}$ solutions.

DISCUSSION

There is a systematic change in the relative positions of the support functions of the various models tested in the two studies which calls for explanation. Comparison of Figs. 8 and 9 reveals that the support functions for the equality and bargaining set solutions changed their relative positions from one study to another. The bargaining set $M_1^{(i)}$ dropped from its most advantageous position in terms of goodness of fit in the first study by Rapoport and Kahan (1976) to the worst position in the second study by Kahan and Rapoport (1980), whereas the equality solution shifted from the last to the second best position. The $\alpha$-power model maintained its relative position, strongly dominating all models except $M_1^{(i)}$ in the first study and all models except the cooperative bargaining set $M_1^{(im)}$ in the second study, and the Shapley value solution, whose predictions in both studies fall midway between the bargaining set $M_1^{(i)}$ and the equality solutions, has retained its position between these two solutions in Figs. 8 and 9.

     This pattern of relations among the models implies, and inspection of the observed payoff vectors substantiates this implication, that between the first and second study the 3-person outcomes 'moved' from the vicinity of the bargaining set $M_1^{(i)}$ in the direction of equal split along the prediction line of the $\alpha$-power model. Because there were no major differences between the two studies with respect to experimental procedure, subject population, and game structure, the more egalitarian division of $v(ABC)$ in the second study is attributed to a different pattern of strength relations among the three players. Taking the ratio $Q = (q_B + q_C)/q_A$ as a rough measure of asymmetry of strength (Kahan and Rapoport, 1980), with $Q = 2$ indicating compete symmetry ($q_A = q_B$

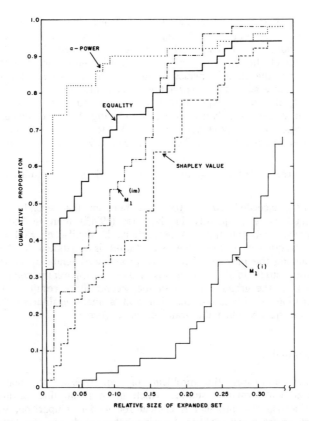

*Figure 9. Support functions for five different models tested competitively in the study by Kahan and Rapoport (1980).*

$= q_C$) and $Q = 0$ complete asymmetry ($q_A > 0$, $q_B = q_C = 0$), Tables I and IV show that $Q$ ranges from 0.685 to 1.569 in the first study and from 0.1 to 0.5 in the second study with no overlap between the two ranges. It is hypothesized that as one of the three players is rendered progressively more power than the other triad members, the two weaker players, because of resentment against the most powerful player, envy, frustration, or a growing solidarity between themselves, tend to join forces against the powerful player and force her to relinquish a larger portion of her $M_1^{(i)}$-prescribed payoff. It is precisely this process that the $\alpha$-power model attempts to capture with its single free parameter $\alpha$ interpreted as a group standard of fairness based on social and moral norms.

When combined over the two studies, the frequency data in Tables II and V seem inconsistent with findings from previous experiments on coalition formation in 3-person CF games.   One would expect that as the difference between the value of the grand coalition and the sum of the three quotas grows, thereby enhancing the attractiveness of the grand coalition vs. the three 2-person coalitions, the incidence of formation of the grand coalition will increase.   This expectation was confirmed in a previous study by Medlin (1976) using the same experimental procedure, subject population, and game structure as the two studies reanalyzed above.  Employing the same quotas as in the five games in Table I, but varying systematically $v(ABC)$, Medlin reported that the frequency of the grand coalition increased from 2.5% to 32.5%, 65%, and 77.5% as the difference

$$v(ABC) - \sum_{i\epsilon N} q_i \text{ increased from } - q_C \text{ to } - q_C/2, 0, \text{ and } q_C/2.$$ Tables II and V show

that although $v(ABC)$ exceeded $\Sigma q_i$ in the first but not the second study, the grand coalition was formed more frequently in the first (69.4%) than in the second (55.6%) study.   The difference between the two proportions is significant $\chi^2(1) = 5.6$, $p < .05$. The difference in frequency between the two studies is attributed to the difference in strength relations among the players.   The more pronounced tendency of the two weaker players in the second study to coalesce against player $A$ apparently compensated for the greater attractiveness of the grand coalition in the second study resulting in both a lower frequency of formation of the grand coalition and a more egalitarian disbursement of $v(ABC)$ relative to the quotas when the grand coalition formed.


## Summary and Conclusion

The present paper addresses the problem of comparison of models of payoff disbursement in coalition formation studies which make point, line, or area predictions. A satisfactory solution to this problem is critical for model comparison, which has been the major focus of research on coalition forming behavior during the last decade.   The goal of this paper is to devise and subsequently apply a test procedure which, in comparing the models to each other, offsets the advantage that the less specific model has over its competitor.   In addition, the test procedure should employ measures of error which yield intuitive results and are consistent with the principles underlying present coalition theories.
        It was contended that both the error measure of Bonacich and the net rate of success of Selten and Krischker suffer from serious deficiencies.   Bonacich's approach allows for degrees of confirmation of a model but employs an index of error which yields counterintuitive results.   The approach of Selten and Krischker also defies intuition and common practice by treating all payoff vectors that do not fall in the model's prediction set in exactly the same manner.   The test procedure proposed in the present paper allows the prediction set of a model to expand uniformly in all the directions (dimensions) of the outcome space until it encompasses all the observed payoff vectors which lie in this space.   In doing so it generates a function, called a support function, which relates the cumulative proportion of observed payoff vectors within the expanded

set of predictions against the relative size of this set. By comparing to each other the cumulative proportions for two different models when the relative sizes of their expanded predictions sets are held equal, the procedure offsets the advantage possessed by the less specific model which initially prescribes a larger or more dispersed prediction set.

Like the index of error $E$ devised by Bonacich, the procedure proposed in the present paper incorporates the intuitive idea that different outcomes differentially confirm a theory if they are not contained in its prediction set. Error is allowed to be continuous even if the theory under consideration is algebraic. Statistical tests of algebraic theories in other areas of psychology are almost always based on this assumption. The procedure also incorporates the shortest rather than the mean squared distance between a payoff vector and a set of predicted payoff vectors as the appropriate measure of error. The shortest distance is appropriate because coalition theories are mute with respect to the degree of 'importance,' 'representativeness,' or 'typicality' of the predictions they make.

The procedure seems to yield satisfactory results. When applied to the two studies by Rapoport and Kahan (1976) and Kahan and Rapoport (1980) it has not favored models making line predictions over models making point predictions. It has established either strong or weak dominance relations between all pairs of models tested in these two studies. And it has confirmed the major conclusions of the two studies, which had been originally reached by less rigorous tests of a smaller number of models.

## Acknowledgment

This paper was written while the author was a George A. Miller Visiting Professor at the University of Illinois. I wish to thank the Department of Psychology and the Miller Endowment at the University of Illinois for their generous support.

## References

Aumann, R. J. and M. Maschler: 1964, 'The Bargaining Set for Cooperative Games,' in M. Dresher, L. S. Shapley, and A. W. Tucker (eds.), *Advances in Game Theory*, Princeton: Princeton University Press, pp. 443–476.

Bonacich, P.: 1979, 'A Single Measure for Point and Interval Predictions of Coalition Theories,' *Behavioral Science* 24, 85–93.

Brams, S. J., A. Schotter, and Schwödiauer (eds.): 1979, *Applied Game Theory*, Physica-Verlag, Würzburg-Wein.

Caplow, T.: 1956, 'A Theory of Coalitions in the Triad,' *American Sociological Review* 21, 489–493.

Caplow, T.: 1968, *Two Against One: Coalitions in Triads*, Prentice Hall, Englewood-Cliffs, NJ.

Chertkoff, J. M.: 1967, 'A Revision of Caplow's Coalition Theory,' *Journal of Experimental Social Psychology* 3, 172-177.

Chertkoff, J. M.: 1971, 'Coalition Formation as a Function of Differences in Resources,' *Journal of Conflict Resolution* 15, 371-383.

Crott, H. W. and W. Albert: 1981, 'The Equal Division Kernel: An Equity Approach to Coalition Formation and Payoff Distribution in *N*-person Games,' *European Journal of Social Psychology* 11, 285-306.

Davis, J. H., P. R. Laughlin, and S. S. Komorita: 1976, 'The Social Psychology of Small Groups,' *Annual Review of Psychology* 27, 501-541.

Davis, M. and M. Maschler: 1965, 'The Kernel of a Cooperative Game,' *Naval Research Logistics Quarterly* 12, 223-259.

Fishburn, P. C. and R. G. Vickson: 1978, 'Theoretical Foundations of Stochastic Dominance,' in G. A. Whitmore and M. L. Findlay (eds.), *Stochastic Dominance*, D. C. Heath, Lexington, MA, pp. 37-113.

Gamson, W. A.: 1961, 'A Theory of Coalition Formation,' *American Sociological Review* 26, 373-382.

Gamson, W. A.: 1964, 'Experimental Studies of Coalition Formation,' in L. Berkowitz (ed.), *Advanced in Experimental Social Psychology*, Academic Press, NY, pp. 82-110.

Gillies, D. B.: 1953, 'Some Theorems on *n*-Person Games,' unpublished doctoral dissertation, Princeton University.

Horowitz, A. D.: 1973, 'The Competitive Bargaining Set for Cooperative *n*-Person Games,' *Journal of Mathematical Psychology* 10, 265-289.

Kahan, J. P., A. W. Coston, R. W. Helwig, Am. Rapoport, and T. S. Wallsten: 1976, 'A PDP-11/45 Program for Playing *N*-Person Characteristic Function games,' *Behavioral Research Methods and Instrumentation* 8, 165-169.

Kahan, J. P., and Am. Rapoport: 1974, 'Test of the Bargaining Set and Kernel Models in Three-Person Games,' in An. Rapoport (ed.), *Game Theory as a Theory of Conflict Resolution*, D. Reidel, Dordrecht, Holland, pp. 119-160.

Kahan, J. P., and Am. Rapoport: 1977, 'When You Don't Need to Join: The Effects of Guaranteed Payoffs on Bargaining in Three-Person Cooperative games,' *Theory and Decision* 8, 97-126.

Kahan, J. P., and Am. Rapoport: 1980, 'Coalition Formation in the Triad When Two are Weak and One is Strong,' *Mathematical Social Sciences* 1, 11-38.

Kahan, J. P., and Am. Rapoport: 1984, *Theories of Coalition Formation*, L. Erlbaum, Hillsdale, NJ.

Kalisch, G. K., J. W. Milnor, J. F. Nash, and E. D. Nering: 1954, 'Some Experimental *N*-Person Games,' in R. M. Thrall, C. H. Coombs and R. S. Davis (eds.), *Decision Processes*, Wiley, NY, pp. 301-327.

Komorita, S. S.: 1978, 'Evaluating Coalition Theories: Some Indices,' *Journal of Conflict Resolution* 22, 691-706.

Komorita, S. S. and J. M. Chertkoff: 1973, 'A Bargaining Theory of Coalition Formation,' *Psychological Review* 80, 149-162.

Komorita, S. S., T. P. Hamilton, and D. A. Kravitz: 1984, 'Effects of Alternatives in Coalition Bargaining,' *Journal of Experimental Social Psychology* **20**, 116-136.

Maschler, M. 1963, 'The Power of a Coalition,' *Management Science* **10**, 8-29.

Medlin, S. M.: 1976, 'Effects of Grand Coalition Payoffs on Coalition Formation in 3-Person Games,' *Behavioral Science* **21**, 48-61.

Michener, H. A., J. A. Fleishman, and J. J. Vaske: 1976, 'A Test of the Bargaining Theory of Coalition Formation in Four-Person Groups,' *Journal of Personality and Social Psychology* **34**, 1114-1126.

Michener, H. A., K. Potter, and M. M. Sakurai: 1983, 'On the Predictive Efficiency of the Core Solution in Side-Payment Games,' *Theory and Decision* **15**, 11-28.

Michener, H. A., K. Yuen, and S. B. Geisheker: 1980, 'Nonsymmetry and Core Size in *N*-Person Side-Payment Games,' *Journal of Conflict Resolution* **24**, 495-523.

Murnighan, J. K.: 1978, 'Models of Coalition Behavior: Game Theoretic, Social, Psychological, and Political Perspectives,' *Psychological Bulletin* **85**, 1130-1153.

Murnighan, J. K.: 1982, 'Evaluating Theoretical Predictions in the Social Sciences: Coalition Theories and Other Models,' *Behavioral Science* **27**, 125-130.

Ordeshook, P. C. (ed.).: 1978, *Game Theory and Political Science*, New York University Press, NY.

Raiffa, H. and R. Schlaifer: 1961, *Applied Statistical Decision Theory*, The MIT Press, MA.

Rapoport, Am. and J. P. Kahan: 1974, 'Computer Controlled Research on Bargaining and Coalition Formation,' *Behavior Research Methods and Instrumentation* **6**, 87-93.

Rapoport, Am. and J. P. Kahan: 1976, 'When Three Isn't Always Two Against One: Coalitions in Experimental Three-Person Games,' *Journal of Experimental Social Psychology* **12**, 253-273.

Rapoport, Am. and J. P. Kahan: 1982, 'The Power of a Coalition and Payoff Disbursement in 3-Person Negotiable Conflicts,' *Journal of Mathematical Sociology* **8**, 193-224.

Rapoport, An. (ed.).: 1974, *Game Theory as a Theory of Conflict Resolution*, D. Reidel, Dordrecht, Holland.

Riker, W. H.: 1967, 'Bargaining in a Three-Person Game,' *American Political Science Review* **61**, 642-656.

Schmeidler, D.: 1969, 'The Nucleolus of a Characteristic Function Game,' *SIAM Journal of Applied Mathematics* **17**, 1163-1170.

Selten, R.: 1972, 'Equal Share Analysis of Characteristic Function Games,' in H. Sauermann (ed.), *Beiträge zur experimentellen Wirtschaftsforschung, Vol. III: Contributions to experimental economics*, J. C. B. Mohr (Siebeck), Töbingen, pp. 130-165.

Selten, R.: 1983, 'Equal Division Payoff Bounds for 3-Person characteristic Function Experiments,' in R. Tietz (ed.), *Aspiration Levels in Bargaining and Economic Decision Making*, Springer-Verlag, Berlin, pp. 265-275.

Selten, R. and W. Krischker: 1983, 'Comparison of Two Theories for Characteristic Function Experiments,' in R. Tietz (ed.), *Aspiration Levels in Bargaining and Economic Decision Making*, Springer-Verlag, Berlin, pp. 259-264.

Shapley, L. S.: 1953, 'A Value for $N$-Person Games,' in H. W. Kuhn and A. W. Tucker
    (eds.), *Contributions to the Theory of Games II. Annals of Mathematical Studies 28*,
    Princeton University Press, Princeton, NJ, pp. 307-317.
Vinacke, W. E. and A. Arkoff: 1957, 'An Experimental Study of Coalitions in the
    Triad,' *American Sociological Review* 22, 406-415.

# CHAPTER 16

# ASSESSMENT OF POLITICAL POWER IN THE ISRAELI KNESSET

**ABSTRACT**: Immediately after the election to the tenth Israeli parliament (Knesset), 21 students of political science, 24 Knesset members, and 7 parliamentary correspondents were each asked (a) to assess the political power ratios of the 10 parties represented in the Knesset and (b) to judge the ideological similarity between them. As ascertained by Saaty's analytic hierarchy scaling technique, the power ratio judgments proved sufficiently consistent to justify the construction of individual ratio scales of perceived political power. The ideological proximities were adequately represented by two-dimensional ideological spaces. Analyses of the derived power measures showed that the higher the political sophistication of the subject, the higher the combined power attributed to the religious parties and the lower the combined power assigned to the two largest parties *Likud* and *Labor*. The derived power measures were then compared to the predictions of six power indices, three of which only consider the seat distributions. Of the six models, the generalized Banzhaf power index best accounted for the perceived power of 62% of the subjects, whereas the classical Shapley-Shubik index provided the best fit for 31% of the subjects. The generalized power indices were found only partly satisfactory with a need for further revision.

There is general agreement among social scientists that the study of power is central to the understanding of conflicts and their resolution. This agreement encompasses conflict situations ranging from dyadic interactions to the formation and dissolution of conflicts in large weighted voting bodies. Thibaut and Kelley (1959) placed power in the center of their psychological investigation of the intricate and often subtle bargaining behavior in mixed-motive dyadic conflicts. Examining large social bodies, Parsons (1963) suggested that power is one of the key concepts in the Western tradition of thought about political phenomena, and Lasswell and Kaplan stated more than 30 years ago that "the concept of power is perhaps the most fundamental in the whole political science; the political process is the shaping, distribution, and exercise of power" (1950, p. 75). Yet despite this general consensus, there have been no attempts to study how people actually assess power in political voting bodies. Because the perception of political power in parliamentary democracies and in other political voting bodies may affect bargaining and influence policy decisions, the outcomes of such an empirical study, besides shedding light on an important aspect of human behavior, are potentially useful for answering questions about the formation of coalitions and the allocation of cabinet ministries among coalition parties.

In discussing the conceptual intractability of the concept of power, Parsons observed that "there is, on analytical levels, a notable lack of agreement both about its specific definition, and about many features of the conceptual context in which it should be placed" (1963, p. 235). Increasingly, Riker's (1962) cutting of the gordian knot of the notion of power, which replaces it by the more concrete notion of winning, has come to be adopted in the special and restricted domain of the distribution of power in weighted voting bodies. In correspondence with Riker's view, political scientists and other researchers have developed numerical indices of power for social systems that can be adequately modeled as simple games (Shapley, 1962), or cooperative $n$-person enterprises in which "winning" is the only goal and a specification of which coalitions are capable of doing so is the only structure.

Although numerical power indices have gained much popularity, our contention is that in their present form they are too limited for modeling perceived voting power. Theoretical developments in the related and more familiar area of coalition formation, which started about a dozen years ago, may prove useful for descriptive purposes and point the way for constructing more adequate models. As is well known, Riker's seminal work on the size principle (1962) inspired the construction of models that proposed alternative criteria for the formation of coalitions in weighted majority games such as the formation of minimum winning coalitions (Riker, 1962), coalitions of minimum size (Gamson, 1961), and coalitions with a minimum number of members. Like the classical power indices of Shapley and Shubik (1954) and Banzhaf (1965), these criteria have all presupposed only knowledge of the distribution of weights (e.g., seat distributions in parliamentary systems). About a dozen years ago these models were successfully challenged by coalition theories which, in addition to the distribution of weights, incorporate notions like ideological space or party distance and postulate the minimization of some form of ideological diversity of the coalition (Axelrod, 1970; DeSwaan, 1973). For example, in his "conflict of interest" theory, Axelrod (1970) predicted the formation of "minimal connected winning coalitions." Connected coalitions consist of coalitions of parties that are adjacent in a one-dimensional ideological ordering and, hence, minimize the "conflict of interest." Minimal connected winning coalitions are connected coalitions for which the deletion of either extreme member renders the coalition losing. Extensions to multidimensional ideological spaces, which remove the constraint imposed by Axelrod, have been proposed more recently by Winer (1979) and Grofman (1982).

Empirical studies (DeSwaan, 1973; Taylor & Laver, 1973) have shown that coalition-formation theories that incorporate information about ideological proximity are descriptively more adequate than theories that disregard this information. The major purpose of the present study is to test the hypothesis that this same conclusion also holds in the area of perceived voting power. Specifically, we use an experimental approach to measure perceived voting power in the Israeli Knesset in order to test competitively six models of perceived voting power. Three of these six models are the power indices of Shapley and Shubik (1954), Banzhaf (1965), and Deegan and Packel (1979), which in general yield different predictions. The other three models generalize the first three power indices by accounting for both the party seat distribution and the ideological proximities between the political parties in the Knesset.

Two additional questions are addressed in an attempt to assess the validity and generality of our conclusions. The first issue is methodological. We attempt to ascertain how—if at all—voting power is perceived at a time when a political coalition is about to be formed. To measure perceived voting power, we use and test a recently proposed scaling procedure (Saaty, 1977, 1980) which possesses several desirable properties, among them an index of the consistency of the subject's responses and a ratio scale of perceived power. The ratio scale properties are required because the predictions of all six models are only unique up to a multiplication by a positive constant. The second question concerns the effects of political sophistication and experience of the respondents on their perception of power. To this end we have collected data from three groups of respondents, namely, graduate students of political science, Knesset members, and Knesset correspondents.

The second section defines several basic concepts of game theory and describes briefly the three power indices of Shapley and Shubik (1954), Banzhaf (1965), Deegan and Packel (1979), and their respective generalizations. The third section provides information about the subjects and the experimental procedure used to elicit their responses, and the remaining sections report the results of the study and discuss their implications.

## Power Indices for Simple Games

As mentioned above, measuring perceived voting power requires examining two sets of power indices, each set consisting of three indices. To understand these six indices and the predictions they make in our Knesset study, several basic concepts from game theory must first be reviewed.

### SIMPLE GAMES

$n$-person cooperative games that model weighted voting bodies in which each coalition that might form can either "win" of "lose" are called *simple* (von Neumann & Morgenstern, 1947). Simple games are attractive because they constitute appropriate models for many $n$-person conflict situations, particularly in political structures such as parliaments and committees, but they are also appealing because the sparseness of their structure enables in-depth analyses of the game.

Consider a set $N = \{1,...,n\}$ of $n$ players. Let $N$ be the power set of $N$ (the set of all $2^n$ possible coalitions), and define a partition of $N$ into two mutually exclusive and exhaustive sets: $W$, the set of all *winning* coalitions; and $L$, the set of all *losing* coalitions. Meaning is assigned to "winning" and "losing" by three requirements for this partition"

1) $\emptyset \in L$,
2) $N \in W$,
3) if $R \in W$ and $R \subset S$, then $S \in W$ .

Conditions (1) and (2) guarantee that the null coalition of no players cannot win and that the grand coalition of all players must win, respectively. The heart of the definition is condition (3), which expresses the intuitive electoral meaning of "winning" in that no losing coalition may contain a winning coalition. A *simple game* can then be defined as a pair $(N, W)$, where $N$ is the set of players and $W$ is the set of all winning coalitions.

A further, almost universally applied, restriction is the condition

4) If $S \in W$, then $(N - S) \in L$.

Condition (4) guarantees that at most one coalition extracted at any single time from the body of $n$ players can be winning. Simple games satisfying condition (4) as well as conditions (1) through (3) are called *proper* (Shapley, 1962).

There are two types of player in simple games, which deserve mentioning. Player $i \in N$ is called a *dictator* if every coalition of which he or she is a member wins, and every coalition he or she is not in loses. A *dummy* is a player in a simple game who can never, by joining a losing coalition, change it to a winning one.

Interest in proper simple games most often centers on a subset of the winning coalitions called minimal winning coalitions, and denoted by $W^m$. A coalition $S$ is said to be *minimal winning* if every proper subset of $S$ is losing, whereas $S$ itself is winning.

A proper simple game can be completely specified by its set of minimal winning coalitions. Alternatively, it is sometimes possible to specify the set of winning coalitions by assigning non-negative integer "weights" (e.g., delegation votes and parliamentary seats) $w_1, w_2, ..., w_n$ to the players, and then specifying a criterion $W$ such that

$$S \in W \leftrightarrow \sum_{i \in S} w_i \geq W.$$

Games in which this specification is possible are termed *weighted majority games*; often, but not necessarily, $W$ is the integer just greater than $(w_1 + w_2 = ... + w_n)/2$. It is convenient to use a shorthand notation $[W; w_1, w_2, ..., w_n]$ to describe weighted majority games. This notation is known as a *weighted majority representation* of a simple game. A simple game may have more than one weighted majority representation. But when the weights have natural interpretations, as in parliamentary seats, there can be little quarrel about their nature.

**The Shapley–Subik Power Index.** The Shapley–Shubik (SS) power index is a specialization of the Shapley (1953) value, which measures a player's power in terms of the relative expected frequency with which he or she turns a losing coalition into a winning coalition by casting the deciding vote. Consider all possible orderings of the $n$ players in a simple game, which may be taken as all of the potential ways of building up toward the grand coalition. For each of these $n!$ permutations, some unique player joins and thereby turns what was a losing coalition into a winning one; this unique player is called the *pivot*. The SS power index of any player $i$, denoted by $\phi_i$, is defined as the number of permutations in which player $i$ is the pivot divided by the total number of alignments. The SS index (Shapley & Shubik, 1954) is computed from

$$\phi_i = \Sigma \, [(s - 1)! \, (n - s) \, !] \, /n!,$$

where $s = |S|$ is the number of players in coalition $S$, and the summation is taken over all winning coalitions $S$ for which Coalition $S - \{i\}$ is losing. The power index for a simple game will be stated as the vector of power indices of its players, $(\phi_1, \phi_2, ..., \phi_n)$.

Although the pivotal-player interpretation leading to the SS index is sufficient grounds for entertaining it, interest is increased because it may be uniquely derived from an axiomatic characterization (Dubey, 1975) and may be given additional interpretations (Roth, 1977; Straffin, 1978).

**The Banzhaf Power Index.** Banzhaf (1965) introduced another index for measuring power in simple games, in which all combinations of voters are considered in constructing the index, rather than all permutations as with the SS index. The Banzhaf (BZ) index of power may be developed in much the same manner as the SS index. For a simple game $(N, W)$ define a *swing* for player $i$ to be a coalition $S$, where player $I$ is a member of coalition $S$, $S$ is winning, and coalition $(S - \{i\})$ is losing. Let $\eta_i$ denote the number of swings for player $i$; $\eta_i$, the "raw" BZ index, counts the number of times player $i$ could change a coalition from losing to winning. Define

$$\beta_i' = \eta_i / 2^{n-1},$$

where $2^{n-1}$ is the total number of coalitions containing player $i$, and therefore, the maximum number of swings player $i$ could possibly have. The vector $(\beta_i, ..., \beta_n)$ is called the *absolute* BZ index. In general, $\sum_{i=1}^{n} \beta_i' \neq 1$. However, as stated by Banzhaf, it is the ratio of "raw" Banzhaf indices which is of importance. It is common, therefore, to use the normalized BZ index $(\beta_1, ..., \beta_n)$ where

$$\beta_1 = \beta_i' / \sum_{i=1}^{n} \beta_i', \quad i \in N.$$

Like the SS index, the BZ index has also been given an axiomatic characterization (Dubey, 1975; Dubey & Shapley, 1979) and alternative interpretations (Roth, 1977; Straffin, 1978).

**The Deegan-Packel Power Index.** Unlike the SS and BZ indices, which are based on a priori notions of power as the ability to be the decisive voter in an abstract legislative body, the Deegan-Packel (DP) index is an attempt to characterize power based on the observed ways in which voters in such legislatures supposedly behave. Deegan and Packel (1979, p. 122) intend "to reflect what we consider to be realistic dimensions of participant behavior and spoils distribution in certain game type situations; notably the exercising of power through interpersonal interactions that may be characterized as being 'political' in nature with all participants in victorious coalitions sharing equally in the spoils."

Following Riker (1962), the model assumes that only minimal winning coalitions will emerge. Formally, given a simple game $(N, W)$, define the collection of all minimal winning coalitions that contain player $i$ by

$$W^m(i) = \{S \in W^m \mid i \in S\}.$$

The DP power index for player $i$, denoted by $\rho_i$, is defined by

$$\rho_i = \frac{1}{|W^m|} \sum_{S \in W^m(i)} 1/s, \tag{1}$$

where $|W^m|$ is the total number of minimal winning coalitions in the game and $s = |S|$ is as before.   The DP power index is then the vector of individual player power indices, $(\rho_1, ..., \rho_n)$.

Three assumptions regarding the behavior of players in simple games give rise to this definition of power:

1.   Only minimal winning coalitions will form.
2.   Players in a minimal winning coalition will divide the coalition payoff equally.
3.   Each minimal winning coalition has an equal probability of forming.

Deegan and Packel (1979) show that the power index $\rho_i$ in Eq. (1) is consistent with and determined by these assumptions.   They have also given their power index an axiomatic characterization.   The resulting axiom set is similar to that for the SS index, but admittedly (Deegan & Packel, 1979, p. 117) lacks the compelling universality of earlier sets.

**Example.**   To illustrate the three power indices above, consider a parliamentary legislation with four parties $A$, $B$, $C$, and $D$ controlling 30, 20, 10, and 40 seats, respectively.   Suppose that to pass a piece of legislation a two-thirds majority is required.   Then this system may be represented as a weighted majority game

$$\begin{array}{cccc} A & B & C & D \\ [67; \ 30, & 20, & 10, & 40] \end{array}$$

This game has neither a dictator nor dummy players.

There are altogether $4! = 24$ permutations of the four parties.   Parties $A$, $B$, $C$, and $D$ occupy pivotal positions in 6, 2, 2, and 14 permutations (orderings), respectively. Hence,

$$(\phi_A, \phi_B, \phi_C, \phi_D) = \frac{1}{24} (6, 2, 2, 14)$$

$$= (0.250, 0.083, 0.083, 0.583).$$

To compute the Banzhaf values, consider all the winning coalitions in the game: $AD$, $ABD$, $ACD$, $BCD$, and $ABCD$.   Counting the number of swings yields $\eta_A = 3$, $\eta_B = \eta_C = 1$, and $\eta_D = 5$.   Therefore,

$(\beta_A, \beta_B, \beta_C, \beta_D) = \frac{1}{10} (3, 1, 1, 5)$

$= (0.333, 0.100, 0.100, 0.500)$.

To compute the DP power values, note that there are two minimal winning coalitions in the game: $W^m = \{AD, BCD\}$. Equation (1) yields directly

$\rho_A = 1/2 \ (1/2) = 1/4, \ \rho_b = \rho_C = 1/2 \ (1/3)$

$= 1/6, \ \rho_D = 1/2 \ (1/2 + 1/3) = 5/12$.

The DP values are given by:

$(\rho_A, \rho_B, \rho_C, \rho_D) = \frac{1}{12} (3, 2, 2, 5)$

$= (0.250, 0.167, 0.167, 0.417)$.

In the present example the DP index provides the most egalitarian results, the SS index gives the least egalitarian results, and the BZ index falls in between. Each of the three power indices assigns the same voting power to parties $B$ and $C$ despite the 10 seat difference between them.

NONSYMMETRIC GENERALIZATIONS OF POWER INDICES

Even a cursory examination of the three power indices shows that the analysis of political voting situations they provide is in many ways insufficient or superficial. The power indices described above ignore the realities of political, economic, or psychological life where alliances, cohesive blocs, discrimination, favoritism, and partisan actions are the rule rather than the exception. Although it is possible that some or perhaps most of these factors will play only insignificant roles in the perception of voting power, it seems unlikely that all of them will be ignored. Experience suggests that some voting combinations or coalitions are more likely to form than others. Notwithstanding individual differences in weights, this asymmetry is most likely to be caused by ideological proximity in parliamentary systems.

Recognizing the seriousness of the limitation of the power indices described above, Owen (1971) proposed a generalization of the Shapley (1953) value, which explicitly considers the affinity among players. In a subsequent article, Shapley (1977) generalized the SS power index to account for asymmetry in preferences, habits, or outlooks of the players. Shenoy (1980) later proposed a similar generalization of the BZ index. And the DP index, too, may be generalized in a straightforward manner. All three generalizations are computational schemes that consider both the weight distribution and ideological proximity between all pairs of players. In all three generalizations, the $n$ players are assumed to be represented as $n$ points in some politically interpretable multidimensional Euclidean space, and the ideological proximity is assumed to be proportional to the Euclidean distance in this space.

**The Generalized Shapley-Shubik Power Index.** To allow for proximities between players, Shapley (1977) proposes representing the players as $n$ points in an $m$-dimensional Euclidean space, $R^m$. This representation is quite common in psychological studies of cognition and nonmetric multidimensional representations of similarity data (Kruskal & Wish, 1978). It leaves ample scope for capturing many kinds of parameters without an excess of arbitration, including the intuitive ideas of "modernization" and "extremism" which are prominent in political analyses (Shapley, 1977).

Both political issues and profiles are represented in the generalized model by $m$-dimensional vectors regarded as belonging to different, dual spaces. Figure 1 illustrates this representation for $n = 5$ and $m = 2$. The two arrows indicate the directions associated with two typical issues. Figure 1 shows that each arrow determines an order of the five players by the simple process of dropping perpendiculars to the shafts of the arrows. As an arrow turns, different player-orders are produced; a $180^0$ turn reverses the order. Turning an arrow $360^0$ may not generate all $n!$ possible orders. For example, in Fig. 1 player $B$ will never appear in any order as the initial or final element. When $m$ is small and $n$ is relatively large, as will be the case in many applications, the model envisages that only a very small fraction of the possible alignments of players will actually be ideologically consistent.

It is assumed that all issue directions are equally likely—"that the 'political winds' blow across the ideological space in a perfectly random way" (Shapley, 1977, p. 20). An arrow $\xi$ can be chosen that represents an issue according to the uniform probability distribution over the unit sphere defined by

$$S^m = \{\xi \in R^m | (\xi_1^2 + \xi_2^2 + \dots + \xi_m^2)^{1/2} = 1\}. \tag{2}$$

Then the probability that $\xi$ lies in any given region in $S^m$ is proportional to the area of that region.

Now, for each player $i \in N$ and each issue (arrow) $\xi$ define $P_i(\xi)$ as the set of players who are more enthusiastic about the issue direction $\xi$ than $i$ is. By "more enthusiastic" is meant that these players are ranked below player $i$ in the player order generated by $\xi$. Also define $S_i^m$ to be the set of issue directions in $S^m$ for which $P_i(\xi) \in L$ and $P_i(\xi) \cup \{i\} \in W$. In other words, $S_i^m$ is the set of issue directions for which player $i$ serves as pivot in the simple game. Then the generalized Shapley-Shubik (GSS) power index is given by

$$\phi_i^g = \frac{\text{area of } S_i^m}{\text{area of } S^m}, \text{ for every } i \in N.$$

As expected, $\sum_{i \in N} \phi_i^g = 1$. When $m = n$ and the $n$ points are the unit vectors of $R^m$, GSS reduces to SS. Examples show that the GSS model has the desirable property that if player $i$ occupies a "central" position in $R^m$ his or her power is enhanced relative to the SS model.

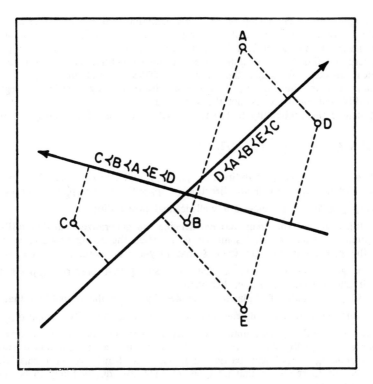

*Figure 1.* A two-dimensional representation of five players with two different issue directions.

**The Generalized Banzhaf Power Index.** Shenoy (1980) proposed a generalization of the BZ power index, which combines elements of Shapley's generalization of the SS index and Straffin's (1978) probabilistic interpretation of both the SS and BZ indices. Shenoy's nonsymmetric generalization may be described as a sequence of three steps.

The first step assumes that the players are presented as $n$ points in $R^m$. Each dimension of $R^m$ is interpretable in terms of psychological, economic, or political parameters, exactly as in the traditional factor analysis and nonmetric multidimensional scaling techniques. The ideological space is a subspace of $R^m$ defined by

$$B^m_{1/2} = \{\mathbf{x}^i \in R^m \mid ((x^i_1)^2 + \ldots + (x^i_m)^2)^{1/2} \leq 1/2\}, \quad i \in N.$$

Each player $i$ is thus represented by a point $\mathbf{x}^i$ in $B^m_{1/2}$, which is called the *profile* of player $i$.

To implement the second step of Shenoy's computational scheme, it is assumed that the assembly of players will be called to vote on a series of proposals or bills called *issues*. An issue in the model is a linear function on $R^m$ represented by a point $\xi$ on the unit sphere $S^m$ (Eq. 2). An issue, then, is some combination of the parameters of the ideological space. Although the players' profiles $\mathbf{x}^i$ and the issues $\xi$ are both $m$-dimensional, like in the Shapley (1977) generalization, they should be regarded as belonging to different, dual spaces, not the same space.

Let $p^i_\xi$ denote the probability that player $i$ will vote "yes" for issue $\xi$, where

$$p^i_\xi = \xi_1 x^i_1 + \xi_2 x^i_2 + \dots + \xi_m x^i_m + 1/2. \tag{3}$$

Equation (3) shows that the probability that player $i$ will support issue $\xi$ is proportional to his or her distance from the issue direction $\xi$. $p^i_\xi$ satisfies $0 \le p^i_\xi \le 1$ for every $\mathbf{x}^i \in B^m_{1/2}$ and every $\xi \in S^m$, and hence is a well-defined probability.

In the third step of the computational scheme the generalized Banzhaf (GBZ) power index is computed. Consider first some issue $\xi$. Then the swing probability for player i, $\Pi^i_\xi(p)$, is the probability that an issue $\xi$ that player $i$ supports passes but would fail were $i$ to change his or her vote, or that the issue $\xi$ that player $i$ opposes fails but would pass if player $i$ changes his or her vote.

The GBZ power index for player $i$, denoted by $\beta^g_i$, is the probability that player $i$ will make a difference in the outcome summed over all issues. To compute $\beta^g_i$, Shenoy makes the same simplifying assumption as Shapley, namely, that all issue directions in the unit sphere are equally likely. If the model is assigned a political interpretation with players corresponding to political parties and issues to legislative proposals, this latter assumption amounts to requiring that all types of bills are equally likely to be introduced to the multi-party parliament.

**The Generalized Deegan–Packel Power Index.** A nonsymmetric generalization of the DP power index, which utilizes information about the ideological proximity between the players may take one of several forms. To allow comparison with the two generalized indices GSS and GBZ, the approach that we propose also represents the players as $n$ points in $R^m$. Assumptions (1) and (2) of the original DP model are retained, but the third, and to our mind more controversial, assumption of equiprobability of minimal winning coalitions is replaced by the assumption that the probability of forming a minimal winning coalition is inversely proportional to the mean of the Euclidean distances between all members of this coalition. Thus, the more cohesive is the minimal winning coalition in the political space, the more likely it is to form.

Formally, let $p(S)$ denote the probability that some minimal winning coalition $S \in W^m$ will form. Whereas in the original DP model $p(S) = 1/|W^m|$, in the present model $p(S)$ depends on the inter-player distances $d(i,j)$, where

$$d(i,j) = \left[ \sum_{k=1}^{m} (x_k^i - x_k^j)^2 \right]^{1/2}, \text{ for } i,j \in S.$$

Denote the mean distance for coalition $S$ by

$$d(S) = \sum_{i,j \in S} d(i,j)/h, \text{ for } i < j,$$

where $h$ is the number of pairs of players in the coalition $S$. Then the non-normalized probability that coalition $S$ will form is given by $p'(S) = 1/d(S)$, which after normalization becomes

$$p(S) = p'(S)/ \sum_{S \in W^m} p'(S).$$

Finally, the generalized Deegan-Packel (GDP) power index for player $i$, denoted by $\rho_i^g$, is defined by

$$\rho_i^g = \sum_{S \in W_{(i)}^m} p(S)/s, \quad \text{for } i \in N.$$

**Example.** To illustrate the effect of ideological centrality on the three generalized power indices and to compare them to each other, consider a political voting body with three parties $A$, $B$, and $C$ controlling 20, 10, and 10 votes, respectively. Assuming a regular majority for passing legislation, this voting body can be represented by the weighted majority game [21; 20, 10, 10]. Party $A$ is a veto player in this game; no coalition may form without it.

Suppose that in terms of their ideological positions the three parties are represented in a 2-dimensional ideological space $B_{1/2}^2$ such that party $A$ is in the center of this space and parties $B$ and $C$ are located on its edge. Specifically, assume that the profiles of the three parties satisfy $x_1^A = x_2^A = 0$, $(x_1^B)^2 + (x_2^B)^2 = (1/2)^2$, and $(x_1^C)^2 + (C_2^C)^2 = (1/2)^2$. This assumption implies that $A$, $B$, and $C$ form an isosceles triangle in which $d(A,B) = d(A,C) = 1/2$, whereas the distance $d(B,C)$ may vary from zero to one depending on the angle $\measuredangle BAC$, which will be denoted by $\alpha$ ($0^0 \le \alpha \le 180^0$). If $\alpha = 0^0$, parties $B$ and $C$ occupy the same position in the ideological space, whereas if $\alpha = 180^0$, parties $C$, $A$, and $B$ form a single ideological dimension with $d(B,C) = 1$. Hence $\alpha$ measures the centrality of $A$ with respect to the ideological positions of $B$ and $C$.

The upper part of Table 1 presents the GSS, GBZ, and GDP values for selected values of $\alpha$. Consider first the GSS power index. Table 1 shows that for the present example $\phi_A^g$ increases linearly in $\alpha$, assuming the value 0.5 when $\alpha = 0^0$ and 1 when $\alpha = 180^0$. When $\alpha = 60^0$, $A$, $B$, and $C$ form an equilateral triangle. In this case,

$$(\phi_A^g, \phi_B^g, \phi_C^g) = (\phi_A, \phi_B, \phi_C) = (2/3, 1/6, 1/6).$$

*Table 1. Generalized power indices for two 3-person weighted majority games*

| | GSS | | | GBZ | | | GDP | | |
|---|---|---|---|---|---|---|---|---|---|
| $\alpha$ | $\phi_A^g$ | $\phi_B^g$ | $\phi_C^g$ | $\beta_A^g$ | $\beta_B^g$ | $\beta_C^g$ | $\rho_A^g$ | $\rho_B^g$ | $\rho_C^g$ |
| | A B C | | | | | | | | |
| Game: [21;20,10,10] | | | | | | | | | |
| $0^0$ | 0.500 | 0.250 | 0.250 | 0.555 | 0.222 | 0.222 | 0.500 | 0.250 | 0.250 |
| $30^0$ | 0.583 | 0.208 | 0.208 | 0.562 | 0.219 | 0.219 | 0.500 | 0.250 | 0.250 |
| $60^0$ | 0.667 | 0.167 | 0.167 | 0.579 | 0.211 | 0.211 | 0.500 | 0.250 | 0.250 |
| $90^0$ | 0.750 | 0.125 | 0.125 | 0.600 | 0.200 | 0.200 | 0.500 | 0.250 | 0.250 |
| $120^0$ | 0.833 | 0.083 | 0.083 | 0.619 | 0.190 | 0.190 | 0.500 | 0.250 | 0.250 |
| $150^0$ | 0.917 | 0.042 | 0.042 | 0.632 | 0.184 | 0.184 | 0.500 | 0.250 | 0.250 |
| $180^0$ | 1.000 | 0 | 0 | 0.636 | 0.182 | 0.182 | 0.500 | 0.250 | 0.250 |
| | A B C | | | | | | | | |
| Game: [21;10,20,10] | | | | | | | | | |
| $0^0$ | 0 | 0.750 | 0.250 | 0.111 | 0.667 | 0.222 | 0 | 0.500 | 0.500 |
| $30^0$ | 0.083 | 0.709 | 0.208 | 0.124 | 0.657 | 0.219 | 0.171 | 0.500 | 0.329 |
| $60^0$ | 0.167 | 0.667 | 0.167 | 0.158 | 0.632 | 0.211 | 0.250 | 0.500 | 0.250 |
| $90^0$ | 0.250 | 0.625 | 0.125 | 0.200 | 0.600 | 0.200 | 0.293 | 0.500 | 0.207 |
| $120^0$ | 0.333 | 0.584 | 0.083 | 0.238 | 0.571 | 0.190 | 0.317 | 0.500 | 0.183 |
| $150^0$ | 0.417 | 0.541 | 0.042 | 0.264 | 0.552 | 0.184 | 0.330 | 0.500 | 0.170 |
| $180^0$ | 0.500 | 0.500 | 0 | 0.273 | 0.545 | 0.182 | 0.333 | 0.500 | 0.167 |

Consider next the GBZ index. As before, the voting power of party $A$ is enhanced as the centrality of $A$ increases. However, the effect of centrality on $\beta_A^g$ is weaker than its effect on $\phi_A^g$ : $\beta_A^g$ varies from 5/9 for $\alpha = 0^0$ to 7/11 for $\alpha = 180^0$. When $\alpha = 90^0$, the GBZ and BZ values coincide for the present example.

The degree of centrality of player $A$ has no effect on the GDP values for the game [21; 20, 10, 10] because the GDP power index, as well as the DP index, only considers minimal winning coalitions in assessing power. In the present example there are only two minimal winning coalitions, $AB$ and $AC$, and the distance between their members is unaffected by varying the ideological positions of parties $B$ and $C$.

To construct the lower part of Table 1, we exchanged the number of votes controlled by parties $A$ and $B$ without changing the parties' profiles. The result is a new game [21; 10, 20, 10] in which $A$ maintains its ideological centrality though not its veto power. Parties $A$ and $C$ are symmetrical in terms of the number of votes they control but not in their ideological profiles. Table 1 shows that for all three generalized power indices, the power of the central party $A$ is enhanced as its centrality increases. The strongest effect of ideological centrality is obtained for the GSS index and the weakest for the GBZ index. Because the set of minimal winning coalitions now includes coalition $BC$ as well as $AB$, the centrality of $A$ affects the GDP as well as the GSS and GBZ values.

The two example games above, as well as other examples not reported here, show that for weighted majority games of the kind discussed in the present article, the three generalized power indices are all sensitive to the ideological profiles of the players, albeit in different degrees. They generally enhance the power of the ideologically more central parties and reduce the power of the ideologically more extreme parties.

## Method

### THE TENTH KNESSET

The institutional framework of the Israeli political system was largely established by the provisional government, founded on April 12, 1948, by the Zionist General Council. The provisional Council chose universal suffrage and a simple proportional representation system, which treats the entire nation as a single constituency for the 120-member *Knesset* (parliament). The task of forming a government is entrusted by the president to a member of the Knesset, typically but not necessarily the leader of the party commanding the largest number of seats. The composition of the government is a topic for party negotiations; it is only partially defined as consisting of a prime minister and an unspecified number of ministers, who may or may not be parliament members. Once a government is formed, it should immediately present itself to the Knesset and be regarded as constituted when it has received from the Knesset its vote of confidence.

The election to the tenth Knesset took place on July 1981 after a long and bitter campaign. Table 2 lists the ten parties that elected members to the Knesset together with the seat distribution. For a detailed description of the Israeli political system, see Arian (1966, 1973) and Seliktar (1982). Here we only present a brief characterization of the ten parties.

*Hadash*, which is an acronym for *Hazit Democratit Leshalom* (Democratic Front for Peace, or DFP), is an orthodox, pro-Russian, anti-Zionist Communist party, committed to an aggressive class struggle and identified with the Arab stand in the Middle East conflict.

*Hatnua Hademocratit Leshinui* (Democratic Movement for Change, or DMC) favors liberal economic and welfare policies and a moderate approach to the Israeli-Arab conflict.

*Table 2.  Frequency distributions of party membership for the tenth Knesset and for group K*

|  | Knesset | | Group K | |
|---|---|---|---|---|
| Party | Frequency | Proportion | Frequency | Proportion |
| DFP | 4 | 0.033 | 1 | 0.042 |
| DMC | 2 | 0.017 | 1 | 0.042 |
| CRM | 1 | 0.008 | 0 | 0 |
| LP | 47 | 0.392 | 9 | 0.375 |
| MNR | 2 | 0.017 | 1 | 0.042 |
| U | 48 | 0.400 | 11 | 0.458 |
| MIT | 3 | 0.025 | 0 | 0 |
| NRP | 6 | 0.050 | 1 | 0.042 |
| AI | 4 | 0.033 | 0 | 0 |
| R | 3 | 0.025 | 0 | 0 |
| Total | 120 | 1.00 | 24 | 1.00 |

*Hatnua Lezhuiot Haezrah* (the Civil Rights Movement, or CRM) is primarily interested in protecting the secular character of the State of Israel and the civil rights of its citizens.  The CRM advocates a liberal economic policy and a dovish stand in the Israeli-Arab conflict.

The *Labor Party* (LP) was established in 1968 by a merger of three parties—*Mapai, Ahdut-ha-Avoda, and Rafi*.  The LP is the most pluralistic party in Israeli politics. Undergoing an evolutionary development since 1948 by perceptibly shifting its position from a pronounced left-wing ideology to a more left-of-center position, the LP professed in 1981 a moderate socialistic and welfare-state orientation toward socioeconomic issues without negating the role of a capitalistic economy.  It accepted a modern degree of nonseparation between state and religion.  Adopting a pro-Western orientation in foreign affairs, it steered a middle course between the maximalist and minimalist demands by evolving a program that seeks a peace settlement with the Arabs while maintaining control of part of the occupied territories (Seliktar, 1982).

*Hatnua Lehithadshut Mamlacit* (Movement for National Revival, or MNR) espouses the superiority of the state mechanism over its sectional components like the *Histadrut*— the general trade union organization in Israel.  It opposes the imposition of a rigid wage structure by the *Histadrut* and its protection of labor rights to the detriment of efficient management, and it advocates a right-to-center stand on the Arab-Israeli conflict.

*Likud* (Union, or U) is a bloc of right-wing parties led by *Herut*, which for 30 years has been the main opposition party.  Reflecting conservative principles, *Likud* calls for a laissez-faire economic policy and the abolition of *Histadrut* controls. Adhering to a highly nationalistic foreign policy, most of the party's activity has been directed toward promoting its national policy, which includes territorial demands and a militant stand toward the Palestinian issue. The *Likud* has maintained control of the Knesset from 1977.

*Tenuat Masoret Israel* (Movement for Israeli Tradition, of MIT) is a religious party primarily interested in improving the socioeconomic conditions and enhancing the political power of Oriental Jews.

*Miflaga Datit Leumit* (National Religious Party, or NRP) is primarily concerned with incorporating religious laws into the law of the state, especially in education, with defining the Jewish status of individuals, and with family laws. The party is committed to a liberal economy; it promotes a nationalistic foreign policy which includes territorial demands, although to a less extent than *Likud*.

*Agudat Israel* (Association of Israel, or AI) is an extremely religious party, rigidly committed to the rule of the Jewish religion. It is an antiestablishment party that, though participating in secular coalitions highly incompatible with its stand, has endeavored to impose its philosophy through an extreme opposition.

*Hathia* (Renaissance, or R) is an ultranationalist right-wing party, which left the Likud because of its maximal territorial demands and extremely nationalistic foreign policy.

SUBJECTS

Three groups of subjects participated in the study. Group S includes 21 undergraduate and graduate students of political science at the University of Haifa, who had to satisfy three requirements: They had taken at least one course on the structure of the Israeli political system, they were present on campus on the day the study was conducted (during the final examination period), and they agreed to participate in the study before taking their final examination.

Group K contains 24 Knesset members who were selected as follows. Immediately after the official announcement of the outcomes of the election to the tenth Knesset, letters were hand delivered to the 120 newly elected members, asking them to participate in a study on the assessment of political power and ideological similarity between parties. The Knesset members were each asked to devote approximately 90 minutes to an individual interview to take place at the time and location of his or her choosing. No response to the letter was required. One to two days later attempts were made to contact the Knesset member and secure the desired interview, which could only take place between the fifth and eighth day after the elections. Several Knesset members could not be located or approached, many refused to be interviewed for personal or political reasons, and others would not or could not work the interview into their schedule, typically mentioning the very short notice as the reason for their refusal.

Table 2 shows the distribution of the members of group K by party affiliation. The difference between the relative frequency distribution for group K and the population frequency distribution, shown on the left-hand side of Table 2, is statistically insignificant ($x^2(2) = 0.42$). Although the subjects of group K were not chosen randomly, there is no reason to doubt their representativeness.

Group R includes seven senior parliamentary correspondents of the Israeli media, who have been covering parliamentary events in the Knesset for some time. Group R consists of all the parliamentary reporters who agreed to the interview and succeeded in working it into their very tight schedule.

EXPERIMENTAL PROCEDURE

Ideological spaces and party distance matrices have been typically constructed from party voting records or from proximity data collected while a particular government was in power. The ideological positions obtained by either of these methods are not entirely suitable for use in any attempt to assess perceived voting power because the parties' voting power is itself partially determined by the membership of the government (Taylor & Laver, 1973). To overcome this methodological difficulty, the timing of the study was chosen with much care. By having subjects assess ratios of voting power and subsequently ideological similarity between pairs of parties after the election to the tenth Knesset but before the formation of a coalition government, we have ensured as much as possible that the membership of the government has no effect on the subjects' responses.

Within a brief period of four days, two practiced experimenters delivered the instructions, elaborated on them when necessary, and collected the data. Whereas the subjects of group S were tested collectively in a classroom, the subjects of groups K and R were tested individually either in their offices or in the Knesset building. For all three groups, the study lasted between 60 and 90 minutes.

The task consisted of two separate parts. The first part used the scaling technique of Saaty (1977, 1980) for measuring political power on a ratio scale (see the Appendix). Each subject was given written instructions which told him or her that the purpose of the study was to assess the political power of the parties in the tenth Knesset. Although the notion of power was not defined, three examples of a hypothetical Knesset with only four parties were presented in weighted majority form to illustrate its complexity.

After the written instructions and their verbal elaboration, the subject was given a response sheet and a list of the ten parties in the Knesset with the number of seats they control. Then all 45 pairs of parties were randomly presented to the subject, one at a time. The subject was asked to attend to each pair separately and to indicate on the response sheet 1) which of the two parties was politically more powerful, and 2) by how much. No constraints were placed on the response scale; all rational numbers equal or larger than 1 were permitted. No time constraint was imposed; the experiment was self-paced.

In the second part of the tasks, similarity judgments were collected to be later subjected to non-metric multidimensional scaling (Coxon, 1982; Davison, 1983) for recovering the subject's political space. The task was again self-paced. All 45 pairs of parties were presented to the subject in a different random order, one at a time. For each pair the subject was asked to specify the degree of political or ideological similarity on a 0-100 response scale.

## Results

CONSISTENCY OF POWER RATIO JUDGMENTS

The matrix **A** was constructed for each subject separately from the $n(n-1)/2$ power ratio judgments (see the Appendix), and then the maximal eigenvalue (denoted hereafter by $\lambda$ rather than $\lambda_{max}$) of A was extracted and the consistency index was computed from Eq. (A2). The values of $\lambda$ and $\mu$ are presented in Table 3, which also shows the response scales of 1 to $r$ used by the individual subjects.

Of the 52 subjects, 45 chose to use numbers (mostly integers but occasionally fractions) between 1 and 10, 5 used numbers between 1 and 9, one subject between 1 and 8, and another subject between 1 and 50. Because almost all the subjects restricted themselves to a 1-9 or 1-10 response scale, the Monte Carlo results reported by Saaty and mentioned in the Appendix are applicable to our data. Table 3 shows that none of the eigenvalues exceeded or even approached the critical level 19.66. The largest value of $\lambda$ in Table 3 is 14.16 (K20), and only 9 of the 52 $\lambda$'s exceed 12. Turning next to the consistency index $\mu$ (Eq. (A2)), Table 3 shows that for only 10 of the 52 subjects $\mu \geq 0.2$.

Combining the results of the two consistency tests, we concluded that for most of the subjects a meaningful ratio scale of political voting power could be constructed. Although the consistency of the responses of 10 subjects may be suspect, it was decided not to omit any subjects from subsequent analyses.

ANALYSIS OF PERCEIVED POWER

Having established the consistency of the subjects' pairwise comparisons, the eigenvectors of A were next extracted, one for each subject. We shall refer to the eigenvector **w** ($w_i \geq 0$, $i = 1, ..., n$; $w_1 + ... + w_n = 1$) as the vector of perceived power. Table 4 presents the means and standard deviations of the perceived power of the ten parties, computed separately for each group and over all 52 subjects.

A comparison of Tables 2 and 4 shows that the four mean vectors of perceived power differ from the vector of proportions of Knesset seats controlled by the parties. Perceived power in the present study cannot be solely accounted for in terms of the distribution of seats. The comparison shows that the mean perceived power of the Labor and Likud parties was considerably lower than their proportion of seats. On the other hand, the perceived power of each of the three religious parties MIT, NRP, and AI exceeded their proportion of seats by a factor of 3 or 4; the three religious parties marshal together only 10.8% of the Knesset seats, whereas their combined perceived power averaged over all the subjects equals 34.7%.

The discrepancy between objective power, as measured by the proportion of seats, and subjective or perceived power may be explained in terms of the likelihood of being included in a winning coalition and thereby sharing the spoils. Several observations of parties with the same number of seats but different perceived power support this explanation. DFP, which had no chance of entering a coalition, even a coalition of national unity, was assigned a mean power of 0.022, whereas AI, which had the same number of seats, but was considered by most analysts as a highly likely candidate for

*Table 3.*    *Eigenvalues, consistency measures, response range, and two goodness-of-fit measures for subjects of all groups*

| Subject | $\lambda$ | $\mu$ | $r$ | RSQ | STR | Subject | $\lambda$ | $\mu$ | $r$ | RSQ | STR |
|---------|------|------|----|------|------|---------|-------|------|----|------|------|
| S01 | 11.08 | 0.12 | 10 | 0.90 | 0.15 | K06 | 10.35 | 0.04 | 10 | 0.93 | 0.12 |
| S02 | 10.25 | 0.03 | 10 | 0.86 | 0.17 | K07 | 10.22 | 0.03 | 10 | 0.90 | 0.16 |
| S03 | 10.21 | 0.02 | 10 | 0.81 | 0.17 | K08 | 10.51 | 0.06 | 10 | 0.93 | 0.12 |
| S04 | 11.30 | 0.14 | 10 | 0.84 | 0.16 | K09 | 11.24 | 0.14 | 10 | 0.85 | 0.19 |
| S05 | 10.47 | 0.05 | 9 | 0.96 | 0.09 | K10 | 11.51 | 0.17 | 10 | 0.92 | 0.14 |
| S06 | 10.95 | 0.11 | 10 | 0.91 | 0.15 | K11 | 10.56 | 0.06 | 10 | 0.84 | 0.15 |
| S07 | 11.18 | 0.13 | 10 | 0.89 | 0.18 | K12 | 12.53 | 0.28 | 10 | 0.77 | 0.18 |
| S08 | 10.85 | 0.10 | 10 | 0.86 | 0.16 | K13 | 13.89 | 0.43 | 10 | 0.94 | 0.12 |
| S09 | 10.56 | 0.06 | 10 | 0.82 | 0.17 | K14 | 10.49 | 0.06 | 10 | 0.80 | 0.21 |
| S10 | 10.30 | 0.03 | 10 | 0.83 | 0.17 | K15 | 10.96 | 0.11 | 10 | 0.88 | 0.15 |
| S11 | 11.06 | 0.12 | 10 | 0.93 | 0.13 | K16 | 10.36 | 0.04 | 10 | 0.95 | 0.11 |
| S12 | 10.94 | 0.11 | 10 | 0.92 | 0.12 | K17 | 12.98 | 0.33 | 10 | 0.90 | 0.15 |
| S13 | 10.71 | 0.08 | 50 | 0.78 | 0.19 | K18 | 10.64 | 0.07 | 10 | 0.88 | 0.19 |
| S14 | 10.96 | 0.11 | 10 | 0.77 | 0.22 | K19 | 10.95 | 0.11 | 9 | 0.87 | 0.15 |
| S15 | 10.62 | 0.07 | 10 | 0.76 | 0.21 | K20 | 14.16 | 0.46 | 10 | 0.92 | 0.17 |
| S16 | 12.12 | 0.24 | 10 | 0.86 | 0.16 | K21 | 13.45 | 0.38 | 10 | 0.87 | 0.14 |
| S17 | 12.53 | 0.28 | 10 | 0.95 | 0.10 | K22 | 10.97 | 0.11 | 10 | 0.86 | 0.15 |
| S18 | 10.96 | 0.11 | 10 | 0.82 | 0.17 | K23 | 11.16 | 0.13 | 9 | 0.94 | 0.12 |
| S19 | 10.71 | 0.08 | 10 | 0.85 | 0.20 | K24 | 11.85 | 0.21 | 10 | 0.79 | 0.18 |
| S20 | 10.43 | 0.05 | 10 | 0.90 | 0.13 | R01 | 11.35 | 0.15 | 10 | 0.85 | 0.17 |
| S21 | 11.28 | 0.14 | 9 | 0.81 | 0.18 | R02 | 11.22 | 0.14 | 10 | 0.92 | 0.15 |
| K01 | 12.21 | 0.25 | 10 | 0.91 | 0.15 | R03 | 11.18 | 0.13 | 10 | 0.88 | 0.16 |
| K02 | 11.65 | 0.18 | 10 | 0.94 | 0.13 | R04 | 11.05 | 0.12 | 10 | 0.93 | 0.11 |
| K03 | 10.64 | 0.07 | 9 | 0.88 | 0.15 | R05 | 10.64 | 0.07 | 10 | 0.87 | 0.16 |
| K04 | 12.59 | 0.29 | 10 | 0.84 | 0.17 | R06 | 11.50 | 0.17 | 10 | 0.88 | 0.17 |
| K05 | 10.29 | 0.03 | 8 | 0.88 | 0.15 | R07 | 11.36 | 0.15 | 10 | 0.95 | 0.09 |

membership in the coalition, was assigned a mean power approximately six times larger. Perhaps less dramatic but more important is the comparison between the two major parties U and LP, which controlled 48 and 47 seats, respectively. Probably sharing the general consensus that U was more likely to form a winning coalition that LP, a consensus that proved true later, the subjects in the present study judged on the average that U was twice as politically powerful as LP.

Table 4 also shows group differences in the mean perceived power of several parties. As the political sophistication of the group members grows, the mean perceived power of LP drops from 0.187 for group S through 0.162 for group K to 0.109 for group R. The mean perceived power of U also decreased in the same direction, although at a slower rate, from 0.338 for group S through 0.323 for group K to 0.292 for group R. Owing to large within-group variability, neither of these two group differences was statistically significant by a one-way ANOVA ($p \geq .05$). However, when the perceived powers of both dominant parties were combined, a one-way ANOVA yielded a significant group effect ($F(2,49) = 3.51$, $p \leq 0.5$). In a similar fashion, the powers assigned to MIT, NRP, and AI were combined to get a general measure of religious power. The mean religious power was 0.308, 0.350, and 0.451 for groups S, K, and R, respectively. A one-way ANOVA resulted in a significant group effect ($F(2,49) = 5.18$, $p \leq 0.5$), showing that as the political sophistication increases more political power is attributed to the religious parties in Israel.

*Table 4. Means and standard deviations of perceived voting power*

| Party | Group S Mean | SD | Group K Mean | SD | Group R Mean | SD | Overall Mean | SD |
|-------|------|-----|------|-----|------|-----|------|-----|
| DPF | .026 | .010 | .020 | .012 | .018 | .006 | .022 | .010 |
| DMC | .029 | .009 | .026 | .012 | .020 | .004 | .027 | .010 |
| CRM | .025 | .009 | .022 | .010 | .020 | .005 | .023 | .009 |
| LP | .187 | .091 | .162 | .082 | .109 | .080 | .165 | .087 |
| MNR | .044 | .017 | .045 | .016 | .038 | .016 | .044 | .015 |
| U | .338 | .059 | .323 | .091 | .292 | .081 | .325 | .065 |
| MIT | .060 | .024 | .072 | .031 | .104 | .031 | .071 | .030 |
| NRP | .139 | .045 | .149 | .042 | .175 | .055 | .149 | .043 |
| AI | .108 | .046 | .130 | .049 | .173 | .047 | .127 | .048 |
| R | .043 | .016 | .052 | .057 | .052 | .014 | .048 | .018 |

Better understanding of the perception of political power may be gained by studying the relationship between the perceived power of different parties over individual subjects. Party size, political ideology, or the history of conflict and cooperation between the parties may result in a positive relationship between the perceived power of certain pairs of parties or a negative relationship for others. To investigate these relationships, all 45 pairwise correlations between perceived power were computed over all 52 subjects. Because the ten weights for each subject sum up to the same constant, the null expectation is for a low negative correlation between parties. Consequently, we chose the significance level of 0.01 for testing the correlations. The results are presented in Table 5.

Table 5 shows several patterns of correlations which are politically interpretable.

1. Regardless of their political ideology, small parties with three or fewer parliament seats (DMC, CRM, MNR, MIT, R) are perceived to resemble one another because of their size. Of the ten correlations in Table 5 between the five "small" parties, eight are positive and the remaining two (between DMC and MIT and between

*Table 5.   Correlations between measures of perceived power*

|       | DFP   | DMC   | CRM   | LP    | MNR   | U     | MIT   | NRP   | AI    | R    |
|-------|-------|-------|-------|-------|-------|-------|-------|-------|-------|------|
| DFP   | 1.00  |       |       |       |       |       |       |       |       |      |
| DMC   | .38*  | 1.00  |       |       |       |       |       |       |       |      |
| CRM   | .60*  | .78*  | 1.00  |       |       |       |       |       |       |      |
| LP    | .43*  | .14   | .18   | 1.00  |       |       |       |       |       |      |
| MNR   | -.03  | .52*  | .34   | -.33  | 1.00  |       |       |       |       |      |
| U     | -.26  | -.35  | -.45* | .09   | -.26  | 1.00  |       |       |       |      |
| MIT   | -.18  | -.01  | -.03  | -.70* | .27   | -.47* | 1.00  |       |       |      |
| NRP   | -.29  | -.25  | -.19  | -.72* | .08   | -.43* | .56*  | 1.00  |       |      |
| AI    | -.42* | -.22  | -.20  | -.78* | .13   | -.40* | .59*  | .73*  | 1.00  |      |
| R     | -.09  | .20   | .24   | -.32  | .31   | -.38* | .41*  | .11   | .20   | 1.00 |

$p < 0.01.$

CRM and MIT) are practically zero.    Of the eight positive correlations, five are significant.

2.    Like the five small parties mentioned immediately above, the three religious parties MIT, NRP, and AI are also positively correlated with one another.    All three correlations between the religious parties are significant (0.56, 0.59, and 0.73 for MIT and NRP, MIT and AI, and NRP and AI, respectively).    Although the three religious parties may compete with one another for the religious vote, they do not compete with each other for power.    Rather, they are perceived as constituting one bloc with a relatively high or low power depending on the importance and attention given by the subject to the bargaining tactics used by the religious parties and their ability to satisfy their political demands.

3.    The perceived power of each of the religious parties is negatively and significantly correlated with the perceived power of the LP.    The correlations between LP and MIT, LP and NRP, and LP and AI are -0.70, -0.72, and -0.78, respectively, each of which accounts for 50% or more of the response variability.    Similarly, the correlations between U and each of the three religious parties are also negative and significant (-0.47, -0.43, and -0.40).    Finally, the correlation between U and LP (0.09) is practically zero.    Politically, this pattern of seven correlations makes much sense because immediately after the 1981 elections a coalition between U and the religious bloc or between LP and the religious bloc was considered much more    likely than any other coalition, in particular a national unity coalition including U and P.

Inspection of Table 5 shows that 14 of the 18 significant correlations are accounted for by patterns 1, 2, and 3 above; the remaining four significant correlations all concern the DFP.

SPATIAL ANALYSIS OF PROXIMITY DATA

In addition to the power ratio judgments, each subject assessed the ideological similarity between any two parties on a 0-100 response scale. The resulting 10 × 10 symmetric proximity matrix of each subject was subjected to a nonmetric multidimensional scaling (Coxon, 1982; Davison, 1983; Kruskal & Wish, 1978; Schiffman, Reynolds, & Young, 1982). A version of ALSCAL (Young & Lewyckyj, 1979) in the SAS computer package was used. For any prespecified value of $m$, the ALSCAL algorithm computes and prints two measures of goodness-of-fit in addition to the $m \times n$ coordinates of the configuration. The RSQ measure is the squared linear correlation between the proximity measures and the corresponding Euclidean distances in the $m$-dimensional configuration. The other measure of goodness-of-fit, denoted by STR, is known as S-STRESS. The present study employed S-STRESS formula one, which is defined in terms of squared distances and squared disparities and is recommended (Davison, 1983) for proximity data. Both the RSQ and STR measures for the two-dimensional spatial solutions are presented in Table 3.

The common criteria of fit, reproducibility, and interpretability were used to determine the appropriate dimensionality of the spatial configurations. For most subjects, a dimension by STR plot began to level off at two dimensions, suggesting that the appropriate solution may be the two-dimensional configuration. Three-dimensional solutions had to be rejected in any case, not because of any belief that political spaces are appropriately interpretable in terms of one or two dimensions only, but because of the recommendation (Young & Lewyckyj, 1979) always to keep the $n/m$ ratio no smaller than 4. With $n = 10$ in the present study, $m \leq 2$. The RSQ results also supported the decision that $m = 2$. The mean RSQ measures for groups S, K, and R.were 0.857, 0.881, and 0.897, respectively, showing that more than 85% of the variability in the similarity judgments could be explained by the linear relationship between the proximities and the two-dimensional Euclidean distances.

Reproducibility dictates that the spatial solution be composed of dimensions that emerge consistently across subgroups (Davison, 1983). In analyses not reported here the proximity matrices of all the subjects in each group were jointly subjected to an individual differences nonmetric multidimensional scaling, using the ALSCAL program to fit the weighted Euclidean model. The resulting three two-dimensional configurations for groups S, K, and R were practically identical to one another (Golan, 1984, Chap. 6). Moreover, approximately 50% of the individual two-dimensional solutions exhibited more or less the same shape, with most of the parties maintaining their relative positions in the configuration.

Most of the individual two-dimensional configurations as well as the three configurations for groups S, K, and R mentioned above were shaped like a horseshoe, with the ordering of the ten parties on this horseshoe corresponding more or less to their left to right ordering in Table 2. The ordinal positions of adjacent parties in the ordering were often reversed, though, particularly between AI and R and Between DMC and CRM. Because no systematic differences among the three group configurations were discovered, all the 52 proximity matrices were jointly subjected to the ALSCAL program. As before, the weighted Euclidean model for individual differences was applied.    The resulting two-dimensional solution, also shaped like the same horseshoe, is depicted in Fig. 2.    Based on several arguments, which are presented elsewhere (Golan, 1984), it was concluded that the solution in Fig. 2 (as well as most individual solutions which have a similar shape) is politically interpretable.    The horizontal axis may be interpreted in terms of the joint and highly correlated effects of three dimensions, namely, defense policy, economic ideology, and attitude towards religion.    The vertical axis is interpreted as a moderation-radicalism dimension, with the more moderate parties placed at the top of the configuration and the more aggressive, traditionally anti-establishment parties placed at the bottom.

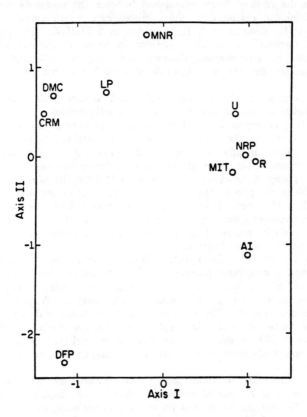

*Figure 2.    A two-dimensional representation of the ten parties yielded by the INDSCAL program.*

*Model Testing*

In addition to the vector of perceived power **w**, which was derived from the subject's power ratio judgments, six theoretical vectors were computed. The vectors $\phi$, $\beta$, and $\rho$ are the predictions of the SS, BZ, and DP power indices, respectively. As these indices only consider the seat distribution, they do not allow for individual differences. The other three vectors are $\phi^g$, $\beta^g$, and $\rho^g$. As they also consider the political space, which differs in general from one subject to another, the generalized indices each yield different predictions for different subjects.

Table 6 presents the predicted vectors $\phi$, $\beta$, and $\rho$ for the tenth Knesset. When compared to each other, the two vectors $\phi$ and $\beta$ are seen to be quite similar; the difference $|\phi_i - \beta_i|$ never exceeds 3.5%. The Banzhaf index, though, yields more egalitarian predictions than the Shapley-Shubik index: $\beta_i \leq \phi_i$ for the two dominant parties LP and U, and $\beta_i > \phi_i$ for the remaining eight, smaller parties. Both these power indices differ radically from the DP index, which predicts more egalitarian results than both. Political considerations would tend to reject the DP offhand, as it prescribes higher voting power to each of the two religious parties NRP and AI and even to the Communist party DFP than to the dominant party U! Clearly the assumptions underlying the DP index do not apply to the tenth Knesset.

*Table 6. Predicted voting power by the Shapley-Shubik, Banzhaf, and Deegan-Packel power indices.*

| Party | SS Value $\phi$ | BZ Value $\beta$ | DP Value $\rho$ |
|---|---|---|---|
| DFP | 0.070 | 0.080 | 0.106 |
| DMC | 0.031 | 0.040 | 0.091 |
| CRM | 0.016 | 0.019 | 0.062 |
| LP | 0.264 | 0.229 | 0.105 |
| MNR | 0.031 | 0.037 | 0.091 |
| U | 0.300 | 0.268 | 0.104 |
| MIT | 0.050 | 0.058 | 0.103 |
| NRP | 0.118 | 0.134 | 0.129 |
| AI | 0.070 | 0.080 | 0.106 |
| R | 0.050 | 0.058 | 0.103 |
| Total | 1.000 | 1.003 | 1.000 |

Table 7 displays the means and standard deviations of the voting power prescribed by the generalized indices GSS, GBZ, and GDP. Attending first to the GBZ and GDP indices, Table 7 shows relatively small standard deviations of predicted power for each of the ten parties. The ratio of mean to standard deviation for each of these two generalized indices is about 20, indicating very tight frequency distributions of power with small between-subject variability. A comparison of the mean vectors $\beta^g$ and $\rho^g$ in Table 7 with their respective vectors $\beta$ and $\rho$ in Table 6 shows only small discrepancies. The maximal difference between $\beta_i^g$ and $\beta_i$ is 2% (party LP) and the maximal difference between $\rho_i^g$ and $\rho_i$ is 1.7% (party DFP). We conclude from this comparison and the relatively small standard deviations of predicted power that the generalizations of the two power indices BZ and DP had only a marginal effect.

*Table 7. Means and standard deviations of predicted voting power by the generalized power indices*

| Party | GSS | | GBZ | | GDP | |
|---|---|---|---|---|---|---|
| | Mean | SD | Mean | SD | Mean | SD |
| DPF | 0.008 | 0.019 | 0.071 | 0.003 | 0.089 | 0.007 |
| DMC | 0.010 | 0.018 | 0.036 | 0.002 | 0.085 | 0.005 |
| CRM | 0.007 | 0.014 | 0.019 | 0.001 | 0.056 | 0.003 |
| LP | 0.123 | 0.087 | 0.209 | 0.011 | 0.102 | 0.006 |
| MNR | 0.015 | 0.033 | 0.036 | 0.002 | 0.090 | 0.004 |
| U | 0.421 | 0.246 | 0.272 | 0.011 | 0.111 | 0.006 |
| MIT | 0.054 | 0.099 | 0.060 | 0.003 | 0.109 | 0.004 |
| NRP | 0.165 | 0.201 | 0.148 | 0.007 | 0.139 | 0.005 |
| AI | 0.147 | 0.104 | 0.088 | 0.004 | 0.111 | 0.006 |
| R | 0.049 | 0.080 | 0.060 | 0.003 | 0.108 | 0.004 |
| Total | 0.999 | | 0.999 | | 1.000 | |

The generalization of the SS index, however, had more pronounced effects. Table 7 shows relatively large standard deviations for the GSS, which exceed the respective means of most of the parties, and a comparison of Tables 7 and 6 also shows marked differences, with the GSS index assigning more power than the SS index to the right-of-the-center parties U, MIT, NRP, and AI and less power to the remaining parties. On the average, the GSS index concentrated most of the voting power (78.7%) in the hands of four parties which, only a short time after the study, actually joined forces to form a minimal winning coalition.

Predicted and observed measures of perceived power were next compared to each other by computing for each subject and each power index the root mean squared deviation

$$\sqrt{\sum_{i=1}^{n} (z_i - w_i)^2},$$

where $z = (z_1, ..., z_n)$ indicates a theoretical vector. The resulting deviation scores, six for each subject, were first used to determine whether the generalizations of the SS, BZ, and DP indices improved the goodness-of-fit. For 49 of the 52 subjects the SS index yielded smaller deviation scores than GSS. A comparison of BZ and GBZ, however, resulted in smaller deviation scores associated with the GBZ index for 39 of the 52 subjects, and in the case of the DP index, the generalization improved the fit in 51 of the 52 cases. We next marked for each subject the power index with the smallest deviation score and compared the best models across all the subjects. The GBZ index provided the best fit for 32 of the 52 subjects (61.5%). Figure 3, which plots the mean perceived power for all subjects in Table 4 against the mean predicted power by the GBZ index in Table 7, provides a general idea of how good the fit is. The results of 10 more subjects (30.8%) were best accounted for by the SS index. The two generalized indices GSS and GDP were the most appropriate models for only one and two subjects, respectively.

## Discussion

Political power, like beauty, is in the eye of the beholder. It depends on, but is probably not solely determined by, the distribution of parliamentary seats, the ideological space, the personalities involved, party cohesiveness, resources controlled by the party, or the history of conflict and cooperation among the parties involving promises, threats, pressures, horsetrading, betrayal, and loyalty. Although power is inherently a multidimensional attribute, an implicit assumption of the present study is that individuals can and do integrate some or all of these facets, albeit in different ways, to form a unidimensional scale of political power. Tests of scale reliability, which have not been undertaken in the present study, are required to determine the stability of the integrating function for a given individual over time. The six power indices examined in the present study might be considered, then, as preliminary attempts to model this integrating process. There may be two major reasons for the failure of any of these models to account for perceived political power. The person may not use exactly the same factor or factors that the model postulates, or he or she may use the same factors as postulated but combine them in a different way.

The results support the underlying assumption of the six models that perceived political power is measurable on a ratio scale. Depending on the criterion used to determine deviations from consistency, most of our subjects exhibited an acceptable level

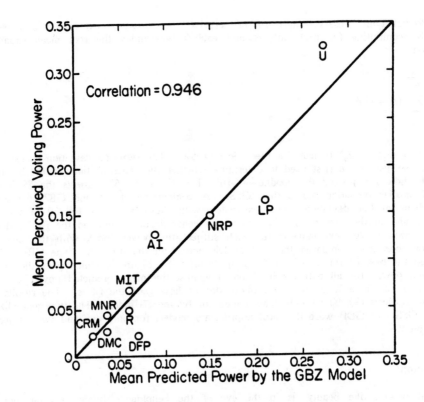

*Figure 3.   Mean perceived power plotted against the mean predicted power by the GBZ power index.*

of imprecision in their power ratio judgments, which has only a small effect on the derived weights.   The analytic hierarchy process was developed by Saaty for the derivation of priorities or weights which reflect the relative importance of the options in a multi-attribute judgment task.   There are several advantages to this technique: it is based on pairwise comparisons, which subjects generally find easy to make; it shares with Thurstonian psychophysical scaling technique and signal detectability theory the indirect approach to the analysis of sensory experience and other subjective phenomena; and it yields a numerical measure of response consistency.   The null hypothesis which it rejects in measuring consistency is too weak; there is a need for statistically defined or justified measures of response uncertainty based on stronger assumptions about the null hypothesis than sheer randomness.   It also appears (Belton & Gear, 1983) that under certain circumstances the technique may yield anomalous results arising from a misunderstanding of what is required in specifying the outputs. Because of these shortcomings, additional studies are required, which apply concurrently several scaling techniques for the measurement of voting power.

Another finding was that as the political sophistication of the subjects grew, less power was jointly attributed to the two largest parties U and LP, and more power was assigned to the three religious parties MIT, NRP, and AI. The loss of power inflicted on the two dominant parties was approximately equal to the joint gain of power by the religious parties. The mean combined power of U and LP decreased significantly from 0.525 for group S to 0.401 for group R, a drop of 12.4%, compared to an increase of 14.% in the mean combined power of the three religious parties from 0.308 for group S to 0.451 for group R. We attribute these two compensatory effects to the political experience of the subjects, their historical orientation, and their understanding of parliamentary politics. More research is required to find out whether the effects of political sophistication or experience are restricted to the three populations of subjects examined in the present study or are more general and apply to other segments of the Israeli population.

It was pointed out above that the power indices SS, BZ, and DP share a simple, experimentally testable property, namely, parties with equal numbers of seats are prescribed equal power. The observed results are inconsistent with this prediction. Table 2 shows three pairs of parties with the same number of seats: DFP and AI, MIT and R, and DMC and MNR. But Table 4 shows that for each group separately and over all groups, the AI was attributed between four to six times more power than DFP. Similarly, the mean perceived power of MIT exceeded the mean perceived power of R by about 50%, and the mean perceived power of MNR was almost twice as large as that of DMC. Also noted is the difference between these two parties. All of these comparisons show that within each pair more power was attributed to the party believed to be the more likely candidate to enter a coalition. They strongly suggest that seat distribution alone cannot account for perceived power and that additional factors, which determine the likelihood of entering a winning coalition, must be considered.

It was, therefore, natural to test the three generalized power indices GSS, GBZ, and GDP, which take into consideration both the seat distribution and the ideological similarities between the parties but combine them in different ways. When compared to the indices SS, BZ, and DP, the generalized indices behaved as expected, prescribing more power to the right-of-center parties and less power to the remaining parties. The DP index and its generalized version GDP are clearly rejected as descriptive models, probably because the assumption of equal division of spoils is untenable. The GSS and GBZ indices "move" in the same direction as the observed results. But although the direction of movement is right, its magnitude is wrong, with the GSS attributing too much power to each of the five right-of-center parties (except MNR), compared with the mean perceived power, and the GBZ index assigning each of them too little power.

Of the different approaches that may be considered in revising the GSS and GBZ indices, one warrants special attention. It may be recalled that both of these indices incorporate the assumption that all issue directions in the ideological space are equally likely. Despite its obvious advantages of simplicity and mathematical tractability, this assumption makes very little political sense. Inspection of voting records in the Knesset shows that the political winds do not blow across the ideological space in a perfectly random way.  Rather, the directional distribution of political issues introduced to the Knesset is largely, although not exclusively, determined by the coalition and tends to concentrate around issues which are of major interest to the government.  An empirical classification of issues actually voted on by the parliament may help to estimate the distribution of issues in $R^m$, which would then replace the uniform distribution in the computation of the two generalized power indices.

## Appendix: Saaty's Ratio Scaling Procedure

Because most social scientists are unlikely to be familiar with Saaty's Analytic Hierarchy Process, a brief discussion is in order.  Suppose we wish to compare a set of $n$ objects or activities in pairs according to their relative weights (assumed to belong to a ratio scale).  The weights may designate levels of different attributes or dimensions such as importance, desirability, brightness, pleasantness, or power.  Denote the objects (political parties in our study) by $C_1$, $C_2$, ..., $C_n$, and their relative weights (political power) by $w_1$, $w_2$, ..., $w_n$.  The $n \times n$ pairwise comparisons between the $n$ objects may be represented by a matrix $A$ of order $n$, known as a *reciprocal* matrix, in which $a_{ij} = w_i/w_j$ denotes the ratio of the weights of objects $C_i$ and $C_j$, $a_{ji} = w_j/w_i$ is enforced, and 1's are placed along the main diagonal.  Thus, only the $n(n - 1)/2$ pairwise comparisons $a_{ij}$ are required to construct $A$.

Suppose $A$ is known but $\mathbf{w} = (w_1, ..., w_n)$ is not, and we wish to recover $\mathbf{w}$.  To do so, we have to solve the system of equations (in matrix form) $(A - n\mathbf{I})\mathbf{w} = 0$ in the $n$ unknowns $w_1$, $w_2$, ..., $w_n$, where $\mathbf{I}$ is the identity matrix and $0$ is a (column) vector of 0's.  This system has a nonzero solution if and only if $n$ is an eigenvalue (characteristic root) of $A$.  Moreover, all the $n$ eigenvalues $\lambda_i$, $i = 1$, ..., $n$, of $A$ are zero, except one, called $\lambda_{max}$, which is equal to $n$.  The solution $\mathbf{w}$ is any column of $A$.  The various solutions differ from one another by a multiplicative constant.  However, it is desirable to have the solution normalized so that $w_1 + w_2 + ... + w_n = 1$.

When the matrix $A$ is generated from the known weights (without error), it satisfies the property

$$a_{ik} = a_{ij} \times a_{jk}, \text{ for all } i, j, k = 1, ..., n.$$

A matrix $A$ that satisfies this property is called *consistent*.

In realistic situations the ratio judgments $a_{ij}$ will be inconsistent to some degree. One subject may judge $a_{ij} = 2$, $a_{jk} = 3$, and $a_{ik} = 5$, where another may respond with $a_{ij} = 2$, $a_{jk} = 3$, and $a_{ik} = 4$.  We say that the second subject is less consistent than the first.  We wish to account for the inconsistency in ratio judgments by deriving from $A$ a single numerical index of the degree of inconsistency in the subject's ratio judgments. Mathematically, this is achieved through the solution of the system of $n$ equations

$$A \, \mathbf{w} = \lambda_{max} \, \mathbf{w}, \tag{A1}$$

where both the scalar $\lambda_{max}$—the maximal eigenvalue of A—and the corresponding eigenvector $\mathbf{w}$ are unknown.  It can be shown that a reciprocal matrix with positive entries is consistent if and only if $\lambda_{max} = n$. With inconsistency, $\lambda_{max} \geq n$ always. Saaty has observed that in any square matrix, small perturbations in its coefficients imply small perturbations in the eigenvalues. Hence, the higher the degree of inconsistency in the pairwise comparisons, the higher the difference $\lambda_{max} - n$.

This observation leads to the next and final step of the scaling procedure, which determines whether the degree of inconsistency observed in the $n(n - 1)/2$ pairwise comparisons of the subject is sufficiently small to justify the derivation of a ratio scale. No analytical solution to this ill-defined problem is known, but two different answers have been proposed by Saaty. The first is based on equating inconsistency with randomness. Reverting to Monte Carlo techniques, Saaty (1980, p. 61) computed the sampling distribution of $\lambda_{max}$ from 500 randomly generated matrices. As in the present study, each matrix was of order 10 × 10 with 1's in the main diagonal entries and with reciprocity enforced. The entries were filled in at random from the scale 1 to 9 (integers only), which is very close to the response scale actually adopted by the subjects of the present study. Saaty reported a truncated normal frequency distribution for $\lambda_{max}$. For a 1 to 9 response scale and significance level of 0.01, the critical level for rejecting the null hypothesis (by a one-tailed test) is 19.66. The decision rule of this approach is to reject the matrix **A** of pairwise ratio judgments as inconsistent if $\lambda_{max} > 19.66$ and accept it otherwise. If $\lambda_{max} < 19.66$, the associated eigenvector--the vector of weights **w**--is computed from Eq. (A1).

Saaty's second answer is to compute the consistency index

$$\mu = (\lambda_{max} - n)/(n - 1),$$                                        (A2)

and to reject **A** as inconsistent if $\mu \geq \mu_{crit}$ and accept it, otherwise. There is presently no statistical theory that underlies the measure $\mu$. Based on his rich and versatile experience with the procedure, Saaty proposed to fix $\mu_{crit}$ at 0.1 (1977, 1980) or 0.2 (1983).

## Acknowledgment

The authors especially wish to thank James P. Kahan for his contribution to the design and analysis of the present study. Thanks are also due to James Kuklinski and David M. Messick for their comments and criticisms throughout the writing of this article, to Asher Arian and Gideon Doron for their support and many helpful suggestions, and to Eythan Weg for his assistance in data analysis.

## References

Arian, A. *The choosing people: Voting behavior in Israel.* Cleveland:  Case Western Reserve University Press, 1973.

Arian, A. Voting and ideology in Israel. *Midwest Journal of Political Science,* 1966, *10,* 265-287.

Axelrod, R. *Conflict of interest: A theory of divergent goals with applications to politics.* Chicago: Markham, 1970.

Banzhaf, J. F. III. Weighted voting doesn't work: A mathematical analysis. *Rutgers Law Review*, 1965, *19*, 317-343.

Belton, V., & Gear, T. On a shortcoming of Saaty's method of analytic hierarchies. *Omega*, 1983, *11*, 228-230.

Coxon, A. P. M. *The user's guide to multidimensional scaling.* London: Heinemann Educational Books, 1982.

Davison, M. L. *Multidimensional Scaling.* New York: Wiley, 1983.

Deegan, J., & Packel, E. W. A new index of power for simple n-person games. *International Journal of Game Theory*, 1979, *7*, 113-123.

DeSwaan, A. *Coalition theories and cabinet formation.* Amsterdam: Elsevier, 1973.

Dubey, P. On the Uniqueness of the Shapley value. *International Journal of Game Theory*, 1975, *4*, 131-139.

Dubey, P., & Shapley, L. S. Mathematical properties of the Banzhaf power index. *Mathematics of Operations Research*, 1979, *4*, 99-131.

Gamson, W. A. A theory of coalition formation. *American Sociological Review*, 1961, *26*, 373-382.

Golan, E. Assessment of voting power and ideological similarity between parties in the *Knesset.* Unpublished Ph.D. dissertation, Tel Aviv University, Israel, 1984.

Grofman, B. A dynamic model of protocoalition formation in ideological N-space. *Behavioral Science*, 1982, *27*, 77-90.

Kruskal, J. B., & Wish, M. *Multidimensional scaling.* Beverly Hills, Calif.: Sage, 1978.

Lasswell, H. D., & Kaplan, A. *Power and society: A framework for political inquiry.* New Haven, Conn.: Yale University Press, 1950.

Owen, G. Political games. *Naval Research Logistics Quarterly*, 1971, *18*, 345-355.

Parsons, T. On the concept of political power. *Proceedings of the American Philosophical Society*, 1963, *107*, 232-262.

Riker, W. H. *The theory of political coalitions.* New Haven, Conn.: Yale University Press, 1962.

Roth, A. E. The Shapley value as a von Neumann-Morgenstern utility. *Econometrica*, 1977, *45*, 657-664.

Saaty, T. L. A scaling method for priorities in hierarchical structures. *Journal of Mathematical Psychology*, 1977, *15*, 234-281.

Saaty, T. L. *The analytic hierarchy process.* New York: McGraw-Hill, 1980.

Saaty, T. L. What is the analytic hierarchy process? Unpublished manuscript, 1983.

Schiffman, S. S., Reynolds, M. L., & Young, F. W. *Introduction to multidimensional scaling.* New York: Academic Press, 1982.

Seliktar, O. Israel: Fragile coalitions in a new nation. In E. C. Browne and J. Dreijmanis (Eds.), *Government coalitions in Western democracies.* New York: Longman, 1982, pp. 283-314.

Shapley, L. S. A comparison of power indices and a nonsymmetric generalization. Rand Corporation Paper No. P-5872, The Rand Corporation, Santa Monica, Calif., 1977.

Shapley, L. A. A value for n-person games. In H. W. Kuhn and W. W. Tucker (Eds.), *Contributions to the theory of games, II. Annals of mathematics studies No. 28.* Princeton, N.J.: Princeton University Press, 1953, pp. 307-317.

Shapley, L. S. Simple games: An outline of the descriptive theory. *Behavioral Science*, 1962, *7*, 59-66.

Shapley, L. S., & Shubik, M. A method for evaluating the distribution of power in a committee system. *American Political Science Review*, 1954, *48*, 787-792.

Shenoy, P. P. The Banzhaf index for political games. Presented at the Annual Meeting of the Public Choice Society, San Francisco, Calif., 1980.

Straffin, P. D., Jr. Probability models for power indices. In P. C. Ordeshook (Ed.), *Game theory and political science.* New York: New York University Press, 1978, pp. 477-510.

Taylor, M., & Laver, M. Government coalitions in western Europe. *European Journal of Political Research*, 1973, *1*, 205-248.

Thibaut, J., & Kelley, H. H. *The social psychology of groups.* New York: Wiley, 1959.

von Neumann, J., & Morgenstern, O. *Theory of games and economic behavior* (2nd ed.). Princeton, N.J.: Princeton University Press, 1947.

Winer, M. Cabinet coalition formation: A game-theoretic analysis. In S. Brams, A. Schotter, & G. Schwödiauer (Eds.), *Applied game theory.* Vienna: Physica-Verlag, 1979, pp. 133-151.

Young, F. W., & Lewyckyj, R. *ALSCAL-4: User's guide* (2nd ed.). Chapel Hill, N.C.: Data Analysis and Theory Associates, 1979.

# CHAPTER 17

# DOMINATED, CONNECTED, AND TIGHT COALITIONS IN THE ISRAELI KNESSET

**ABSTRACT:**    Considered in the present paper are parliamentary systems in which a single party is given a mandate to form a coalition after the elections. A multi-criteria model is proposed postulating the formation of coalitions that are dominated by the party given the mandate to form a coalition, are ideologically connected in the multidimensional politically interpretable space, and have minimal ideological distances between their members. The model is then tested with ideological proximity measures from 52 parliament members, reporters, and students of political science collected immediately after the 1981 elections to the tenth Israeli Knesset but before the formation of a coalition government. Theoretical implications of the model are briefly discussed.

## 1. Introduction

Elections in a parliamentary democracy are followed by attempts to form a controlling coalition. To this end, representatives of the political parties engage in face-to-face and often quite lengthy bargaining, which is constrained by ideologies, political programs, and previous commitments, on the one hand, and by legislative laws or procedures concerning the bargaining process, on the other. Politics in this world of multi-party parliaments has been aptly characterized as a "parliamentary game" (Duverger, 1951), the object of which is to form and subsequently control the government. Therefore, it is natural to employ the conceptual tools of game theory in an attempt to gain an understanding of the game's logic, structure, and outcomes. A primary objective of this endeavor has been to predict the likelihood of the formation of particular coalitions.

     A number of models of political coalition formation grounded in the game-theoretic tradition have been proposed (e.g., Axelrod, 1970; DeSwaan, 1973; Dodd, 1974; Gamson, 1961; Grofman, 1982; Hinckley, 1972; Leiserson, 1968; McKelvey, Ordeshook, and Winer, 1978; Riker, 1962). The multiplicity of these models testifies to the variety and complexity of the coalition formation situations they attempt to describe. Most of these models assume that each of the political parties involved employs a single criterion – such as the size of the coalition, the number of members it contains, its ideological diversity, or the distribution of a finite and transferable set of benefits, such as cabinet posts, within a coalition – in choosing between alternative coalitions (Taylor, 1972). However, it seems likely that in the context of government coalition formation some of the parties will be guided in their choices among competitive coalitions by several, partially conflicting, criteria giving rise to different preference orders (Taylor, 1972). In addition, even if the same criterion is used by all the parties in a given situation, different criteria may be employed in different political contexts.

     The political context we have in mind in the present paper is of a parliamentary system (e.g., Israel) in which a particular party, typically the one with the largest number of votes, is singled out after the elections and given a mandate to form a coalition. Often, such a mandate is assigned according to tradition or legislation by an official authority like a president or a king. Singling out a particular party and assigning it the task of forming a coalition is politically significant because it imposes nontrivial restrictions on the process of forming a coalition (Peleg, 1981).

The purpose of the present paper is to present and empirically test a multi-criteria model for predicting coalition formation in parliamentary systems in which a party is singled out and given a mandate to form a coalition. The model draws on Peleg's (1981) work regarding dominant players in simple games and Grofman's (1982) dynamic model of proto-coalition formation in ideological multidimensional spaces. Its predictive power is tested experimentally with data collected individually from politically sophisticated respondents immediately after the 1981 election to the tenth Knesset in Israel. Section 2 introduces the model and explores the relationships with the models of Peleg and Grofman. Section 3 describes the tenth Israeli Knesset. Section 4 provides information about the subjects who participated in the tenth Knesset study and the experimental procedure employed. Section 5 presents the results of the study, and Section 6 discusses methodological and substantive implications.

## 2. The Model

DOMINATED COALITIONS

It is natural to model our parliamentary system as a weighted majority game. Formally, let $N = \{1,2,...,n\}$ be a set of $n$ parties in a parliament. Denote the number of seats party $i$ controls ($i \in N$) by $w(i)$ and the number of seats controlled by coalition $S$ by

$$w(S) = \sum_{i \in S} w(i), \ S \subseteq N.$$

For a given parliament, let $q$ be the quota, or the number of seats a coalition requires to win. Simple majority rule is usually used, so that $q$ is the smallest integer strictly greater than $w(N)/2$. We shall say that coalition $S$ is winning if and only if $w(S) > q$, and denote the set of all winning coalitions by $W$. The resulting weighted majority game $G$ will be denoted by $[q;w(1),w(2),...,w(n)]$.

Peleg (1981) noted that a player holding a strict majority within a winning coalition plays an important role in the coalition formation process. Having defined the notion of a dominant player, Peleg proceeded to build a theory of dominated coalitions and then illustrated it using empirical data from several parliaments. Several definitions are required in order to describe his theory.

Let $G$ be a weighted majority game. A coalition $S$ is *at least as desirable* as coalition $T$ (with respect to the game $G$) if whenever $B \subset N$ is such that $B \cap (S \cup T) = \phi$ and $B \cup T$ is winning, it follows that $B \cup S$ is winning too. In other words, $S$ is at least as desirable as $T$ if out of the set of coalitions disjoint from both coalitions $S$ and $T$, the set winning with $T$ is a subset of the set winning with $S$.

When $S$ is at least as desirable as $T$, we shall write $S \succeq T$.    If $S \succeq T$, but $T \succeq S$ does not hold, we shall write $S \rightarrow T$ and say that $S$ is *more desirable than* $T$.

Several remarks concerning the relation of desirability are useful:    (1) $\succeq$ is complete and $\rightarrow$ is acyclic on the set of all coalitions; (2) every winning coalition is more desirable than a losing one; (3) in weighted majority games the following does not hold:

$$w(T) > w(S) \text{ implies } T \rightarrow S.$$

For example, in the three-person game $[5; 2,3,4]$, the second and third players are of unequal weight but of equal desirability; finally (4) $S \succeq T$ $(S \rightarrow T)$ implies $S \succeq T_1$ $(S \rightarrow T_1)$ for every $T_1 \subset T$ and $S_1 \succeq T$ $(S_1 \rightarrow T)$ for every $S_1 \supset S$.

Continuing with our definitions, player $i$ in coalition $S$ is said to *dominate* (*weakly dominate*) $S$ if $\{i\} \rightarrow S - \{i\}$ $(\{i\} \succeq S - \{i\})$.    Player $i$ is *dominant* if he or she dominates some winning coalition.    Peleg (1981) showed that the set of dominant players in weighted majority games consists of at most one player.    This leads us to single out those weighted majority games that have a single dominant player and that are not dictatorial, i.e., in which the winning coalitions are not determined by a lone player. Here such games will be called *dominated* games.[1]

Why should political scientists studying coalition formation in parliamentary democracies be interested in dominated games?    The answer seems to reside in the prevalence of these games.    Reanalyzing the information contained in Chapters 9 through 11 of DeSwaan (1973) about nine parliamentary democracies, Peleg (1981) showed that of 105 nondictatorial assemblies in the present century, 81 (77 percent) were dominated.    In particular, the Israeli Knesset was dominated during the years 1949 to 1977 by the Labor party and from 1977 to 1981 by the Likud party, rendering the theory of dominated games highly relevant to our study.

Let $G$ be a dominated weighted majority game.    Denote the dominant player by $i$ and assume that he or she is provided with a mandate to form a coalition.    Peleg proposed the following hypothesis:

HYPOTHESIS D:    In a dominated game in which the dominant player is given a mandate to form a coalition, only winning coalitions weakly dominated by $i$ will result. The set of winning coalitions weakly dominated by player $i$ will also be denoted by $D$.

Peleg provides strong evidence in support of Hypothesis D.    Analyzing data from 67 assemblies of Denmark, Israel, Italy, The Netherlands, and Sweden, he showed that type D coalitions formed in 56 cases (84 percent).    This evidence notwithstanding, Hypothesis D appears to us incomplete as a descriptive model of coalition formation in parliamentary democracies.    The first difficulty is that it incorporates information only about the weights of the $n$ parties and disregards information about the ideological relationships among them.    However, there is much empirical evidence to suggest that information about ideological diversity cannot be ignored.    Indeed, Peleg himself considered information about policy order in testing Axelrod's (1970) hypothesis

---

[1]The definition of dominated games given here differs slightly from Peleg's (1981).    His definition refers to more general simple games.

concerning connected coalitions. However, he did not incorporate the notion of connectedness in Hypothesis D, nor did he attempt to generalize unidimensional connectedness to multidimensional policy spaces. The second difficulty is that the predictive power of hypothesis D is weak. As we show below, the set D may include so many coalitions as to be of little predictive value.

## CONNECTED COALITIONS

Because we wish to incorporate information about ideological proximities in our model of coalition formation, it seems reasonable to represent the parties' most preferred positions (political policies) as points in some multidimensional space. As is common in the field (McKelvey, Ordeshook, and Winer, 1978; Grofman, 1982), it is assumed that each party evaluates the relative desirability of alternatives in terms of their distances from its most preferred point, and that these alternatives are always sufficiently distinct so that ties cannot occur. We assume that the $m$-dimensional ideological space is Euclidean and denote it by $R^m$. This choice leaves ample scope for capturing many kinds of parliaments without an excess of abstraction and generality (Shapley, 1977). If $m = 1$, $R$ is often considered to be the simple left-right spectrum of popular political analysis. If $m = 2$, one dimension may again be interpreted as the left-right spectrum, whereas the other dimension may reflect degrees of religious involvement or amount of radicalism. Typically, the representation will be determined from observed measures of ideological proximity by some multidimensional scaling technique.

We have interpreted $R^m$ as a political policy or issue space with each of the $m$ issues represented by a single dimension. A point $x_i \in R^m$ represents the description of the "political profile" of party $i$, and the distance $d(x_i, x_j)$ between any two points $x_i$ and $x_j$ in $R^m$ represents the ideological dissimilarity between the two corresponding parties $i$ and $j$. A generalization of the notion of connectedness to a multidimensional policy space is straightforward (see Grofman, 1982). Let $G$ be a weighted majority game. A coalition $S$ in $G$ is *connected* if there is no point $x_j$, $j \notin S$, in the convex hull of the points $\{x_i | i \in S\}$. We shall denote by $C = C(G)$ the set of all connected coalitions in $G$.[2]

---

[2]To check connectedness in $R^m$ of a coalition $S$ of size $s$, we take note of the following: Let the configuration of $S$ in $R^m$ be represented by an $m$ by $s$ matrix $X$, and let $Z$ be a column vector representing a party $j$ not in $S$. Then $Z$ is in the convex hull of the vectors representing $S$ if and only if the following linear program has a zero optimal solution:

$$\min(1_m^T \cdot Y)$$

subject to $\begin{bmatrix} X & I_m \\ 1_s^T & 0 \end{bmatrix} \begin{bmatrix} \lambda \\ Y \end{bmatrix} = \begin{bmatrix} Z \\ 1_1 \end{bmatrix}$, $Y \geq 0$, $\lambda \geq 0$,

where $\lambda$ is a matrix of unknowns ($s$ by 1), $I_m$ identity ($m$ by $m$), $Y$ is a matrix of unknowns ($m$ by 1), and $1_k$ is a matrix of units ($k$ by 1). Also if $S \subset T$ and $T$ is connected, then one should check only $T - S$ for possible violations of the connectedness of $S$.

Figure 1 illustrates the notion of connectedness in $R^2$. It portrays ten parties, labeled alphabetically from $A$ through $J$, in a two-dimensional space. Coalition $ABC$ in Figure 1 is connected; none of the seven points $x_D$ through $x_J$ is contained in the triangle formed by the points $x_A$, $x_B$, and $x_C$. Similarly, coalition $DEFHJ$ is connected. However, coalition $DEFJ$ is not connected because party $H$, which is not a member, is contained in the convex hull generated by the four points $x_D$, $x_E$, $x_F$, and $x_J$.

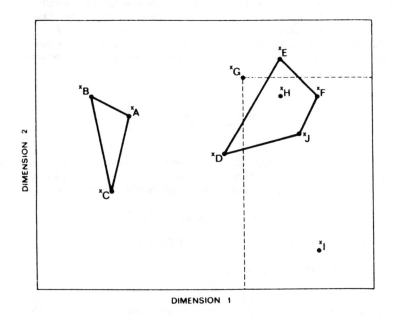

*Figure 1. Ten Hypothetical Parties in a Two-Dimensional Policy Space.*

Connectedness is not preserved under projections. For example, in Figure 1 coalition $DEFHJ$ is connected, although point $x_G$ falls within the range of that coalition on the horizontal as well as the vertical dimensions.

Two separate sources of information have been assumed to play a decisive role in the formation of political coalitions. Hypothesis D requires only information about voting weights of the players, whereas connectedness requires only dimensional representation of ideological proximity. The following hypothesis combines both sources of information:

HYPOTHESIS DC: In a dominated coalition game embedded in an ideologically interpretable Euclidean space in which the dominant player $i$ is given a mandate to form a coalition, only connected and winning coalitions, weakly dominated by $i$, will form.

TIGHT COALITIONS

To achieve ideological homogeneity and therefore prolong coalition durability, connected and weakly dominated coalitions tend to look at their members' relative ideological proximity as a measure of stability. We contend that a coalition $S$ in $C \cap D$ whose members are relatively close to one another ideologically is less fractionalized and more stable than another coalition $T$ in $C \cap D$ whose members are ideologically further apart. Distances in the ideological space may affect cabinet durability (Dodd, 1974) and therefore render the formation of coalition $S$ more likely than that of $T$.

To formalize these ideas, let $d(x_i,x_j)$ denote the Euclidean distance between points $x_i$ and $x_j$ in $R^m$ as before, and define $d(S)$ to be the mean distance between every two members of coalition $S$:

$$d(S) = \sum_i \sum_j d(x_i,x_j) / \binom{s}{2}$$

where $s = |S|$ is the cardinality of $S$ and summation is over $i$ and $j$ in $S$ such that $i < j$. We interpret $d(S)$ as the *degree of ideological tightness* of coalition $S$. Coalition $S$ in $C \cap D$ is *tight* if the mean distance between its members is minimal:

$$d(S) = \min \{d(T)|T \in C \cap D\}.$$

Our third and most stringent hypothesis is the following:

HYPOTHESIS DCT:   Only tight coalitions will form.

As demonstrated below, Hypothesis DC is not easily refutable because it often allows too many coalitions to form. On the other hand, Hypothesis DCT, which in general predicts only a single coalition, is too stringent because of the extreme sensitivity of the degree of tightness of coalition $S$ to the exact positions of its members in $R^m$. Although the assumption of a multidimensional representation of political parties is common (e.g., Grofman, 1982; Kruskal and Wish, 1978; Rapoport and Golan, 1985; Rattinger, 1982; Shapley, 1977), the exact determination of the coordinates of the points $x_i$ is problematic. Scaling procedures such as factor analysis or nonmetric multidimensional scaling, which are commonly used for the analysis of ideological proximity data, yield spatial configurations that trade variability in the data for low dimensionality. Criteria for achieving the highly desirable goal of low dimensionality are subjective. Additionally, some change in the positions of the $n$ points in the spatial configuration may result from technical features of these scaling methods such as the starting configuration, the criterion of badness-of-fit minimized by the numerical program, the number of iterations allowed, and the like. Also, small perturbations of the configuration might not change the badness-of-fit at all. Nevertheless, these sources of variability may affect the ordering of the coalitions in $C \cap D$ by their degree of tightness. Consequently, we will test a weaker version of Hypothesis DCT, asserting that one of the first $k$ coalitions in $C \cap D$ ranked by degree of tightness will form.

## 3. The Tenth Knesset Study

The form and practice of the Israeli national government is parliamentary. Authority is centered in the Knesset and power is distributed among the parties holding its 120 seats. A winning coalition controls such valued objects as the prime-ministership, cabinet posts, and government funds, which allow it to determine and implement policy.

Negotiations for forming a coalition government start immediately after election day. Traditionally, the president has asked the largest party to form a coalition government within an extendable period of three weeks. The period between the announcement of the election results and the formation of a new government is ideal for (1) the collection of data about voting power and ideological similarities between parties, and (2) eliciting predictions regarding the coalition that will eventually form and the allocation of cabinet ministerships among its members. During this time, information concerning voting power and, particularly, ideological similarities between parties, is not contaminated by the coalition government to be eventually formed. Consequently, support for political theories of coalition formation at this time can justifiably be based on prediction rather than "postdiction" (Murnighan, 1978).

COMPOSITION OF THE TENTH KNESSET

Following four years of rule by a coalition government dominated by the Likud party, elections for the tenth Knesset were held in July 1981. Thirty-one parties participated in the elections, but only ten parties each gained more than 1 percent of the total vote and thereby Knesset representation. The results of the 1981 elections were as follows: Hadash ($A$), 4 seats; Shinui ($B$), 2 seats; Ratz ($C$), 1 seat; Labor ($D$), 47 seats; Telem ($E$), 2 seats; Likud ($F$), 48 seats; Tami ($G$), 3 seats; Mafdal ($H$), 6 seats; Agudat Israel ($I$), 4 seats; Tehiya ($J$), 3 seats.

A brief description of these ten parties is in order. Hadash is an orthodox Communist party with a strong pro-Russian line. Shinui, Ratz, and Telem are liberal parties differing from one another in their positions on moral values, civil and human rights, economic policy, and settlement in the West Bank. Labor is an alignment of left, right, and middle-of-the-road socialist parties and factions. Likud is a liberal-conservative party that gains much of its support from the lower and middle classes, and promotes free enterprise, nationalism, and expansionism. Tami, Mafdal, and Agudat Israel are primarily religious parties, the first representing the social and religious interests of Jews of eastern origin, the second placing relatively great weight on settlement in the West Bank and maintenance of Jewish tradition and values, and the third ardently defending orthodox Jewish law. Finally, the Tehiya party is the strongest supporter of nationalism, territorial expansionism, and aggressive foreign policy.

## 4. Method

SUBJECTS

Three groups of subjects, differing from one another in their age, experience, political sophistication, and knowledge of political events, participated in the study. The student group consisted of 21 undergraduate and graduate students of political science at the University of Haifa, who had taken at least one course about the political system of Israel. Their political sophistication and knowledge of the parties' program were thought to be above the national average but below that of the other two groups of subjects.

The second group consisted of recently elected parliament members who were selected in the following manner. After the elections, individual letters were mailed to all the 120 members of the newly elected Knesset asking them to participate in a study concerning electoral power and ideological similarities between parties. The ninety-minute interviews were individual, kept anonymous, and conducted at the subject's convenience. Twenty-four parliament members, most of whom were veterans of previous Knessets, agreed to take part in the study. The Parliament members consisted of 1 member of party $A$, 1 member of party $B$, 9 members of party $D$, 1 member of party $E$, 11 members of party $F$, and 1 member of party $H$. Although no attempt was made to choose a representative sample (we gladly would have interviewed all 120 members), the composition of Parliament members corresponded closely to the composition of the tenth Knesset.

Reporters included seven Knesset-based reporters of the Israeli media (newspaper, radio, and television), who regularly cover the Knesset. These reporters were approached because of their reputation, political sophistication, knowledge of the Knesset, and experience in covering political events and coalition negotiations.

PROCEDURE

There were two parts to the experimental procedure. The first employed a scaling technique proposed by Saaty (1977) to measure political power on a ratio scale; the results of this part are reported elsewhere (Rapoport and Golan, 1985). The second part employed a paired comparison method to obtain measures of ideological similarity between parties, which were later submitted to nonmetric multidimensional scaling analyses. All 45 pairs of parties were presented to the subject in a random order one at a time, with no time limit. The subject was asked to rate the ideological similarity of the two members of each pair using a 0-100 rating scale.

Following the second part, the subjects in the student group only were presented with a list of the ten parties in the tenth Knesset and the distribution of seats among them. The subjects were then asked to predict which coalition would eventually form.

## 5. Results

In order to test Hypothesis DCT, the ten parties in the tenth Knesset must be represented as ten points in a finite-dimensional Euclidean space amenable to political interpretation.

Classical nonmetric multidimensional scaling (MDS) was applied to each of the 52 individual symmetric matrices of ideological similarity judgments for the purpose of deriving spatial configurations in low dimensionality. The results of the MDS analysis are presented in the first part of this section; they are followed by individual tests of the DCT hypothesis, which make use of the spatial configurations from the first part.

## MDS ANALYSIS

The individual similarity judgments were converted to dissimilarity judgments. Each subject's 10 by 10 symmetric matrix of dissimilarities was then subjected to classical nonmetric MDS realized through the ALSCAL procedure included in the 1980 version of the Statistical Analysis System (SAS) package. Results were obtained in one or two dimensions ($m = 1, 2$); spatial configurations with three or more dimensions were unreliable due to the low ratio of data points to the number of parameters that needed to be estimated (Kruskal and Wish, 1978; Schiffman, Reynolds, and Young, 1981).

Multidimensional scaling of the dissimilarity matrices in $R^1$ yielded uniformly poor results. This led us to the conclusion that a single dimension was not sufficient to account for the dissimilarity data. Consequently, two-dimensional configurations were derived for each of the 52 individual subjects. Goodness-of-fit was assessed by the RSQ measure, which is the squared correlation between the Euclidean distances in $R^2$ (between the members of each of the 45 pairs of parties) and the corresponding disparities (monotonically transformed dissimilarity judgments).[3]

The RSQ scores ranged from .757 to .964. The mean RSQ scores for the student group, Parliament members, and reporters were .857, .881, and .897, respectively. A one-way ANOVA conducted on the RSQ scores yielded nonsignificant results, suggesting no differences among the three groups in terms of the goodness-of-fit index. On the average, more than 85 percent of the variance in the similarity judgments was accounted for by the linear relation between the 45 Euclidean distances in $R^2$ and the corresponding 45 disparities, leading us to conclude that two-dimensional solutions were satisfactory for most of our subjects.[4]

---

[3]Goodness-of-fit was also measured by Kruskal's (1964) STRESS index. Specifically, we employed S-STRESS formula one, which measures badness-of-fit of the solution in terms of the squared distances and squared disparities. S-STRESS is recommended for proximity data (Davison, 1983). The mean S-STRESS scores for the student group, the Parliament members, and the reporters were .161, .151, and .145, respectively, indicating moderate, though by no means perfect, fit in two dimensions.

[4]In analyses reported elsewhere (Golan, 1984), the proximity matrices of all the subjects in each group separately were subjected to an individual differences nonmetric multidimensional scaling (INDSCAL), using the ALSCAL computer program to fit the weighted Euclidean model (Davison, 1983; Schiffman, Reynolds, and Young, 1981). The resulting three two-dimensional configurations for the student group, the Parliament members, and the reporters were practically identical to one another. Because our interest is primarily in individual rather than group tests of the DCT model, no further use is made of the group configurations.

Problems of indeterminacy arise whenever the ratio of the number of dimensions ($m$) to the number of objects scaled ($n$) is relatively high, as it is in the present study. In addition, the high RSQ scores indicate a high degree of stability of the points in the configurations. Consequently, low values of $k$ are required in this case to test the DCT Hypothesis. No attempt has been made here to fit different values of $k$ to different subjects according to their RSQ scores. Rather, because the ratio $m/n$ was relatively high and the fit in terms of $R^2$ was generally good but not perfect, we settled initially on the value $k = 5$ for all subjects.

Only a brief description of the results of the individual MDS analyses will be attempted here. Complete details may be found in Golan (1984), in which the coordinates of the 52 two-dimensional configurations are presented and discussed. Figure 2 depicts the spatial configuration of three subjects: one (M14) with a relatively low RSQ score (.774), another (M3) with a relatively moderate RSQ score (.884), and yet another (R7) with a relatively high RSQ score (.952). All three configurations are shaped like a horseshoe; the differences among them are marginal. The configurations are also typical (Golan, 1984); 39 of the 52 subjects yielded horseshoe-shaped configurations although not necessarily with the ten parties in the same order. The horizontal axis was interpreted as the traditional left-right dimension representing the attitudes of the parties to religious matters, economic policy, and foreign affairs, whereas the vertical axis was interpreted as a moderation-radicalism continuum (see Rapoport and Golan, 1985).

TESTS OF THE DCT HYPOTHESIS

Immediately following the 1981 elections, the tenth Knesset was representable by the weighted majority game:

$$
\begin{array}{ccccccccccc}
 & A & B & C & D & E & F & G & H & I & J \\
[61; & 4, & 2, & 1, & 47, & 2, & 48, & 3, & 6, & 4, & 3].
\end{array}
$$

The tenth Knesset game is dominated; it is nondictatorial and has player $F$ (Likud) as the sole dominant player. Hypothesis D, which depends only on the players' weights, is therefore applicable.

As assumed by Hypothesis D, the president gave player $F$ a mandate to form a coalition government. After lengthy negotiations about the allocation of cabinet posts and compromises concerning a long list of policy issues, the Likud, Tami, Mafdal, and Agudat Israel formed a minimal winning coalition with 61 seats (coalition $FGHI$). Several months later, the Tehiya joined the former four parties to form a nonminimal winning coalition, $FGHIJ$.

Being weakly dominated by player $F$, both $FGHI$ and $FGHIJ$ are type D coalitions. However, the support they provide for Hypothesis D is very weak, since they are only two of a total of 130 possible winning coalitions in the tenth Knesset weakly dominated by player $F$.

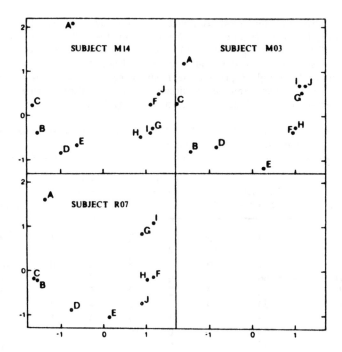

*Figure 2. Two-Dimensional Configurations for Three Typical Subjects with Relatively Low (M14), Medium (M3), and High (R7) RSQ Scores.*

The DCT Hypothesis was tested in three stages. First, the individual two-dimensional configurations yielded by the MDS procedure together with the set D (which is the same for all subjects) were jointly used to compute for each subject the set $C \cap D$ of connected and weakly dominated coalitions. Because of the differences among the individual spatial configurations, the sets $C \cap D$ differ in general from subject to subject. Next, the coalitions in the set $C \cap D$ for each subject were rank ordered in terms of their degree of tightness. Lastly, Hypothesis DCT was tested for each individual, first with the five ($k = 5$) tightest coalitions and then with the first three ($k = 3$).

The number of winning, connected, and weakly dominated coalitions for Parliament members ranged between 8 and 130 with a mean of 42.9. Thus, imposing connectedness reduced the number of candidates by a factor of three on the average. Of the 120 coalitions (24 subjects by 5 ranks), four consisted of two parties, 38 consisted of four parties, 59 consisted of five parties, 18 consisted of six parties, and one consisted of seven parties. In general, the number of parties in a coalition S in $C \cap D$ increased as the degree of tightness decreased, but the correlation between $d(S)$ and $|S|$ was far from perfect.

Table 1 shows the ten most frequent coalitions ranked by the frequency of occurrence within the five tightest coalitions over all the subjects in the Parliament members group (first column on the right). The first column on the left shows the coalition, and the second shows the total number of Knesset members belonging to this coalition. Columns 3 through 7 present the frequencies of each coalition as a function of its tightness rank. For example, coalition $FGHI$ was ranked first in degree of tightness by seven of the 24 subjects and second by only four.

TABLE 1. Frequencies of the five tightest coalitions in the parliament members group over subjects

| Coalition | Knesset Seats | Frequency of Rank | | | | | Total |
|---|---|---|---|---|---|---|---|
| | | 1 | 2 | 3 | 4 | 5 | |
| FGHIJ | 64 | 5 | 12 | 2 | 2 | 1 | 22 |
| FGHI | 61 | 7 | 4 | 7 | 0 | 2 | 20 |
| FHIJ | 61 | 9 | 3 | 6 | 0 | 0 | 18 |
| EFGHIJ | 66 | 1 | 0 | 2 | 7 | 7 | 17 |
| EFGHJ | 62 | 2 | 2 | 2 | 5 | 5 | 16 |
| EFGHI | 63 | 0 | 2 | 1 | 4 | 4 | 11 |
| EFHIJ | 63 | 0 | 1 | 4 | 4 | 1 | 10 |
| DF | 95 | 0 | 0 | 0 | 2 | 2 | 4 |
| BEFGHJ | 64 | 0 | 0 | 0 | 0 | 1 | 1 |
| BEFGHIJ | 68 | 0 | 0 | 0 | 0 | 1 | 1 |
| Total | | 24 | 24 | 24 | 24 | 24 | 120 |

Ten coalitions accounted collectively for the five tightest coalitions for the 24 Parliament members. The three most frequent coalitions were $FGHIJ$, $FGHI$, and $FHIJ$ with total frequencies of 22, 20, and 18, respectively. Table 1 shows that these three coalitions differ from the remaining seven coalitions not only in the frequencies of occurrence among the first five tightest coalitions, but also with respect to the number of times they occupy the first position. Thus, coalitions $FGHIJ$, $FGHI$, and $FHIJ$ are ranked as tightest by five, seven, and nine subjects, respectively. Of the seven remaining coalitions, only one ($EFGHJ$) is ranked tightest twice, another coalition ($EFGHJ$) is ranked once, and the remaining five never occupy the first rank. If only the first three ($k = 3$) tightest coalitions for each subject are examined, the difference between coalitions $FGHIJ$, $FGHI$, and $FHIJ$ and the rest is even more pronounced. Among the three tightest coalitions for each subject, coalitions $FGHIJ$, $FGHI$, and $FHIJ$ occurred 19, 18, and 18 times respectively, whereas the next most frequent coalition ($EFGHJ$) occurred only six times.

The results in Table 1 support the DCT Hypothesis and the assumptions underlying it. The first coalition that actually formed in the tenth Knesset — *FGHI* — is among the three coalitions that Hypothesis DCT clearly favors. And the coalition that succeeded it a few months later — *FGHIJ* — has the highest total frequency of occurrence, regardless of whether the first two, three, four, or five tightest coalitions for each subject are examined. Moreover, the first seven coalitions that appear in Table 1, each with a total frequency of 10 or more, were judged by the media to be the most likely to form following the elections to the tenth Knesset. Table 1 shows that these seven coalitions all include both the Likud (*F*) and Mafdal (*H*) parties that together have constituted the backbone of the coalition government in the tenth Knesset.

The social sciences are abundant with examples of models faring well with one population of subjects but failing miserably with another. Since political sophistication and experience of the same subjects have been shown by Rapoport and Golan (1985) to result in different assessments of political power, tests of the DCT Hypothesis for the remaining two groups of subjects are warranted.

The number of winning, connected, and weakly dominated coalitions for the reporters ranged from 23 to 84 with a mean of 44.1. The difference between the means of the number of connected and weakly dominated coalitions of Parliament members and reporters was not significant ($t < 1$, $p > 0.05$). The reporters, like the Parliament members, showed a tendency for coalition size to grow as the degree of tightness decreased. Table 2 presents the same information of reporters as Table 1 for Parliament members. Seven coalitions accounted for the five tightest coalitions generated for the seven reporters. Tables 1 and 2 are very similar. The seven coalitions in Table 2 are identical to and ordered in the same way as the seven most frequent coalitions in Table 1.

TABLE 2. *Frequencies of the five tightest coalitions in the reporters group over subjects*

| Coalition | Knesset Seats | Frequency of Rank | | | | | Total |
|---|---|---|---|---|---|---|---|
| | | 1 | 2 | 3 | 4 | 5 | |
| FGHIJ | 64 | 0 | 3 | 4 | 0 | 0 | 7 |
| FGHI | 61 | 2 | 2 | 2 | 1 | 0 | 7 |
| FHIJ | 61 | 4 | 2 | 1 | 0 | 0 | 7 |
| EFGHIJ | 66 | 0 | 0 | 0 | 0 | 4 | 4 |
| EFGHJ | 62 | 1 | 0 | 0 | 3 | 0 | 4 |
| EFGHI | 63 | 0 | 0 | 0 | 2 | 1 | 3 |
| EFHIJ | 63 | 0 | 0 | 0 | 1 | 2 | 3 |
| Total | | 7 | 7 | 7 | 7 | 7 | 35 |

The information about the five tightest coalitions for the student group is summarized in Table 3. Altogether eight coalitions accounted for the five tightest coalitions in 86 (81.9 percent) of a total of 105 cases. These eight coalitions are the same as the eight most frequently found coalitions in Table 1. As in Tables 1 and 2, *FGHIJ, FGHI*, and *FHIJ* are the three most frequent coalitions with a total frequency of 18, 18, and 16, respectively. The difference between the three most frequent coalitions and the remaining five coalitions is again most clearly visible when only ranks 1 through 3 are examined. Among the three tightest coalitions for each subject, coalitions *FGHIJ, FGHI*, and *FHIJ* occur 16, 15, and 14 times, respectively, whereas the next most frequent coalition in Table 3 (*DF*) occurs only four times.

TABLE 3.        *Frequencies of the five tightest coalitions in the student group over subjects*

| Coalition | Knesset Seats | Frequency of Rank | | | | | Total |
|-----------|---------------|---|----|---|----|----|-------|
|           |               | 1 | 2  | 3 | 4  | 5  |       |
| FGHIJ     | 64            | 1  | 10 | 5 | 2  | 0  | 18 |
| FGHI      | 61            | 10 | 1  | 4 | 2  | 1  | 18 |
| FHIJ      | 61            | 7  | 2  | 5 | 2  | 0  | 16 |
| EFGHJ     | 62            | 0  | 2  | 1 | 3  | 4  | 10 |
| EFGHI     | 63            | 0  | 3  | 0 | 3  | 3  | 9  |
| EFGHIJ    | 66            | 0  | 0  | 2 | 3  | 2  | 7  |
| DF        | 95            | 2  | 1  | 1 | 0  | 1  | 5  |
| EFHIJ     | 63            | 0  | 1  | 0 | 0  | 2  | 3  |
| Total     |               | 20 | 20 | 18 | 15 | 13 | 86 |

Subsequent to making their similarity judgments, the subjects of the student group were each asked to predict which coalition would eventually form. These predictions were collected on the fifth day after the elections, when the coalition negotiations were very intense. During this period, the election results and the subsequent negotiations were the most publicized and hotly debated topic in the Israeli media. Despite disagreements among reporters and commentators about the outcome of the negotiations, there was an almost unanimous agreement that the next coalition government would not include parties *A, B,* and *C,* or *J.* Presumably these speculations affected the predictions made by the students.

Table 4 presents the predictions of the student group regarding the forthcoming coalition. Column 1 on the left shows the students' identities, and column 2 presents their predicted coalitions. We examined each predicted coalition to determine whether it was winning and weakly dominated and whether it was connected. The results of these two tests are shown in columns 3 and 4, respectively. Column 5 presents the number of winning, weakly dominated, and connected coalitions for each student separately. Finally, the right–hand column of Table 4 shows for each student the tightness ranking of his or her predicted coalition within the set $C \cap D$.

TABLE 4. *Coalitions predicted by subject in the student group*

| Subject | Predicted Coalition | D | C | \|C ∩ D\| | Tightness Ranking |
|---------|---------------------|---|---|-----------|-------------------|
| ST1  | FGHI   | + | + | 63 | 1  |
| ST2  | EFGHI  | + | + | 39 | 4  |
| ST3  | EFGHI  | + | + | 22 | 13 |
| ST4  | EFGHI  | + | + | 34 | 22 |
| ST5  | EFGHI  | + | + | 27 | 4  |
| ST6  | FGHI   | + | + | 34 | 7  |
| ST7  | EFGHI  | + | + | 74 | 2  |
| ST8  | FGHI   | + | − | 31 | *  |
| ST9  | EFHI   | − | − | 16 | *  |
| ST10 | EFGHIJ | + | + | 73 | 6  |
| ST11 | EFGHI  | + | + | 91 | 6  |
| ST12 | EFGHI  | + | + | 80 | 7  |
| ST13 | FGHI   | + | − | 31 | *  |
| ST14 | EFHI   | − | − | 55 | *  |
| ST15 | EFGHI  | + | + | 30 | 2  |
| ST16 | FGHI   | + | + | 83 | 1  |
| ST17 | EFGHI  | + | − | 36 | *  |
| ST18 | EFHIJ  | + | + | 38 | 5  |
| ST19 | FGHI   | + | + | 36 | 2  |
| ST20 | EFGHI  | + | + | 26 | 5  |
| ST21 | EFGHI  | + | − | 12 | *  |

*The coalition is not a member of $C \cap D$

Two students (ST9 and ST14) predicted the formation of a nonwinning coalition (EFHI) and were therefore eliminated from further analysis. All of the remaining 19 students predicted the formation of a type $D$ coalition, weakly dominated by the Likud (player $F$), and 15 of these 19 students predicted a connected coalition. Table 4 shows that the degree of agreement among the students' predictions is higher than observed in Tables 1, 2, and 3. Of the 19 students, 11 predicted the formation of coalition $EFGHI$, which does not include player J. Only two students predicted a winning coalition including player J - student ST10 ($EFGHIJ$) and student ST18 ($EFHIJ$). The four predicted coalitions $EFGHI$, $FGHI$, $EFGHIJ$, and $EFHIJ$ are among the seven most frequent coalitions in Tables 1, 2, and 3. Conspicuous in their absence are coalitions *FGHIJ*, *FHIJ*, and *EFGHJ*, each of which contains player *J*; preceding analyses showed that these coalitions have a relatively high incidence of occurrence among the tightest coalitions. We attribute their absence to the strong effects of the media.

For nine (60 percent) of the 15 students who predicted the formation of a weakly dominated and connected coalition, the predicted coalition was among their five tightest coalitions. The coalitions predicted by four additional students ranked sixth or seventh in degree of tightness. Only students ST3 and ST4 predicted a coalition of a relatively low ranking in $C \cap D$, in contradiction to hypothesis DCT.

## 6. Discussion

The major hypothesis presented and experimentally tested in the present study is that only winning, weakly dominated, connected, and relatively tight coalitions will form. Proximity matrices from 52 subjects, who differed from one another in their political affiliation and political sophistication, were employed to test this hypotheses. The individual tests predicted for the most part the formation of three coalitions in the tenth Israeli Knesset. In descending order of tightness they were: *FGHIJ*, *FGHI*, and *FHIJ*. What in fact happened was that the minimal winning coalition *FGHI* formed for a short time, and was followed by coalition *FGHIJ*, as a result of the entrance of the Tehiya party (*J*). Hypothesis DCT adequately predicted the government which actually formed in Israel after the 1981 election, and also accounted for the prediction of most of the individual students in the student group who had been asked to predict the forthcoming coalition.

The DCT model is not intended to provide insight into Israeli politics, or, for that matter, any other parliamentary system. A detailed political analysis of the parliamentary system under consideration is required to achieve this purpose. Rather, the model follows previous attempts to predict the formation of political coalitions, and combines two criteria for predicting the formation of coalitions in parliamentary systems in which a single party is given a mandate to form a coalition. One criterion – the formation of dominated coalitions – is based solely on *structural* properties of the coalition game and the constraints imposed on it by the legislative procedure for forming a coalition. The other criterion – the formation of connected coalitions – is based on the *ideological* constraints imposed on the coalition game as reflected by the desire to form ideologically compatible coalitions. With respect to the former criterion, dominated coalitions play an analogous role in our model to minimal winning coalitions in the early theories of coalition formation by Riker (1962) and Gamson (1961). With respect to the latter criterion, our notion of connectedness is a generalization to multidimensional policy space of the same notion in the context of policy order in Axelrod's theory (1970). An important advantage of this generalization is that it does not depend on the particular interpretation given to the dimensions of the policy space. As defined in our model, connectedness is invariant under rotation, translation, and contraction of the spatial configuration in $R^m$.

Both criteria are required because neither the model of dominated coalitions nor the model of protocoalition formation accounts for the data of the present study. Hypothesis D is too weak, predicting a total of 130 different dominated coalitions in the tenth Israeli Knesset. Grofman's model, for other reasons, is also inadequate. First, the multistage model of protocoalition formation that Grofman proposes, which may be appropriate for cabinet negotiations conducted secretly, sequentially, and bilaterally, seems inappropriate for the coalition formation process in the Knesset, since it ignores the particular role assigned by the president to the dominant party. Second and most important, despite the importance assigned by Grofman to the notion of connectedness ("$N$-connectedness" in his terminology), the multistage process of coalition formation that he postulates need not produce connected coalitions when the dimensionality of the ideological space is equal to or larger than two (Grofman, 1982, p. 81). Third, Grofman's model seems too sensitive to the exact positions of the parties in the ideological space; small perturbations in these positions may change the single predicted coalition. It should be noted that the assumption that the ideological space is Euclidean has remained essentially untested. Moreover, even if this assumption is valid, it is difficult if not impossible to determine the positions of the $n$ parties in $R^m$ exactly. Consequently, we contend that the prediction set of any model of coalition formation that incorporates the notion of ideological diversity and measures ideological proximities by Euclidean distances should include more than a single element. The size of this prediction set should be inversely related to the goodness of fit of the spatial configuration.

The DCT model is founded on several suppositions. It supposes that resources (e.g., Gamson, 1961) or size (e.g., Riker, 1962) models cannot by themselves accurately predict coalitional alignments. Like the coalition formation models of Axelrod (1970), McKelvey, Ordeshook, and Winer (1978), and Grofman (1982), it supposes that ideological proximity correlates strongly and positively with coalitional choice. Another supposition is that the nature of the coalitional process, whether expressed in the coalitional dynamics or in the constraints imposed on the negotiation process, has important consequences for the nature of the expected outcomes. All of these suppositions together suggest that the emphasis in coalition research should be shifted from searching for a universal "best" model to examining the political circumstances and empirical conditions in parliamentary systems which favor one model over another.

Although the political circumstances that prevailed in Israel in the summer of 1981 seem to favor our model, we do not know in general the conditions favoring or disfavoring hypothesis DCT. We can only note that for certain vote distributions or patterns of ideological proximities between parties the set $C \cap D$ may be empty. The set $C \cap D$ will be empty if either the nondictatorial weighted majority game has no dominant player, or if connectedness is incompatible with Hypothesis D (see Peleg, 1981, and Einy, 1985, for examples of incompatibility of connectedness in $R^1$ with Hypothesis D). The case $|C \cap D| = 0$ should be interpreted to mean that the requirements specified by our model cannot be satisfied; rather, alternative principles of coalition formation in weighted majority games have to be invoked and empirically tested. Technically, there remains the problem of specifying which weighted majority games always have a dominant player and, for this class of games, of determining which spatial configurations in $R^m$ are always compatible with Hypothesis D.

A final methodological remark is in order.  Grofman pointed out that the data used to test his model suffer from the problem of circularity – parties included in the same coalition may be judged to be ideologically closer than they really are.  We are not familiar with studies that compared the ideological similarities between the same parties when they are in coalition and when they are not.  However, the Israeli experience indicates that the problem of circularity is potentially serious; ideologies may shift rather quickly with parties modifying their political postures often to the dismay of their supporters, once they have joined a winning coalition and assumed new responsibilities. A partial resolution of the problem of circularity may be achieved – as we did in the present study – by assessing ideological similarities immediately after the elections but before a coalition government actually formed.

## Acknowledgement

We would like to thank Dan Felsenthal and Zeev Maoz for a critical reading of the manuscript and Esther Golan for help in data collection.

## References

Axelrod, R. 1970.  *Conflict of interest:  A theory of divergent goals with applications to politics*.  Chicago: Markham.
Davison, M. L. 1983.  *Multidimensional scaling*.  New York: Wiley.
DeSwaan, A. 1973.  *Coalition theories and cabinet formation*.  San Francisco: Jossey-Bass.
Dodd, L. C. 1974.  Party coalitions in multiparty parliaments:  A game theoretic analysis. *American Political Science Review*, 68 (September):  1093-1117.
Duverger, M. 1951.  *Political parties*.  London: Methuen.
Einy, E. 1985.  On connected coalitions in dominated simple games.  *International Journal of Game Theory*, 14 (2): 103-25.
Gamson, W. A. 1961.  A theory of coalition formation. *American Sociological Review*, 26 (June): 373-82.
Golan, E. 1984.  *Assessment of voting power and ideological similarity between parties in the Knesset*.  Ph.D. Diss., Tel Aviv University, Israel.
Grofman, B. 1982.  A dynamic model of protocoalition formation in ideological N-space. *Behavioral Science*, 27 (January): 77-90.
Hinckley, B. 1972.  Coalitions in Congress:  Size and ideological distance.  *Midwest Journal of Political Science*, 16 (May): 197-207.
Kruskal, J. B. 1964.  Multidimensional scaling by optimizing goodness of fit to a nonmetric hypothesis. *Psychometrika*, 29 (March): 1-27.
Kruskal, J. B. and M. Wish. 1978.  *Multidimensional scaling*.  Beverly Hills: Sage.
Leiserson, M. 1968.  Faction and coalitions in one-party Japan:  An interpretation based on the theory of games.  *American Political Science Review*, 62 (September): 770-87.
McKelvey, R. D., P. C. Ordeshook, and M. Winer. 1978.  The competitive solution for n-person games without sidepayments.  *American Political Science Review*, 72 (June): 599-615.

Murnighan, J. K. 1978. Models of coalition behavior: Game theoretic, social psychological and political perspectives. *Psychological Bulletin*, 85 (5): 1130-53.
Peleg, B. 1981. Coalition formation in simple games with dominant players. *International Journal of Game Theory*, 10 (1): 11-33.
Rapoport, A., and E. Golan. 1985. Assessment of political power in the Israeli Knesset. *American Political Science Review*. 79 (September): 673-92.
Rattinger, H. 1982. Measuring power in voting bodies: Linear constraints, spatial analysis and computer program. In M. J. Holler, Ed., *Power, voting, and voting power*. Würzburg: Physica-Verlag.
Riker, W. H. 1962. *The theory of political coalitions*. New Haven: Yale University Press.
Saaty, T. L. 1977. A scaling method for priorities in hierarchical structures. *Journal of Mathematical Psychology*, 15 (3): 234-81.
Schiffman, S. S., M. L. Reynolds, and F. W. Young. 1981. *Introduction to multidimensional scaling*. New York: Academic.
Shapley, L. S. 1977. A comparison of power indices and nonsymmetric generalization. Paper number P-5872. Santa Monica: The Rand Corporation.
Statistical Analysis System (SAS) Institute, Inc. *SAS Supplemental Library User's Guide*. Cary, N.C.
Taylor, M. 1972. On the theory of government coalition formation. *British Journal of Political Science*, 2 (July): 361-86.

# AUTHOR INDEX

427

# SUBJECT INDEX

433

# THEORY AND DECISION LIBRARY

SERIES C:   GAME THEORY, MATHEMATICAL PROGRAMMING AND
            OPERATIONS RESEARCH

*Already published:*

**Compromise, Negotiation and Group Decision**
*Edited by Bertrand R. Munier and Melvin F. Shakun*
ISBN 90–277–2625–6

**Models of Strategic Rationality**
*by Reinhard Selten*
ISBN 90–277–2663–9

**Cooperative Games, Solutions and Applications**
*by Theo Driessen*
ISBN 90–277–2729–5

**Additive Representations of Preferences**
*by Peter P. Wakker*
ISBN 0–7923–0050–5